The Inkwell Handbook of Business and Economics Quotations

The Inkwell Handbook of Business and Economics Quotations

James A. Barham
Editor

Inkwell
PRESS

Description

The Inkwell Handbooks of Business and Economics are a series of extensive and rigorously researched reference works covering the fields of business, industry, entrepreneurship, finance, and economics from various angles. The present volume in this series, *The Inkwell Handbook of Business and Economics Quotations,* provides a large number of insightful and witty quotations by a range of thought leaders in the above fields, as well as several philosophers and well-known authors from other fields. In all, the volume contains 152 articles, organized by author, from Aga Khan to Mark Zuckerberg. Each article presents a brief biographical sketch, before listing some of the author's most noteworthy and elegant comments. Within each article, the quotations are organized by topic.

Library Cataloging Data

The Inkwell Handbook of Business and Economics Quotations by James A. Barham

Trim size: 7 × 10 inches

Library of Congress Control Number: 2026936188

ISBN: 979-8-89946-033-3 (Paperback), 979-8-89946-032-6 (Kindle)

BISAC: BUS055000 BUSINESS & ECONOMICS / Reference

BISAC: BUS024000 BUSINESS & ECONOMICS / Education

BISAC: REF019000 REFERENCE / Quotations

Book Cover Design

By Chloe Dembski. Image is a detail of Frants Henningsen's *At the Pawnbroker* (1893).

Inkwell PRESS

2321 Sir Barton Way
Suite 140-1032
Lexington, KY 40509
https://press.inkwell.net

Why This Book?

The world of business and economics has always been made up of famous men and women with uncommon ability and shrewdness. That is hardly surprising, given that we do not remember the names of run-of-the-mill individuals—the foot-soldiers, if you will, of any field of endeavor. It is the generals who make their mark on history and whose names are known to us.

But being famous as an innovator in the field of commerce, finance, economics, and enterprise is one thing; having the gift of speaking about one's vision is something very different.

The Inkwell Handbook of Business and Economics Quotations is a collection of inspiring insights put into pithy and memorable language.

We know very well there are many collections of intriguing quotations on the markets, organized according to all manner of different principles. However, we believe ours supplies a real need: We might have called our volume *The Wit and Wisdom of the Robber Barons, Tycoons, and Worldly Philosophers*. It is not a title we have seen elsewhere.

Therefore, we present here a unique collection of 152 of our favorite quotations by well-known businessmen, financiers, economists, and entrepreneurs. We have also added some observations on human nature and society made by individuals from other walks of life—just because we could not resist including them.

—James A. Barham, Editor

Table of Contents

Aga Khan

Shāh Karīm al-Ḥusaynī, Āghā Khān IV / b. 1936 / Geneva, Switzerland / Spiritual Leader, Businessman, Philanthropist, Founder and Chairman of the Aga Khan Development Network

Note: The fourth Aga Khan's father (who did not assume the office) was born in Italy, while his mother was English. His grandfather, the third Aga Khan, was born in Karachi, in what is now Pakistan. The family are the hereditary imāms (religious leaders) of the Nizārī Ismā'īlī community, an important Shīʿite sub-group prevalent in Pakistan, Afghanistan, Iran, and, formerly, central Africa. In the mid-nineteenth century, the Shāh of Persia bestowed the additional title of "*Āghā Khān*" (meaning, approximately, "Venerable Leader") upon the Nizārī imām of that time, who lived in Iran. The present imām, Aga Khan IV, is 49th in the overall line of succession.

Canada

Canada is today the most successful pluralist society on the face of our globe, without any doubt in my mind. . . . That is something unique to Canada. It is an amazing global human asset.

Reported in "Canada: 'A model for the world,'" The Globe and Mail, Toronto, Canada, February 2, 2002.

Canada has an experience of governance of which much of the world stands in dire need. It is a world of increasing dissension and conflict in which a significant contribution is the failure of different ethnic, tribal, religious, or social groups to search for, and agree upon, a common space for harmonious co-existence.

Address, Leadership and Diversity Conference, Gatineau, Quebec, Canada, May 19, 2004.

Education

What students know is no longer the most important measure of an education. The true test is the ability of students and graduates to engage with what they do not know, and to work out a solution. They must also be able to reach conclusions that constitute the basis for informed judgements. The ability to make judgements that are grounded in solid information, and employ careful analysis, should be one of the most important goals for any educational endeavor. As students develop this capability, they can begin to grapple with the most important and difficult step: to learn to place such judgements in an ethical framework. For all these reasons, there is no better investment that individuals, parents, and the nation can make than an investment in education of the highest possible quality. Such investments are reflected, and endure, in the formation of the kind of social conscience that our world so desperately needs.

Vision statement, agakhanacademies.org, 2020.

A secure pluralistic society requires communities that are educated and confident both in the identity and depth of their own traditions and in those of their neighbours.

Address, Leadership and Diversity Conference, Gatineau, Quebec, Canada, May 19, 2004.

Pluralist societies are not accidents of history. They are a product of enlightened education and continuous investment by governments and all of civil society in recognizing and celebrating the diversity of the world's peoples.

Speech, Democratic Development, Pluralism, and Civil Society, Nobel Institute, Oslo, Norway, April 7, 2005; transcript accessible at the.akdn.

Global Development

There are those . . . who enter the world in such poverty that they are deprived of both the means and the motivation to improve their lot. Unless these unfortunates can be touched with the spark which ignites the spirit of individual enterprise and determination, they will only sink back into renewed apathy, degradation, and despair. It is for us, who are more fortunate, to provide that spark.

Speech, inauguration of the Aga Khan Baug [Co-op Housing Society], Versova [Bombay], India, January 17, 1983; accessible at ismaili.net.

A proper home can provide the bridge across that terrible gulf between poverty and a better future.

Reported by Princess Zahra in her acceptance speech upon receiving the World Habitat Award, Kazan, Russian Federation, October 4, 2006.

You start with an idea, and then you let it grow. I think at the moment, there is a tendency to want to see political change occur in the developing world very rapidly, and I think this notion of consultation and democracy is all excellent, but I simply don't believe that Western forms of democracy are necessarily replicable throughout the developing world that I know, and indeed I would go so far as to say that, at the moment, one of our risks is to see democracies fail. . . . I think you have to be patient, careful, analytical, thoughtful, prudent, and build step-by-step. I don't think it can be done like mixing a glass of Nescafé.

Interview with BBC Two NewsNight, London, November 14, 2007; accessible at nanowisdoms.org.

International Relations

Tolerance, openness, and understanding towards other peoples' cultures, social structures, values and faiths are now essential to the very survival of an interdependent world.

Speech, Inauguration of the Restored Humayun's Tomb Gardens, New Delhi, India, April 15, 2003.

Pluralism is no longer simply an asset or a prerequisite for progress and development, it is vital to our existence.

Speech, Inauguration of the Restored Humayun's Tomb Gardens, New Delhi, India, April 15, 2003.

Conflict situations are driven by concepts of victory, power, and elimination of inherited culture, and not by the underlying values of civilization. There are many interpretations of Islam within the wider Islamic community, but generally we are instructed to leave the world a better place than it was when we came into it. The Aga Khan Award for Architecture seeks to make a better place in physical terms. This means trying to bring values into environments, buildings, and contexts that improve the quality of life for future generations.

Interview with Robert Ivy (FAIA), architecturalrecord.com, February, 2002.

I believe leadership everywhere must continuously work to ensure that pluralism, and all its benefits, become top global priorities. In this effort, civil society has a vital role. By its very nature, civil society is pluralist because it seeks to speak for the multiple interests not represented by the state. I refer, for example, to organisations which ensure best practices such as legal societies and associations of accountants, doctors and engineers. The meritocracy they represent is the very foundation of pluralism. And meritocracy is one of the principles of democracy itself.

Speech, Democratic Development, Pluralism, and Civil Society, Nobel Institute, Oslo, Norway, April 7, 2005; transcript accessible at the.akdn.

Civil society organisations make a major contribution to human development, particularly when democracies are failing, or have failed; for it is then that the institutions of civil society can, and often do, carry an added burden to help sustain improvements in quality of life. I believe strongly that a critical part of any development strategy should include support for civil society. I know that Norway supports this approach and works actively with its own civil society organizations to build capacity in the developing world.

Speech, Democratic Development, Pluralism, and Civil Society, Nobel Institute, Oslo, Norway, April 7, 2005; transcript accessible at the.akdn.

We cannot make the world safe for democracy unless we also make the world safe for diversity.

Address, School of International and Public Affairs, Columbia University, New York, May 15, 2006.

Islam

I think there is a massive gulf in the understanding and knowledge between Muslims and non-Muslims—I mean particularly the West and the Islamic world. What we are talking about in reality is a strong minority of people committed to their own particular interpretation of Islam, who seek to impose it on others. I do not believe that the totality of the Islamic world recognizes the Taliban interpretation of the faith as being representative of its own view. There is no unanimity in Islam with regard to this interpretation. Generally you will see as much diversity in the Islam as you do in the Christian world today. But the West does not really understand the pluralism of the Islamic world.

Interview with Robert Ivy (FAIA), architecturalrecord.com, February, 2002.

If we judge from Islamic history, there is much to encourage us. For century after century, the Arabs, the Persians, the Turks and many other Islamic societies achieved powerful leadership roles in the world—not only politically and economically but also intellectually. . . . The fundamental reason for the pre-eminence of Islamic civilizations lay neither in accidents of history nor in acts of war, but rather in their ability to discover new knowledge, to make it their own, and to build constructively upon it. They became the Knowledge Societies of their time.

Address, 2006 Convocation of the Aga Khan University, Karachi, Pakistan, December 2, 2006.

Philosophical Vision

The right to hope is the most powerful human motivation I know.

Commencement Address, Brown University, Providence, Rhode Island, USA, May 26, 1996; accessible at brown.edu.

If our animosities are born out of fear, then confident generosity is born out of hope. One of the central lessons I have learned after a half century of working in the developing world is that the replacement of fear by hope is probably the single most powerful trampoline of progress.

Address upon receiving the "Tolerance" Award, Tutzing Evangelical Academy, Tutzing, Germany, May 20, 2006.

The spirit of the Knowledge Society is the spirit of Pluralism—a readiness to accept the Other, indeed to learn from him, to see difference as an opportunity rather than a threat.

Address, 2006 Convocation of the Aga Khan University, Karachi, Pakistan, December 2, 2006.

The search for justice and security, the struggle for equality of opportunity, the quest for tolerance and harmony, the pursuit of human dignity—these are moral imperatives which we must work towards and think about on a daily basis.

Remarks, University of Évora, Évora, Portugal, February 12, 2006.

The Muslim world, with its history and cultures, and indeed its different interpretations of Islam, is still little known in the West. . . . The two worlds, Muslim and non-Muslim, Eastern and Western, must, as a matter of urgency, make a real effort to get to know one another, for I fear that what we have is not a clash of civilisations, but a clash of ignorance on both sides.

Closing Address, "Musée–Musées" Roundtable, Louvre Museum, October 17, 2007.

Muhammad Ali

Muhammad Ali (Cassius Marcellus Clay, Jr.) / 1942–2016 / Kentucky, USA / Boxing

Float like a butterfly, sting like a bee. Your hands can't hit what your eyes can't see.

Source: Various news reports prior to then-Clay's heavyweight title bout against Sonny Liston on February 24, 1964.

The man who views the world at 50 the same as he did at 20 has wasted 30 years of his life.

Source: Interview, Playboy magazine, November, 1975.

I hated every minute of it [training]. But I said to myself, 'Suffer now, and live the rest of your life as a champion.

Source: Interview, Newsweek, September 25,1978.

Age is whatever you think it is. You are as old as you think you are.

Source: Interview, Jet magazine, August, 1992.

If Ali says a mosquito can pull a plow, don't ask how. Hitch him up.

Source: Interview, Time magazine, June 14, 1999.

Religions all have different names, but they all contain the same truths. ... I think the people of our religion should be tolerant and understand people believe different things.

Source: Interview, CNN, September 20, 2001.

Allah is the Greatest. I'm just the greatest boxer.

Source: Interview, Soundvision.com, April 3, 2002.

Spirituality is recognizing the divine light that is within us all. It doesn't belong to any particular religion; it belongs to everyone.

Source: The Soul of a Butterfly (2004).

Paul Gardner Allen

Paul Gardner Allen / 1953–2018 / Washington, USA / Computer Programmer, Businessman, Investor, Entrepreneur, Co-Founder of Microsoft Corporation

Allen on Allen

I'm trying to transmit the visions of creativity and build institutions that are incredibly catalytic to their fields.

Reported by Quentin Hardy in "Paul Allen's Philanthropy Mirrors His Passions and Business Approach," nytimes.com, November 2, 2015.

I simply wanted to advance the field of artificial intelligence so that computers could do what they do best (organize and analyze information) to help people do what they do best, those inspired leaps of intuition that fuel original ideas and breakthroughs.

Reported in "Thought process: Building an artificial brain," washingtonpost.com, September 30, 2015.

[**Q**: Why Allen is so interested in the brain.]
A: We're just starting to understand the outlines of how things work. . . . It's so completely different than the way a computer works, and as someone who programs computers, that fascinates me. The brain was designed by evolution, so each part of it is optimized for what it does, and it's incredibly, incredibly complex. . . . Then there's trying to understand, at a chemical level, at a biological level, how the different parts of the brain work, and if you understood that, and those aspects of the brain, then you could possibly bring forward treatments to neurodegenerative diseases.

Interview with Clare McGrane, "Hear Microsoft co-founder Paul Allen reflect on his life and legacy in rare public interview," geekwire.com, October 15, 2018.

I'm always interested in finding ways to innovate. . . . It's a blend; it's not a point focus.

Reported by Kristi Heim in "Passion for arts and science drives Paul Allen's eclectic approach," seattletimes.com, July 29, 2007.

Others might have found us eccentric, but I didn't care. I had discovered my calling. I was a programmer.

Paul Allen, Idea Man: A Memoir by the Cofounder of Microsoft(2011).

My style was to absorb all the data I could to make the best-informed decision possible, sometimes to the point of over-analysis.

Paul Allen, Idea Man: A Memoir by the Cofounder of Microsoft(2011).

I've also seen what can happen when the right team isn't in place, how the best ideas can founder. . . . I often failed to find the right people to help me execute my vision. My own history probably swayed me to take a flier on some with slim track records and to entrust them with too much too soon. Since then I have learned to be more careful.

Paul Allen, Idea Man: A Memoir by the Cofounder of Microsoft(2011).

. . . any crusade requires optimism and the ambition to aim high. For as long as I can remember, I've wanted to find my own challenges, see them through to fruition, and—if everything breaks right—change the world for the better.

Paul Allen, Idea Man: A Memoir by the Cofounder of Microsoft(2011).

[**Q**: Why Allen wrote his book, *Idea Man*, the way he did.]

A: You are faced with a decision when you do something like this. Are you going to make it unvarnished, warts and all? Are you going to tell things as best as you could recollect them. And that was the decision that I made, but it was an easy one, based on who I am and how I've been brought up. That's just what you do. I wanted something of substance, something that was accurate, something that was honest, and I believe we achieved something like that.

Interview with Clare McGrane, "Hear Microsoft co-founder Paul Allen reflect on his life and legacy in rare public interview," geekwire.com, October 15, 2018.

[**Q**: How Allen's second bout with cancer made him both more and less patient.]

A: Whenever you go through one of these treatment regimens there are many things that are completely out of your control. You just have to be patient and hope things work out for the best, and be optimistic. Take a positive attitude. On the other hand, [you] realize that if there isn't a positive outcome, your time may be limited so it makes you that much more focused on realizing your dreams and hopes, because all of our times on this planet are limited.

Interview with Clare McGrane, "Hear Microsoft co-founder Paul Allen reflect on his life and legacy in rare public interview," geekwire.com, October 15, 2018.

[**Q**: On Allen's contribution to the funding of the Search for Extra-Terrestrial Intelligence.]

A: It's a very, very long shot, and if they do hear something, they're supposed to call me. But my Blackberry, nothing. It's not even vibrating. No, imagine how all of our lives would be stimulated and changed if there were other societies out there beyond our solar system. It's a very, very long shot. But I thought it was worth it.

Interview with Clare McGrane, "Hear Microsoft co-founder Paul Allen reflect on his life and legacy in rare public interview," geekwire.com, October 15, 2018.

Business Philosophy

There's going to be reversals. You have to be ready, to be philosophical about that.

Reported by Sally Deneen in "Paul Allen is No Second Act," success.com, January 29, 2009.

Few things worth doing can be done alone. To get past the conceptual stage, ideas need to become crusades; you've got to convince people to join you.

Paul Allen, Idea Man: A Memoir by the Cofounder of Microsoft(2011).

It's very challenging to carve back market share,

Reported by Nick Wingfield in "40 Busy Years Later, Paul Allen, a Microsoft Founder, Considers His Creation," nytimes.com, May 3, 2015.

In my experience, each failure contains the seeds of your next success—if you are willing to learn from it.

Paul Allen, Idea Man: A Memoir by the Cofounder of Microsoft(2011).

Talent is indeed essential, but seasoning and maturity are not to be underestimated. Above all, I've learned the pitfalls of getting so locked in to looking ahead that you miss the pothole that makes you stumble, or the iceberg that sinks you.

Paul Allen, Idea Man: A Memoir by the Cofounder of Microsoft(2011).

Facebook

[**Q**: On the rise of Facebook.]

A: It's amazing, if you think about it, why wasn't something like Facebook done years earlier? It could have been. There was nothing stopping that from occurring. It's just you have to have the idea. So there's always things that come down the pike, that you don't expect that suddenly affect all of our lives in a great way, and I think that's one of the wonderful aspects of technology.

Interview with Clare McGrane, "Hear Microsoft co-founder Paul Allen reflect on his life and legacy in rare public interview," geekwire.com, October 15, 2018.

Future of Information Technology

Here's what the death knell for the personal computer will sound like: Mainly I use my phone/pad, but I still use my PC to write long e-mails and documents. Most people aren't there yet, but that's where we're headed.

Paul Allen, Idea Man: A Memoir by the Cofounder of Microsoft(2011).

History shows that you ignore emerging platforms at your peril, because one of them might make you irrelevant.

Paul Allen, Idea Man: A Memoir by the Cofounder of Microsoft(2011).

Bill Gates

I was lucky right off the bat to find Bill Gates, whose passion for business matched mine for tracking technology.

Paul Allen, Idea Man: A Memoir by the Cofounder of Microsoft(2011).

[**Q**: Whether Allen's book. *Idea Man*, had jeopardized his friendship with Bill Gates.]

A: I don't think so, but I'm sure there are things in the book that Bill wants to discuss, and he'll have a different slant about them. Bill and I have had many intense discussions over the years. We haven't had a chance to talk about the book since it was published. I gave him a copy months ahead of publication. So he had a head start on it. That discussion will be very, very intense, and he'll be very direct, as will I.

Interview with Clare McGrane, "Hear Microsoft co-founder Paul Allen reflect on his life and legacy in rare public interview," geekwire.com, October 15, 2018.

Bill and I would actually dive in the dumpsters (at a local computer lab) to try to find listings of the secret inner code of the operating system, and try to figure out how it worked. That's how passionate we were.

Interview with Lesley Stahl, "Paul Allen and the birth of the PC, Microsoft," 60 Minutes, cbsnews.com, October 15, 2018.

You had to fight back intensely to stand your ground and make your position and your convictions expressed, but [Gates] didn't like to back down, so these fights would go on. They could go on for hours. You're just screaming at each other for hours. And that's exhausting. It's exhausting. But that was Bill's style.

Interview with Lesley Stahl, "Paul Allen and the birth of the PC, Microsoft," 60 Minutes, cbsnews.com, October 15, 2018.

Microsoft

What we did was unprecedented, but what is less well understood is that we had no choice.

Paul Allen, Idea Man: A Memoir by the Cofounder of Microsoft(2011).

Our great string of successes had married my vision to [Bill Gates's] unmatched aptitude for business.

Paul Allen, Idea Man: A Memoir by the Cofounder of Microsoft(2011).

For the most part, the best opportunities now lie where your competitors have yet to establish themselves, not where they're already entrenched. Microsoft is struggling to adapt to that new reality.

Paul Allen, Idea Man: A Memoir by the Cofounder of Microsoft(2011).

In a company where tech decisions were still ultracentralized, the repercussions of a distracted CEO had to be damaging.

Paul Allen, Idea Man: A Memoir by the Cofounder of Microsoft(2011).

Mukesh Dhirubhai Ambani

Mukesh Dhirubhai Ambani / b. 1957 / Aden, Yemen / Businessman, Chairman and Managing Director of Reliance Industries
Note: Though born in Yemen, Ambani's father (the founder of Reliance Industries) and mother were from the Indian state of Gujarat. The family returned to India in 1958, when the younger Ambani was only one-year-old. He was raised mostly in Mumbai (Bombay).

Ambani on Ambani

My first memories are of the early '60s at Mount Road which was then an emerging area. We were a close-knit family and the four of us—Dipti, Nina, Anil, and I—were left to do what we wanted. There were boundaries, of course, but within those, we were not micro-managed. Things have changed so much now. When my kids, Isha and Akash, were in the third standard, we behaved as though it was our exam.

Reported in "Always invest in businesses of the future and in talent," Rediff News, January 17, 2007; accessible at rediff.com.

Our own childhood was totally different. I guess when you are left on your own, you find your true potential. I remember my father never came to our school even once. Nevertheless, he was hugely interested in our all-round development for which he did some amazing things.

Reported in "Always invest in businesses of the future and in talent," Rediff News, January 17, 2007; accessible at rediff.com.

A third track running at that time, apart from academics and the fun stuff, was that my father shared with me his passion for business and entrepreneurship from very early on. Even when I was in high school, I used to spend long hours at office on weekends.

Reported in "Always invest in businesses of the future and in talent," Rediff News, January 17, 2007; accessible at rediff.com.

So, these were the four components of my upbringing—the academic stuff where I was left to myself, Mahendrabhai [Vyas—one of Ambani's teachers], my father's passion for creating Reliance, and the last piece was his deep links with the family.

Reported in "Always invest in businesses of the future and in talent," Rediff News, January 17, 2007; accessible at rediff.com.

It is easy to be with your kids and say "let's do homework together." But we try to do things, beyond doing lunches and dinners. I learnt that from my father. He was a big nature lover and during our school days, we went to different places every Sunday—we walked through the forest or had a bath in streams.

Reported in "Always invest in businesses of the future and in talent," Rediff News, January 17, 2007; accessible at rediff.com.

I have turned into a big nature fan as well. . . . I can afford it more today. These childhood influences have shaped me into what I am today.

Reported in "Always invest in businesses of the future and in talent," Rediff News, January 17, 2007; accessible at rediff.com.

Even when I was doing chemical engineering, I was working almost full time for Reliance. I finished college at 2:30 pm and went straight to the office.

Reported in "Always invest in businesses of the future and in talent," Rediff News, January 17, 2007; accessible at rediff.com.

When we started work on setting up a polyester filament yarn project, my chemical engineering and business school background helped me in organizing the work, creating reporting structures, motivating people. . . . [I]n all this, my father and Rasikbhai [Meswani—Ambani's first boss] were two steps ahead of me.

Reported in "Always invest in businesses of the future and in talent," Rediff News, January 17, 2007; accessible at rediff.com.

The first 200-odd people who built Patalganga [industrial park] with me are still around, running different businesses. It has gone into their psyche that we do things differently here. We have taken money from ordinary Indians and we are their trustees. When this is drilled into thousands of people, you automatically get performance.

Reported in "Always invest in businesses of the future and in talent," Rediff News, January 17, 2007; accessible at rediff.com.

For me, this is a moment of re-dedication to the values, vision and goals of my father, teacher and mentor, Dhirubhai Ambani. To lead by love, by trust, and by example, I learnt these principles from him with humility.

Reported by Rahul Singhal in The Legacy Continues: Ambani Brothers: Life & Times of Mukesh Dhirajlal Ambani & Anil Dhirajlal Ambani (out of print) (2002).

[A] leader is only recognized when he can resolve all differences. My father had the veto power over all decisions and that veto power is mine. But in the last ten years, he never used his veto power. He would say, once you have fired you gun you no longer have the bullet with you. . . . My father's biggest legacy was his leadership. He used to say, a leader must have followers. Respect can not be demanded . I have to get others to say what I want to say.

Reported by Rahul Singhal in The Legacy Continues: Ambani Brothers: Life & Times of Mukesh Dhirajlal Ambani & Anil Dhirajlal Ambani (out of print) (2002).

Business Philosophy

In the journey of an entrepreneur, the most important thing is self-belief and the ability to convert that belief into reality.

Reported in "Always invest in businesses of the future and in talent," Rediff News, January 17, 2007; accessible at rediff.com.

Always invest in businesses of the future and in talent.

Reported in "Always invest in businesses of the future and in talent," Rediff News, January 17, 2007; accessible at rediff.com.

One of my biggest obsessions today is that senior people must give bright 25-year-olds the opportunity to contribute meaningfully.

Reported in "Always invest in businesses of the future and in talent," Rediff News, January 17, 2007; accessible at rediff.com.

In the journey of an entrepreneur, the most important thing is self-belief and the ability to convert that belief into reality.

Reported in "Always invest in businesses of the future and in talent," Rediff News, January 17, 2007; accessible at rediff.com.

India

As my father was privileged to have witnessed in 1947, independence of India from Britain, I was privileged to have seen in 1991 India embracing economic reforms that liberated our country's entrepreneurial energies. These two transitions set India on the path of development and had a profound on the world both political economic terms.

Mukesh Ambani, "Making the Next Leap," in McKinsey & Company, Inc., eds., Reimagining India: Unlocking the Potential of Asia's Next Superpower (2013).

The performance of Reliance shows an amazing trend when mapped against time. The inflection point was 1991. We grew exponentially, eventually becoming India's biggest private enterprise, on the basis of freedom to compete against the best in the world.

Mukesh Ambani, "Making the Next Leap," in McKinsey & Company, Inc., eds., Reimagining India: Unlocking the Potential of Asia's Next Superpower (2013).

I believe India today is potentially poised for another even more stupendous leap on its upward trajectory. India's relative weight in the global economy and in world affairs in general, is bound to grow for many reasons. By 2030, India is projected to overtake China as the most populous country in the world, with the third largest economy in US dollar terms. Furthermore India is a very young nation with nearly two thirds of its population below the age of thirty-five.

Mukesh Ambani, "Making the Next Leap," in McKinsey & Company, Inc., eds., Reimagining India: Unlocking the Potential of Asia's Next Superpower (2013).

I am very bullish on India because it is really the aspiration of a billion people and ours is a county where all the billion count. There are some countries in the world where one person counts, there are some where the Politburo or 12 people count.

Reported in "Aspiration of countrymen to ensure growth: Mukesh Ambani," Hindustan Times, February 10, 2013.

I dream of India becoming one of four most powerful economies of the world. I believe this dream can be made a reality within our life times.

Reported by Rahul Singhal in The Legacy Continues: Ambani Brothers: Life & Times of Mukesh Dhirajlal Ambani & Anil Dhirajlal Ambani (out of print) (2002).

Reliance Industries

In the '80s, when I came in, the ground rules were made clear to me. 'Build this business from scratch, without taking anyone from Reliance.' That forced you to be very disciplined. I looked around and figured out in three months that this industry runs on heroes.

Reported in "Mukesh Ambani on how Reliance was built," Rediff News, January 18, 2007; accessible at rediff.com.

Even the managers. It was all a feudal style of management. If we had accepted that style, we would not have grown. It was simply not a scalable model. Of course, the easiest thing would have been to follow it. But we had a disruptive style of management. So we said, "we don't want people carrying their wisdom in notebooks as if it is some kind of secretive operation."

Reported in "Mukesh Ambani on how Reliance was built," Rediff News, January 18, 2007; accessible at rediff.com.

We were clear that we had to be internationally competitive and were passionate about building competencies that were the best in the world even when the tariffs were very high. It was an obsession with me to beat the Taiwanese and the Koreans who dominated the polyester business in the '70s.

Reported in "Mukesh Ambani on how Reliance was built," Rediff News, January 18, 2007; accessible at rediff.com.

My reference points were US companies. We were hugely influenced by large US chemical companies, especially DuPont. It was a very open company and we could take advantage of their learnings. The US is also a very open society. I could to go the US Association of Chemical Engineers and get the standards, data, etc.

Reported in "Mukesh Ambani on how Reliance was built," Rediff News, January 18, 2007; accessible at rediff.com.

I was very focussed on building various competencies in Reliance and we were not ready to do two things at the same time. It was a big risk for us to get into IT, especially because it was hugely effort-intensive. In my language, I said we have too much soap on our body and we need to take a bath in the chemicals business.

Reported in "Mukesh Ambani on how Reliance was built," Rediff News, January 18, 2007; accessible at rediff.com.

Then, we stumbled on human and plant biotech. We were fortunate to have some good people and decided that Reliance can build this business over 5–10 years without any great revenue pressures. In the mainstream business, there was telecom or what I call infocom.

Reported in "Mukesh Ambani on how Reliance was built," Rediff News, January 18, 2007; accessible at rediff.com.

We got into telecom in the '90s by bidding for cellular licences. But I felt that the real value is in the convergence of information and communication; pure communication will not deliver a sustainable value; that is why we called ourselves infocomm. It was learning a whole new domain. We brought in experts from the outside but we essentially did it with proven Reliance people

Reported in "Mukesh Ambani on how Reliance was built," Rediff News, January 18, 2007; accessible at rediff.com.

Technology

I am a big believer that technology shapes mankind.

Reported in "5 things you may not know about Mukesh Ambani," Profit NDTV, October 15, 2012; accessible at ndtv.com.

[The] Internet: the biggest discovery after [the] printing press.

Reported in "5 things you may not know about Mukesh Ambani," Profit NDTV, October 15, 2012; accessible at ndtv.com.

Mahatma Gandhi's dream of self-reliance can be attained by making use of Internet and technology.

Reported in "5 things you may not know about Mukesh Ambani," Profit NDTV, October 15, 2012; accessible at ndtv.com.

Broadband and digital services will no longer be a luxury item—a scarce commodity—to be rationed amongst the privileged few,

Reported in "Ambani bets on 4G broadband in India, but risks abound," CNBC, June 23, 2013.

Thomas Aquinas

Thomas Aquinas / 1225–1274 / Latium, Kingdom of Italy / Theologian, Philosopher
Note: All quotations are taken from *Summa Theologiae* [Summary of Theology], written between 1265 and 1274.

Action

It is natural to a man to love his own work (thus it is to be observed that poets love their own poems); and the reason is that we love to be and to live, and these are made manifest especially in our action.

Part II-II, Q. 26.

Chastity

The virtue of chastity most of all makes man apt for contemplation, since sexual pleasures most of all weigh the mind down to sensible objects.

Part II-II, Q. 180.

Death

Now among all passions inflicted from without, death holds the first place, just as sexual concupiscences are chief among internal passions. Consequently, when a man conquers death and things directed to death, his is a most perfect victory.

Part III, Supplement, Q. 96.

Friendship

When our friends fall into sin, we ought not to deny them the benefits of friendship so long as there is hope of their mending their ways, and we ought to help them more readily to regain virtue than to recover money, had they lost it, since vir- tue is more akin than money to friendship. When, however, they fall into very great wickedness, and become incurable, we ought no longer to show them friendliness.

Part II-II, Q. 25.

Because the friendship of comrades originates through their own choice, love of this kind takes precedence of the love of kindred in matters where we arc free to do as we choose, for instance in matters of action. Yet the friendship of kindred is more stable, since it is more natural, and preponderates over others in matters touching nature. Consequently we are more bound to them in the providing of necessities.

Part II-II, Q. 26.

Good and Bad

The good is what should be done and pursued, and the bad is what should be avoided.

Part I-II, Q. 94.

Happiness

Therefore man ought, out of charity, to love God, Who is the common good of all. more than himself, since happiness is in God as in the universal and fountain-head principle of all who are able to have a share of that happiness.

Part II-II, Q. 26.

Honor

Honour is not that reward of virtue, for which the virtuous work, but they receive honour from men by way of reward, as from those who have nothing greater to offer. But virtue's true reward is happiness itself, for which the virtuous work, whereas if they worked for honour, it would no longer be virtue, but ambition.

Part I-II, Q. 2.

Human Nature

Man's nature may be looked at in two ways: first, in its integrity, as it was in our first parent before sin; secondly, as it is corrupted in us after the sin of our first parent. . . . man by his natural endowments could will and do the good proportionate to his nature, such as the good of acquired virtue, but not surpassing good, as the good of infused virtue. But in the state of corrupt nature, man falls short even of what he could do by his nature, so that he is unable to fulfil it by his own natural powers. Yet because human nature is not altogether corrupted by sin, so as to be shorn of every natural good, even in the state of corrupted nature it can, by virtue of its natural endowments, work some particular good, as to build dwellings, plant vineyards, and the like; yet it cannot do all the good natural to it, so as to fall short in nothing, just as a sick man can of himself make some movements, yet he cannot be perfectly moved with the movements of one in health, unless by the help of medicine he be cured.

Part I-II, Q. 109.

Love

Charity signifies not only the love of God but also a certain friendship with Him; and this implies, besides love, a certain mutual return of love, together with mutual communion . . . Therefore just as friendship with a person would be impossible if one disbelieved in, or despaired of, the possibility of his fellowship or familiar intercourse, so too, friendship with God, which is charity, is impossible without faith, so as to believe in this fellowship and intercourse with God, and to hope to attain to this fellowship. Therefore charity is altogether impossible without faith and hope.

Part I-II, Q. 65.

Now it is evident that through every mortal sin which is contrary to God's commandments, an obstacle is placed to the outpouring of charity, since from the very fact that a man chooses to prefer sin to God's friendship, which requires that we should follow His will, it follows that the habit of charity is lost at once through one mortal sin.

Part II-II, Q. 24.

Relationships

If however we compare union with union, it is evident that the union arising from natural origin is prior to, and more stable than, all others, because it is something affecting the very substance, while other unions are something added above and may cease altogether. Therefore the friendship of kindred is more stable, while other friendships may be stronger in respect of that which is proper to each of them.

Part II-II, Q. 26.

Youth

Youth is a cause of hope for three reasons. . . . youth has much of the future before it, and little of the past; and therefore since memory is of the past, and hope of the future, it has little to remember and lives very much in hope. Again, youths, on account of the heat of their nature, are full of spirit, so that their heart expands, and it is owing to the heart being expanded that one tends to that which is arduous; therefore youths are spirited and hopeful. Likewise they who have not suffered defeat, nor had experience of obstacles to their efforts, are prone to count a thing possible to them. Therefore youths, through inexperience of obstacles and of their own shortcomings, easily count a thing possible, and consequently are of good hope.

Part I-II, Q. 40.

Hannah Arendt

Hannah Arendt / 1906–1975 / Hanover, German Empire (now Germany) / Philosopher

Collective Guilt

When all are guilty, no one is; confessions of collective guilt are the best possible safeguard against the discovery of culprits, and the very magnitude of the crime the best excuse for doing nothing.

Source: On Violence (Harcourt Brace Jovanovich, 1970).

Education

Education is the point at which we decide whether we love the world enough to assume responsibility for it, and by the same token save it from that ruin which except for renewal, except for the coming of the new and the young, would be inevitable. And education, too, is where we decide whether we love our children enough not to expel them from our world and leave them to their own devices, nor to strike from their hands their chance of undertaking something new, something unforeseen by us, but to prepare them in advance for the task of renewing a common world.

Source: "The Crisis in Education" (1959), in Hannah Arendt on Educational Thinking and Practice in Dark Times (Bloomsbury Academic, 2020).

Love

Love, by its very nature, is unworldly, and it is for this reason rather than its rarity that it is not only apolitical but antipolitical, perhaps the most powerful of all antipolitical forces.

Source: The Human Condition (University of Chicago Press, 1970).

Perpetrators of Evil

The sad truth is that most evil is done by people who never make up their minds to be good or evil.

Source: The Life of the Mind (Harcourt, Brace, 1978).

Propaganda

In an ever-changing, incomprehensible world the masses had reached the point where they would, at the same time, believe everything and nothing, think that everything was possible and that nothing was true… Mass propaganda discovered that its audience was ready at all times to believe the worst, no matter how absurd, and did not particularly object to being deceived because it held every statement to be a lie anyhow. The totalitarian mass leaders based their propaganda on the correct psychological assumption that, under such conditions, one could make people believe the most fantastic statements one day, and trust that if the next day they were given irrefutable proof of their falsehood, they would take refuge in cynicism; instead of deserting the leaders who had lied to them, they would protest that they had known all along that the statement was a lie and would admire the leaders for their superior tactical cleverness.

Source: The Origins of Totalitarianism (Harcourt Brace Jovanovich, 1973).

Radical Revolution

The most radical revolutionary will become a conservative the day after the revolution.

Source: New Yorker, September 12, 1970.

Totalitarian Rule

The ideal subject of totalitarian rule is not the convinced Nazi or the convinced Communist, but people for whom the distinction between fact and fiction (i.e., the reality of experience) and the distinction between true and false (i.e., the standards of thought) no longer exist.

Before mass leaders seize the power to fit reality to their lies, their propaganda is marked by its extreme contempt for facts as such, for in their opinion fact depends entirely on the power of man who can fabricate it.

Source: The Origins of Totalitarianism (Harcourt Brace Jovanovich, 1973).

Aristotle

Aristotle / 384–322 BC / Kingdom of Macedonia / Philosopher

Causes of Action

Every action must be due to one or other of seven causes: chance, nature, compulsion, habit, reasoning, anger, or appetite.

Rhetoric.

Divine in Man

Of all living beings with which we are acquainted man alone partakes of the divine, or at any rate partakes of it in a fuller measure than the rest.

Parts of Animals.

God (Unmoved Mover)

But since there is something which moves while itself unmoved, existing actually, this can in no way be otherwise than as it is. . . . On such a principle, then, depend the heavens and the world of nature. . . . If, then, God is always in that good state in which we sometimes are, this compels our wonder; and if in a belter this compels it yet more. And God is in a better state. And life also belongs to God; for the actuality of thought is life, and God is that actuality; and God's self-dependent actuality is life most good and eternal. We say therefore that God is a living being, eternal, most good, so that life and duration continuous and eternal belong to God; for this is God.

Metaphysics.

Does it matter, then, or not, whether it [the Unmoved Mover] thinks of the good or of any chance thing? . . . Evidently, then, it thinks of that which is most divine and precious, and it does not change; for change would be change for the worse, ... For both thinking and the act of thought will belong even to one who thinks of the worst thing in the world, so that if this ought to be avoided (and it ought, for there are even some things which it is better not to see than to see), the act of thinking cannot be the best of things. Therefore it must be of itself that the divine thought thinks (since it is the most excellent of things), and its thinking is a thinking on thinking.

Metaphysics.

Human Nature

All men naturally desire knowledge. An indication of this is our esteem for the senses; for apart from their use we esteem them for their own sake, and most of all the sense of sight. Not only with a view to action, but even when no action is contemplated, we prefer sight, generally speaking, to all the other senses. The reason of this is that of all the senses sight best helps us to know things, and reveals many distinctions.

Metaphysics.

Natural Purpose

Now a corpse has the same shape and fashion as a living body; and yet it is not a man. Again, a hand constituted in any and every manner, e.g., a bronze or wooden one, is not a hand except in name; and the same applies to a physician depicted on canvas, or a flute carved in stone. None of these can perform the functions appropriate to the things that bear those names. Likewise, the eye or the hand (or any other part) of a corpse is not really an eye or a hand. Democritus's statement, therefore, needs to be qualified, or a carpenter might as well claim that a hand made of wood really was a hand. The physiologers, however, when they describe the formation and the causes of the shape of animal bodies, talk in this selfsame vein. Suppose we ask the carver "By what agency was this hand fashioned?" Perhaps his answer will be "By my axe" or "By my auger," just as if we ask the physiologer "By what agency was this body fashioned?" he will say "By air " and "By earth." But of the two the craftsman will give a better answer, because he will not feel it is sufficient to say merely that a cavity was created here, or a level surface there, by a blow from his tool. He will state the cause on account of which, and the purpose for the sake of which, he made the strokes he did; and that will be, in order that the wood might finally be formed into this or that shape.

Parts of Animals.

If purpose, then, is inherent in art, so is it in Nature also. The best illustration is the case of a man being his own physician, for Nature is like that—agent and patient at once.

Physics.

Nature

In all things of nature there is something of the marvelous.

Parts of Animals.

Origin of Philosophy

It is through wonder that men now begin and originally began to philosophize; wondering in the first place at obvious perplexities, and then by gradual progression raising questions about the greater matters too, e.g. about the changes of the moon and of the sun, about the stars and about the origin of the universe.

Metaphysics.

Political Animal

No one would choose the whole world on condition of being alone, since man is a political creature and one whose nature is to live with others.

Nicomachean Ethics.

Man, when perfected, is the best of animals, but, when separated from law and justice, he is the worst of all; since armed injustice is the more dangerous, and he is equipped at birth with arms, meant to be used by intelligence and virtue, which he may use for the worst ends. Wherefore, if he have not virtue, he is the most unholy and the most savage of animals, and the most full of lust and gluttony.

Politics.

Rational Animal

That which is proper to each thing is by nature best and most pleasant for each thing; for man, therefore, the life according to reason is best and pleasantest, since reason more than anything else is man.

Nicomachean Ethics.

Three-Part Soul

Of the psychic powers . . . some kinds of living things . . . possess all, some less than all, others one only. Those we have mentioned are the nutritive, the appetitive, the sensory, the locomotive, and the power of thinking. Plants have none but the first, the nutritive, while another order of living things has this plus the sensory. If any order of living things has the sensory it must also have the appetitive; for appetite is the genus of which desire, passion, and wish are the species; now all animals have one sense at least, viz. touch. . . . Certain kinds of animals possess in addition the power of locomotion, and still another order of animate beings, that is, man and possibly another order like man or superior to him, the power of thinking, that is, mind.

On the Soul (De anima).

Truth

The least initial deviation from the truth is multiplied later a thousandfold.

On the Heavens (De caelo).

Virtue

. . . men must do just actions to become just, and those of self-mastery to acquire the habit of self-mastery . . . these virtues are formed in a man by his doing the actions; . . .

Nicomachean Ethics.

Bernard Jean Étienne Arnault

Bernard Jean Étienne Arnault / b. 1949 / Roubaix, France / Businessman, Investor, Art Collector, Founder and CEO of LVMH Moët Hennessy Louis Vuitton

Arnault on Arnault

I've never sought success in order to get fame and money; it's the talent and the passion that count in success.

Interview with Forbes magazine, 2014.

I have no doubt that the success of the Louis Vuitton brand is linked to the fact that we have always remained faithful to our heritage while keeping an eye on the future.

Interview with the New York Times, 2018.

I have always believed that the best way to predict the future is to invent it.

Interview with the New York Times, 2018.

Re: a trip to Mongolia:

I like to see the reaction of the people in the shops. I also like to see the competition. I am quite competitive. I want to stay ahead and increase our advance.

Reported in "Master of the Brand: Bernard Arnault," Forbes magazine, November 4, 2010; accessible at forbes.com.

I see myself as an ambassador of French heritage and French culture. What we create is emblematic. It's linked to Versailles, to Marie Antoinette.

Reported in "Master of the Brand: Bernard Arnault," Forbes magazine, November 4, 2010; accessible at forbes.com.

I remember precisely the first time I met [John Galliano] in my office. My assistant said, "There is a very strange guy in the lobby with rasta hair and a T-shirt."

Reported in "Master of the Brand: Bernard Arnault," Forbes magazine, November 4, 2010; accessible at forbes.com.

Not long ago, I said to one of our designers, "Why don't you take a trip to Japan and see what the teenage girls are wearing on the streets at night?" These girls are very leading-edge in fashion; they create trends years before they hit the mainstream, like with those very high shoes, and it makes very good sense to watch them. I did not say to the designer, "Go and see what kinds of shoes they are wearing and copy them," although I was hoping he would notice their shoes. I just suggested, "Go look." And in fact, he came home very inspired. That's all a manager can hope to do, or should do, in my opinion.

Reported by Suzy Wetlaufer in "The Perfect Paradox of Star Brands: An Interview with Bernard Arnault of LVMH," Harvard Business Review, October, 2001; accessible at hbr.org.

Business Philosophy

My definition of luxury is not necessarily about price, it's about the rarity, the quality, and the uniqueness of a product.

Interview with the New York Times, 2018.

A brand for a company is like a reputation for a person. You earn reputation by trying to do hard things well.

Interview with the Financial Times, 2007.

The luxury business is about creating desire. Desire for a product, desire for a brand, desire for a lifestyle.

Interview with the Financial Times, 2017.

Q: So, is heritage the main characteristic of a star brand?

A: I would say that there are four characteristics required. A star brand is timeless, modern, fast-growing, and highly profitable.

Q: Can a brand be all four at once?

A: It is rare. In my opinion, there are fewer than ten star brands in the luxury world. It is very hard to balance all four characteristics at once—after all, fast growth is often at odds with high profitability—but that is what makes them stars. If you have a star brand, then basically you can be sure you have mastered a paradox.

Reported by Suzy Wetlaufer in "The Perfect Paradox of Star Brands: An Interview with Bernard Arnault of LVMH," Harvard Business Review, October, 2001; accessible at hbr.org.

The key to success is this duality—timelessness and the utmost modernity.

Reported in "Master of the Brand: Bernard Arnault," Forbes magazine, November 4, 2010; accessible at forbes.com.

Mastering the paradox of star brands is very difficult and rare. Fortunately.

Reported by Suzy Wetlaufer in "The Perfect Paradox of Star Brands: An Interview with Bernard Arnault of LVMH," Harvard Business Review, October, 2001; accessible at hbr.org.

One key element of management of a group like this is decentralization. You need the right team of inspired managers.

Reported in "Master of the Brand: Bernard Arnault," Forbes magazine, November 4, 2010; accessible at forbes.com.

The responsibility of the manager in a company dependent on innovation, then, very much becomes picking the right creative people—the ones who want to see their designs on the street.

Reported by Suzy Wetlaufer in "The Perfect Paradox of Star Brands: An Interview with Bernard Arnault of LVMH," Harvard Business Review, October, 2001; accessible at hbr.org.

And just as important, to allow creativity to happen, a company has to be filled with managers who have a certain love of artists and designers—or whatever kind of creative person you have in your company. If you deeply appreciate and love what creative people do and how they think, which is usually in unpredictable and irrational ways, then you can start to understand them. And finally, you can see inside their minds and DNA.

Reported by Suzy Wetlaufer in "The Perfect Paradox of Star Brands: An Interview with Bernard Arnault of LVMH," Harvard Business Review, October, 2001; accessible at hbr.org.

Leadership

Innovation distinguishes between a leader and a follower.

Interview with Forbes magazine, 2014.

My job is not to be easy on people. My job is to make them better.

Interview with Harvard Business Review, October 1, 2010.

LVMH

Our goal for the group is to remain a family company.

Reported in "Master of the Brand: Bernard Arnault," Forbes magazine, November 4, 2010; accessible at forbes.com.

Today it's clear that the world is driven by the growth of Asia and emerging countries. Vuitton has always been a pioneer. We were the first to arrive in China. There were only bicycles when we opened there, no cars.

Reported in "Master of the Brand: Bernard Arnault," Forbes magazine, November 4, 2010; accessible at forbes.com.

So, [LVMH] keeps spending in emerging markets, which are on the forefront of growth.

Reported in "Master of the Brand: Bernard Arnault," Forbes magazine, November 4, 2010; accessible at forbes.com.

Louis Vuitton should be run as if [CEO] Yves Carcelle owns the brand.

Reported in "Master of the Brand: Bernard Arnault," Forbes magazine, November 4, 2010; accessible at forbes.com.

Re: John Galliano's dresses made of newspaper:

So, you see, with certain techniques, everyone can win, the company, the designer, and the customer.

Reported by Suzy Wetlaufer in "The Perfect Paradox of Star Brands: An Interview with Bernard Arnault of LVMH," Harvard Business Review, October, 2001; accessible at hbr.org.

I don't have alarm bells when it comes to creativity. If you think and act like a typical manager around creative people—with rules, policies, data on customer preferences, and so forth—you will quickly kill their talent. Our whole business is based on giving our artists and designers complete freedom to invent without limits.

Reported by Suzy Wetlaufer in "The Perfect Paradox of Star Brands: An Interview with Bernard Arnault of LVMH," Harvard Business Review, October, 2001; accessible at hbr.org.

Our philosophy is quite simple, really. If you look over a creative person's shoulder, he will stop doing great work. Wouldn't you, if some manager were watching your every move, clutching a calculator in his hand? So that is why LVMH is, as a company, so decentralized. Each brand very much runs itself, headed by its own artistic director. Central headquarters in Paris is very small, especially for a company with 54,000 employees and 1,300 stores around the world. There are only 250 of us, and I assure you, we do not lurk around every corner, questioning every creative decision.

Reported by Suzy Wetlaufer in "The Perfect Paradox of Star Brands: An Interview with Bernard Arnault of LVMH," Harvard Business Review, October, 2001; accessible at hbr.org.

Some companies are very marketing-driven; they follow the consumer. And they succeed with that strategy. They go out, they test what people want, and then they make it. But that approach has nothing to do with innovation, which is the ultimate driver, we believe, of growth and profitability. You can't charge a premium price for giving people what they expect, and you won't ever have break-out products that way—the kinds of products that people line up around the block for. We have those, but only because we give our artists freedom.

Reported by Suzy Wetlaufer in "The Perfect Paradox of Star Brands: An Interview with Bernard Arnault of LVMH," Harvard Business Review, October, 2001; accessible at hbr.org.

Our strategy is to trust the creators. You have to give them leeway. When a creative team believes in a product, you have to trust the team's gut instinct.

Reported by Suzy Wetlaufer in "The Perfect Paradox of Star Brands: An Interview with Bernard Arnault of LVMH," Harvard Business Review, October, 2001; accessible at hbr.org.

The fact is, star brands take time to grow. Take some of the small makeup companies we have acquired recently, like Bliss and Urban Decay. When we bought them, they were little start-ups run by their founders —very simple businesses, but with a lot of originality in the products. So now we know we must nurture them until they have some history. But even if it takes ten or 15 years for them to become stars, that has been an amazing investment, right?

Reported by Suzy Wetlaufer in "The Perfect Paradox of Star Brands: An Interview with Bernard Arnault of LVMH," Harvard Business Review, October, 2001; accessible at hbr.org.

Personal Philosophy

When you're a creative person, you constantly need to be challenged, and as you have more and more success, it becomes harder to find those challenges.

Interview with the Wall Street Journal, 2012.

I believe that in life, you have to give before you can receive.

Interview with the Wall Street Journal, 2012.

Raymond Claude Ferdinand Aron

Raymond Claude Ferdinand Aron / 1905–1983 / Paris, France / Sociologist, Political Philosopher, Historian, Journalist

Democracy

Democracy, like any non-coercive relationship, rests on a shared understanding of limits.

Plaidoyer pour l'Europe décadente (1977) / In Defense of Decadent Europe (1977).

The democracy of the rich and the democracy of the poor have this in common: both accept a certain inequality as compatible with democracy.

L'opium des intellectuels (1955) / The Opium of the Intellectuals(1957).

We are all convinced that 'democratic' means, as a matter of course, good. We are all convinced that "totalitarian: means, as a matter of course, bad."

Les guerres en chaîne (1951) / The Century of Total War (1954).

Doubt

If tolerance is born of doubt, let us teach everyone to doubt all the models and utopias, to challenge all the prophets of redemption and the heralds of catastrophe.

L'opium des intellectuels (1955) / The Opium of the Intellectuals(1957).

Foreign Policy

The test of a country's greatness is its attitude towards small nations.

Source unknown.

Anyone who does not see that there is a "struggle for power" element is naïve; anyone who sees nothing but this aspect is a false realist.

Démocratie et totalitarisme (1965) / Democracy and Totalitarianism (1968).

Yesterday's enemy is today's friend. There is no reasonable politics without the ability to forget.

La Paix et la guerre entre les nations (1962) / Peace and War: A Theory of International Relations (1966).

In politics, shared hatreds are almost always the basis of friendships.

L'opium des intellectuels (1955) / The Opium of the Intellectuals(1957).

Freedom

Liberty is not the power of doing what we like, but the right to do what we ought.

Démocratie et totalitarisme (1965) / Democracy and Totalitarianism (1968).

Freedom flourishes in temperate zones; it does not survive the burning faith of prophets and crowds.

Thinking Politically: Liberalism in the Age of Ideology (1997).

French Politics

I did not deny the fact that there was a distinction between the right and the left in the National Assembly. What I denied was that there was an eternal left, the same in various historical circumstances, inspired by the same values, united by the same aspirations.

Mémoires: 50 ans de réflexion politique (1983) / Memoirs: Fifty Years of Political Reflection (1997).

History

History teaches us that men and nations behave wisely once they have exhausted all other alternatives.

La Paix et la guerre entre les nations (1962) / Peace and War: A Theory of International Relations (1966).

History is the science of what never happens twice.

Introduction à la philosophie de l'histoire: Essai sur les limites de l'objectivité historique (1938) / Introduction to the Philosophy of History: An Essay on the Limits of Historical Objectivity (1961).

Europeans would like to escape from their history, a "great" history written in letters of blood. But others, by the hundreds of millions, are taking it up for the first time, or coming back to it.

Source unknown.

The idolater of history . . . convinced that it acts with a view to achieving the only future which is worthwhile, sees, and wants to see, the other merely as an enemy to be eliminated, and a contemptible enemy at that since he is incapable of wanting the good or of recognizing it.

L'opium des intellectuels (1955) / The Opium of the Intellectuals(1957).

The historian is an expert, not a physicist. He does not seek the causes of the explosion in the expansive force of gases, but in the smoker's match.

Source unknown.

Human Nature

Every great crisis reveals the excessive preoccupations of men.

L'opium des intellectuels (1955) / The Opium of the Intellectuals (1957).

Men accept servility in order to acquire wealth; as if they could acquire anything of their own when they cannot even acquire their own judgment.

L'opium des intellectuels (1955) / The Opium of the Intellectuals (1957).

There is no apprenticeship to misfortune. When it strikes us, we still have everything to learn.

Source unknown.

Ideology

The man who no longer expects miraculous changes either from a revolution or from an economic plan is not obliged to resign himself to the unjustifiable. It is because he likes individual human beings, participates in communities, and respects the truth, that he refuses to surrender his soul to an abstract ideal of humanity, a tyrannical party, and an absurd scholasticism.

L'opium des intellectuels (1955) / The Opium of the Intellectuals (1957).

Intellectuals

The intellectual . . . must try never to forget the arguments of the adversary, or the uncertainty of the future, or the faults of one's own side, or the underlying fraternity of ordinary men everywhere.

L'opium des intellectuels (1955) / The Opium of the Intellectuals (1957).

Rationalism

The rationalist is not unaware of the animal impulses in man, and of the passions of man in society. The rationalist has long since abandoned the illusion that men, alone or in groups, are reasonable. He bets on the education of humanity, even if he is not sure he will win his wager."

Politics and History: Selected Essays (1978).

Revolutionaries

Profoundly moralistic in regard to the present, the revolutionary is cynical in action. He protests against police brutality, the inhuman rhythm of industrial production, the severity of bourgeois courts, the execution of prisoners whose guilt has not been proved beyond doubt. Nothing, short of a total "humanization," can appease his hunger for justice. But as soon as he decides to give his allegiance to a party which is as implacably hostile as he is himself to the established disorder, we find him forgiving, in the name of the Revolution, everything he has hitherto relentlessly denounced. The revolutionary myth bridges the gap between moral intransigence and terrorism.

L'opium des intellectuels (1955) / The Opium of the Intellectuals (1957).

Are revolutions worthy of so much honor? The men who conceive them are not those who carry them out. Those who begin them rarely live to see their end, except in exile or in prison. Can they really be the symbol of a humanity which is the master of its own destiny if no man recognizes his handiwork in the achievement which results from the savage free-for-all struggle?

L'opium des intellectuels (1955) / The Opium of the Intellectuals(1957).

Skepticism

If they can abolish fanaticism, let us pray for the advent of the sceptics.

L'opium des intellectuels (1955) / The Opium of the Intellectuals(1957).

Skepticism cannot be revolutionary, even though it speaks the language of revolution.

Source unknown.

Mary Kay Ash

Mary Kay Ash (née Wagner) / 1918–2001 / Texas, USA / Businesswoman, Founder of Mary Kay Cosmetics, Inc.

Ash on Ash

There are four kinds of people in this world:

- those who make things happen
- those who watch things happen
- those who wonder what happened
- those who don't know that anything happened!

I knew from a very early age that I wanted to be first on that list.

Mary Kay Ash, Mary Kay: The Success Story of America's Most Dynamic Businesswoman, revised edition (1986).

Never forget, your family should always have priority over your work.

Mary Kay Ash, Mary Kay: You Can Have It All (1995).

To the age of 14, a woman needs good parents and good health. And then, from 14 to 40, she needs good books. From 40 to 60, she needs personality. And after 60, I'm here to tell you, what you need is cash.

Interview with Morley Safer, 60 Minutes, CBS, youtube.com, October 28, 1979.

The goal, and for us as a company, is to become the largest and the best skin care company in the world.

Interview, "The Spirit of Freedom," 1985; reported in "Lessons and Legends," you.tube.com, September 13, 2016.

I read that aerodynamics had proven that the bumblebee body was too heavy to fly and the wings were too weak, but it went right on flying, and I thought; "That's just like women. They just don't know how great they are."

Interview, "People Are Talking," 1984; reported in "Lessons and Legends," you.tube.com, September 13, 2016.

Re: Ash's 1985 leveraged buyout of Mary Kay, Inc., publicly held since 1976, returning the company to private ownership:
And how nice that no more shareholders are telling us that, now that we have become a "more mature" company, we should change our pink cadillacs to blue.

Reported in "Lessons and Legends," you.tube.com, September 13, 2016.

It's my heartfelt wish that every single person who had anything to do with Mary Kay would be the richer for it, not only financially, but spiritually, and every other way.

Reported in "Lessons and Legends," you.tube.com, September 13, 2016.

Business Philosophy

Pretend that every single person you meet has a sign around his or her neck that says, "Make me feel important." Not only will you succeed in sales, you will succeed in life.

Mary Kay Ash, Mary Kay on People Management (1984).

A mediocre idea that generates enthusiasm will go further than a great idea that inspires no one.

Mary Kay Ash, Mary Kay on People Management (1984).

People are definitely a company's greatest asset. It doesn't make any difference whether the product is cars or cosmetics. A company is only as good as the people it keeps.

Mary Kay Ash, Mary Kay on People Management (1984).

A company is only as good as the people it keeps.

Mary Kay Ash, Mary Kay: You Can Have It All (1995).

We treat our people like royalty. If you honor and serve the people who work for you, they will honor and serve you.

Mary Kay Ash, Mary Kay: You Can Have It All (1995).

There is a way: Up, Around, Over, or Through.

Mary Kay Ash, Mary Kay on People Management (1984).

The speed of the leader is the speed of the gang.

Quoted by David Holl, CEO of Mary Kay, Inc.; Mary Kay website, marykay.com.

God

God does not ask your ability or your inability. He asks only your availability.

Widely quoted; however, attribution unconfirmed.

I really feel that our company is where it is today, and has been blessed beyond all belief, by the fact that God is using our company as a vehicle to help women to become the beautiful creatures that He created.

Interview with Morley Safer, 60 Minutes, CBS, youtube.com, October 28, 1979.

Personal Philosophy

There are three types of people in this world: those who make things happen, those who watch things happen, and those who wonder what happened.

Mary Kay Ash, Mary Kay on People Management (1984).

Don't limit yourself. Many people limit themselves to what they think they can do. You can go as far as your mind lets you. What you believe, you can achieve.

Mary Kay Ash, Mary Kay on People Management (1984).

There are two things people want more than sex and money: recognition and praise.

Mary Kay Ash, Mary Kay: You Can Have It All (1995).

Note: In an article in its "Business Day" section, the *New York Times* asked several business leaders to name the book that most influenced their careers.

Ash's Reponse: *The Power of Positive Thinking* by Norman Vincent Peale is still a classic. Especially in business, if you think you can, you can. And if you think you can't, you're right.

Interview with New York Times, October 20, 1985.

Most people live and die with their music still unplayed. They never dare to try.

Mary Kay Ash, Mary Kay: The Success Story of America's Most Dynamic Businesswoman, revised edition (1986).

Don't limit yourself. Many people limit themselves to what they think they can do. You can go as far as your mind lets you. What you believe, you can achieve.

Widely quoted; however, attribution unconfirmed.

The greatest pollution problem we face today is negativity.

Widely quoted; however, attribution unconfirmed.

For every failure, there's an alternative course of action. You just have to find it.

When you come to a roadblock, take a detour.

Mary Kay Ash, Mary Kay: The Success Story of America's Most Dynamic Businesswoman, revised edition (1986).

A good goal is like a strenuous exercise—it makes you stretch. Goals should be slightly out of reach to be of maximum value.

Mary Kay Ash, Mary Kay (1981).

The only difference between successful people and unsuccessful people is extraordinary determination.

Mary Kay Ash, Mary Kay: The Success Story of America's Most Dynamic Businesswoman, revised edition (1986).

Women

While clothes may not make the woman, they certainly have a strong effect on her self-confidence, which, I believe, does make the woman.

Mary Kay Ash, Mary Kay: You Can Have It All (1995).

I want women to earn money commensurate with men. I want them to be paid on the basis of what they have between their ears, in their brains, and not because they're male or female. But at the same time, I would like women to remain feminine, because I have found that it's an asset to be female in a man's world.

Interview with Morley Safer, 60 Minutes, CBS, youtube.com, October 28, 1979.

Augustine of Hippo

Augustine of Hippo / 354–430 AD / Roman Province of Numidia (in modern Algeria) / Rhetorician, Christian prelate, Bishop of Hippo Regius

Beauty

Late have I loved you, O Beauty ever ancient and ever new! Late have I loved you! And, behold, you were within me, and I out of myself, and there I searched for you.

Source: Confessions, Book X.

Beauty grows in you to the extent that love grows, because charity itself is the soul's beauty.

Source: Homilies on the First Epistle of John, Ninth Homily.

Christianity

Nowhere in the Gospel do we read that the Lord said: "I am sending you a Paraclete who will teach you about the course of the sun and moon." For He wanted to make Christians, not mathematicians.

Source: A Debate with Felix the Manichean.

Conversion

The confession of evil works is the first beginning of good works.

Source: Tractates on the Gospel of John, Tractate XII on John 3:6–21.

Faith and Understanding

Therefore do not seek to understand in order to believe, but believe that thou mayest understand.

Source: Tractates on the Gospel of John, Tractate XXIX on John 7:14–18.

Freedom

Therefore the good man, although he is a slave, is free; but the bad man, even if he reigns, is a slave, and that not of one man, but, what is far more grievous, of as many masters as he has vices.

Source: City of God, Book IV.

God

You have made us for yourself, O Lord, and our hearts are restless until they rest in you.

Source: Confessions, Book I.

Interpretation

In matters that are so obscure and far beyond our vision, we find in Holy Scripture passages which can be interpreted in very different ways without prejudice to the faith we have received. In such cases, we should not rush in headlong and so firmly take our stand on one side that, if further progress in the search for truth justly undermines this position, we too fall with it.

Source: The Literal Meaning of Genesis.

Knowledge

We both are, and know that we are, and delight in our being, and our knowledge of it. Moreover, in these three things no true-seeming illusion disturbs us; for we do not come into contact with these by some bodily sense, as we perceive the things outside of us of all which sensible objects it is the images resembling them, but not themselves which we perceive in the mind and hold in the memory, and which excite us to desire the objects. But, without any delusive representation of images or phantasms, I am most certain that I am, and that I know and delight in this. In respect of these truths, I am not at all afraid of the arguments of the Academicians, who say, What if you are deceived? For if I am deceived, I am.

Source: City of God, Book XI.

Doubt is the origin of wisdom.

Source: City of God, Book XV.

Law

An unjust law is no law at all.

Source: On the Free Choice of the Will.

Love

I was not yet in love, yet I loved to love…I sought what I might love, in love with loving.

Source: Confessions, Book II.

As a youth I prayed, "Give me chastity and continence, but not right now."

Source: Confessions, Book VIII.

Man

People travel to wonder at the height of mountains, at the huge waves of the sea, at the long courses of rivers, at the vast compass of the ocean, at the circular motion of the stars; and they pass by themselves without wondering.

Source: Confessions, Book X.

Political Authority

Without justice what are kingdoms but great bands of robbers? And what is a band of robbers but such a kingdom in miniature?

Source: City of God, Book IV.

Political Community

A people is an assemblage of reasonable beings bound together by a common agreement as to the objects of their love,

Source: City of God, Book XIX.

Theodicy

God judged it better to bring good out of evil than to suffer no evil to exist.

Source: Enchiridion [Manual], Chapter 27.

Time

What then is time? If no one asks me, I know what it is. If I wish to explain it to him who asks, I do not know.

Source: Confessions, Book XI.

Truth

If there is something more excellent than the truth, then that is God; if not, then truth itself is God.

Source: On the Free Choice of the Will.

The Will

Will is to grace as the horse is to the rider.

Source: On the Free Choice of the Will.

Marcus Aurelius

Marcus Aurelius Antoninus / 121–180 AD / Latium, Province of Italy, Roman Empire / Emperor, Philosopher
Note: All quotes from MEDITATIONS.

Behavior

Let it be thy earnest and incessant care as a Roman and a man to perform whatsoever it is that thou art about, with true and unfeigned gravity, natural affection, freedom and justice: and as for all other cares, and imaginations, how thou mayest ease thy mind of them. Which thou shalt do; if thou shalt go about every action as thy last action, free from all vanity, all passionate and wilful aberration from reason, and from all hypocrisy, and self-love, and dislike of those things, which by the fates or appointment of God have happened unto thee.

Book II.

Brevity of Life

Worship the Gods, procure the welfare of men, this life is short. Charitable actions, and a holy disposition, is the only fruit of this earthly life.

Book VI.

If thou shouldst live three thousand, or as many as ten thousands of years, yet remember this, that man can part with no life properly, save with that little part of life, which he now lives: and that which he lives, is no other, than that which at every instant he parts with. . . . For how should a man part with that which he hath not? . . . that life which any the longest liver, or the shortest liver parts with, is for length and duration the very same, for that only which is present, is that, which either of them can lose, as being that only which they have; for that which he hath not, no man can truly be said to lose.

Book II.

Death and the Fear of Death

It is but an ordinary coarse one, yet it is a good effectual remedy against the fear of death, for a man to consider in his mind the examples of such, who greedily and covetously (as it were) did for a long time enjoy their lives. What have they got more, than they whose deaths have been untimely? Are not they themselves dead at the last? . . . For if thou shalt look backward; behold, what an infinite chaos of time doth present itself unto thee; and as infinite a chaos, if thou shalt look forward. In that which is so infinite, what difference can there be between that which liveth but three days, and that which liveth three ages?

Book IV.

Alexander of Macedon, and he that dressed his mules, when once dead both came to one. For either they were both resumed into those original rational essences from whence all things in the world are propagated; or both after one fashion were scattered into atoms.

Book VI.

Divine Part of Man

What is the present estate of my understanding? For herein lieth all indeed. As for all other things, they are without the compass of mine own will: and if without the compass of my will, then are they as dead things unto me, and as it were mere smoke.

Book XII.

If therefore whensoever the time of thy departing shall come, thou shalt readily leave all things, and shalt respect thy mind only, and that divine part of thine, and this shall be thine only fear, not that some time or other thou shalt cease to live, but thou shalt never begin to live according to nature: then shalt thou be a man indeed, worthy of that world, from which thou hadst thy beginning.

Book XII.

Of things that are external, happen what will to that which can suffer by external accidents. Those things that suffer let them complain themselves, if they will; as for me, as long as I conceive no such thing, that that which is happened is evil, I have no hurt; and it is in my power not to conceive any such thing.

Book VII.

If therefore it be a thing external that causes thy grief, know, that it is not that properly that doth cause it, but thine own conceit and opinion concerning the thing: which thou mayest rid thyself of, when thou wilt. But if it be somewhat that is amiss in thine own disposition, that doth grieve thee, mayest thou not rectify thy moral tenets and opinions. But if it grieve thee, that thou doest not perform that which seemeth unto thee right and just, why doest not thou choose rather to perform it than to grieve?

Book VIII.

Such is the nature of thy reasonable commanding part, as that if it exercise justice, and have by that means tranquillity within itself, it doth rest fully satisfied with itself without any other thing.

Book VII.

Fate and the Course of Nature

Either fate, (and that either an absolute necessity, and unavoidable decree; or a placable and flexible Providence) or all is a mere casual confusion, void of all order and government. If an absolute and unavoidable necessity, why doest thou resist? If a placable and exorable Providence, make thyself worthy of the divine help and assistance. If all be a mere confusion without any moderator, or governor, then hast thou reason to congratulate thyself; that in such a general flood of confusion thou thyself hast obtained a reasonable faculty, whereby thou mayest govern thine own life and actions.

Book XII.

How ridiculous and strange is he, that wonders at anything that happens in this life in the ordinary course of nature!

Book XII.

Whatsoever it be that happens unto thee, it is that which from all time was appointed unto thee. For by the same coherence of causes, by which thy substance from all eternity was appointed to be, was also whatsoever should happen unto it, destinated and appointed.

Book X.

Purpose of Life

In the morning, when thou risest sore against thy will, summon up this thought: “I am arising to do the work of a man. Why then this peevishness, if the way lies open to perform the tasks which I exist to perform, and for whose sake I was brought into the world? Or am I to say I was created for the purpose of lying in blankets and keeping myself warm?”

Book II.

Vanity of Fame

And as for fame. This life is short. Both he that praiseth, and he that is praised; he that remembers, and he that is remembered, will soon be dust and ashes. Besides, it is but in one corner of this part of the world that thou art praised; and yet in this corner, thou hast not the joint praises of all men; no nor scarce of any one constantly. And yet the whole earth itself, what is it but as one point, in regard of the whole world?

Book VIII.

Simone de Beauvoir

Simone de Beauvoir / 1908–1986 / France / Philosopher, Essayist, Novelist, Memoirist

Aging

Work almost always has a double aspect: it is a bondage, a wearisome drudgery; but it is also a source of interest, a steadying element, a factor that helps to integrate the worker with society. Retirement may be looked upon either as a prolonged holiday or as a rejection, a being thrown on to the scrap-heap.

La vieillesse [Old Age] (1970).

Society cares about the individual only in so far as he is profitable. The young know this. Their anxiety as they enter in upon social life matches the anguish of the old as they are excluded from it.

La vieillesse [Old Age] (1970).

Artists

In order for the artist to have a world to express he must first be situated in this world, oppressed or oppressing, resigned or rebellious, a man among men.

Pour une morale de l'ambiguïté [Towards an Ethics of Ambiguity] (1947).

Conscience

There is only one good. And that is to act according to the dictates of one's conscience.

Tous les hommes sont mortels [All Men Are Mortal] (1946].

Freedom

To will freedom and to will to disclose being are one and the same choice.

Pour une morale de l'ambiguïté [Towards an Ethics of Ambiguity] (1947).

. . . the individual is defined only by his relationship to the world and to other individuals; he exists only by transcending himself, and his freedom can be achieved only through the freedom of others.

Pour une morale de l'ambiguïté [Towards an Ethics of Ambiguity] (1947).

Generosity

That's what I consider true generosity. You give your all, and yet you always feel as if it costs you nothing.

Tous les hommes sont mortels [All Men Are Mortal] (1946).

Genius

One is not born a genius, one becomes a genius; and the feminine situation has up to the present rendered this becoming practically impossible.

Le deuxième sexe [The Second Sex] (1949).

Human Life

I wish that every human life might be pure transparent freedom.

Le sang des autres [The Blood of Others] (1945).

What has value in their eyes is never what is done for them; it's what they do for themselves.

Tous les hommes sont mortels [All Men Are Mortal] (1946).

It is impossible to do anything for anyone.

Tous les hommes sont mortels [All Men Are Mortal] (1946).

If you live long enough, you'll see that every victory turns into a defeat.

Tous les hommes sont mortels [All Men Are Mortal] (1946).

After wars peace, after peace, another war. Every day men are born and others die.

Tous les hommes sont mortels [All Men Are Mortal] (1946).

Men of today seem to feel more acutely than ever the paradox of their condition. They know themselves to be the supreme end to which all action should be subordinated, but the exigencies of action force them to treat one another as instruments or obstacles, as means. The more widespread their mastery of the world, the more they find themselves crushed by uncontrollable forces.

Pour une morale de l'ambiguïté [Towards an Ethics of Ambiguity] (1947).

The fact that we are human beings is infinitely more important than all the peculiarities that distinguish human beings from one another.

Le deuxième sexe [The Second Sex] (1949).

One's life has value so long as one attributes value to the life of others, by means of love, friendship, indignation and compassion.

La vieillesse [Old Age] (1970).

Liberation

To emancipate woman is to refuse to confine her to the relations she bears to man, not to deny them to her; let her have her independent existence and she will continue none the less to exist for him also: mutually recognising each other as subject, each will yet remain for the other an other. The reciprocity of their relations will not do away with the miracles—desire, possession, love, dream, adventure—worked by the division of human beings into two separate categories; and the words that move us—giving, conquering, uniting—will not lose their meaning. On the contrary, when we abolish the slavery of half of humanity, together with the whole system of hypocrisy that it implies, then the "division" of humanity will reveal its genuine significance and the human couple will find its true form.

Le deuxième sexe [The Second Sex] (1949).

It is for man to establish the reign of liberty in the midst of the world of the given. To gain the supreme victory, it is necessary, for one thing, that by and through their natural differentiation men and women unequivocally affirm their brotherhood.

Le deuxième sexe [The Second Sex] (1949).

Marriage

To "catch" a husband is an art; to "hold" him is a job.

Le deuxième sexe [The Second Sex] (1949).

The curse which lies upon marriage is that too often the individuals are joined in their weakness rather than in their strength, each asking from the other instead of finding pleasure in giving.

Le deuxième sexe [The Second Sex] (1949).

Maternal Instinct

It was said that I refused to grant any value to the maternal instinct and to love. This was not so. I simply asked that women should experience them truthfully and freely, whereas they often use them as excuses and take refuge in them, only to find themselves imprisoned in that refuge when those emotions have dried up in their hearts.

La force des choses [The Force of Circumstance] (two volumes) (1963).

Metaphysics

At the present time there still exist many doctrines which choose to leave in the shadow certain troubling aspects of a too complex situation. But their attempt to lie to us is in vain. Cowardice doesn't pay. Those reasonable metaphysics, those consoling ethics with which they would like to entice us only accentuate the disorder from which we suffer.

Pour une morale de l'ambiguïté [Towards an Ethics of Ambiguity] (1947).

From the very beginning, existentialism defined itself as a philosophy of ambiguity.

Pour une morale de l'ambiguïté [Towards an Ethics of Ambiguity] (1947).

Parenting

It's frightening to think that you mark your children merely by being yourself. . . . It seems unfair. You can't assume the responsibility for everything you do—or don't do.

Les Belles Images [The Beautiful Images] (1966).

Rape

To be gazed at is one danger; to be manhandled is another. Women as a rule are unfamiliar with violence, they have not been through the tussles of childhood and youth as have men; and now the girl is laid hold of, swept away in a bodily struggle in which the man is the stronger. She is no longer free to dream, to delay, to maneuver: she is in his power, at his disposal.

Le deuxième sexe [The Second Sex] (1949).

Revolutionary Politics

What did today's sacrifices matter: the Universe lay ahead in the future. What did burnings at the stake and massacres matter? The Universe was somewhere else, always somewhere else! And it isn't anywhere: there are only men, men eternally divided.

Tous les hommes sont mortels [All Men Are Mortal] (1946].

Sahara Desert

. . . the Sahara was a spectacle as alive as the sea. The tints of the dunes changed according to the time of day and the angle of the light: golden as apricots from far off, when we drove close to them they turned to freshly made butter; behind us they grew pink; from sand to rock, the materials of which the desert was made varied as much as its tints.

La force des choses [The Force of Circumstance] (two volumes) (1963).

Sartre

We were two of a kind, and our relationship would endure as long as we did: but it could not make up entirely for the fleeting riches to be had from encounters with different people.

Reported by Lisa Appignanesi in "Did Simone de Beauvoir's Open 'Marriage' Make Her Happy?," The Guardian, June 9, 2005.

Self-Knowledge

Self-knowledge is no guarantee of happiness, but it is on the side of happiness and can supply the courage to fight for it.

La force des choses [The Force of Circumstance] (two volumes) (1963).

Sexual Intercourse

From primitive times to our own, intercourse has always been considered a "service" for which the male thanks the woman by giving her presents or assuring her maintenance; but to serve is to give oneself a master; there is no reciprocity in this relation.

Le deuxième sexe [The Second Sex] (1949).

Solitude

They were walking side by side, but each was alone.

Tous les hommes sont mortels [All Men Are Mortal] (1946).

Truth

I tore myself away from the safe comfort of certainties through my love for truth—and truth rewarded me.

Tout compte fait [All Said and Done] (1972).

In spite of so many stubborn lies, at every moment, at every opportunity, the truth comes to light, the truth of life and death, of my solitude and my bond with the world, of my freedom and my servitude, of the insignificance and the sovereign importance of each man and all men. There was Stalingrad and there was Buchenwald, and neither of the two wipes out the other. Since we do not succeed in fleeing it, let us therefore try to look the truth in the face. Let us try to assume our fundamental ambiguity. It is in the knowledge of the genuine conditions of our life that we must draw our strength to live and our reason for acting.

Pour une morale de l'ambiguïté [Towards an Ethics of Ambiguity] (1947).

Women

Insects were scurrying about in the shade cast by the grass, and the lawn was a huge monotonous forest of thousands of little green blades, all equal, all alike, hiding the world from each other. Anguished, she thought, "I don't want to be just another blade of grass."

Tous les hommes sont mortels [All Men Are Mortal] (1946]; Regina.

He walks in the street, a picture of modesty in his felt hat and his gabardine suit, and all the while he's thinking, "I'm immortal." The world is his, time is his, and I'm nothing but an insect.

Tous les hommes sont mortels [All Men Are Mortal] (1946]; Regina.

All agree in recognising the fact that females exist in the human species; today as always they make up about one half of humanity. And yet we are told that femininity is in danger; we are exhorted to be women, remain women, become women. It would appear, then, that every female human being is not necessarily a woman; to be so considered she must share in that mysterious and threatened reality known as femininity.

Le deuxième sexe [The Second Sex] (1949).

One is not born, but rather becomes, a woman.

Le deuxième sexe [The Second Sex] (1949).

Samuel Beckett

Samuel Beckett / 1906–1989 / Ireland (then the United Kingdom of Great Britain and Ireland) / Poet, Short Story Writer, Literary Critic, Dramatist, Novelist
Note: Beckett lived most of his adult life in France and wrote many of his most important works in French; he translated most of these works into English himself.

Absurdity

But he had hardly felt the absurdity of those things, on the one hand, and the necessity of those others, on the other (for it is rare that the feeling of absurdity is not followed by the feeling of necessity), when he felt the absurdity of those things of which he had just felt the necessity (for it is rare that the feeling of necessity is not followed by the feeling of absurdity).

Watt (1943).

Day and Night

The sun shone, having no alternative, on the nothing new.

Murphy (1938).

One night as he sat at his table head on hands he saw himself rise and go. One night or day. For when his own light went out he was not left in the dark. Light of a kind came then from the one high window. Under it still the stool on which till he could or would no more he used to mount to see the sky. Why he did not crane out to see what lay beneath was perhaps because the window was not made to open or because he could or would not open it. Perhaps he knew only too well what lay beneath and did not wish to see it again. So he would simply stand there high above the earth and see through the clouded pane the cloudless sky. Its faint unchanging light unlike any light he could remember from the days and nights when day followed hard on night and night on day. This outer light then when his own went out became his only light till it in its turn went out and left him in the dark. Till it in its turn went out.

"Stirrings Still" (1988).

Death

"Christ!" he said, "it's alive."
His aunt looked at the lobster. It moved again. It made a faint nervous act of life on the oilcloth. They stood above it, looking down on it, exposed cruciform on the oilcloth. It shuddered again. Belacqua felt he would be sick.
"My God," he whined, "it's alive, what'll we do?"
The aunt simply had to laugh. She bustled off to the pantry to fetch her smart apron, leaving him goggling down at the lobster, and came back with it on and her sleeves rolled up, all business.
"Well," she said, "it's to be hoped so, indeed."
"All this time," muttered Belacqua. Then suddenly aware of her hideous equipment: "What are you going to do?" he cried.
"Boil the beast," she said, "what else?"

"But it's not dead," protested Belacqua, "you can't boil it like that."
She looked at him in astonishment. Had he taken leave of his senses?
"Have sense," she said sharply, "lobsters are always boiled alive. They must be." She caught up the lobster and laid it on its back. It trembled. "They feel nothing," she said.
In the depths of the sea it had crept into the cruel pot. For hours, in the midst of its enemies, it had breathed secretly. It had survived the Frenchwoman's cat and his witless clutch. Now it was going alive into scalding water. It had to. Take into the air my quiet breath.
Belacqua looked into the old parchment of her face, grey in the dim kitchen.
"You make a fuss," she said angrily, "and upset me and then lash into it for your dinner."
She lifted the lobster clear of the table. It had about thirty seconds to live.
Well, thought Belacqua, it's a quick death, God help us all.
It is not.

"Dante and the Lobster," in More Pricks Than Kicks (1934).

I shall soon be quite dead at last in spite of all. Perhaps next month. Then it will be the month of April or of May. For the year is still young, a thousand little signs tell me so. Perhaps I am wrong, perhaps I shall survive Saint John the Baptist's Day and even the Fourteenth of July, festival of freedom. Indeed I would not put it past me to pant on to the Transfiguration, not to speak of the Assumption. But I do not think so, I do not think I am wrong in saying that these rejoicings will take place in my absence, this year.

Malone meurt [Malone Dies] (1951).

Birth was the death of him.

"A Piece of Monologue" (1979).

Failure

All of old. Nothing else ever. Ever tried. Ever failed. No matter. Try again. Fail again. Fail better.

"Worstward Ho" (1983).

God

God is a witness that cannot be sworn.

Watt (1943).

Language

Every word is like an unnecessary stain on silence and nothingness.

Reported by John Gruen in "Samuel Beckett Talks About Beckett," Vogue, December, 1969.

The expression that there is nothing to express, nothing with which to express, nothing from which to express, no power to express, no desire to express, together with the obligation to express.

"Three Dialogues," with Georges Duthuit, transition 49, 1949.

Life

Personally of course I regret everything. Not a word, not a deed, not a thought, not a need, not a grief, not a joy, not a girl, not a boy, not a doubt, not a trust, not a scorn, not a lust, not a hope, not a fear, not a smile, not a tear, not a name, not a face, no time, no place, that I do not regret, exceedingly. An ordure, from beginning to end.

Watt (1943).

In me there have always been two fools, among others, one asking nothing better than to stay where he is and the other imagining that life might be slightly less horrible a little further on.

Molloy [Molloy] (1951).

Estragon: Nothing to be done.
Vladimir: I'm beginning to come round to that opinion.

En attendant Godot (Waiting for Godot) (1952).

. . . it will be the silence, where I am, I don't know, I'll never know, in the silence you don't know, you must go on, I can't go on, I'll go on.

L'Innomable [The Unnamable] (1953).

Curtain.
1. Faint light on stage littered with miscellaneous rubbish. Hold for about five seconds.
2. Faint brief cry and immediately inspiration and slow increase of light together reaching maximum together in about ten seconds. Silence and hold about five seconds.
3. Expiration and slow decrease of light together reaching minimum together (light as in 1.) in about ten seconds and immediately cry as before. Silence and hold for about five seconds.

"Breath" (1969).

Man

For the only way one can speak of nothing is to speak of it as though it were something, just as the only way one can speak of God is to speak of him as though he were a man, which to be sure he was, in a sense, for a time, and as the only way one can speak of man, even our anthropologists have realized that, is to speak of him as though he were a termite.

Watt (1943).

Nothing

Nothing is more real than nothing.

Malone meurt [Malone Dies] (1951).

Sin

The only sin is the sin of being born.

Reported by John Gruen in "Samuel Beckett Talks About Beckett," Vogue magazine, December, 1969.

Unhappiness

Nell: Nothing is funnier than unhappiness.
Nagg: Oh?
Nell: Yes, yes, it's the most comical thing in the world. And we laugh, we laugh, with a will, in the beginning. But it's always the same thing. Yes, it's like the funny story we have heard too often, we still find it funny, but we don't laugh any more.

Fin de partie [Endgame] (1957).

Thomas Bernhard

Thomas Bernhard / 1931–1989 / The Netherlands / Poet, Short Story Writer, Novelist, Dramatist
Note: Though born in the Netherlands, from infancy Bernhard lived mainly in Austria.

Ambition

My ambition has always been greater than my strength.

Ein Kind [A Child] (1982).

Death

The world is the school of death. At first the world is the *elementary school* of death, then the *middle school* of death, then, *for very few, . . .* it is the *university of death.*

Verstörung [Disturbance] (1967).

Our whole life is but an approach to the extreme limits of life itself.

Verstörung [Disturbance] (1967).

Distraction

I try to distract myself from myself, but now I only succeed sporadically.

Verstörung [Disturbance] (1967).

Existence

We are not even able to live, we are not able to exist, since in truth we do not exist, but rather are being existed.

Der Untergeher [The Loser] (1983).

Exaggeration

We often go so far into an exaggeration . . . that we end up considering that exaggeration the only coherent fact, and we no longer even perceive the real fact, but only the exaggeration pushed to the extreme beyond measure.

Auslöschung: Ein Zerfall [Extinction: A Disintegration] (1986).

Happiness

He would have been even more unhappy if overnight he had lost his unhappiness.

Der Untergeher [The Loser] (1983).

Humanity

He hated people who talk without having finished thinking, so he hated almost all of humanity.

Der Untergeher [The Loser] (1983).

Wertheimer was not capable of seeing himself as a unique being in the world, while in fact this is how each of us can and must allow himself to see himself if he does not want to fall prey to despair, every human being, however he is made, is a unique being in the world, I tell myself this constantly and with this I am saved.

Der Untergeher [The Loser] (1983).

Illness

The patient is a seer, no one has a clearer picture of the world than his.

Der Atem: Eine Entscheidung [The Breath: A Decision] (1978).

There is no more widespread hypocrisy than that of the healthy towards the sick. Basically, the healthy no longer want to have anything to do with the sick and they are not at all happy that the sick, I'm talking about the real sick, that is to say the seriously ill, suddenly demand to return to good health, or at least to normalize or at least to improve their health conditions. The healthy, if he is a sincere person, will admit that he no longer wants to have anything to do with the sick, he does not want anyone to remind him of disease and, through disease, logically and forcibly, death.

Wittgensteins Neffe: Eine Freundschaft [Wittgenstein's Nephew: A Friendship] (1982).

Knowledge

Real clarity is not possible, but only a generic, approximate clarity, effective knowledge is not possible, but only approximate, everything is always only approximate and can always be only approximate.

Korrektur [Correction] (1975).

We are wrong when we believe we are right and vice versa. The path of the absurd is the only practicable one.

Die Kälte: Eine Isolation [The Cold: A Confinement] (1981).

Men walk together, talk together, sleep together, but they don't know each other. If men knew each other they wouldn't walk together, they wouldn't talk together, they wouldn't sleep together.

Verstörung [Disturbance] (1967).

Language

Language is of no use when it comes to telling the truth, to communicating something, language allows the writer only approximation, always and only the desperate and therefore also dubious approximation to the object, language only reproduces a counterfeit authenticity, a terrifyingly deformed picture, although the writer takes a great deal of effort, the words trample and deform everything, and on paper they transform the absolute truth into a lie.

Die Kälte: Eine Isolation [The Cold: A Confinement] (1981).

I speak a language that I alone understand, no one else, just as everyone speaks only their own language, and those who think they understand are imbeciles or charlatans.

Der Keller: Eine Entziehung [The Cellar: A Withdrawal] (1976).

Life

Life is a penitentiary with very little freedom of movement. Hopes turn out to be misunderstandings.

Die Kälte: Eine Isolation [The Cold: A Confinement] (1981).

After all, I haven't traveled a road, probably because I've always been afraid of taking an endless and therefore meaningless road. If I wanted, I said to myself every time, I could do it. But I didn't take any road. Something happened, I got older, I didn't stand still, but I didn't take any road.

Der Keller: Eine Entziehung [The Cellar: A Withdrawal] (1976).

There are men [...] who are content with life in its raw state and don't bother working with it, the raw material is enough for them.

Verstörung [Disturbance] (1967).

Vulgarity is all around us, and every day, inevitably, we suffocate in imbecility.

Ein Kind [A Child] (1982).

Life was a tragedy, and we could at best turn it into a comedy.

Ein Kind [A Child] (1982).

Love

There is no person in the world that we have the right to bind to us against his will.

Der Untergeher [The Loser] (1983).

Marriage

. . . contracting a marriage, like making a friendship, means deciding to bear in full awareness a situation of double despair and double exile, it means passing from the antehell of solitude to the hell of life in common.

Das Kalkwerk [The Lime Works] (1970).

Parents

The child had been thrown into this cog of existence by the mother, the father kept this cog of existence constantly going, which relentlessly tore the child to pieces. Parents know perfectly well that the unhappiness inherent in them is perpetuated in their children, but in their cruelty they go on to have children and throw them into the machinery of existence.

Der Untergeher [The Loser] (1983).

Perception

We force ourselves not to perceive our abyss. Yet, throughout our lives, we do nothing but look *down* at our physical and psychic abyss, even without perceiving it.

Verstörung [Disturbance] (1967).

Poetry and Philosophy

Poets . . . use that truth that philosophers cannot use.

Verstörung [Disturbance] (1967).

Questions

We keep our questions in reserve because we fear them ourselves, then suddenly it's too late to ask them. We want to leave the questioned alone, we don't want to hurt him deeply because we want to leave ourselves alone and not hurt ourselves deeply. We postpone the decisive questions and ask ridiculous, useless and petty questions over and over again, and when we ask the decisive questions it is already too late.

Die Kälte: Eine Isolation [The Cold: A Confinement] (1981).

School

I was shaking going into school, crying out of school. I went to school as one goes to the gallows, my beheading was always only postponed, and this was torture for me.

Ein Kind [A Child] (1982).

Schools are only factories of imbecility and depravity.

Ein Kind [A Child] (1982).

It is the school itself . . . that murders the child.

Ein Kind [A Child] (1982).

Solitude

On the one hand we, people like us, are unable to be alone, on the other we can't stand company.

Beton [Concrete] (1982).

Every man, regardless of what he is and totally regardless of what he does, is continually driven back into himself, every man is a nightmare left only to himself.

Der Keller: Eine Entziehung [The Cellar: A Withdrawal] (1976).

Each of us is completely isolated in himself, even if the bond between us is very close. The whole of life is nothing but an uninterrupted attempt to find each other.

Verstörung [Disturbance] (1967).

Titles

The bigger the title sounds, the bigger the imbecile who bears it.

Auslöschung: Ein Zerfall [Extinction: A Disintegration] (1986).

Words

I've always taken big words and high-sounding phrases for what they are: manifestations of incompetence that shouldn't be ignored.

Der Keller: Eine Entziehung [The Cellar: A Withdrawal] (1976).

Work

To fight the nonsense, get out of bed, work and think immersed in nothing but nonsense. . . . Waking up, starting work and continuing until you drop, until your eyes can't and don't want to see anymore, stop, turn off the light, fall at the mercy of nightmares, surrender to them as if to an unparalleled ceremony. And the next morning do the same thing again, with the utmost precision, with the utmost concentration, *pretending that it all means something.*

Die Kälte: Eine Isolation [The Cold: A Confinement] (1981).

Françoise Bettencourt Meyers

Françoise Bettencourt Meyers / b. 1953 / Neuilly-sur-Seine, France / Businesswoman, Entrepreneur, Author, Heiress to the L'Oréal fortune

Beauty

Beauty is a reflection of inner balance, and the more we take care of our health, the more beautiful we become.

Interview with Forbes magazine, 2017.

Diversity

It is also important to recognize the value of diversity and inclusivity in achieving success. By embracing diverse perspectives and experiences, we can come together to create innovative solutions and drive positive change in the world.

Statement, "Françoise Bettencourt Meyers: the billionaire heiress who wants to change the world!," youtube.com, March 14, 2023.

Education

I believe that education is the key to a better future for everyone.

Interview with Vanity Fair, 2020.

I believe that knowledge and intellectual curiosity are essential qualities for a successful life.

Interview with Women's Wear Daily, 2016.

Reading has always been a very important part of my life. It allows us to travel through time, to discover other cultures, and to open our minds to new ideas.

Interview with Le Point magazine, 2020.

For me, [making a positive impact] starts with a deep commitment to lifelong learning and personal growth. I believe that we are all capable of achieving incredible things, but it requires a willingness to continually push ourselves out of our comfort zones and expand our knowledge and skills.

Statement, "Françoise Bettencourt Meyers: the billionaire heiress who wants to change the world!," youtube.com, March 14, 2023.

Environment

I believe that businesses have a responsibility to be environmentally sustainable and socially responsible.

Interview with The Guardian, 2019.

Family Feud

These accusations are unbearable! And totally groundless. There is a perfect continuity in the family's attachment to L'Oréal across generations.

Reported by Miles Socha in "Le Monde's M Magazine Interviews Françoise Bettencourt Meyers," Women's Wear Daily, March 12, 2012; accessible at wwd.com.

Re: Bettencourt Meyers's mother, Liliane Bettencourt:

[François-Marie Banier's] objective is clear: break away my mother from our family to profit from her. I will not let it happen.

Reported by Avery Hartmans in "Meet billionaire L'Oréal heiress Françoise Bettencourt Meyers, the richest woman in the world, who has a net worth of $82.1 billion," businessinsider.com, February 12, 2023.

[It felt as if Liliane] was pulled into a sect by a guru who cut me off from my family.

Reported by Rob Wile in "Meet the New 'World's Richest Woman,' a 64-Year-Old Expert on Greek Gods Who Shuns the Spotlight," money.com, September 29, 2017.

Inherited Wealth

Inheritance is a responsibility. You have to make sure that what you inherited will last for the next generation.

Interview with The New York Times, 2019.

Giving back to society is a fundamental value of our family.

Interview with Forbes magazine, 2019.

L'Oréal

Re: Impact of Liliane's death:

In this painful moment for us, I would like to reiterate, on behalf of our family, our entire commitment and loyalty to L'Oréal and to renew my confidence in its President Jean-Paul Agon and his teams worldwide," she said in a statement on Thursday.

*Reported by **Tom Metcalf** and **Devon Pendleton** in "Piano-loving L'Oreal heiress Francoise Bettencourt Meyers becomes world's richest woman," Sydney Morning Herald, September 23, 2017; accessible at smh.com.*

As the Chairwoman of the family holding company for L'Oréal, I have been fortunate to witness firsthand the power of innovation, dedication, and collaboration. But beyond just business success, what inspires me most is the potential that we all have to make a positive impact.

Statement, "Françoise Bettencourt Meyers: the billionaire heiress who wants to change the world!," youtube.com, March 14, 2023.

Personal Philosophy

Money doesn't make you happy. It can help, of course, but happiness comes from within.

Interview with Forbes magazine, 2019.

Money doesn't bring happiness. What brings happiness is being able to do good things for other people.

Interview with Marie Claire magazine, 2020.

The greatest gift you can give yourself is the gift of knowledge.

Interview with The Guardian, 2019.

The best way to help others is to lead by example.

Interview with Forbes magazine, 2019.

The more people you help, the more successful you are.

Interview with The New York Times, 2019.

Success is not measured by wealth or power, but by the impact we have on the world around us.

Interview with The Guardian, 2021.

Generosity is an essential part of our human nature, and we should embrace it as a virtue that makes the world a better place.

Interview with Le Figaro, 2016.

. . . I believe that success is not just about achieving financial wealth or status. True success comes from living a meaningful and purpose-driven life, and using our resources and abilities to make a positive impact on the world around us.

Statement, "Françoise Bettencourt Meyers: the billionaire heiress who wants to change the world!," youtube.com, March 14, 2023.

I want to encourage all of you to embrace your own unique abilities and passions, and to use them to create positive change in the world. Each and every one of us has the potential to make a difference, and it is up to us to embrace this potential and bring our ideas and visions to life.

Statement, "Françoise Bettencourt Meyers: the billionaire heiress who wants to change the world!," youtube.com, March 14, 2023.

In closing, I want to express my deep gratitude for the opportunity to speak with you today, and I wish you all the best on your own personal journeys of growth, learning, and making a positive impact in the world.

Statement, "Françoise Bettencourt Meyers: the billionaire heiress who wants to change the world!," youtube.com, March 14, 2023.

Philanthropy

Philanthropy is a natural extension of my family's values, which place great importance on generosity and on taking responsibility for others.

Interview with The New York Times, 2019.

The power of money is not in the money itself, but in what we do with it.

Interview with Madame Figaro newspaper supplement, 2020.

Philanthropy is not just about giving money; it's about using our resources to create positive change in the world.

Interview with the Financial Times, 2020.

One of the key lessons that I have learned over the years is the importance of giving back to others. Whether it is through philanthropy, volunteer work, or simply showing kindness and compassion to those around us, giving back is essential to living a fulfilling life.

Statement, "Françoise Bettencourt Meyers: the billionaire heiress who wants to change the world!," youtube.com, March 14, 2023.

Technology

Technology has the power to transform our lives, but it's important to ensure that it's being used for good.

Interview with CNBC, 2020.

We have to be very careful about the way we use technology. It can be very helpful, but it can also be very harmful.

Interview with BBC News, 2018.

Women

Women have always played a crucial role in society, but their contributions have often been overlooked or undervalued. It's time to change that

Speech, Women in Science Awards Ceremony, UNESCO, Paris, March 22, 2018.

Women have a responsibility to support each other and work together to achieve our goals.

Interview with Elle magazine, 2019.

The world is changing, and so are the needs and aspirations of women.

Interview with The New York Times, 2019.

Jeffrey Preston Bezos

Jeffrey Preston Bezos (né Jorgensen) / b. 1964 / New Mexico, USA / Entrepreneur, Founder of Amazon.com

Amazon

What I would really like people to say about Amazon is that we raised the bar on customer experience for every industry all over the world. Some companies have missions that are even bigger than the company; an example of that would be Sony. Sony, coming out of World War II, said that their mission was, "We are going to make Japan known for quality." They had a mission that was bigger than Sony. It was a mission for Japan. And we have a similar mission.

Reported by Cal Fussman, "Jeff Bezos: What I've Learned," Esquire, January 1, 2002.

If everything you do needs to work on a three-year time horizon, then you're competing against a lot of people. But if you're willing to invest on a seven-year time horizon, you're now competing against a fraction of those people, because very few companies are willing to do that. Just by lengthening the time horizon, you can engage in endeavors that you could never otherwise pursue. At Amazon we like things to work in five to seven years. We're willing to plant seeds, let them grow—and we're very stubborn. . . . We've had three big ideas at Amazon that we've stuck with for 18 years, and they're the reason we're successful: Put the customer first. Invent. And be patient.

Reported by Tren Griffin, "A Dozen Things I have Learned from Jeff Bezos," 25iq.com, April 26, 2014.

We will make bold rather than timid investment decisions where we see a sufficient probability of gaining market leadership advantages. Some of these investments will pay off, others will not, and we will have learned another valuable lesson in either case.

Reported by Tren Griffin, "A Dozen Things I have Learned from Jeff Bezos," 25iq.com, April 26, 2014.

Bezos on Bezos

I'm certainly the kind of person that has to grow on a woman. It takes repeated exposure to wear down her defenses.

Reported by Cal Fussman, "Jeff Bezos: What I've Learned," Esquire, January 1, 2002.

I wear the same thing every weekday, and I have for ten years. I don't like to think about what I want to wear in the morning. You should definitely stay away from asking me fashion questions.

Reported by Cal Fussman, "Jeff Bezos: What I've Learned," Esquire, January 1, 2002.

Sometimes I think the *Time* Person of the Year is chosen for the man, and I think sometimes they are chosen as a symbol of something, and my selection was clearly that. They weren't choosing Jeff Bezos so much as they were choosing me as a symbol for the Internet. Yeah, my parents were very proud. I mean, they are parents. They are not objective.

Reported by Cal Fussman, "Jeff Bezos: What I've Learned," Esquire, January 1, 2002.

Business

What characteristics do I look for when hiring somebody? That's one of the questions I ask when interviewing. I want to know what kind of people they would hire.

Reported by Cal Fussman, "Jeff Bezos: What I've Learned," Esquire, January 1, 2002.

Debt is a useful invention. It's why people can afford houses before they reach seventy. They can actually have the house while they need it and then work and pay for it. That's very, very useful.

Reported by Cal Fussman, "Jeff Bezos: What I've Learned," Esquire, January 1, 2002.

Morale comes not from things that you layer on to make people happy. It comes from being able to build. People like to build. The question is, Could it be done? The answer is, Absolutely.

Reported by Cal Fussman, "Jeff Bezos: What I've Learned," Esquire, January 1, 2002.

Percentage margins are not one of the things we are seeking to optimize. . . . What matters always is dollar margins: the actual dollar amount. Companies are valued not on their percentage margins, but on how many dollars they actually make, and a multiple of that. . . . When forced to choose between optimizing the appearance of our GAAP accounting and maximizing the present value of future cash flows, we'll take the cash flows.

Reported by Tren Griffin, "A Dozen Things I have Learned from Jeff Bezos," 25iq.com, April 26, 2014.

Your margin is my opportunity.

Reported by Tren Griffin, "A Dozen Things I have Learned from Jeff Bezos," 25iq.com, April 26, 2014.

Market leadership can translate directly to higher revenue, higher profitability, greater capital velocity, and correspondingly stronger returns on invested capital.

Reported by Tren Griffin, "A Dozen Things I have Learned from Jeff Bezos," 25iq.com, April 26, 2014.

The balance of power is shifting toward consumers and away from companies . . . the individual is empowered. . . . The right way to respond to this if you are a company is to put the vast majority of your energy, attention and dollars into building a great product or service and put a smaller amount into shouting about it, marketing it. . . . Your brand is formed primarily, not by what your company says about itself, but what the company does.

Reported by Tren Griffin, "A Dozen Things I have Learned from Jeff Bezos," 25iq.com, April 26, 2014.

The great thing about fact-based decisions is that they overrule the hierarchy.

Reported by Tren Griffin, "A Dozen Things I have Learned from Jeff Bezos," 25iq.com, April 26, 2014.

Freedom

People think of liberty or freedom as being happiness, but it's not. Those very smart people who wrote "Life, liberty, and the pursuit of happiness" had it right.

Reported by Cal Fussman, "Jeff Bezos: What I've Learned," Esquire, January 1, 2002.

Human Nature

It's impossible to interact with an eighteen-month-old child and not come away with the impression that people are fundamentally good.

Reported by Cal Fussman, "Jeff Bezos: What I've Learned," Esquire, January 1, 2002.

I really think very, very deep in the human psyche there is this need to explore. The pre-Einstein people didn't know that there were any limits to speed. And one of the things that comes out of Einstein's theory is that the speed of light is an absolute limit, that you can't go faster than that. And that seems unfair to me.

Reported by Cal Fussman, "Jeff Bezos: What I've Learned," Esquire, January 1, 2002.

Innovation

There'll always be serendipity involved in discovery. . . . If you double the number of experiments you do per year you're going to double your inventiveness.

Reported by Tren Griffin, "A Dozen Things I have Learned from Jeff Bezos," 25iq.com, April 26, 2014.

I believe you have to be willing to be misunderstood if you're going to innovate.

Reported by Tren Griffin, "A Dozen Things I have Learned from Jeff Bezos," 25iq.com, April 26, 2014.

I think frugality drives innovation, just like other constraints do. One of the only ways to get out of a tight box is to invent your way out.

Reported by Tren Griffin, "A Dozen Things I have Learned from Jeff Bezos," 25iq.com, April 26, 2014.

If you decide that you're going to do only the things you know are going to work, you're going to leave a lot of opportunity on the table. Companies are rarely criticized for the things that they failed to try. But they are, many times, criticized for things they tried and failed at.

Reported by Tren Griffin, "A Dozen Things I have Learned from Jeff Bezos," 25iq.com, April 26, 2014.

Internet Commerce

On the Internet, companies are scale businesses, characterized by high fixed costs and relatively low variable costs. You can be two sizes: You can be big, or you can be small. It's very hard to be medium. A lot of medium-sized companies had the financing rug pulled out from under them before they could get big.

Reported by Tren Griffin, "A Dozen Things I have Learned from Jeff Bezos," 25iq.com, April 26, 2014.

Life Lessons

My grandfather taught me that it is harder to be kind than it is to be clever. That has always stuck with me.

Reported by Cal Fussman, "Jeff Bezos: What I've Learned," Esquire, January 1, 2002.

Go to bed early and wake up early. The morning hours are good.

Reported by Cal Fussman, "Jeff Bezos: What I've Learned," Esquire, January 1, 2002.

Everyone always says that parenting is not a popularity contest. I think that grandparenting is.

Reported by Cal Fussman, "Jeff Bezos: What I've Learned," Esquire, January 1, 2002.

At the end of the day, when you're eighty years old and looking back on your life, you want to have minimized the number of regrets you have. That's what should drive people. Not how much money they have. It's regrets that I think haunt people at the end of their life.

Reported by Cal Fussman, "Jeff Bezos: What I've Learned," Esquire, January 1, 2002.

Love

Love and sex? People will die for love.

Reported by Cal Fussman, "Jeff Bezos: What I've Learned," Esquire, January 1, 2002.

When you're a little kid, you have no idea how much your parents love you.

Reported by Cal Fussman, "Jeff Bezos: What I've Learned," Esquire, January 1, 2002.

Prediction

The landscape is littered with the corpses of people who have made predictions, so I won't try to predict what America will look like a hundred years from now. Nobody remembers what you said anyway, unless you're Nostradamus.

Reported by Cal Fussman, "Jeff Bezos: What I've Learned," Esquire, January 1, 2002.

Virtue

When you're young, deferring gratification is not a honed skill. As you get older, you get better at the marathon mentality.

Reported by Cal Fussman, "Jeff Bezos: What I've Learned," Esquire, January 1, 2002.

People need to think of themselves as fortunate.

Reported by Cal Fussman, "Jeff Bezos: What I've Learned," Esquire, January 1, 2002.

Ambrose Bierce

Ambrose Bierce / 1842–c. 1914 / Ohio, USA / Poet, Short Story Author, Journalist
Note: All quotations taken from The Devil's Dictionary (1911).
Achievement, n. The death of endeavor and the birth of disgust.
Admiration, n. Our polite recognition of another's resemblance to ourselves.
Applause, n. The echo of a platitude.
Back, n. That part of your friend which it is your privilege to contemplate in your adversity.
Blackguard, n. A man whose qualities, prepared for display like a box of berries in a market—the fine ones on top—have been opened on the wrong side. An inverted gentleman.
Bore, n. A person who talks when you wish him to listen.
Childhood, n. The period of human life intermediate between the idiocy of infancy and the folly of youth—two removes from the sin of manhood and three from the remorse of age.
Christian, n. One who believes that the New Testament is a divinely inspired book admirably suited to the spiritual needs of his neighbor. One who follows the teachings of Christ in so far as they are not inconsistent with a life of sin.
Consul, n. In American politics, a person who having failed to secure an office from the people is given one by the Administration on condition that he leave the country.
Conversation, n. A fair for the display of minor mental commodities, each exhibitor being too intent upon the arrangement of his own wares to observe those of this neighbor.
Cynic, n. A blackguard whose faulty vision sees things as they are, not as they ought to be.
Dog, n. A kind of additional or subsidiary Deity designed to catch the overflow and surplus of the world's worship. This Divine Being in some of his smaller and silkier incarnations, takes, in the affection of Woman, the place to which there is no human male aspirant.
Edible, adj. Good to eat, and wholesome to digest, as a worm to a toad, a toad to a snake, a snake to a pig, a pig to a man, and a man to a worm.
Education, n. That which discloses to the wise and disguises from the foolish their lack of understanding.
Exile, n. One who serves his country by residing abroad, yet is not an ambassador.
Handkerchief, n. A small square of silk or linen, used in various ignoble offices about the face and especially serviceable at funerals to conceal the lack of tears.
Hearse, n. Death's baby-carriage.
Idleness, n. A model farm where the devil experiments with seeds of new sins and promotes the growth of staple vices.
Kilt, n. A costume sometimes worn by Scotchmen in America and Americans in Scotland.
Labor, n. One of the processes by which A acquires property for B.
Litigation, n. A machine which you go into as a pig and come out as a sausage.

Marriage, n. A community consisting of a master, a mistress, and two slaves, making in all, two.

Notoriety, n. The fame of one's competitor for public honors. The kind of renown most accessible and acceptable to mediocrity.

Prejudice, n. A vagrant opinion without visible means of support.

Telescope, n. A device having a relation to the eye similar to that of the telephone to the ear, enabling distant objects to plague us with a multitude of needless details.

Conrad Moffat Black

Conrad Moffat Black / b. 1944 / Montreal, Quebec, Canada / Businessman, Newspaper Publisher, Author, Owner of Argus Corporation, Ravelston Corporation, and Hollinger International, among others

Argus Corporation

Bud [McDougald] was a true Darwinist, so in his view, when he died—to the winner should go the spoils. It was a free-for-all. A lot of people, Nelson Davis for one, used to ask me what Bud would have thought of the somewhat unseemly scramble that went on after he died. I suspect it would have flattered him. Had he wanted an orderly succession, he would have organized one. He certainly told Monte and me that he wanted us to take over—but he told a few other people the same thing. Bud was very skillful at presenting the carrot and making sure it wasn't within anyone's grasp.

Statement, 1978; reported by Peter C. Newman in The Establishment Man: A Portrait of Power (1982).

Black on Black

I tended, even from my early years, to look at the world from a slightly different vantage point. Although I might have had trouble articulating it at the age of 10, I wasn't unduly convinced of the durability of the Anglo-Saxon world as we had come to know it in the postwar period, a world of latter-day materialism advancing around the globe on the wings of the English language and the American dollar. I had a sneaking suspicion that we were living in a bit of a fool's paradise.

Interview with Peter C. Newman, reported in The Establishment Man: A Portrait of Power (1982).

All those who, by their docility or obsequiousness, legitimized the excesses of the school's penal system, the several sadists and few aggressively fondling homosexuals on the faculty, and the more numerous swaggering boobies who had obviously failed in the real world and retreated to Lilliput where they could maintain their exalted status by constant threat of battery: all gradually produced in me a profound revulsion.

Conrad Black, A Life In Progress (1993).

I have always felt it was the compulsive element in Napoleon that drew him into greater and greater undertakings, until he was bound to fail.

Interview with Peter C. Newman, reported in The Establishment Man: A Portrait of Power (1982).

Re: The reviewer of one of Black's books:
I had never heard of [Walter] Young before, and I do not expect to hear from him again.

Interview with Peter C. Newman, reported in The Establishment Man: A Portrait of Power (1982).

Perhaps [Montreal] Archbishop Paul-Émile Léger suffered from what they call in French a taste for the sensational. He was like one of those matadors who, as the cadence of the olé's gets more and more rapid, are always trying to find something more daring to do. He grew hasty in his desire to produce new spectacles and maybe did a few ill-considered things. But on the whole I remain impressed with him.

Interview with Peter C. Newman, reported in The Establishment Man: A Portrait of Power (1982).

All those pent-up forces of envy and disbelief finally showed their true colours instead of masquerading in the deceitful fashion they have used since I took over at Argus. . . . There is something about the Canadian mentality that cannot stand an unbroken string of successes, unless it comes after a long life or after evident ordeal. No one begrudged Terry Fox getting the Order of Canada and no one boos any more when E.P. Taylor wins the Queen's Plate. But present Canadians with too much success too soon and it's just unbearable. That's how it works in this country.

Interview with Peter C. Newman, reported in The Establishment Man: A Portrait of Power (1982).

I'm reasonably upwardly mobile, but I'm not the ravening megalomaniac you read in the press.

Statement, 1978; reported by Peter C. Newman in The Establishment Man: A Portrait of Power (1982).

I am amazed by the number of so-called financial experts who are luxuriating in the view that I am some sort of punch-drunk prizefighter on the ropes. Well, screw them.

Interview with Canadian Business magazine, July, 1981; reported by Peter C. Newman in The Establishment Man: A Portrait of Power (1982).

Business Philosophy

Like all fads, corporate governance has its zealots.

Statement, May, 2003; reported by David Olive in "The World According to Conrad Black," Toronto Star, March 11, 2007; accessible at thestar.com.

Guardian

I have long regarded *The Guardian* as the most nauseating newspaper in the English language.

Conrad Black, "A Magnificent Phenomenon," Claremont Review of Books, Winter 2022/23, p. 106.

Journalists

We must express the view, based on our empirical observations, that a substantial number of journalists are ignorant, lazy, opinionated, and intellectually dishonest. The profession is heavily cluttered with aged hacks toiling through a miasma of mounting decrepitude and often alcoholism, and even more so with arrogant and abrasive youngsters who substitute "commitment" for insight.

Conrad Black, F. David Radler, and Peter G. White, "A Brief to the Special Senate Committee on the Mass Media"; reported by the Sherbrooke Record, Sherbrooke, Quebec, November 7, 1969.

[The] swarming, grunting masses of jackals calling themselves "investigative journalists."

Op-ed column, Toronto Sun, 1989; reported by David Olive in "The World According to Conrad Black," Toronto Star, March 11, 2007; accessible at thestar.com.

Re: Norman Mailer:

The bedraggled warhorse of American blowhardism.

Statement, 1969; reported by David Olive in "The World According to Conrad Black," Toronto Star, March 11, 2007; accessible at thestar.com.

Stewart Alsop, one of the more torrential snivelers of the American press . . .

Statement, 1969; reported by David Olive in "The World According to Conrad Black," Toronto Star, March 11, 2007; accessible at thestar.com.

Philosophy of Life

Since biblical times, and probably before, the wealthy have been envied and condemned.

Reported by Andrew Clark in "At some level, he's still asking the same question as he was when he was seven or eight —Who am I?," theguardian.com, March 16, 2007.

Greed has been severely underestimated and denigrated—unfairly so, in my opinion. There is nothing wrong with avarice as a motive, as long as it doesn't lead to dishonest or anti-social conduct.

Interview with Peter C. Newman, reported in The Establishment Man: A Portrait of Power (1982).

Politics

Re: Canada's welfare system:

An overgenerous reinsurance policy for an underachieving people.

Reported by David Plotz in "Conrad Black," slate.com, August 31, 2001.

Re: The resignation of the UK Minister of Defence for the Navy to protest the government's decision to scrap its aircraft carriers:

. . . the last resonance of good sense in that country until Maggie Thatcher came in.

Interview with Peter C. Newman, reported in The Establishment Man: A Portrait of Power (1982).

Re: the Black Panther Party:

Eldridge Cleaver, Bobby Seale, and other members of the criminal lunatic fringe.

Statement, 1968; reported by David Olive in "The World According to Conrad Black," Toronto Star, March 11, 2007; accessible at thestar.com.

Re: Eugene J. McCarthy:

His . . . recent erratic conduct has caused many to wonder if he is even fit to continue as a mediocre, lazy, and temperamental Senator, let alone preside over the nation.

Statement, 1969; reported by David Olive in "The World According to Conrad Black," Toronto Star, March 11, 2007; accessible at thestar.com.

Re: Robert F. Kennedy:

Bobby Kennedy, as the inimitable opportunist of contemporary American affairs, bubbled naturally to the top of this political cesspool—the wartime President's traditional cup of hemlock.

Statement, 1969; reported by David Olive in "The World According to Conrad Black," Toronto Star, March 11, 2007; accessible at thestar.com.

Re: Hearings on Robert H. Bork's nomination to the Supreme Court:

It is galling to see such mendacious hypocrites as [Edward] Kennedy and [Joseph] Biden at the Senate Judiciary Committee sitting in judgment on distinguished jurists.

Statement, 1988; reported by David Olive in "The World According to Conrad Black," Toronto Star, March 11, 2007; accessible at thestar.com.

Re: Franklin Delano Roosevelt:

Thanks to Eleanor, Roosevelt was probably the only president in American history who had any direct familiarity with urban poverty.

Conrad Black, Franklin Delano Roosevelt: Champion of Freedom (2003).

Quebec

The present government of Quebec is the most financially and intellectually corrupt in the history of the province. There are the shady deals, brazenly conducted, and the broken promises, most conspicuously that of last October to retain Bill 63. . . . The government dragged out the ancient and totally fictitious spectre of assimilation to justify Bill 22 and its rejection of the right of free choice in education, its its reduction of English education to the lowest echelon of ministerial whim, its assault upon freedom of expression through the regulation of the internal and external language of businesses and other organizations, and its creation of a fatuous new linguistic bureaucracy that will conduct a system of organized denunciation, harassment, and patronage.

Radio broadcast, July 26, 1974; reported by Peter C. Newman in The Establishment Man: A Portrait of Power (1982).

There is a paralytic social sickness in Quebec. In all this debate, not a single French Quebecker has objected to Bill 22 on the grounds that it was undemocratic or a reduction of liberties exercised in the province. The Quebec Civil Liberties Union, founded by Pierre Trudeau, from which one might have expected such sentiments, has instead demanded the abolition of English education, and this through the spokemanship of Jean-Louis Roy, who derives his income from McGill University.

Radio broadcast, July 26, 1974; reported by Peter C. Newman in The Establishment Man: A Portrait of Power (1982).

It is clear that Mr. Bourassa . . . is now going to try to eliminate the Parti Quebecois by a policy of gradual scapegoatism directed against the non-French elements in the province. . . . The English community here, still deluding itself with the illusion of Montreal as an incomparably fine place to live, is leaderless and irrelevant, except as the hostage of a dishonest government. Last month one of the most moderate ministers, Guy St-Pierre, told an English businessman's group, "If you don't like Quebec, you can leave it." With sadness but with certitude, I accept that choice.

Radio broadcast, July 26, 1974; reported by Peter C. Newman in The Establishment Man: A Portrait of Power (1982).

Michael Rubens Bloomberg

Michael Rubens Bloomberg / b. 1942 / Massachusetts, USA / Businessman, Co-Founder and CEO of Bloomberg, LP, politician, Mayor of New York City

Banks and Venture Capitalists

Banks and venture capitalists can be the worst enemies of entrepreneurs. They create doubt in entrepreneurs' minds, with their insistence on detailed game plans before they lend. They want five-year projections in a world that makes six-month forward planning difficult, even for stable and mature businesses, and they insist on "revenue budgeting" when no one knows what the new product will look like or who'll buy how much. And worst of all, they think an originator will be helped by their oh-so-insightful views on how he or she should run the new business. Often, they kill off what's different, special, and full of potential.

Michael Bloomberg, Bloomberg by Bloomberg, revised and updated edition (2019).

Bloomberg on Bloomberg

Re: Bloomberg's performance in college:
I was the one of those students who made the top half of the class possible.

Reported by Clea Simon in "Bloomberg extols 'moral leadership' at Business School," Harvard Gazette, harvard.edu, May 30, 2019.

We've been down that path before. Every year, the first $500 million of city sales tax revenue still goes to retiring Big MAC [Municipal Assistance Corporation] bonds issued to bail the city out from the fiscal crisis of the 1970s. And that dead weight of debt will burden the city budget through fiscal 2008.

No, we're not going to repeat that mistake. I have read that history, and it's not pleasant. Like all parents, I love my children dearly. I want to leave them: hope and opportunity, not our problems. We will not borrow our way out this time. I was elected to stand up and face the music now. And rest assured, I'll do exactly that.

Reported in "Mayor Michael Bloomberg's 2003 State of the City Address," gothamgazette.com, January 23, 2003.

And, as I would learn later on in my life—at Salomon Brothers and in my own company—it's the "doers," the lean and hungry ones, those with ambition in their eyes and fire in their bellies and no notions of social caste, who go the furthest and achieve the most.

Michael Bloomberg, Bloomberg by Bloomberg, revised and updated edition (2019).

Did I want to risk an embarrassing and costly failure? Absolutely. Happiness for me has always been the thrill of the unknown, trying something that everyone says can't be done, feeling that gnawing pit in my stomach that says "Danger ahead". Would it be nice not to have uncertainty, to sit back and "veg out"? When the phone rings constantly, when people keep demanding attention, when I desperately need time to myself, it seems an attractive notion just to "chuck it all." But then nobody calls, nobody stops by, and soon I'm nibbling my nails and getting irritable, and I realize that's not what I want. It sounds good. In reality though, I want action, I want challenge.

Michael Bloomberg, Bloomberg by Bloomberg, revised and updated edition (2019).

Every morning when we get up, we relish the day's upcoming battles. They keep us alive, and they keep Bloomberg's corporate family thriving. We can't wait for tomorrow. Who says we can't do that? What do you mean they'll beat us? Have them put on their boxing gloves, and send them into the ring. We're ready!

Michael Bloomberg, Bloomberg by Bloomberg, revised and updated edition (2019).

Business Philosophy

Those enterprises that see new needs and react more quickly, win!

Michael Bloomberg, Bloomberg by Bloomberg, revised and updated edition (2019).

If you have to compete based on capital, the giant always wins. If you can compete based on smarts, flexibility, and willingness to give more for less, then small companies like Bloomberg clearly have an advantage.

Michael Bloomberg, Bloomberg by Bloomberg, revised and updated edition (2019).

A better way to evaluate a company is to talk to the experts. No, I don't mean journalists or analysts. I mean those who really know what's going on and what the potential.

Michael Bloomberg, Bloomberg by Bloomberg, revised and updated edition (2019).

If you're going to succeed, you need a vision, one that's affordable, practical, and fills a customer need. Then, go for it. Don't worry too much about the details. Don't second-guess your creativity. Avoid overanalyzing the new project's potential. Most importantly, don't strategize about the long term too much.

Michael Bloomberg, Bloomberg by Bloomberg, revised and updated edition (2019).

When I saw that screen light up that day in the Merrill Lynch offices, I lost any residual doubt that Bloomberg could make it. We had picked just the right project. It was big enough to be useful, small enough to be possible. Start with a small piece; fulfill one goal at a time, on time. Do it with all things in life. Sit down and learn to read one-syllable words. If you try to read Chaucer in elementary school, you'll never accomplish anything. You can't jump to the end game right away, in computers, politics, love, or any other aspect of life.

Michael Bloomberg, Bloomberg by Bloomberg, revised and updated edition (2019).

Energy

Any friend of fossil is a friend of mine.

Reported by Tim McLaughlin in "New York's Bloomberg takes SUV to green car event," reuters.com, June 14, 2007.

Guns

We've made New York the safest big city in the nation, in part by adopting tough gun laws and proactively enforcing them. Every state in the Union has citizens killed by guns coming from other another state, and every state is powerless to stop the mayhem. Until Congress gets tough on trafficking, guns will continue flowing to our streets from states with much looser gun laws.

Speech, Bloomberg School of Public Health at Johns Hopkins University in Baltimore; reported in "Mayor Bloomberg Delivers Opening Address at Johns Hopkins University Summit on Reducing Gun Violence in America," nyc.gov, January 14, 2013.

Higher Education

The whole purpose of college is to learn how to deal with difficult situations, not to run away from them. A micro-aggression is exactly that: micro. But in a macro sense, one of the most dangerous places on a college campus is the so-called "safe space," because it creates a false impression that we can isolate ourselves from those who hold different views. We can't, and we shouldn't try—not in politics or in the workplace. Graduates, in the global economy, and in a democratic society, an open mind is the most valuable asset you can possess.

Commencement Address, University of Michigan at Ann Arbor, April 30, 2016; accessible on youtube.com, posted May 24, 2016.

New York City

We've shown the world that New York can never be defeated, because of its dynamic and diverse population and because it embodies the spirit of enterprise and the love of liberty. And because no matter who you are, if you believe in yourself and your dream, New York will always be the place for you.

Address, Republican National Convention; reported in "Text of Mayor Michael Bloomberg's Speech at the Republican National Convention," washingtonpost.com, August 30, 2004.

We're the world's second home, the place where every religion is practiced and every culture is celebrated.

Address, Republican National Convention; reported in "Text of Mayor Michael Bloomberg's Speech at the Republican National Convention," washingtonpost.com, August 30, 2004.

New York State

Government by three men in a room has turned New York State into a national symbol of governmental dysfunction. Enough is enough!

Reported in "Mayor Bloomberg's 2007 State of the City address," gothamgazette.com, January 17, 2007.

Social Security

I don't know if Bernie Madoff got his idea from there, but if there's ever a Ponzi scheme, people say Madoff was the biggest? Wrong. Social Security is, far and away.

Reported by Zack Budrick in "Bloomberg called Social Security a 'Ponzi scheme' as mayor," thehill.com, February 26, 2020.

Technology

The key questions are more important than ever: What is the problem? How valuable is the solution? Can we provide it profitably? Where will our competition come from? When I started out with computers, I believed what the manufacturers' promotional materials promised. I grew into a skeptical, non-trusting cynic, but one who believes more than most in the potential technology has to improve our lives. What I learned on the journey was that we are all humans, and technology exists to serve us, not the reverse. The challenge is to resolve people issues, not software ones.

Michael Bloomberg, Bloomberg by Bloomberg, revised and updated edition (2019).

Daniel John Bongino

Daniel John Bongino / b. 1974 / New York, New York, USA / Secret Service Special Agent, Author, Radio Host, Political Commentator, Podcaster, Candidate for US Congress

Note: The sources of the following quotations are provided where known; however, the specific sources of the great majority of the quotations are unknown, presumably deriving from Bongino's many writings, online commentaries, interviews, and podcasts

The American Dream

The American Dream is not about free stuff; it's about freedom.

Bongino on Bongino

I didn't want to be a man of words but of action.

Talk is cheap if it doesn't motivate action.

As a proud former Secret Service agent, it's tough to stand by and watch the agency struggle.

I joined the Secret Service in June 1999 as a special agent and vividly remember an agency brimming with pride.

I don't live like liberals in a 5,000 square foot mansion.

I've had problems with the Republican establishment in the past.

Being a Secret Service agent, I have an obligation not to disclose personal conversations and security details. But that doesn't prevent me from speaking generally about foundational principles and the system of patronage and punishment I saw in the Obama administration.

The big umbrella issue is, do I make a bigger difference on the outside of political process or on the inside?

But it was becoming more and more difficult to accompany the president and listen to another speech whose content was contrary to the principles I believe make this country exceptional.

> *Life Inside the Bubble: Why a Top-Ranked Secret Service Agent Walked Away from It All (2021).*

What we are fighting are not just random, off-the-shelf bad guys. It is genuine, generational evil. This is the real fight.

> *The Gift of Failure: (And I'll rethink the title if this book fails!)(2023).*

I failed to comprehend just how destructive and malevolent they are. It's ironic that they tweet about fascism all the time, claiming that they are warriors against it, when in reality they emulate the tactics of these generationally destructive fascists and totalitarians themselves.

> *The Gift of Failure: (And I'll rethink the title if this book fails!)(2023).*

The Constitution

The Constitution was written to protect your freedoms, not your feelings.

The Constitution is not an à la carte menu. You can't pick and choose the parts you like and ignore the ones you don't.

This Constitution was not a suggestion.

Culture War

We are now living through peak stupid with the left, and this "toxic masculinity," "white patriarch" nonsense, where they've now devolved to judging people exclusively by their gender and their skin color is a marker of the total intellectual collapse of the radical left.

Economics

Wealth is not determined by how much you earn; it's determined by how much you save.
Capitalism is not about how you divide the pie; it's about how you grow the pie.
No good libertarian I know wants us to completely isolate ourselves from the rest of the world. It's not even possible. I mean there are economic ties – there are trade routes that need to be secured. You know international trade can't happen if you don't have open oceans.
If we had a flat tax code rather than a 70,000-page document full of cronyism and favors, bureaucrats and elected officials wouldn't have the power to do you any favors. That's what we need. You would have to compete on your own on a level playing field, but that's not what the government permits now.

Education

The battle for the future of this country will be won or lost on the field of education.

Foreign Policy

I can't think of a more powerful message to send to the world when we act as one nation, one team, one fight.
Israel is one of our staunchest allies in an increasingly volatile world.

Freedom

Liberty isn't a menu option, it's the whole damn meal.
Freedom isn't just a privilege; it's a responsibility.
In the battle between government control and individual liberty, I will always choose liberty.

Free Speech

Your right to speak your mind should never be subject to someone else's feelings.

Government

The government does not solve problems. It subsidizes them.
When you're a hammer, everything looks like a nail. When you're a government, everything looks like a program.
The government's not your mommy or your daddy. The government's not there to feed you, to clothe you, to give you shelter. The government's there to protect you and to protect your rights.
The government doesn't have any money. It only has your money.
That's why we don't give the government extra money as conservatives because government generally stinks at spending money. That's why!
In Washington, DC, perception is reality and managing perceptions is a lucrative business for those who are skilled at it.

> *The Fight: A Secret Service Agent's Inside Account of Security Failings and the Political Machine (2016).*

Always remember that men and women of character are a direct threat to those politicians who are only in the game for the power.

> *Life Inside the Bubble: Why a Top-Ranked Secret Service Agent Walked Away from It All (2021).*

Principled men and women in politics often walk alone in Washington, but they attract legions of dedicated supporters in the real world of grassroots politics.

Life Inside the Bubble: Why a Top-Ranked Secret Service Agent Walked Away from It All (2021).

Gun Control

It's not about "commonsense gun laws." It's about commonsense liberals.

There is no such thing as gun control. Only people control.

History

History picks interesting messengers.

Judicial System

We have a problem with judicial activism in this country.

The left loves the courts. They hate constitutional limited government.

A law has to have teeth.

Law Enforcement

Assessing any possible threat is one thing, but pressing into a full investigation without facts of a crime or national security threat violates standard procedure.

In the United States, authorities are supposed to investigate crimes and find the people who have committed them.

Leadership

No amount of government spending can buy quality leadership.

Being an effective leader means having the ability to tell those you like that they are wrong and those you don't that they are right, and to show your human failings when there is a lesson to be transmitted.

Life Inside the Bubble: Why a Top-Ranked Secret Service Agent Walked Away from It All (2021).

Life

You can't live a perfect day without doing something for someone who will never be able to repay you.

Making a Difference

You can make a difference if you commit yourself to action. The only power in words is to motivate people to action. A better tomorrow awaits your response.

Life Inside the Bubble: Why a Top-Ranked Secret Service Agent Walked Away from It All (2021).

The Media

The media is done, they don't do journalism anymore, it's activism, nothing more, right? What's "straight news?" I guess a lot of people out there in the general public would probably say the *New York Times*and Reuters. I just disagree that is straight news. I definitely have a real frustration with the media, especially having dealt with them as an agent.

Obama

I'm done with President Obama, and frankly, so are my law enforcement friends.

There are no figures in the Trump campaign who colluded with Russia—but there were at least five in the Obama administration who helped push the bogus narratives of collusion and obstruction, and they have plenty of questions to answer.

The Solyndra scandal occurred because of people with money who have influence and power.

Politics

Liberals believe that the state is the solution to problems. Conservatives believe that the state is the problem.

Conservatives think liberals are people with bad ideas; liberals think conservatives are bad people with ideas.

Liberals confuse the cost of government for the value of government.

The Left believes that you're too stupid to make decisions for yourself.

Liberalism is an ideology of feelings, not facts.

The Democrats want to destroy the country immediately.

Liberalism is a cancer; it's a forest fire; it destroys every single thing it touches.

Democratic socialists, why don't you open your eyes, *Clockwork Orange*–style, and look at the truth.

New York Democrat Rep. Alexandria Ocasio-Cortez relies on a lot of economic ignorance to get you to believe what's not true could be true.

Conservatism is about empowering people to make choices, not the government.

Conservatism is about freedom, liberty, and personal responsibility.

You want to spend more of the money you earn? You want to control your own healthcare, and you want to pick where your kid goes to school? Then, welcome to the new Republican party. That's us.

Here's the deal: when conservatives lose elections, they change their strategy. When liberals lose elections, they want to change the rules.

Government grows and liberty dies when apathy flourishes.

Only after the people get involved and support the politicians who want to move this country forward—with our founding principles as a stepping-stone—will our government be returned to its rightful owner: you.

Life Inside the Bubble: Why a Top-Ranked Secret Service Agent Walked Away from It All (2021).

. . . but voting without a properly informed electorate has become a poor mechanism for limiting the growing role of government in our lives.

The Fight: A Secret Service Agent's Inside Account of Security Failings and the Political Machine (2016).

The President

Accessibility and openness are good politics but bad security.

One wrong move that appears to reveal a president ensconced in a White House bubble can lose an election, such as when President George H.W. Bush was criticized for expressing interest in the capabilities of a grocery-store scanner in the early 1990s.

White House staff spends enormous amounts of time planning a president's every move so that his public persona reflects the mood of the public.

The average guy doesn't have an army of lobbyists and lawyers working on his behalf every day in the White House.

Secret Service

The President can't go around in a steel box, as much as the Secret Service would like him to. Protection is an art form, keeping the President available to the public while protecting. Most of the hard protection is done by the police, the perimeter work.

"Because we've always done it that way." During my 12-year tenure as a special agent with the U.S. Secret Service, I heard those words all too often. The agency, in my experience, has an entrenched management culture resistant to change.

The mission of the Secret Service (to keep the president of the United States safe and secure) is, by its very nature, pivotal to the proper functioning of the country, and any failure to accomplish this mission has the potential to cause an immediate international crisis.

When you're a federal agent you don't get to arrest people for like $5.00 petty crimes or anything like that, they'll throw you right out of there.

Socialism

Socialism is a disease of the mind that convinces people that theft is compassion and force is love.

It's ironic that socialism and similar left-wing ideas appeal to people who fashion themselves as "anti-establishment," when you can't have socialism without political repression.

Ironically, socialist countries do tend to have immediate short-term decreases in poverty before collapsing.

While no famine has ever taken place in a democracy, they're the rule rather than the exception in socialist countries.

When everybody owns something, nobody owns it, and nobody has a direct interest in maintaining or improving its condition.

Success

Success is never owned; it's only rented, and the rent is due every day.

Success is not final, failure is not fatal: it is the courage to continue that counts.

The Gift of Failure: (And I'll rethink the title if this book fails!)(2023).

Venezuela

Nicolás Maduro is a fraud. He is a fake. He is a charlatan.

Tom Brady

Tom Brady (Thomas Edward Patrick Brady, Jr.) / (b. 1977) / California, USA / Football

I have always believed the sport of football is an 'all-in' proposition—if a 100% competitive commitment isn't there, you won't succeed, and success is what I love so much about our game.

Source: Instagram post, February 1, 2022.

I believe that what we get out of our bodies is a direct result of what we put in. I (mostly) follow a plant-based diet of whole foods that helps my body stay in balance and limits additional inflammation. I try to surround myself with positive people, and I work to minimize distractions whenever possible. My lifestyle has helped me stay physically and mentally fit.

Source: MariaShriver.com (2017).

When things don't go your way—or, rather, what you don't *think* of as your way—there can be a variety of opportunities that may not be obvious in the moment but that through hard work, preparation, and persistence can present themselves over time and make you better.

Source: The TB12 Method (2017).

You can make life a lot harder for yourself by focusing on negative things in your path or making excuses for why things didn't go your way. Or, you can refuse to take things personally, let them go, learn from them, and become the best version of yourself. It's a *choice*. It's actually *your choice*.

Source: The TB12 Method (2017).

Wisdom, someone said, is about knowing the difference between the things you can control and the things you can't. Today, if things go my way, great; and if they don't, that's okay, too, since I always have the chance to overcome them in the future. Whenever my team loses a game, it's an opportunity to learn something. A game is always an experiment.

Source: The TB12 Method (2017).

Stewart Brand

Stewart Brand / b. 1938 / Illinois, USA / Music Producer, Author, Publisher

A realm of intimate, personal power is developing—power of the individual to conduct his own education, find his own inspiration, shape his own environment, and share his adventure with whoever is interested.

Source: Whole Earth Catalog (1968).

Science is the only news. When you scan through a newspaper or magazine, all the human interest stuff is the same old he-said-she-said, the politics and economics the same sorry cyclic dramas, the fashions a pathetic illusion of newness, and even the technology is predictable if you know the science. Human nature doesn't change much; science does, and the change accrues, altering the world irreversibly.

Source: Whole Earth Discipline (2009).

On the one hand information wants to be expensive, because it's so valuable. The right information in the right place just changes your life. On the other hand, information wants to be free, because the cost of getting it out is getting lower and lower all the time. So you have these two fighting against each other.

Source: Whole Earth Review (May, 1985).

Every interview with a public figure should include the question "What have you been wrong about, and how did that change your views?" The answer will tell us if the person is intellectually honest or a tale spinner with delusions of infallibility.

Source: Whole Earth Discipline (2009).

When environmentalists are wrong, it is frequently technology that they are wrong about, and they wind up supporting parochial Green goals at the cost of comprehensive ones.

Source: Whole Earth Discipline (2009).

Redundancy of function is always more reliable than attempts at perfect, which time treats cruelly.

Source: How Buildings Learn (1994).

We ***are*** as gods and might as well get good at it.

Source: Whole Earth Catalog (1968).

Richard Charles Nicholas Branson

Richard Charles Nicholas Branson / b. 1950 / London, UK / Businessman, Entrepreneur, Venture Capitalist, Founder of Virgin Group, Ltd.

Brands

Good brands reflect the histories of the time and the group of people that made them. They can not be copied. They can not be recycled.

Richard Branson, Business Stripped Bare: Adventures of a Global Entrepreneur (2010).

Branson on Branson

My general attitude to life is to enjoy every minute of every day. I never do anything with a feeling of, "Oh God, I've got to do this today."

Interview with the Guardian, September 20, 2008.

I became an entrepreneur by mistake. Ever since then I've gone into business, not to make money, but because I think I can do it better than it's been done elsewhere. And, quite often, just out of personal frustration about the way it's been done by other people.

Interview with Martyn Lewis, reported in Reflections on Success(1997).

Making money never was my incentive. I just want to fight big companies.

Interview with the Sunday Mirror, January 16, 2000.

If you want to be a Millionaire, start with a billion dollars and launch a new airline.

Interview with Peter Greenberg in "Why JetBlue will be different," reported on MSNBC, 2001.

. . . I was born under a lucky star, and I have nothing whatsoever to regret. I wouldn't change a thing about my life.

Interview with Nina Myskow, reported in Saga magazine, saga.co.uk, July, 2007.

Respect is how to treat everyone, not just those you want to impress.

Richard Branson, Screw It, Let's Do It: Lessons In Life (2006).

The brave may not live forever—But the cautious do not live at all.

Richard Branson, Like a Virgin: Secrets They Won't Teach You at Business School (2012).

I can honestly say that I have never gone into any business purely to make money. If that is the sole motive then I believe you are better off not doing it. A business has to be involving, it has to be fun, and it has to exercise your creative instincts.

Richard Branson, Like a Virgin: Secrets They Won't Teach You at Business School (2012).

As soon as something stops being fun, I think it's time to move on. Life is too short to be unhappy. Waking up stressed and miserable is not a good way to live.

Richard Branson, Screw It, Let's Do It: Lessons In Life (2006).

There have been times when I could have succumbed to some form of bribe, or could have had my way by offering one. But ever since that night in Dover prison I have never been tempted to break my vow. . . . My Parents always drummed into me that all you have life is your reputation: you may be very rich, but if you lose your good name you'll never be happy.

Richard Branson, Losing My Virginity: How I've Survived, Had Fun, and Made a Fortune Doing Business My Way (2005).

Business Philosophy

There's only one thing that is an absolute certainty in business—we all make mistakes.

Richard Branson blog, virgin.com, accessed March 15, 2023.

My philosophy is that if I have any money I invest it in new ventures and not have it sitting around.

Interview with the Sunday Mirror, January 16, 2000.

To be associated with industry no longer carries the stigma of profiteering, exploitation and of being uncaring as it did when I was at school.

Richard Branson, "Foreword," in Ian Marcouse, Understanding Industry (1996).

If somebody offers you an amazing opportunity but you are not sure you can do it, say yes—then learn how to do it later!

Reported by Ruth Umoh in "Billionaire Richard Branson reveals why he's such a huge fan of always saying 'yes,'" cnbc.com, December 18, 2017.

Train people well enough so they can leave, treat them well enough so they don't want to.

Richard Branson tweet, March 27, 2014.

Throwing yourself into a job you enjoy is one of the life's greatest pleasures.

Richard Branson, Business Stripped Bare: Adventures of a Global Entrepreneur (2010).

Only a fool never changes his mind.

Richard Branson, Like a Virgin: Secrets They Won't Teach You at Business School (2012).

It is only by being bold that you get anywhere. If you are a risk-taker, then the art is to protect the downside.

Richard Branson, Losing My Virginity: How I've Survived, Had Fun, and Made a Fortune Doing Business My Way (2005).

You get the idea. Every business, like a painting, operates according to its own rules. There are many ways to run a successful company. What works once may never work again. What everyone tells you never to do may just work, once. There are no rules. You don't learn to walk by following rules. You learn by doing, and by falling over, and it's because you fall over that you learn to save yourself from falling over. It's the greatest thrill in the world and it runs away screaming at the first sight of bullet points.

Richard Branson, Business Stripped Bare: Adventures of a Global Entrepreneur (2010).

In the same way that I tend to make up my mind about people within thirty seconds of meeting them, I also make up my mind about whether a business proposal excites me within about thirty seconds of looking at it. I rely far more on gut instinct than researching huge amounts of statistics.

Richard Branson, Losing My Virginity: How I've Survived, Had Fun, and Made a Fortune Doing Business My Way (2005).

I have always believed that the only way to cope with a cash crisis is not to contract but to try to expand out of it.

Richard Branson, Losing My Virginity: How I've Survived, Had Fun, and Made a Fortune Doing Business My Way (2005).

Clients and Employees

Clients do not come first. Employees come first. If you take care of your employees, they will take care of the clients.

Reported widely; for example, by Alex Bourgeois in "Clients don't come first—employees do," medium.com, February 20, 2018.

Courage

Courage is what it takes to stand up and speak; courage is also what it takes to sit down and listen.

Richard Branson, The Virgin Way: If It's Not Fun, It's Not Worth Doing (2014).

Education

The talents of young people must not be stifled. Education is not just about getting the right grades in exams but it should encourage all students to develop their optimum capacity, whatever that may be. Schools and colleges should prepare young people for life.

Richard Branson, "Foreword," in Ian Marcouse, Understanding Industry (1996).

Government Bail-Outs

I think other companies need to stand on their own two feet, and the weak ones need to go to the wall.

Interview with BBC, reported in "Branson opposes wider bail-outs," news.bbc.co.uk, February 21, 2009.

Luck

Luck is what happens when preparation meets opportunity.

Richard Branson, The Virgin Way: If It's Not Fun, It's Not Worth Doing (2014).

Necessary Evils

Most "necessary evils" are far more evil than necessary.

Richard Branson, Losing My Virginity: How I've Survived, Had Fun, and Made a Fortune Doing Business My Way (2005).

Public Relations

A good PR story is infinitely more effective than a front page ad.

Richard Branson blog, virgin.com [attribution unconfirmed].

Safety

If you opt for a safe life, you will never know what it's like to win.

Richard Branson, Screw It, Let's Do It: Lessons In Life (2006).

Virgin Galactic

We're here to make space more accessible to all. We want to turn the next generation of dreamers into the astronauts of today and tomorrow. We've all us on this stage have had the most extraordinary experience, and we'd love it if a number of you can have it, too. . . . If you ever had a dream, now is the time to make it come true—and I'd like to end by saying welcome to the dawn of a new space age.

Reported by Jackie Wattles, Fernando Alfonso, III, and Mike Hayes in "Richard Branson goes to space," cnn.com, July 11, 2021.

Virgin's Success

Fun is at the core of the way I like to do business and it has been key to everything I've done from the outset. More than any other element, fun is the secret of Virgin's success. I am aware that the ideas of business as being fun and creative goes right against the grain of convention, and it's certainly not how the they teach it at some of those business schools, where business means hard grind and lots of "discounted cash flows" and "net present values."

Richard Branson, Losing My Virginity: How I've Survived, Had Fun, and Made a Fortune Doing Business My Way (2005).

Sergey Mikhailovich Brin

Sergey Mikhailovich Brin / b. 1973 / Russia (then USSR) / Computer Scientist, Entrepreneur

Administrative State

. . . whenever I have met with our elected officials they are invariably thoughtful, well-meaning people. And yet collectively 90% of their effort seems to be focused on how to stick it to the other party.

Reported by Kevin Hall, "Google's Sergey Brin calls on U.S. politicians to ditch their parties," Dvice.com blog, Syfy website, November 6, 2012.

Entrepreneurship and the Economy

When it's too easy to get money, then you get a lot of noise mixed in with the real innovation and entrepreneurship. Tough times bring out the best parts of Silicon Valley.

Reported by Jessica Guynn, "Google's Schmidt, Page and Brin hold court at Zeitgeist,"Los Angeles Times, September 17, 2008.

Gmail

. . . great user experience has helped other email systems (others have increased storage, etc.). There are areas that have been overlooked in industry, much as search was overlooked in the 90's.

Reported by Richard MacManus, "Conversation: Sergey Brin of Google," readwriteweb.com, October 7, 2005.

Liberty

Having come from a totalitarian country, the Soviet Union, and having seen the hardships that my family endured—both while there and trying to leave—I certainly am particularly sensitive to the stifling of individual liberties.

Reported by Josh Horwitz, "Without Sergey Brin, Google has lost its healthy fear of authoritarianism," qz.com, August 6, 2018.

Ranking

We came up with the notion that not all web pages are created equal. People are – but not web pages.

Lecture, University of California, Berkeley, October 5, 2005.

Technology

Technology is an inherent democratizer. Because of the evolution of hardware and software, you're able to scale up almost anything. It means that in our lifetime everyone may have tools of equal power.

Lecture, University of California, Berkeley, October 5, 2005.

If what you're doing is not seen by some people as science fiction, it's probably not transformative enough.

Reported by Catherine Mayer, "Meet 'Schmeat': Say Hello to the Stem-Cell Hamburger," Time magazine, August 5, 2013.

Warren Edward Buffett

Warren Edward Buffett / b. 1930 / Nebraska, USA / Businessman, Investor, CEO of Berkshire Hathaway, Inc.

Berkshire Hathaway

Note: Responding to a question why Buffett does not deal in tech stocks:

We're more comfortable in that kind of business. It means we miss a lot of very big winners. But we wouldn't know how to pick them out anyway. It also means we have very few big losers—and that's quite helpful over time. We're perfectly willing to trade away a big payoff for a certain payoff.

Buffett statement, 1999; reported in "Why Won't Buffett Invest in Tech Stocks?," The Motley Fool, March 6, 2000.

Buffett on Buffett

I wouldn't mind going to jail if I had three cellmates who played bridge.

Reported by Robert G. Hagstrom in The Warren Buffett Portfolio: Mastering the Power of the Focus Investment Strategy (1999).

I happen to have a talent for allocating capital. But my ability to use that talent is completely dependent on the society I was born into. If I'd been born into a tribe of hunters, this talent of mine would be pretty worthless. I can't run very fast. I'm not particularly strong. I'd probably end up as some wild animal's dinner.

Reported by Barack Obama in The Audacity of Hope: Thoughts on Reclaiming the American Dream (2006).

Business Philosophy

Someone's sitting in the shade today because someone planted a tree a long time ago.

Buffett statement, 1991; reported by Andrew Kilpatrick in Of Permanent Value: The Story of Warren Buffett (1996).

I like thinking big. I always have. To me it's very simple: if you're going to be thinking anyway, you might as well think big.

Reported by Roger Lowenstein in Buffett: The Making of an American Capitalist (1995).

There's class warfare, all right, but it's my class, the rich class, that's making war, and we're winning.

Reported by Ben Stein in "In Class Warfare, Guess Which Class Is Winning," nytimes.com, November 26, 2006.

It takes 20 years to build a reputation and five minutes to ruin it. If you think about that, you'll do things differently.

Reported by Dan Robert Anderson in Corporate Survival: The Critical Importance of Sustainability Risk Management (2005).

The free market's the best mechanism ever devised to put resources to their most efficient and productive use. . . . The government isn't particularly good at that. But the market isn't so good at making sure that the wealth that's produced is being distributed fairly or wisely.

Reported by Barack Obama in The Audacity of Hope: Thoughts on Reclaiming the American Dream (2006).

People will always try to stop you doing the right thing if it is unconventional.

Reported by Guy Spier in "My $650,100 Lunch with Warren Buffett," time.com, June 30, 2008.

Rule No. 1: Never lose money. Rule No. 2: Never forget rule No. 1.

Reported by Stephanie Loiacono in "Rules That Warren Buffett Lives By," Yahoo Finance, yahoo.com, February 23, 2010.

You don't find out who's been swimming naked until the tide goes out.

Buffett statement, 1994 annual meeting; reported by CNBC, April 25, 1994.

Investing

I call investing the greatest business in the world . . . because you never have to swing. You stand at the plate, the pitcher throws you General Motors at 47! U.S. Steel at 39! and nobody calls a strike on you. There's no penalty except opportunity lost. All day you wait for the pitch you like; then when the fielders are asleep, you step up and hit it.

Reported in "The Money Men," Forbes magazine, November 1, 1974.

You're dealing with a lot of silly people in the marketplace; it's like a great big casino and everyone else is boozing. If you can stick with Pepsi, you should be O.K.

Reported in "The Money Men," Forbes magazine, November 1, 1974.

If you understood a business perfectly and the future of the business, you would need very little in the way of a margin of safety. So, the more vulnerable the business is, assuming you still want to invest in it, the larger margin of safety you'd need. If you're driving a truck across a bridge that says it holds 10,000 pounds and you've got a 9,800 pound vehicle, if the bridge is 6 inches above the crevice it covers, you may feel okay, but if it's over the Grand Canyon, you may feel you want a little larger margin of safety. . . .

Buffett statement, 1997; reported by Andrew Kilpatrick in Of Permanent Value: The Story of Warren Buffett, revised edition (2000).

Success in investing doesn't correlate with I.Q. once you're above the level of 125. Once you have ordinary intelligence, what you need is the temperament to control the urges that get other people into trouble in investing.

Reported by Amy Stone in "Homespun Wisdom from the 'Oracle of Omaha,'" Businessweek, June 5, 1999.

If I was running $1 million today, or $10 million for that matter, I'd be fully invested. Anyone who says that size does not hurt investment performance is selling. The highest rates of return I've ever achieved were in the 1950s. I killed the Dow. You ought to see the numbers. But I was investing peanuts then. It's a huge structural advantage not to have a lot of money. I think I could make you 50% a year on $1 million. No, I know I could. I guarantee that.

Reported by Amy Stone in "Homespun Wisdom from the 'Oracle of Omaha,'" Businessweek, June 5, 1999.

We don't get paid for activity, just for being right. As to how long we'll wait, we'll wait indefinitely.

Buffett statement, 1998; reported by Frank Partnoy, Wait: The Art and Science of Delay (2012).

You want to be greedy when others are fearful. You want to be fearful when others are greedy. It's that simple. . . . They're pretty fearful. In fact, in my adult lifetime, I don't think I've ever seen people as fearful economically as they are right now.

Interview with Charlie Rose, PBS, October 1, 2008.

I try to buy stock in businesses that are so wonderful that an idiot can run them. Because sooner or later, one will.

Buffett statement, panel discussion, DVD extra, Patrick Creadon, I.O.U.S.A. (2008).

Money

I don't have a problem with guilt about money. The way I see it is that my money represents an enormous number of claim checks on society. It is like I have these little pieces of paper that I can turn into consumption. If I wanted to, I could hire 10,000 people to do nothing but paint my picture every day for the rest of my life. And the GNP would go up. But the utility of the product would be zilch, and I would be keeping those 10,000 people from doing AIDS research, or teaching, or nursing. I don't do that though. I don't use very many of those claim checks. There's nothing material I want very much. And I'm going to give virtually all of those claim checks to charity when my wife and I die.

Reported by Janet C. Lowe in Warren Buffett Speaks: Wit and Wisdom from the World's Greatest Investor (1997).

Parenting

Love is the greatest advantage a parent can give.

Reported by Richard I. Kirkland, Jr., in "Should You Leave It All to the Children?," Fortune magazine, cnn.com, September 29, 1986.

Value

Draw a circle around the businesses you understand and then eliminate those that fail to qualify on the basis of value, good management and limited exposure to hard times. . . . Buy into a company because you want to own it, not because you want the stock to go up. . . . People have been successful investors because they've stuck with successful companies. Sooner or later, the market mirrors the business.

Reported in "The Money Men," Forbes magazine, November 1, 1974.

Investors making purchases in an overheated market need to recognize that it may often take an extended period for the value of even an outstanding company to catch up with the price they paid.

Warren Buffett, The Essays of Warren Buffett: Lessons for Corporate America, edited by Lawrence A. Cunningham (1998).

Wall Street

Wall Street is the only place that people ride to work in a Rolls Royce to get advice from those who take the subway.

Reported by Egbert Sukop in The Money Adventure (1998).

Edmund Burke

Edmund Burke / 1729–1797 / Ireland (then, Kingdom of Ireland) / Politician, Member of Parliament, Philosopher

Atheists

The writers against religion, whilst they oppose every system, are wisely careful never to set up any of their own.

A Vindication of Natural Society (1756).

Boldness formerly was not the character of Atheists as such. … But of late they are grown active, designing, turbulent, and seditious.

"Thoughts on French Affairs" (1791).

Change

Nothing in progression can rest on its original plan. We may as well think of rocking a grown man in the cradle of an infant.

"A Letter to the Sheriffs of Bristol on the Affairs of America" (1777).

A state without the means of some change is without the means of its conservation.

Reflections on the Revolution in France (1790).

Chivalry

The age of chivalry is gone.—That of sophisters, economists, and calculators, has succeeded; and the glory of Europe is extinguished for ever.

Reflections on the Revolution in France (1790).

I thought ten thousand swords must have leapt from their scabbards to avenge even a look that threatened her [Marie-Antoinette] with insult.

Reflections on the Revolution in France (1790).

The unbought grace of life, the cheap defence of nations, the nurse of manly sentiment and heroic enterprise, is gone!

Reflections on the Revolution in France (1790).

Compromise

All government—indeed, every human benefit and enjoyment, every virtue and every prudent act—is founded on compromise and barter.

"Speech on Conciliation with the Colonies" (1775).

Curiosity

The first and the simplest emotion which we discover in the human mind is Curiosity.

A Philosophical Enquiry into the Origin of Our Ideas of the Sublime and Beautiful (1757).

Entrepreneurs

There is a sort of enthusiasm in all projectors [entrepreneurs], absolutely necessary for their affairs, which makes them proof against the most fatiguing delays, the most mortifying disappointments, the most shocking insults; and, what is severer than all, the presumptuous judgement of the ignorant upon their designs.

An Account of the European Settlements in America (1757).

Habit

Custom reconciles us to every thing.

A Philosophical Enquiry into the Origin of Our Ideas of the Sublime and Beautiful (1757).

International Affairs

Whenever our neighbour's house is on fire, it cannot be amiss for the engines to play a little on our own.

Reflections on the Revolution in France (1790).

Law

There is but one law for all, namely, that law which governs all law, the law of our Creator, the law of humanity, justice, equity—the law of nature, and of nations.

"Speech on the Impeachment of Warren Hastings" (1794).

Liberty

Liberty too must be limited in order to be possessed.

"A Letter to the Sheriffs of Bristol on the Affairs of America" (1777).

Among a people generally corrupt, liberty cannot long exist,

"A Letter to the Sheriffs of Bristol on the Affairs of America" (1777).

Abstract liberty, like other mere abstractions, is not to be found.

"Speech on Conciliation with the Colonies" (1775).

Natural Reason

A good parson once said, that where mystery begins, religion ends. Cannot I say, as truly at least, of human laws, that where mystery begins, justice ends? It is hard to say whether the doctors of law or divinity have made the greater advances in the lucrative business of mystery. The lawyers, as well as the theologians, have erected another reason besides natural reason; and the result has been, another justice besides natural justice.

A Vindication of Natural Society (1756).

We are indebted for all our miseries to our distrust of that guide, which Providence thought sufficient for our condition, our own natural reason, which rejecting both in human and Divine things, we have given our necks to the yoke of political and theological slavery. We have renounced the prerogative of man, and it is no wonder that we should be treated like beasts.

A Vindication of Natural Society (1756).

Order

Good order is the foundation of all good things.

Reflections on the Revolution in France (1790).

Society cannot exist unless a controlling power upon will and appetite be placed somewhere, and the less of it there is within, the more there must be without. It is ordained in the eternal constitution of things, that men of intemperate minds cannot be free. Their passions forge their fetters.

"A Letter to a Member of the National Assembly" (1791).

Past and Future Generations

People will not look forward to posterity, who never look backward to their ancestors.

Reflections on the Revolution in France (1790).

Society is indeed a contract...it becomes a partnership not only between those who are living, but between those who are living, those who are dead, and those who are to be born.

Reflections on the Revolution in France (1790).

Politics

Kings are ambitious; the nobility haughty; and the populace tumultuous and ungovernable.

A Vindication of Natural Society (1756).

We scarce ever had a prince, who by fraud, or violence, had not made some infringement on the constitution. We scarce ever had a parliament which knew, when it attempted to set limits to the royal authority, how to set limits to its own. Evils we have had continually calling for reformation, and reformations more grievous than any evils. Our boasted liberty sometimes trodden down, sometimes giddily set up, and ever precariously fluctuating and unsettled; it has only been kept alive by the blasts of continual feuds, wars, and conspiracies.

A Vindication of Natural Society (1756).

People must be governed in a manner agreeable to their temper and disposition; and men of free character and spirit must be ruled with, at least, some condescension to this spirit and this character.

"Observations on a Late Publication Entitled 'The Present State of the Nation'" (1769).

. . . and politics ought to be adjusted, not to human reasonings, but to human nature; of which the reason is but a part; and by no means the greatest part.

"Observations on a Late Publication Entitled 'The Present State of the Nation'" (1769).

It is a general popular error to suppose the loudest complainers for the publick to be the most anxious for its welfare.

"Observations on a Late Publication Entitled 'The Present State of the Nation'" (1769).

The conduct of a losing party never appears right: at least it never can possess the only infallible criterion of wisdom to vulgar judgements—success.

"A Letter to a Member of the National Assembly" (1791).

Because half a dozen grasshoppers under a fern make the field ring with their importunate chink, whilst thousands of great cattle, reposed beneath the shadow of the British oak, chew the cud and are silent, pray do not imagine that those who make the noise are the only inhabitants of the field.

Reflections on the Revolution in France (1790).

Power

Those who have been once intoxicated with power, and have derived any kind of emolument from it, even though for but one year, can never willingly abandon it.

"A Letter to a Member of the National Assembly" (1791).

Public Positions

I need not excuse myself to your Lordship, nor, I think, to any honest man, for the zeal I have shown in this cause; for it is an honest zeal, and in a good cause. I have defended natural religion against a confederacy of atheists and divines. I now plead for natural society against politicians, and for natural reason against all three. When the world is in a fitter temper than it is at present to hear truth, or when I shall be more indifferent about its temper, my thoughts may become more public. In the mean time, let them repose in my own bosom, and in the bosoms of such men as are fit to be initiated in the sober mysteries of truth and reason.

A Vindication of Natural Society (1756).

Radical Egalitarianism

This barbarous philosophy, which is the offspring of cold hearts and muddy understandings.

Reflections on the Revolution in France (1790).

In the groves of *their* academy, at the end of every vista, you see nothing but the gallows.

Reflections on the Revolution in France (1790).

As much injustice and tyranny has been practised in a few months by a French democracy, as in all the arbitrary monarchies in Europe in the forty years of my observation.

"A Letter to Captain Thomas Mercer," February 26, 1790.

State of Nature

In a state of nature, it is an invariable law, that a man's acquisitions are in proportion to his labours. In a state of artificial society, it is a law as constant and as invariable, that those who labour most enjoy the fewest things; and that those who labour not at all have the greatest number of enjoyments. A constitution of things this, strange and ridiculous beyond expression! We scarce believe a thing when we are told it, which we actually see before our eyes every day without being in the least surprised.

A Vindication of Natural Society (1756).

Consider the ravages committed in the bowels of all commonwealths by ambition, by avarice, envy, fraud, open injustice, and pretended friendship; vices which could draw little support from a state of nature, but which blossom and flourish in the rankness of political society.

A Vindication of Natural Society (1756).

Sublimity of Nature

A great profusion of things, which are splendid or valuable in themselves, is *magnificent*. The starry heaven, though it occurs so very frequently to our view, never fails to excite an idea of grandeur. This cannot be owing to the stars themselves, separately considered. The number is certainly the cause. The apparent disorder augments the grandeur, for the appearance of care is highly contrary to our idea of magnificence. Besides, the stars lie in such apparent confusion, as makes it impossible on ordinary occasions to reckon them. This gives them the advantage of a sort of infinity.

A Philosophical Enquiry into the Origin of Our Ideas of the Sublime and Beautiful (1757).

James Burnham

James Burnham / 1905–1987 / Chicago, Illinois, USA / Political Scientist

Democracy

Democracy is not a good in itself; it is a political technique, a means to an end.

The Managerial Revolution: What is Happening in the World(1941).

A genuinely democratic political system requires a democratic culture, and the development of such a culture is a slow and difficult process.

The Struggle for the World (1947).

Geopolitics

In the realm of geopolitics, nations act in their own self-interest, and power is the ultimate currency.

Source unknown.

Ideology

Political ideologies often serve as rationalizations for the pursuit of power.

Source unknown.

Intellectuals

Intellectuals like to imagine themselves as the clerks of society, but they are more often its critics, parasites, and saboteurs.

The Managerial Revolution: What is Happening in the World(1941).

The intellectuals who complain that the system does not live up to its principles are, in fact, complaining that it does not live up to their misconceptions and fantasies.

Source unknown.

Liberalism

Liberalism can do nothing to cleanse or halt this Augean wave; can only, in fact, smooth its advance. The secular relativism and permissiveness to which liberalism is committed provides no metaphysical foothold on which a stand might be taken.

"Notes on Authority, Morality, Power," National Review, December 1, 1970.

The Managerial Revolution

Private-capitalist ownership of the economy meant a dispersion of economic power and a partial separation between economic and other social forces in a manner that prevented the concentration of an overwhelming single social force. Today the advance of the managerial revolution is everywhere concentrating economic power in the state apparatus, where it tends to unite with control over the other great social forces—the army, education, labor, law, the political bureaucracy, art, and science even. This development, too, tends to destroy the basis for those social oppositions that keep freedom alive.

The Machiavellians: Defenders of Freedom (1943).

Morality

The line between good and evil is not a fixed, immoveable barrier between the two, but a shifting one.

The Machiavellians: Defenders of Freedom (1943).

Power

In the real world, power is always on the side of the strongest.

The Machiavellians: Defenders of Freedom (1943).

The struggle for power and influence is the driving force behind political dynamics.

The Machiavellians: Defenders of Freedom (1943).

The instability of all governments and political forms follows in part from the limitless human appetite for power.

The Machiavellians: Defenders of Freedom (1943).

For a nation, the supreme moral task and responsibility is to make the right use of power.

"Ideology and Common Sense," National Review, October 8, 1960.

The Machiavellians are the only ones who have told us the full truth about power. . . . The primary object, in practice, of all rulers is to serve their own interest, to maintain their own power and privilege. . . . No theory, no promises, no morality, no amount of good will, no religion will restrain power. Neither priests nor soldiers, neither labor leaders nor businessmen, neither bureaucrats nor feudal lords will differ from each other in the basic use which they will seek to make of power. . . . Only power restrains power. . . . When all opposition is destroyed, there is no longer any limit to what power may do. A despotism, any kind of despotism, can be benevolent only by accident.

The Machiavellians: Defenders of Freedom (1943).

The Ruling Class

From the point of view of the theory of the ruling class, a society is the society of its ruling class. A nation's strength or weakness, its culture, its powers of endurance, its prosperity, its decadence, depend in the first instance upon the nature of its ruling class. More particularly, the way in which to study a nation, to understand it, to predict what will happen to it, requires first of all and primarily an analysis of the ruling class. Political history and political science are thus predominantly the history and science of ruling classes, their origin, development, composition, structure, and changes.

The Machiavellians: Defenders of Freedom (1943).

Herman Cain

Herman Cain / 1945–2020 / Tennessee, USA / Businessman, Chairman and CEO of Godfather's Pizza, Political Activist, Candidate for 2012 Republican Presidential Nomination

Abortion

Re: origins of Planned Parenthood:

One of the motivations was killing black babies, because they didn't want to deal with the problems of illiteracy and poverty.

Reported by Manuel Roig-Franzia in "Cain Makes Inroads in Ga. Senate Bid," Washington Post, July 18, 2004; accessible at washingtonpost.com.

I do not think abortion should be legal in this country. Abortion should not be legal. That is clear. But if a family made the decision to break the law, that's that family's decision.

Reported by "America Live," Fox News, October 21, 2011.

Cain on Cain

I'm not a professional politician. I'm a professional problem solver.

Reported by Sam Stein in "Herman Cain's 2004 Campaign: 'Godless' Gays and Planned Parenthood Eugenics," huffpost.com, October 5, 2011.

I am an American. Black. Conservative. I don't use "African American", because I'm American, I'm black and I'm conservative. I don't like people trying to label me. "African American" is socially acceptable for some people, but I am not some people. . . .

Reported by Jeffrey Goldberg in "Herman Cain on Why 'The Black Guy Is Winning,'" Bloomberg View, March 6, 2011; accessible at bloomberg.com.

So we get to the fountain, my brother and I, and we look around, there wasn't a lot of people there and I said to my brother, "*You* go first." He tasted the white water and then we looked around and says, "Your turn." We tasted—I taste the white water. Then we both taste the colored water, and we looked at each other, six and seven years old. *The water tastes the same!* What's the big deal? We had not been taught segregation at the age of six and seven. We wondered what the big deal was about.

Now, that being said and growing in the segregated South, I am not *mad* at America. I don't have a *grudge* against America, because one of the things that has made this nation great in the short 235-year history, Sean, is its ability to change. A lot of other countries don't have that ability. We ought to be appreciative of the fact that this country has that kind of resilience.

Interview with Sean Hannity, on "Hannity," Fox News, October 4, 2011.

I well remember, as a young teenager, seeing signs printed in large black letters at the fronts of buses: "White seat from front, colored seat from rear." One day when I was thirteen, my friends and I were riding home from school in a half-empty bus — this was at the time that the civil rights movement was just getting off the ground and some police officers were just looking for a reason to shoot a black person who "got out of line." So, counter to our real feelings, we decided to avoid trouble by moving to the back of the bus when the driver told us to.

By that time, the sit-ins and the Freedom Rides had kind of broken the ice, even though things hadn't fully changed. So we saw it every day on TV and read about it in the news. Dad always said, "Stay out of trouble," and we did.

Herman Cain, This is Herman Cain!: My Journey to the White House (2011).

And in November 2012, the day after the election, when we wake up that morning and all the votes are counted, and they declare not only all of the local election results, the statewide election results, the senatorial results, and when we wake up and they declare the presidential results, and Herman Cain has been elected, we'll be able to say: "Free at last, free at last, thank God almighty this nation is free at last again.

Herman Cain, This is Herman Cain!: My Journey to the White House (2011).

Federal Reserve

Some people say that we ought to audit the Fed. Here's what I do know. The Federal Reserve already has so many internal audits it's ridiculous. I don't know why people think we're gonna learn this great amount of information by auditing the Federal Reserve. I think a lot of people are calling for this audit of the Federal Reserve because they don't know enough about it. There's no hidden secrets going on in the Federal Reserve to my knowledge.

Reported by Neal Boortz on the Neal Boortz Show (nationally syndicated radio talk show), December 29, 2010.

Healthcare Policy

If Obamacare had been fully implemented when I caught cancer, I'd be dead and here's why. Here's why. I was able to go to the doctors that I wanted to go to. As fast as they could do the test. I didn't have to wait six months like you do in other countries to get a CAT scan, and sometimes people die before they get the CAT scan, because the cancer in my body was spreading so fast. But because I was able to get the treatment as soon as I could, and to get the quality care that I did, that's what has me alive today. You ought to be able to make those choices if you get a serious illness, not some bureaucrat in Washington, DC.

Remarks at campaign stop, Lexington, South Carolina, August 18, 2011; reported by Geneva Sands in "Herman Cain says he'd 'be dead' under 'ObamaCare,'" thehill.com, August 19, 2013.

Israel

Let me be clear. I am, you know, exploring this whole Presidential run. Let me just tell you what the *Cain* Doctrine would be as it relates to Israel, if I were President: You mess with Israel, you are messing with the United States of America. It's that simple. I want to protect that relationship because they have been our only consistent ally in that part of the world.

Interview on Fox News, May 20, 2011.

Q: Do you think the Palestinian refugees, the people who were kicked out of the land in 1948, should be able or should have any right to return to Israeli land?

A: Yes. They should have a right to come back if that is a decision that Israel wants to make. Back to—it's up to Israel to determine the things they will accept. Prime Minister Benjamin Netanyahu made it real clear in his statement following the statement that President Obama made. They are wiling to make some concessions. They are willing to give on a lot of things. They are willing to be compassionate. I don't think they have a big problem with people returning.

Interview with Chris Wallace on "Fox News Sunday," May 22, 2011.

Muslims

One percent of the practicing religious believers in this country are Muslim. And so I push back and reject them trying to convert the rest of us. And based upon the little knowledge that I have of the Muslim religion, you know, they have an objective to convert all infidels or kill them. Now, I know that there are some peaceful Muslims who don't go around preaching or practicing that. Well, unfortunately, we can't sit back and tolerate the radical ones simply because we know that there are some of them who don't believe in that aspect of the Muslim religion.

Reported by Trevor Persaud in "Q & A: Herman Cain on Faith, Calling, and Presidential Aspirations," christianitytoday.org, March 21, 2011.

There are tons of capable people in this country, and while I have been in this exploratory phase, yes, I have been considering who would I put in various roles, who do I consider to be some of the true patriots of this country that could help a Herman Cain cabinet if I were to run and to become president. And so yes, so far I have not come across or I don't have acquaintances with people who have professed the Muslim religion who are on a list of people I would consider. We are—we have become a nation of crises, Neil. And being politically correct is not something I'm going to spend a whole lot of time worrying about when we've got all of these other problems that we are facing right here in this country.

Reported by Neil Cavuto on "Your World with Neil Cavuto," Fox News, March 28, 2011.

Barack Obama

Barack Obama is more of an international. I think he's out of the mainstream and always has been. Look, he was raised in Kenya, his mother was white from Kansas and her family had an influence on him, it's true, but his dad was Kenyan, and when he was going to school he got a lot of fellowships, scholarships, he stayed in the academic environment for a long time. He spent most of his career as an intellectual.

Reported by Jeffrey Goldberg in "Herman Cain on Why 'The Black Guy Is Winning,'" Bloomberg View, March 6, 2011; accessible at bloomberg.com.

Political Philosophy

We have a war on our moral fiber. We will not allow the godless few to destroy our moral foundation.

Reported by Chattanooga Times Free Press, February 2, 2004.

Q: For what possible reason would [Barack Obama] *possibly* want to destroy America's economy and place in the world. Where is that coming from?

A: Where I'm coming from is if you weaken the United States *militarily*, *economically*, and *culturally*, then America is gonna suffer from the same problems that all of—a lot of the other countries suffer from, and that opens the door to some *dramatic change* in how we run this country.

Q: Would that fit into black liberation theology, social, Marxism, redistribution, "G.D. America," "America's chickens have come home to roost"?

A: It fits into what I would call anti-American, anti-Constitutional, anti-Declaration of Independence. That's what it fits into.

Interview with Sean Hannity, Fox News, April 14, 2010.

The American dream is under attack because our government has been hijacked by the liberals in Washington, D.C. . . . They want you to believe that they're going to drag out enough prisoners and dead people to win the election. Well, let me tell you a little secret. Conservatives that are alive outnumber the dead people and prisoners. ... I have a message for the political elites in Washington, D.C.: The United States of America is not going to become the United States of Europe, not on our watch.

Reported by Lynn Hulsey in "Tea Party speaker: 'Stupid people' running country," Dayton Daily News, October 15, 2010.

The objective of the liberals is to destroy this country. The objective of the liberals is to make America mediocre like everybody else who aspire to be like America. That's their objective. And so the liberals, they have an objective: destroy America, make it mediocre, become part of what they call this world order stuff.

Interview with David Gregory, "Cain on the liberal 'mission' to destroy America," NBC News, October 16, 2011.

They have only three tactics: S.I.N. They shift the subject, they ignore the facts, and they name-call. Am I right? That's all they do.

Reported by Kyle Mantyla in "Herman Cain: 'Stupid People Are Ruining America,'" righwingwatch.org, February 11, 2011.

We don't need to rewrite the Constitution of the United States of America, we need to re-*read* the Constitution and *enforce* the Constitution. We don't need to re-*write*, let's *reread!* And I know that there are some people that are not going to do that. So for the benefit of those who are not going to read it because they don't want us to go by the Constitution, there's a little section in there that talks about "life, liberty and the pursuit of happiness." You know, those ideals that we live by, we believe in, your parents believed in, they instilled in you. When you get to the part about "life, liberty and the pursuit of happiness," don't stop right there, keep reading. 'Cause that's when it says "when any form of government becomes destructive of those ideals, it is the right of the people to alter or abolish it." We've got some *altering* and some *abolishing* to do!

Rally stump speech, Centennial Olympic Park, Atlanta, Georgia, May 21, 2011; reported by Willoughby Mariano in "Cain mistakes Declaration of Independence language for Constitution," politifact.com, May 25, 2011.

Racism

I don't believe racism in this country today holds anybody back in a big way. Are there some elements of racism? Yes, it gets back to if we don't grow this economy, that is a ripple effect for every economic level, and because blacks are more disproportionately unemployed, they get hit the worst when economic policies don't work. That's where it starts.

Interview, "Cain: Racism not holding anyone back," State of the Nation, CNN, October 9, 2011; accessible at cnn.com.

Elias Canetti

Elias Canetti / 1905–1994 / Principality of Bulgaria (then under the suzerainty of the Ottoman Empire) / Social Theorist, Novelist, Dramatist, Essayist, Memoirist, Aphorist
Note: Though born into a Sephardic Jewish family in Bulgaria during the last years of the Ottoman Empire, Canetti's family moved to Vienna in 1912, when he was seven years old. He lived there until the *Anschluss* in 1938, when he was 33. He was thus Viennese by upbringing and culture.
Note: All quotations are taken from *Das Geheimherz der Uhr* [The Secret Heart of the Clock] (1987), unless otherwise indicated.

Books

There are books, that one has for twenty years without reading them, that one always keeps at hand, that one takes along from city to city, from country to country, carefully packed, even when there is very little room, and perhaps one leafs through them while removing them from a trunk; yet one carefully refrains from reading even a complete sentence. Then after twenty years, there comes a moment when suddenly, as though under a high compulsion, one cannot help taking in such a book from beginning to end, at one sitting: it is like a revelation. Now one knows why one made such a fuss about it. It had to be with one for a long time; it had to travel; it had to occupy space; it had to be a burden; and now it has reached the goal of its voyage, now it reveals itself, now it illuminates the twenty bygone years it mutely lived with one. It could not say so much if it had not been there mutely the whole time, and what idiot would dare to assert that the same things had always been in it.

Die Provinz des Menschen: Aufzeichnungen 1942–1972 [The Province of Man: Notebooks 1942–1972] (1973).

What proof have we that inorganic objects can feel no pain? Who knows if a book may not yearn for other books, its companions of many years, in some way strange to us and therefore never yet perceived?

Die Blendung [The Blinding] (1935).

Death

I repulse death with all my strength. If I accepted it, I would be a murderer.
He will not do death the honor of taking it into account.

Experience

"Life experience" does not amount to very much and could be learned from novels alone, e.g., from Balzac, without any help from life.
Relearn astonishment.

Experimental Literature

I was never drawn to experiment with language; I take note of such experiments, but avoid them in my own writing. The reason is that the substance of life claims me completely. To indulge in linguistic experiments is to ignore the greater part of this substance, leaving all but a tiny portion untouched and unused, as if a musician were to ceaselessly play an instrument with his little finger only.

Fear

Fear thrives strongest; there is no telling how little we would be without having suffered fear. An intrinsic characteristic of humanity is the tendency to give in to fear. No fear is lost, but its hiding places are a riddle. Perhaps, of all things, fear is the one that changes least.

Die gerettete Zunge: Geschichte einer Jugend [The Tongue Set Free: Story of a Youth] (1977).

When I think back on my early years, the very first things I recognize are the fears, of which there was an inexhaustible wealth.

Die gerettete Zunge: Geschichte einer Jugend [The Tongue Set Free: Story of a Youth] (1977).

Forgetting

Everything one has forgotten screams for help in dreams.

Die Provinz des Menschen: Aufzeichnungen 1942–1972 [The Province of Man: Notebooks 1942–1972] (1973).

Happiness

Kien was almost tempted to believe in happiness, that contemptible life-goal of illiterates. If it came of itself, without being hunted for, if you did not hold it fast by force and treated it with a certain condescension, it was permissible to endure its presence for a few days.

Die Blendung [The Blinding] (1935).

Home

Yes, this was his home. Here no harm could come to him. . . . Every human creature needed a home, not a home of the kind understood by crude knock-you-down patriots, not a religion either, a mere insipid foretaste of a heavenly home: no, a real home, in which space, work, friends, recreation, and the scope of a man's ideas came together into an orderly whole, into—so to speak—a personal cosmos. The best definition of a home was a library.

Die Blendung [The Blinding] (1935).

Humankind

There is almost nothing bad that I couldn't say about humans and humankind. And yet my pride in them is so great that there is only one thing I really hate: their enemy, death.

Die gerettete Zunge: Geschichte einer Jugend [The Tongue Set Free: Story of a Youth] (1977).

Knowledge

For I believe that part of knowledge is its desire to show itself and its refusal to put up with a merely hidden existence. I find mute knowledge dangerous, for it grows ever more mute and ultimately secret, and must then avenge itself for being secret.

Die gerettete Zunge: Geschichte einer Jugend [The Tongue Set Free: Story of a Youth] (1977).

Life

Any life is laughable if one knows it well enough. It is something serious and terrible if one knows it even better.

Der andere Prozeß: Kafkas Briefe an Felice [Kafka's Other Trial: The Letters to Felice] (1969).

Literature

It amazes me how a person to whom literature means anything can take it up as an object of *study*.

Love

Nothing among all human emotions is more beautiful and more hopeless than the wish to be loved for oneself alone. Who are you anyway, next to countless others, to deserve such preference? . . . As though the earth had only one heaven, and heaven only one earth, we lay claim to the validity of both and, if we have one, we want to be the other. In reality, however, we are filled with planets, and countless heavens open their doors to us.

Die Provinz des Menschen: Aufzeichnungen 1942–1972 [The Province of Man: Notebooks 1942–1972] (1973).

Music

One single beautiful sound is more beautiful than a long discourse.

Old Age

I noticed in the front row a small, very pale, almost white man, old, tremendously alert, old in the only way I love old age, namely more alive for all the years, more attentive, more unrelenting, expectant and ready, as though he still had to make up his mind about most things and must not disregard anything.

Public Discourse

Is there still a possibility of public truth?

The prime condition for that would be that you pose your own questions, not just answer them. The questions of others have a distorting influence, one adapts to them, accepts words and concepts that should be avoided at all costs.

Ideally, you should use only words which you have filled with new meaning.

There is something *impure* in the laments about the dangers of our time, as if they could serve to excuse our personal failure.

Reading and Research

You can tirelessly keep on reading the same author, revere, admire, praise him, exalt him to the skies, know and recite each of his sentences by heart, and yet remain completely unaffected by him, as if he had never demanded anything of you and not said anything at all.

You keep taking note of whatever confirms your ideas—better to write down what refutes and weakens them!

Technology

The hand which scoops up the water is the first vessel. The fingers of both hands intertwined are the first basket.

Masse und Macht [Crowds and Power] (1960).

Thought

Whenever the truth threatens, he hides behind a thought.

Ambition is the death of thought.

You don't have to know a philosopher's every syllable to know why he rubs you the wrong way. You may know it best after a few of his sentences, and less and less well after that. The important thing is to see his web and move away before you tear it.

One needs time to free oneself of wrong convictions. If it happens too suddenly, they go on festering.

His meals were always punctual. Whether she cooked well or badly he did not know; it was a matter of total indifference to him. During his meals, which he ate at his writing desk, he was busy with important considerations. As a rule he would not have been able to say what precisely he had in his mouth. He reserved consciousness for real thoughts; they depend upon it; without consciousness, thoughts are unthinkable. Chewing and digestion happen of themselves.

Die Blendung [The Blinding] (1935).

Everything you rejected and pushed aside—take it up again.

Writing

He sometimes tells himself that there is nothing more to be said, simply because he won't get around to saying it.—How contemptible! You need the rhetoric of others, the aversion it inspires, in order to find the way out of your own.

Say the most personal thing, say it, nothing else matters, don't be ashamed, the generalities can be found in the newspaper.

The process of writing has something infinite about it. Even though it is interrupted each night, it is one single notation, and it seems most true when it eschews artistic devices of any sort.

Karl Kraus

Karl Kraus / 1874–1936 / Kingdom of Bohemia, Austro-Hungarian Empire / Journalist, Publisher, Lecturer, Poet, Dramatist, Essayist, Aphorist

Note: Though born into an Ashkenazi Jewish family in what is now the Czech Republic, Kraus's family moved to Vienna in 1877, when he was three years old. He lived there for the rest of his life.

Note: Unless indicated otherwise, all quotations are taken from *Die Fackel* [The Torch], the newspaper that Kraus published, edited, and contributed to between 1899 and 1936. After 1911, he contributed essentially all of the copy for the magazine himself. English translations of most, but not all, of the quotations from *Die Fackel* reproduced here may also be found in Half-Truths and One-and-a-Half Truths: Selected Aphorisms (1976).

Aphorisms

An aphorism can never be the whole truth; it is either a half-truth or a truth-and-a-half.

Someone who can write aphorisms should not fritter away his time writing essays.

Art

Only he is an artist who can make a riddle out of a solution.

Love and art do not embrace what is beautiful but what is made beautiful by this embrace,

Beim Wort genommen [Taken at His Word] (1955).

Berlin and Vienna

In Berlin, things are serious but not hopeless. In Vienna, they are hopeless but not serious.

Books and Writers

Where will I ever find the time not to read so much?

Sprüche und Widersprüche [Sayings and Gainsayings] (1909).

One must read all writers twice—the good as well as the bad. The one kind will be recognized; the other, unmasked.

There are two kinds of writers. With the first, content and form belong together like soul and body; with the second, they match each other like body and clothes.

Consumerism

We are sacrificing ourselves for our ready-made goods; we are consumers and live in such a way that the means may consume the end.

"In dieser grossen Zeit" [In This Great Time] (1914).

Criminal Justice

Squeeze human nature into a straitjacket of criminal justice and crime will appear!

Culture

Culture is the tacit agreement to let the means of subsistence disappear behind the purpose of existence.

"In dieser grossen Zeit" [In This Great Time] (1914).

When the sun of culture is low, even dwarves will cast long shadows.

Democracy

Democracy means the opportunity to be everyone's slave.

Equality

Nothing is more narrow-minded than chauvinism or race hatred. To me all men are equal: there are jackasses everywhere, and I have the same contempt for them all.

Esthetes

The esthete stands in the same relation to beauty as the pornographer stands to love, and the politician stands to life.

Freedom

The tyranny of necessity grants its slaves three kinds of freedom: opinion free from intellect, entertainment free from art, and orgies free from love,

"In dieser grossen Zeit" [In This Great Time] (1914).

Greetings

If I return some people's greetings, I do so only to give them their greeting back.

Humanity

The devil is an optimist if he thinks he can make people worse than they are.

The superman is a premature ideal, one that presupposes a man.

To be human is erroneous.

Lord, forgive them, for they know what they do!

A weak man has doubts before a decision, a strong man has them afterwards.

Jealousy

Jealousy is a dog's bark which attracts thieves.

Journalists

The making of a journalist: no ideas and the ability to express them.

Kraus's Public

I and my public understand each other very well: it does not hear what I say, and I don't say what it wants to hear.

I trim my opponents to fit my arrows.

Many desire to kill me, and many wish to spend an hour chatting with me. The law protects me from the former.

Life

Life is an effort that deserves a better cause.

You don't even live once.

Literature

Today's literature: prescriptions written by patients.

It is better not to express what one means than to express what one does not mean.

Love

There is no more unfortunate creature under the sun than a fetishist who yearns for a woman's shoe and has to settle for the whole woman.

A “seducer” who boasts of initiating women into the mystery of love is like a stranger who arrives at a railroad station and offers to show the sights to a tourist guide.

Prejudice

I have often been asked to be fair and view a matter from all sides. I did so, hoping something might improve if I viewed all sides of it. But the result was the same. So I went back to viewing things only from one side, which saves me a lot of work and disappointment. For it is comforting to regard something as bad and be able use one’s prejudice as an excuse.

Progress

Progress celebrates Pyrrhic victories over nature.

Pro Domo et Mundo [For Home and World] (1912).

Progress … has subordinated the purpose of life to the means of subsistence and turned us into the nuts and bolts for our tools.

“In dieser grossen Zeit” [In This Great Time] (1914).

Psychoanalysis

My unconscious knows more about the consciousness of the psychologist than his consciousness knows about my unconscious.

Psychoanalysis is that mental illness for which it regards itself as therapy.

So-called psychoanalysis is the occupation of lustful rationalists who trace everything in the world to sexual causes – with the exception of their occupation.

Reason and Passion

Keep your passions in check, but beware of giving your reason free rein.

Solitude

Solitude would be an ideal state if one were able to pick the people one avoids.

The world is a prison in which solitary confinement is preferable.

Technology

The development of technology will leave only one problem: the infirmity of human nature.

War

War: first, one hopes to win; then one expects the enemy to lose; then, one is satisfied that the enemy too is suffering; in the end, one is surprised that everyone has lost.

When the word “peace” was uttered for the first time, there was panic at the stock exchange. They screamed in pain: “We’ve been earning! Leave us the war! We’ve earned the war!”

How is the world ruled and led to war? Diplomats lie to journalists and believe these lies when they see them in print.

Women

There are women who are not beautiful but only look that way.

Sprüche und Widersprüche [Dicta and Contradictions] (1909).

Women at least have elegant dresses. But what can men use to cover their emptiness?

Nicolas Chamfort

Nicolas **Chamfort** / 1741–1794 / France / Dramatist, Poet, Essayist, Critic, Aphorist
Note: All quotations are taken from *Maximes et pensées* [Maxims and Thoughts] (first published posthumously in 1796).

Common Decency

A decent man plays his part to the best of his ability, regardless of the taste of the gallery.

Contemplation

Contemplation often makes life miserable. We should act more, think less, and stop watching ourselves live.

Happiness

Pleasure can be supported by an illusion, but happiness rests upon truth.

Last Words

And so I leave this world, where the heart must either break or turn to lead.

Laughter

The most wasted day of all is that on which we have not laughed.

Life

In order not to find life unbearable, you must accept two things: the ravages of time and the injustices of man.

Living is a sickness to which sleep provides relief every sixteen hours. It's a palliative. The remedy is death.

Love

There are more people who wish to be loved than there are who are willing to love.

Misanthropy

Whoever is not a misanthrope at forty can never have loved mankind.

Opposing Virtues

We ought to be able to combine opposites: the love of goodness with indifference to other people's opinions, a liking for work with indifference to fame, concern for our health with indifference to life.

Passion

It is passion that makes man live; wisdom makes one only last.

Public Opinion

Public opinion is the worst of all opinions. One can be certain that every generally held idea, every received notion, will be an idiocy, because it has been able to appeal to a majority.

Society

It is commonly supposed that the art of pleasing is a wonderful aid in the pursuit of fortune; but the art of being bored is infinitely more successful.

When you want to be well-liked in the world, you have to let a lot of people teach you things that you know and they don't.

M. de Lassay, a very mild-mannered man, but with a great knowledge of society, used to say that we should swallow a toad every morning to avoid being disgusted for the rest of the day, when we have to spend it in society.

Coco Chanel

Gabrielle Bonheur Chanel / 1883–1971 / France / Fashion Designer, Businesswoman

Art vs. Fashion

A work of art is something that at first seems ugly and becomes beautiful. Fashion first seems beautiful and then becomes ugly.

Reported in "France: Dictator by Demand," TIME magazine, March 4, 1957; accessible at time.com.

We don't need genius, just a little skill and a lot of taste.

Reported in "High Priestess of High Fashion: Gabrielle Chanel," TIME magazine, August 22, 1960; accessible at time.com.

Chanel on Chanel

In 1919 I woke up famous. I'd never guessed it. If I'd known I was famous, I'd have stolen away and wept. I was stupid. I was supposed to be intelligent. I was sensitive and very dumb.

Reported by Marcel Haedrich in Coco Chane: Her Life, Her Secrets (1972); originally published in French in 1971.

Re: Chanel's friendship with Misia Sert:

In 1919 I woke up famous and with a new friend who was to give its full meaning to my success.

In conversation with Salvador Dalí; reported by Meredith E. Smith in The Persistence of Memory: A Biography of Dalí (1992).

Re: In response to the question who she dressed:

Ask me who I don't dress!

Reported by David Downie in Paris, Paris: Journey Into the City of Light (2005).

I was a rebellious child, a rebellious lover, a rebellious *couturière*—a real devil.

Reported by David Downie in Paris, Paris: Journey Into the City of Light (2005).

Re: imitations Chanel dresses:

Thirty years ago, I went to dinner at Giro's. I remember counting 23 Chanel dresses in the room. But I was sure of only one: mine. I found that a very pretty compliment.

Reported in "High Priestess of High Fashion: Gabrielle Chanel," TIME magazine, August 22, 1960; accessible at time.com.

Re: Chanel's rejection of the Duke of Westminster's marriage proposal:

There have been several duchesses of Westminster. There is only one Chanel.

Reported in "High Priestess of High Fashion: Gabrielle Chanel," TIME magazine, August 22, 1960; accessible at time.com.

Fashion

There is nothing more comfortable than a caterpillar and nothing more made for love than a butterfly. We need dresses that crawl and dresses that fly. Fashion is at once a caterpillar and a butterfly, caterpillar by day, butterfly by night.

Statement from 1920s; reported by Jean Leymari in Chanel(2011); originally published in French in 1987.

Fashion is made to become unfashionable.

Interview, LIFE magazine, August 19, 1957.

Fashion is architecture. It is a matter of proportions.

Reported by Marcel Haedrich in Coco Chane: Her Life, Her Secrets (1972); originally published in French in 1971.

Elegance is not the prerogative of those who have just escaped from adolescence, but of those who have already taken possession of their future.

Reported by Marcel Haedrich in Coco Chane: Her Life, Her Secrets (1972); originally published in French in 1971.

Dress shabbily and they remember the dress; dress impeccably and they remember the woman.

Reported by Marcel Haedrich in Coco Chane: Her Life, Her Secrets (1972); originally published in French in 1971.

Fashion fades, only style remains the same.

Widely cited; however, attribution unconfirmed.

Fashion is not something that exists in dresses only. Fashion is in the sky, in the street, fashion has to do with ideas, the way we live, what is happening.

Reported by Axel Madsen in Chanel: A Woman of Her Own (1990).

The best colour in the whole world is the one that looks good on you.

Reported by Natalie Bloom in Beauty in Bloom: A Collection of Beautiful Inspirations (2009).

Men and Women

As long as you know that most men are like children, you know everything.

Widely cited; however, attribution unconfirmed.

A girl should be two things: classy and fabulous.

Reported by Marcel Haedrich in Coco Chane: Her Life, Her Secrets (1972); originally published in French in 1971.

Women think of all colors except the absence of color. I have said that black has it all. White too. Their beauty is absolute. It is the perfect harmony.

Reported by Jean Leymari in Chanel (2011); originally published in French in 1987.

Philosophy of Life

How many cares one loses when one decides not to be something, but to be someone.

Widely cited; however, attribution unconfirmed.

Youth is something very new: Twenty years ago no one mentioned it.

Reported by Marcel Haedrich in Coco Chane: Her Life, Her Secrets (1972); originally published in French in 1971.

Nothing is ugly as long as it is alive.

Reported by Marcel Haedrich in Coco Chane: Her Life, Her Secrets (1972); originally published in French in 1971.

In order to be irreplaceable one must always be different.

Reported by Marcel Haedrich in Coco Chane: Her Life, Her Secrets (1972); originally published in French in 1971.

Don't spend time beating on a wall, hoping to transform it into a door.

Reported by Marcel Haedrich in Coco Chane: Her Life, Her Secrets (1972); originally published in French in 1971.

The most courageous act is still to think for yourself. Aloud.

Reported by Marcel Haedrich in Coco Chane: Her Life, Her Secrets (1972); originally published in French in 1971.

The best things in life are free. The second best are very expensive.

Widely cited; however, attribution unconfirmed.

Some people think luxury is the contrary of being poor. No, it is the contrary of vulgarity.

Reported in "High Priestess of High Fashion: Gabrielle Chanel," TIME magazine, August 22, 1960; accessible at time.com.

World War II

Re: Charles De Gaulle:

I wholeheartedly welcomed his eulogy of French valour, to which he attributed the liberation of Paris. Have you listened to him lately? He will soon be claiming that the Resistance has liberated the world.

Interview with Malcolm Muggeridge (then working for British intelligence, MI6), September, 1944; accessible at muggeridge.co.uk.

One should refrain from contempt for the baser specimens of humanity, for whom liberation amounts to shaving the heads of women who have slept with Germans.

Interview with Malcolm Muggeridge (then working for British intelligence, MI6), September, 1944; accessible at muggeridge.co.uk.

A major shortcoming of the Resistance is the outnumbering, before long, of the genuine warriors by camera-carrying midgets intent on leaving a record of their purported heroism.

Interview with Malcolm Muggeridge (then working for British intelligence, MI6), September, 1944; accessible at muggeridge.co.uk.

Q: . . . Which side were you on?

A: On neither side, of course. I stood up for myself as I always have done. Nobody has ever told Coco Chanel what to think.

Interview with Malcolm Muggeridge (then working for British intelligence, MI6), September, 1944; accessible at muggeridge.co.uk.

. . . I have learned to dissemble my true feelings. I have misled people, so many people, that I too could have worked in espionage.

Interview with Malcolm Muggeridge (then working for British intelligence, MI6), September, 1944; accessible at muggeridge.co.uk.

A: Your allies accommodate with Stalin, a mass-murderer. The Germans, on the other hand, fought against the mass-murderer, but are set on destroying civilisation. How, in these circumstances, can I be expected to choose between the two?

Q: Perhaps because those circumstances to which you allude have not always prevailed. For the first two years of the war, I remind you that Stalin was opposed to the Allies. Why did you not support us then?

A: My dear Mr. Muggeridge, during the first two years of the war, your Allies did not even exist. The fate of the world hinged on one man—a friend of mine, Winston Churchill. He, and he alone, stood up to Hitler. Sadly, though, Churchill has already lost the war.

Q: With great respect, he is winning the war, actually.

A: Far from it. Can you possibly conceive appeasing Stalin as a victory for Winston, proud of his forebears as he is? Winston is a dandy and a visionary. Unfortunately, in winning wars, principles are inevitably debased. That's politics. As early as the 1930s, when Winston confronted Hitler on his own, he must have realised that, with war looming sooner or later, he would be forced to make compromises. Unlike him, I have steadfastly refused to make concessions that would undermine my ideals.

Interview with Malcolm Muggeridge (then working for British intelligence, MI6), September, 1944; accessible at muggeridge.co.uk.

Amy Chua

Amy Lynn Chua / b. 1962 / Illinois, USA / Attorney, Legal Scholar, Author

Asian vs. European Culture and Parenting Practices

There are all kinds of psychological disorders in the West that don't exist in Asia.

Amy Chua, Battle Hymn of the Tiger Mother (2011).

The fact is that Chinese parents can do things that would seem unimaginable-even legally actionable-to Westerners. Chinese mothers can say to their daughters, "Hey fatty-lose some weight." By contrast, Western parents have to tiptoe around the issue, talking in terms of "health" and never ever mentioning the f-word, and their kids still end up in therapy for eating disorders and negative self image.

Amy Chua, Battle Hymn of the Tiger Mother (2011).

Western parents try to respect their children's individuality, encouraging them to pursue their true passions, supporting their choices, and providing positive reinforcement and a nurturing environment. By contrast, the Chinese believe that the best way to protect their children is by preparing them for the future, letting them see what they're capable of, and arming them with skills, work habits, and inner confidence that no one can ever take away.

Amy Chua, Battle Hymn of the Tiger Mother (2011).

All decent parents want to do what's best for their children. The Chinese just have a totally different idea of how to do that.

Amy Chua, Battle Hymn of the Tiger Mother (2011).

Chinese parents believe that their kids owe them everything.

Amy Chua, Battle Hymn of the Tiger Mother (2011).

Western parents worry a lot about their children's self-esteem. But as a parent, one of the worst things you can do for your child's self-esteem is to let them give up. On the flip side, there's nothing better for building confidence than learning you can do something you thought you couldn't.

Amy Chua, Battle Hymn of the Tiger Mother (2011).

All these Western parents with the same party line about what's good for children and what's not—I am not sure that they are making choices at all. They just do what every one else does. They are not questioning anything either, which is what Westerners are supposed to be so good at doing. They just keep repeating things like "You have to give your children the freedom to pursue their passion" when it is obvious that the "passion" is just going to be Facebook for ten hours which is a total waste of time and eating all that disgusting junk food. I am telling you, this country is going to go straight downhill.

Amy Chua, Battle Hymn of the Tiger Mother (2011).

Chua on Chua

But just because you love something, I added to myself, doesn't mean you'll ever be great. Not if you don't work. Most people stink at the things they love.

Amy Chua, Battle Hymn of the Tiger Mother (2011).

Everything I've ever done that's valuable is something I was afraid to try.

Amy Chua, Battle Hymn of the Tiger Mother (2011).

The truth is I'm not good at enjoying life.

Amy Chua, Battle Hymn of the Tiger Mother (2011).

Unlike Western parents, reminding my child of Lord Voldemort didn't bother me.

Amy Chua, Battle Hymn of the Tiger Mother (2011).

Once when I was young—maybe more than once—when I was extremely disrespectful to my mother, my father angrily called me "garbage" in our native Hokkien dialect. It worked really well. I felt terrible and deeply ashamed of what I had done. But it didn't damage my self esteem or anything like that. I knew exactly how highly he thought of me. I didn't actually think I was worthless or feel like a piece of garbage. As an adult, I once did the same thing to [Chua's daughter] Sophie, calling her garbage in English when she acted extremely disrespectful toward me. When I mentioned I had done this at a dinner party, I was immediately ostracized. One guest named Marcy got so upset she broke down in tears and had to leave early.

Amy Chua, Battle Hymn of the Tiger Mother (2011).

One of my greatest fears is family decline. There's an old Chinese saying that "prosperity can never last for three generations."

Amy Chua, Battle Hymn of the Tiger Mother (2011).

My goal as a parent is to prepare you for the future, not to make you like me.

Amy Chua, Battle Hymn of the Tiger Mother (2011).

My dogs can't do anything–and what a relief. I don't make any demands of them, and I don't try to shape them or their future. For the most part, I trust them to make the right choices for themselves. I always look forward to seeing them, and I love just watching them sleep. What a great relationship.

Amy Chua, Battle Hymn of the Tiger Mother (2011).

Philosophy of Life

Do you know what a foreign accent is? It's a sign of bravery. Those are people who crossed an ocean to come to this country.

Amy Chua, Battle Hymn of the Tiger Mother (2011).

Nothing is fun until you're good at it.

Amy Chua, Battle Hymn of the Tiger Mother (2011).

As a purely mathematical fact, people who sleep less live more.

Amy Chua, Battle Hymn of the Tiger Mother (2011).

Every day that you don't practice is a day you're getting worse.

Amy Chua, Battle Hymn of the Tiger Mother (2011).

Be modest, be humble, be simple.Make sure you come in first so that you have something to be humble about.

Amy Chua, Battle Hymn of the Tiger Mother (2011).

Never complain or make excuses. If something seems unfair, just prove yourself by working twice as hard and being twice as good.

Amy Chua, Battle Hymn of the Tiger Mother (2011).

Humans are tribal. We need to belong to groups. We crave bonds and attachments, which is why we love clubs, teams, fraternities, family. Almost no one is a hermit. Even monks and friars belong to orders. But the tribal instinct is not just an instinct to belong. It is also an instinct to exclude.

Amy, Chua, Political Tribes: Group Instinct and the Fate of Nations (2018).

A life that doesn't include hard-won accomplishment and triumph over obstacles may not be a satisfying one. There is something deeply fulfilling—even thrilling—in doing almost anything difficult extremely well. There is a joy and pride that come from pushing yourself to another level or across a new frontier. A life devoted only to the present—to feeling good in the now—is unlikely to deliver real fulfillment. The present moment by itself it too small, too hollow. We all need a future. Something beyond and greater than our own present gratification, at which to aim or feel we've contributed.

Amy Chua and Jed Rubenfeld, The Triple Package: How Three Unlikely Traits Explain the Rise and Fall of Cultural Groups in America (2014).

Politics

Today, no group in America feels comfortably dominant. Every group feels attacked, pitted against other groups not just for jobs and spoils but for the right to define the nation's identity. In these conditions, democracy devolves into zero-sum group competition—pure political tribalism.

Amy, Chua, Political Tribes: Group Instinct and the Fate of Nations (2018).

America's continued existence as a supergroup is under tremendous strain today. America is beginning to display destructive political dynamics much more typical of developing and non-Western countries: ethnonationalist movements; backlash by elites against the masses; popular backlash against both "the establishment" and "outsider minorities" viewed as disproportionately powerful; and, above all, the transformation of democracy into an engine of zero-sum political tribalism.

Amy, Chua, Political Tribes: Group Instinct and the Fate of Nations (2018).

When groups feel threatened, they retreat into tribalism. They close ranks and become more insular, more defensive, more punitive, more us-versus-them. In America today, every group feels this way to some extent. Whites and blacks, Latinos and Asians, men and women, Christians, Jews, and Muslims, straight people and gay people, liberals and conservatives—all feel their groups are being attacked, bullied, persecuted, discriminated against. Of course, one group's claims to feeling threatened and voiceless are often met by another group's derision because it discounts their own feelings of persecution—but such is political tribalism.

Amy, Chua, Political Tribes: Group Instinct and the Fate of Nations (2018).

Winston Churchill

Winston Leonard Spencer Churchill / 1874–1965 / England (United Kingdom of Great Britain and Ireland) / Politician, Prime Minister, Historian

WORLD WAR II

Blood, Toil, Tears, and Sweat

I would say to the House, as I said to those who have joined this Government, I have nothing to offer but blood, toil, tears and sweat. We have before us an ordeal of the most grievous kind. We have before us many long months of toil and struggle.

You ask what is our policy. I will say, it is to wage war with all our might, with all the strength that God can give us, to wage war against a monstrous tyranny never surpassed in the dark, lamentable catalogue of human crime.

You ask what is our aim? I can answer in one word: Victory. Victory at all costs. Victory in spite of all terror. Victory however long and hard the road may be. For without victory there is no survival.

Source: Speech, House of Commons, May 13, 1940.

Be Ye Men of Valour

. . . side by side, the British and French peoples have advanced to rescue not only Europe but mankind from the foulest and most soul-destroying tyranny which has ever darkened and stained the pages of history. Behind them—behind us—behind the Armies and Fleets of Britain and France—gather a group of shattered States and bludgeoned races . . . upon all of whom the long night of barbarism will descend, unbroken even by a star of hope, unless we conquer, as conquer we must; as conquer we shall.

Today is Trinity Sunday. Centuries ago words were written to be a call and a spur to the faithful servants of Truth and Justice: "Arm yourselves, and be ye men of valour, and be in readiness for the conflict; for it is better for us to perish in battle than to look upon the outrage of our nation and our altar. As the Will of God is in Heaven, even so let it be." (1 Maccabees 3:58–60)

Source: BBC speech to the nation, May 19, 1940.

Never Surrender

We shall not flag or fail. We shall go on to the end. We shall fight in France, we shall fight on the seas and oceans, we shall fight with growing confidence and growing strength in the air. We shall defend our island, whatever the cost may be. We shall fight on the beaches, we shall fight on the landing-grounds, we shall fight in the fields and in the streets, we shall fight in the hills. We shall never surrender!

Source: Speech, House of Commons, June 4, 1940.

Preparing for the Battle of Britain

What General Weygand called the Battle of France is over. I expect that the battle of Britain is about to begin. Upon this battle depends the survival of Christian civilisation. Upon it depends our own British life, and the long continuity of our institutions and our Empire. The whole fury and might of the enemy must very soon be turned on us. . . . Let us therefore brace ourselves to our duties, and so bear ourselves that if the British Empire and its Commonwealth last for a thousand years, men will still say, "This was their Finest Hour."

Source: Speech, House of Commons, June 18, 1940.

Winning the Battle of Britain

The gratitude of every home in our island, in our Empire, and indeed throughout the world, except in the abodes of the guilty, goes out to the British airmen who, undaunted by odds, unwearied in their constant challenge and mortal danger, are turning the tide of the world war by their prowess and by their devotion. Never in the field of human conflict was so much owed by so many to so few.

Source: Speech, House of Commons, August 20, 1940.

The Tide Turns

The Germans have received back again that measure of fire and steel which they have so often meted out to others. Now this is not the end. It is not even the beginning of the end. But it is, perhaps, the end of the beginning.

Source: Speech, Lord Mayor's Luncheon, Mansion House, London, November 10, 1942.

THE COLD WAR

A shadow has fallen upon the scenes so lately lighted by the Allied victory. Nobody knows what Soviet Russia and its Communist international organization intends to do in the immediate future, or what are the limits, if any, to their expansive and proselytizing tendencies. . . . It is my duty however, for I am sure you would wish me to state the facts as I see them to you, to place before you certain facts about the present position in Europe.

From Stettin in the Baltic to Trieste in the Adriatic, an iron curtain has descended across the Continent. Behind that line lie all the capitals of the ancient states of Central and Eastern Europe. . . .

Source: Speech, Westminster College, Fulton, Missouri, March 5, 1946.

MISCELLANEOUS

Success is not final, failure is not fatal: it is the courage to continue that counts.

Source: doubtful attribution.

Never give in, never give in, never, never, never, never—in nothing, great or small, large or petty—never give in except to convictions of honour and good sense.

Source: Speech, Harrow School, October 29, 1941.

Success consists of going from failure to failure without loss of enthusiasm.

Source: doubtful attribution.

It is a mistake to look too far ahead. Only one link of the chain of destiny can be handled at a time.

Source: Speech, House of Commons, February 27, 1945.

If you are going through hell, keep going.

Source: doubtful attribution.

I cannot forecast to you the action of Russia. It is a riddle wrapped in a mystery inside an enigma.

Source: Speech, BBC, October 1, 1939.

The empires of the future are the empires of the mind.

Source: Speech, Harvard University, September 6, 1943.

E.M. Cioran

Emil Mihai Cioran / 1911–1995 / near Hermannstadt [Nagyszeben], Kingdom of Hungary (now Sibiu, Romania) / Novelist, Essayist, Aphorist

Absurdity

On the heights of despair, the passion for the absurd is the only thing that can still throw a demonic light on chaos. When all the current reasons—moral, esthetic, religious, social, and so on—no longer guide one's life, how can one sustain life without succumbing to nothingness? Only by a connection with the absurd, by love of absolute uselessness, loving something which does not have substance but which simulates an illusion of life. *I live because the mountains do not laugh and the worms do not sing.*

Sur les cimes du désespoir [On the Heights of Despair] (1934).

Cities

Whenever I happen to be in a city of any size, I marvel that riots do not break out everyday: Massacres, unspeakable carnage, a doomsday chaos. How can so many human beings coexist in a space so confined without hating each other to death?

Histoire et utopie [History and Utopia] (1960).

Consciousness

Knowledge is the plague of life, and consciousness, an open wound in its heart.

Sur les cimes du désespoir [On the Heights of Despair] (1934).

Haven't people learned yet that the time of superficial intellectual games is over, that agony is infinitely more important than syllogism, that a cry of despair is more revealing than the most subtle thought, and that tears always have deeper roots than smiles?

Sur les cimes du désespoir [On the Heights of Despair] (1934).

Consciousness is nature's nightmare.

Des larmes et des saints [Tears and Saints] (1937).

Better to be an animal than a man, an insect than an animal, a plant than an insect, and so on. Salvation? Whatever diminishes the kingdom of consciousness and compromises its supremacy.

De l'inconvénient d'être né [The Trouble with Being Born] (1973).

Convictions

We have convictions only if we have studied nothing thoroughly.

De l'inconvénient d'être né [The Trouble with Being Born] (1973).

Courage

Every act of courage is the work of an unbalanced man. Animals, normal by definition, are always cowardly except when they know themselves to be stronger, which is cowardice itself.

Écartelèment [Drawn and Quartered] (1983).

Death

Tell me how you want to die, and I'll tell you who you are.

Des larmes et des saints [Tears and Saints] (1937).

As long as I live I shall not allow myself to forget that I shall die; I am waiting for death so that I can forget about it.

Des larmes et des saints [Tears and Saints] (1937).

We must live, you used to say, as if we were never going to die.—Didn't you know that's how everyone lives, including those obsessed with Death?

Écartelèment [Drawn and Quartered] (1983).

Education

The only thing the young should be taught is that there is virtually nothing to be hoped for from life. One dreams of a *Catalogue of Disappointments* which would include all the disillusionments reserved for each and every one of us, to be posted in the schools.

De l'inconvénient d'être né [The Trouble with Being Born] (1973).

Epiphany

I was walking late one night along a tree-lined path; a chestnut fell at my feet. The noise it made as it burst, the resonance it provoked in me, and an upheaval out of all proportion to this insignificant event thrust me into miracle, into the rapture of the definitive, as if there were no more questions —only answers. I was drunk on a thousand unexpected discoveries, none of which I could make use of. This is how I nearly reached the Supreme. But instead I went on with my walk.

De l'inconvénient d'être né [The Trouble with Being Born] (1973).

Eros

No one should forget: Eros alone can fulfill life; knowledge, never.

Le livre des leurres [The Book of Delusions] (1936).

Existence

I am absolutely persuaded that I am nothing in this universe; yet I feel that mine is the only real existence.

Sur les cimes du désespoir [On the Heights of Despair] (1934).

Can it really be that for us existence means exile, and nothingness, home?

Sur les cimes du désespoir [On the Heights of Despair] (1934).

What am I, other than a chance in the infinite probabilities of not having been!

Le livre des leurres [The Book of Delusions] (1936).

This world was created from God's fear of solitude. In other words, us, the creatures, have no other meaning but to distract the Creator.

Des larmes et des saints [Tears and Saints] (1937).

By capitulating to life, this world has betrayed nothingness. . . .

Précis de décomposition [Précis of Decomposition] (1949].

I used to ask myself, over a coffin: "What good did it do the occupant to be born?," I now put the same question about anyone alive.

De l'inconvénient d'être né [The Trouble with Being Born] (1973).

I do not forgive myself for being born. It is as if, creeping into this world, I had profaned a mystery, betrayed some momentous pledge, committed a fault of nameless gravity. Yet in a less assured mood, birth seems a calamity I would be miserable not having known.

De l'inconvénient d'être né [The Trouble with Being Born] (1973).

Not to be born is undoubtedly the best plan of all. Unfortunately, it is within no one's reach.

De l'inconvénient d'être né [The Trouble with Being Born] (1973).

What to think of other people? I ask myself this question each time I make a new acquaintance. So strange does it seem to me that we exist, and that we consent to exist.

Écartelèment [Drawn and Quartered] (1983).

Fear

To fear is to die every minute.

Des larmes et des saints [Tears and Saints] (1937).

Freedom

If we would regain our freedom, we must shake off the burden of sensation, no longer react to the world by our senses, break our bonds. For all sensation is a bond, pleasure as much as pain, joy as much as misery. The only free mind is the one that, pure of all intimacy with beings or objects, plies its own vacuity.

La tentation d'exister [The Temptation to Exist] (1956).

No one can enjoy freedom without trembling.

Histoire et utopie [History and Utopia] (1960).

For you who no longer possess it, freedom is everything, for us who do, it is merely an illusion.

Histoire et utopie [History and Utopia] (1960).

One is and remains a slave as long as one is not *cured* of hoping.

Écartelèment [Drawn and Quartered] (1983).

God

I am displeased with everything. If they made me God, I would immediately resign.

Sur les cimes du désespoir [On the Heights of Despair] (1934).

I don't understand how people can believe in God, even when I myself think of him every day.

Le livre des leurres [The Book of Delusions] (1936).

The more one is obsessed with God, the less one is innocent. Nobody bothered about him in paradise. The fall brought about this divine torture. It's not possible to be conscious of divinity without guilt. Thus God is rarely to be found in an innocent soul.

Des larmes et des saints [Tears and Saints] (1937).

Obviously God was a solution, and obviously none so satisfactory as that will ever be found again.

De l'inconvénient d'être né [The Trouble with Being Born] (1973).

History

Isn't history ultimately the result of our fear of boredom?

Histoire et utopie [History and Utopia] (1960).

Human Condition

As far as I am concerned, I resign from humanity. I no longer want to be, nor can still be, a man. What should I do? Work for a social and political system, make a girl miserable? Hunt for weaknesses in philosophical systems, fight for moral and aesthetic ideals? It's all too little. I renounce my humanity even though I may find myself alone. But am

I not already alone in this world from which I no longer expect anything?

Sur les cimes du désespoir [On the Heights of Despair] (1934).

He who has never envied the vegetable has missed the human drama.

La chute dans le temps [The Fall into Time] (1964).

What are you waiting for in order to give up?

De l'inconvénient d'être né [The Trouble with Being Born] (1973).

Ideas

Ideas should be neutral. But man animates them with his passions and folly. Impure and turned into beliefs, they take on the appearance of reality.

Précis de décomposition [Précis of Decomposition] (1949].

Once man loses his faculty of indifference he becomes a potential murderer; once he transforms his idea into a god the consequences are incalculable. We kill only in the name of a god or of his counterfeits: the excesses provoked by the goddess Reason, by the concept of nation, class, or race are akin to those of the Inquisition or of the Reformation.

Précis de décomposition [Précis of Decomposition] (1949].

Life

One of the greatest delusions of the average man is to forget that life is death's prisoner.

Sur les cimes du désespoir [On the Heights of Despair] (1934).

If I were to be totally sincere, I would say that I do not know why I live and why I do not stop living. The answer probably lies in the irrational character of life which maintains itself without reason.

Sur les cimes du désespoir [On the Heights of Despair] (1934).

Why do you lack the strength to escape the obligation to breathe?

Précis de décomposition [Précis of Decomposition] (1949).

Love

Love, a tacit agreement between two unhappy parties to overestimate each other.

La chute dans le temps [The Fall into Time] (1964).

Memory

One of the biggest paradoxes of our world: memories vanish when we want to remember, but fix themselves permanently in the mind when we want to forget.

Sur les cimes du désespoir [On the Heights of Despair] (1934).

Music

A heart without music is like beauty without melancholy.

Des larmes et des saints [Tears and Saints] (1937).

If there is anyone who owes everything to Bach, it is certainly God.

Syllogismes de l'amertume [Syllogisms of Bitterness] (1952).

Old Age

Old age, after all, is merely the punishment for having lived.

Écartelèment [Drawn and Quartered] (1983).

Patriotism

What every man who loves his country hopes for in his inmost heart: the suppression of half his compatriots.

Histoire et utopie [History and Utopia] (1960).

Philosophers

. . . all of the philosophers put together are not worth a single saint.

Des larmes et des saints [Tears and Saints] (1937).

It has been a long time since philosophers have read men's souls. It is not their task, we are told. Perhaps. But we must not be surprised if they no longer matter much to us.

De l'inconvénient d'être né [The Trouble with Being Born] (1973).

Religion

Religion comforts us for the defeat of our will to power. It adds new worlds to ours, and thus brings us hope of new conquests and new victories. We are converted to religion out of fear of suffocating within the narrow confines of this world.

Des larmes et des saints [Tears and Saints] (1937).

Let us speak plainly: everything which keeps us from self-dissolution, every lie which protects us against our unbreathable certitudes is religious.

La tentation d'exister [The Temptation to Exist] (1956).

Sleep

Anyone can escape into sleep, we are all geniuses when we dream, the butcher's the poet's equal there.

La tentation d'exister [The Temptation to Exist] (1956).

Suffering

To suffer is the great modality of taking the world seriously.

Le livre des leurres [The Book of Delusions] (1936).

Suicide

No one commits suicide for external reasons, only because of inner disequilibrium. Under similar adverse circumstances, some are indifferent, some are moved, some are driven to suicide.

Sur les cimes du désespoir [On the Heights of Despair] (1934).

Why don't I commit suicide? Because I am as sick of death as I am of life.

Sur les cimes du désespoir [On the Heights of Despair] (1934).

In a single second we do away with all seconds; God himself could not do as much.

Précis de décomposition [Précis of Decomposition] (1949].

I live only because it is in my power to die when I choose to: without the *idea* of suicide, I'd have killed myself right away.

Syllogismes de l'amertume [Syllogisms of Bitterness] (1952).

When people come to me saying they want to kill themselves, I tell them, "What's your rush? You can kill yourself any time you like. So calm down. Suicide is a positive act." And they do calm down.

De l'inconvénient d'être né [The Trouble with Being Born] (1973).

Tears

Tears do not burn except in solitude.

Sur les cimes du désespoir [On the Heights of Despair] (1934).

. . . my tears would drown the world, as my inner fire would reduce it to ashes.

Sur les cimes du désespoir [On the Heights of Despair] (1934).

Thinking

Only those are happy who never think or, rather, who only think about life's bare necessities, and to think about such things means not to think at all. True thinking resembles a demon who muddies the spring of life or a sickness which corrupts its roots. To think all the time, to raise questions, to doubt your own destiny, to feel the weariness of living, to be worn out to the point of exhaustion by thoughts and life, to leave behind you, as symbols of your life's drama, a trail of smoke and blood—all this means you are so unhappy that reflection and thinking appear as a curse causing a violent revulsion in you.

Sur les cimes du désespoir [On the Heights of Despair] (1934).

The moment we believe we've understood *everything* grants us the look of a murderer.

Syllogismes de l'amertume [Syllogisms of Bitterness] (1952).

The first thinker was, without a doubt, the first man obsessed by why.

De l'inconvénient d'être né [The Trouble with Being Born] (1973).

Every thought derives from a thwarted sensation.

De l'inconvénient d'être né [The Trouble with Being Born] (1973).

Each of us believes, quite unconsciously of course, that we alone pursue the truth, which the rest are incapable of seeking out and unworthy of attaining. This madness is so deep-rooted and so useful that it is impossible to realize what would become of each of us if it were someday to disappear.

De l'inconvénient d'être né [The Trouble with Being Born] (1973).

Time and Eternity

Time is heavy sometimes; imagine how heavy eternity must be.

Le livre des leurres [The Book of Delusions] (1936).

Truth

If truth were not boring, science would have done away with God long ago. But God as well as the saints is a means to escape the dull banality of truth.

Des larmes et des saints [Tears and Saints] (1937).

Truths begin by a conflict with the police—and end by calling them in.

Précis de décomposition [Précis of Decomposition] (1949].

We live in the false as long as we have not suffered. But when we begin to suffer, we enter the truth only to regret the false.

Écartelèment [Drawn and Quartered] (1983).

Utopia

Utopia is a mixture of childish rationalism and secularized angelism.

Histoire et utopie [History and Utopia] (1960).

Albert Cohen

Albert Cohen / 1895–1981 / Corfu, Kingdom of Greece / International Administrator, Novelist, Memoirist

Babies

A baby staggers like a drunkard. Charming, this baby, not dangerous, doesn't judge Jews. Makes me feel like kissing him. No. Too blond. An anti-Semite in twenty years.

Belle du Seigneur [The Master's Beauty] (1968).

Eternal Life

Brothers, my human brothers, force me to believe in eternal life.

Le livre de ma mère [The Book of My Mother] (1954).

Fatherland

Yes, the words, the land of my birth, they console me and compensate, but they would not bring me my mother back.

Le livre de ma mère [The Book of My Mother] (1954).

Habit

Having become protocol and polite ritual, the words of love glided along on the oilcloth of habit.

Belle du Seigneur [The Master's Beauty] (1968).

Happiness

Suddenly, at my work table, because all is in order and I have a cup of hot coffee and have just lit a cigarette and because I have a lighter that works and my fountain pen works well and I am near the fire and my cat, I experience a moment of great happiness that moves me. I pity myself for this childish capacity for immense joy which foretells nothing good. How much pity I feel to see myself so contented on account of a fountain pen that works well, pity for this poor bastard of a heart which wants to stop suffering and to grab onto some reason to live.

Le livre de ma mère [The Book of My Mother] (1954).

More words, fast, if we stop speaking unhappiness insinuates itself.

Belle du Seigneur [The Master's Beauty] (1968).

Human Race

The human race will expire from cruelty.

Belle du Seigneur [The Master's Beauty] (1968).

Life and Death

. . . man lives for the blink of an eye and then rots forever, and every day you take another step closer to the hole in the ground where you will molder in great stupidity and silence with nothing for company but worms, white and fat like those in flour or cheese, which penetrate all your orifices to feed.

Belle du Seigneur [The Master's Beauty] (1968).

Quite alone we are, the two of us, you in the earth, me in my bedroom. Me, a little bit dead among the living, you, a little bit alive among the dead.

Le livre de ma mère [The Book of My Mother] (1954).

Loneliness

Alone dwells every man and everyone mocks everyone else, and a deserted island is our pain.

Le livre de ma mère [The Book of My Mother] (1954).

With her alone I was not alone. Now I am alone with everyone.

Le livre de ma mère [The Book of My Mother] (1954).

In my solitude I sing to myself a sweet lullaby, as sweet as my mother used to sing to me.

Le livre de ma mère [The Book of My Mother] (1954).

Love

This happened in the blink of an eye and she looked at me without seeing me, and it was glory and spring and the sun and the warm sea and her diaphanous presence on the shore and my youth restored, and the world was born.

Belle du Seigneur [The Master's Beauty] (1968).

Solemn among the loveless couples, preoccupied by themselves alone, they tasted each other, careful, profound, abandoned. Feeling blessed to be held and guided, she disregarded everyone else, listened to the happiness in her veins, sometimes admiring them in the high mirrors on the walls, elegant, moving, exceptional, a woman loved, sometimes craning her head to see him better as he murmured marvels she did not always understand, for she watched him too much, but which she always approved with her whole soul . . . she whispered that they had their whole lives, and suddenly she was afraid she had displeased him, too sure of herself, but no, O happiness, he smiled at her and kept on holding her close to him . . .

Belle du Seigneur [The Master's Beauty] (1968).

Whoever wishes to be loved religiously makes a pact with the devil, because he loses his soul. Women have forced me to pretend to be cruel. I will never forgive them!

Belle du Seigneur [The Master's Beauty] (1968).

Others take weeks and months to arrive at loving, and at loving a little, and they require discussions and shared tastes and crystallizations. Me, it was the time of the blink of an eye.

Belle du Seigneur [The Master's Beauty] (1968).

She did not doubt that he was coming to adore her awkwardness and that he remained silent to make it last.

Belle du Seigneur [The Master's Beauty] (1968).

Kneeling, men were ridiculous, they were proud and handsome, and to live was sublime.

Belle du Seigneur [The Master's Beauty] (1968).

If poor Romeo had suddenly had his nose cut clean off in an accident, when Juliet next saw him she would have fled in horror. Thirty grams less meat and Juliet's soul is no longer nobly stirred. Thirty grams less and that is the end of sublime moonlit babble, of "It is not yet near day: it was the nightingale, and not the lark."

Le livre de ma mère [The Book of My Mother] (1954).

Marseille

She had loved everything about Marseille, noisy Longue-des-Capucins Street with its foodstuffs on display and its criers, the fish market with its strapping, loud-mouthed lads, Rome Street, Saint-Férréol Street, la Canebière, the Old Port with its narrow, sinister, yet friendly streets filled with feline, sway-hipped, and pock-marked gentlemen driving dangerously.

Belle du Seigneur [The Master's Beauty] (1968).

Memory

Go away, image of my living mother, full of life, as I saw her in France for the last time. Go away! My mother's ghost.

Le livre de ma mère [The Book of My Mother] (1954).

I say to myself that her little hands are no longer warm, and that never again will I carry them so soft to my forehead.

Le livre de ma mère [The Book of My Mother] (1954).

Mother and Son

Human friends, friends in hardship and in life, this is our pure love, love of mother and son.

Le livre de ma mère [The Book of My Mother] (1954).

My true single consolation is that she is not present to see me in my agony at her death.

Le livre de ma mère [The Book of My Mother] (1954).

In my sleep, which is the song of the tombs, I have just seen her again, as beautiful as in her youth.

Le livre de ma mère [The Book of My Mother] (1954).

She answers no more, the one who used to answer always.

Le livre de ma mère [The Book of My Mother] (1954).

She does not talk anymore, the one who used to talk so pleasantly.

Le livre de ma mère [The Book of My Mother] (1954).

She waited three hours for me in that square. Three hours which I could have spent with her. While she was waiting for me, wreathed in patience, I chose to concern myself, stupidly enthralled, with some poetic amber damsel, abandoning the wheat for the chaff. I missed three hours of my mother's life. And for whom, good God? For an Atalanta, an attractive arrangement of flesh. I dared to prefer an Atalanta to the most sacred goodness, to my mother's love, my mother's incomparable love.

Incidentally, if some sudden illness had deprived me of my strength or merely all my teeth, the poetic damsel would have pointed me out and ordered her maid to sweep away that toothless garbage. . . . Her soul would have made off on wings of scorn. Those noble creatures love men who are strong, energetic, and assertive—in other words, gorillas. Toothless or not, strong or weak, young or old, our mothers love us. And the weaker we are, the more they love us. Our mothers' incomparable love.

Le livre de ma mère [The Book of My Mother] (1954).

Nobility

Nobility is a matter of vocabulary.

Belle du Seigneur [The Master's Beauty] (1968).

Poverty

Not to become poor with a poor man's soul. Poverty debases us. The poor man becomes ugly and takes the bus, washes less, smells of perspiration, counts his change, loses his nobility and can no longer despise sincerely.

One hardly despise what one possesses and dominates. Goethe was better than Rousseau at despising.

Belle du Seigneur [The Master's Beauty] (1968).

Power

How great the suffering we can inflict on those who love us and how frightful the power to do harm that we have over them. And how we make use of that power.

Le livre de ma mère [The Book of My Mother] (1954).

Purposelessness

Outside, everywhere, a relentless rain recounted their unhappiness. Caught in a mousetrap of love, condemned for life to the labor of love, they were lying next to each other, beautiful, tender lovers and purposeless. Purposeless.

Belle du Seigneur [The Master's Beauty] (1968).

Taste

. . . the poor are vulgar, not interested in beauty, in what elevates the soul, very different indeed from Queen Marie of Romania who in her memoirs blessed the faculty that God, it seems, gave her "of feeling deeply the beauty of things and of rejoicing in it." Exquisite attentiveness by the Everlasting.

Belle du Seigneur [The Master's Beauty] (1968).

Writing

What a strange little happiness, sad and limping but sweet as a sin or a hidden bottle, what happiness it is, after all, to write in this moment, alone in my kingdom and far from the bastards.

Le livre de ma mère [The Book of My Mother] (1954).

Tim Cook

Timothy Donald Cook / b. 1960 / Alabama, USA / Business Executive, former COO and current CEO of Apple, Inc.

Apple

You can converge a toaster and refrigerator, but these things are probably not going to be pleasing to the user.

Reported by Nick Wingfield in "Apple Chief's Offhand Comment Spawns Internet Quip," nytimes.com, April 24, 2012.

Our base philosophy is to never fear cannibalization. If we do, somebody else will just cannibalize it. We never fear it.

Reported by Megan Geuss in "Tim Cook on the iMac: 'cannibalization is a huge opportunity for us,'" arstechnica.com, January 23, 2013.

When we work on making our devices accessible by the blind, I don't consider the bloody ROI.

Reported by Steve Denning in "Why Tim Cook Doesn't Care About 'The Bloody ROI,'" forbes.com, March 7, 2014.

The things we should be doing at Apple are things that others can't.

Reported by Brad Stone and Adam Satariano in "The iPhone 6, the Apple Watch, and Remaking a Company's Culture," blomber.com, September 17, 2014.

If you want me to only do things for ROI reasons, then you should get out of this stock.

Reported by Siimon Reynolds in "Lessons You Can Learn From Apple's CEO," forbes.com, March 25, 2015.

It was like a total revelation for me that a company could run like this, because I was used to these layers and bureaucracies and studies—the sort of paralysis that companies could get into—and Apple was totally different.

Reported by Don Reisinger in "Apple CEO Tim Cook Says Working for Steve Jobs Was 'Liberating,'" fortune.com, August 23, 2018.

Apple Music

There are very few content owners that believe that the existing model will last forever, I think the most forward-thinking ones are looking and saying, "I'd rather have the first-mover advantage."

Reported by Julia Love in "Apple Music hits 6.5 million paid users: Tim Cook," investing.com, October 20, 2015.

We worry about the humanity being drained out of music, about it becoming a bits-and-bytes kind of world instead of the art and craft.

Reported by Cal Jeffrey in "Tim Cook thinks Spotify is 'draining the humanity out of music,'" techspot.com, August 8, 2018.

Apple Watch

If there were any doubts, I think that they should be put to bed.

Reported by Brad Stone and Adam Satariano in "The iPhone 6, the Apple Watch, and Remaking a Company's Culture," blomber.com, September 17, 2014.

Business Philosophy

Don't just accept the world you inherit today. Don't just accept the status quo. No big challenge has ever been solved, and no lasting improvement has ever been achieved, unless people dare to try something different. Dare to think different.

Reported by Nina Zipkin in "From Oprah Winfrey to Tim Cook, Leaders Offer Gems of Wisdom to the Class of 2018," entrepreneur.com, May 24, 2018.

I don't think business should only deal in commercial things. Business, to me, is nothing more than a collection of people. If people have values, then companies should.

Reported by Karen Gilchrist in "Apple's Tim Cook shares a rule that leaders should live by," cnbc.com, June 26 2018.

When I think of ethics, I think of leaving things better than you found them. And to me, that goes from everything from environmentally, to how you work with suppliers with labor questions, to the carbon footprint of your products, to the things you choose to support, to the way you treat your employees. . . . Your whole persona fits under that umbrella.

Leander Kahney, Tim Cook: The Genius Who Took Apple to the Next Level (2019).

. . . the power of human creativity can solve even the biggest challenges—and that the people who are crazy enough to think they can change the world are the ones who do.

Leander Kahney, Tim Cook: The Genius Who Took Apple to the Next Level (2019).

Cook on Cook

I don't consider myself an activist, but I realize how much I've benefited from the sacrifice of others, . . . So if hearing that the CEO of Apple is gay can help someone struggling to come to terms with who he or she is, or bring comfort to anyone who feels alone, or inspire people to insist on their equality, then it's worth the trade-off with my own privacy.

Reported by Daisuke Wakabayashi and Lisa Fleisher in "Apple CEO Tim Cook: 'I'm Proud to Be Gay,'" wsj.com, October 30, 2014.

Steve was a genius and a visionary, and I've never viewed that my role was to replace him. Steve was an original. I've never really felt the weight of trying to be Steve. It's not my goal in life. I am who I am. I am focused on that. On being a great CEO of Apple.

Reported by Dan Farber in "Tim Cook: 'I've never really felt the weight of trying to be Steve,'" cnet.com, May 29, 2012.

Re: Cook's decision to leave Compaq to take the job at Apple:

I don't think that you're born with a gut, I think the gut matures and gets better and better over time, and the struggle that most people have, I think, is learning to listen to it and figuring out how to access it in some way. For me, what I found is that even though I'm an engineer and an analytical person at heart. the most important decisions I've made had nothing to do with any of that. They were always based on intuition. The Apple one is the prime example of that. I remember, actually, forming my list of pluses and minuses and I could not get the chart to work out the way I wanted it to. Because I wanted something to say this says I should go to Apple. But it would not. Nothing financially would do that, I talked to people I trusted, that knew me, and they said: "This is not what you should do." It wasn't so easy. People said, "you're just crazy, you're working for the top PC company in the world, how could you even think of doing it, you've lost your mind." And, yet, that voice said, "Go West young man, Go West." And sometimes you just have to go for it.

Interview at Fuqua School of Business, Duke University, "Apple CEO Tim Cook on Intuition," youtube.com.

Impact of Technology

All of these things are great conveniences of life. They change your daily life in a great way. But if you're getting bombarded by notifications all day long, that's probably a use of the system that might not be so good anymore.

Interview with Laura Sydell and Steve Inskeep in "Apple Requested 'Zero' Personal Data In Deals With Facebook, CEO Tim Cook Says," npr.org, June 4, 2018.

Coding gives people the ability to change the world and from my perspective, it's the most important second language and the only language that is global.

Leander Kahney, Tim Cook: The Genius Who Took Apple to the Next Level (2019).

International Trade

The countries that embrace openness do exceptional and the countries that don't, don't. It's not a matter of carving things up between sides. I'm going to encourage that calm heads prevail.

Reported by Mark Gurman in "Apple's Cook to Meet With Trump Amid China Trade Tensions," bloomberg.com, April 24, 2018.

iPhone

Re: The introduction of iPhone 6 and Apple Watch:

If there was a lot of emotion in my voice today, it's because we've all been waiting for this day for a long time. It felt so great, . . . the people at this company are doing the best work of their lives, the best work that Apple has ever done.

Reported by Marco della Cava in "Tim Cook tells USA TODAY: 'This is epic,'" usatoday.com, September 9, 2014.

Privacy

We reject the excuse that getting the most out of technology means trading away your right to privacy. So we choose a different path, collecting as little of your data as possible, being thoughtful and respectful when it's in our care because we know it belongs to you.

Reported by Jackie Wattles in "Apple's Tim Cook urges Duke graduates to think hard about data privacy," cnn.com, May 13, 2018.

The privacy thing has gotten totally out of control. I think most people are not aware of who is tracking them, how much they're being tracked and sort of the large amounts of detailed data that are out there about them.

Reported by Seth Fiegerman in "Tim Cook reveals his tech habits: I use my phone too much," cnn.com, June 4, 2018.

Stephen R. Covey

Stephen Richards Covey / 1932–2012 / Utah, USA / Businessman, Educator, Author

Accusations

Give no answer to contentious arguments or irresponsible accusations. Let such things "fly out open windows" until they spend themselves.

Stephen R. Covey, Principle-Centered Leadership (1990).

Character

Our capacity for production and enjoyment is a function, in the last analysis, of our character, our integrity.

Stephen R. Covey, The 8th Habit: From Effectiveness to Greatness (2004).

Communicating

In the last analysis, what we are communicates far more eloquently than anything we say or do.

Stephen R. Covey, Principle-Centered Leadership (1990).

Prepare your mind and heart before you prepare your speech. What we say may be less important than how we say it.

Stephen R. Covey, Principle-Centered Leadership (1990).

The power to distinguish between person and performance and to communicate intrinsic worth flows naturally out of our own sense of intrinsic worth.

Stephen R. Covey, Principle-Centered Leadership (1990).

Courage

Courage is not the absence of fear but the awareness that something else is more important.

Stephen R. Covey, "Foreword," in Alex Pattakos, Prisoners of Our Thoughts: Viktor Frankl's Principles at Work (2004).

Free Will

Unless we exercise our power to choose wisely, our actions will be determined by conditions. Our ultimate freedom is the right and power to decide how anybody or anything outside ourselves will affect us.

Stephen R. Covey, Principle-Centered Leadership (1990).

Integrity in the Moment of Choice: Quality of life depends on what happens in the space between stimulus and response.

Stephen R. Covey, A. Roger Merrill, and Rebecca R. Merrill, First Things First (1994).

The Moment of Choice: A moment of choice is a moment of truth. It's the testing point of our character and competence.

Stephen R. Covey, A. Roger Merrill, and Rebecca R. Merrill, First Things First (1994).

Because of the space between stimulus and response, people have the power of choice;

therefore, leaders are neither born nor made —meaning environmentally trained and nurtured. They are self-made through chosen responses, and if they choose based on principles and develop increasingly greater discipline, their freedom to choose increases.

Stephen R. Covey, The 8th Habit: From Effectiveness to Greatness (2004).

Leadership and Management

Effective leadership is putting first things first. Effective management is discipline, carrying it out.

Reported by Paul G. Schempp in Teaching Sport and Physical Activity: Insights on the Road to Excellence (2003).

Management is efficiency in climbing the ladder of success; leadership determines whether the ladder is leaning against the right wall.

Stephen R. Covey, (1989).

Learning and Teaching

Remember, to learn and not to do is really not to learn. To know and not to do is really not to know.

Stephen R. Covey, (1989).

Let natural consequences teach responsible behavior. One of the kindest things we can do is to let the natural or logical consequences of people's actions teach them responsible behavior. They may not like it or us, but popularity is a fickle standard by which to measure character development. Insisting on justice demands more true love, not less. We care enough for their growth and security to suffer their displeasure.

Stephen R. Covey, Principle-Centered Leadership (1990).

Life Mission

We don't invent our missions, we detect them.

Reported by Hyrum W. Smith, What Matters Most: The Power of Living Your Values (2000).

Listening

Most people do not listen with the intent to understand; they listen with the intent to reply.

Stephen R. Covey, (1989).

Love

Live the law of love. We encourage obedience to the laws of life when we live the laws of love.

Stephen R. Covey, Principle-Centered Leadership (1990).

Personal Growth

Live out of your imagination, not your history.

Reported by Eric Allenbaugh in Wake-Up Calls: You Don't Have to Sleepwalk Through Your Life, Love, or Career! (1992).

Self growth is tender; it's holy ground. There's no higher investment.

Stephen R. Covey, (1989).

Principles

Principles are *universal*—that is, they transcend culture and geography. They're also *timeless,* they never change—principles such as fairness, kindness, respect, honesty, integrity, service, contribution. Different cultures may translate these principles into different practices and over time may even totally obscure these principles through the wrongful use of freedom. Nevertheless, they are present. Like the law of gravity, they operate constantly.

Stephen R. Covey, The 8th Habit: From Effectiveness to Greatness (2004).

Prioritizing

The key is not to prioritize what's on your schedule, but to schedule your priorities.

Stephen R. Covey, (1989).

Retirement

Retire from your job but never from meaningful projects. If you want to live a long life, you need *eustress,* that is, a deep sense of meaning and contribution to worthy projects and causes, particularly your intergenerational family.

Stephen R. Covey, The 8th Habit: From Effectiveness to Greatness (2004).

Selfless Service

Perform anonymous service. Whenever we do good for others anonymously, our sense of intrinsic worth and self-respect increases. . . . Selfless service has always been one of the most powerful methods of influence.

Stephen R. Covey, Principle-Centered Leadership (1990).

Spiritual Intelligence

Spiritual Intelligence represents our drive for meaning and connection with the infinite.

Stephen R. Covey, The 8th Habit: From Effectiveness to Greatness (2004).

Time Management

We present a dramatically different approach to time management. This is a principle-centered approach. It transcends the traditional prescriptions of faster, harder, smarter, and more. Rather than offering you another clock, this approach provides you with a compass—because more important than how fast you're going, is where you're headed.

Stephen R. Covey, A. Roger Merrill, and Rebecca R. Merrill, First Things First (1994).

Trust

Trust is the glue that holds everything together. It creates the environment in which all of the other elements—win-win stewardship agreements, self-directing individuals and teams, aligned structures and systems, and accountability—can flourish.

Stephen R. Covey, A. Roger Merrill, and Rebecca R. Merrill, First Things First (1994).

Vision and Values

It's not enough to have values without vision; you want to be good, but you want to be good for something. On the other hand, vision without values can create a Hitler. An empowering mission statement deals with both character and competence; what you want to be and what you want to do in your life.

Stephen R. Covey, A. Roger Merrill, and Rebecca R. Merrill, First Things First (1994).

Values are social norms — they're personal, emotional, subjective, and arguable. All of us have values. Even criminals have values. The question you must ask yourself is, *Are your values based upon principles?* In the last analysis, principles are natural laws — they're impersonal, factual, objective and self-evident. Consequences are governed by principles and behavior is governed by values; therefore, value principles!

Stephen R. Covey, The 8th Habit: From Effectiveness to Greatness (2004).

Michael Dell

Michael Saul Dell / b. 1965 / Texas, USA / Businessman, Entrepreneur, Founder of Dell Technologies

Artificial Intelligence

Every technology creates good and bad. You can sit here and say, "AI is really bad, we shouldn't have AI"—that's nonsense. We have to figure out how to use it in a responsible way, that's our job.

Reported by Chris Duckett, "AI shouldn't be held back by scaremongering: Michael Dell," zdnet.com, May 1, 2018.

Change

Real transformations of major tech companies are extremely rare: I think because companies develop a particular capability, and a set of customers, and change is hard. You can't take the stripes off a tiger. If you're born a dog, you don't die a cat.

Play Nice But Win: A CEO's Journey from Founder to Leader(2021).

Climate

If you think about decarbonization and climate and the environment, technology is the fulcrum. All of these problems, opportunities, challenges I believe are at some level tied to technology because their opportunities were computational power and networks and communications and all the ingredients of technology would go into solving the problems.

Report by John Simons, "Michael Dell Has Been a Tech CEO for 34 Years. He Has Some Advice For Younger Founders," Time, October 31, 2021.

Dell on Dell

I don't know why people aren't more curious, and why curiosity isn't considered a more important leadership trait. A journalist once asked me if I was ever bored as a kid. I only had to think about it for a second: I never was, not even for a minute, because I was so curious. Every day I'd wake up excited by all the new things there were to learn about.

Play Nice But Win: A CEO's Journey from Founder to Leader(2021).

Sometimes it's better not to ask—or to listen—when tell you something can't be done. I didn't ask for permission or approval. I just went ahead and did it.

Direct From Dell: Strategies That Revolutionized an Industry, with Catherine Fredman (1999).

And with a forty-five-year-old genuine grown-up and experienced entrepreneur as president and CFO, we now had access to all kinds of working-capital credit we couldn't get before. Unlike the twenty-one-year-old CEO, Lee Walker could go to people like Frank Phillips at Texas Commerce Bank and say, "Look, Texaco, Exxon, Monsanto—all these companies, not to mention the US government—they all owe this company money. Give us a loan based on all these receivables." And the bankers would say, "Okay, Lee, we don't know about the kid, but we trust you."

Play Nice But Win: A CEO's Journey from Founder to Leader(2021).

Q: When you talk to these younger founders, what are they most interested to hear from you? What are they asking you about?

A: It's interesting. They ask about how you grow and evolve a team, because they're struggling with that—the hyper growth. And then they get into how you raise your kids and how do you make sure your kids don't turn out to be horrible and stuff like that. They want to know a lot about how you raise a family and manage that balance.

Report by John Simons, "Michael Dell Has Been a Tech CEO for 34 Years. He Has Some Advice For Younger Founders," Time, October 31, 2021.

Our business is about technology, yes. But it's also about operations and customer relationships. There are a lot of things that go into creating success. I don't like to do just the things I like to do. I like to do things that cause the company to succeed. I don't spend a lot of time doing my favorite activities.

Reported by William J. Holstein in "Dell's CEO Michael Dell: Exclusive Interview with Dell's Michael Dell," chiefexecutive.com.

Dell Technologies

I started the business with a simple question: How can we make the process of buying a computer better? The answer was: Sell computers directly to the end customer. Eliminate the reseller's markup and pass those savings on to the customer.

Direct From Dell: Strategies That Revolutionized an Industry, with Catherine Fredman (1999).

The magic formula in our business is figuring out what stage of the evolution a given technology is at and when it's right for Dell to use its business model and customer relationships to make a product that is much higher in volume and lower in cost. Some would call it commoditization or standardization, but we constantly look at our business and say, "Well, where are these new technologies on the continuum? And when is it the right time for us to start a new activity? When is the right time to go after a new type of customer, a new geography? Should we be focusing more on large businesses vs. small businesses vs. consumers? What about services? What about professional services or financial services? We have many more choices than we could ever execute on. We're not constrained by capital. We're constrained by, "How many of these things can you actually achieve with a high degree of success and profit?" We've got that paradox.

Reported by William J. Holstein in "Dell's CEO Michael Dell: Exclusive Interview with Dell's Michael Dell," chiefexecutive.com.

This is a 19-year-old company, so we've gone through some pretty dynamic changes in a pretty short period of time. In that sense, it wasn't all that different from other periods of change. Except here, while we might not have made our financial goals, we were still pretty nicely profitable and our business was pretty healthy. Whenever you adjust your strategy for the times, say for industry consolidation, a kind of logical follow-on to that is, "What is the right structure?" We consolidated some things.

We kind of started off with "Where are you growing, where are you expanding?" The right creative tension in the business is to examine those on a constant basis. So that you say, "Okay, we're trying to expand into these nine areas, but the market is contracting, so maybe we should scale that back and only do three of those and save the other six for later because that's what the times dictate."

Reported by William J. Holstein in "Dell's CEO Michael Dell: Exclusive Interview with Dell's Michael Dell," chiefexecutive.com.

Direct Business Model

You actually get to have a relationship with the customer and that creates valuable information, which, in turn, allows us to leverage our relationships with both suppliers and customers. Couple that information with technology, and you have the infrastructure to revolutionize the fundamental business models of major global companies.

Reported by Joan Magretta, "The Power of Virtual Integration: An Interview with Dell Computer's Michael Dell," Harvard Business Review, March-April, 1998.

Ecological Ramifications

Let me back up to the early '90s. We were producing enormous numbers of computers and it's doubling every year. And at some point, you kind of figure out wow, this is a machine with a defined lifespan. At some point, it's no longer useful. What the heck happens then? We better think about this pretty carefully, because if you make a million of these things, eventuality there's a million that are no longer being used. Then you make 10 million, you make 100 million, et cetera. You start to think deeply about the lifecycle and the materials and the ingredients that go in these things. What if these things end up in a stream somewhere or a dumpster or a ditch? So I challenged our team. Let's really do a molecular level look at everything we're putting in our machines to say which of any of these ingredients could possibly, over time, be dangerous or harmful. How do we eliminate those? So we started thinking about how do we use the cleanest, greenest materials. We started thinking about recycling and life cycle. When I was going to sleep at night, putting the head on the pillow, I'm thinking, "Holy *bleep*, all these things have my name on them."

Report by John Simons, "Michael Dell Has Been a Tech CEO for 34 Years. He Has Some Advice For Younger Founders," Time, October 31, 2021.

Excellence

If you want to sustain excellence over a long time, you'd better come up with a system that works well. Anyone can sprint for a little while, but you can't sprint for forty years.

Attribution unconfirmed.

Try never to be the smartest person in the room. And if you are, I suggest you invite smarter people . . . or find a different room.

Commencement address, University of Texas at Austin, 2003.

For-Profit vs. Philanthropy

I had a dinner at my house on Friday night with about 10 founders of companies, and they were all, I'll say, 10 to 15 years younger than I am. A lot of super interesting companies, some of them are already public, some are about to go public. And these companies were born more with the purpose orientation that we now have. I'm investing in a lot of these companies that have a deep belief that they can make a positive impact in the world. Philanthropy is great, and I support philanthropy and do a lot there, but actually I think the for-profit enterprises that have an intention of doing things that benefit society are driving a lot more progress than philanthropy by itself. And you've seen this time and time again in finance for example, and microfinance, with microlending. You see for-profit enterprises making a huge impact.

Report by John Simons, "Michael Dell Has Been a Tech CEO for 34 Years. He Has Some Advice For Younger Founders," Time, October 31, 2021.

Founders

I do think a founder has special permission to make sweeping changes across an organization.

Reported by Connie Guglielmo, "A Private Conversation with Michael Dell, 'The Man In The Arena,'" October 30, 2013.

Growth

Growth covers up a lot of sins.

Play Nice But Win: A CEO's Journey from Founder to Leader(2021).

Ideas vs. Execution

Ideas are commodity. Execution of them is not.

Attribution unconfirmed.

Our lean beginnings created the strategic management principles that define our culture: Less is more. Information is better than inventory. Ingenuity is better than investment. Execution is everything. No excuses.

Direct From Dell: Strategies That Revolutionized an Industry, with Catherine Fredman (1999).

Innovation and Risk Aversion

At the root of it, you have to erase risk and you have to raise experimentation and incubating new ideas and testing things. You have to be explicit about the desire to go after these new opportunities, with the knowledge that they're not all going to work. Risk is not a bad thing. One of the things that happens in companies as they get bigger is they become risk averse. Nobody wants to take a risk. Well, turns out, if you want to innovate, you're going to have risk. So we make heroes of the innovators. We celebrate the patent awardees. We have, I think, 32,000 patents now. You want to see an exciting thing, come to our patent awards celebrations that we have and see somebody get an award for getting 50 patents or 100 patents during their career. It's always experiment, test, fail, try again, and then eventually, hopefully you get some success. You want to encourage that.

Report by John Simons, "Michael Dell Has Been a Tech CEO for 34 Years. He Has Some Advice For Younger Founders," Time, October 31, 2021.

Investment

We have lots of hack-a-thons and contests inside the company, those kinds of things. We have a pretty developed process to fund internal new ventures. And of course innovation occurs not just within the boundaries of the company. You have partners and alliances that you're always collaborating with. You have companies you acquire because they're at the bleeding edge of experimenting with new things and so that can accelerate innovation. And then we have another thing which is very important: Dell Technologies Capital, which has invested in about 130 companies [since 2012]. It's all about 5G and AI and machine learning and cybersecurity, and things that are relevant to our future. And these companies are experimenting and some of them will be successful. Most of them will fail. That's just the way the ventures work, but we'll learn a lot from those companies.

Report by John Simons, "Michael Dell Has Been a Tech CEO for 34 Years. He Has Some Advice For Younger Founders," Time, October 31, 2021.

Milestones

We have this history of setting outrageous targets internally and occasionally will talk about those externally. You have to be careful about doing them externally because they become a forecast and have a very different implication.

But we find that our people are very motivated by big goals, whether it's providing customers with absolutely the best value or entering a new market with great success or achieving a particular milestone. I think of them as milestones. You have plenty along the way. It does focus the attention of the organization on what we're trying to achieve.

Reported by William J. Holstein in "Dell's CEO Michael Dell: Exclusive Interview with Dell's Michael Dell," chiefexecutive.com.

Opportunity

People have often told us that what we wanted to do couldn't be done. Our success is due, in part, to not just an ability but a willingness to look at things differently. I believe opportunity is part instinct and part immersion—in an industry, a subject, or an area of expertise. Dell is proof that people can learn to recognize and take advantage of opportunities that others are convinced don't exist.

Direct From Dell: Strategies That Revolutionized an Industry, with Catherine Fredman (1999).

Personnel

One of the things I learned early on was that not everyone had the same values and beliefs. We had to be very explicit about what was OK and what wasn't OK. As you expand a company, especially around the world—this is maybe not the most elegant way to put it, but—there are places in the world where if they didn't catch you doing it, it's OK. Well, that's not OK in our company. So we had to be super explicit about that and I think by being explicit, we hopefully didn't attract people that wanted to operate in a different way. And when there were things that were consistent with that, it wasn't like a, "Hey, I'm sorry, I'll never do it again." It's like, "No, no. You don't do that. You're gone." And I think having an extremely clear boundary around what's acceptable and what's not acceptable . . . some might say wow, it's really harsh.

Report by John Simons, "Michael Dell Has Been a Tech CEO for 34 Years. He Has Some Advice For Younger Founders," Time, October 31, 2021.

Social Issues

I don't want to be known as the guy that created an environmental catastrophe, right? When all we were trying to do was make computers.

Report by John Simons, "Michael Dell Has Been a Tech CEO for 34 Years. He Has Some Advice For Younger Founders," Time, October 31, 2021.

You've probably seen some of the same data I have, but the Gen-Zers… I think a high percentage of them believe that companies should aim to do good in the world. I don't think that was the case 40 years ago. And maybe this is because organizations have a bigger role in the world than they used to. Maybe it's because other organizations have a lesser role. I don't really know. We don't feel compelled to weigh in on every issue, but there are certainly issues that we feel sort of intersect with our business and our stakeholders and our shareholders and also things that we can do something about, and meaningfully impact.

Report by John Simons, "Michael Dell Has Been a Tech CEO for 34 Years.

He Has Some Advice For Younger Founders," Time, October 31, 2021.

Success and Failure

You don't have to be a genius or a visionary or even a college graduate to be successful. You just need a framework and a dream.

Reported in "Michael Dell: Taking the Direct Approach," Entrepreneur, October 9, 2008.

How successful you are is really a function of how well you deal with failure—and how much you learn from it.

Play Nice But Win: A CEO's Journey from Founder to Leader(2021).

Technology

We have a long history here of integrating the technologies closer together. This is what customers have been asking us to do. It is what we are doing. It is working extremely well. There is much, much more to come here.

Reported by Mark Haranas, "Michael Dell: 'Much, Much More To Come' on Dell EMC VMware Integration," crn.com, June 11, 2018.

The way I describe this when talking with businesspeople is that the domain of technology is no longer in the IT department; the whole company is technology. I'm talking about all companies. If you're trying to make cars or medical devices or any kind of product at all, and you want to have new customers, technology is the fulcrum of progress in everything you're doing.

Play Nice But Win: A CEO's Journey from Founder to Leader(2021).

I think we're going to see a whole new wave of rapid industry transition—unlike the slow transition of, say, transportation, in which it took many years to go from rail to air travel. In this transition, you will see traditionally structured companies being seriously challenged by new, smaller, more efficient entrants—right away. The logical extension of the Internet's cost efficiencies means that market share will flow to the most efficient companies, not the largest or the richest—companies that can deliver the greatest value to their customers will earn a higher profit while requiring far fewer assets. The productivity of their capital will be significantly improved over the traditional model because they will have replaced physical assets with information assets.

Direct From Dell: Strategies That Revolutionized an Industry, with Catherine Fredman (1999).

Transhumanism

I love this idea of human-machine partnerships because in my mind it's always been very clear. It's not about humans *or* machines, it's about humans *and* machines.

Reported by Jessica Lyons Hardcastle, "Michael Dell Says Robopocalypse Is Fake News, Future Is Software Defined," sdxcentral.com, April 30, 2018.

Virtual Integration

When the company started, I don't think we knew how far the direct model could take us. It has provided a consistent underlying strategy for Dell despite a lot of change in our industry. Along the way, we have learned a lot, and the model has evolved. Most important, the direct model has allowed us to leverage our relationships with both suppliers and customers to such an extent that I believe it's fair to think of our companies as being virtually integrated. That allows us to focus on where we add value and to build a much larger firm much more quickly. I don't think we could have created a $12 billion business in 13 years if we had tried to be vertically integrated.

Reported by Joan Magretta, "The Power of Virtual Integration: An Interview with Dell Computer's Michael Dell," Harvard Business Review, March-April, 1998.

Alan Dershowitz

Alan Morton Dershowitz / b. 1938 / New York, New York, USA / Attorney, Law Professor, Legal Analyst, Political Commentator, Author, Podcaster

Note: The sources of the following quotations are provided where known; while the specific sources of most quotations are not known, they presumably derive from Dershowitz's numerous writings, online interviews, commentaries, and podcasts

Abortion

I can't find anything in the Constitution that says you prefer the life of the mother, or the convenience of the mother if it's an abortion by choice, over the potential life of the fetus.

Look, I think women, if they're required to not have abortions, could die—so I favor a woman's right to choose.

Civil Disobedience

Civil disobedience, as I put it to the audience, was not the problem, despite the warnings of some that it threatened social stability, that it led to anarchy. The greatest danger, I argued, was civil obedience, the submission of individual conscience to governmental authority.

Civil Liberties

Civil liberties had their origin and must find their ultimate guaranty in the faith of the people. If that faith should be lost, five or nine men in Washington could not long supply its want. The greatest protections of liberty are found in local self-government and in the representative character of our institutions.

Being a civil libertarian means I don't have to taste your soup to know it's too hot.

The concept of civil liberties is not an American concept; it is a universal concept. It's the concept of the rights of the individual against the state.

Constitution

One of the great things about the United States is that we have a constitution that guarantees everybody equal protection of the laws. And that is not just word; that is a constitutional principle.

The framers of the Constitution were very clear. They were to be a government, not of men, but of laws. They recognized that people who are given authority will abuse it.

Democracy

In a democracy, it's your vote that counts. In feudalism, it's your count that votes.

Dershowitz on Dershowitz

I'm a very tough guy, and I fight hard, and I don't give up. And that makes me friends and that makes me enemies, and I know that.

It's every lawyer's dream to help shape the law, not just react to it.

Aspirations don't disappoint, so long as you realize that the struggle for liberty, justice and anything else worth pursuing never stays won.

. . . despite finishing first in my class at Yale Law School, I was rejected by all 32 of the law firms to which I applied.

The Case Against BDS: Why Singling Out Israel for Boycott Is Anti-Semitic and Anti-Peace (2018).

I learned at that time, for an absolute certainty, that I did not believe in an intervening God, since I did not spend one second praying or trying to make a deal with God.

Taking the Stand: My Life in the Law (2013).

I have always considered "Pascal's Wager" a questionable bet to place. Any God worth "believing in" would surely prefer an honest agnostic to a calculating hypocrite.

Euphemisms

Asymmetrical warfare is a euphemism for terrorism, just like collateral damage is a euphemism for killing innocent civilians.

Extremism

The greatest dangers to liberty lurk in insidious encroachment by men of zeal, well-meaning but without understanding.

I am for civil liberties, and I am against extremism on both sides. I think extremism on both sides is dangerous.

Free Society

The test of a free society is how it treats its dissidents and nonconformists.

You can't pick and choose which types of freedom you want to defend. You must defend all of it or be against all of it.

The right to be let alone is indeed the beginning of all freedom.

The case for a free society is not that it is perfect; there is no such thing. It is that it is better than any alternative.

Free Speech

Censorship is antithetical to democracy. It is essential that information flow freely and without censorship. Even when people are acting irresponsibly, information about their activities should be available to the public.

If you don't have freedom of speech, then democracy is meaningless. If you can't express your views, democracy is just a façade.

The threat or fear of violence should not become an excuse or justification for restricting freedom of speech.

Freedom of speech means freedom for those who you despise, and freedom to express the most despicable views. It also means that the government cannot pick and choose which expressions to authorize and which to prevent.

Israel and Palestine

I'm not against criticizing Israel. I think Israel is a legitimate target for criticism. But it has to be legitimate criticism, it has to be fact-based criticism, it has to be fair criticism. It has to be criticism that recognizes that Israel does have a right to exist, does have a right to defend itself.

You can't think about terrorism without thinking about Palestinian terrorism. Palestinians began international terrorism. It started with them in 1968. They used it as the first resort, not the last resort. They invented it, they perfected it, they benefited from it and they taught the world how to use it and that it would be successful.

Those primarily responsible for the current desperate situation of the Palestinian people have been their own leaders, from Haj Hussaini (the late Grand Mufti of Jerusalem) to Yassir Arafat, to the leaders of Hamas and the other terrorist groups. These leaders have placed a higher priority on the destruction of Israel than on the construction of Palestine.

The Case for Israel (2003).

It is fair to say that although Israeli actions in combating terrorism have been far from perfect, Israel has been in greater compliance with the rule of law than any other country facing comparable dangers.

The Case for Israel (2003).

Yet the world, including many in the media, academia, and even diplomacy, seems to accept Palestinian violence as cultural. On the other hand, something different is expected from Israelis. This is cultural relativism bordering on racism. To expect less of Palestinians, regardless of their grievances, is to diminish their humanity.

The Case for Israel (2003).

The Palestinians will eventually have a state, but it should not come as a reward for terrorism.

The Case for Israel (2003).

Justice System

The courtroom is not a place where truth and innocence inevitably triumph; it is only an arena where contending lawyers fight not for justice but to win.

When you have high-profile cases, there are always going to be negative things that are going to come out, whether it's about my clients or my cases or my ethics or whatever.

The distinction between self-defense and aggression is not a moral one, but a legal one. It's a line in the sand that separates lawful violence from unlawful violence.

Justice is not always an outcome. It is a process.

Juries are not computers. They are composed of human beings who evaluate evidence differently.

Judges are the weakest link in our system of justice, and they are also the most protected.

Morality

Hypocrisy is not a way of getting back to the moral high ground. Pretending you're moral, saying you're moral is not the same as acting morally.

Public Good

I have spent my career trying to strike the balance between protecting civil liberties on the one hand and protecting national security on the other. And as I have said, it is not easy to strike that balance, and it's hard to do it right.

Individual rights must be balanced with collective responsibilities. In some cases, the greater good might require individuals to make sacrifices for the benefit of society.

Rule of Law

The challenge for democracy is to make sure that the rule of law becomes stronger than the rule of violence.

The Second Amendment

Foolish liberals who are trying to read the Second Amendment out of the Constitution by claiming it's not an individual right or that it's too much of a public safety hazard don't see the danger in the big picture. They're courting disaster by encouraging others to use the same means to eliminate portions of the Constitution they don't like.

Tolerance

The mark of a truly civilized society is the ability to recognize and respect the rights of people with whom we disagree.

If you deny that any principle or any principle of law is infallible, then you must drive to distinguish what is fallible from what is infallible. This is a much more difficult and dangerous task than is commonly supposed.

In the end, it is not what we believe, but how we believe that is most important.

Trump

. . . if a president did something that he believes will help him get elected, in the public interest, that cannot be the kind of quid pro quo that results in impeachment.

Reported in Nikki Carvajal, Paul LeBlanc, and Marshall Cohen, "Alan Dershowitz argues presidential quid pro quos aimed at reelection are not impeachable," cnn.com, January 29, 2020.

The essence of justice is that it must be equally applicable to all. . . . No one is above the law but digging to find crimes in order to influence an election does not constitute the equal application of the law.

Get Trump: The Threat to Civil Liberties, Due Process, and Our Constitutional Rule of Law (2023).

Truth

Winston Churchill reportedly quipped that "A lie travels around the globe while the truth is putting on its shoes." That was before the internet. Today, the truth can't even find its shoes.

Cancel Culture: The Latest Attack on Free Speech and Due Process (2020).

Charles Dickens

Charles Dickens / 1812–1870 / England (United Kingdom of Great Britain and Ireland) / Novelist

Ambition

Quadruped lions are said to be savage, only when they are hungry; biped lions are rarely sulky longer than when their appetite for distinction remains unappeased.

Nicholas Nickleby, Chapter 15 (1839).

Americans

Dollars! All their cares, hopes, joys, affections, virtues, and associations seemed to be melted down into dollars. Whatever the chance contributions that fell into the slow cauldron of their talk, they made the gruel thick and slab with dollars. Men were weighed by their dollars, measures were gauged by their dollars; life was auctioneered, appraised, put up, and knocked down for its dollars.

Martin Chuzzlewit, Chapter 16 (1844).

Babies

It is a pleasant thing to reflect upon, and furnishes a complete answer to those who contend for the gradual degeneration of the human species, that every baby born into the world is a finer one than the last.

Nicholas Nickleby, Chapter 36 (1839).

Beer

"Did you ever taste beer?" "I had a sip of it once," said the small servant. "Here's a state of things!" cried Mr Swiveller, raising his eyes to the ceiling. "She *never* tasted it—it can't be tasted in a sip!"

The Old Curiosity Shop, Chapter 57 (1841).

Bureaucracy

The Circumlocution Office was (as everybody knows without being told) the most important Department under Government. No public business of any kind could possibly be done at any time without the acquiescence of the Circumlocution Office. Its finger was in the largest public pie, and in the smallest public tart. It was equally impossible to do the plainest right and to undo the plainest wrong without the express authority of the Circumlocution Office. . . .
Whatever was required to be done, the Circumlocution Office was beforehand with all the public departments in the art of perceiving—HOW NOT TO DO IT.

Little Dorrit, Book I, Chapter 10 (1857).

Children

It is said that the children of the very poor are not brought up, but dragged up.

Bleak House, Chapter 6 (1853).

Christmas

Christmas time! That man must be a misanthrope indeed, in whose breast something like a jovial feeling is not roused—in whose mind some pleasant associations are not awakened—by the recurrence of Christmas.

Sketches by Boz, "Characters," Chapter 2 (1836).

Education

Now, what I want is, Facts. Teach these boys and girls nothing but Facts. Facts alone are wanted in life. Plant nothing else, and root out everything else. You can only form the minds of reasoning animals upon Facts: nothing else will ever be of any service to them. This is the principle on which I bring up my own children, and this is the principle on which I bring up these children. Stick to Facts, sir!

Hard Times, Book I, Chapter 1 (1854).

I took a good deal o' pains with his eddication, sir; let him run in the streets when he was wery young, and shift for his-self. It's the only way to make a boy sharp, sir.

The Pickwick Papers, Chapter 20 (1836).

Equality

But death, fires, and burglary, make all men equals.

Oliver Twist, Chapter 28 (1838).

There are many pleasant fictions of the law in constant operation, but there is not one so pleasant or practically humorous as that which supposes every man to be of equal value in its impartial eye, and the benefits of all laws to be equally attainable by all men, without the smallest reference to the furniture of their pockets.

Nicholas Nickleby, Chapter 46 (1839).

Evidence

Take nothing on its looks; take everything on evidence. There's no better rule.

Great Expectations, Chapter 40 (1861).

Flatterers

Although a skilful flatterer is a most delightful companion if you can keep him all to yourself, his taste becomes very doubtful when he takes to complimenting other people.

Nicholas Nickleby, Chapter 28 (1839).

Freedom

I only ask to be free. The butterflies are free. Mankind will surely not deny to Harold Skimpole what it concedes to the butterflies!

Bleak House, Chapter 6 (1853).

Gentlemen

He is a gentleman of strict conscience, disdainful of all littleness and meanness and ready on the shortest notice to die any death you may please to mention rather than give occasion for the least impeachment of his integrity. He is an honourable, obstinate, truthful, high-spirited, intensely prejudiced, perfectly unreasonable man.

Bleak House, Chapter 2 (1853).

Habits

I never could have done what I have done, without the habits of punctuality, order, and diligence, without the determination to concentrate myself on one object at a time.

David Copperfield, Chapter 42 (1850).

Happiness

Annual income twenty pounds, annual expenditure nineteen nineteen and six, result happiness. Annual income twenty pounds, annual expenditure twenty pounds ought and six, result misery.

David Copperfield, Chapter 12 (1850).

Humanity

"No one is useless in this world," retorted the Secretary, "who lightens the burden of it for any one else."

Our Mutual Friend, Book III, Chapter 9 (1865).

Inwardness

When a man bleeds inwardly, it is a dangerous thing for himself; but when he laughs inwardly, it bodes no good to other people.

The Pickwick Papers, Chapter 31 (1836).

Law

Jarndyce and Jarndyce drones on. This scarecrow of a suit, has, in course of time, become so complicated that no man alive knows what it means. The parties to it understand it least; but it has been observed that no two Chancery lawyers can talk about it for five minutes, without coming to total disagreement as to all the premises.

Bleak House, Chapter 1 (1853).

"It was all Mrs. Bumble. She *would* do it," urged Mr. Bumble; first looking round, to ascertain that his partner had left the room.

That is no excuse," returned Mr. Brownlow. "You were present on the occasion of the destruction of these trinkets, and, indeed, are the more guilty of the two, in the eye of the law; for the law supposes that your wife acts under your direction."

If the law supposes that," said Mr. Bumble, squeezing his hat emphatically in both hands, "the law is a ass—a idiot. If that's the eye of the law, the law is a bachelor; and the worst I wish the law is, that his eye may be opened by experience—by experience."

Oliver Twist, Chapter 51 (1838).

Hard it is upon the part of the law that it should be so confoundedly down upon us unfortunate victims; when it takes such amazing good interest for itself from all its clients. But charity begins at home, and justice begins next door.

Martin Chuzzlewit, Chapter 27 (1844).

Life

. . . trifles make the sum of life.

David Copperfield, Chapter 53 (1850).

A man must take the fat with the lean.

David Copperfield, Chapter 51 (1850).

London

It is strange with how little notice, good, bad, or indifferent, a man may live and die in London.

Sketches by Boz, "Characters," Chapter 1 (1836).

Love

Mystery and disappointment are not absolutely indispensable to the growth of love, but they are very often its powerful auxiliaries.

Nicholas Nickleby, Chapter 40 (1839).

Marriage

My experience teaches me, Lady Dedlock, that most of the people I know would do far better to leave marriage alone. It is at the bottom of three fourths of their troubles.

Bleak House, Chapter 41 (1853).

Mother Love

Pride is one of the seven deadly sins; but it cannot be the pride of a mother in her children, for that is a compound of two cardinal virtues—faith and hope.

Nicholas Nickleby, Chapter 43 (1839).

New Testament

I put a New Testament among your books, for the very same reasons, and with the very same hopes that made me write an easy account of it for you, when you were a little child; because it is the best book that ever was or will be known in the world.

Letter to Edward Dickens, September 26, 1868.

Parting

Pip, dear old chap, life is made of ever so many partings welded together.

Great Expectations, Chapter 27 (1861).

The pain of parting is nothing to the joy of meeting again.

Nicholas Nickleby, Chapter 3 (1839).

Patriotism

In love of home, the love of country has its rise.

The Old Curiosity Shop, Chapter 38 (1841).

Philosophers

"I am ruminating," said Mr. Pickwick, "on the strange mutability of human affairs." "Ah! I see—in at the palace door one day, out at the window the next. Philosopher, Sir?" "An observer of human nature, Sir," said Mr. Pickwick. "Ah, so am I. Most people are when they've little to do and less to get."

The Pickwick Papers, Chapter 2 (1836).

Although Oliver had been brought up by philosophers, he was not theoretically acquainted with the beautiful axiom that self-preservation is the first law of nature.

Oliver Twist, Chapter 10 (1838).

Pride

"And if it's proud to have a heart that never hardens, and a temper that never tires, and a touch that never hurts," Miss Jenny struck in, flushed, "she is proud."

Our Mutual Friend, Book III, Chapter 2 (1865).

Prison

A prison taint was on everything there. The imprisoned air, the imprisoned light, the imprisoned damps, the imprisoned men, were all deteriorated by confinement. As the captive men were faded and haggard, so the iron was rusty, the stone was slimy, the wood was rotten, the air was faint, the light was dim. Like a well, like a vault, like a tomb, the prison had no knowledge of the brightness outside; and would have kept its polluted atmosphere intact, in one of the spice islands of the Indian Ocean.

Little Dorrit, Book I, Chapter 1 (1857).

Regret

Of all fruitless errands, sending a tear to look after a day that is gone is the most fruitless.

Nicholas Nickleby, Chapter 10 (1839).

Self-Assurance

. . . always sure that what he thought or said or did was right, and holding it as a thing quite settled and ordained by the laws of nature and Providence, that anybody who said or did or thought otherwise must be inevitably and of necessity wrong.

Barnaby Rudge, Chapter 1 (1841).

Self-Sacrifice

It is a far, far better thing that I do, than I have ever done; it is a far, far better rest that I go to than I have ever known.

A Tale of Two Cities, Book III, Chapter 15 (1859).

Unrequited Love

If you could see my legs when I take my boots off, you'd form some idea of what unrequited affection is.

Dombey and Son, Chapter 48 (1848).

Virtues and Vices

. . . vices are sometimes only virtues carried to excess.

Dombey and Son, Chapter 48 (1848).

Wealth

Money and goods are certainly the best of references.

Our Mutual Friend, Book I, Chapter 4 (1865).

Wine

What is the odds so long as the fire of soul is kindled at the taper of conwiviality, and the wing of friendship never moults a feather! What is the odds so long as the spirit is expanded by means of rosy wine, and the present moment is the least happiest of our existence!

The Old Curiosity Shop, Chapter 2 (1841).

Wine in; truth out.

Nicholas Nickleby, Chapter 27 (1839).

Christian Dior

Christian Ernest Dior / 1905–1957 / Granville, France / Fashion Designer, Businessman, Founder of Christian Dior SE (now a part of LVMH)

America

What alarmed me most in the course of my stay in the United States was the habit of spending enormous sums of money in order to achieve so little real luxury. America represents the triumph of quantity over quality. Mass production triumphs; men and women both prefer to buy a multitude of mediocre things rather than a smaller number, carefully chosen. The American woman, faithful to the ideal of optimism with the United States seems to have made its rule of life, spends money entirely in order to gratify the collective need to buy. She prefers three new dresses to one beautiful one and does not linger over a choice, knowing perfectly well that her fancy will be of short duration and the dress which she is in the process of buying will be discarded very soon.

Christian Dior, Christian Dior and I (1957).

Beauty

Zest is the secret of all beauty. There is no beauty that is attractive without zest.

Reported in Ladies' Home Journal, Vol. 73, April, 1956.

Business

Gossip, even malicious rumors, are worth more than the most expensive publicity campaign in the world.

Christian Dior, Christian Dior and I (1957).

Since there is no patience where vanity is concerned, any client who is kept waiting considers it a personal insult.

Christian Dior, Christian Dior and I (1957).

The dresses of this collection may be worn by only a few of the thousands of women who read and dream about them, but high fashion need not be directly accessible to everyone: it need only exist in the world for its influence to be felt.

Christian Dior, Christian Dior and I (1957).

Dior on Dior

I'm a mild man, but I have violent tastes.

Reported by Jeanne Perkins in "Dior," Life magazine, Vol. 24, No. 9, March 1, 1948, pp. 85–90; accessible at books.google.com.

I wanted to be considered a good craftsman. I wanted my dresses to be constructed like buildings, molded to the curves of the female form, stylizing its shape.

Cited in statement in "The Master of Haute Couture" exhibition, Cristóbal Balenciaga Museum, Getaria, Spain, 2011.

We were emerging from the period of war, of uniforms, of women-soldiers built like boxers. I drew women-flowers, soft shoulders, fine waists like liana, and wide skirts like corolla.

Reported by Shirley Miles O'Donnol in American Costume, 1915–1970: A Source Book for the Stage Costumer (1982).

If my poor maman had still been alive, I would never have tried.

Reported by Marie-France Pochna in Christian Dior: The Man Who Made the World Look New (1996).

I used to have frequent arguments with my father which ended in doors slamming and the ultimate expletive, "filthy bourgeois!"

Reported by Marie-France Pochna in Christian Dior: The Man Who Made the World Look New (1996).

Re: Dior's childhood fear of his father's fertilizer factory:

This was certainly at the root of my intense dislike of machinery, and my firm determination never to work in an office or anything of that nature.

Reported by Marie-France Pochna in Christian Dior: The Man Who Made the World Look New (1996).

My mother whom I adored, secretly wasted away and died of grief. . . . Her death . . . marked me for life.

Reported by Marie-France Pochna in Christian Dior: The Man Who Made the World Look New (1996).

We went from losses to goods seized by creditors, while continuing to organize surrealist or abstract exhibitions.

Reported by Marie-France Pochna in Christian Dior: The Man Who Made the World Look New (1996).

I think I would be more suited to the couture side of the business!

Reported by Marie-France Pochna in Christian Dior: The Man Who Made the World Look New (1996).

Fashion

I know very well the women. The short skirt was never a good fashion—very vulgar. The American women will accept the new fashions. You can never stop the fashions.

Reported by Malcolm P. McNair and Harry L. Hansen in Problems in Marketing (out of print) (1949).

[Black is] the most popular and the most convenient and the most elegant of all colors.

Reported by Akiko Fukai in Fashion in Colors (2004).

Colour is what gives jewels their worth. They light up and enhance the face. Nothing is more elegant than a black skirt and sweater worn with a sparkling multi-stoned necklace.

Reported by Maria Doulton in "Simply brilliant: Cher Dior lights up Paris," The Telegraph (UK), August 16, 2011.

Bright reds—scarlet, pillar-box red, crimson, or cherry—are very cheerful and youthful.

Reported by Maria Doulton in "Simply brilliant: Cher Dior lights up Paris," The Telegraph (UK), August 16, 2011.

A dress is a piece of ephemeral architecture, designed to enhance the proportions of the female body.

Reported by Marie-France Pochna in Christian Dior: The Man Who Made the World Look New (1996).

You can wear black at any time. You can wear it at any age. You may wear it for almost any occasion; a "little black frock" is essential to a woman's wardrobe.

Reported by Nancy MacDonell Smith in The Classic Ten: The True Story of the Little Black Dress and Nine Other Fashion Favorites (2003).

Much has been written about fashion, in all its aspects, but i do not think any couturier has ever before attempted to compile a dictionary on the subject.

Christian Dior, The Little Dictionary of Fashion: A Guide to Dress Sense for Every Woman (1954).

Many people dismiss haute couture as being something that is only for those who are very wealthy… simplicity, good taste, and grooming are the three fundamentals of good dressing and these do not cost money.

Reported by Alison Marie Behnke in The Little Black Dress and Zoot Suits: Depression and Wartime Fashions from the 1930s to the 1950s (2011).

The prime need of fashion is to please and attract. Consequently this attraction cannot be born of uniformity, the mother of boredom.

Christian Dior, Christian Dior and I (1957).

Contemporary elegance is at once simple and natural.

Christian Dior, Christian Dior and I (1957).

The best bargain in the world is a successful dress. It brings happiness to the woman who wears it and it is never too dear for the man who pays for it. The most expensive dress in the world is a dress which is a failure. It infuriates the woman who wears it and it is a burden to the man who pays for it. In addition, it practically always involves him in the purchase of a second dress much more expensive—the only thing that can blot out the memory of the first failure.

Christian Dior, Christian Dior and I (1957).

Personal Philosophy

It is unforgivable to do what one doesn't love, especially if one succeeds.

Cited in statement in "The New Look" exhibition, The Metropolitan Museum of Art, New York, 1947; reported by Judith Miller in Costume Jewelry (2007).

In a machine age, dressmaking is one of the last refuges of the human, the personal, the inimitable.

Reported in Rotunda: The Magazine of the Royal Ontario Museum, Volume 34, 2001.

Don't buy much but make sure that what you buy is good.

Christian Dior, The Little Dictionary of Fashion: A Guide to Dress Sense for Every Woman (1954).

Living in a house which does not suit you is like wearing someone else's clothes.

Christian Dior, Christian Dior and I (1957).

The need for display, which is dormant in all of us, can express itself nowadays in fashion and nowhere else.

Christian Dior, Christian Dior and I (1957).

It is astonishing how the passing of one night permits one to isolate that which one did not really like, from that which one adores!

Christian Dior, Dior by Dior: The Autobiography of Christian Dior(1964).

Women

My dream is to save women from nature.

Reported in Newsweek magazine, Vol. 50, No. 19, November 4, 1957.

Women are most fascinating between the ages of 35 and 40, after they have won a few races and know how to pace themselves. Since few women ever pass 40, maximum fascination can continue indefinitely.

Reported in the Philippines Free Press, Vol. 62, 1969.

Women, with their sure instincts, realized that my intention was to make them not just more beautiful but also happier.

Reported by Marie-France Pochna in Christian Dior: The Man Who Made the World Look New (1996).

A woman's perfume tells more about her than her handwriting.

Reported by D.R. Schneider in Saving the Whales (2008).

There will always be women who cling to a particular style of dress because they wore it during the time of their greatest happiness, but white hair is the only excuse for this type of eccentricity.

Christian Dior, Christian Dior and I (1957).

Jack Dorsey

Jack Patrick Dorsey / b. 1976 / Missouri, USA / Computer Programmer, Entrepreneur, Co-Founder of Twitter

Bitcoin

For me Bitcoin changes absolutely everything. What I'm drawn to the most about it is the ethos, is what it represents, are the conditions that created it, which are so rare and so special and so precious. I don't think there's anything more important in my lifetime to work on and I don't think there's anything more enabling for people around the world.

Interview with Alex Gladstein, Bitcoinmagazine.com, June 4, 2021.

Whatever I can do, whatever my companies can do to make Bitcoin accessible to everyone is how I'm going to spend the rest of my life. If I were not at Square or Twitter, I'd be working on Bitcoin. If it needed more help than Square and Twitter, I would leave them for Bitcoin. But I believe both companies have a role to play and I think anything we can do as companies to help find the right intersection between a corporate narrative and a community open narrative is for the best.

Interview with Alex Gladstein, Bitcoinmagazine.com, June 4, 2021.

. . . we don't need the banks anymore.

Interview with Alex Gladstein, Bitcoinmagazine.com, June 4, 2021.

My belief in bitcoin is that it's an amazing asset, but my belief is that the internet needs a native currency, and we need to be able to transact with this every single day. And everyone around the world needs to transact with it every single day. So the only reason Square got into Bitcoin is to that end. It's not just to be an exchange. And that's why we don't deal with any other "currencies" or "coins" because we're so focused on making bitcoin the native currency for the internet.

Interview with Alex Gladstein, Bitcoinmagazine.com, June 4, 2021.

Again, the conditions that created Bitcoin—everything that went into it from the proof-of-work model to the development model—no single points of failure—everything about it is why we're into it. There's nothing else that compares to it. And we have no interest other than making sure that we are building a native currency for the internet and helping in every way that we can. So all the other coins to me don't factor in at all.

Interview with Alex Gladstein, Bitcoinmagazine.com, June 4, 2021.

. . . I think Bitcoin benefits the entire world. That's what makes it incredible. Is that every single person in the world will benefit and get value from utilizing this. And the more accessible we can make it — just that realization that we finally have a currency that can be traded to any single point on the planet — is pretty incredible and what that enables going forward is mind-blowing. And I'm going to do everything in my power to make sure that happens.

Interview with Alex Gladstein, Bitcoinmagazine.com, June 4, 2021.

Censorship

. . . we have been bad at communication, we haven't been as forthright as we need to, we certainly haven't been as transparent. We do care deeply. But we need to do it in scalable ways. this work doesn't happen overnight.

Interview with Brian Hiatt, Rolling Stone, January 23, 2019.

Dorsey on Dorsey

I am a citizen in this world. I feel the weight of how our tool is used in society and how it's been used for good and how it's used for stuff I'm not proud of.

Interview with Brian Hiatt, Rolling Stone, January 23, 2019.

We can only show that we care through how we change our product and fix things. Nothing I say is going to do that. And, look, I have a lot of people who care about the world and society and our impacts reading my tweets, a lot of shareholders reading my tweets. But I also have a lot of entrepreneurs reading my tweets. And my mom reading my tweets. I don't want to model a behavior where I'm up 20 hours a day working nonstop to fix something, 'cause I don't think it's long-term healthy. Like, it's delusional.

Interview with Brian Hiatt, Rolling Stone, January 23, 2019.

I know who I am. The people around me know who I am. I was not taken aback by the focus on meditation versus Myanmar. I was taken aback by people being upset that I did a meditation in the first place. Or saw it as bragging. Yeah, I'm trying to learn. I'm upset by that because I think it shuts off something for pople in that they won't try it themselves. I wanted to share my experience, it's going to resonate with some, because what else do we do?

Interview with Brian Hiatt, Rolling Stone, January 23, 2019.

I loved drawing. I loved making music. I loved creating. It was more in that angle. I didn't really love business. I didn't want to be a CEO. I didn't want to be an entrepreneur. I wanted to create stuff.

Interview with Brian Hiatt, Rolling Stone, January 23, 2019.

Yeah, I had a [speech] impediment. I couldn't pronounce any of my words. I went to speech therapy for two years. It made me shy. I didn't want to talk with anyone, even my family. Then I had this speech therapy, and they fixed most of it. I still am very mindful of it—in this conversation, I mispronounced at least four words.

Interview with Brian Hiatt, Rolling Stone, January 23, 2019.

I love Twitter. I was always willing to do whatever it took to make it reach its potential. As long as I'm useful to the company, then I'll be there. If I become irrelevant, and at some point I will, then hopefully I've built other choices for the company in people.

Interview with Brian Hiatt, Rolling Stone, January 23, 2019.

Fear of Big Tech

There's a lot of distrust. There's a lot of fear. It's fear of companies like ours. It's fear of power, and it's completely, 100 percent natural. People are afraid of what technology has become and what it can do. . . . If we can't be transparent about our intentions and what our technology is doing, we're feeding into that fear of irrelevance. We need to communicate in a way that is understandable to people, which today we're not.

Interview with Brian Hiatt, Rolling Stone, January 23, 2019.

Impact of Internet and Social Media

This vision to stream money to people that you care about, in a way that the government cannot stop . . . well guess what, it's coming, and nobody can stop it.

Interview with Alex Gladstein, Bitcoinmagazine.com, June 4, 2021.

Expression is messy. It has unpredicted outcomes. It has so many people coming in and adding their voice. The song just keeps going on and on. Looking back, 50 years in the future when it's still here and I'm gone, my impact will be nothing compared to the impact that people using the platform in those 50 years will have on it. We all have time to add to the song. Then we depart, and it continues to go on.

Interview with Brian Hiatt, Rolling Stone, January 23, 2019.

Musk

[Elon Musk[*is* ridiculous. You have to be. You have to be to think that big. I love him. I love what he's trying to do, and I want to help in whatever way. . . . I understand what he wants to do, and I want to help. That's the role of any toolmaker. We're making tools.

Interview with Brian Hiatt, Rolling Stone, January 23, 2019.

Programming

Programming is an amazing field. I like painting, I like drawing, and I like programming because those are the arts where you literally start from absolutely nothing and suddenly something can emerge.

Interview with Brian Hiatt, Rolling Stone, January 23, 2019.

. . . the thing that pushed me away wasn't an interest in massage therapy or botanical illustration or fashion. It was that programming is so abstract. I got lost in it constantly because you were so much in your head all the time. It affects your dreams. You start programming in your dreams. You can actually control your dreams. At least that was my experience. It's so abstract, and nothing feels real. Every time I wanted to do something different, I wanted to do something with my hands.

Interview with Brian Hiatt, Rolling Stone, January 23, 2019.

Public Square

People see Twitter as a public square, and therefore they have expectations that they would have of a public square. Washing Square Park, for instance—I just had an hour and a half there, today. I sat, and I did my phone calls, and I watched people, filmmakers, musicians, street hustlers, weed dealers, chess players. And there's people talking out in the open. The park itself is completely neutral to whatever happens on top of it. But if you stop there, you don't realize what I believe the park actually is. It does come with certain expectations of freedom of expression, but everyone is watching one another.

Interview with Brian Hiatt, Rolling Stone, January 23, 2019.

Twitter

I know that there's a lot of you out there who disagree with a lot of actions that Twitter has taken. I know there's a lot of you out there who disagree with our policies and the way we have evolved them. I appreciate that and recognize it. I also recognize the fact that there is an incentive and a corporate incentive and a business incentive that is different than what might be needed for global communication and for a public conversation. And my goal in my life in this moment is to remove as much as I can the corporateness of our companies and find better intersections with the open-source community.

Interview with Alex Gladstein, Bitcoinmagazine.com, June 4, 2021.

Peter Drucker

Peter Ferdinand Drucker / 1909–2005 / Vienna, Austro-Hungarian Empire / Journalist, Economist, Professor, Business Consultant, Author

Administrative/Corporate State

In the modern corporation the decisive power, that of the managers, is derived from no one but the managers themselves controlled by nobody and nothing and responsible to no one. It is in the most literal sense unfounded, unjustified, uncontrolled and irresponsible power.

The Future of Industrial Man (1942).

Unless the power of the corporation can be organized on an accepted principle of legitimacy, it will... be taken over by a central government.

The Future of Industrial Man (1942).

Aims of Politics

. . . the basic decisions are... about aims. . . . what is desirable... the greater good or the lesser evil in the case of conflicting aims. . . . what sacrifice we are willing to make for a certain achievement, and at what point the sacrifice outweighs the advantages.

The Future of Industrial Man (1942).

Anti-Semitism

Equally striking is the fact that racial anti-Semitism was not taken seriously even by the great majority of Nazis. "It is just a catchword to attract voters" was a standing phrase which everybody repeated and believed, and that I took it seriously was more than once regarded as definite proof of my stupidity and gullibility.

The End of Economic Man: The Origins of Totalitarianism(1939).

Business

There is only one valid definition of a business purpose: *to create a customer.*

The Practice of Management (1954).

Success always obsoletes the very behavior that achieved it.

Management: Tasks, Responsibilities, Practices (1973).

One cannot hire a hand; the whole man always comes with it.

Management: Tasks, Responsibilities, Practices (1973).

Capitalism

Capitalism as a social order and as a creed is the expression of the belief in economic progress as leading toward the freedom and equality of the individual in a free and open society. Marxism expects this society to result from the abolition of private profit. Capitalism expects the free and equal society to result from the enthronement of private profit as supreme ruler of social behavior...

The End of Economic Man: The Origins of Totalitarianism(1939).

Capitalism is being attacked not because it is inefficient or misgoverned but because it is cynical. And indeed a society based on the assertion that private vices become public benefits cannot endure, no matter how impeccable its logic, no matter how great its benefits.

The Practice of Management (1954).

Civic Education

We need in this modern world . . . an incredible number of very highly trained technicians and professional men. . . . But nothing will be gained unless [they] are also educated as citizens . . . to know about the ends, the beliefs, the purposes . . . to which their craft and skill is to contribute . . . about the basic issues which . . . every generation of free men has had to decide. . . . it is the liberal arts . . . that is our lighthouse in the dark and uncharted waters of the postwar world.

"An Economist Looks at the Peace," Southwestern Bulletin, n.s.,1945, ***32****(3): 3–11.*

Communism

Fascism is the stage reached after communism has proved an illusion. And it has been proven as much of an illusion in Stalinist Russia as it proven an illusion in pre-Hitler Germany. Communism in anything but name was abandoned in Russia when the Five-Year Plan was substituted for the New Economic Policy (NEP) after Lenin's death.

The End of Economic Man: The Origins of Totalitarianism(1939).

Economists

It is not enough for the economist in a free society to be a good economic craftsman; he must also think and act as a citizen.

"An Economist Looks at the Peace," Southwestern Bulletin, n.s.,1945, ***32****(3): 3–11.*

Fascism

As for the explanation that fascism is a last desperate attempt of capitalism to delay the socialist revolution, it simply is not true. It is not true that 'big business' promoted fascism. On the contrary, both in Italy and in Germany the proportion of fascist sympathizers and backers was smallest in the industrial and financial classes. It is equally untrue that "big business" profits from fascism; of all the classes it probably suffers most from totalitarian economics and *Wehrwirtschaft* [economics of the military state].

The End of Economic Man: The Origins of Totalitarianism(1939).

. . . the 'total state' of fascism is not a political alignment *within* the existing political and social setup, but that it is a revolution which, like all revolutions, works from *without*.

The End of Economic Man: The Origins of Totalitarianism(1939).

Of course, every revolution repudiates what went on before and considers itself a conscious break with the past; it is only posterity that sees, or imagines it sees, the historical continuity. Fascism, however, goes much further in its negation of the past than any earlier political movement, because it makes this negation its main platform. What is even more important, it denies simultaneously ideas and tendencies which are in themselves antithetic. It is antiliberal, but it is also anticonservative; antireligious and antiatheist; anticapitalist and antisocialist; antiwar and antipacifist…

The End of Economic Man: The Origins of Totalitarianism(1939).

Freedom

Freedom rests on ethical decisions. But the political sphere deals with power. …Individually, power may well be the goal of personal ambition. But socially it is a servant; its organization is only a means to a social end. . . . power distributes rank and determines relations within society; it is a means of internal organization. But the end of society is always an ethical purpose.

The Future of Industrial Man (1942).

. . . freedom cannot be legislated into existence—though it can be legislated out of existence if the necessary minimum of free government is destroyed. . . . freedom rests upon beliefs and social institutions and not upon laws. . . . legislative enactment does not create or determine institutional structure, social beliefs and human nature.

The Future of Industrial Man (1942).

There can be no freedom if one man or one group of men . . . is assumed . . . inherently perfect or perfectible. Its claim to perfection or perfectibility is a claim to absolute rule.

The Future of Industrial Man (1942).

Today we know that a free society is not the product of nature, but of man; that it is not self-maintaining and self-winding, but demands the vigilant and constant support of responsible citizens. . . . freedom is not inevitable and easy . . . but the product of a long, hard struggle of man's reason and man's faith that has to be fought over and won again by every generation.

*"An Economist Looks at the Peace," Southwestern Bulletin, n.s.,1945, **32**(3): 3–11.*

Future

The only thing we know about the future is that it is going to be different.

Management: Tasks, Responsibilities, Practices (1973).

Industrial Society

We have only one alternative: either to build a functioning industrial society or see freedom itself disappear in anarchy and tyranny.

The Future of Industrial Man (1942).

No society can function as a society, unless it gives the individual member social status and function, and unless the decisive social power is legitimate.

The Future of Industrial Man (1942).

Unless we realize that the essence of Nazism is also an attempt to solve a universal problem of Western civilization—that of the industrial society—and that the basic principles on which the Nazis base this attempt are also in no way confined to Germany, we do not know what we fight for or what we fight against. . . . The war is being fought for the structure of industrial society—its basic principles, its purposes, and its institutions.

The Future of Industrial Man (1942).

Innovation

All economic activity is by definition "high risk." And defending yesterday—that is, not innovating—is far more risky than making tomorrow.

Innovations and Entrepreneurship (1984).

Knowledge Society

This society in which knowledge workers dominate is in danger of a new "class conflict" between the large minority of knowledge workers and the majority of workers who will make their livings through traditional ways, either by manual work . . . or by service work. The productivity of knowledge work—still abysmally low—will predictably become the economic challenge of the knowledge society. On it will depend the ability of the knowledge society to give decent incomes, and with them dignity and status, to non knowledge people.

Managing in a Time of Great Change (1995).

Management

The better a man is, the more mistakes will he make—for the more new things he will try. I would never promote a man into a top level job who had not made mistakes, and big ones at that. Otherwise he is sure to be mediocre.

The Practice of Management (1954).

Nazism

The Nazi agitator whom, many years ago, I heard proclaim to a wildly cheering peasants' meeting: "*We don't want lower bread prices, we don't want higher bread prices, we don't want unchanged bread prices—we want National-Socialist bread prices,*" came nearer explaining fascism than anybody I have heard since.

The End of Economic Man: The Origins of Totalitarianism(1939).

Power

Of these denials of European tradition one is especially important: that is the refutation of the demand that the political and social order and the authority set up under it have to justify themselves as benefiting their subjects. Hardly any other concept or idea of our past is held up to so much ridicule by fascism as that of the justification of power. 'Power is its own justification' is regarded as self-evident. Nothing shows better how far the totalitarian revolution has already gone than the general acceptance of this new maxim throughout Europe as a matter of course… [I]t is the most startling innovation. For the last two thousand years… justification of power and authority has been the central problem of European political thought and… political history. And since Europe became Christian there has never been any other approach… than… seeking justification in the benefit which the exercise of power confers upon its subjects… Not even the most fanatical advocates of absolute monarchy would have dared to justify the sovereign otherwise.

The End of Economic Man: The Origins of Totalitarianism(1939).

Propaganda

The most dangerous and at the same time most stupid explanation of fascism is the propaganda theory. In the first place, I have never been able to find anyone who could reconcile it with the fact that right up to the fascist victory—and in Italy beyond it —literally all means of propaganda were in the hands of uncompromising enemies of fascism. There was not one widely-read newspaper but poured ridicule on Hitler and Mussolini while the Nazi and the fascist press were unread and on the verge of bankruptcy. The radio in Germany, owned by the government, issued one anti-Nazi broadside after the other. More powerful than both, the established churches used all the enormous direct influence of the pulpit and the confessional to fight fascism and Nazism.

The End of Economic Man: The Origins of Totalitarianism(1939).

Spiritual Collapse

Fascism is the result of the collapse of Europe's spiritual and social order… catastrophes broke through the everyday routine which makes men accept existing forms, institutions and tenets as unalterable natural laws. They suddenly exposed the vacuum behind the facade of society.

The End of Economic Man: The Origins of Totalitarianism(1939).

Truth

. . . in a free society each individual has a responsibility towards the beliefs of his society —a responsibility on which all the rights and duties of citizenship are founded.

"An Economist Looks at the Peace," Southwestern Bulletin, n.s.,1945, ***32****(3): 3–11.*

War

If war production should remain the only way out of a long-term depression, industrial society would be reduced to the choice between suicide through total war or suicide through total depression.

The Concept of the Corporation (1945).

For if this country—or any other of the great powers—were to make its defense program a function of its domestic employment situation, it would become impossible to conduct a constructive and well-thought out foreign policy or to develop any lasting collaboration.

The Concept of the Corporation (1945).

Ree Drummond (Pioneer Woman)

Anne Marie "Ree" Drummond / b. 1969 / Bartlesville, Oklahoma, USA / Children's book author, Autobiographer, Television Host, Founder of *The Pioneer Woman* blog and product line
Note: Sources of all quotations are unknown.

Cooking

I prefer cooking to baking. Baking, to me, is very precise, and it's about perfection.

Daily Life

My days are spent wrangling children, chipping dried manure from boots, washing jeans, and frying calf nuts.

Drummond on Drummond

I'm not a chef, and I'm not an expert at anything. I'm just a mom and a wife.
I'm a thirty-something ranch wife, mother of four, moderately agoraphobic middle child who grew up on a golf course in the city.
I'm a writer and a photographer – I'm totally aware that doesn't always translate to TV.
If I were a single person living in a city, I could support myself, but I probably wouldn't have a blog, because I would have nothing to blog about.
I was the last person that any of my friends would have pictured moving to the boonies.
The truth of the matter is that I live on an isolated cattle ranch in the middle of Oklahoma and that's not going to change.

Holidays

Christmas and Thanksgiving are the two days of the year where we know the spurs are going to stay off the boots because the family doesn't have to work. It's such a nice – and rare – treat!

Home

I'm so boring. My idea of a great day is just to be home with absolutely nothing to do.

Inspiration

I'm as flawed as the next person. But maybe I inspire women because I'm an example that you should never assume that where you are in life or what you're doing is going to remain exactly as it is forever.

Pioneer Woman

I didn't even know any cowboys growing up. When my friends heard that I was marrying a cattle rancher and moving to the country, they literally could not believe it. They started calling me the Pioneer Woman as a joke.
Now I live in the middle of nowhere on a working cattle ranch.

I think people are drawn to 'The Pioneer Woman,' not because I am some fascinating person but because I present things that a lot of people can relate to.

Small Towns

I think a common misconception about a small town in rural America is that everyone believes the same way, and nothing could be further from the truth.

Larry Elder

Laurence Allen Elder / b. 1952 / Los Angeles, California, USA / Political Commentator, Radio Host, Podcaster, Gubernatorial Candidate
Note: The specific sources of the following quotations are unknown.

America

America traditionally represents the greatest possibility of someone's going from nothing to something. Why? In theory, if not practice, the government stays out of the way and lets individuals take risks and reap rewards or accept the consequences of failure. We call this capitalism—or, at least, we used to.
But did the Founding Fathers ever intend for the federal government to involve itself in education, health care or retirement benefits? The answer, quite clearly, is no. The Constitution, in Article I, Section 8—which contains the general welfare clause—seeks to restrain federal government, not expand it.

Child-Raising

To bring a child into the world that you cannot feed, clothe, house, and educate is the moral equivalent, in my opinion, of a drive-by shooting.
Raising a child is an on-the-job kind of thing. There aren't a whole lot of manuals for that.

Divorce

Studies show that children of divorced parents can have outcomes as positive as those coming from intact homes, provided the father remains financially supportive and active in his children's lives.

Drugs

The war on drugs is wrong, both tactically and morally. It assumes that people are too stupid, too reckless, and too irresponsible to decide whether and under what conditions to consume drugs. The war on drugs is morally bankrupt.
Once brave politicians and others explain the war on drugs' true cost, the American people will scream for a cease-fire. Bring the troops home, people will urge. Treat drugs as a health problem, not as a matter for the criminal justice system.

Economics

Government cannot control the economy without controlling people.
Outsourcing and globalization of manufacturing allows companies to reduce costs, benefits consumers with lower cost goods and services, causes economic expansion that reduces unemployment, and increases productivity and job creation.
Lower taxes, less government spending on domestic programs, and fewer regulations mean a better economy for everybody.

According to the Social Security Administration, in 1945, 41.9 workers supported each individual retiree, while today only 3.3 workers support each retiree. This system cannot continue.

Most people work for the private sector, which cannot exist without profit.

Elder on Elder

Raised by an irresponsible mother during the Great Depression in the Jim Crow south, my father was on his own from the age of 13.

My dad was a Marine. He was one of the Montford Point Marines. Those are the equivalent of the Tuskegee Airmen for Marines. He's a tough, tough guy. When I was 15 we had a fight, and I didn't speak to him for 10 years.

My mom and my dad were married 56 years, and the fact that I reconciled with my dad I think made their marriage a little bit better as well.

If anybody had a reason to become a delinquent, to become a criminal, to be angry at the man, to be angry at the white man, to be angry at America, it's my dad, but he did not feel that way at all.

Nobody ever worked as hard as my father. My father averaged maybe four hours of sleep at night, and when you're a kid, you don't realize that. The man was tired. He was tired.

Families

The welfare state is an assault on families.

Racism is not a major problem in America today. The number one problem facing black Americans today is the lack of fathers in the home.

The welfare state has done to black Americans what slavery couldn't do, what Jim Crow couldn't do, what the harshest racism couldn't do. And that is to destroy the black family.

Freedom

Freedom is not empowerment. Empowerment is what the Serbs have in Bosnia. Anybody can grab a gun and be empowered. It's not entitlement. An entitlement is what people on welfare get, and how free are they? It's not an endlessly expanding list of rights—the "right" to education, the "right" to health care, the "right" to food and housing. That's not freedom, that's dependency. Those aren't rights, those are the rations of slavery—hay and a barn for human cattle.

I'd rather be free than equal.

Government

I believe in limited government, fiscal responsibility, individual liberty, a strong national defense, and free market capitalism.

The government is not your mommy or your daddy. It's not supposed to take care of you.

Individuals can spend their money more wisely, efficiently, and more humanely than can government.

Only in Washington does a decrease in the proposed increase equal a spending cut.

Gun Control

This battle for "common-sense" gun control laws pits emotion and passion against logic and reason. All too often in such a contest, logic loses. So, expect more meaningless, if not harmful, "gun control" legislation. Good news—if you're a crook.

A woman who demands further gun control legislation is like a chicken who roots for Colonel Sanders.

Human Nature

Doing what you want to do is easy. Doing what you have to do is hard.

You are not what you think you are. You are not what they think you are. You are what you think they think you are.

Victimhood is not a strategy for success.

People value and spend their money more wisely when they acquire it by their own efforts—also known as work.

The Media

Because Fox News is allegedly biased in favor of conservatives, critics whine like children whose lunch money got snatched. Conservatives have been pummeled for decades. Now that Fox News and conservative talk radio give people alternatives, critics squeal as if being sodomized.

Politics

The No. 1 cause of preventable death for young black men is not auto accidents or accidental drowning, but homicide.

Bad schools, crime, drugs, high taxes, the social security mess, racism, the health care ? crisis? unemployment, welfare state dependency, illegitimacy, the gap between rich and poor. What do these issues have in common? Politicians, the media, and our so-called leaders lie to us about them. They lie about the cause. They lie about the effect. They lie about the solutions.

Conservatives consider liberals well-intentioned but misguided. Liberals consider conservatives not only wrong, but really, really bad people.

Rent Control

Rent-control laws disproportionately benefit the non-poor because the elite pull strings, work the system, and are better connected than the non-poor.

Responsibility

A free market punishes irresponsibility. Government rewards it.

Success

The formula for achieving middle-class success is simple: Finish high school; don't have a child before the age of 20; and get married before having the child.

A goal without a plan is just a wish.

Optimism. It's not just a mind-set, it is behavior.

Tradition

Just because something is a tradition doesn't make it right.

Welfare

Welfare distorts behavior, makes one less personally responsible, and reduces the role of private charity. This principle applies to corporate welfare.

White Liberals

Good motives aside, white condescension does more damage than good. White condescension says to a black child, "The rules used by other ethnic groups don't apply to you. Forget about work hard, get an education, possess good values. No, for you, we'll alter the rules by lowering the standards and expecting less." Expect less, get less.

Larry Ellison

Lawrence Joseph Ellison / b. 1944 / New York, USA / Computer Engineer, Entrepreneur, Investor, Co-Founder and CEO of Oracle Corporation

Business Philosophy

Really great blogs do not take the place of great microprocessors. Great blogs do not replace great software. Lots and lots of blogs does not replace lots and lots of sales.

Reported by Jim Finkle in "Special Report: Can that guy in Ironman 2 whip IBM in real life?," reuters.com, May 12, 2010.

. . . when people start telling you that you're crazy, you just might be on to the most important innovation in your life.

Commencement address, University of Southern California, Los Angeles, 2016.

. . . in a constantly changing world, what is possible is a moving target.

Commencement address, University of Southern California, Los Angeles, 2016.

Ellison on Ellison

When I started Oracle, what I wanted to do was to create an environment where I would enjoy working. That was my primary goal. Sure, I wanted to make a living. I certainly never expected to become rich, certainly not this rich. I mean, rich does not even describe this. This is surreal.

Interview, Oral and Visual Histories, Smithsonian Institution, October 24, 1995.

I had all the disadvantages necessary for success.

Interview with Maria Bartiromo, Fox Business, youtube.com, October 25, 2018.

My dream was to go to the USC Medical School, get married, raise a family, and practice medicine in Los Angeles.

Commencement address, University of Southern California, Los Angeles, 2016.

I just could not make myself study something that didn't interest me. At the time, I thought I lacked discipline and that I was selfish. Maybe so. But whatever the underlying reason, I was unable to make myself into the person that I thought I should be. So, I decided to stop trying. I was 21 years old when I dropped out of college . . .

Commencement address, University of Southern California, Los Angeles, 2016.

My work week is down to 50 hours—I work less. In the beginning it was insane, I would leave the office at [1am]. I'm too old to do that.

I still sail competitively—I'm not too old to sail. I like to spend time with my family, I read I lot, I sail and play tennis and play basketball. I spend a lot of time at Oracle thinking about things. Thinking through all the open source stuff is something we've done relatively recently—making sure we understand what all the implications are. Is it disruptive, is it a risk, how do we respond to it, can it hurt us, how can we take advantage of it?

Interview with Richard Waters, "FT interview with Larry Ellison (Part Two)," Financial Times, April 17, 2006.

Q: So have you thought about retiring?

A: I love my job. I don't need the money.

Interview with Richard Waters, "FT interview with Larry Ellison (Part Two)," Financial Times, April 17, 2006.

Industry Standards

Microsoft doesn't adhere to standards. This is an Achilles heel—IBM in the early days wasn't standards-based, Microsoft isn't standards-based. The biggest companies, the leaders—IBM in the old days, Microsoft now, SAP now—think they can set their own standards. It's really an interesting element of hubris. Being number one, you think the rules don't quite apply to you. We became number one in database, but always based on standards. We don't think we can compete outside of the area of standards.

Interview with Richard Waters, "FT interview with Larry Ellison (Part Two)," Financial Times, April 17, 2006.

Information Technology

Q: Why have companies in many cases got less benefit from their information systems than they expected during the period of big technology spending in the 1990s?

A: Companies are still using information in a siloed away. The information inside companies is fragmented in so many separate databases, so many separate systems.

The trouble is, large organisations are themselves divisionalised and fragmented. If you look at some of these large companies that grew as a result of acquisition, they never threw away the old systems, they never really integrated the businesses. When a company like Citibank wants to ask, who are my customers, that's really in lots and lots of systems. Each one of those businesses is run by a different general manager. Each of those people makes a decision about what sort of systems he or she wants in the division.

It's really astounding, the organisational complexity of these big companies, which devolves into systems complexity. To unify all this is not really a technology issue, it's an organisational issue. How much do you want to unify your organisation? There are very few companies with very strong centralised leadership that will mandate these things. Most large companies are highly decentralised. . . .

These problems tend to be self-correcting—the inefficient operators tend to disappear. But it's not merely a systems issue, it's a corporate culture issue, its an organisational operations issue. But gradually we're going to move towards these modern information systems—it's just going to take a whole lot longer than I ever imagined.

Interview with Richard Waters, "FT interview with Larry Ellison (Part Two)," Financial Times, April 17, 2006.

Q: When will companies get more radical in overhauling their systems?

A: It's going to happen when the risks of not doing something are greater than the risks of doing something. In a lot of industries, it's too risky to do nothing. Telecoms, for instance, is changing so much—the wireline business is declining so rapidly—if you're not moving aggressively into wireless, you're putting your business at risk. They've got to be in those businesses, it's too risky not to.

Interview with Richard Waters, "FT interview with Larry Ellison (Part Two)," Financial Times, April 17, 2006.

Internet Commerce

If the Internet turns out not to be the future of computing, we're toast. But if it is, we're golden.

Reported by Jeff Sweat in "Oracle's Talking: Should You Be Listening?," informationweek.com, February 7, 2000.

Open Source Software

If an open source product gets good enough, we'll simply take it. . . . the great thing about open source is nobody owns it—a company like Oracle is free to take it for nothing, include it in our products and charge for support, and that's what we'll do. So it is not disruptive at all—you have to find places to add value. Once open source gets good enough, competing with it would be insane. . . . We don't have to fight open source, we have to exploit open source.

Interview with Richard Waters, "FT interview with Larry Ellison (Part One)," Financial Times, April 17, 2006.

Oracle

Twenty minutes compared to never, that's a lot.

Reported in "Ellison: Oracle remains unbreakable," CNN, January 21, 2002.

Q: Where do you go from here?

A: We want to make sure we beat Amazon in cloud database. . . . It's very simple. It's just like playing basketball. If you're playing basketball, you want to beat the Warriors, you want to win the championship. So, our job—we have the best database in the world, we've got to deliver it in the context of a cloud that's as easy to use as Amazon, but secure.

Interview with Maria Bartiromo, Fox Business, youtube.com, October 25, 2018.

Personal Computers

I hate the PC, with a passion.

Cited in the documentary film, The Triumph of the Nerds, directed by Paul Sen (VHS format, 1996; DVD format 2002).

It's Microsoft versus mankind, with Microsoft having only a slight lead.

Reported by Kara Swisher in "The Company Therapist Message Board (Closed)," Wall Street Journal, March 5, 1998.

The computer industry is the only industry that is more fashion-driven than women's fashion. Maybe I'm an idiot, but I have no idea what anyone is talking about. What is [cloud computing]? It's complete gibberish. It's insane. When is this idiocy going to stop?

Speech, Oracle OpenWorld, reported in "Oracle's Ellison nails cloud computing," cnet.com, September 26, 2008.

Philosophy of Life

You cannot measure a man by his riches but by the quality of the woman holding his hand.

Reported by Avra Amar Filion in The Ellison Effect (2014).

Great achievers are driven, not so much by the pursuit of success, but by the fear of failure.

Attribution unconfirmed.

"The moral high ground," I said [to Steve Jobs], "well that just might be the most expensive real estate on earth."

Commencement address, University of Southern California, Los Angeles, 2016.

. . . deep inside of all of us—all of us—there's a primal desire to do something important with our lives.

Commencement address, University of Southern California, Los Angeles, 2016.

Scale Advantage

The more of the footprint we have, the happier customers are, up to the point where they say, "Gee Oracle, you're all over the place." As long as we do a good job and we don't price gouge them—that would be self-defeating. We make plenty of money now, we don't need to gouge people on prices. In fact, the bigger we become, the more we can lower our prices. With volume comes the ability to lower price.

Interview with Richard Waters, "FT interview with Larry Ellison (Part Two)," Financial Times, April 17, 2006.

Social and Political Issues

Modernization, socialization, and progression doesn't alter nor permit discarding the morals and the laws one should abide themselves too.

Reported by Avra Amar Filion in The Ellison Effect (2014).

Nigel Farage

Nigel Paul Farage / b. 1964 / Farnborough, England, United Kingdom / Former Leader of the UK Independence Part (UKIP), former Member of the European Parliament, Television News Presenter, Author, Podcaster

Note: The sources of the following quotations are unknown, but presumably derive from Farage's very numerous writings, online comments, interviews, and podcasts

Brexit

Brexit was a victory for ordinary people who wanted to take back control of their country.

Brexit is the most important political event in the last 50 years. It's about whether we govern our own country and make our own laws.

Brexit is the beginning, not the end. It's a chance for Britain to reset and redefine its role in the world.

I am convinced that the "we want our country back, we want our borders back" message that we took across the country on an open-top double decker energised non-voters to back Brexit.

Democracy

I've always believed in the power of democracy. It's the people who should have the final say.

I believe in the values of democracy and freedom. That's why I've dedicated my political career to fighting for them.

Democracy is the most important thing. It's the people who should be in control, not distant bureaucrats.

We used to fight for democracy. Democracy used to matter. We now treat it with contempt. We have turned our backs on values that we built up over hundreds of years, for the benefit of politicians in Europe. To me, that is heartbreaking.

Economics

I believe that if you have a strong economic plan and good governance, you can build a strong country and a strong society.

I want to see a strong, prosperous, and sovereign Britain that can trade freely with the world.

I believe in a Britain that is open to trade with the world and that takes control of its own destiny.

We shouldn't measure everything in terms of GDP figures or economics. There is something called quality of life.

It's a European Union of economic failure, of mass unemployment and of low growth.

I'm not a fan of the euro. It's a flawed currency that has caused a lot of economic problems in Europe.

The euro *Titanic* has now hit the iceberg—and there simply aren't enough lifeboats to go round.

European Union

I'm not anti-European, but I am against the concept of being forced under a political structure called the European Union. I'm happy to be friendly with Europe, to trade with Europe, to cooperate with Europe. But I don't want to be governed by Europe.

The European Union is an outdated, failing project that needs to be consigned to history.

I don't want to be part of a European superstate. I want Britain to be a proud, independent nation.

I want my country back. I want my passport back. I want my identity back.

I'm not anti-European, I just want us to be self-governing.

I've always been a critic of the European Union, but I'm also a realist. We have to work with our European neighbors, but not be ruled by them.

I'm not against Europe, I'm against the European Union. I want a Europe of sovereign nations, not a European superstate.

The European Union is a political project that has gone far beyond what was originally intended. It's time for Britain to reclaim its sovereignty.

The EU is a club for politicians, not for the people. It's time for the people to take back control.

We want our country back. And we want our country back not because we don't like the French or the Germans or the Spanish. We want our country back because we love it and we're proud of it.

I love Europe! France is wonderful. It should be. We've subsidised it for 40 years.

Are we the same? Good lord, no! That's why Europe's fun—it's fun because it's different. A political project that seeks to make it all the same—it's ghastly.

Farage on Farage

I've been called a maverick, a troublemaker, and a disruptor. But I'm just someone who speaks my mind and stands up for what I believe in.

I want to see a Britain that is open to the world, but not controlled by it.

I've been called all sorts of names, but I don't care. I'm not in this for popularity; I'm in it for the principles I believe in.

I'm not a career politician. I'm just a regular guy who got involved in politics because I wanted to make a difference.

I've spent my whole political career fighting against the establishment, and I'll continue to do so.

I'm not interested in being part of the political elite. I'm interested in representing the concerns of ordinary people.

I've always believed that if you have the courage to stand up for what you believe in, you can make a difference.

I've never been part of the establishment. I've always been an outsider, and I'm proud of that.

I'm not interested in being a career politician. I'm interested in achieving my political goals and then getting back to the real world.

I've always believed in putting my country first and standing up for what I believe in, no matter the opposition.

I'm proud to have played a part in the Brexit campaign. It was a victory for democracy and self-determination.

I've spent my political career fighting for what I believe in, and I have no intention of stopping now.

I suppose, being in politics, it wasn't a job—it was almost a calling. It dominated my life, so I do think that probably a lot of people around me have paid quite a big price for that.

I am married to a girl from Hamburg, so no one need tell me about the dangers of living in a German-dominated household.

Free Speech

I believe in free speech, even when it's uncomfortable. Political correctness is a threat to our freedom of expression.

Global Warming

We may have made one of the biggest and most stupid collective mistakes in history by getting so worried about global warming.

Immigration

We're not against immigration, but we believe in managed immigration. We're not against people coming to Britain to work, but we believe they should have a job.

I want us to be able to control our own borders, make our own laws, and trade with the world.

I have never said anything anti-immigrant. I've said we should have a proper immigration policy and we should be able to control the numbers.

In Britain, what we've done is say to 485 million people, "You can all come, every one of you. You're unemployed? You've got a criminal record? Please come. You've got 19 children? Please come." We've lost any sense of perspective on this.

Politics

The global political establishment is out of touch with ordinary people. I've made it my mission to represent their views.

I think it's essential that people in politics have a sense of humor and an ability to laugh at themselves. Otherwise, you end up taking yourself too seriously.

Politics is about conviction and principle. It's not about pandering to the latest opinion polls.

I do think that a degree of polarization has helped the political debate. When people stand up and are counted and say, "This is what I believe, and this is what I think we should do," then it helps the electorate to make a decision.

I've always believed that the best decisions are made by those closest to the people, not by distant bureaucrats.

There are two kinds of people in politics: there are those who want to be something, and there are those who want to do something.

I think what's happened in the last couple of years is that the political class in Britain have been shaken to their core, and they now realize that the people are not going to be browbeaten.

Trump

I would say that in many ways, Donald Trump is the most important political figure in the West.

UKIP

I want to lead a political party that is not simply a pressure group, that is not simply putting ideas on the table for others to pick up and run with. I want us as a political party to be absolutely at the heart of the national debate.

Quite simply, without UKIP, there would not have been a referendum.

No deals with the Tories; it's war.

United Kingdom

I think we should be an independent, self-governing, democratic nation, making our own laws in our own country.

I think the political class has let us down, and let us down badly. I think we have a group of people in Westminster, not just in the Labour Party, the Conservative Party too, who do not understand ordinary people's lives.

I've never been a fan of big government. I believe in small government and individual liberty.

I'm not a fan of the nanny state. People should have the freedom to make their own choices.

The real question is, at the end of the day, do we want to run our country? Are we proud of who we are? Are we happy to be just a star on somebody else's flag, or do we want to be an independent nation?

I want to live in a country where our laws are made by people we elect, not by unelected bureaucrats in Brussels.

There are two completely different Britains. There's London, and there's the rest of Britain.

We do have, I'm sad to say, a fifth column that is living within our own countries that is utterly opposed to our values, we're going to have to be a lot braver . . . in standing up for our Judaeo-Christian culture.

Carly Fiorina

Cara Carleton Fiorina (née Sneed) / b. 1954 / Texas, USA / Businesswoman, CEO of Hewlett-Packard

Abortion

Liberals and progressives will spend inordinate amounts of time and money to protect fish, frogs, and flies. But they do not think a 17-week-old, a 20-week-old, a 24-week-old is worth saving?

Reported by Jay Hobbs in "Carly Fiorina: 'Liberals Protect Fish and Frogs, Don't Think a 20-Week Unborn Baby Worth Saving," lifenews.com, October 21, 2015.

Business Philosophy

Alignment and collaboration need not be fuzzy, ill-defined concepts for "let's just all get along." Effective teamwork is more than good manners and good will, although both help an organization function more effectively. Alignment results from shared goals. Collaboration results from shared measures of success.

Carly Fiorina, Tough Choices: A Memoir (2006).

We are a nation founded on a visionary and, at the time, radical idea. That visionary idea is that every human life has potential, and everyone has the right to fulfill his or her potential. That is what the Founders meant when they wrote "life, liberty and the pursuit of happiness.

Carly Fiorina, Rising to the Challenge: My Leadership Journey(2015).

All triumphs are made of the same stuff: the right support, the right team, the determination to achieve the goal, lots of really hard work. And all triumphs are much more about choice than they are about chance.

Carly Fiorina, Tough Choices: A Memoir (2006).

[Women] are neither the helpless victims nor the unthinking drones nor the single-issue hysterics our politics treated them as. I know from being a CEO that any company needs as much talent around the table as it can possibly muster. Failing to take advantage of the talents of women—half the population—is corporate malpractice as far as I'm concerned.

Carly Fiorina, Rising to the Challenge: My Leadership Journey(2015).

Believe me, if it can be digitized, it will be.

Address, "The Transformation Accelerates," CTEA [Convergence Transportation Electronics Association] 2000 conference, Detroit, Michigan, October 17, 2000; accessible at hp.com.

Capitalism and History

If you look at history, you see that human flourishing exploded beginning about the time two things first appeared: the new American republic and free market capitalism. If you plot the history of human prosperity going back over a thousand years, what you see is a flat line hovering just above zero until the late eighteenth century; then the line turns upward, and it hasn't turned back.

Carly Fiorina, Rising to the Challenge: My Leadership Journey(2015).

China

They're not terribly imaginative. They're not entrepreneurial. They don't innovate. That's why they're stealing our intellectual property.

Reported by Lydia O'Connor in "Carly Fiorina Calls the Chinese Unimaginative Idea Thieves," huffpost.com, May 26, 2015.

Fiorina on Fiorina

Childhood is precious. The hardest part of growing up is growing up, I think.

Interview with David Webb; reported by Alex Swoyer in "Ohio Male RNC Member Calls Carly Fiorina 'Hot Babe,'" breitbart.com, August 5, 2015.

Re: a male coworker who wanted to conduct his first business meeting with Fiorina in a strip club:

I have to stand up for myself. . . . I learned something that I could and should stand up for myself, and he learned something, which was she will stand up for herself.

Interview with David Webb; reported by Alex Swoyer in "Ohio Male RNC Member Calls Carly Fiorina 'Hot Babe,'" breitbart.com, August 5, 2015.

If you've had to overcome an obstacle or insecurity or fear, . . . genuinely you can bet on that person because they have gathered themselves and found through their inner strength, they have determination, they have grit.

Interview with David Webb; reported by Alex Swoyer in "Ohio Male RNC Member Calls Carly Fiorina 'Hot Babe,'" breitbart.com, August 5, 2015.

When I think of something that really is me, that I'm proud of, is honestly, I would have to say, I've never sold my soul along the way… All those things, you're selling your soul, and I don't think I have.

Interview with David Webb; reported by Alex Swoyer in "Ohio Male RNC Member Calls Carly Fiorina 'Hot Babe,'" breitbart.com, August 5, 2015.

For me, business is a story about people—what they are capable of when supported and challenged; what they can envision and create—which is why I like the business world.

Carly Fiorina, Rising to the Challenge: My Leadership Journey(2015).

I need debate and dialogue with others to test my own thinking and to make a decision. I test others' convictions or opinions by pushing on their arguments and seeing how strongly they will defend them. When challenged, do people shrink away from their own views, or do they stand behind them? When pressed, do people offer more data to support their position, or do they simply repeat the same things in a louder voice?

Carly Fiorina, Tough Choices: A Memoir (2006).

Global Economy

There is no job that is America's God-given right anymore. We have to compete for jobs as a nation. Our competitiveness as a nation is not inevitable. It will not just happen.

Press conference; reported by Drew Cullen in "US tech industry stands up for overseas jobs," theregister.com, January 8, 2004.

Government

. . . of all the things I resent most about out-of-control government and the politicians who support it, grow it, or simply fail to deal with it, what angers me above all else is the knowledge that all of this waste and ruin is entirely preventable.

Carly Fiorina, Rising to the Challenge: My Leadership Journey(2015).

Hewlett-Packard (HP)

HP's goal is to bring the most compelling entertainment content and experiences to our customers, ... We explored a range of alternatives to deliver a great digital music experience and concluded Apple's iPod music player and iTunes music service were the best by far. By partnering with Apple, we have the opportunity to add value by integrating the world's best digital music offering into HP's larger digital entertainment system strategy.

HP press release, January 1, 2004.

Leadership

Leadership is all about unlocking the potential in others.

Speech, University of Maryland, October 10, 2003.

The hard truth about leadership and success is that it can never be taken for granted. It must always be invested in. When companies—or countries for that matter—begin to rest on their laurels and take comfort in their past triumphs or their present performance, the future begins to dim just a bit. The past is not prologue to the future. The future must always be built.

Carly Fiorina, Rising to the Challenge: My Leadership Journey (2015).

. . . what have I learned about leadership? The first thing that I would say is I think we're really confused about leadership. . . . What I used to think was that a leader was whoever had the big office, the big title. I thought leadership was the same as position, title. If you have a big position, if you have a big title, if you have perks, if you've got a big budget, you must be a leader. Then I looked around and I noticed that there were people with big offices, big titles, sometimes big egos to go along with it, and they were not leading. Leadership is not about position or title. There are people with position and title who lead, but it's not because of their position and title.

Lecture, "A Lesson in Leadership," Busch School of Business and Economics, Catholic University of America, October 24, 2017.

Second thing I've learned about leadership, so you got to be courageous. The second thing I've learned about leadership is, you have to have character. You know about character, it's why you're here, but character is such an old-fashioned word these days and honestly, I think our culture writ large, celebrates anything but character. We celebrate controversy, we celebrate conflict, we celebrate outrageous, the more outrageous the better, but character, character is knowing there is a difference between right and wrong, and there is. Character is knowing that two wrongs don't make a right. Character is knowing that the ends do not always justify the means. Character is knowing that how you get things done is as important as what you get done, and says as much about you. Character is also knowing the difference between a short-term win and a long-term victory, and leaders without character are focused on solving the wrong problems, or they're focused on themselves, because the final aspect of character is a willingness to accept that there is something bigger than ourselves, more important than ourselves.

Lecture, "A Lesson in Leadership," Busch School of Business and Economics, Catholic University of America, October 24, 2017.

The third thing that leadership takes is collaboration. Collaboration. Working with others to solve a problem. There is nothing worth doing in this life that can be done with one person acting alone. Nothing. Everything worth doing is a collaboration. Everything. To collaborate, by the way, to solve problems, frequently means that we're collaborating with people that might be different than we are. One of the things about human nature I think is we are all most comfortable with people like ourselves. We're most comfortable with people that look like us, that have the same background as us, that sound like us. It's just human nature it doesn't make us bad, but unfortunately, when we hang out with only people like us or only people who agree with us, then we actually aren't able to collaborate effectively to solve a problem. We have to reach out.

Lecture, "A Lesson in Leadership," Busch School of Business and Economics, Catholic University of America, October 24, 201

Personal Philosophy

What you are is God's gift to you, what you make of yourself is your gift to God.

Interview, Robert J. Dole Institute of Politics, University of Kansas, April 14, 2019.

Everyone truly does have God given gifts. . . . Find them and use them, and don't let anyone else tell you that you are less than who you are.

Interview with David Webb; reported by Alex Swoyer in "Ohio Male RNC Member Calls Carly Fiorina 'Hot Babe,'" breitbart.com, August 5, 2015.

Presidential Nomination Campaign, Republican Party, 2016

Donald Trump is Hillary Clinton's Christmas gift wrapped up under a tree. I am the lump of coal in her stocking.

Tweet; reported by Eric Bradner in "A Trump-driven conspiracy to elect Clinton?," cnn.com, December 10, 2015.

Trump says a lot of things that are crazy. . . . Trump's a moron.

Reported by Ben Gittleson in "Carly Fiorina Repeats After Girl: 'Donald Trump's a Moron,'" abcnews.com, January 15, 2016.

When people get to know me, they tend to support me. . . . That's what you see in the polls.

Interview with Jimmy Fallon, The Tonight Show, NBC; reported by Ali Vitali in "Carly Fiorina Talks Trump and Religion, Rocks for Fallon on 'Tonight Show,'" nbcnews.com, Sept. 21, 2015.

From my travels around the country, I've noticed that the GOP has two distinct but related problems with women voters. First, many GOP-leaning women are apathetic. They may have previously voted with Republicans, but they've become disenchanted or perhaps have just disengaged.

Second, many women are open to voting for Republicans but have to be persuaded. Neither group much likes the tone and tenor of politics. They are put off by the vitriol, the arguing, the seemingly endless posturing, and the paucity of results. Women tend to be both doers and collaborators—their complicated, busy lives require both skill sets. They get frustrated when they don't see much of either in the political process. This is a tragedy, because women—every bit as much as men, maybe more so—have the potential to contribute to our party.

Carly Fiorina, Rising to the Challenge: My Leadership Journey(2015).

Religious Faith

I actually believe that people of faith make better leaders. . . . Whether they are Christians, as I am—my faith has sustained me through some very bad times; I've battled cancer, I've lost a child, I've been tested—but whether it's a person of Christian faith or Jewish faith or Muslim faith or other faiths, I think faith gives us humility, and empathy and optimism. And I think those are important things.

Interview with Jimmy Fallon, The Tonight Show, NBC; reported by Ali Vitali in "Carly Fiorina Talks Trump and Religion, Rocks for Fallon on 'Tonight Show,'" nbcnews.com, Sept. 21, 2015.

Steve Forbes

Malcolm Stevenson ("Steve") Forbes, Jr. / b. 1947 / New Jersey, USA / Business Executive, Author, Political Candidate, Publisher of*Forbes* Magazine

Church and State

There's nothing wrong with posting the Ten Commandments in our schools today, because they are the basis of Western civilization. Also, when you look to what's happened in the last 40 years to the quality of life in this country, when prayer was barred from school, I think it's fitting and proper that we have voluntary prayer.

Republican Party Presidential Nomination Debate, Johnston, Iowa, January 16, 2000.

[We should] protect people of all faiths—or of no faith—from encroachments by the state that violate their consciences and most deeply held beliefs. The Founders never intended the separation of church from state to become a separation of religion from public and civic life. There is no reason why a child should be denied the right to hold a Bible study before or after school, or write an essay about a biblical figure during school.

A New Birth of Freedom: Vision for America (1999).

Federal Reserve

The central bank's bond purchases or sales are also an important indication of where the value of the dollar is headed. Is the Fed continuing its bond purchases and further expanding the money supply? Or, is it shrinking the monetary base by selling those securities? The answers may be found on the Federal Reserve balance sheet.

Inflation: What It Is, Why It's Bad, and How to Fix It, with Nathan Lewis and Elizabeth Ames (2022).

The foundations for today's prosperity were laid by Ronald Reagan in the early 1980's. [Fed Chairman Alan] Greenspan did a very good job in the early 1990's. But recently he's fallen prey to this crazy theory that prosperity causes inflation. So they're trying to slow the economy down by raising interest rates. It's like a doctor saying you're in great health, so we have to make you sick a little bit. It's a bizarre theory. It's going to hurt our economy.

Republican Party Presidential Nomination Debate, Phoenix, Arizona, December 7, 1999.

Financial Crisis of 2008

To appreciate the depth of political upheaval created by the 2008 financial crisis, just tally the power shifts that occurred in its wake. In addition to the turmoil in the Middle East, 13 out of 17 European governments changed over as a result of the initial financial crisis. In the United States, the stock market panic in September 2008 reversed the slight lead of John McCain and helped sweep the far-left Barack Obama into office.

Money: How the Destruction of the Dollar Threatens the Global Economy—and What We Can Do About It, with Elizabeth Ames (2014).

Flat Tax

Twenty-five countries have tried it, and it's succeeded everywhere it's been tried.

Interview with Crystal Lu, Wharton Magazine, November 7, 2014.

Well, what a flat tax does is jump the current tax code, all 9 million gory words of it, and replaces it with a single rate, with generous exemptions for adults and for kids. A family of four, for instance, would pay no federal income tax on your first $46,000 of income, no tax on your savings, no death taxes. On the business side, it would reduce the rate from 35 percent to 17 percent. My flat rate would be 17 percent. It would also get rid of depreciation schedules. So, if you make a capital investment—you know, build a plant or buy a computer or truck—you would expense it in the year in which you make it, instead of over several years. . . . You'd see the economy take off like a rocket.

Interview with Crystal Lu, Wharton Magazine, November 7, 2014.

Gay Rights

My father {Malcolm Forbes] had his life. We respected it. What he meant to us and to others I think speaks for itself. You don't have to approve of something that someone does to have compassion and love.

Reported by Stephen McFarland, New York Daily News, March 1, 1996.

Q: Would you hire qualified men and women to work in your administration, who are openly gay?

A: I will hire people who are qualified for the job, people who can do the work at hand; people who are there to get something done. If a person wants a job to make a statement, they're not going to get it. If a person wants a job because they're qualified and [share my] principles and philosophy, they will be actively considered for it. I believe in equal rights for all, special rights for none.

Republican Party Presidential Nomination Debate, Dartmouth College, Hanover, New Hampshire, October 29, 1999.

Government Spending

Don't back down in the face of mounting surpluses. Hold the line. Keeping the budget caps is the right way to provide a dramatic tax cut and to save Social Security.

Reported in "Economic Security," Forbes, May 21, 1999.

Great Depression

The real cause of the beginning of the Great Depression was the Smoot-Hawley Tariff Act. This shocking and totally unprecedented legislation ended up imposing an average 60 percent tax on more than 3,000 import items. It was the equivalent of exploding a bomb that devastated the global trading system.

Inflation: What It Is, Why It's Bad, and How to Fix It, with Nathan Lewis and Elizabeth Ames (2022).

Health Care

Q. Going back to healthcare, you don't believe there should be a public option?

A. Well that's government, and I've seen what the government has done to Medicare, Medicaid, Social Security, housing. And what they should do, instead, is remove barriers to people buying insurance around the country. If you live here in Philadelphia, it's illegal for you to buy insurance in New York or New Jersey. You're allowed to buy cars there. You're allowed to open up brokerage accounts, banks accounts. Why can't you buy health insurance? That way you'd get real competition. Right now each state erects its own barriers. A lot of states have very little competition.

Interview with Crystal Lu, Wharton Magazine, November 7, 2014.

Inflation

How do you end inflation? The good news is that a nation doesn't need tax hikes, super-high interest rates, horrible recessions —or even fishing restrictions. The way to do it, very simply, is to stabilize the value of money. How to achieve this? When a currency begins to slide, the first step should be for a government to publicly declare its intention to support its money, i.e., maintain its value. The way to do so is, very simply, by shrinking the monetary base.

Inflation: What It Is, Why It's Bad, and How to Fix It, with Nathan Lewis and Elizabeth Ames (2022).

Imagine how tricky it would be to bake a cake if the recipe called for 45 minutes in the oven, and you had to figure out if those were nominal minutes or inflation-adjusted minutes.

Money: How the Destruction of the Dollar Threatens the Global Economy—and What We Can Do About It, with Elizabeth Ames (2014).

At the G-20 meeting in Paris in 2011, finance ministers expressed fears that U.S.-driven global inflation was threatening global stability. George Melloan was among those who made the connection between this unrest and QE. He acknowledged in the *Wall Street Journal*: "Probably few of the protesters in the streets connect their economic travail to Washington. But central bankers do."

Money: How the Destruction of the Dollar Threatens the Global Economy—and What We Can Do About It, with Elizabeth Ames (2014).

Money

The ultimate lesson of history—and of this book—is that no nation has ever gotten rich by eroding the value of its money.

Inflation: What It Is, Why It's Bad, and How to Fix It, with Nathan Lewis and Elizabeth Ames (2022).

We need to keep the Federal Reserve from lurching into deflation or inflation. Remember, prosperity does not cause inflation. It's time to link the value of our money to something stable and secure, like the price of gold. That will ensure that the Fed does not inadvertently put its thumb on the world's windpipe, cause global currency turbulence, and cause commodity prices to be devastatingly low.

A New Birth of Freedom: Vision for America (1999).

The only reliable compass [for monetary policy] is one using the gold price. This does not mean you buy the yellow metal. All you do is look at the price. If it [goes up], you're printing too much money. If it [goes down], you're being too tight. Is it a perfect compass? No. Is it better than the others? Yes. So I propose using gold as a compass. In this imperfect world, it is the most reliable one, whether you're doing it right or doing it wrong. And that way we will get lower interest rates.

Speech, Kennedy School of Government, Harvard University, November 27, 1995.

Morality and Politics

Crime is not new. But Americans have rarely been so confused about right and wrong, about what is acceptable and what is to be forcefully condemned.

- A free society cannot survive the collapse of the two-parent family or the absence of fathers

- A free society cannot survive an unchecked explosion in violent crime
- Nor can a free society survive a generation of crack babies and teenagers whose minds and bodies have been destroyed by illegal drugs.

A New Birth of Freedom: Vision for America (1999).

Obama Administration

The stimulus plan was a nice waste of money, most of it. If they wanted a true stimulus, they would have cut the payroll tax for a couple of years, which would have given people money instantly and also lowered the cost of employing people. So the dollar, taxes, trade, healthcare—I think we should be going [in] the opposite direction. Instead of a government takeover, we should have more patients control healthcare resources, not bureaucracies. And on energy, why not move to promote exploration for natural gas and developing nuclear energy? They are very slow so far in proposals to modernize the grid and if you want wind power, you better have transmission lines to move the electricity. They haven't done that.

Interview with Crystal Lu, Wharton Magazine, November 7, 2014.

"Third Way" or Mixed Economy

Where some speak of a "Third Way," let us pursue the right way—free markets, free elections, free trade—because these are the tools of a free people. It is time to show the world that the Reagan-Thatcher-Forbes model offers true economic liberation for those who languish in poverty and economic stagnation.

Speech, London, reported by Reuters , October 13, 1999.

Wealth Creation vs. Redistribution

[We should] give all Americans the freedom to create real personal wealth for themselves and their families. Creating personal wealth —not redistributing it—should be one of America's highest priorities as we move into the new century. The real source of wealth and capital in this new era is not material things—it is the human mind, the human spirit, the human imagination, and our faith in the future. That's the magic of a free society—everyone can move forward and prosper because wealth comes from within.

A New Birth of Freedom: Vision for America (1999).

Benjamin Franklin

Benjamin Franklin / 1706–1790 / Province of Massachusetts Bay / Printer, Author, Diplomat

Freedom and Virtue

Only a virtuous people are capable of freedom. As nations become more corrupt and vicious, they have more need of masters.

Source: Letter to Messrs., the Abbés Chalut and Arnaud, April 17, 1787.

Freedom of Thought and Speech

Without Freedom of Thought, there can be no such Thing as Wisdom; and no such Thing as publick Liberty, without Freedom of Speech; which is the Right of every Man, as far as by it, he does not hurt or controul the Right of another: And this is the only Check it ought to suffer, and the only Bounds it ought to know.

Source: "Silence Dogood, No. 8," New-England Courant, July 9, 1722.

Liberty vs. Safety

Those who would give up essential liberty, to purchase a little temporary safety, deserve neither liberty nor safety.

Source: Letter to Pennsylvania Governor Robert Hunter Morris on behalf of the colonial Assembly, 1755.

Uncertainty of Human Life

Our new Constitution is now established, everything seems to promise it will be durable; but, in this world, nothing is certain except death and taxes.

Source: Letter to Jean-Baptiste Le Roy, November, 1789.

Virtue and Constitutional Self-Government

I agree to this Constitution with all its faults, if they are such; because I think a general Government necessary for us, and there is no form of Government but what may be a blessing to the people if well administered, and believe farther that this is likely to be well administered for a course of years, and can only end in Despotism, as other forms have done before it, when the people shall become so corrupted as to need despotic Government, being incapable of any other.

Source: Speech to Constitutional Convention, Philadelphia, September 17, 1787.

Warfare Between the Governing & Governed

Reasons will never be wanting for proposed augmentations. And there will always be a party for giving more to the rulers, that the rulers may be able in return to give more to them. -Hence as all history informs us, there has been in every State & Kingdom a constant kind of warfare between the governing & governed: the one striving to obtain more for its support, and the other to pay less. And this has alone occasioned great convulsions, actual civil wars, ending either in dethroning of the Princes, or enslaving of the people. Generally indeed the ruling power carries its point, the revenues of princes constantly increasing, and we see that they are never satisfied, but always in want of more. The more the people are discontented with the oppression of taxes; the greater need the prince has of money to distribute among his partizans and pay the troops that are to suppress all resistance, and enable him to plunder at pleasure. There is scarce a king in a hundred who would not, if he could, follow the example of Pharoah [sic], get first all the peoples money, then all their lands, and then make them and their children servants for ever.

Source: Speech to Constitutional Convention, Philadelphia, June 2, 1787.

From Poor Richard's Almanack

Lost Time is never found again.
Love your Enemies, for they tell you your Faults.
If you would not be forgotten, as soon as you are dead and rotten, either write things worth reading, or do things worth writing.
Speak little, do much.
A friend in need is a friend indeed!
Experience keeps a dear school, but fools will learn in no other, and scarce in that.
Fish and Visitors stink in 3 days.
Search others for their virtues, thyself for thy vices.
There are three faithful friends: an old wife, an old dog, and ready money.
A stitch in time may save nine.
Today is Yesterday's Pupil.
He that's content, hath enough; He that complains, has too much
Fools need Advice most, but wise Men only are the better for it
If you would persuade, appeal to interest and not to reason.

Source: Poor Richard's Almanack, published annually, 1732–1758.

Lex Fridman

Lex Fridman, né Alexei Fedotov / b. 1983 / Chkalovsk (now Buston), Tajikistan, USSR / Computer Scientist, AI Researcher, Podcaster
Note: The following quotations lack specific sources; however, they probably derive from Fridman's numerous podcasts and tweets.

Artificial Intelligence

We will become AI. AI will become us.

Curiosity

Curiosity is the spark that ignites the fire of knowledge.

Disagreement

I believe disagreement is an art. It requires care. It requires skills, it requires compassion and respect. When there's underlying respect you get to play, there's humor, there's wit. Ultimately you arrive at something profound as a result.

Education

School should inspire not just educate.

Fridman on Fridman

Being an adult is overrated. I refuse to grow up.
Writing music and poetry have been a part of my life for many years, along with science and martial arts. I've written a lot of songs, almost all of which no one has ever heard, including close friends.

History

Don't cancel history. Learn from it.
Now is the best time to be alive. I'm grateful for this moment and for the entire history of life on Earth that led up to it.

The Human Mind

The quest for understanding the human mind is a journey without a final destination.

Human Nature

We humans are better at pointing out the elephants in other rooms than in our own.
Kindness and empathy is not weakness, it's strength.
No one is perfect. If you look for the bad you will find it. If you look for the good, you will find it. Choose wisely what you look for.

Ideas

Sometimes it feels like ideas come from outside the mind.
Good execution is more important than a good idea. But one helps the other.

Life

Life can end at any moment.

Listening

The most profound conversations often arise from a willingness to listen and learn from others.

Love

People need love more than they need advice. Most people know the right thing to do, they just need someone to believe in them.

When you turn your back on the voices of those who are in pain and who are angry, you breed hate. Love is the way out, not hate.

Every love story ends in loss. The deeper the love, the more painful the loss. This is a feature not a bug. It's all worth it.

The Military-Industrial Complex

Beware of the military-industrial complex and the warmongers who exploit tragedy to advocate for more war. A global war would lead to immeasurable suffering. Diplomacy, conversation between leaders is the way out.

Optimism

Resentment and cynicism suffocate the human spirit. Choose optimism, and fight for the best possible future you can imagine.

I look for the good in people. Sometimes I get hurt for it, but it's rare and it's worth it. You may hear me say optimistic things that sound naive. I'm not naive. I've read too much history to be naive. I just think love wins out over the darker parts of human nature in the end.

Everything is possible.

Politics

Most of us are politically in the middle. Don't let the far left or far right convince you otherwise.

Propaganda machines are hard at work stoking the fires of outrage and division, while more and more innocent people suffer.

One person can change the world. That person can be you.

Science

All scientific articles should be free and accessible to everyone.

Self-Improvement

Complain less. Build more.

Technology

Technology has the power to both heal and harm; it depends on how we choose to use it.

Time

There are a lot of hours in a day, plenty to get stuff done if you focus

Truth

Truth is a process not a final destination. The former requires humility and curiosity. The latter dogmatic certainty. There's always more nuance and wisdom to discover, through empathy and reason.

Truth. If you're struggling, stay strong and keep fighting! We're in this together.

Silencing "wrong" ideas will eventually destroy our ability to discover the truth.

Milton Friedman

Milton Friedman / 1912–2006 / New York, USA / Economist

Equality and Freedom

A society that aims for equality before liberty will end up with neither equality nor liberty, and a society that aims for liberty will not end up with equality, but it will end up with a closer approach to equality than any other kind of system that has ever been developed.

Source: "Milton Friedman Speaks: The Role of Government in a Free Society" (in the Q&A section, at about 1:13), 1978.

Freedom and Free Markets

Underlying most arguments against the free market is a lack of belief in freedom itself.

Source: Capitalism and Freedom (University of Chicago Press, 1962).

Government Programs

Nothing is as permanent as a temporary government program.

Source: Tyranny of the Status Quo (Houghton Mifflin Harcourt, 1984).

Inflation

Inflation is always and everywhere a monetary phenomenon.

Source: "The Counter-Revolution in Monetary Theory," IEA Occasional Paper No. 33 (London: Institute of Economic Affairs, 1970).

Intentions vs. Results

One of the great mistakes is to judge policies and programs by their intentions rather than their results.

Source: "Living within Our Means," interview with Richard Heffner, December 7, 1975.

Property Rights

I think that nothing is so important for freedom as recognizing in the law each individual's natural right to property, and giving individuals a sense that they own something that they're responsible for, that they have control over, and that they can dispose of.

Source: "Free to Choose," interview with Larry Arnn, July, 2006.

Self-Interest and Free Enterprise

The world runs on individuals pursuing their separate interests. The great achievements of civilization have not come from government bureaus. Einstein didn't construct his theory under order from a bureaucrat. Henry Ford didn't revolutionize the automobile industry that way. In the only cases in which the masses have escaped from the kind of grinding poverty you're talking about, the only cases in recorded history, are where they have had capitalism and largely free trade. If you want to know where the masses are worse off, worst off, it's exactly in the kinds of societies that depart from that. So that the record of history is absolutely crystal clear, that there is no alternative way so far discovered of improving the lot of the ordinary people that can hold a candle to the productive activities that are unleashed by the free-enterprise system.

Source: "Your Greed or Their Greed?," interview with Phil Donahue, 1979.

Bill Gates

Bill Gates (William Henry Gates III) / b. 1950 / Washington state, USA / Computer Scientist, Entrepreneur, Co-Founder of Microsoft Corporation

Big Pharma

This leads to the paradox, that because the disease is only in the poor countries, there is not much investment. For example, there is more money put into baldness drugs, than are put into malaria. Now, baldness, it is a terrible thing [audience laughter] and rich men are afflicted, so that is why that priority is set.

Bill Gates, "Mosquitos, Malaria, and Education," TED Talk, February, 2009.

Browsers

Any operating system without a browser is going to be f***ing out of business. Should we improve our product, or go out of business?

"In Search of the Real Bill Gates," Time, January 13, 1997.

Bugs

There are no significant bugs in our released software that any significant number of users want fixed. . . . I'm saying we don't do a new version to fix bugs. We don't. Not enough people would buy it. You can take a hundred people using Microsoft Word. Call them up and say "Would you buy a new version because of bugs?" You won't get a single person to say they'd buy a new version because of bugs. We'd never be able to sell a release on that basis.

Focus Magazine, number 43, October 23, 1995.

Business Strategy

One thing we have got to change in our strategy—allowing Office documents to be rendered very well by other peoples browsers is one of the most destructive things we could do to the company. We have to stop putting any effort into this and make sure that Office documents very well depend on PROPRIETARY IE capabilities.

Memo to the Office product group, 1998.

About three million computers get sold every year in China, but people don't pay for the software. Someday they will, though. As long as they are going to steal it, we want them to steal ours. They'll get sort of addicted, and then we'll somehow figure out how to collect sometime in the next decade.

Speech at the University of Washington, reported in "Gates, Buffett a bit bearish," CNET News, July 2, 1998.

Sometimes we do get taken by surprise. For example, when the Internet came along, we had it as a fifth or sixth priority. It wasn't like somebody told me about it and I said, "I don't know how to spell that." I said, "Yeah, I've got that on my list, so I'm okay." But there came a point when we realized it was happening faster and was a much deeper phenomenon than had been recognized in our strategy.

Speech at the University of Washington, reported in "Gates, Buffett a bit bearish," CNET News, July 2, 1998.

We don't have the user centricity. Until we understand context, which is way beyond presence—presence is the most trivial notion, just am I on this device or not; it doesn't say am I meeting with something, am I focused on writing something.

Speech, NET Briefing Day, July 24, 2002.

Consumers

If you show people the problems and you show people the solutions they will be moved to act.

Interview, Live8, July 2, 2005, as reported on BBC News, July 24, 2005.

COVID-19

Most governments take advantage of their scientists and listen to them. They don't undermine them and attack them.

Matthew J. Belvedere, "Bill Gates slams U.S. on Covid: 'Most governments listen to their scientists, not attack them,'" October 14, 2020.

We always have to be serious about public health in a global sense and surveillance for "the next one", because we don't know where it will emerge.

Lisa M. Krieger, "Coronavirus: Bill Gates describes what we did wrong, and how to do better," Mercury News, October 21, 2020.

Education Policy

Just giving people devices has a really horrible track record. You really have to change the curriculum and the teacher. And it's never going to work on a device where you don't have a keyboard-type input. Students aren't there just to read things. They're actually supposed to be able to write and communicate. And so it's going to be more in the PC realm—it's going to be a low-cost PC that lets them be highly interactive.

"A Conversation with Bill Gates about the Future of Higher Education," Chronicle of Higher Education, June 25, 2012.

Equality

One of the wonderful things about the information highway is that virtual equity is far easier to achieve than real-world equity… We are all created equal in the virtual world and we can use this equality to help address some of the sociological problems that society has yet to solve in the physical world,

Bill Gates, The Road Ahead (1995).

Film Media

Understand that [Blu-ray] is the last physical format there will ever be.

Interview, The Daily Princetonian, Oct 14, 2000.

Gates on Gates

It's possible, you can never know, that the universe exists only for me. If so, it's sure going well for me, I must admit.

"In Search of the Real Bill Gates," Time, January 13, 1997.

I wish I wasn't [the world's richest man] . . . There's nothing good that comes out of that. You get more visibility as a result of it.

Online advertising conference in Redmond, Washington, reported in The Guardian, May 5, 2006.

The best way to prepare [to be a programmer] is to write programs, and to study great programs that other people have written. In my case, I went to the garbage cans at the

Computer Science Center and fished out listings of their operating system.

Suzanne Lammers, Programmers at Work: Interviews With 19 Programmers Who Shaped the Computer Industry (1989).

Global Warming

The only way you can get to the very positive scenario is by great innovation. Innovation really does bend the curve.

Christopher Adams and John Thornhill, "Gates to double investment in renewable energy projects: Microsoft cofounder takes interest in new areas of research like in solar, high wind and new nuclear," Financial Times, June 25, 2015.

I [have become] convinced of three things: 1. To avoid a climate disaster, we have to get to get to zero {net emissions by the year 2050}. 2. We need to deploy the tools we already have, like solar and wind, faster and smarter. 3. And we need to create and roll out breakthrough technologies that can take us the rest of the way.

Bill Gates, How to Avoid a Climate Disaster: The Solutions We Have and the Breakthroughs We Need (2021).

Immigration Policy

I'm a big believer that as much as possible, and there's obviously political limitations, freedom of migration is a good thing.

"Bill Gates backs immigration reform on Mexico trip," Reuters, March 21, 2007.

Microchip Capacity

I have to say that in 1981, making those decisions, I felt like I was providing enough freedom for 10 years. That is, a move from 64 K to 640 K felt like something that would last a great deal of time. Well, it didn't—it took about only 6 years before people started to see that as a real problem.

Speech on the history of the microcomputer industry, 1989.

I laid out memory so the bottom 640 K was general purpose RAM and the upper 384 I reserved for video and ROM, and things like that. That is why they talk about the 640 K limit. It is actually a limit, not of the software, in any way, shape, or form, it is the limit of the microprocessor. That thing generates addresses, 20-bits addresses, that only can address a megabyte of memory. And, therefore, all the applications are tied to that limit. It was ten times what we had before. But to my surprise, we ran out of that address base for applications within—oh five or six years people were complaining.

Interview: Winner of the 1993 Price Waterhouse Leadership Award for Lifetime Achievement, Computerworld Smithsonian Awards, National Museum of American History—Smithsonian Institution, 1993.

Microsoft

Instead of buying airplanes and playing around like some of our competitors, we've rolled almost everything back into the company.

Comment to reporters during the IBM PC launch, 1981.

As soon as I learned about this miracle of chip making I thought, what is the key missing element? . . . I'd been working on software so I decided that maybe that was what was necessary to bring all this power to life. I talked about that with a friend, Paul Allen, and we kept saying, "What can we do? Can we start our own software company?" It seemed impossible at the time because software was not done by independent companies. The companies that built the computers—IBM and DEC—they did all the software. And when we called them up and said, "We would like to do an operating system," they said, "who are you?" to which we said, "we're high-school students." That was s, uh—that was the end of that conversation.

Speech to the Economic Club of Detroit, 1997.

We've done some good work, but all of these products become obsolete so fast. . . . It will be some finite number of years, and I don't know the number—before our doom comes.

Daniel Gross, Forbes Greatest Business Stories of All Time (1997).

Microsoft has had clear competitors in the past. It's a good thing we have museums to document that.

Speech at the Computer History Museum, reported in InfoWorld magazine, October, 2001.

Before Paul and I started the company, we had been involved in some large-scale software projects that were real disasters. They just kept pouring people in, and nobody knew how they were going to stabilize the project. We swore to ourselves that we would do better.

Suzanne Lammers, Programmers at Work: Interviews With 19 Programmers Who Shaped the Computer Industry (1989).

OS/2 Operating System

I believe OS/2 is destined to be the most important operating system, and possibly program, of all time.

OS/2 Programmers Guide, November, 1987.

Personal Computing

Personal computing today is a rich ecosystem encompassing massive PC-based data centers, notebook and Tablet PCs, handheld devices, and smart cell phones. It has expanded from the desktop and the data center to wherever people need it—at their desks, in a meeting, on the road or even in the air.

Bill Gates, "The PC Era Is Just Beginning," Business Week, March 22, 2005.

Gary Kildall was one of the original pioneers of the PC revolution. He was a very creative computer scientist who did excellent work. Although we were competitors, I always had tremendous respect for his contributions to the PC industry. His untimely death was very unfortunate and he and his work will be missed.

"Gary Kildall," special edition of The Computer Chronicles, 1995.

If you just want to say, "Steve Jobs invented the world, and then the rest of us came along," that's fine. If you're interested, [Vista development chief] Jim Allchin will be glad to educate you feature by feature what the truth is. . . . Let's be realistic, who came up with "File/Edit/View/Help"? Do you want to go back to the original Mac and think about where those interface concepts came from?

Interview with Steven Levy, "Finally, Vista Makes Its Debut. Now What?," Newsweek, January 31, 2007.

Product Development

If something is expensive to develop, and somebody's not going to get paid, it won't get developed. So you decide: Do you want software to be written, or not?

Interview with Dennis Bathory-Kitsz in 80 Microcomputing, 1980.

Science and Religion

In terms of doing things I take a fairly scientific approach to why things happen and how they happen. I don't know if there's a god or not, but I think religious principles are quite valid.

Interview with David Frost, PBS, November, 1995.

Just in terms of allocation of time resources, religion is not very efficient. There's a lot more I could be doing on a Sunday morning.

"In Search of the Real Bill Gates," Time, January 13, 1997.

The moral systems of religion, I think, are superimportant. We've raised our kids in a religious way; they've gone to the Catholic church that Melinda goes to and I participate in. I've been very lucky, and therefore I owe it to try and reduce the inequity in the world. And that's kind of a religious belief. I mean, it's at least a moral belief.

Interview, Rolling Stone, March 27, 2014.

Software Development

It's not manufacturers trying to rip anybody off or anything like that. There's nobody getting rich writing software that I know of.

Interview with Dennis Bathory-Kitsz in 80 Microcomputing, 1980.

There's only one trick in software, and that is using a piece of software that's already been written.

Interview with Electronics magazine, 1989.

What we're saying to people is that every idea about ease-of-use, we can develop in software, for the PC, without asking them to buy new hardware, without asking them to throw away their old applications.

Interview with Charlie Rose, PBS, November 25, 1996.

It's easier for our software to compete with Linux when there's piracy than when there's not.

Fortune, July 17, 2007.

Spam

Like almost everyone who uses e-mail, I receive a ton of spam every day. Much of it offers to help me get out of debt or get rich quick. It would be funny if it weren't so irritating.

Bill Gates, "Why I Hate Spam," Microsoft PressPass, 2003.

Spam will be a thing of the past in two years' time.

Reported on BBC News, January 24, 2004.

Success

Success is a lousy teacher. It seduces smart people into thinking they can't lose.

Bill Gates, The Road Ahead (1995).

Unhappy Customers

Your most unhappy customers are your greatest source of learning.

Bill Gates, Business @ The Speed of Thought: Succeeding in the Digital Economy (1999).

Viruses

When I was a kid, the disaster we worried about most was a nuclear war. . . . If anything kills over 10 million people in the next few decades, it's most likely to be a highly infectious virus rather than a war. Not missiles, but microbes.

Bill Gates, "The next outbreak? We're not ready," TED talk, April 3, 2015.

George Gilder

George Franklin Gilder / b. 1939 / New York, USA / Economist, Investor, Author

Artificial Intelligence

The blind spot of AI is that consciousness does not emerge from thought; it is the source of it.

Life After Google: The Fall of Big Data and the Rise of the Blockchain Economy (2018).

Big Data

In the age of Big Data, the von Neumann bottleneck has philosophical implications. The more knowledge that is put into a von Neumann machine, the bigger and more crowded its memory, the further away its average data address, and the slower its functioning.

Life After Google: The Fall of Big Data and the Rise of the Blockchain Economy (2018).

Capitalism

If the government controls, guarantees, channels, or directs investment, it is not capitalism.

The Scandal of Money: Why Wall Street Recovers but the Economy Never Does (2016).

DNA

The analogy between [Claude] Shannon and codes in biology isn't something that sprang from my belief in God . . . except maybe on some deeper or more transcendent level.

Interview with the Boston Globe, July 27, 2005.

Entrepreneurs

Far from being greedy, America's leading entrepreneurs—with some exceptions—display discipline and self-control, hard work and austerity, excelling those found in any college of social work, Washington think tank, or congregation of bishops.

Knowledge and Power: The Information Theory of Capitalism and How it is Revolutionizing our World (2013).

Evolution

Academic scientists of any sort expect to be struck by lightning if they celebrate real creation *de novo* in the world.

Knowledge and Power: The Information Theory of Capitalism and How it is Revolutionizing our World (2013).

I'm not pushing to have [ID] taught as an alternative to Darwin, and neither are they. . . . What's being pushed is to have Darwinism critiqued, to teach there's a controversy. Intelligent design itself does not have any content. . . . Much of what I've written about has been in reaction to the materialist superstition, the belief that the universe is a purely material phenomenon that can be reduced to physical and chemical laws. It's a concept that's infected the social sciences as well.

Interview with the Boston Globe, July 27, 2005.

Excellence

The envy of excellence leads to perdition; the love of it leads to the light.

The Israel Test: Why the World's Most Besieged State is a Beacon of Freedom and Hope for the World Economy (2012).

Family

The question thus becomes: Will the scientists and women's liberationists be able to unleash on the world a generation of kinless children to serve as the Red Guards of a totalitarian state? Will we try to reproduce the Nazi experiment, when illegitimacy was promoted by the provision of lavish nursing homes and the state usurped the provider male. Or will we manage to maintain our most indispensable condition of civilization —and obstacle to totalitarian usurpation— the human marriage and family.

Sexual Suicide (1973).

Friedman's Errors

In 1976 [Milton] Friedman suffered a crippling intellectual trauma that for the rest of his life seriously affected his thinking. The king of Sweden awarded him a Nobel Prize for economic science, specifically for his errors—his monetary theory and his permanent income hypothesis.

The Scandal of Money (2016).

Genius

The most precious resource in the world economy is human genius.

The Israel Test: Why the World's Most Besieged State is a Beacon of Freedom and Hope for the World Economy (2012).

God

[Kurt] Gödel demonstrated that every logical scheme, including mathematics, is dependent upon axioms that it cannot prove and that cannot be reduced to the scheme itself. In an elegant mathematical proof, introduced to the world by the great mathematician and computer scientist John von Neumann in September 1930, Gödel demonstrated that mathematics was intrinsically incomplete. Gödel was reportedly concerned that he might have inadvertently proved the existence of God, a *faux pas* in his Viennese and Princeton circle. It was one of the famously paranoid Gödel's more reasonable fears. As the economist Steven Landsberg, an academic atheist, put it, "Mathematics is the only faith-based science that can prove it."

Knowledge and Power: The Information Theory of Capitalism and How it is Revolutionizing our World (2013).

Government Philosophy

If it moves tax it. If it keeps moving regulate it. If it stops moving subsidize it.

Life After Google: The Fall of Big Data and the Rise of the Blockchain Economy (2018).

Light

Let there be light, says the Bible. All the firmaments of technology, all our computers and networks, are built with light, and of light, and for light, to hasten its spread around the world.

Telecosm: How Infinite Bandwidth Will Revolutionize Our World(2000).

Love and Marriage

Marriage is not simply a ratification of an existing love. It is the conversion of that love into a biological and social continuity transcending any two individuals.

Sexual Suicide (1973).

The natural fulfillment of love is a child, and the fantasies and projects of the childless couple may well be considered as surrogate children.

Sexual Suicide (1973).

The essential pattern is clear. Women manipulate male sexual desire in order to teach them the long-term cycles of female sexuality and biology on which civilization is based. When men learn, their view of the woman as an object of their own sexuality succumbs to an image of her as the bearer of a richer and more extended eroticism and as the keeper of the portals of social immorality. She becomes a way to lend elaborate continuity and meaning to the limited erotic compulsions of the male.

Sexual Suicide (1973).

At the deepest level, therefore, love and marriage are based on this complementary pattern. The man's most profound and indispensable life must be experienced through the woman; she is the master of their sexuality. Meanwhile the woman's external existence will to some extent be sustained and protected by the man; he gives space for their worldly haven. This may be the very essence of a closed marriage but it is the essence of the institution itself.

Sexual Suicide (1973).

Materialism

Much of what I've written about has been in reaction to the materialist superstition, the belief that the universe is a purely material phenomenon that can be reduced to physical and chemical laws. It's a concept that's infected the social sciences as well.

Interview with the Boston Globe, July 27, 2005.

Money

Money is not a magic wand but a measuring stick, not wealth but a gauge of it.

Life After Google: The Fall of Big Data and the Rise of the Blockchain Economy (2018).

Religion

Futurists falter because they belittle the power of religious paradigms, deeming them either too literal or too fantastic.

Telecosm: How Infinite Bandwidth Will Revolutionize Our World(2000).

Sex

Nonetheless, a kind of Gresham's law applies. Bad sex drives out the good, and the worst of all—philandering and homosexuality—are exalted. Gay liberation, pornographic glut, and one-night trysts are all indices of sexual frustration; all usually disclose a failure to achieve profound and loving sexuality. When a society deliberately affirms these failures: contemplates legislation of homosexual marriage, celebrates the women who denounce the family, and indulges pornography as a manifestation of sexual health and a release from repression-the culture is promoting a form of erotic suicide. For it is destroying the cultural preconditions of profound love and sexuality; the durable heterosexual relationships necessary to a community of emotional investments and continuities in which children can find a secure place.

Sexual Suicide (1973).

In the most elemental sense, the sex drive is the survival instinct: the primal tie to the future. When people lose faith in themselves and their prospects, they also lose their procreative energy. They commit sexual suicide. They just cannot bear the idea of "bringing children into the world." But it is a kind of aimless copulation having little to do with the deeper currents of sexuality and love that carry a community into the future.

Sexual Suicide (1973).

Welfare

The welfare culture tells the man he is not a necessary part of the family; he feels dispensable, his wife knows he is dispensable, his children sense it.

Wealth and Poverty: A New Edition for the Twenty-First Century, second edition (2012).

Rudy Giuliani

Rudolph William Louis Giuliani / b. 1944 / New York, New York, USA / Lawyer, US Associate Attorney General, US Attorney for the Southern District of New York, Mayor of New York City, Political Commentator and Activist, Author, Podcaster

Note: Sources of quotations are provided where known; otherwise, quotes may be assumed to derive from Giuliani's extremely prolific public statements, both in print and online, over many years

9/11

The attacks of September 11 were intended to break our spirit, instead we have emerged stronger and more unified. We feel renewed devotion to the principles of political, economic, and religious freedom, the rule of law, and respect for human life. We are more determined than ever to live our lives in freedom.

Remarks, Dedication for the exhibit, "After September 11: Images from Ground Zero," December 31, 2001.

I don't need Michael Moore to tell me about September 11.

Press conference, July 29, 2004.

In the 9/11 Commission Report, one of the things they point out is that firefighters saved just about everybody below the fire. I don't think they realize how proud the fire department is of that. Because, conceivably, that's all they could have done. They could not have gotten above that fire.

The lesson of 9/11 is that America is truly exceptional. We withstood the worst attack of our history, intended by our enemies to destroy us. Instead, it drew us closer and made us more united. Our love for freedom and one another has given us a strength that surprised even ourselves.

2020 Election

To all those patriots challenging the fraudulent election . . . You are on the right side of the law and history.

Tweet, January 6, 2021.

America First Movement

The idea of "America First" is back and stronger than ever.

Authority

We look upon authority too often and focus over and over again, for thirty or forty or fifty years, as if there is something wrong with authority. We see only the oppressive side of authority. Maybe it comes out of our history and our background. What we don't see is that freedom is not a concept in which people can do anything they want, be anything they can be. Freedom is about authority. Freedom is about the willingness of every single human being to cede to lawful authority a great deal of discretion about what you do.

Cited in the New York Times, March 20, 1994.

COVID-19 Restrictions

America is about freedom. We should respect that freedom, even if it means taking risks to defend it.

Interview, Fox News, May, 2021.

The way you deal with these situations is to be honest with the American people. Let them know what you know and what you don't know.

Interview, "Meet the Press," NBC, April, 2020.

Criminal Justice System

You know, as a lawyer, I've defended an awful lot of people. And I know how easy it is, even for innocent people, to get into a jam.

Interview, ABC News, April, 2018.

It's about time law enforcement got as organized as organized crime.

Cited in TIME magazine, October 15, 1984

Democracy

Aspiring dictators sometimes win elections, and elected leaders sometimes govern badly and threaten their neighbors. . . . History demonstrates that democracy usually follows good governance, not the reverse.

Cited in "Giuliani": Too much stress on two-state plan," Jewish Telegraph Agency, August 15, 2007.

We can determine America's future. After all, that's what an election is all about. So, let's decide for optimism, not pessimism; for hope, not despair; for strength, not weakness; for victory, not defeat.

December 15, 2007.

Education

Schools exist in America and have always existed to train responsible citizens of the United States of America. If they don't do that, it's very hard to hold us together as a country, because it's shared values that hold us together.

When I was mayor of New York, my views changed. I began as mayor of New York City thinking that I could reform the New York City school system. After two or three years, four years, I became an advocate of choice, of scholarships, and vouchers, and parental choice, because I thought that was the only way to really change the school system.

Equality Under the Law

I think the president has to be treated like everyone else. 'Cause I think under the criminal law everybody should be treated the same. I know there are people who would say that the president should be treated stricter. We used to have an era in which the president was treated much more leniently. But I think the right answer is: the president should be treated the same; as far as the criminal law is concerned the president is a citizen.

Interview, "Charlie Rose," PBS, July, 1998.

Freedom

The idea of freedom and liberty and democracy is very contagious.

Interview, CNN, April, 2005.

Giuliani on Giuliani

I don't sit around thinking about me and my legacy.

Interview, New Yorker, October 2019.

The reality is, I'm a lawyer. I'm not an investigator. I'm not a special agent.

Interview, Fox News, May, 2018.

I'm the mayor of New York City. I've got a job to do. I've got to protect the people of the city. And I've got to do something about the crime problem.

Speech, National Press Club, January, 1995.

Re: 9/11

I'm not a hero, I just did my job.

Interview, "Larry King Live," CNN, October, 2001.

I have been in the eye of the storm from September 11 forward. And I have never left the eye of the storm.

Speech, Republican National Convention, New York, August 30, 2004.

I've always been a Republican. But I've always been a Republican because the Republican Party stood for individual freedom.

Interview, CNN, May, 2021.

I don't back down. I don't cave under pressure.

Interview, CNN, November, 2020.

I was at Ground Zero as often, if not more, than most of the workers. I was there working with them. I was there guiding things. I was there bringing people there. But I was exposed to exactly the same things they were exposed to. So, in that sense, I'm one of them.

Cited in the New York Times, August 11, 2007.

The most important lesson my dad taught me was how to manage fear. Early on, he taught me that in a time of emergency, you've got to become deliberately calm.

You never begin a new life. It's a mistake to think that you end one part of your life and start another as if there's no continuity.

I was very serious about being a priest, twice in my life. Almost joined the Montfort Seminary after I graduated from high school. Almost went back in the seminary during college.

You have to keep a strong sense of who you really are—and I have a pretty strong sense of myself. It gets me in trouble when I say this, but I don't think of myself as a politician. I've always tried to be honest when communicating with people.

When I became mayor of New York City, I had a $2.4 billion deficit. And everybody wanted me to raise taxes. I said, "If I raise taxes, I'll drive people out of New York City, and then I'll be raising taxes again." So, what I did was, I cut expenses by 15 percent.

There are terrible, terrible memories of September 11th, things that I saw, people that I lost, the devastation, the identification of bodies. I mean, all these memories come back to you at different times. And then the other side of it this tremendous response with the firefighters and the police officers saving people, the rescue workers.

I'll tell you what makes me feel worthwhile: organizing and solving other people's problems. It makes me feel good to go to Mexico City and figure out theories on how you can reorganize and reduce crime. To me, it's one of the more fulfilling ways to spend a day.

You never agree with any one candidate 100 percent. I don't agree with myself 100 percent.

Immigration Policy

If you're not in favor of border security, I don't see how you can call yourself a citizen of the United States of America.

Interview, Fox News, June, 2018.

Leadership

Leadership is not about being popular. It's about being right and being strong.

Leadership is not about being in charge. It is about taking care of those in your charge.

Speech, Republican National Convention, New York, August 30, 2004.

There are many qualities that make a great leader but having strong beliefs, being able to stick with them through popular and unpopular times, is the most important characteristic of a great leader.

Speech, Republican National Convention, New York, August 30, 2004.

Leaders must be optimists. Their vision was beyond the present and set on a future of real peace and true freedom.

Speech, Republican National Convention, New York, August 30, 2004.

In choosing a president, we really don't choose a Republican or Democrat, a conservative or liberal. We choose a leader.

Speech, Republican National Convention, New York. August 30, 2004.

When you confront a problem, you begin to solve it.

Cited in RFID Journal, February 28, 2005.

. . . the sky's the limit for all Americans if we have the right kind of leadership.

Republican debate, Univision, December 9, 2007.

When I said the city would be stronger, I didn't know that. I just hoped it. There are parts of you that say, "Maybe we're not going to get through this." You don't listen to them.

When you're in a crisis of, you know, tremendous proportions, it's beyond any human capability to control, you just make the best decisions you can, and you just hope that your intuition is correct.

Obama

Change is not a destination as hope is not a strategy.

Speech, Republican National Convention, 2008.

I do not believe, and I know this is a horrible thing to say, but I do not believe that the president loves America. He doesn't love you. And he doesn't love me. He wasn't brought up the way you were brought up and I was brought up through love of this country.

Cited by Darren Samuelsohn in "Rudy Giuliani: President Obama doesn't love America," Politico, February 18, 2015.

Policing

Blacks commit murder eight times more per capita than any other group in our society. If I had put all of my police officers on Park Avenue and none in Harlem, thousands and thousands more blacks would've been killed during the eight years that I was mayor.

Protest

The rule is, you can protest all you want. Make all the noise you want. Carry all the signs you want. The minute you throw a rock, you get arrested. The minute you break a window, you get arrested. The minute you break into a store, you get arrested.

Public Opinion Polls

We have too many politicians who are poll-driven to excess. Polls are important. You've got to know what the public is thinking, but you can't let them drive you completely.

Racism

There's no room for intolerance or racism in the Republican Party or in America. That's not what I believe, that's not what I practiced, that's not what I taught when I was mayor of New York City.

Trump

I do not believe that any President has accomplished as much as this one in the first two and a half years of his presidency.

The spirit of America has revived because of President Trump.

Interview, Fox News, October, 2020.

I do not believe that any president . . . has had as much respect for religious freedom and for the role of religious institutions in our society as this president.

Speech, National Catholic Prayer Breakfast, September, 2020.

I was one of the first people to support Trump. I supported him when there was no one else around him.

Interview, Wall Street Journal, June, 2018.

I believe the Democrats do not want this president to have a fair trial. I believe they want a political trial.

Interview, Fox News, December, 2019.

When you say "interfere," it's a very vague word. I want to know what you mean by "interfere." It's not a crime to talk to the Russians."

Interview, "State of the Union," CNN, July 2018.

I think people are tired of politicians who dither around and don't get things done.

Interview, Fox News, June, 2018.

I have known Donald Trump for almost 30 years. And he has created and accomplished great things. But beyond that, this is a man with a big heart.

Every time New York City suffered a tragedy, Donald Trump was there to help. And he did it anonymously.

There is no more time for us left to revive our great country. No more time to repeat our mistakes of the past. Washington needs a complete turnaround, and Donald Trump is the agent of change, and he will be the leader of the change we need.

It's time to make America safe again. It's time to make America one again. I know it can be done because I did it by changing New York City from "the crime capital of America" to—according to the FBI—the safest large city in America. What I did for New York City, Donald Trump will do for America.

Truth

Truth will always come out. It will always find a way to make itself known. The truth always eventually emerges, no matter how many people try to hide it.

Speech, Republican National Convention, New York, August 30, 2004.

Utopianism

I think one of the biggest mistakes that America has made—and maybe the world because this is, sort of, the core of communism and socialism—is that you can have perfect solutions to social problems like poverty, like crime. You're not going to eliminate all crime. Maybe you'll never eliminate all poverty.

Johann Wolfgang von Goethe

Johann Wolfgang von Goethe / 1749–1832 / Free Imperial City of Frankfurt, Holy Roman Empire (now Germany) / Poet, Novelist, Dramatist, Memoirist, Naturalist

Architecture

I call architecture frozen music.

Source: J.P. Eckermann, Conversations with Goethe, March 23, 1829 (1836).

Art is Long

Ah, God! how long is art!
And soon it is we die.
Oft when my critical pursuits I ply,
I truly grow uneasy both in head and heart.
How hard to gain the means whereby
A man mounts upward to the source!
And ere man's ended barely half the course.
Poor devil! I suppose he has to die.

Source: Faust, Part One, Scene I (1808); Wagner.

Children

We can't form our children on our own concepts; we must take them and love them as God gives them to us.

Source: Hermann and Dorothea (1797).

Death

O'er all the hilltops
Is quiet now,
In all the treetops
Hearest thou
Hardly a breath;
The birds are asleep in the trees:
Wait; soon like these
Thou too shalt rest.

Source: "Wanderer's Nightsong II" (1780).

Freedom without Responsibility

Everything that emancipates the spirit without giving us control over ourselves is harmful.

Source: Proverbs in Prose (1819).

How to Live

One ought, every day at least, to hear a little song, read a good poem, see a fine picture, and, if it were possible, to speak a few reasonable words.

Source: Wilhelm Meister's Apprenticeship (1795–96).

Inspiring Others

"When we take people," thou wouldst say, "merely as they are, we make them worse; when we treat them as if they were what they should be, we improve them as far as they can be improved."

Source: Wilhelm Meister's Apprenticeship (1795–96).

Knowledge vs. Action

Knowing is not enough; we must apply. Willing is not enough; we must do.

Source: Wilhelm Meister's Journeyman Years (1821).

Life vs. Theory

Dear friend, all theory is gray,
And green the golden tree of life.

Source: Faust, Part One, Scene IV (1808); Mephistopheles.

Love

If I love you, what business is it of yours?

Source: Wilhelm Meister's Apprenticeship (1795–96).

Manhood

For I have been a man, and that means to have been a fighter.

Source: West-Eastern Divan (1819).

Marriage

The sum which two married people owe to one another defies calculation. It is an infinite debt, which can only be discharged through all eternity.

Source: Elective Affinities (1809).

Negativity

I am the Spirit that always denies!

Source: Faust, Part One, Scene III (1808); Mephistopheles.

Seize the Day

What's left undone to-day, To-morrow will not do.
Waste not a day in vain digression:
With resolute, courageous trust
Seize every possible impression,
And make it firmly your possession;
You'll then work on, because you must.

Source: Faust, Part One, "Prelude at the Theater" (1808); Manager.

Striving

He only earns his Freedom and Existence,
Who's forced to win them freshly every day.

Source: Faust, Part Two, Act V, Scene VI (1832); Faust.

Talent

One must **be** something to be able to **do** something.

Source: J.P. Eckermann, Conversations with Goethe, October 20, 1828 (1836).

A talent is formed in stillness, a character in the world's torrent

Source: Torquato Tasso (1790).

Teaching

A teacher who can arouse a feeling for one single good action, for one single good poem, accomplishes more than he who fills our memory with rows on rows of natural objects, classified with name and form.

Source: Elective Affinities (1809).

Truth

Nothing is great but truth, and the smallest truth is great. The other day I had a thought, which I put like this: Even a harmful truth is useful, for it can be harmful only for the moment and will lead to other truths, which must always become useful, very much so. Conversely, even a useful error is harmful, for it can be useful only for the moment, enticing us into other errors, which become more and more harmful.

Source: Letter to Charlotte von Stein (1787).

Nothing is more damaging to a new truth than an old error.

Source: Proverbs in Prose (1819).

First and last, what is demanded of genius is love of truth.

Source: Proverbs in Prose (1819).

Woman

Woman, eternal,
Beckons us on.

Source: Faust, Part Two, Act V, Scene VII (1832); Mystic Choir.

Words and Deeds

The words you've bandied are sufficient;
'Tis deeds that I prefer to see:

Source: Faust, Part One, "Prelude at the Theater" (1808); Manager.

Baltasar Gracián

Baltasar Gracián / 1601–1658 / Aragón, Spain / Jesuit Priest, Novelist, Essayist, Aphorist
Note: All quotations are taken from *Oráculo Manual y Arte de Prudencia* [*The Oracle, a Manual of the Art of Discretion*] (1647); also translated as *The Art of Worldly Wisdom: A Pocket Oracle* (1892).

Action

Do something well, and that is quickly enough.
Don't live by generalities, unless it be to act virtuously, and don't ask desire to follow precise laws, for you will have to drink tomorrow from the water you scorn today.

Beginnings

Honorable beginnings should serve to awaken curiosity, not to heighten people's expectations. We are much better off when reality surpasses our expectations, and something turns out better than we thought it would

Complaints

Complaints will always discredit you.

Counsel

When you counsel someone, you should appear to be reminding him of something he had forgotten, not of the light he was unable to see.

Deceit

Not believing others implies that you yourself are deceitful.

Flattery

Many owe their greatness to their enemies. Flattery is fiercer than hatred, for hatred corrects the faults flattery had disguised.

Freedom

Freedom is more precious than the gift that makes us lose it

Friendship

Knowing how to keep a friend is more important than gaining a new one.

Ignorance

Because the ignorant do not know themselves, they never know for what they are lacking. Some would be sages if they did not believe they were so already.

Knowledge

If you cannot make knowledge your servant, make it your friend.

Pleasing

The one rule for pleasing: whet the appetite, keep people hungry.

Politeness

Politeness and a sense of honor have this advantage: we bestow them on others without losing a thing.

Readiness

Readiness is the mother of luck.

Regret

Some die because they feel everything, others because they feel nothing. Some are fools because they suffer no regrets, and others because they do.

Royal Confidant

To hear a prince's secrets is not a privilege but a burden. Many smash the mirror that reminds them of their ugliness.

Tolerance

The person who does not know how to put up with others should retire into himself, if indeed he can suffer even himself.

Truth

Some marry the first information they receive, and turn what comes later into their concubine. Since deceit is always first to arrive, there is no room left for truth.

Valuation

To overvalue something is a form of lying.

Virtue

Virtue alone is for real; all else is sham. Talent and greatness depend on virtue, not on fortune. Only virtue is sufficient unto herself.

Workers

Those who want to look like hard workers give the impression that they aren't up to their jobs.

Katharine Graham

Katharine Graham, née Meyer / 1917–20011 / New York, New York, USA / Newspaper Publisher, Memoirist

Capitalism

I believed—and believe—that capitalism works best for a freedom-loving society, that it brings more prosperity to more people than any other social-economic system, but that somehow we have to take care of people.

Source unknown.

Competitiveness

To be competitive, you have to be pretty ruthless.

Interview, cited in Sue Ellen Moncrief, "The Last Publisher," New York Times Magazine, March 18, 1973.

Democracy

The greatest threat to democracy is the notion that it has already been achieved.

Source unknown.

There are some things the general public does not need to know and shouldn't. I believe democracy flourishes when the government can take legitimate steps to keep its secrets, and when the press can decide whether to print what it knows.

Source unknown.

Graham on Graham

One of my principal childhood memories is hearing one of the Liszt Hungarian Rhapsodies waft throughout the house.

Source unknown.

Those first few years of marriage, before the war interrupted all our lives, Phil and I had a very happy time. I grew up considerably, mostly thanks to him.

Source unknown.

Mistakes

A mistake is simply another way of doing things.

Interview, cited in William Safire, "The Power of the Press," New York Times Magazine, October 17, 1971.

The only way to guarantee you won't make a mistake is not to do anything. And that leads you to make mistakes out of omission rather than commission.

Interview, cited in William Safire, "The Power of the Press," New York Times Magazine, October 17, 1971.

Motivation

People are motivated by the desire to make a difference, to make a mark. Otherwise, why wake up in the morning?

Personal History: A Memoir (1997).

News

News is what someone wants suppressed. Everything else is advertising.

Source unknown.

The Press

Family ownership provides the independence that is sometimes required to withstand governmental pressure and preserve freedom of the press.

Source unknown.

The press these days should be rather careful about its role. We may have acquired some tendencies about over-involvement that we had better overcome.

Source unknown.

Truthfulness

To be persuasive, we must be believable; to be believable, we must be credible; to be credible, we must be truthful. It is as simple as that.

Commencement address, Stanford University, June 17, 1984.

Washington

One doesn't soon forget the natural beauty of Washington, although those of us who live here do sometimes take it for granted.

Source unknown.

Watergate

If we had failed to pursue the facts as far as they led, we would have denied the public any knowledge of an unprecedented scheme of political surveillance and sabotage.

Source unknown.

Women

The thing women must do to rise to power is to redefine their femininity. Once, power was considered a masculine attribute. In fact, power has no sex.

Source unknown.

So few grown women like their lives.

Source unknown.

Work

To love what you do and feel that it matters—how could anything be more fun?

Personal History: A Memoir (1997).

Alan Greenspan

Alan Greenspan / b. 1926 / New York, USA / Economist, Chairman of the Federal Reserve

Antitrust

The world of antitrust is reminiscent of Alice's Wonderland: everything seemingly is, yet apparently isn't, simultaneously. It is a world in which competition is lauded as the basic axiom and guiding principle, yet "too much" competition is condemned as "cutthroat." It is a world in which actions designed to limit competition are branded as criminal when taken by businessmen, yet praised as "enlightened" when initiated by the government. It is a world in which the law is so vague that businessmen have no way of knowing whether specific actions will be declared illegal until they hear the judge's verdict—after the fact.

> *"Antitrust," address to the National Association of Business Economists, Cleveland, Ohio, September 25, 1961; published in Ayn Rand, ed., Capitalism: The Unknown Ideal (1966).*

Capitalism

Capitalism is based on self-interest and self-esteem; it holds integrity and trustworthiness as cardinal virtues and makes them pay off in the marketplace, thus demanding that men survive by means of virtue, not vices. It is this superlatively moral system that the welfare statists propose to improve upon by means of preventative law, snooping bureaucrats, and the chronic goad of fear.

> *"The Assault on Integrity," in Ayn Rand, ed., Capitalism: The Unknown Ideal (1966).*

Intensive research in recent years into the sources of economic growth among both developing and developed nations generally point to a number of important factors: the state of knowledge and skill of a population; the degree of control over indigenous natural resources; the quality of a country's legal system, particularly a strong commitment to a rule of law and protection of property rights; and yes, the extent of a country's openness to trade with the rest of the world. For the United States, arguably the most important factor is the type of rule of law under which economic activity takes place. When asked abroad why the United States has become the most prosperous large economy in the world, I respond, with only mild exaggeration, that our forefathers wrote a constitution and set in motion a system of laws that protects individual rights, especially the right to own property. Nonetheless, the degree of state protection is sometimes in dispute. But by and large, secure property rights are almost universally accepted by Americans as a critical pillar of our economy. While the right of property in the abstract is generally uncontested in all societies embracing democratic market capitalism, different degrees of property protection do apparently foster different economic incentives and outcomes.

Address, "The critical role of education in the nation's economy," 2004 Annual Meeting, Greater Omaha Chamber of Commerce, Omaha, Nebraska, February 20, 2004; accessible on federalreserve.gov.

In general, corruption tends to exist whenever governments have favors to extend, or something to sell.

Alan Greenspan, The Age of Turbulence: Adventures in a New World (2008).

We are going through a period with no precedent in American history.

Reported by Nicholas Lemann in "The Hand on the Lever," newyorker.com, July 21, 2014.

Gold

An almost hysterical antagonism toward the gold standard is one issue which unites statists of all persuasions. They seem to sense—perhaps more clearly and subtly than many consistent defenders of laissez-faire—that gold and economic freedom are inseparable, that the gold standard is an instrument of laissez-faire and that each implies and requires the other.

"Gold and Economic Freedom," in Ayn Rand, ed., Capitalism: The Unknown Ideal (1966).

In the absence of the gold standard, there is no way to protect savings from confiscation through inflation. There is no safe store of value. If there were, the government would have to make its holding illegal, as was done in the case of gold. If everyone decided, for example, to convert all his bank deposits to silver or copper or any other good, and thereafter declined to accept checks as payment for goods, bank deposits would lose their purchasing power and government-created bank credit would be worthless as a claim on goods. The financial policy of the welfare state requires that there be no way for the owners of wealth to protect themselves. This is the shabby secret of the welfare statists' tirades against gold. Deficit spending is simply a scheme for the confiscation of wealth. Gold stands in the way of this insidious process. It stands as a protector of property rights. If one grasps this, one has no difficulty in understanding the statists' antagonism toward the gold standard.

"Gold and Economic Freedom," in Ayn Rand, ed., Capitalism: The Unknown Ideal (1966).

The reason there is very little support for the gold standard is the consequences of those types of market adjustments are not considered to be appropriate in the 20th and 21st century. I am one of the rare people who have still some nostalgic view about the old gold standard, as you know, but I must tell you, I am in a very small minority among my colleagues on that issue.

Testimony, US House of Representatives Committee on Financial Services, July 22, 1998.

Greenspan on Greenspan

Since becoming a central banker, I have learned to mumble with great incoherence. If I seem unduly clear to you, you must have misunderstood what I said.

Testimony, US Senate Committee; reported by the Los Angeles Times, September 27, 1987.

Well, first of all, the Federal Reserve is an independent agency, and that means, basically, that there is no other agency of government which can overrule actions that we take. So long as that is in place and there is no evidence that the administration or the Congress or anybody else is requesting that we do things other than what we think is the appropriate thing, then what the relationships are don't, frankly, matter. And I've had very good relationships with presidents.

Interview with Jim Lehrer, "The NewsHour with Jim Lehrer," pbs.org, September 18, 2007.

We generally did not talk about the stock market very much at the Fed.

Alan Greenspan, The Age of Turbulence: Adventures in a New World (2008).

Housing Bubble of 2008

Without calling the overall national issue a bubble, it's pretty clear that it's an unsustainable underlying pattern.

Reported by Edmund L. Andrews in "Greenspan is Concerned About 'Froth' in Housing," nytimes.com, May 21, 2005.

. . . there can be little doubt that exceptionally low interest rates on ten-year Treasury notes, and hence on home mortgages, have been a major factor in the recent surge of homebuilding and home turnover, and especially in the steep climb in home prices. Although a "bubble" in home prices for the nation as a whole does not appear likely, there do appear to be, at a minimum, signs of froth in some local markets where home prices seem to have risen to unsustainable levels.

Testimony, "The economic outlook," Joint Economic Committee, U.S. Congress, June 9, 2005; accessible on federalreserve.gov.

I really didn't get it until very late in 2005 and 2006.

Reported by Mark Felsenthal in "Greenspan says didn't see subprime storm brewing," reuters.com, September 13, 2007.

I was aware that the loosening of mortgage credit terms for subprime borrowers increased financial risk. But I believed then, as now, that the benefits of broadened home ownership are worth the risk.

Alan Greenspan, The Age of Turbulence: Adventures in a New World (2008).

Those of us who have looked to the self-interest of lending institutions to protect shareholder's equity—myself especially—are in a state of shocked disbelief.

Reported by Stephen Foley in "Greenspan says crisis left him in 'shocked disbelief,'" independent.co.uk, October 24, 2008.

Re: US Representative Henry Waxman's question whether Greenspan had discovered a flaw in his free-market ideology.

Yes, I've found a flaw. I don't know how significant or permanent it is. But I've been very distressed by that fact.

Testimony, US House of Representatives Oversight Committee; reported by Michael M. Grynbaum in "Greenspan Concedes Error on Regulation," nytimes.com, October 23, 2008.

Much of the securitization took the form of collateralized debt obligations (CDOs) with senior credit tranches certified by rating agencies as AAA. It was the failure to properly price such risky assets that characterized the crisis.

Alan Greenspan, The Age of Turbulence: Adventures in a New World (2008).

Inflation

We are obviously all hurt by inflation. Everybody is hurt by inflation. If you really wanted to examine who percentage-wise is hurt the most in their incomes, it is the Wall Street brokers. I mean their incomes have gone down the most.

Address, Washington, DC, September 19, 1974; published in US Government Printing Office, The Conference on Inflation—Health, Education, Income Security, and Social Services (1974).

Irrational Exuberance

We can see that in the inverse relationship exhibited by price/earnings ratios and the rate of inflation in the past. But how do we know when irrational exuberance has unduly escalated asset values, which then become subject to unexpected and prolonged contractions as they have in Japan over the past decade?

Lecture, American Enterprise Institute, Washington, DC, December 5, 1996.

Market Forces

It hardly makes any difference who will be the next president. The world is governed by market forces.

Interview with Tages-Anzeiger, Zurich, Switzerland, 2007; reported by Adam Tooze in "Beyond the Crash," theguardian.com, July 29, 2018.

Risk Premium

History has not dealt kindly with the aftermath of protracted periods of low risk premiums.

Address, "Reflections on central banking," symposium, Federal Reserve Bank of Kansas City, Jackson Hole, Wyoming, August 26, 2005; accessible on federalreserve.gov.

Values

The need for values is inbred. Their content is not.

Alan Greenspan, The Age of Turbulence: Adventures in a New World (2008).

Wayne Gretzky

Wayne Gretzky / b. 1961 / Ontario, Canada / Ice Hockey

You miss 100% of the shots you don't take.

Source: Interview, Hockey News, 1983.

I skate to where the puck is going to be, not where it has been.

Source: Numerous interviews; inspired by Gretzky's father, Walter Gretzky.

The highest compliment that you can pay me is that I work hard every day, that I never dog it.

Source: Attribution unconfirmed.

No matter who you are, we're creatures of habit. The better your habits are, the better they will be in pressure situations.

Source: Attribution unconfirmed.

You know, I've held women and babies and jewels and money, but nothing will ever feel as good as holding that Cup.

Source: Attribution unconfirmed.

Andrew Grove

Andrew Stephen Grove (András István Gróf) / 1936–2016 / Budapest, Hungary / Chemical Engineer, Entrepreneur, CEO of Intel Corporation
Note: Grove escaped from Communist Hungary in 1956, when he was 20 years old, and lived in the US from 1957 until his death.

Business Cycle

I have this vague feeling that, just as every generation thinks it invented sex, every generation thinks it created a new economy. The economy has always had cycles of supply and demand, undercapacity and overcapacity, boom and bust. Maybe a year ago someone could have argued that we have eliminated cycles. Well, that's obviously wrong now. All you can argue is different is that this new technology has increased productivity and therefore nudged up the noninflationary growth rate.

Interview with John Heilemann, "Andy Grove's Rational Exuberance," wired.com, June 1, 2001.

Business Philosophy

Your career is your business, and you are its CEO.

Statement from 1999, reported by George M. Dupuy and David H. Dupuy in (2003).

You need to try to do the impossible, to anticipate the unexpected. And when the unexpected happens, you should double the efforts to make order from the disorder it creates in your life. The motto I'm advocating is—Let chaos reign, then rein chaos. Does that mean that you shouldn't plan? Not at all. You need to plan the way a fire department plans. It cannot anticipate fires, so it has to shape a flexible organization that is capable of responding to unpredictable events.

High Output Management (1983).

You have no choice but to operate in a world shaped by globalization and the information revolution. There are two options: adapt or die.

High Output Management (1983).

A corporation is a living organism; it has to continue to shed its skin. Methods have to change. Focus has to change. Values have to change. The sum total of those changes is transformation.

Reported by Mike Sager, "Andy Grove: What I've Learned," esquire.com, January 29, 2007.

I think it is very important for you to do two things: act on your temporary conviction as if it was a real conviction; and when you realize that you are wrong, correct course very quickly.

Interview with Clayton M. Christensen, press conference, Harvard Business School, October 3, 2002; cited by Roger Martin and Karen Christensen in Rotman on Design: The Best on Design Thinking from Rotman Magazine (2013).

Growth is kinda built into everyone's genes. It's built into management's genes, the salesman's genes, the investors' desires.

People expect companies to grow. Management measures its performance by growth. Employees measure their opportunities by potential to grow. Growth is the fertilizer for the tree that a company becomes. Why do you get up in the morning if all you do is serve exactly the same market with the same customers and the same products? It's not a healthy state not to grow—from the investment, employee, or strategic standpoint.

Interview with John Heilemann, "Andy Grove's Rational Exuberance," wired.com, June 1, 2001.

Challenge of Success

Success breeds complacency. Complacency breeds failure. Only the paranoid survive.

Reported by William J. Baumol, Robert E. Litan, and Carl J. Schramm in Good Capitalism, Bad Capitalism, and the Economics of Growth (2007).

Crises

Bad companies are destroyed by crisis, Good companies survive them, Great companies are improved by them.

Statement from 1994, reported by Albert Yu, Creating the Digital Future: The Secrets of Consistent Innovation at Intel(1998).

Dot-com Bubble

In the 1980s, the Japanese almost buried the US manufacturing industry. Belatedly, the US manufacturers embraced the Japanese manufacturing techniques—just-in-time techniques, inventory-control techniques, supplier relationships, quality control—and escaped extinction. But it only happened after the better part of a decade of denials. So now here come the dotcoms, and the same US management reacted a lot quicker, because it's still in our memories that not reacting to the Japanese nearly cost us our livelihood. I really think there is an instinctive relationship between what happened in the 1980s and what happened in the 1990s. The threats were only 10 years apart, so it's still the same generation of managers. Clay Christensen's disruptive technology concept—the attack from below destroying existing businesses and technologies—really resonates with everyone, if imprecisely and vaguely, because that's what happened to so many of us in our businesses in the 1980s. And now it was about to happen again! And people said, By golly, we are not going to let that happen again, and so we all reacted a lot more aggressively.

Interview with John Heilemann, "Andy Grove's Rational Exuberance," wired.com, June 1, 2001.

Electric Cars

The drumbeat of the electrical transportation is accelerating like nothing I've ever seen in my life.

Interview with Ken Thomas, reported in "Ex-Intel head Grove: Electric transportation 'has to be done,'" usatoday.com, June 30, 2008.

The personal computer… went to individuals first before it went to corporations. . . . The corporations are sitting, wishing this whole friggin' thing [electric cars] to go away. Which is exactly what the computer companies' attitude was to personal computers.

Interview with Ken Thomas, reported in "Ex-Intel head Grove: Electric transportation 'has to be done,'" usatoday.com, June 30, 2008.

Grove on Grove

When I came to Intel, I was scared to death. I left a very secure job where I knew what I was doing and started running R&D for a brand new venture in untried territory. It was terrifying.

Statement from 1993, reported by Ian King in "Andy Grove, Valley Veteran Who Founded Intel, Dies at 79," bloomberg.com, March 21, 2016.

By the time I was twenty, I had lived through a Hungarian Fascist dictatorship, German military occupation, the Nazis' "Final Solution," the siege of Budapest by the Soviet Red Army, a period of chaotic democracy in the years immediately after the war, a variety of repressive Communist regimes, and a popular uprising that was put down at gunpoint . . . [where] many young people were killed; countless others were interned. Some two hundred thousand Hungarians escaped to the West. I was one of them.

Swimming Across: A Memoir (2001).

And try not to get too depressed in the part of the journey, because there's a professional responsibility. If you are depressed, you can't motivate your staff to extraordinary measures. So you have to keep your own spirits up even though you well understand that you don't know what you're doing.

Interview with Clayton M. Christensen, press conference, Harvard Business School, October 3, 2002; cited by Bob Sutton in "Andy Grove Tells the Truth About What Great Leaders Do," bobsutton.typepad.com, March 11, 2007.

I think of myself as somebody who has the luxury to speak his mind more of the time than many other people in the industry. And with that luxury comes a certain responsibility to say what I think is true, even if it isn't all what the industry collectively thinks. I certainly wasn't speaking for the industry when I said that Internet commerce should be taxed in a neutral fashion. I got a whole lot of complimentary emails about that—but not from anyone in the industry! But I just couldn't hold up my head and argue with a straight face that it's in the public's interest to give tax advantages to ecommerce. If I had been a spokesman for the industry, I would have been constrained by the lowest common denominator. On that deal, I was a spokesman only for myself.

Interview with John Heilemann, "Andy Grove's Rational Exuberance," wired.com, June 1, 2001.

I've had a fantastic life. I arrived in the Valley and my first assignment in my first job, at Fairchild, was to analyze the characteristics of MOS capacitors. In six weeks, I was one of the world's experts in a field that was a cornerstone of this industry—I mean, how lucky can you get? And it's gone like that ever since. At Fairchild, in the scientific sense; at Intel, in the industrial sense—I was there at the right moment and I made, if not the most of it, pretty close to the most of those opportunities. So I feel very fortunate to have had those opportunities and very satisfied with what I made of them. But I'm also very mindful that had I made a different choice—had I gone to a different university, or decided to work back east instead of here in the west, or if my timing had been off by just two years—the same me would not have accomplished nearly so much. Oh, I would have had a good career. But I did have certain lucky breaks in terms of timing that was not my merit.

Interview with John Heilemann, "Andy Grove's Rational Exuberance," wired.com, June 1, 2001.

Intel Corporation

In various bits and pieces, we have steered Intel from a start-up to one of the central companies of the information economy.

Reported by John H. Sheridan in "1997 Technology Leader of the Year," industryweek.com, December 15, 1997.

In the 1980s, our existing core business—memory chips—was in disarray. We were putting about 40 percent of our developmental capital spending into a business that represented only 3 to 4 percent of our revenue and in which we had a market share of 3 to 4 percent. There was nothing wrong with that business in terms of growth potential, but we had become marginalized by our Japanese competitors. There really was no viable option for us to work our way out. We had a situation where the defining business of the company had hit not a pothole but an ultimate wall, and we had to make a very desperate move. It was fortunate that we had made investments in microprocessors, secondary though they were, which had been going on for a long time. So we gave up the memory business and committed to microprocessors as our new path. It was a very dramatic, complete shift of emphasis, and it entailed a very major retrenchment to resize the company; roughly speaking, one-third of the company was shut down and laid off, with factories closing and all of that. And then the PC really took off, and we were positioned to benefit from that, and the rest is history.

Interview with John Heilemann, "Andy Grove's Rational Exuberance," wired.com, June 1, 2001.

Q: Intel has made more than 30 acquisitions in the past three years. Is there a limit to how big you can get?

A: We can be a lot bigger than we are now. That is the significance of communications as a field. We are probably as big as we can get in computing, approximately speaking. We can pick up graphics in our chipsets and this and that, but we're not going to double our size, given the size of the computer industry. In communications, we are already a fairly significant player, but our share of that business is a fraction of what it is in computing, and the business itself is as big as computing or maybe bigger. There may be a theoretically derivable size that is impossible to manage—that's bigger than a $100 billion technology company. I don't know. It hasn't been tested. But that's not what's limiting us. Had we put the same investment into communications that we put into videoconferencing, and done it at the same time, we probably would be twice the size in communications that we are today.

Interview with John Heilemann, "Andy Grove's Rational Exuberance," wired.com, June 1, 2001.

Q: Do you still see yourself when you look at the new generation of leaders of Intel?

A: Yeah, I do. The management team works almost without a conductor instructing them on what music to play. It works almost as well as it ever has.

Interview with John Heilemann, "Andy Grove's Rational Exuberance," wired.com, June 1, 2001.

Internet Commerce

I have been quoted saying that, in the future, all companies will be Internet companies. I still believe that. More than ever, really.

Interview with John Heilemann, "Andy Grove's Rational Exuberance," wired.com, June 1, 2001.

Scaling Up

Each company, ruggedly individualistic, does its best to expand efficiently and improve its own profitability. However, our pursuit of our individual businesses, which often involves transferring manufacturing and a great deal of engineering out of the country, has hindered our ability to bring innovations to scale at home. Without scaling, we don't just lose jobs—we lose our hold on new technologies. Losing the ability to scale will ultimately damage our capacity to innovate.

Reported in "Andy Grove: How America Can Create Jobs,"bloomberg.com, July 1, 2010.

Social Responsibility

All of us in business have a responsibility to maintain the industrial base on which we depend and the society whose adaptability—and stability—we may have taken for granted.

Reported by Teresa Tritch in "Andy Grove's Warning to Silicon Valley," nytimes.com, March 26, 2016.

Technology

Technology happens, it's not good, it's not bad. Is steel good or bad?

Reported by Walter Isaacson, "Man of the Year: Andrew Grove," Time magazine, cnn.com, December 22, 1997.

Technology will always win. You can delay technology by legal interference, but technology will flow around legal barriers.

Reported by Michael Kanellos in "Andy Grove Coins His Own Law," cnet.com, May 18, 2005.

A fundamental rule in technology says that whatever can be done will be done.

Reported by Ciarán Parker in The Thinkers 50: The World's Most Influential Business Writers and Leaders (2006).

Time Management

Just as you would not permit a fellow employee to steal a piece of office equipment worth $2,000, you shouldn't let anyone walk away with the time of his fellow managers.

Computer Decisions, Vol. 16 (1984).

Victor Davis Hanson

Victor Davis Hanson / b. 1953 / Fowler, California, USA / Classicist, Military Historian, Farmer, Author, Political Commentator, Podcaster
Note: Sources of quotations are supplied where known; however, many sources are unknown, likely due to their multiple occurrence in Hanson's very numerous writings and online essays, interviews, and podcasts.

Academia

Let me be blunt. . . . Academia does not attract the top brains in the country.

"The Backwardness of Modern Progressives," The Victor Davis Hanson Show, January 18, 2024.

Adversity

In the face of adversity, the resilience of individuals and nations is often revealed.

America

Behind every American soldier, dozens of their countrymen tonight sleep soundly — and hundreds more in their shadow abroad will wake up alive and safe.

Even in its third century, America is still the most meritocratic nation in the world.

Americans spend more money on Botox, face lifts and tummy tucks than on the age-old scourges of polio, smallpox, and malaria.

California

[H]ow does a state manage to achieve, all at once, the highest basket of gas, sales, and income taxes, yet rate nearly dead last in roads and highways, or school performance tests, and have the nation's greatest number of billionaires, and one-sixth of America's welfare recipients, and the largest percentage of any state population below the poverty line.

The Decline and Fall of California: From Decadence to Destruction, ebook (2015).

Citizenship

This revolutionary idea of Western citizenship—replete with ever more rights and responsibilities—would provide superb manpower for growing legions and a legal framework that would guarantee that the men who fought felt that they themselves in a formal and contractual sense had ratified the conditions of their own battle service. The ancient Western world would soon come to define itself by culture rather than by race, skin color, or language. That idea alone would eventually bring enormous advantages to its armies on the battlefield.

Carnage and Culture Landmark Battles in the Rise to Western Power (2001).

In a 2017 poll taken by the University of Pennsylvania's Annenberg Public Policy Center, most Americans appeared ignorant of the fundamentals of the US Constitution. Thirty-seven percent could not name a single right protected by the First Amendment. Only one out of four Americans could name all three branches of government. One in three could not name any branch of government. In a 2018 survey conducted by the Woodrow Wilson National Fellowship Foundation, almost 75 percent of those polled were not able to identify the thirteen original colonies. Over half had no idea whom the United States fought in World War II. Less than 25 percent knew why colonists had fought the Revolutionary War. Twelve percent thought Dwight D. Eisenhower commanded troops in the Civil War.

The Dying Citizen: How Progressive Elites, Tribalism, and Globalization Are Destroying the Idea of America (2021).

Democratic citizenship requires knowledge of war—and now, in the age of weapons of mass annihilation, more than ever.

The Father of Us All: War and History, Ancient and Modern(2010).

Economics

The great hatred of capitalism in the hearts of the oppressed, ancient and modern, I think, stems not merely from the ensuing vast inequality in wealth, and the often unfair and arbitrary nature of who profits and who suffers, but from the silent acknowledgement that under a free market economy the many victims of the greed of the few are still better off than those under the utopian socialism of the well-intended. It is a hard thing for the poor to acknowledge benefits from their rich moral inferiors who never so intended it.

Carnage and Culture Landmark Battles in the Rise to Western Power (2001).

History has shown that a government's redistribution of shrinking wealth, in preference to a private sector's creation of new sources of it, can provide more destruction than even the most deadly enemy.

Freedom

Freedom is not free; it requires vigilance, sacrifice, and the defense of shared values.

Globalization

Globalization has enriched the planet beyond belief, leading to ever-increased demands of perfection. And thanks to 24/7 communications, we all instantaneously know when these expectations aren't met.

History

The study of history is not just about the past; it's about understanding the present and preparing for the future.

A civilization that forgets its past is doomed to repeat its mistakes.

Evil is ancient, unchanging, and with us always. The more postmodern the West becomes — affluent, leisured, nursed on moral equivalence, utopian pacifism, and multicultural relativism — the more premodern the evil among us seems to arise in nihilistic response.

General George Patton and others lamented that the Second World War had broken out in 1939 over saving the free peoples of Eastern Europe from totalitarianism—only to end, through the broken 1945 Yalta accords, ensuring their enslavement by an erstwhile Soviet ally whose military we had supplied lavishly.

The Father of Us All: War and History, Ancient and Modern(2010).

For a capitalist system to work, the state had to protect, not regulate or interfere with, free markets. Both for political and religious reasons, this the sultan could not do: The Ottomans had then no idea of the balance of trade. . . . Originated from an age-old tradition in the Middle East, the Ottoman trade policy was that the state had to be concerned above all that the people and craftsmen in the cities in particular would not suffer a shortage of necessities and raw material. Consequently, the imports were always welcomed and encouraged, and exports discouraged.

Carnage and Culture Landmark Battles in the Rise to Western Power (2001).

We forget that even worse choices than those have confronted us in the past—like sending billions of dollars of aid to Joseph Stalin to stop Adolf Hitler, just a few years after the former had slaughtered or starved to death twenty million Soviets, invaded hapless Finland, carved up Poland with Hitler, and sent strategic materials daily to the Third Reich as it firebombed London.

The Father of Us All: War and History, Ancient and Modern(2010).

Military history reminds us that those who died on behalf of democratic freedom to stop totalitarian killing were a different sort than totalitarians who died fighting against it to perpetuate killing. The sacrifice of the former meant that generations yet born might have a greater likelihood of opportunity, security, and freedom; the latter fought for a cause that would have increased the suffering of future generations.

The Father of Us All: War and History, Ancient and Modern(2010).

Given the Western ability to produce deadly weapons, its propensity to create cheap, plentiful goods, and its tradition of seeing war in pragmatic rather than ritual terms as a mechanism to advance political ends, it is no surprise that Mesoamericans, African tribes, and native North Americans all joined European forces to help kill off Aztecs, Zulus, and Lakotas.

Carnage and Culture Landmark Battles in the Rise to Western Power (2001).

The gradual decline of a society is often a self-induced process of trying to meet ever-expanding appetites, rather than a physical inability to produce past levels of food and fuel, or to maintain adequate defense.

Human Nature

[H]uman character is unchanging and thus its conduct in calamitous times is always predictable.

A War Like No Other: How the Athenians and Spartans Fought the Peloponnesian War (2005).

To assert that military history suggested that wars broke out because bad men, in fear or in pride, sought material advantage or status, or because sometimes good but naive men had done too little to deter them, was understandably seen as antithetical to a more enlightened understanding of human nature.

The Father of Us All: War and History, Ancient and Modern(2010).

International Affairs

Apologizing for our past sins may reveal character and for a time lessen anti-Americanism abroad, but if it is done without acknowledging that the sins of America are the sins of mankind, and that our remedies are so often exceptional, then it only earns transitory applause—and a more lasting contempt that we ourselves do not believe in the values we profess.

The Father of Us All: War and History, Ancient and Modern(2010).

Athens's disastrous 415 B.C. expedition against Sicily, the largest democracy in the Greek world, may not prefigure our war in Iraq. (A hypothetical parallel to democratic Athens's preemptive attack on the neutral, distant, far larger, and equally democratic Syracuse in the midst of an ongoing though dormant war with Sparta would be America's dropping its struggle with al-Qaeda to invade India).

The Father of Us All: War and History, Ancient and Modern(2010).

The United States is often criticized as interventionist, but in fact America's traditional propensity has been more isolationist—willing to act forcefully in the world when absolutely necessary, but preferring to be unencumbered.

The Father of Us All: War and History, Ancient and Modern(2010).

States are like people. They do not question the awful status quo until some dramatic event overturns the conventional and lax way of thinking.

Politics

Often the white elite signaled their disgust of the "white privilege" of the disintegrating middle class as a means of exempting their own quite genuine white privilege of insider contacts, professional degrees, wealth, inheritance, and influence.

The Case for Trump (2019).

In Trump's mind, the problem with federal agencies was not just that they overreached and were weaponized, but that their folds of bureaucracy led to incompetency.

The Case for Trump (2019).

Popular Culture

Entertainers wrongly assume that their fame, money, and influence arise from broad knowledge rather than natural talent, looks, or mastery of a narrow skill.

Popular culture is simply a reflection of what the majority seems to want.

War

War seems to come out of nowhere, like rust that suddenly pops up on iron after a storm.

War is a tragic and often necessary part of the human experience, but it should never be romanticized or glamorized.

This bloody past suggests to us that enemies cease hostilities only when they are battered enough to acknowledge that there is no hope in victory – and thus that further resistance means only useless sacrifice.

But wars—or the threat of war—at least put an end to American chattel slavery, Nazism, Fascism, Japanese militarism, and Soviet Communism. It is hard to think of any democracy—Afghan, American, Athenian, contemporary German, Iraqi, Italian, Japanese, ancient Theban—that was not an outcome of armed struggle and war.

The Father of Us All: War and History, Ancient and Modern(2010).

If Westerners deem themselves too smart, too moral, or too soft to stop aggressors in this complex nuclear age, then—as Socrates and Aristotle alike remind us—they can indeed become real accomplices to evil through inaction.

The Father of Us All: War and History, Ancient and Modern(2010).

Victory may now require a level of force deemed objectionable by civilized peoples, meaning that some, for justifiable reasons, may be reluctant to pursue it. But victory has not become an ossified concept altogether.

The Father of Us All: War and History, Ancient and Modern(2010).

Again, wars do not really end until the conditions that started them–a bellicose government, an aggressive leader, a national policy of brinksmanship–are eliminated. Otherwise, there remains a *bellum interruptum*, much like the so-called Peace of Nicias, when Athens and Sparta agreed to a time-out in 421 B.C., before going at each other with renewed and deadly fury in 415 B.C.

It was the horror of the two world wars—Verdun, the Somme, Hiroshima—that led to our own era's questioning of the tragic view of war. Such a reaction was certainly true and understandable in a Europe that nearly destroyed itself in two devastating industrial wars within a roughly twenty-year period. Yet out of such numbing losses we may have missed the lesson of the horror. The calamity of sixty million dead was not just because nationalistic Westerners went to war in an industrial age of weaponry of mass annihilation, but rather because the liberal democracies were unwilling to make moderate sacrifices to keep the peace well before 1914 and 1939—when real resolve could have stopped Prussian militarism, and then Nazism without millions of the blameless perishing.

The Father of Us All: War and History, Ancient and Modern(2010).

A public that's illiterate about the conflicts of the past can easily find itself confused during wartime. Without standards of historical comparison, people prove ill-equipped to make informed judgments when the dogs of war are unleashed. Neither U.S. politicians nor most citizens seem to recall the incompetence and terrible decisions that, in December 1777, December 1941, and November 1950, led to massive American casualties and, for a time, public despair.

The Father of Us All: War and History, Ancient and Modern(2010).

Military history teaches us, contrary to popular belief, that wars are not necessarily the most costly of human calamities. The allied coalition lost few lives in getting Saddam out of Kuwait during the Gulf War of 1991, yet doing nothing in Rwanda allowed savage gangs and militias to murder hundreds of thousands with impunity. Bill Clinton stopped a Balkan holocaust through air strikes, without sacrificing American soldiers. His supporters argued, with some merit, that the collateral damage from the NATO bombing of Belgrade resulted in far fewer innocents killed, in such a "terrible arithmetic," than if the Serbian death squads had been allowed to continue their unchecked cleansing of Islamic communities.

The Father of Us All: War and History, Ancient and Modern(2010).

Friedrich A. Hayek

Friedrich A. Hayek / 1899–1992 / Vienna, Austr0-Hungarian Empire (now Austria) / Economist, Political Philosopher

Centralized Control

Economic control is not merely control of a sector of human life which can be separated from the rest; it is the control of the means for all our ends. And whoever has sole control of the means must also determine which ends are to be served, which values are to be rated higher and which lower, in short, what men should believe and strive for.

Source: The Road to Serfdom (University of Chicago Press, 1944).

Coercion

Coercion occurs when one man's actions are made to serve another man's will, not for his own but for the other's purpose.

Source: The Constitution of Liberty (University of Chicago Press, 1960).

Coercion implies . . . that I still choose but that my mind is made someone else's tool, because the alternatives before me have been so manipulated that the conduct that the coercer wants me to choose becomes for me the least painful one.

Source: The Constitution of Liberty (University of Chicago Press, 1960).

Once wide coercive powers are given to governmental agencies for particular purposes, such powers cannot be effectively controlled by democratic assemblies.

Source: The Constitution of Liberty (University of Chicago Press, 1960).

If one objects to the use of coercion in order to bring about a more even or more just distribution, this does not mean that one does not regard these as desirable. But if we wish to preserve a free society, it is essential that we recognize that the desirability of a particular object is not sufficient justification for the use of coercion.

Source: The Constitution of Liberty (University of Chicago Press, 1960).

It is indeed probable that more harm and misery have been caused by men determined to use coercion to stamp out a moral evil than by men intent on doing evil.

Source: The Constitution of Liberty (University of Chicago Press, 1960).

Freedom and Governance

What a free society offers to the individual is much more than what he would be able to do if only he were free.

Source: The Constitution of Liberty (University of Chicago Press, 1960).

Our faith in freedom does not rest on the foreseeable results in particular circumstances, but on the belief that it will, on balance, release more forces for the good than for the bad … Freedom granted only when it is known beforehand that its effects will be beneficial is not freedom.

Source: The Constitution of Liberty (University of Chicago Press, 1960).

Perhaps the fact that we have seen millions voting themselves into complete dependence on a tyrant has made our generation understand that to choose one's government is not necessarily to secure freedom.

Source: The Constitution of Liberty (University of Chicago Press, 1960).

Freedom and Justice

We must face the act that the preservation of individual freedom is incompatible with a full satisfaction of our views of distributive justice.

Source: Individualism and Economic Order (University of Chicago Press, 1948).

Freedom and Merit

A free society will not function or maintain itself unless its members regard it as right that each individual occupy the position that results from his action and accept it as due to his own action.

Source: The Constitution of Liberty (University of Chicago Press, 1960).

Freedom and Responsibility

Liberty not only means that the individual has both the opportunity and the burden of choice; it also means that he must bear the consequences of his actions ... Liberty and responsibility are inseparable.

Source: The Constitution of Liberty (University of Chicago Press, 1960).

Limits to Knowledge

The curious task of economics is to demonstrate to men how little they really know about what they imagine they can design.

Source: The Fatal Conceit: The Errors of Socialism (University of Chicago Press, 1991).

The case for individual freedom rests chiefly on the recognition of the inevitable and universal ignorance of all of us concerning a great many of the factors on which the achievement of our ends and welfare depends.

Source: The Constitution of Liberty (University of Chicago Press, 1960).

No human mind can comprehend all the knowledge which guides the actions of society.

Source: The Constitution of Liberty (University of Chicago Press, 1960).

Most of the advantages of social life, especially in the more advanced forms that we call "civilization" rest on the fact that the individual benefits from more knowledge than he is aware of. It might be said that civilization begins when the individual in the pursuit of his ends can make use of more knowledge than he has himself acquired and when he can transcend the boundaries of his ignorance by profiting from knowledge he does not himself possess.

Source: The Constitution of Liberty (University of Chicago Press, 1960).

Majority and Minority

It is always from a minority acting in ways different from what the majority would prescribe that the majority in the end learns to do better.

Source: The Constitution of Liberty (University of Chicago Press, 1960).

The Tyranny of Experts

The first need is to free ourselves of that worst form of contemporary obscurantism which tries to persuade us that what we have done in the recent past was all either wise or unavoidable. We shall not grow wiser before we learn that much that we have done was very foolish.

Source: The Road to Serfdom (University of Chicago Press, 1944).

There is no reason why a man who has made a distinctive contribution to economic science should be omnicompetent on all problems of society—as the press tends to treat him till in the end he may himself be persuaded to believe.

Source: Speech, Nobel Prize banquet, Stockholm, Sweden, 1974.

I confess that I prefer true but imperfect knowledge, even if it leaves much indetermined and unpredictable, to a pretence of exact knowledge that is likely to be false.

Source: "The Pretence of Knowledge," Nobel Prize Lecture, Stockholm, Sweden, December 11, 1974.

It would scarcely be an exaggeration to say that the greatest danger to liberty today comes from the men who are most needed and most powerful in modern government, namely, the efficient expert administrators exclusively concerned with what they regards as the public good.

Source: The Constitution of Liberty (University of Chicago Press, 1960).

Unlimited Government

The chief evil is unlimited government, and nobody is qualified to wield unlimited power.

Source: The Constitution of Liberty (University of Chicago Press, 1960).

Hewlett and Packard

William Redington Hewlett / 1913–2001 / Michigan, USA / Electrical Engineer, Entrepreneur, Co-Founder of the Hewlett-Packard Company
David Packard / 1912–1996 / Colorado, USA / Electrical Engineer, Entrepreneur, Co-Founder of the Hewlett-Packard Company
Note: Most of these quotations were originally articulated by Dave Packard. However, Packard acknowledges he developed his business philosophy—which came to be known as "the HP Way"—in close cooperation with Hewlett. For this reason, we have chosen not to attempt to differentiate between the contributions of the two founders of Hewlett-Packard [HP] to the ideas expressed in the quotations below.

Future of Mankind

The most important question we have to deal with, is a combination of population control and the control of our environment—how to utilize the world in as effective a way as we can for the future of mankind.

Statement by Packard, reported by Rushworth M. Kidder, An Agenda for the 21st Century (1987).

Growth

[Hewlett] said that more businesses die from indigestion than starvation. I have observed the truth of that advice many times since then.

David Packard, The HP Way: How Bill Hewlett and I Built Our Company (1995).

Marketing

Marketing is far too important to be left only to the marketing department!

Statement by Packard, reported by Philip Kotler in Marketing Management, Millennium Edition (1999).

Purpose

I want to discuss why a company exists in the first place. In other words, why are we here? I think many people assume, wrongly, that a company exists simply to make money. While this is an important result of a company's existence, we have to go deeper and find the real reasons for our being. . . . Purpose (which should last at least 100 years) should not be confused with specific goals or business strategies (which should change many times in 100 years). Whereas you might achieve a goal or complete a strategy, you cannot fulfill a purpose; it's like a guiding star on the horizon—forever pursued but never reached. Yet although purpose itself does not change, it does inspire change. The very fact that purpose can never be fully realized means that an organization can never stop stimulating change and progress.

Statement by Packard from 1960, reported by Bruce Jones in "The Difference Between Purpose and Mission,"

Harvard Business Review, hbr.com, February 2, 2016.

Responsibility

A company has a responsibility beyond making a profit for stockholders; it has a responsibility to recognize the dignity of its employees as human beings, to the well-being of its customers, and to the community at large.

David Packard, The HP Way: How Bill Hewlett and I Built Our Company (1995).

Rules for Business Development

1. The greatest success goes to the person who is not afraid to fail in front of even the largest audience.
2. Set out to build a company and make a contribution, not an empire and a fortune.
3. The best possible company management is one that combines a sense of corporate greatness and destiny, with empathy for, and fidelity to, the average employee.
4. The biggest competitive advantage is to do the right thing at the worst time.
5. A company that focuses solely on profits ultimately betrays both itself and society.
6. Corporate reorganisations should be made for cultural reasons more than financial ones.
7. A frustrated employee is a greater threat than a merely unhappy one.
8. The job of a manager is to support his or her staff, not vice versa and that begins by being among them.
9. The best business decisions are the most humane decisions. And, all other talents being even, the greatest managers are also the most human managers.
10. Investing in new product development and expanding the product catalogue are the most difficult things to do in hard times, and also among the most important.

Reported by Michael S. Malone in Bill and Dave: How Hewlett and Packard Built the World's Greatest Company (2007).

Rules for Personnel Management

1. **Think first of the other fellow.** This is THE foundation—the first requisite—for getting along with others. And it is the one truly difficult accomplishment you must make. Gaining this, the rest will be "a breeze."
2. **Respect the other man's personality rights.** Respect as something sacred the other fellow's right to be different from you. No two personalities are ever molded by precisely the same forces.
3. **Give sincere appreciation.** If we think someone has done a thing well, we should never hesitate to let him know it. WARNING: This does not mean promiscuous use of obvious flattery. Flattery with most intelligent people gets exactly the reaction it deserves—contempt for the egotistical "phony" who stoops to it.
4. **Eliminate the negative.** Criticism seldom does what its user intends, for it invariably causes resentment. The tiniest bit of disapproval can sometimes cause a resentment which will rankle—to your disadvantage—for years.
5. **Avoid openly trying to reform people.** Every man knows he is imperfect, but he doesn't want someone else trying to correct his faults. If you want to improve a person, help him to embrace a higher working goal—a standard, an ideal—

and he will do his own "making over" far more effectively than you can do it for him.

6. **Try to understand the other person.** How would you react to similar circumstances? When you begin to see the "whys" of him you can't help but get along better with him.
7. **Check first impressions.** We are especially prone to dislike some people on first sight because of some vague resemblance (of which we are usually unaware) to someone else whom we have had reason to dislike. Follow Abraham Lincoln's famous self-instruction: "I do not like that man; therefore I shall get to know him better."
8. **Take care with the little details.** Watch your smile, your tone of voice, how you use your eyes, the way you greet people, the use of nicknames and remembering faces, names and dates. Little things add polish to your skill in dealing with people. Constantly, deliberately think of them until they become a natural part of your personality.
9. **Develop genuine interest in people.** You cannot successfully apply the foregoing suggestions unless you have a sincere desire to like, respect and be helpful to others. Conversely, you cannot build genuine interest in people until you have experienced the pleasure of working with them in an atmosphere characterized by mutual liking and respect.
10. **Keep it up.** That's all—just keep it up!

Presentation by Packard at HP's second annual management conference, Sonoma, California, 1958.

Arianna Huffington

Arianna Huffington, née Ariadnē-Anna Stasinopoulou / b. 1950 / Athens, Greece / Businesswoman, Publisher, Political Commentator, Author

Charity

Imagine how our culture, how our lives, will change when we begin valuing go-givers as much as we value go-getters.

Thrive: The Third Metric to Redefining Success and Creating a Life of Well-Being, Wisdom, and Wonder (2014).

Child-Rearing

If you look at the best research on parenting, it comes down to one thing and one thing only. Not what you teach your children or how much time you spend with them, or if you read to them or not. What it comes down to is who you are, because we teach who we are.

On Becoming Fearless . . . in Love, Work, and Life (2006).

Employees

Treat people like family, and they will be loyal and give their all.

Thrive: The Third Metric to Redefining Success and Creating a Life of Well-Being, Wisdom, and Wonder (2014).

Fear

Fearlessness is not the absence of fear. It's the mastery of fear. It's about getting up one more time than we fall down.

Thrive: The Third Metric to Redefining Success and Creating a Life of Well-Being, Wisdom, and Wonder (2014).

Forgiving and Forgetting

There is nothing more draining than holding grudges.

Thrive: The Third Metric to Redefining Success and Creating a Life of Well-Being, Wisdom, and Wonder (2014).

Health

On the importance of getting enough sleep: Sleep your way to the top.

Source unknown.

Huffington on Huffington

My mother was a continual source of wisdom and great advice. . . . [S]he taught me that there is always a way around a problem —you've just got to find it. Keep trying doors; one will eventually open. She also taught me to accept failure as part and parcel of life.

Thrive: The Third Metric to Redefining Success and Creating a Life of Well-Being, Wisdom, and Wonder (2014).

I do not try to dance better than anyone else. I only try to dance better than myself.

Thrive: The Third Metric to Redefining Success and Creating a Life of Well-Being, Wisdom, and Wonder (2014).

And whenever I'd complain or was upset about something in my own life, my mother had the same advice: "Darling, just change the channel. You are in control of the clicker. Don't replay the bad, scary movie."

Thrive: The Third Metric to Redefining Success and Creating a Life of Well-Being, Wisdom, and Wonder (2014).

Leadership

The essence of leadership is being able to see the iceberg before it hits the *Titanic.*

Interview, Forbes, August, 2014.

Whenever we look around the world, we see smart leaders—in politics, in business, in media—making terrible decisions. What they're lacking is not IQ, but wisdom. Which is no surprise; it has never been harder to tap into our inner wisdom, because in order to do so, we have to disconnect from all our omnipresent devices—our gadgets, our screens, our social media—and reconnect with ourselves.

Thrive: The Third Metric to Redefining Success and Creating a Life of Well-Being, Wisdom, and Wonder (2014).

Iagos

Never let life's Iagos—flatterers, dissemblers—onto your train.

Thrive: The Third Metric to Redefining Success and Creating a Life of Well-Being, Wisdom, and Wonder (2014).

Life

Money and power by themselves are a two-legged stool—you can balance on them for a while, but eventually you're going to topple over.

Thrive: The Third Metric to Redefining Success and Creating a Life of Well-Being, Wisdom, and Wonder (2014).

It's not "What do I want to do?," it's "What kind of life do I want to have?"

Thrive: The Third Metric to Redefining Success and Creating a Life of Well-Being, Wisdom, and Wonder (2014).

We may not be able to witness our own eulogy, but we're actually writing it all the time, every day.

Thrive: The Third Metric to Redefining Success and Creating a Life of Well-Being, Wisdom, and Wonder (2014).

Today we often use deadlines—real and imaginary—to imprison ourselves.

Thrive: The Third Metric to Redefining Success and Creating a Life of Well-Being, Wisdom, and Wonder (2014).

A purpose of human life, no matter who is controlling it, is to love whoever is around to be loved.

Thrive: The Third Metric to Redefining Success and Creating a Life of Well-Being, Wisdom, and Wonder (2014).

Motherhood

The fastest way to break the cycle of perfectionism and become a fearless mother is to give up the idea of doing it perfectly—indeed to embrace uncertainty and imperfection.

On Becoming Fearless . . . in Love, Work, and Life (2006).

Self-Confidence

The more we refuse to buy into our inner critics—and our external ones too—the easier it will get to have confidence in our choices, and to feel comfortable with who we are—as women and as mothers.

On Becoming Fearless . . . in Love, Work, and Life (2006).

Life is shaped from the inside out. The more we embrace our own ordinariness, the more extraordinary our lives become.

Thrive: The Third Metric to Redefining Success and Creating a Life of Well-Being, Wisdom, and Wonder (2014).

If you take care of your mind, you take care of the world.

Thrive: The Third Metric to Redefining Success and Creating a Life of Well-Being, Wisdom, and Wonder (2014).

We all have within us the ability to move from struggle to grace.

Thrive: The Third Metric to Redefining Success and Creating a Life of Well-Being, Wisdom, and Wonder (2014).

Success

We need to accept that we won't always make the right decisions, that we'll screw up royally sometimes—understanding that failure is not the opposite of success, it's part of success.

Thrive: The Third Metric to Redefining Success and Creating a Life of Well-Being, Wisdom, and Wonder (2014).

We think, mistakenly, that success is the result of the amount of time we put in at work, instead of the quality of time we put in.

Thrive: The Third Metric to Redefining Success and Creating a Life of Well-Being, Wisdom, and Wonder (2014).

Have you noticed that when we die, our eulogies celebrate our lives very differently from the way society defines success?

Thrive: The Third Metric to Redefining Success and Creating a Life of Well-Being, Wisdom, and Wonder (2014).

David Hume

David Hume / 1711–1776 / Scotland (Great Britain) / Philosopher, Historian, Essayist

Equality of Means

But historians, and even common sense, may inform us, that, however specious these ideas of *perfect* equality may seem, they are really, at bottom, *impracticable*; and were they not so, would be extremely *pernicious* to human society. Render possessions ever so equal, men's different degrees of art, care, and industry will immediately break that equality. Or if you check these virtues, you reduce society to the most extreme indigence; and instead of preventing want and beggary in a few, render it unavoidable to the whole community.

Source: An Enquiry Concerning the Principles of Morals (1751).

Equality Under the Law

The government, which, in common appellation, receives the appellation of free, is that which admits of a partition of power among several members, whose united authority is no less, or is commonly greater, than that of any monarch; but who, in the usual course of administration, must act by general and equal laws, that are previously known to all the members, and to all their subjects. In this sense, it must be owned, that liberty is the perfection of civil society.

Source: Essays, Moral, Political and Literary: Part I, Essay V, "Of the Origin of Government" (1758).

Experience and Belief

A wise man, therefore, proportions his belief to the evidence. In such conclusions as are founded on an infallible experience, he expects the event with the last degree of assurance, and regards his past experience as a full proof of the future existence of that event. In other cases, he proceeds with more caution: He weighs the opposite experiments: He considers which side is supported by the greater number of experiments: to that side he inclines, with doubt and hesitation; and when at last he fixes his judgement, the evidence exceeds not what we properly call *probability*.

Source: An Enquiry Concerning Human Understanding, Section X: Of Miracles" (1748).

No testimony is sufficient to establish a miracle, unless the testimony be of such a kind, that its falsehood would be more miraculous than the fact which it endeavors to establish.

Source: An Enquiry Concerning Human Understanding, Section X: "Of Miracles" (1748).

Liberty vs. Authority

In all governments, there is a perpetual intestine struggle, open or secret, between Authority and Liberty; and neither of them can ever absolutely prevail in the contest. A great sacrifice of liberty must necessarily be made in every government; yet even the authority, which confines liberty, can never, and perhaps ought never, in any constitution, to become quite entire and uncontroulable.

Source: Essays, Moral, Political and Literary: Part I, Essay V, "Of the Origin of Government" (1758).

Loss of Liberty

It is a very comfortable reflection to the lovers of liberty that this peculiar privilege of *Britain* [freedom of the press] is of a kind that cannot easily be wrested from us and must last as long as our government remains in any degree free and independent. It is seldom that liberty of any kind is lost all at once. Slavery has so frightful an aspect to men accustomed to freedom that it must steal in upon them by degrees and must disguise itself in a thousand shapes in order to be received.

Source: Essays, Moral, Political and Literary: Part I, Essay II, "Of the Liberty of the Press" (1758).

Private Property

For when men, from their early education in society, have become sensible of the infinite advantages that result from it (property), and have besides acquir'd a new affection to company and conversation; and when they have observ'd, that the principal disturbance in society arises from those goods, which we call external, and from their looseness and easy transition from one person to another; they must seek for a remedy, by putting these goods, as far as possible, on the same footing with the fix'd and constant advantages of the mind and body. This can be done after no other manner, than by a convention enter'd into by all the members of the society to bestow stability on the possession of those external goods, and leave every one in the peaceable enjoyment of what he may acquire by his fortune and industry.

Source: A Treatise of Human Nature (1739–1740).

And as to practical arts, which encrease the commodities and enjoyments of life, it is well known, that men's happiness consists not so much in an abundance of these, as in the peace and security with which they possess them; and those blessings can only be derived from good government.

Source: Essays, Moral, Political and Literary: Part I, Essay VIII, "Of Parties in General" (1758).

I observe, that it will be for my interest to leave another in the possession of his goods, *provided* he will act in the same manner with regard to me.

Source: A Treatise of Human Nature (1739–1740).

A man's property is some object related to him. This relation is not natural, but moral, and founded on justice.

Source: A Treatise of Human Nature (1739–1740).

No one can doubt, that the convention for the distinction of property, and for the stability of possession, is of all circumstances the most necessary to the establishment of human society, and that after the agreement for the fixing and observing of this rule, there remains little or nothing to be done towards settling a perfect harmony and concord.

Source: A Treatise of Human Nature (1739–1740).

Reason vs. the Passions

We speak not strictly and philosophically when we talk of the combat of passion and of reason. Reason is, and ought only to be the slave of the passions, and can never pretend to any other office than to serve and obey them.

Source: A Treatise of Human Nature (1739–1740).

. . . as nothing can be contrary to truth or reason, except what has a reference to it, and as the judgments of our understanding only have this reference, it must follow, that passions can be contrary to reason only so far as they are accompanyed with some judgment or opinion. . . . Where a passion is neither founded on false suppositions, nor chuses means insufficient for the end, the understanding can neither justify nor condemn it. It is not contrary to reason to prefer the destruction of the whole world to the scratching of my finger.

Source: *A Treatise of Human Nature* *(1739–1740).*

Lee Iacocca

Lido Anthony Iacocca / 1924–2019 / Pennsylvania, USA / Corporate Executive, Developer of the Ford Mustang, CEO of Chrysler Corporation

Automobile Industry

Safety doesn't sell.

Reported by Mark Dowie in "Pinto Madness," Mother Jones, September/October, 1977; accessible at motherjones.com.

Business Philosophy

In the end, all business operations can be reduced to three words: people, product, and profits. People come first. Unless you've got a good team, you can't do much with the other two.

Lee Iacocca, with William Novak, Lee Iacocca: An Autobiography (1986).

If I had to sum up in one word the qualities that make a good manager, I'd say that it all comes down to decisiveness.

Lee Iacocca, with William Novak, Lee Iacocca: An Autobiography (1986).

I began by reducing my own salary to $ 1.00 a year. Leadership means setting an example. When you find yourself in a position of leadership, people follow your every move. I don't mean they invade your privacy, although there's some of that, too. But when the leader talks, people listen. And when the leader acts, people watch. So you have to be careful about everything you say and everything you do.

Lee Iacocca, with William Novak, Lee Iacocca: An Autobiography (1986).

You can aim at a duck and get it in your sights, but the duck is always moving. In order to hit the duck, you have to move your gun. But a committee faced with a major decision can't always move as quickly as the events it's trying to respond to. By the time the committee is ready to shoot, the duck has flown away.

Lee Iacocca, with William Novak, Lee Iacocca: An Autobiography (1986).

By their very nature, financial analysts tend to be defensive, conservative, and pessimistic. On the other side of the fence are the guys in sales and marketing—aggressive, speculative, and optimistic. They're always saying, "Let's do it," while the bean counters are always cautioning you on why you shouldn't do it. In any company you need both sides of the equation, because the natural tension between the two groups creates its own system of checks and balances.

Lee Iacocca, with William Novak, Lee Iacocca: An Autobiography (1986).

In the end, all business operations can be reduced to three words: people, product, and profits. People come first. Unless you've got a good team, you can't do much with the other two.

Lee Iacocca, with William Novak, Lee Iacocca: An Autobiography (1986).

Chrysler

Re: Chrysler's filing of bankruptcy:
This is a sad day for me. It pains me to see my old company, which has meant so much to America, on the ropes. But Chrysler has been in trouble before, and we got through it, and I believe they can do it again. . . . Let's face it, if your car breaks down, you're not going to take it to the White House to get fixed. But, if your company breaks down, you've got to go to the experts on the ground, not the bureaucrats.

Reported by Julie Halpert in "Lee Iacocca on Chrysler's Bankruptcy," newsweek.com, April 29, 2009.

But one thing was perfectly clear: John (Riccardo) was sacrificing himself to save the company. He was over his head and he knew it. Although it meant the end of his own career, he bent over backward to make sure that the transition would go as smoothly as possible. He blew himself out of the water to bring Chrysler back to life. And that is the test of a real hero.

Lee Iacocca, with William Novak, Lee Iacocca: An Autobiography (1986).

Energy

We were on a joyride, on free energy almost. . . . It seems to me we need something like the Manhattan Project. We need some urgency saying, "Here's what we should be doing. We've got to get off fossil fuels."

Interview, "Iacocca Says Detroit is Living in the Past," Morning Edition, npr.org, April 26, 2007.

Ford

But [Ford General Manager Robert S.] McNamara knew more than the actual facts—he also knew the hypothetical ones. When you talked with him, you realized that he had already played out in his head the relevant details for every conceivable option and scenario.

Lee Iacocca, with William Novak, Lee Iacocca: An Autobiography (1986).

"The trouble with you, Phil [Ford CEO Philip Caldwell], is that you went to Harvard, where they taught you not to take any action until you've got all the facts. You've got ninety-five percent of them, but it's going to take you another six months to get that last five percent. And by the time you do, your facts will be out of date because the market has moved on you. That's what life is all about—timing."

Lee Iacocca, with William Novak, Lee Iacocca: An Autobiography (1986).

Iacocca on Iacocca

I always kept in mind my father's warning: "If he's bigger than you are, don't fight back. Use your head instead of your fists.

Lee Iacocca, with William Novak, Lee Iacocca: An Autobiography (1986).

Although I was never a candidate, I learned a lot from all the presidential talk. Shortly after the whole business began, I was having a conversation with a guy in advertising. He said something interesting: "I've decided why everybody talks about you as a presidential candidate. It's very simple. They don't believe anybody anymore. You talk to them and you make them believe that you stand for something and then you pursue it. You don't bullshit them, and the American public has been bullshitted too often.

Lee Iacocca, with William Novak, Lee Iacocca: An Autobiography (1986).

. . . after reaching the presidency I experienced a certain letdown. I had spent years climbing the mountain. When I finally made it to the top, I started to wonder why I had been in such a hurry to get there.

Lee Iacocca, with William Novak, Lee Iacocca: An Autobiography (1986).

You can go a long way with some integrity.

Lee Iacocca, with William Novak, Lee Iacocca: An Autobiography (1986).

Philosophy of Life

Get all the education you can then go out and do something—do anything.

Lee Iacocca, with William Novak, Lee Iacocca: An Autobiography (1986).

It's a good thing God doesn't let you look a year or two into the future, or you might be sorely tempted to shoot yourself. But He's a charitable Lord: He only lets you see one day at a time. When times get tough, there's no choice except to take a deep breath, carry on, and do the best you can.

Lee Iacocca, with William Novak, Lee Iacocca: An Autobiography (1986).

It looks bad right now, but remember, this too shall pass.

Lee Iacocca, with William Novak, Lee Iacocca: An Autobiography (1986).

Mistakes are a part of life; you can't avoid them. All you can hope is that they won't be too expensive and that you don't make the same mistake twice.

Lee Iacocca, with William Novak, Lee Iacocca: An Autobiography (1986).

No matter what you've done for yourself or for humanity, if you can't look back on having given love and attention to your own family, what have you really accomplished?

Lee Iacocca, with William Novak, Lee Iacocca: An Autobiography (1986).

I learned about the strength you can get from a close family life. I learned to keep going, even in bad times. I learned not to despair, even when my world was falling apart. I learned that there are no free lunches. And I learned the value of hard work.

Lee Iacocca, with William Novak, Lee Iacocca: An Autobiography (1986).

Politics and Economics

We've got a gang of clueless bozos steering our ship of state right over a cliff, we've got corporate gangsters stealing us blind, and we can't even clean up after a hurricane much less build a hybrid car. But instead of getting mad, everyone sits around and nods their heads when the politicians say, "Stay the course." Stay the course? You've got to be kidding. This is America, not the damned *Titanic*.

Lee Iacocca, Where Have All the Leaders Gone? (2007).

Why don't we pass a law that says when you borrow money to buy somebody else and cannibalize him, the interest payments on those loans are not deductible? That would get the excesses out of the system pretty fast. Right now, if you want to buy up a competitor, generally you can't. That would violate the antitrust laws. But if you want to buy a company that does something else entirely, that's okay. Where's the sense in that?

Lee Iacocca, Where Have All the Leaders Gone? (2007).

But I do think that our national leadership consists of too many lawyers and not enough people from business. I'd like to see a system where we brought in twenty top managers to run the business side of the country and maybe even paid them $1 million a year, tax-free. That would be a real incentive, and then we'd see a lot more talented people interested in public life.

Lee Iacocca, Where Have All the Leaders Gone? (2007).

It seems that in the United States the one thing you can count on is that even during a depression, the rich get richer.

Lee Iacocca, Where Have All the Leaders Gone? (2007).

Steve Jobs

Steven Paul Jobs / 1955–2011 / California, USA / Entrepreneur, C0-Founder of Apple Computer, Inc.

Apple and Macintosh

We're gambling on our vision, and we would rather do that than make "me too" products. Let some other companies do that. For us, it's always the next dream.

"Steve Jobs Unveiling the Macintosh," January 24, 1984; available on HistoryvsHollywood, YouTube.

. . . Bell filed the patents for the telephone. It performed basically the same function as the telegraph, but people already knew how to use it. Also, the neatest thing about it was that besides allowing you to communicate with just words, it allowed you to sing. . . . It allowed you to intone your words with meaning beyond the simple linguistics. And we're in the same situation today. Some people are saying that we ought to put an IBM PC on every desk in America to improve productivity. It won't work. The special incantations you have to learn this time are "slash q-zs" and things like that. The manual for WordStar, the most popular word-processing program, is 400 pages thick. To write a novel, you have to read a novel—one that reads like a mystery to most people. They're not going to learn slash q-z any more than they're going to learn Morse code. That is what Macintosh is all about. It's the first "telephone" of our industry. And, besides that, the neatest thing about it, to me, is that the Macintosh lets you sing the way the telephone did. You don't simply communicate words, you have special print styles and the ability to draw and add pictures to express yourself.

Interview with Philip Elmer-Dewitt, Playboy magazine, February, 1985.

My opinion is that the only two computer companies that are software-driven are Apple and NeXT, and I wonder about Apple.

Cited in Fortune, August 26, 1991.

John Sculley ruined Apple and he ruined it by bringing a set of values to the top of Apple which were corrupt and corrupted some of the top people who were there, drove out some of the ones who were not corruptible, and brought in more corrupt ones and paid themselves collectively tens of millions of dollars and cared more about their own glory and wealth than they did about what built Apple in the first place — which was making great computers for people to use.

Interview, "Advice for Future Entrepreneurs," Computerworld Smithsonian Awards Program Oral History, April 20, 1995.

Business Philosophy

Real artists ship.

Cited in Frank Rose, West of Eden: The End of Innocence at Apple Computer (1989).

If, for some reason, we make some big mistake and IBM wins, my personal feeling is that we are going to enter a computer Dark Ages for about twenty years.

Cited in Jeffrey S. Young, Steve Jobs: The Journey is the Reward (1988).

You can't just ask customers what they want and then try to give that to them. By the time you get it built, they'll want something new.

Interview, "The Entrepreneur of the Decade Award," Inc. Magazine, 1 April 1, 1989.

It's rare that you see an artist in his 30s or 40s able to really contribute something amazing.

Interview with Philip Elmer-Dewitt, Playboy magazine, February, 1985.

[A computer is] actually pretty simple. . . . It takes these very, very simple-minded instructions—"Go fetch a number, add it to this number, put the result there, perceive if it's greater than this other number"—but executes them at a rate of, let's say, 1,000,000 per second. At 1,000,000 per second, the results appear to be magic... Most people have no concept of how an automatic transmission works, yet they know how to drive a car. You don't have to study physics to understand the laws of motion to drive a car. You don't have to understand any of this stuff to use Macintosh.

Interview with Philip Elmer-Dewitt, Playboy magazine, February, 1985.

How come the Mac group produced Mac and the people at IBM produced the PCjr? We think the Mac will sell zillions, but we didn't build Mac for anybody else. We built it for ourselves. We were the group of people who were going to judge whether it was great or not. We weren't going to go out and do market research. We just wanted to build the best thing we could build. When you're a carpenter making a beautiful chest of drawers, you're not going to use a piece of plywood on the back, even though it faces the wall and nobody will ever see it. You'll know it's there, so you're going to use a beautiful piece of wood on the back. For you to sleep well at night, the aesthetic, the quality, has to be carried all the way through.

Interview with Philip Elmer-Dewitt, Playboy magazine, February, 1985.

I'm convinced that about half of what separates the successful entrepreneurs from the non-successful ones is pure perseverance.

Interview, "Advice for Future Entrepreneurs," Computerworld Smithsonian Awards Program Oral History, April 20, 1995.

We have always been shameless about stealing great ideas.

Cited in "Triumph of the Nerds," PBS, 1996.

You've got to start with the customer experience and work backwards to the technology.

World Wide Developers Conference, May, 1997.

Innovation has nothing to do with how many R&D dollars you have. When Apple came up with the Mac, IBM was spending at least 100 times more on R&D. It's not about money. It's about the people you have, how you're led, and how much you get it.

Cited in Fortune, November 9, 1998.

I think if you do something and it turns out pretty good, then you should go do something else wonderful, not dwell on it for too long. Just figure out what's next.

Brian Williams, "Jobs: Iconoclast and salesman," MSNBC, May 25, 2006.

Computers

What a computer is to me is it's the most remarkable tool that we have ever come up with. It's the equivalent of a bicycle for our minds.

Cited in Michael Lawrence, "Memory and Imagination: New Pathways to the Library of Congress, YouTube, 1991.

The desktop computer industry is dead. Innovation has virtually ceased. Microsoft dominates with very little innovation. That's over. Apple lost. The desktop market has entered the dark ages, and it's going to be in the dark ages for the next 10 years, or certainly for the rest of this decade.

Interview with Gary Wolf, "Steve Jobs: The Next Insanely Great Thing," WIRED magazine, February, 1996.

The world's clearly a better place. Individuals can now do things that only large groups of people with lots of money could do before.

Interview with Jeff Goodell, Rolling Stone, June 16, 1994.

We think basically you watch television to turn your brain off, and you work on your computer when you want to turn your brain on.

Interview, Macworld magazine, February, 2004.

Creativity

Creativity is just connecting things. When you ask creative people how they did something, they feel a little guilty because they didn't really *do* it, they just *saw* something. It seemed obvious to them after a while. That's because they were able to connect experiences they've had and synthesize new things. And the reason they were able to do that was that they've had more experiences or they have thought more about their experiences than other people.

Interview with Gary Wolf, "Steve Jobs: The Next Insanely Great Thing," WIRED magazine, February, 1996.

Human minds settle into fixed ways of looking at the world. That's always been true and it's probably always going to be true and I think… I've always felt that death is the greatest invention of life. I'm sure that life evolved without death at first, and found that without death life didn't work very well. Because it didn't make room for the young, who didn't know how the world was fifty years ago, who didn't know how the world was twenty years ago. Who saw it as it is today without any preconceptions, and saw and dreamed how it could be based on that. . . . Without death there would be very little progress.

Interview with Daniel Morrow, Computer World, April, 1995.

God

Sometimes I believe in God, sometimes I don't. I think it's 50–50 maybe.

Reported in Walter Isaacson, Steve Jobs (2011).

Jobs on Jobs

I feel like somebody just punched me in the stomach and knocked all my wind out. I'm only 30 years old and I want to have a chance to continue creating things. I know I've got at least one more great computer in me. And Apple is not going to give me a chance to do that.

Cited in Playboy magazine, September, 1987; regarding Jobs's expulsion from Apple.

Do you want to spend the rest of your life selling sugared water or do you want a chance to change the world?

Cited in John Sculley and John A. Byrne, Odyssey: Pepsi to Apple: A Journey of Adventure, Ideas, and the Future (1987); regarding Sculley's leaving Pepsi to join Apple.

It's more fun to be a pirate than to join the Navy.

Cited in John Sculley and John A. Byrne, Odyssey: Pepsi to Apple: A Journey of Adventure, Ideas, and the Future (1987).

Woz and I very much liked Bob Dylan's poetry, and we spent a lot of time thinking about a lot of that stuff. This was California. You could get LSD fresh made from Stanford. You could sleep on the beach at night with your girlfriend. California has a sense of experimentation and a sense of openness —openness to new possibilities.

Interview with Philip Elmer-Dewitt, Playboy magazine, February, 1985.

Being the richest man in the cemetery doesn't matter to me ... Going to bed at night saying we've done something wonderful... that's what matters to me.

Cited in The Wall Street Journal, 1993.

I would trade all of my technology for an afternoon with Socrates.

Cited in "The Classroom of the Future," Newsweek, October 29, 2001.

We used to dream about this stuff. Now we get to build it. It's pretty great.

Steve Jobs, Keynote Address, Apple Worldwide Developers Conference, June, 2004.

I'm the only person I know that's lost a quarter of a billion dollars in one year. . . . It's very character-building.

Reported by Owen W. Linzmayer, Apple Confidential 2.0: The Definitive History of the World's Most Colorful Company (2004).

I didn't see it then, but it turned out that getting fired from Apple was the best thing that could have ever happened to me. The heaviness of being successful was replaced by the lightness of being a beginner again, less sure about everything. It freed me to enter one of the most creative periods of my life.

Steve Jobs, Commencement Address, Stanford University, June 12, 2005.

Remembering that I'll be dead soon is the most important tool I've ever encountered to help me make the big choices in life.

Steve Jobs, Commencement Address, Stanford University, June 12, 2005.

Pixar

We believe it's the biggest advance in animation since Walt Disney started it all with the release of Snow White 50 years ago.

Cited in Fortune, September 18, 1995; regarding Toy Story(1995).

If I knew in 1986 how much it was going to cost to keep Pixar going, I doubt if I would have bought the company.

Cited in Fortune, September 18, 1995.

Television

When you're young, you look at television and think, There's a conspiracy. The networks have conspired to dumb us down. But when you get a little older, you realize that's not true. The networks are in business to give people exactly what they want. That's a far more depressing thought. Conspiracy is optimistic! You can shoot the bastards! We can have a revolution! But the networks are really in business to give people what they want. It's the truth.

Interview with Gary Wolf, "Steve Jobs: The Next Insanely Great Thing," WIRED magazine, February, 1996.

Samuel Johnson

Samuel Johnson / 1709–1784 / England (Great Britain) / Poet, Novelist, Essayist, Lexicographer, Raconteur

Enterprise

Nothing . . . will ever be attempted if all possible objections must first be overcome.

The History of Rasselas, Prince of Abissinia: A Tale (1759).

Fear of Death

Boswell. "Foote, Sir, told me, that when he was very ill he was not afraid to die." *Johnson.* "It is not true. Sir. Hold a pistol to Foote's breast, or to Hume's breast, and threaten to kill them, and you'll see how they behave."

James Boswell, The Life of Samuel Johnson, LL.D.; October 26, 1769 (1791).

Genius

The errors and follies of a great genius are seldom without some radiations of understanding, by which meaner minds may be enlightened.

Rambler No. 29 (1750).

Keep always in your mind, that, with due submission to Providence, a man of genius has been seldom ruined but by himself.

Letter to Giuseppe ("Joseph") Baretti, December 21, 1762.

Habit

It was the peculiar artifice of Habit not to suffer her power to be felt at first. Those whom she led, she had the address of appearing only to attend, but was continually doubling her chains upon her companions; which were so slender in themselves, and so silently fastened, that while the attention was engaged by other objects, they were not easily perceived. Each link grew tighter as it had been longer worn, and when, by continual additions, they became so heavy as to be felt, they were very frequently too strong to be broken.

"The Vision of Theodore, the Hermit of Teneriffe, Found in His Cell" (1748).

Hope

A gentleman who had been very unhappy in marriage, married immediately after his wife died: Johnson said, it was the triumph of hope over experience.

James Boswell, The Life of Samuel Johnson, LL.D.; 1770 (1791).

No place affords a more striking conviction of the vanity of human hopes, than a publick library.

Rambler No. 106 (1751).

Human Life

Human life is everywhere a state in which much is to be endured, and little to be enjoyed.

The History of Rasselas, Prince of Abissinia: A Tale (1759).

Idleness

We would all be idle if we could.

James Boswell, The Life of Samuel Johnson, LL.D.; April 3, 1776 (1791).

Knowledge and Integrity

Integrity without knowledge is weak and useless, and knowledge without integrity is dangerous and dreadful.

The History of Rasselas, Prince of Abissinia: A Tale (1759).

London

Why, Sir, you find no man, at all intellectual, who is willing to leave London. No, Sir, when a man is tired of London, he is tired of life; for there is in London all that life can afford.

James Boswell, The Life of Samuel Johnson, LL.D.; September 20, 1777 (1791).

Mental Concentration

Depend upon it, sir, when a man knows he is to be hanged in a fortnight, it concentrates his mind wonderfully.

James Boswell, The Life of Samuel Johnson, LL.D.; September 19, 1777 (1791).

Money-Making

There are few ways in which a man can be more innocently employed than in getting money.

James Boswell, The Life of Samuel Johnson, LL.D.; March 27, 1775 (1791).

Old Age

Every old man complains of the growing depravity of the world, of the petulance and insolence of the rising generation. He recounts the decency and regularity of former times, and celebrates the discipline and sobriety of the age in which his youth was passed; a happy age which is now no more to be expected, since confusion has broken in upon the world, and thrown down all the boundaries of civility and reverence.

Rambler No. 50 (1750).

He that would pass the latter part of life with honour and decency, must, when he is young, consider that he shall one day be old; and remember, when he is old, that he has once been young.

Rambler No. 50 (1750).

Patriotism

Patriotism is the last refuge of a scoundrel.

James Boswell, The Life of Samuel Johnson, LL.D.; April 7, 1775 (1791).

Politics

And I have always said, the first Whig was the Devil.

James Boswell, The Life of Samuel Johnson, LL.D.; April 28, 1778 (1791).

Reading

A man ought to read just as inclination leads him; for what he reads as a task will do him little good.

James Boswell, The Life of Samuel Johnson, LL.D.; July 14, 1763 (1791).

Refutation of Idealism

After we came out of the church, we stood talking for some time together of Bishop Berkeley's ingenious sophistry to prove the nonexistence of matter, and that every thing in the universe is merely ideal. I observed, that though we are satisfied his doctrine is not true, it is impossible to refute it. I never shall forget the alacrity with which Johnson answered, striking his foot with mighty force against a large stone, till he rebounded from it—"I refute it *thus*."

James Boswell, The Life of Samuel Johnson, LL.D.; August 6, 1763 (1791).

Self-Reproach

All censure of a man's self is oblique praise. It is in order to shew how much he can spare. It has all the invidiousness of self-praise, and all the reproach of falsehood.

James Boswell, The Life of Samuel Johnson, LL.D.; April 25, 1778 (1791).

Most men seem rather inclined to confess the want of virtue than of importance.

Rambler No. 13 (1750).

Writing

No man but a blockhead ever wrote, except for money.

James Boswell, The Life of Samuel Johnson, LL.D.; April 5, 1776 (1791).

Read over your compositions, and where ever you meet with a passage which you think is particularly fine, strike it out.

James Boswell, The Life of Samuel Johnson, LL.D.; April 30, 1773 (1791).

A man will turn over half a library to make one book.

James Boswell, The Life of Samuel Johnson, LL.D.; April 6, 1775 (1791).

Michael Jordan

Michael Jordan / b. 1963 / New York, USA / Basketball

I can accept failure. Everyone fails at something. But I can't accept not trying. Talent wins games, but teamwork and intelligence wins championships.

Source: I Can't Accept Not Trying (1994).

Enjoy every minute of life. Never second-guess life.

Source: How to Be Like Mike (2005).

Limits, like fears, are often just an illusion.

Source: Address upon induction into the National Baseball Hall of Fame, 2009.

I was raised by parents who taught me to love and respect people regardless of their race or background, so I am saddened and frustrated by the divisive rhetoric and racial tensions that seem to be getting worse as of late. I know this country is better than that, and I can no longer stay silent. We need to find solutions that ensure people of color receive fair and equal treatment AND that police officers—who put their lives on the line every day to protect us all—are respected and supported.

Source: Andscape.com (previously, The Undefeated), July 25, 2016.

Joseph Joubert

Joseph Joubert / 1754–1824 / France / Essayist, Memoirist, Aphorist
Note: All quotations are taken from *Pensées* [Thoughts] (posthumously published in 1838).

Ambition

When you go in search of honey you must expect to be stung by bees.

Art and Speech

Drawing is speaking to the eye; talking is painting to the ear.

Children

Children need models rather than critics.

Discussion

The aim of argument, or of discussion, should not be victory, but progress.
It is better to debate a question without settling it than to settle a question without debating it.

Imagination

Imagination is the eye of the soul.

Kindness

A part of kindness consists in loving people more than they deserve.

Learning

He who has imagination without learning has wings but no feet.

Life

How many people eat, drink, and get married; buy, sell, and build; make contracts and attend to their fortune; have friends and enemies, pleasures and pains, are born, grow up, live and die—but asleep!

Misery

Misery is almost always the result of thinking.

Poetry

You will find poetry nowhere unless you bring some of it with you.

Teaching

To teach is to learn twice.

Truth

What is true by lamplight is not always true by sunlight.

Worries

Our worries always come from our weaknesses.

Bill Joy

Bill Joy / b. 1954 / Michigan, USA / Computer Engineer, Venture Capitalist

Given the incredible power of these new technologies, shouldn't we be asking how we can best coexist with them? And if our own extinction is a likely, or even possible, outcome of our technological development, shouldn't we proceed with great caution?

Source: "Why the Future Doesn't Need Us," Wired, April 1, 2000.

. . . the smartest people in the world don't all work for us. Most of them work for someone else. The trick is to make it worthwhile for the great people outside your company to support your technology. Innovation moves faster when the people elsewhere are working on the problem with you.

Source: Cited by Brent Schlender in "Whose Internet Is It, Anyway?," 1995, Fortune, ***132****(12): p. 130.*

Our most powerful 21st-century technologies—robotics, genetic engineering, and nanotech—are threatening to make humans an endangered species.

Source: "Why the Future Doesn't Need Us," Wired, April 1, 2000.

We have to encourage the future we want rather than trying to prevent the future we fear.

Source: Attribution unconfirmed.

John Maynard Keynes

John Maynard Keynes / 1883–1946 / England (United Kingdom of Great Britain and Ireland) / Economist, Mathematician, Biographer

Capitalism

Capitalism is the astonishing belief that the nastiest motives of the nastiest men somehow or other work for the best results in the best of all possible worlds.

Source: attribution in George Schuster, Christianity and Human Relations (Epworth Press, 1951); multiple versions.

Communism

How can I accept the Communist doctrine, which sets up as its bible, above and beyond criticism, an obsolete textbook which I know not only to be scientifically erroneous but without interest or application to the modern world? How can I adopt a creed which, preferring the mud to the fish, exalts the boorish proletariat above the bourgeoisie and the intelligentsia, who with all their faults, are the quality of life and surely carry the seeds of all human achievement? Even if we need a religion, how can we find it in the turbid rubbish of the red bookshop? It is hard for an educated, decent, intelligent son of Western Europe to find his ideals here, unless he has first suffered some strange and horrid process of conversion which has changed all his values.

Marxian Socialism must always remain a portent to the historians of opinion — how a doctrine so illogical and so dull can have exercised so powerful and enduring an influence over the minds of men, and, through them, the events of history.

Source: The End of Laissez-Faire (Hogarth Press, 1926); chapter 3.

Economists

The ideas of economists and political philosophers, both when they are right and when they are wrong are more powerful than is commonly understood. Indeed, the world is ruled by little else. Practical men, who believe themselves to be quite exempt from any intellectual influences, are usually slaves of some defunct economist. Madmen in authority, who hear voices in the air, are distilling their frenzy from some academic scribbler of a few years back.

If economists could manage to get themselves thought of as humble, competent people, on a level with dentists, that would be splendid!

Source: Essays in Persuasion (Macmillan, 1931).

German Reparations for WWI

I cannot leave this subject as though its just treatment wholly depended either on our own pledges or economic facts. The policy of reducing Germany to servitude for a generation, of degrading the lives of millions of human beings, and of depriving a whole nation of happiness should be abhorrent and detestable — abhorrent and detestable, even if it were possible, even if it enriched ourselves, even if it did not sow the decay of the whole civilized life of Europe. Some preach it in the name of Justice. In the great events of man's history, in the unwinding of the complex fates of nations Justice is not so simple. And if it were, nations are not authorized, by religion or by natural morals, to visit on the children of their enemies the misdoings of parents of rulers.

Source: The Economic Consequences of the Peace (Macmillan, 1919).

Ideas

The difficulty lies not so much in developing new ideas as in escaping from old ones.
Soon or late, it is ideas, not vested interests, which are dangerous for good or evil.

Source: The General Theory of Employment, Interest, and Money (Palgrave Macmillan, 1936).

Liquidity

Of the maxims of orthodox finance, none, surely, is more antisocial than the fetish of liquidity.... It forgets that there is no such thing as liquidity of investment for the community as a whole.

Source: The General Theory of Employment, Interest, and Money (Palgrave Macmillan, 1936); chapter 12.

Long Run

Long run is a misleading guide to current affairs. In the long run we are all dead.

Source: A Tract on Monetary Reform (Macmillan, 1923); chapter 3.

Love of Money

The love of money as a possession—as distinguished from the love of money as a means to the enjoyments and realities of life—will be recognized for what it is, a somewhat disgusting morbidity, one of those semi-criminal, semi-pathological propensities which one hands over with a shudder to the specialists in mental disease.

Source: Essay in Persuasion (Macmillan, 1931); part V.

Negotiation

When the final result is expected to be a compromise, it is often prudent to start from an extreme position.

Source: The Economic Consequences of the Peace (Macmillan, 1919).

Solvency

Markets can remain irrational longer than you can remain solvent.

Source: misattribution; coined by financial analyst Gary Shilling in an oral presentation to AmSouth Bank in Montgomery, AL, in 1986, as reported in the Montgomery Advertiser.

Thrift

The engine which drives Enterprise is not Thrift, but Profit.
If enterprise is afoot, wealth accumulates, whatever may be happening to thrift; and if enterprise is asleep, wealth decays, whatever thrift may be doing.

Source: A Treatise on Money (two volumes) (Macmillan, 1930).

Words

Words ought to be a little wild for they are the assault of thoughts on the unthinking.

Source: New Statesman and Nation, July 15, 1933.

Charlie Kirk

Charles J. Kirk / b. 1993 / Arlington Heights, Illinois, USA / Political Commentator and Activist / Founder and CEO of Turning Point, USA, Author, Podcaster
Note: The sources of the following quotes are unknown, but presumably derive from Kirk's many writings, commentaries, interviews, and podcasts.

America

The United States is the greatest country in the history of the world, and we should be proud of our heritage and values.
The American Dream is not about what the government can give you, but about what you can achieve through hard work and freedom.
The American spirit is about resilience, self-reliance, and the pursuit of happiness.
American exceptionalism is not a myth, it's a reality.
Conservatism is about preserving the values and principles that have made America exceptional.
America is a land of opportunity, where success is determined by your choices and efforts.
The American Dream is not about guaranteed outcomes, but about the chance to succeed through hard work and determination.
America is a beacon of freedom and opportunity, and we should never take that for granted.
This silent majority are the Americans who love God, their family, and our amazing country. They don't want their morals, their job, or their lifestyle threatened by the government or any candidates.

Capitalism

Capitalism creates more wealth, more prosperity, more freedom, and more opportunity than any other economic system ever created by man.
Capitalism has lifted more people out of poverty than any other system in history.
Capitalism rewards hard work and innovation, while socialism rewards complacency.

Conservatism

Conservatism is the antidote to tyranny precisely because its principles are the founding principles.
Conservatives believe in empowering individuals, not government.
Conservatism is the only ideology that embraces the individual and their God-given rights.
Conservatives believe in limited government because we believe in unlimited potential for individuals.
Conservatives believe in individual responsibility, not government handouts.
Conservatism is the ideology of freedom, liberty, and personal responsibility.
Conservatism is rooted in the belief that the individual is the best steward of their own life.

Conservatives believe in empowering individuals, not creating dependence on the government.

Conservatives believe in the power of the individual to make their own choices and shape their own destiny.

Constitution

The Constitution is not a living, breathing document. It's a contract with the American people.

The Constitution is a shield that protects the rights of individuals from government overreach.

The Constitution is not a menu; you can't pick and choose which rights to protect.

Courage

If you believe in something, you need to have the courage to fight for those ideas—not run away from them or try and silence them.

COVID-19

The Left has viewed the coronavirus pandemic as a political "opportunity" from the start.

Cultural Marxism

Cultural Marxism that has permeated all of Europe and has been the driving force that has brought France—the nation of Liberty, Fraternity and Equality—to the brink.

Americans needs to understand that the election of Donald Trump has forestalled our slide into the abyss of cultural Marxism and the surrendering of our national heritage and identity to that of the global community.

Economics

A healthy economy is a foundation for a healthy future.

Regulation often helps Big Industry remain entrenched in power. The burdensome costs of complying with any new regulation would be a rounding error for the likes of Facebook and Google, but it might completely destroy a promising start-up poised to challenge their dominance.

Education

We should be teaching our kids how to think, not what to think.

Many textbooks fail to present students with both sides of an issue. Students are being pushed toward an education that demonizes free enterprise while advocating top-down government, deficit spending and class warfare.

Yes, college tuition is a problem for many young Americans, but it is a problem exacerbated by government subsidies and an overwhelming demand to get a college degree, despite high dropout rates.

Election Integrity

The real reason Democrats are pushing for universal mail-in balloting has nothing to do with the global pandemic which originated in China; they simply believe it will help them win elections.

I'm concerned about the integrity of American elections.

Letting non-citizens vote jeopardizes our principles as a nation. They vote only for entitlement, not for their own responsibility as citizens.

Requirements for an ID are not voter suppression—they are just commonsense steps to ensure people don't vote if they are ineligible, don't vote using false identities, and don't vote more than once.

Democrats have long been the party of voter fraud.

Letting non-citizens vote jeopardizes our principles as a nation. They vote only for entitlement, not for their own responsibility as citizens.

Equality

In America, we don't believe in equal outcomes, we believe in equal opportunities.

Socialism offers equality of misery, not prosperity.

Freedom

Freedom and liberty are worth defending and preserving at all costs.

Big government is the greatest threat to individual liberty and prosperity.

Freedom of speech is the bedrock of a free society. We must defend it at all costs.

The greatest threat to freedom is the belief that someone else knows what's best for you.

Freedom is the foundation of America, and it's worth defending with everything we have.

The strength of America lies in the diversity of thought and the freedom to express it.

The Left's vision of a utopian society often leads to authoritarianism and loss of individual freedoms.

Liberals like to say there aren't any limitations on speech, and it's true that they can say or do just about anything. But conservatives apparently can't even stand still while wearing a MAGA hat without crossing a line.

Government

The government is not your savior, it is your servant.

The government should be limited in its power, but the individual should be limitless in their potential.

The government should serve the people, not the other way around.

We live in a welfare state society—one that is already bloated and overburdened. We cannot continue to absorb and support an endless stream of people who will inevitably need legal residents to subsidize their lives.

Identity Politics

The Left's obsession with identity politics is dividing our nation instead of uniting it.

The Left's focus on group identity undermines the importance of individual character and merit.

The Left's obsession with identity politics is tearing our country apart.

Immigration

Throwing open our borders to everyone who wants to enter is impractical and could cause grave harm to our nation and the American people.

Once we lose our border protection, the road to citizenship, voting and welfare benefits for a flood of new immigrants will be all but paved.

For years, elites in both political parties have ignored the illegal immigration crisis growing on America's southern border.

Many migrants awaiting asylum hearings in the U.S. never show up for their court dates. And the longer they stay in the U.S., the more sympathy they draw in the media and from many compassionate Americans.

Democrats encouraged a porous southern border because they saw migrants and their American-born children as a source of future political support.

Kirk on Kirk

I founded Turning Point U.S.A. to take the fight for ideological diversity directly to a progressive stronghold: the nation's leading colleges and universities.

I started a college campus-based nonprofit in June 2012 called Turning Point U.S.A. to target millennials in college. Our mission was to create a powerful conservative grassroots activist network on campuses and identify, educate, train and organize students to promote the principles of freedom, free markets and limited government.

Left vs. Right

The Left wants to silence dissent and control the narrative, while conservatives value free speech and open debate.

The Left's ideology is based on envy and resentment, while conservatism is built on personal responsibility and gratitude.

Once we're ignored or dismissed long enough, conservatives seem to just shrug our collective shoulders and accept defeat. It's this type of passivity that has allowed progressives to dominate film and television, universities, and large swaths of the mainstream news media.

Historically, Democrats have shown they are willing to do just about anything to win elections. Republicans must quit taking the high road and fight back with everything we have.

Millennials

I'm urging all my millennial peers and the young people coming up behind us to look for signs and symptoms of them being in a Democrat-induced delusion. Don't confuse the dream state of the socialists with any sort of reality. If you spot any signs of this politically terminal affliction within yourself, please seek help.

Since I started Turning Point U.S.A., almost all millennials are off the college campuses, where the organization and I continue to focus much of our efforts.

Young people in college—many living away from their parents for the first time in their lives—are particularly vulnerable to the leftist propaganda campaign designed to turn them away from supporting president Trump and turning them away from believing in American exceptionalism.

Original Sin

I believe we're broken by sin upon birth.

Political Correctness

Political correctness is the deadliest of political weaponry.

We have been indoctrinated to see the world through a politically correct lens.

Prisons

Prisons are called "correctional facilities" because the goal is to correct the behavior that sent people there.

Imprisoning convicted criminals for longer and longer periods sounds like an appealing and commonsense proposal to many people. After all, when lawbreakers are locked up they can't commit more crimes and law-abiding citizens are safer. Right? Actually, wrong.

The simple truth is that America is locking up too many people, for too long, and spending too much money on them.

In addition to making sense and serving the needs of justice, rehabilitating prisoners and releasing them when they are ready can save taxpayers money.

Socialism

Big government is the oxygen of socialism.

Socialism is a broken system, and it's a system that I think is actually evil.

The Left's ideas are so bad that they have to be mandatory.

The Left loves to play the victim while they victimize everyone else.

Socialism is the belief that you can give away everything for free, and somehow still have everything.

The Left wants to control every aspect of your life, from what you say to what you eat.

Socialism stifles innovation and individual initiative.

How can it possibly be that so many Americans are rallying to support Ocasio-Cortez, when all they need to do is look at Venezuela to see where she is leading them?

The case for socialism is always made based on an ideal and a promise. The ideal is that humans can lovingly coexist in a sharing and peaceful way. The promise is that this time, unlike failed attempts elsewhere, socialism will be implemented properly, and no citizen will suffer as a result.

The Truth

When you deliberately distort and selectively present the truth, you lie.

Konstantin Kisin

Konstantin Vadimovich Kisin / b. 1982 / Moscow, Russia, USSR / Comedian, Author, Political Commentator, Podcaster
Note: The sources of the following quotations are provided where known; the remaining quotes presumably derive from Kisin's extensive online essays, interviews, and podcasts.

Biden

Triggernometry co-host Francis Foster: Everybody knows that Joe Biden isn't in charge. He simply can't be.
Konstantin Kisin: He could be, but that's worse.

> *"Trump Must Win to Avoid Prison," interview with Scott Adams, Triggernometry, September 13, 2023.*

Comedy

Comedy is about pushing boundaries, challenging conventions, and making people think while they laugh.
In comedy, there are no sacred cows. Everything is fair game for humor.
A good comedian can make you see the absurdity in everyday life and make you question the status quo.
Being a comedian means speaking your mind, even if it's uncomfortable or controversial.

COVID-19

I'm against mandates and I'm against mandates of vaccination, right? People are free to have the vaccination, people are free to wear a mask, people are free to do whatever they want, right? But I think, if you look back, the idea that people shouldn't be forcibly injected with medical things that they don't wish to have, came out in 1945 [during the Nuremberg trials—ed.] for very good fucking reason. Very good reason. And the fact that that became a controversial thing to say. . . . No! No, no, no. People came together in Nuremberg for a very good reason and decided we're not going to let this happen again. And the fact that people were willing to just completely overlook that. This is the thing, they flip everything on its head.

> *"Leader of Canadian Freedom Convoy SPEAKS OUT," Triggernometry, September 27, 2023.*

Freedom

Freedom, human rights, tolerance, peace and prosperity are like the eternal flame that must be guarded, nurtured and never, ever taken for granted.

> *An Immigrant's Love Letter to the West (2022).*

We have forgotten that the prosperity, safety, life expectancy, stability and freedoms we enjoy did not just fall out of the sky. They were built, over centuries, on philosophical and moral foundations that have withstood the test of time. They were defended over and over again by our ancestors who bled to defend them. They were refined in the crucible of fierce political and ideological debates.

An Immigrant's Love Letter to the West (2022).

Free Speech

Suppression of free speech is a symptom of tyranny.

It's important for everyone to do their bit in defending free speech. Including you. Yes, technically we already have it. But every successive generation still needs to defend it. Why? Because it's constantly at risk of attack from people who think they know better. And how free is speech if there are serious consequences, such as unemployment and character assassination?

An Immigrant's Love Letter to the West (2022).

Free speech is not some right-wing reframing of whatever; it is the foundation of Western civilization.

Speech to Oxford Union, "Woke Culture HAS Gone Too Far," January 12, 2023.

When you have some kid, who works for Twitter in the Philippines, censoring a Nobel price winning scientist, speaking about his area of expertise, I think we've lost the plot

Interview, "WE'VE LOST THE PLOT!," Bill Maher show, Triggernometry, June 21, 2023.

One of the things people don't say enough about free speech is "Yes, it causes harm but the harm is worth it." And we don't make that argument because it's too honest and complicated and unpleasant.

Interview, "Why Is Everyone Losing Their Minds?," Chris Williamson show, October 23, 2023.

Global Warming

This country is responsible for 2 percent of global carbon emissions, which means that if Britain was to sink into the sea right now it would make absolutely no difference to the issue of climate change. You know why? Because the future of the climate is going to be decided in Asia and in Latin America. By poor people who couldn't give a shit about saving the climate. . . . Do you know why? Because they're poor. . . . 120 million people in China do not have enough food. I don't mean that they don't get dessert, I mean they suffer from malnutrition. That means that their immune system is breaking down because they don't have enough food. You're not going to get them to stay poor.

Speech to Oxford Union, "Woke Culture HAS Gone Too Far," January 12, 2023.

International Affairs

Rather than us exporting liberal democracy to these countries instead we're importing Chinese style authoritarianism.

Interview, "Konstantin Kisin On Free Speech, Vladimir Putin, Jordan Peterson, Greta Thunberg, & Bitcoin," Anthony Pompliano show, January 23, 2023.

Kisin on Kisin

If there is one thing my Soviet childhood taught me, it's that subscribing to someone else's ideology will always inevitably mean having to suspend your own judgment about right and wrong to appease your tribe. I refuse to do so.

An Immigrant's Love Letter to the West (2022).

I actually get invited on TV a lot nowadays, and I don't do as much of it as I used to. And part of the reason is that once you've [got] the heroin of a long term conversation, why would you drop down to methadone? This is so much more fulfilling and satisfying. We're sitting here for a good chunk of time, you're giving me the space to speak, you're not talking over me, you're not trying to make me look bad . . . and [in corporate media] you get three minutes to make one point. And look, there's a market out there for that [but] I enjoy this. I enjoy having a conversation [and] connecting with somebody, getting to know how they think and them getting to know how I think, disagreeing where there's disagreement but doing it in a constructive way as opposed to going for the click bait and all of that. That is a really fulfilling part of doing *Triggernometry* for me. We get to interview fascinating people . . . and we just sit and learn. . . . How many people get the opportunity to sit down with a great mind for an hour and just engage, and speak, and listen, and think about the world? To me, that is incredibly gratifying. And I don't think that if i was hosting something on TV [that] I'd get a chance to do that.

Interview, "Konstantin Kisin On Free Speech, Vladimir Putin, Jordan Peterson, Greta Thunberg, & Bitcoin," Anthony Pompliano show, January 23, 2023.

We come from generations of people who were killed for their beliefs. Well, I'm not going to dishonor them.

"Is It Brave to Say What You Think?," Triggernometry, June 30, 2023.

Laughter

Laughter is a universal language that can bridge cultural divides and bring people together.

The Media

The media . . . is not yours to co-opt or use to spread propaganda. You are merely stewards of the industry.

An Immigrant's Love Letter to the West (2022).

Opinion Polls

You've got to be careful with opinion polls in totalitarian regimes.

Racism

The only way to deal with the problem of racism is to treat people on the content of their character and nothing else, and the fact that woke culture seeks to overturn that is a new form of racism that we must all oppose.

Speech to Oxford Union, "Woke Culture HAS Gone Too Far," January 12, 2023.

Triggernometry

We don't have a budget to employ a bunch of people to do extensive research on things or to do fact checking for us. So we can't do certain things that the mainstream media can do, and should do. The problem is the mainstream media isn't doing it either. . . . There's a really important role for the mainstream media. I just wish they'd play that role. . . . New media has its own problems. It over rewards charisma. It over rewards passion. It massively under rewards any attempts to cling to truth. It encourages people to go off in the pursuit of the most exciting take, and truth isn't always exciting. The truth is we need a vibrant ecosystem in which all of these different pieces play their own different roles, which is why I'm in favour of maximum freedom because that's when you get everybody doing their thing. Over time people who want wholesome content if you like, when it comes to fact or information or whatever, can seek it out. Because people aren't stupid.

Interview, "Why Is Everyone Losing Their Minds?," Chris Williamson show, October 23, 2023.

Women

I think, it doesn't apply to everybody, caveat, for most women the greatest gift their partner can give them is the opportunity, if they want to be at home with the children, to do that.

Interview, "Why Is Everyone Losing Their Minds?," Chris Williamson show, October 23, 2023.

Henry Kissinger

Henry Alfred Kissinger / 1923–2023 / Political Scientist, Public Servant, Diplomat, Author

Diplomacy

A diplomat's task is to represent his country in such a manner as to encourage the respect and trust of the country to which he is accredited.

Diplomacy (1994).

Foreign Policy

The absence of alternatives clears the mind marvelously.

Years of Upheaval (1982).

Each success only buys an admission ticket to a more difficult problem.

White House Years (1979).

The superpowers often behave like two heavily armed blind men feeling their way around a room, each believing himself in mortal peril from the other, whom he assumes to have perfect vision.

Years of Upheaval (1982).

In the absence of an agreed objective, foreign policy and diplomacy resemble a waltz without music.

Source unknown.

No foreign policy—no matter how ingenious—has any chance of success if it is born in the minds of a few and carried in the hearts of none.

Source unknown.

History

History knows no resting places and no plateaus.

Source unknown.

Kissinger on Kissinger

The longer I am out of office, the more infallible I appear to myself.

Cited in Niall Ferguson, Kissinger: 1923–1968: The Idealist(2015).

Leadership

The task of the leader is to get his people from where they are to where they have not been.

American Foreign Policy (1969).

A leader does not deserve the name unless he is willing occasionally to stand alone.

Years of Renewal (1999).

Leaders are responsible not for running public opinion polls but for the consequences of their actions.

Source unknown.

It is, after all, the responsibility of the expert to operate the familiar and that of the leader to transcend it.

American Foreign Policy (1969).

Politicians

Ninety percent of the politicians give the other ten percent a bad reputation.

Source unknown.

Power

Power is the great aphrodisiac.

Interview, in Oriana Fallaci, If the Sun Dies (1965).

Statesmen

The statesman's duty is to bridge the gap between his nation's experience and his vision.

Source unknown.

Warfare

The conventional army loses if it does not win. The guerrilla wins if he does not lose.

Nuclear Weapons and Foreign Policy (1957).

Watergate

The illegal we do immediately; the unconstitutional takes a little longer.

Conversation re: US covert operations in Angola, recorded in the White House Situation Room, March 10, 1975; declassified in 2005.

Karl Kraus

Karl Kraus / 1874–1936 / Kingdom of Bohemia, Austro-Hungarian Empire / Journalist, Publisher, Lecturer, Poet, Dramatist, Essayist, Aphorist

Note: Though born into an Ashkenazi Jewish family in what is now the Czech Republic, Kraus's family moved to Vienna in 1877, when he was three years old. He lived there for the rest of his life.

Note: Unless indicated otherwise, all quotations are taken from *Die Fackel* [The Torch], the newspaper that Kraus published, edited, and contributed to between 1899 and 1936. After 1911, he contributed essentially all of the copy for the magazine himself. English translations of most, but not all, of the quotations from *Die Fackel* reproduced here may also be found in *Half-Truths and One-and-a-Half Truths: Selected Aphorisms* (1976).

Aphorisms

An aphorism can never be the whole truth; it is either a half-truth or a truth-and-a-half.

Someone who can write aphorisms should not fritter away his time writing essays.

Art

Only he is an artist who can make a riddle out of a solution.

Love and art do not embrace what is beautiful but what is made beautiful by this embrace,

> *Beim Wort genommen [Taken at His Word] (1955).*

Berlin and Vienna

In Berlin, things are serious but not hopeless. In Vienna, they are hopeless but not serious.

Books and Writers

Where will I ever find the time not to read so much?

> *Sprüche und Widersprüche [Sayings and Gainsayings] (1909).*

One must read all writers twice—the good as well as the bad. The one kind will be recognized; the other, unmasked.

There are two kinds of writers. With the first, content and form belong together like soul and body; with the second, they match each other like body and clothes.

Consumerism

We are sacrificing ourselves for our ready-made goods; we are consumers and live in such a way that the means may consume the end.

> *"In dieser grossen Zeit" [In This Great Time] (1914).*

Criminal Justice

Squeeze human nature into a straitjacket of criminal justice and crime will appear!

Culture

Culture is the tacit agreement to let the means of subsistence disappear behind the purpose of existence.

"In dieser grossen Zeit" [In This Great Time] (1914).

When the sun of culture is low, even dwarves will cast long shadows.

Democracy

Democracy means the opportunity to be everyone's slave.

Equality

Nothing is more narrow-minded than chauvinism or race hatred. To me all men are equal: there are jackasses everywhere, and I have the same contempt for them all.

Esthetes

The esthete stands in the same relation to beauty as the pornographer stands to love, and the politician stands to life.

Freedom

The tyranny of necessity grants its slaves three kinds of freedom: opinion free from intellect, entertainment free from art, and orgies free from love,

"In dieser grossen Zeit" [In This Great Time] (1914).

Greetings

If I return some people's greetings, I do so only to give them their greeting back.

Humanity

The devil is an optimist if he thinks he can make people worse than they are.

The superman is a premature ideal, one that presupposes a man.

To be human is erroneous.

Lord, forgive them, for they know what they do!

A weak man has doubts before a decision, a strong man has them afterwards.

Jealousy

Jealousy is a dog's bark which attracts thieves.

Journalists

The making of a journalist: no ideas and the ability to express them.

Kraus's Public

I and my public understand each other very well: it does not hear what I say, and I don't say what it wants to hear.

I trim my opponents to fit my arrows.

Many desire to kill me, and many wish to spend an hour chatting with me. The law protects me from the former.

Life

Life is an effort that deserves a better cause.

You don't even live once.

Literature

Today's literature: prescriptions written by patients.

It is better not to express what one means than to express what one does not mean.

Love

There is no more unfortunate creature under the sun than a fetishist who yearns for a woman's shoe and has to settle for the whole woman.

A "seducer" who boasts of initiating women into the mystery of love is like a stranger who arrives at a railroad station and offers to show the sights to a tourist guide.

Prejudice

I have often been asked to be fair and view a matter from all sides. I did so, hoping something might improve if I viewed all sides of it. But the result was the same. So I went back to viewing things only from one side, which saves me a lot of work and disappointment. For it is comforting to regard something as bad and be able use one's prejudice as an excuse.

Progress

Progress celebrates Pyrrhic victories over nature.

Pro Domo et Mundo [For Home and World] (1912).

Progress … has subordinated the purpose of life to the means of subsistence and turned us into the nuts and bolts for our tools.

"In dieser grossen Zeit" [In This Great Time] (1914).

Psychoanalysis

My unconscious knows more about the consciousness of the psychologist than his consciousness knows about my unconscious.

Psychoanalysis is that mental illness for which it regards itself as therapy.

So-called psychoanalysis is the occupation of lustful rationalists who trace everything in the world to sexual causes – with the exception of their occupation.

Reason and Passion

Keep your passions in check, but beware of giving your reason free rein.

Solitude

Solitude would be an ideal state if one were able to pick the people one avoids.

The world is a prison in which solitary confinement is preferable.

Technology

The development of technology will leave only one problem: the infirmity of human nature.

War

War: first, one hopes to win; then one expects the enemy to lose; then, one is satisfied that the enemy too is suffering; in the end, one is surprised that everyone has lost.

When the word "peace" was uttered for the first time, there was panic at the stock exchange. They screamed in pain: "We've been earning! Leave us the war! We've earned the war!"

How is the world ruled and led to war? Diplomats lie to journalists and believe these lies when they see them in print.

Women

There are women who are not beautiful but only look that way.

Sprüche und Widersprüche [Dicta and Contradictions] (1909).

Women at least have elegant dresses. But what can men use to cover their emptiness?

Ray Kroc

Raymond Albert Kroc / 1902–1984 / Illinois, USA / Businessman, CEO of McDonald's

Business Philosophy

Luck is the dividend of sweat. The more you sweat, the luckier you get.

Widely cited; however, attribution unconfirmed.

Look after the customer and the business will take care of itself.

Widely cited; however, attribution unconfirmed.

"Opportunity is dead in the United States!" "The tax structure has destroyed all incentive!" How often we have heard such laments during the past thirty years, when in fact greater fortunes have been made and higher living standards achieved than ever before on earth!

Ray Kroc, Grinding It Out: The Making of McDonald's (1977).

If a corporation has two executives who think alike, one of them is unnecessary.

Reported by John F. Love in McDonald's: Behind the Arches(1986).

. . . the basics have to be stressed over and over. If I had a brick for every time I've repeated the phrase QSC and V (Quality, Service, Cleanliness, and Value), I think I'd probably be able to bridge the Atlantic Ocean with them. And the operators need the stress on fundamentals as much as their managers and crews. This is especially true of a new location.

Ray Kroc, Grinding It Out: The Making of McDonald's (1977).

I believe that if you hire a man to do a job, you ought to get out of the way and let him do it.

Ray Kroc, Grinding It Out: The Making of McDonald's (1977).

Kroc on Kroc

Another piece of paper discovered among my father's effects was a yellowed document dated 1906. It was a phrenologist's report of a reading he had done on the bumps of the head of Raymond A. Kroc, aged four. He had predicted that I would become a chef or work in some branch of food service. I was amazed at the prognostication; after all I was in a food service–related business and felt a real affinity for kitchens. Little did I know how much more accurate that old boy's prophesy would eventually prove to be.

Ray Kroc, Grinding It Out: The Making of McDonald's (1977).

I sold a Multimixer to a guy named Willard Marriott, who had just opened a drive-in called A&W Root Beer. His method of operation fascinated me. I considered myself a connoisseur of kitchens; after all, selling Multimixers took me into thousands of them. I prided myself on being able to tell which operations would appeal to the public and which would fail. Willard Marriott looked like a winner to me from the start. I had no more idea than he did back then, though, of what a giant his Marriott Corporation would become in hotels and restaurants."

Ray Kroc, Grinding It Out: The Making of McDonald's (1977).

There was a lot of nervous tension at that time on all levels of society over the alarming developments in Europe and Asia. Magazines speculated grimly on whether war with Japan was inevitable. Then our attention was diverted from Japanese aggression in China to the Nazi conquests in Europe. On December 7, 1941, we were thrown into war by the Japanese sneak attack on Pearl Harbor, and I was thrown out of the Multimixer business. Supplies of copper, used in winding the motors for Multimixer, were restricted by the war effort.

Ray Kroc, Grinding It Out: The Making of McDonald's (1977).

We started Franchise Realty Corporation with $1,000 paid-in capital, and Harry [Sonneborn] parlayed that cash investment into something like $170 million worth of real estate. His idea, simply put, was that we would induce a property owner to lease us his land on a subordinated basis. That is, he would take back a second mortgage so that we could go to a lending institution (in the early days it was a bank) and arrange a first mortgage on the building; the landlord would subordinate his land to the building. I must admit that I was a bit skeptical.

Ray Kroc, Grinding It Out: The Making of McDonald's (1977).

This was the beginning of real income for McDonald's. Harry devised a formula for the monthly payments being made by our operators that paid our own mortgage and other expenses plus a profit.

Ray Kroc, Grinding It Out: The Making of McDonald's (1977).

[Kroc's first wife] Ethel was incensed by the whole thing. We had no obligations that would be jeopardized by it; our daughter, Marilyn, was married and no longer dependent on us. But that didn't matter to Ethel; she just didn't want to hear about the McDonalds or my plans.

Ray Kroc, Grinding It Out: The Making of McDonald's (1977).

[Ethel] dutifully attended McDonald's gatherings in later years, and she was liked by operators' wives and by women on the staff, but there was nothing more between us. Our thirty-five years of holy matrimony endured another five in unholy acrimony.

Ray Kroc, Grinding It Out: The Making of McDonald's (1977).

I was about to lose one of my biggest accounts, Walgreens, the people I had created a tremendous amount of business for and to whom I was selling five million cups a year. Fred Stoll told me in strictest confidence that a former Walgreen executive who had a lot of pull in the top offices of the company had gone into the paper cup business with a competitor of mine, and he was going to be given all of the Walgreen trade. The rationale would be that this competitor was selling for five percent under my price. I explained this to John Clark and tried to get him to go along with offering Walgreens a price break—after all, they paid their bills on time and there was promotion value in having a big company like that use your product. But all I got was a tongue lashing.

Ray Kroc, Grinding It Out: The Making of McDonald's (1977).

The best part of it for me personally was that every time I saw a new Walgreen's store going up it meant new business. This sort of multiplication was clearly the way to go. I spent less and less time chasing pushcart vendors around the West Side and more time cultivating large accounts where big turnover would automatically winch in sales in the thousands and hundreds of thousands.

Ray Kroc, Grinding It Out: The Making of McDonald's (1977).

There is an old saying that all work and no play makes Jack a dull boy. I never believed it because, for me, work was play. I got as much pleasure out of it as I did from playing baseball.

Ray Kroc, Grinding It Out: The Making of McDonald's (1977).

McDonald's

This historic year of 1976 will see McDonald's Corporation surpass one billion dollars in total revenue for the first time. Casual students of business history may not realize the significance of the fact that this milestone will be reached during the twenty-second year of the company's history.

Ray Kroc, Grinding It Out: The Making of McDonald's (1977).

[Kroc's friend] had a son-in-law named Ed MacLuckie who was looking for a job and who had expressed a liking for the food service business. Ed was working a wholesale hardware territory over in Michigan at the time and it was not going well. So I talked to him. He was one of these whip-lean, nervous types who are often very fussy and fastidious and have great endurance. Just the kind of qualifications I was looking for, so I hired him as a manager of my first store. Art Bender, the McDonald brothers' manager, came to Des Plaines and helped Ed and me open that store on April 15, 1955.

Ray Kroc, Grinding It Out: The Making of McDonald's (1977).

[Richard and Maurice McDonald] were obtuse, they were utterly indifferent to the fact that I was putting every cent I had and all I could borrow into this project. When we sat down with our lawyers in attendance, the brothers acknowledged the problems but refused to write a single letter that would permit me to make changes. . . . It was almost as though they were hoping I would fail. This was a peculiar attitude for them to take because the more successful the franchising, the more money they would make. My attorney gave up on the situation.

Ray Kroc, Grinding It Out: The Making of McDonald's (1977).

Cooking with gas was a popular expression at the time, but it was an in-joke with us. When somebody was cooking with gas around our place it meant that he was really doing everything right. This stemmed from our experience in patterning our stores on the plans provided by the McDonald brothers. Jim Schindler insisted on using gas units for making French fries instead of the electric friers the McDonald boys were using. Gas proved to be more efficient for this purpose. It was cheaper, and we got a better product. So we tried to "cook with gas" in all our operations at McDonald's.

Ray Kroc, Grinding It Out: The Making of McDonald's (1977).

One of the things I did differently was to make my milkshakes with a soft product drawn from a tank, instead of hand-dipping ice cream. This changed the layout and gave us more space. One major problem in adapting the California-style building to the Midwestern climate was ventilation. I brought in architectual consultants one after the other in an attempt to solve the problem of exhausting the stale air and replacing it with fresh cool or heated air.

Ray Kroc, Grinding It Out: The Making of McDonald's (1977).

I had memorized the procedure when I watched the McDonald's operation in San Bernardino, and I had done it exactly the same way. I went through the whole thing once more. The result was the same—bland, mushy French fries. They were as good, actually, as the French fries you could buy at other places. But that was not what I wanted.

Ray Kroc, Grinding It Out: The Making of McDonald's (1977).

. . . when potatoes are dug, they are mostly water. They improve in taste as they dry out and the sugars change to starch. The McDonald brothers had, without knowing it, a natural curing process in their open bins, which allowed the desert breeze to blow over the potatoes. With the help of the potato people, I devised a curing system of my own. I had the potatoes stored in the basement so the older ones would always be next in line for the kitchen. I also put a big electric fan down there and gave the spuds a continuous blast of air, which greatly amused Ed MacLuckie. "We have the world's most pampered potatoes," he said. "I almost feel guilty about cooking them."

Ray Kroc, *Grinding It Out: The Making of McDonald's (1977).*

One of my suppliers told me, "Ray, you know you aren't in the hamburger business at all. You're in the French-fry business. I don't know how the livin' hell you do it, but you've got the best French fries in town, and that's what's selling folks on your place."

Ray Kroc, *Grinding It Out: The Making of McDonald's (1977).*

One day I said, "Mac, the only way in this world that you can increase your soda fountain volume is to sell to people who don't take up a stool. Look, I'll tell you what I'm gonna do. I will give you 200 or 300 containers with covers, however many you need to try this for a month in your store down the street. Now most of your takeout customers will be Walgreen employees from headquarters here, and you can conduct your own marketing survey on them and see how they like it. You get the cups free, so it's not going to cost you anything to try it." Finally he agreed. I brought him the cups, and we set the thing up at one end of the soda fountain. It was a big success from the first day. It wasn't long before McNamarra was more excited about the idea of takeouts than I was.

Ray Kroc, *Grinding It Out: The Making of McDonald's (1977).*

Personal Philosophy

There are things money can't buy and hard work can't win. One of them is happiness.

Ray Kroc, *Grinding It Out: The Making of McDonald's (1977).*

Work is the meat in the hamburger of life.

Ray Kroc, *Grinding It Out: The Making of McDonald's (1977).*

I have always believed that each man makes his own happiness and is responsible for his own problems.

Ray Kroc, *Grinding It Out: The Making of McDonald's (1977).*

Ray Kurzweil

Ray Kurzweil / b. 1948 / New York, USA / Computer Scientist, Inventor, Author

Until such time that computers at least match human intelligence in every dimension, it will always remain possible for skeptics to say the glass is half empty. Every new achievement of AI can be dismissed by pointing out other goals that have not yet been accomplished. Indeed, this is the frustration of the AI practitioner: once an AI goal is achieved, it is no longer considered as falling within the realm of AI and become instead just a useful general technique. AI is thus often regarded as the set of problems that have not yet been solved.

The Singularity Is Near: When Humans Transcend Biology (2005).

The ethical debates are like stones in a stream. The water runs around them. You haven't seen any biological technologies held up for one week by any of these debates.

"The Singularity," in John Brockman, ed., The New Humanists: Science at the Edge (2003).

A primary reason that evolution—of life-forms or technology—speeds up is that it *builds on its own increasing order*.

The Age of Spiritual Machines: When Computers Exceed Human Intelligence (1999).

The power of ideas to transform the world is itself accelerating.

The Singularity Is Near: When Humans Transcend Biology (2005).

One of the advantages of being in the futurism business is that by the time your readers are able to find fault with your forecasts, it is too late for them to ask for their money back.

"The Virtual Book Revisited," The Library Journal, Februrary 1, 1993.

I quickly realized that you had to have a good idea of the future if you were going to succeed as an inventor.

"The Singularity," in John Brockman, ed., The New Humanists: Science at the Edge (2003).

The primary political and philosophical issue of the next century will be the definition of who we are.

The Age of Spiritual Machines: When Computers Exceed Human Intelligence (1999).

Before the next century is over, human beings will no longer be the most intelligent or capable type of entity on the planet. Actually, let me take that back. The truth of that last statement depends on how we define human.

The Age of Spiritual Machines: When Computers Exceed Human Intelligence (1999).

To this day I remain convinced of this basic philosophy: no matter what quandaries we face . . . there is an idea that can enable us to prevail.

The Singularity Is Near: When Humans Transcend Biology (2005).

Jaron Lanier

Jaron Z. Lanier / b. 1960 / New York, USA / Computer Scientist

Advertising

An economy where advertisers thrive while journalists and artists struggle, reflects the values of a society more interested in deception and manipulation than in truth and beauty.

Advertisers and marketers should be looking to bring new experiences to different parts of the brain. It's a more profound idea than just dropping a billboard into a video game.

Source: "A Call to Expand the use of Neuromarketing so Advertisers Can Target our Brain," Center for Digital Democracy, interview with Jeff Chester, September 17, 2011.

If you want to know what's really going on in a society or ideology, follow the money. If money is flowing to advertising instead of musicians, journalists, and artists, then a society is more concerned with manipulation than truth or beauty.

Source: You Are Not a Gadget: A Manifesto (Knopf, 2010).

Funding a civilization through advertising is like trying to get nutrition by connecting a tube from one's anus to one's mouth.

Source: You Are Not a Gadget: A Manifesto (Knopf, 2010).

Facebook says, "Privacy is theft," because they're selling your lack of privacy to the advertisers who might show up one day.

Artificial Intelligence's False Promises

The Turing test cuts both ways. You can't tell if a machine has gotten smarter or if you've just lowered your own standards of intelligence to such a degree that the machine seems smart. If you can have a conversation with a simulated person presented by an AI program, can you tell how far you've let your sense of personhood degrade in order to make the illusion work for you?

Source: You Are Not a Gadget: A Manifesto (Knopf, 2010).

There is no difference between machine autonomy and the abdication of human responsibility.

Source: "One Half of a Manifesto," The Edge, 2003.

We imagine "pure" cybernetic systems, but we can prove only that we know how to build fairly dysfunctional ones. We kid ourselves when we think we understand something, even a computer, merely because we can model or digitize it.

Source: "One Half of a Manifesto," The Edge, 2003.

Big Tech's Enablers

There will always be humans, lots of them, who provide the data that makes the networked realization of any technology better and cheaper.

Source: Who Owns the Future? (Simon & Schuster, 2014).

Companies Under Big Tech

At the height of its power, the photography company Kodak employed more than 140,000 people and was worth $28 billion. They even invented the first digital camera. But today Kodak is bankrupt, and the new face of digital photography has become Instagram. When Instagram was sold to Facebook for a billion dollars in 2012, it employed only thirteen people. Where did all those jobs disappear to?

Source: Who Owns the Future? (Simon & Schuster, 2014).

Feeding the Cloud

The cloud is driven by statistics, and even in the worst individual cases of personal ignorance, dullness, idleness, or irrelevance, every person is constantly feeding data into the cloud these days. The value of such information could be treated as genuine, but it is not. Instead, the blindness of our standards of accounting to all that value is gradually breaking capitalism.

Source: Who Owns the Future? (Simon & Schuster, 2014).

Humanism

We should treat computers as fancy telephones, whose purpose is to connect people.... As long as we remember that we ourselves are the source of our value, our creativity, our sense of reality, then all of our work with computers will be worthwhile and beautiful.

Source: Digerati: Encounters With the Cyber, ed. John Brockman (Hardwired, 1996); Chapter 17: "The Prodigy."

Mob vs. Individual

Human beings either function as individuals or as members of a pack. There's a switch inside us, deep in our spirit, that you can turn one way or the other. It's almost always the case that our worst behaviour comes out when we're switched to the mob setting. The problem with a lot of software designs is that they switch us to that setting.

No Free Lunch

Digital technologies are setting down the new grooves of how people live, how we do business, how we do everything–and they're doing it according to the expectations of foolish utopian scenarios. We want free online experiences so badly that we are happy to not be paid for information that comes from us now or ever. That sensibility also implies that the more dominant information becomes in our economy, the less most of us will be worth.

Source: "Who Owns the Future," Humanities North Dakota, Fall, 2015.

Perils of Total Connectedness

Some of the fantasy objects arising from cybernetic totalism (like the noosphere, which is a supposed global brain formed by the sum of all the human brains connected through the internet) happen to motivate infelicitous technological designs. For instance, designs that celebrate the noosphere tend to energize the inner troll, or bad actor, within humans.

Pop Culture

Pop culture has entered into a nostalgic malaise. Online culture is dominated by trivial mashups of the culture that existed before the onset of mashups, and by fandom responding to the dwindling outposts of centralized mass media. It is a culture of reaction without action.

Source: You Are Not a Gadget: A Manifesto (Knopf, 2010).

Virtual Reality

Back in the 1980s, when the internet was only available to a small number of pioneers, I was often confronted by people who feared that the strange technologies I was working on, like virtual reality, might unleash the demons of human nature. For instance, would people become addicted to virtual reality as if it were a drug? Would they become trapped in it, unable to escape back to the physical world where the rest of us live? Some of the questions were silly, and others were prescient.

Source: You Are Not a Gadget: A Manifesto (Knopf, 2010).

François de La Rochefoucauld

François de La Rochefoucauld / 1613–1680 / France / Memoirist, Aphorist
Note: All quotations are taken from *Maximes* [Maxims] (1665; many later editions).

Advice

Men give away nothing so liberally as their advice.
Old people love to give good advice; it compensates them for their inability to set a bad example.

Bores

We frequently forgive those who bore us, but cannot forgive those whom we bore.

Courage

We are strong enough to bear the misfortunes of others.

Death

Neither the sun nor death can be looked at steadily.

Evil

No man is clever enough to know all the evil he does.

Faults

If we had no faults of our own, we would not take so much pleasure in noticing those of others.
We confess to little faults only to persuade ourselves that we have no great one.
Most of our faults are more pardonable than the means we use to conceal them.

Fortune and Misfortune

We need greater virtues to sustain good fortune than bad.
In the misfortune of our best friends we often find something that is not displeasing.

Good Sense

We rarely find that people have good sense unless they agree with us.

Gratitude

Gratitude is merely the secret hope of further favors.

Happiness

We are never so happy nor so unhappy as we imagine.

Hypocrisy

Hypocrisy is the homage that vice pays to virtue.

Love

There is no disguise which can for long conceal love where it exists or simulate it where it does not.

True love is like ghosts, which everybody talks about and few have seen.

The pleasure of love is in loving. We are happier in the passion we feel than in that we arouse.

Absence diminishes mediocre passions and increases great ones, as the wind blows out candles

and fans fire.

We pardon to the extent that we love.

Passions

If we resist our passions, it is more due to their weakness than our strength.

The mind is always the dupe of the heart.

Philosophy

Philosophy triumphs easily over past evils and future evils; but present evils triumph over it.

Quarrels

Quarrels would not last long if the fault was only on one side.

Self-Regard

We would rather speak ill of ourselves than not talk about ourselves at all.

Self-love is the greatest of all flatterers.

Everyone complains of his memory, and no one complains of his judgment.

We are so accustomed to disguise ourselves to others, that in the end, we become disguised to ourselves.

Understanding

Mediocre minds usually dismiss anything which reaches beyond their own understanding.

Wisdom

The constancy of the wise is the art to contain their excitement in the heart.

Christopher Lasch

Robert Christopher Lasch / 1932–1994 / Omaha, Nebraska, USA / Historian, Social Critic

American Character

Our society is absolutely intolerant of the display of genuine emotion. We avoid it, because it's extremely disturbing.

Interview, The Christian Century, 1990.

The American Dream has become a relentless pursuit of material success, often at the expense of meaningful relationships and a sense of purpose.

"The Culture of Narcissism Revisited," The New York Times, 1990.

In a culture that prizes novelty, celebrity, and success, there is little room for the cultivation of character or the development of a moral sense.

The Revolt of the Elites and the Betrayal of Democracy (1995).

Economics

The obsession with efficiency and productivity has led to a devaluation of the importance of leisure, contemplation, and the pursuit of the higher things in life.

"The Lost Art of Political Argument," The Nation, 1985.

Without a truly moral compass, the economy will disintegrate into purely self-interested actions, unrestrained by any sense of responsibility to the common good.

"The Lost Art of Political Argument," The Nation, 1985.

Expertise

The modern world has created a cult of experts who claim to have all the answers, but true wisdom often resides in the collective wisdom of ordinary people.

"The Eclipse of the Public," Salmagundi, 1978.

Family

The family is not just a social institution. It's also the school of sentiment, the school of emotion.

Interview, Hartford Courant, 1985.

The family is the most effective and important social safety net. It is the first and most important welfare agency.

Haven in a Heartless World: The Family Besieged (1977).

The family is a haven in a heartless world.

Haven in a Heartless World: The Family Besieged (1977).

Lasch on Lasch

The pursuit of happiness, as I conceived it, was a heroic pursuit, and that implied a lifetime vocation.

The Minimal Self: Psychic Survival in Troubled Times (1984).

Moral Psychology

The pursuit of happiness has traditionally been linked to the idea of personal responsibility.

"The Lost Art of Argument," The New Republic, 1985.

Every age develops its own peculiar forms of pathology, which express in exaggerated form its underlying character structure.

The Culture of Narcissism: American Life in an Age of Diminishing Expectations (1979).

Cultural renewal requires a reconnection with our history and traditions, as well as a willingness to confront the moral and social challenges of our time.

Interview, New Perspectives Quarterly, 1992.

Modern society is characterized by an excessive focus on the self and an erosion of a sense of community and shared responsibility.

The Culture of Narcissism: American Life in an Age of Diminishing Expectations (1979).

Nostalgia

Nostalgia for a bygone era has a way of distorting the truth. In any case, there's nothing magical about the past. What's magical is the future.

"Nostalgia and Progress," The Public Interest, 1977.

Public Life

To revitalize American democracy, we need to encourage the formation of public spaces where citizens can come together to discuss common problems and share a sense of community.

"The Lost Art of Argument," The New Republic, 1985.

The history of American politics is littered with bodies of people who took so pure a position that they had no clout at all.

Interview, in Bill Moyers, A World of Ideas (1989).

The Left has shifted its emphasis from economic inequality to issues of identity and representation, but in the process, it has lost touch with the economic realities faced by working-class Americans.

The Revolt of the Elites and the Betrayal of Democracy (1995).

Democracy encourages the formation of self-reliant individuals who can participate actively in public life.

Source unknown.

A democratic society requires a shared moral vision, a set of values that unite its citizens and guide their actions.

The True and Only Heaven: Progress and Its Critics (1991).

The pursuit of individual happiness should not come at the expense of the common good or the well-being of the community.

The True and Only Heaven: Progress and Its Critics (1991).

A just society requires not only the protection of individual rights but also a commitment to social justice and the common good.

The Minimal Self: Psychic Survival in Troubled Times (1984).

Self-Knowledge

The key to self-reliance is self-knowledge.

The Minimal Self: Psychic Survival in Troubled Times (1984).

Therapeutic Culture

The rise of the therapeutic culture has encouraged a preoccupation with self-help and self-improvement, often at the expense of addressing larger societal issues.

"The Eclipse of the Public," Salmagundi, 1978.

Gottfried Wilhelm Leibniz

Gottfried Wilhelm Leibniz / 1646–1716 / Leipzig, Electorate of Saxony, Holy Roman Empire (now Germany) / Philosopher, Mathematician, Historian

Automation

It is unworthy of excellent men to lose hours like slaves in the labor of calculation which could safely be relegated to anyone else if machines were used.

Source: Machina arithmetica in qua non addito[sic] tantum et subtractio sed multiplicatio nullo, divisio vero pœne nullo animi labore peragantur [An arithmetical machine in which not only addition and subtraction, but also multiplication and division, may be carried out with almost no mental labor], unpublished manuscript, 1685 (on the hand-cranked calculating machine he invented in 1673).

Consciousness

If you could blow the brain up to the size of a mill and walk about inside, you would not find consciousness.

Source: Monadology, 1714; section 17.

Cosmic Optimism

God has chosen the best of all possible worlds.

Source: Theodicy, 1695; section 168 et passim.

Interconnectedness of All Things

Now this connexion or adaptation of all created things to each and of each to all, means that each simple substance has relations which express all the others, and, consequently, that it is a perpetual living mirror of the universe.

Source: Monadology, 1714; section 56.

Principle of Sufficient Reason

Nihil est sine ratione.
[There is nothing without a reason.]

Source: Theory of Abstract Motion: Fundamental Principles, 1671; section 24 (earliest of many references to the "Principle of Sufficient Reason" throughout his work).

Giacomo Leopardi

Giacomo Leopardi / 1798–1837 / Marche, Papal States (now Italy) / Poet, Philologist, Essayist

Note: Many quotations are taken from *Zibaldone* [Hodge-Podge, or Miscellany], an enormous work composed between 1817 and 1832, first published *in toto* posthumously in 1898. Various compilations of extracts from the *Zibaldone,* in both Italian and English, are noted below.

Art

. . . the recognition of the irredeemable vanity and falsity of all beauty and all greatness is itself a kind of beauty and greatness that fills the soul when it is conveyed by a work of genius. And the spectacle of nothingness is itself a thing in these works, and seems to enlarge the reader's soul, to raise it up and to make it take satisfaction in itself and its despair.

Zibaldone, complete English version (2013).

Boredom

Boredom is in some ways the most sublime of human feelings. . . . not being able to be satisfied with any earthly thing or, so to speak, with the whole earth; considering the immeasurable extent of space, the number and the wonderful size of the worlds, and finding that everything is small and petty in comparison with the capacity of one's own mind; picturing to oneself the infinite number of worlds, and the infinite universe, and feeling that the soul and our desire must be still greater than such a universe; always accusing things of insufficiency and nothingness; and suffering a huge lack and emptiness, and therefore boredom—all this seems to me the greatest sign of grandeur and nobility which there is in human nature. And so boredom is seldom seen in men of no account, and very seldom or never in other creatures.

Pensieri [Thoughts], selection from the Zibaldone, published in 1837.

Children

Children find everything in nothing, men find nothing in everything.

Zibaldone, complete English version (2013).

Death

Death is not an evil, because it frees us from all evils, and while it takes away good things, it takes away also the desire for them. Old age is the supreme evil, because it deprives us of all pleasures, leaving us only the appetite for them, and it brings with it all sufferings. Nevertheless, we fear death, and we desire old age.

Pensieri [Thoughts], selection from the Zibaldone, published in 1837.

Two truths that most men will never believe: one that we know nothing, the other that we are nothing. Add the third, which depends a lot on the second: that there is nothing to hope for after death.

Passions, English selection from the Zibaldone (2014).

Humanity

In every land the universal vices and ills of mankind and of human society are noted as peculiar to that place. . . . Men are wretched by necessity, and determined to believe themselves wretched by accident.

Pensieri [Thoughts], selection from the Zibaldone, published in 1837.

No one can truthfully boast or say in anger: I cannot be unhappier than I am.

Zibaldone, complete English version (2013).

No one thing shows the greatness and power of the human intellect or the loftiness and nobility of man more than his ability to know and to understand fully and feel strongly his own smallness.

Zibaldone, complete English version (2013).

Laughter

The power of laughter is terrible and awful: anyone who has the courage to laugh is master over others, in the same way as anyone who has the courage to die.

Zibaldone, complete English version (2013).

Leopardi's Philosophy

My philosophy isn't only *not* conducive to misanthropy, as it might appear to a superficial reader, and as many have accused me. It essentially rules out misanthropy, it tends toward healing, to dissolving discontent and hatred. . . . My philosophy holds nature guilty of everything, it acquits mankind completely and directs our hate, or at least our lamentations, to its matrix, to the true origin of the afflictions living creatures suffer, etc.

Pensieri [Thoughts], selection from the Zibaldone, published in 1837.

Pleasure

Pleasure is always in the past or in the future, never in the present.

Zibaldone, complete English version (2013).

Purpose of Life

Icelander: . . . since that which is destroyed suffers, and that which is born from its destruction also suffers in due course, and finally is in its turn destroyed, would you enlighten me on one point, about which hitherto no philosopher has satisfied me? For whose pleasure and service is this wretched life of the world maintained, by the suffering and death of all the beings which compose it?

"Dialogo della Natura e di un Islandese" [Dialogue Between Nature and an Icelander], composed in 1824 and collected in Operette Morali [Little Moral Essays], first published in 1827.

It seems as though death were the essential aim of all things. That which has no existence cannot die; yet all that exists has proceeded from nothing. The final cause of existence is not happiness, for nothing is happy. It is true, living creatures seek this end in all their works, but none obtain it; and during all their life, ever deceiving, tormenting, and exerting themselves, they suffer indeed for no other purpose than to die.

"Cantico del gallo silvestre" [Song of the Wild Cock], composed in 1824 collected in Operette Morali [Little Moral Essays], first published in 1827.

Revenge

Revenge is so sweet one often wishes to be insulted so as to be able to take revenge, and I don't mean just by an old enemy, but anyone, or even (especially when in a really bad mood) by a friend.

Passions, English selection from the Zibaldone (2014).

Value of Existence

Everything is evil. I mean, everything that is, is wicked; every existing thing is an evil; everything exists for a wicked end. Existence is a wickedness and is ordained for wickedness. Evil is the end, the final purpose, of the universe...The only good is nonbeing; the only really good thing is the thing that is not, things that are not things; all things are bad.

Zibaldone, complete English version (2013).

Vision of Vesuvius

And you, gentle broom,
who adorn this despoiled countryside
with fragrant thickets,
you too will soon succumb to the cruel power
of the subterranean fire,
which returns to the place
it already knows, to stretch over your soft copses
its voracious tongue. And you'll bow
beneath its mortal flow without a struggle
your innocent head:
but a head not bent in vain
cowardly begging before
a future oppressor; nor raised
with insane pride to the stars,
nor above the desert,
where your home and birthplace were
not through choice but chance:
far wiser and much less
fallible than man, since you never believed
that your frail species
could, by fate or yourself, become immortal.

"La Ginestra" [The Wild Broom], composed in 1836, and first published in the 1837 edition of Canti [Songs].

Georg Christoph Lichtenberg

Georg Christoph Lichtenberg / 1742–1799 / near Darmstadt, Landgraviate of Hesse-Darmstadt (now Germany) / Physicist, Travel Writer, Publisher, Aphorist
Note: All quotations are taken from *Sudelbücher* [Waste Books] (first published posthumously between 1800 and 1806).

Americans

The American who first discovered Columbus made a bad discovery.

Arguments

A handful of soldiers is always better than a mouthful of arguments.

Belief

With most men, unbelief in one thing springs from blind belief in another.

Books

A book is a mirror: if an ape looks into it an apostle is hardly likely to look out.
There are very many people who read simply to prevent themselves from thinking.
It is almost everywhere the case that soon after it is begotten the greater part of human wisdom is laid to rest in repositories.

God

It is hardly to be believed how spiritual reflections when mixed with a little physics can hold people's attention and give them a livelier idea of God than do the often ill-applied examples of his wrath.

Honesty

Once the good man was dead, one wore his hat and another his sword as he had worn them, a third had himself barbered as he had, a fourth walked as he did, but the honest man that he was—nobody any longer wanted to be that.

Human Nature

Every man has his moral backside which he refrains from showing unless he has to and keeps covered as long as possible with the trousers of decorum.
What is called an acute knowledge of human nature is mostly nothing but the observer's own weaknesses reflected back from others.
That man is the noblest creature may also be inferred from the fact that no other creature has yet contested this claim.
God makes the animals, man makes himself.
Man loves company—even if it is only that of a small burning candle.

Imitation

To do just the opposite is also a form of imitation.

Intelligent Design

The thing that astonished him was that cats should have two holes cut in their coat exactly at the place where their eyes are.

Maturation

Just as we outgrow a pair of trousers, we outgrow acquaintances, libraries, principles, etc., at times before they're worn out and at times—and this is the worst of all—before we have new ones.

. . . the more thoughtful we become the more earnest we grow.

To grow wiser means to learn to know better and better the faults to which this instrument with which we feel and judge can be subject.

Metaphors

We do not think good metaphors are anything very important, but I think that a good metaphor is something even the police should keep an eye on.

Morality

. . . universal morality is to be found in little everyday penny events just as much as in great ones.

Partiality

Man is always partial and is quite right to be. Even impartiality is partial.

Reason and Passion

He was then in his fifty-fourth year, when even in the case of poets reason and passion begin to discuss a peace treaty and usually conclude it not very long afterwards.

Man is to be found in reason, God in the passions.

Scholarship

People often become scholars for the same reason they become soldiers: simply because they are unfit for any other station.

Erudition can produce foliage without bearing fruit.

Much reading has brought upon us a learned barbarism.

Rational free spirits are the light brigade who go on ahead and reconnoitre the ground which the heavy brigade of the orthodox will eventually occupy.

Scientists

The most heated defenders of a science, who cannot endure the slightest sneer at it, are commonly those who have not made very much progress in it and are secretly aware of this defect.

Self-Love

He who is enamored of himself will at least have the advantage of being inconvenienced by few rivals.

Talent

Just as the performance of the vilest and most wicked deeds requires spirit and talent, so even the greatest demand a certain insensitivity which under other circumstances we would call stupidity.

Tranquility

Nothing contributes more to peace of soul than having no opinion at all.

Truth

Even if my philosophy does not extend to discovering anything new, it does nevertheless possess the courage to regard as questionable what has long been thought true.

Even truth needs to be clad in new garments if it is to appeal to a new age.

Soothsayers make a better living in the world than truthsayers.

There are people who believe everything is sane and sensible that is done with a solemn face.

It is almost impossible to bear the torch of truth through a crowd without singeing somebody's beard.

The most dangerous untruths are truths moderately distorted.

Abraham Lincoln

Abraham Lincoln / 1809–1865 / Kentucky, USA / Lawyer, Politician, President

Appeal to the South

In your hands, my dissatisfied fellow-countrymen, and not in mine, is the momentous issue of civil war. The Government will not assail you. You can have no conflict without being yourselves the aggressors. You have no oath registered in heaven to destroy the Government, while I shall have the most solemn one to "preserve, protect, and defend it.

I am loath to close. We are not enemies, but friends. We must not be enemies. Though passion may have strained it must not break our bonds of affection. The mystic chords of memory, stretching from every battlefield and patriot grave to every living heart and hearthstone all over this broad land, will yet swell the chorus of the Union, when again touched, as surely they will be, by the better angels of our nature.

Source: First Inaugural Address, March 1, 1861.

Character

Character is like a tree and reputation its shadow. The shadow is what we think it is and the tree is the real thing.

Source: oral tradition; first published in Anthony Gross, Lincoln's Own Stories (1912).

Limits to Disinformation

You can fool some of the people all of the time, and all of the people some of the time, but you can not fool all of the people all of the time.

Source: doubtful attribution.

Meaning of the Civil War

If we could first know *where* we are, and *whither* we are tending, we could then better judge *what* to do, and *how* to do it. We are now far into the *fifth* year, since a policy was initiated, with the *avowed* object, and *confident* promise, of putting an end to slavery agitation. Under the operation of that policy, that agitation has not only, *not ceased*, but has *constantly augmented*. In *my* opinion, it *will* not cease, until a *crisis* shall have been reached, and passed.

"A house divided against itself cannot stand." (Matthew 12:25)

I believe this government cannot endure, permanently half *slave* and half *free*.

Source: Speech, Republican State Convention, Springfield, Illinois, June 16, 1858.

The fiery trial through which we pass will light us down in honor or dishonor to the latest generation. We say we are for the Union. The world will not forget that we say this. We know how to save the Union. The world knows we do know how to save it. We, even we here, hold the power and bear the responsibility. In giving freedom to the slave we assure freedom to the free–honorable alike in what we give and what we preserve. We shall nobly save or meanly lose the last best hope of earth.

Source: State of the Union address, December 1, 1862.

Four score and seven years ago our fathers brought forth on this continent a new nation, conceived in liberty, and dedicated to the proposition that all men are created equal. “Now we are engaged in a great civil war, testing whether that nation, or any nation so conceived and so dedicated, can long endure. We are met on a great battlefield of that war. We have come to dedicate a portion of that field as a final resting place for those who here gave their lives that that nation might live. It is altogether fitting and proper that we should do this. But in a larger sense we cannot dedicate, we cannot consecrate, we cannot hallow this ground. The brave men, living and dead, who struggled here have consecrated it, far above our poor power to add or detract. The world will little note, nor long remember, what we say here, but it can never forget what they did here. It is for us the living, rather, to be dedicated here to the unfinished work which they who fought here have thus far so nobly advanced. It is rather for us to be here dedicated to the great task remaining before us,that from these honored dead we take increased devotion to that cause for which they gave the last full measure of devotion, that we here highly resolve that these dead shall not have died in vain, that this nation, under God, shall have a new birth of freedom, and that government of the people, by the people, for the people, shall not perish from the earth.

Source: Gettysburg Address, Gettysburg, Pennsylvania, November 19, 1863.

If we shall suppose that American slavery is one of those offenses which, in the providence of God, must needs come, but which, having continued through His appointed time, He now wills to remove, and that He gives to both North and South this terrible war as the woe due to those by whom the offense came, shall we discern therein any departure from those divine attributes which the believers in a living God always ascribe to Him? Fondly do we hope, fervently do we pray, that this mighty scourge of war may speedily pass away. Yet, if God wills that it continue until all the wealth piled by the bondsman’s two hundred and fifty years of unrequited toil shall be sunk, and until every drop of blood drawn with the lash shall be paid by another drawn with the sword, as was said three thousand years ago, so still it must be said “the judgments of the Lord are true and righteous altogether.

Source: Second Inaugural Address, March 4, 1865.

With malice toward none, with charity for all, with firmness in the right as God gives us to see the right, let us strive on to finish the work we are in, to bind up the nation’s wounds, to care for him who shall have borne the battle and for his widow and his orphan, to do all which may achieve and cherish a just and lasting peace among ourselves and with all nations.

Source: Second Inaugural Address, March 4, 1865.

Walter Lippmann

Walter Lippmann / 1889–1974 / New York, New York, USA / Journalist, Commentator, Author

The Civilized State

The first principle of a civilized state is that the power is legitimate only when it is under contract.

An Inquiry into the Principles of the Good Society (1937).

The final test of a civilization is whether or not it can persuade men to take the time and the trouble to think for themselves.

A Preface to Morals (1929).

Freedom

The truth is that men are tired of liberty.

A Preface to Morals (1929).

Most men, after a little freedom, have preferred authority with the consoling assurances and the economy of effort it brings.

A Preface to Morals (1929).

Good Government

The final test of a good government is whether it can protect the interests of the country against the greed and selfishness of powerful private interests.

The Good Society (1937).

Journalism

There can be no higher law in journalism than to tell the truth and to shame the devil.

Liberty and the News (1920).

The art of newspaper paragraphing is to stroke a platitude until it purrs like an epigram.

A Preface to Morals (1929).

The news of the day as it reaches the newspaper office is an incredible medley of fact, propaganda, rumor, suspicion, clues, hopes, and fears, and the task of selecting and ordering that news is one of the truly sacred and priestly offices in a democracy.

Liberty and the News (1920).

The news and truth are not the same thing, and must be clearly distinguished.

Public Opinion (1922).

Leadership

The final test of a leader is that he leaves behind him in other men the conviction and the will to carry on.

Men of Destiny (1927).

Politics

When men are brought face to face with their opponents, forced to listen and learn and mend their ideas, they cease to be children and savages and begin to live like civilized men.

A Preface to Politics (1913).

The opposition is indispensable. A good statesman, like any other sensible human being, always learns more from his opposition than from his fervent supporters.

A Preface to Politics (1913).

People do not want words—they want the sound of battle.

A Preface to Politics (1913).

The very first lesson that ought to be taught us when we are old enough to understand it, is that we live in a world which is so full of interests that we cannot possibly get to know them all.

Public Opinion (1922).

Public Opinion

Where all think alike, no one thinks very much.

Liberty and the News (1920).

The private citizen, beset by partisan appeals for the loan of his Public Opinion, will soon see, perhaps, that these appeals are not a compliment to his intelligence, but an imposition on his good nature and an insult to his sense of evidence.

Public Opinion (1922).

The public is not a blank sheet to be written on. It is a complex and vital organization that takes more time to reach and understand than does a congressman or a senator.

Public Opinion (1922).

The more vigorously the proposition is denied, the more often it is repeated, the more fervently it is believed.

Public Opinion (1922).

It requires wisdom to understand wisdom: the music is nothing if the audience is deaf."

A Preface to Morals (1929).

Public Servants

In government offices which are sensitive to the vehemence and passion of mass sentiment public men have no sure tenure. They are in effect perpetual office seekers, always on trial for their political lives, always required to court their restless constituents.

Public Opinion (1922).

Reform

Unless the reformer can invent something which substitutes attractive virtues for attractive vices, he will fail.

The Phantom Public (1925).

Revolution

In the end, the revolution devours its own children. It creates a new set of vested interests and a new hierarchy of power. It leaves behind a new elite and a new proletariat. It offers new opportunities for greed, deception, and cruelty.

The Phantom Public (1925).

Scientism

The radical novelty of modern science lies precisely in the rejection of the belief, which is at the heart of all popular religion, that the forces which move the stars and atoms are contingent upon the preferences of the human heart.

A Preface to Morals (1929).

Glenn Cartman Loury

Glenn Cartman Loury / b. 1948 / Chicago, Illinois, USA / Professor of Economics, Author, Podcaster
Note: The specific sources of the following quotations are unknown.

Criminal Justice

The land of the free—we've got an army marching around the world under the banner of freedom, and yet, we are the most unfree society, in terms of institutions of the deprivation of liberty, of incarceration. The incidence of incarceration is higher in the United States than elsewhere in the world.
You can put a person in jail for five years, for 10 years, or 20 years, for the same crime. We're deciding on 10 years to 20 years, when five years would be enough. Okay. The deterrent value, the additional amount of leverage that you get over a criminal to keep them from breaking the law in the first place, associated with making the sentences longer, is *de minimis*; it's essentially nothing.
The primary contact between Black men and the government today is the prison system.
Never before has a supposedly free country denied basic liberty to so many of its citizens. In December 2006, some 2.25 million persons were being held in the nearly 5,000 prisons and jails that are scattered across America's urban and rural landscapes. . . . On average, state inmates have fewer than 11 years of schooling. They are also vastly disproportionately black and brown.
Today, 15 years after crime peaked, the American prison system has become a leviathan unmatched in human history. Never has a supposedly 'free country' denied basic liberty to so many of its citizens. . . . We have become a nation of jailers.

Critical Race Theory

[Speaking with John McWhorter]:
I take umbrage at the lionization of lightweight, empty-suited, empty-headed mother*****s like Ibram X. Kendi. Who couldn't carry my book bag. He hasn't read a f*****g thing. If you ask him what Nietzsche said, he would have no idea. He's an unserious, superficial, empty-suited, lightweight—he's not our equal, not even close.

Drugs

We can see in retrospect that criminalizing the consumption of alcohol proves not to be the solution to the very real problem of drunkenness. So to what I want to say is the very real problem of the human susceptibility to addiction isn't best dealt with by building prisons and throwing people into jails.
My mouth is no prayer book, but my view is, I'd view addiction to these substances as a medical problem and I would treat it accordingly. What little I know about the history of drug control policy in the United States leaves me thinking that a hugely important

moment came when the lawyers win out over the doctors on this matter.
The drug problem in this country is a consumption issue.

Education

The pursuit of knowledge and education is a path towards empowerment and progress.

Equality of Opportunity

Equality of opportunity is a fundamental principle of justice, and we must work towards achieving it for all.

Healthcare

America is the only advanced industrial democracy where people can get sick and languish because they can't afford care. Or where people are blocked in access to the system because they don't have access to insurance, which is only available through certain narrow portals and under certain very restricted conditions. We're the only society that hasn't embraced this idea that no one should go without access to these services, regardless of their financial condition. And no one should be saddled with a lifetime of debt because they have the misfortune of falling ill.
If you have a system that says everybody who needs healthcare gets it and we're going to make sure that it gets paid for by raising your taxes and providing the requirements on individuals where they have the ability to pay, such as we determine as appropriate, then the insurance issue doesn't come up.

Human Dignity

True progress can only be achieved when we recognize the dignity and worth of every individual, regardless of their background.

Loury on Loury

I'm left. Okay. And sometimes radically, and sometimes I even shock myself with the degree of radicalness in my own—that I'm allowing to come out in my old age.
[Re: Brown University]:
The facilities are magnificent, the campus is beautiful—I even like living four days a week in Providence, which I never thought I was going to do.
I was a hot commodity . . . Being African-American didn't hurt me—I was one of the leading young theoretical economists of the generation.
What I was wrong about was not realizing that in my saying those things in the way I said them had political consequences . . . It wasn't just a matter about being right. Being right about something isn't good enough. You also have to be smart about it.
[Re: Loury's drug problems during the 1980s]:
I got my life back together and I haven't looked back.

Public Discourse

Every now and then when I hear someone called a racist, I just mentally insert the word "witch." And it almost always works. What they're actually doing is they're calling you a witch.
I object to the soft tyranny of having political postures put forward as self-evident truths to which every decent member of this community should subscribe. I object to that.

Racial Disparity

The persistence of racial inequality in America is a scandal. We must confront it, honestly and forthrightly.
We need to have open and honest discussions about race in order to move forward as a society.

Racial problems can't be easily reconciled with a pat account about racism and discrimination that lets us sort of relax into saying when we finally get this right, when we get rid of racism, when we reach the post-racial society, everything is going to be okay. Well, no, because along the way here, as we've not yet been in this racial nirvana, facts on the ground have been created.

There are many disparities, and for every disparity, there are alternative explanations that one can bring to bear, but structural racism doesn't even attempt to provide an explanation. It attempts to maneuver you into a corner rhetorically so that you must concede it's not the fault of the people who suffered the condition at hand.

I'm not saying that you won't find many patterns or practices of racial mistreatment in history, but I'm saying that the link between them and the contemporary circumstances of African American communities, especially at the bottom end, is woefully inadequate to explain what we see.

Slavery ended a long time ago, but the institution of chattel slavery and the ideology of racial subordination that accompanied it have cast a long shadow. I speak here of the history of lynching throughout the country; the racially biased policing and judging in the South under Jim Crow and in the cities of the Northeast, Midwest, and West to which blacks migrated after the First and Second World Wars; and the history of racial apartheid that ended only as a matter of law with the civil-rights movement. It should come as no surprise that in the post–civil rights era, race, far from being peripheral, has been central to the evolution of American social policy.

Reparations

I don't want to see the issue of Black reparations for slavery close the door to historic memory and continuing responsibility.

War

The fact that we don't' talk about it, that we don't have a politics in which this question of war and peace can even get onto the table, so that we can open up our Orwell, our *1984*, or *Animal Farm*, or whatever, and read the political text that's being spotted to us on the television right off of the page; the fact that we don't have a politics robust enough to actually debate whether or not we want to be a country permanently at war. That's what keeps me from sleeping at night

Welfare

My sermon for us Americans would be to construct the kind of institutions of mutuality and social cooperation that don't leave 15 or 20 percent of our people falling through the cracks. We can do it. It's not like we don't know what to do. It's not like there aren't models there. It's not like this isn't being done elsewhere. It's not like we can't afford to do it. It's a question of political will and it's about our definition as a people.

Glenn Michael Malice

Michael Malice, né Michael Krechmer / b. 1976 / Lviv, Ukraine, USSR / Author, Ghost-writer, Television Commentator, Podcaster
Note: The sources of the following quotations are provided where known. Otherwise, it may be assumed that quotations derive from Malice's numerous writings and online commentaries, interviews, and podcasts

American Society

To realize that we live in an absurd culture where we are taught absurd things by absurd people and threatened with absurd consequences for defying all of it is to achieve a level of contentment.

The New Right: A Journey to the Fringe of American Politics(2019).

Anarchism

The black flag comes in many colors.

The Anarchist Handbook (2021).

What are presented as the best arguments against anarchism are inevitably a description of the status quo,

Twitter, 2020.

Brexit

The Cathedral predicted that Brexit wouldn't pass, and that if it did pass there would be disastrous consequences. Neither of these came true.

The New Right: A Journey to the Fringe of American Politics(2019).

Conservatism

Conservatism is progressivism driving the speed limit.

COVID-19

Intentionally or not, some very, very bad people got some very useful information of how much the populace was willing to put up with. . . . There was clearly a consideration on the parts of the authorities in each country about "What can we do and what [can we] get away with?"

"YOUR WELCOME" with Michael Malice, #198: Lauren Southern, March 16, 2022.

Democracy

. . . in a democracy someone is setting the guidelines for everyone else. Elitist rule is inevitable.

The New Right: A Journey to the Fringe of American Politics(2019).

Democracy entails people who run their businesses well being forced to run their businesses poorly by people who can't run businesses at all.

The New Right: A Journey to the Fringe of American Politics(2019).

Perhaps it will be said that this consent is not a specific, but a general, one, and that the citizen is understood to have assented to everything his representative may do, when he voted for him. But suppose he did not vote for him; and on the contrary did all in his power to get elected someone holding opposite views—what then? The reply will probably be that by taking part in such an election, he tacitly agreed to abide by the decision of the majority. And how if he did not vote at all? Why then he cannot justly complain of any tax, seeing that he made no protest against its imposition. So, curiously enough, it seems that he gave his consent in whatever way he acted—whether he said "Yes," whether he said "No," or whether he remained neutral! A rather awkward doctrine . . .

The Anarchist Handbook (2021).

Free Speech

The claim "hate speech is not free speech" implies "free" is a type of speech, as opposed to how speech is treated in a free society.

History

[T]hrough the centuries men have formed concepts designed to check and limit the exercise of State rule; and, one after another, the State, using its intellectual allies, has been able to transform these concepts into intellectual rubber stamps of legitimacy and virtue to attach to its decrees and actions.

The Anarchist Handbook (2021).

Human Nature

Those driven by emotion (children, the mentally ill, hormonal men and women alike) don't freak out when they get their way; they freak out when they're not getting their way.

The New Right: A Journey to the Fringe of American Politics(2019).

Leaders

Those who need leaders are not qualified to choose them.

The New Right: A Journey to the Fringe of American Politics(2019).

People will say with a straight face that having one choice for dear leader is tyranny —but having two is freedom.

The Anarchist Handbook (2021).

Left vs. Right

The political binary is the dumbest of all. It's based on the seating system in the old French legislature, and I refuse to base my life on anything French.

The New Right: A Journey to the Fringe of American Politics(2019).

Malice on Malice

I have no interest in reaching the general population. The general population are the people who would have been Nazis in the 40s and they would have been jihadis or sympathetic in some of these other countries 20 years ago. So they will always follow the ruling class.

Interview, "A Friendly Chat with Michael Malice," Sargon of Akkad, June 22, 2021.

You have all these choices at the supermarket and then you go to government, which is far more important than what brand of soda you drink, and you're told it's got to be Boris Johnson or Jeremy Corbyn. To hell with that! I want my views and I want to live my life and you setting up this false alternative is completely unacceptable. I'm not playing this game.

Interview, "A Friendly Chat with Michael Malice," Sargon of Akkad, June 22, 2021.

The Media

What corporate media does, which is far more nefarious than the state, is simultaneously it will tell the audience "These are the issues you should be concerned about today, and . . . here's how you should think about it." So very quickly it gives the person, who is often marginally intelligent, both the concerns of the day, which is just kind of like a fashion issue, but also the answer so that not only do they look sympathetic and empathetic they also simultaneously seem informed. . . . If you go to [public places] and you hear how these people talk, you realize they are parroting . . . almost verbatim, if not verbatim, the people that they saw on their own screen . . . and when you have that epiphany you realize this kind of conservative model that "We are just going to teach the population to respect people's rights and in a 100 years we are going to be free" is really not a tenable one.

Interview, "A Friendly Chat with Michael Malice," Sargon of Akkad, June 22, 2021.

If you're dealing with a journalist who you perceive as being engaged in good faith, and there's plenty of them, when you explain a particular view that you know is outside of their worldview, ask them to explain it back to you to see that they got what you meant. And if you have that on tape and they try to mis-characterize you, so much the better, now you have evidence that this was done maliciously.

Interview, "A Friendly Chat with Michael Malice," Sargon of Akkad, June 22, 2021.

The battle is won when the average American regards a corporate journalist exactly as they regard a tobacco executive. Once you realize that's what you're dealing with, everything falls into place. Okay, this guy wants to sell me cancer, he makes money selling me cancer, he knows he's selling me cancer. I'm not going to get him to say that [cigarettes] are cancer, but now I can proceed accordingly knowing that this is going to be about promoting [cigarettes] or parliaments or whatever it is.

Interview, "A Friendly Chat with Michael Malice," Sargon of Akkad, June 22, 2021.

If you read a play, a lot of times at the beginning of the play there will be that cast of characters and it will say like "Jane, a wealthy widow seeking love," "Thomas, her young paramour." When they bring a character onto the scene in a corporate news article, it will say "Joe Rogan, a podcaster known for his history of transphobic remarks," "Scott Adams, the disgraced . . ." They will immediately tell you from their personal perspective how you should feel about this person before they even finish the sentence. And once you spot that this is the technique, you can't unsee it.

"YOUR WELCOME" with Michael Malice, #278: Scott Adams, September 27, 2023.

The New Right

A loosely connected group of individuals united by their opposition to progressivism, which they perceive to be a thinly veiled fundamentalist religion dedicated to egalitarian principles and intent on totalitarian world domination via globalist hegemony.

The New Right: A Journey to the Fringe of American Politics(2019).

The New Right is of the fringe (and I say that as an anarchist), and the fringe is where both innovation and insanity lie.

The New Right: A Journey to the Fringe of American Politics(2019).

For years, the New Right has had little political representation and been treated as beneath notice by the mainstream press. This is no longer an option, especially in a social media world. Its members are smart, they are organized, and, most importantly, they do have a very coherent worldview. Illiterately tweeting "YOUR RACIST" over and over at one's enemies is not enough to silence millions of people.

The New Right: A Journey to the Fringe of American Politics(2019).

Police

Re: the 1993 siege and ultimate attack on the Branch Davidian compound near Waco, Texas.

There is no law so obscene that the police would not be willing to enforce it, up to and including the mass execution of innocent children.

Twitter, 2021.

Politics

"We need" is always code for "I want."

According to [Murray] Rothbard, complete gridlock is the best one can hope for in Washington. A paralyzed government was fairly close to his anarchist ideal.

The New Right: A Journey to the Fringe of American Politics(2019).

Twenty-five years later, Pat Buchanan has been proven correct. There is a religious war going on in our country for the soul of America. On one side of the battlefield is the religion known as progressivism. On the other stands the New Right.

The New Right: A Journey to the Fringe of American Politics(2019).

In a sense, asking people to make political decisions is like asking them to forecast the weather. They're not in a position to do so, and it is silly to expect them to.

The New Right: A Journey to the Fringe of American Politics(2019).

Progressives

"The personal is the political" is a totalitarian progressive decree that I reject entirely.

The New Right: A Journey to the Fringe of American Politics(2019).

. . . the language of these intellectually impoverished young people is larded with ready-made phrases. They quote Stalin instead of thinking for themselves; they derive their opinion from *Pravda* editorials. They are arrogant and complacent, and everything that pertains to them is the greatest thing there is.

The White Pill: A Tale of Good and Evil (2022).

When you have a fundamentalist faith you are certain that you are on the side of the angels.

Interview, The Rubin Report, January 29, 2020.

Come at that conversation appreciating that what they're spouting now has become their identity and also has become their status. So you're asking them to give up something both that matters to them on an emotional and values level, but also from an evolutionary-psychology level.

Interview, "A Friendly Chat with Michael Malice," Sargon of Akkad, June 22, 2021.

Rights

My rights are not up for discussion, let alone a vote, whether it be 75% of the population, the will of one king, or the whim of 100 senators.

Twitter, 2022.

Trump

Here in 2016, when Trump got elected, what happened as a consequence was blue-pilled leftists for a long time were taught that the Trump-world view . . . [was a minority view]. "We have sat you down for a year and told you that voting for Trump is completely unacceptable. That to do so is effectively to decree yourself to be aligned with the Klan and the Nazis." [One of the big newspapers] had a front page of Trump called Antichrist when the Pope criticized him for something during when he was just merely a candidate. And yet Americans went in and flicked the leaver for Hitler-Antichrist. And they didn't know what to do because in their mind there is very few of these lunatics and now there's enough to elect the president . . . They thought "100 percent of the people I know," but obviously it's not 100. At best it's [60 percent]. So this was . . . a moment of panic: "Wait a minute! I don't know who these people are anymore!"

"YOUR WELCOME" with Michael Malice, #198: Lauren Southern, March 16, 2022.

Tyranny of the Experts

There will be a new class, a new hierarchy of real and pretended scientists and scholars, and the world will be divided into a minority ruling in the name of knowledge and an immense ignorant majority. And then, woe betide the mass of ignorant ones!

The Anarchist Handbook (2021).

Gamergate was an important moment in proving the existence of the Cathedral, the idea that what is being presented as fact is actually a carefully coordinated movement by elites to establish and impose their view of what reality is and how it should be.

The Anarchist Handbook (2021).

Marissa Mayer

Marissa Ann Mayer / b. 1975 / Wisconsin, USA / Businesswoman, Investor, Google Executive, Yahoo! CEO, Founder of Sunshine Contacts and Lumi Labs

Burnout

I have a theory that burnout is about resentment. And you beat it by knowing what it is you're giving up that makes you resentful.

Reported by Matthew Toren in "Marissa Explains It All: 5 Motivating Quotes From Yahoo's CEO," entrepreneur.com, July 17, 2014.

Business Philosophy

I always did something I was a little not ready to do. I think that's how you grow. When there's that moment of "Wow, I'm not really sure I can do this," and you push through those moments, that's when you have a breakthrough.

Reported by Matthew Toren in "Marissa Explains It All: 5 Motivating Quotes From Yahoo's CEO," entrepreneur.com, July 17, 2014.

There are different phases of companies. When you're in the tens of people, the idea itself either attracts people or it doesn't. People are there because they think the problem you're trying to solve is just that important.

Reported by David Gelles in "Marissa Mayer is Still Here," nytimes.com, April 18, 2018.

I've heard our strategy described as spreading peanut butter across the myriad opportunities that continue to evolve in the online world. The result: a thin layer of investment spread across everything we do and thus we focus on nothing in particular. I hate peanut butter. We all should.

Reported by Nicholas Carlson in Marissa Mayer and the Fight to Save Yahoo! (2015).

You know, there's some people . . . they're like, "I love it when it's 10 people or less," like working in a garage. And there's some people who are like, "Oh, I just love it when you're a couple hundred people and you're starting to hit that inflection point of growth." And there's, I mean, who are just like, "Look, if it's not operating at scale of thousands or tens of thousands of people and doesn't have, you know, hundreds of millions of users, like, what's it all for?" And I love every phase of that.

I love it when it's small and everyone's [an] individual contributor. I like managing small teams. I like managing large teams. I love the impact and scale of running and being part of a big organization. I love the growth. I even love the challenges.

Interview with Elizabeth Bramson-Boudreau, "Marissa Mayer on the rise of women technology leaders," MIT Technology Review, technologyreview.com, October 3, 2019.

"Cultural DNA"

I think I've always thought of culture as DNA. I don't know a lot about genetics, but I understand some of it and I think that what you really want are the genes that are positive to hyper-express themselves in culture.

Reported by Patricia Sellers in "Transcript: Marissa Mayer at Fortune MPW [Most Powerful Women]," fortune.com, October 17, 2013.

Gender

If you can find something that you're really passionate about, whether you're a man or a woman comes a lot less into play. Passion is a gender-neutralizing force.

Reported by Matthew Toren in "Marissa Explains It All: 5 Motivating Quotes From Yahoo's CEO," entrepreneur.com, July 17, 2014.

Google

I was at Google. And if you looked at Tumblr and Yahoo!, you know when you look at a map and you can see the way that South America and Africa used to fit together, I sort of joked that as we got to know Tumblr we were like we kind of felt like those continents, like our users were older, their users were younger.

Reported by Patricia Sellers in "Transcript: Marissa Mayer at Fortune MPW [Most Powerful Women]," fortune.com, October 17, 2013.

Someone even suggested the insane idea that Google should scan all the libraries in the world and put every book ever written online. But no one laughed the idea off. They started to think about how it could be done.

Reported by Nicholas Carlson in Marissa Mayer and the Fight to Save Yahoo! (2015).

Leadership

I think it's really important to be authentic and true to yourself in terms of what you think the right thing to do is in a particular moment. I think people respect that type of leadership and while certainly some of those moves might be misunderstood outside, to me, I always have looked at how does the organization respond to those moves?

Interview with Elizabeth Bramson-Boudreau, "Marissa Mayer on the rise of women technology leaders," MIT Technology Review, technologyreview.com, October 3, 2019.

Lumi Labs

We're a tech incubator in more of the old school train of thought. We're not an investment firm, so we're not investing in other people's startups, or finding teams to invest in. We have a series of ideas that we'd like to explore, applications we'd like to build. Some of them are theses that we could actually base a product line around. And so we've worked on hiring very capable engineers who could work on any range of products, and have been staffing them to start to build these products. That said, right now we look much more like a traditional startup because we're working on our first idea. It's become fairly well developed and we want to bring it to market.

Interview with Elizabeth Bramson-Boudreau, "Marissa Mayer on the rise of women technology leaders," MIT Technology Review, technologyreview.com, October 3, 2019.

Mayer on Mayer

I didn't set out to be at the top of technology companies. I'm just geeky and shy and I like to code.

Reported by Jacob Weisberg in "Yahoo's Marissa Mayer: Hail to the Chief," vogue.com, August 15, 2013.

It was a very well-rounded childhood, with lots of different opportunities. My mom will say she set out to overstimulate me—surround me with way too many things and let me pick. As a result, I've always been a multitasker; I've always liked a lot of variety.

Reported by Jacob Weisberg in "Yahoo's Marissa Mayer: Hail to the Chief," vogue.com, August 15, 2013.

It was the height of the first boom, so it was 1999. It was a good year to be a graduate in computer science.

Reported by Patricia Sellers in "Transcript: Marissa Mayer at Fortune MPW [Most Powerful Women]," fortune.com, October 17, 2013.

I really like even numbers, and I like heavily divisible numbers. Twelve is my lucky number—I just love how divisible it is. I don't like odd numbers, and I really don't like primes. When I turned 37, I put on a strong face, but I was not looking forward to 37. But 37 turned out to be a pretty amazing year. Especially considering that 36 is divisible by twelve!

Reported by Jacob Weisberg in "Yahoo's Marissa Mayer: Hail to the Chief," vogue.com, August 15, 2013.

One night I looked up and was like, "Oh, my God, it's midnight and I have a husband and I'm, like, eight months pregnant. I need to leave!" I was just here working, having the best possible time. When Zack and I were brushing our teeth in the morning, he was like, "Where were you last night?"

Reported by Jacob Weisberg in "Yahoo's Marissa Mayer: Hail to the Chief," vogue.com, August 15, 2013.

. . . in 2008, I had gotten engaged. It was a great and fun time in my life. Unfortunately for Silicon Valley, Gawker had come to town and had created a blog about us. And there were various characters that made appearances on there. And unfortunately, I was one of them. And it was, you know, it was a caricature of me. It wasn't me. And, you know, they wrote really awful articles. And I was like, you know, wait, it's one thing to criticize my product decisions, my career, my business, the arts and leadership. But it's whole 'nother to go into the personal realm where. My fiancé wasn't a public person. And things like that.

Interview with Elizabeth Bramson-Boudreau, "Marissa Mayer on the rise of women technology leaders," MIT Technology Review, technologyreview.com, October 3, 2019.

Silicon Valley

I've heard both the founding stories of Google and Yahoo, and for both those companies, the founders didn't even have to get into a car. They could literally go to the law office, the venture capitalists, the bank . . . on a bike. It's all that close together.

Reported by Adam Fisher in Valley of Genius: The Uncensored History of Silicon Valley (As Told by the Hackers, Founders, and Freaks Who Made It Boom) (2018).

Technology

You can be good at technology and like fashion and art. You can be good at technology and be a jock. You can be good at technology and be a mom. You can do it your way, on your terms.

Reported by Matthew Toren in "Marissa Explains It All: 5 Motivating Quotes From Yahoo's CEO," entrepreneur.com, July 17, 2014.

It's really wonderful to work in an environment with a lot of smart people.

Reported by Matthew Toren in "Marissa Explains It All: 5 Motivating Quotes

From Yahoo's CEO," entrepreneur.com, July 17, 2014.

. . . when I was starting out, I was an oddity in computer science and women were maybe the minority in computer science. But I was an oddity to the point where, a lot of my schoolmates had been programming since they were 11. You ended up being a programmer if you were a teenage boy, really into video games and science fiction. And I didn't fit that mold. And I think a lot of those stereotypes, because technology has become so much more pervasive and people now understand the kinds of opportunities and applications that can be built on the Internet I think that people have a much better understanding of how becoming a software engineer has can ultimately have an impact on what you're doing day to day. And that helps a lot with people entering computer science overall, both men and women.

Interview with Elizabeth Bramson-Boudreau, "Marissa Mayer on the rise of women technology leaders," MIT Technology Review, technologyreview.com, October 3, 2019.

Tumblr

[Founder] David Karp is just incredibly special. I like to think that I'm good at empathy, but I will say that David Karp is just incredibly empathetic and really in tune with the community of people that he has, that are contributing and creating on Tumblr.

Reported by Patricia Sellers in "Transcript: Marissa Mayer at Fortune MPW [Most Powerful Women]," fortune.com, October 17, 2013.

Yahoo!

Now I think we're on the mobile wave. . . . I think that the big piece here is that it really allows us to partner. Yahoo! has always been a very friendly company.

Reported by Alexis Kleinman in "Marissa Mayer Lays Out Plan To Save Yahoo at Davos," huffpost.com, January 25, 2013.

"Pay-Pal." People wrote down "payments." He said "Google." People wrote down "search." He said "eBay" and they wrote "auctions." After a few more companies, he said "Yahoo!" He collected the thirty pieces of paper on Yahoo! Everybody had a different word. What was Yahoo! trying to be? No one inside the company knew anymore.

Reported by Nicholas Carlson in Marissa Mayer and the Fight to Save Yahoo! (2015).

[Jerry] Yang believed Microsoft made ugly, bad products. Its besuited culture was so the opposite of Yahoo!'s.

Reported by Nicholas Carlson in Marissa Mayer and the Fight to Save Yahoo! (2015).

[Scott] Thompson announced that Yahoo! was going to sue Facebook over patent infringement. The move deeply embarrassed both the engineers at Yahoo, who thought that kind of behavior was for trolls, and the media people at Yahoo! who depended on traffic partnerships with Facebook to build audiences.

Reported by Nicholas Carlson in Marissa Mayer and the Fight to Save Yahoo! (2015).

If Microsoft and Yahoo! didn't combine, Google was going to own the Internet forever.

Reported by Nicholas Carlson in Marissa Mayer and the Fight to Save Yahoo! (2015).

. . . it was becoming unwise to send a résumé from an email address with an "@yahoo.com" at the end.

Reported by Nicholas Carlson in Marissa Mayer and the Fight to Save Yahoo! (2015).

I'm proud of what we achieved at Yahoo! That said, we had a quickly decaying legacy business. All we really managed to do was offset the declines.

Reported by David Gelles in "Marissa Mayer is Still Here," nytimes.com, April 18, 2018.

One of my key learnings from Yahoo! is that timing is everything. There was a time when Yahoo!'s offerings could consume hours a day, and trying to regain that moment in time was really hard. We could make the products really good, but regaining that contextual relevance that was afforded to Yahoo! in 1999 and the early 2000s was difficult.

Reported by David Gelles in "Marissa Mayer is Still Here," nytimes.com, April 18, 2018.

John McAfee

John David McAfee / 1945–2021 / Gloucestershire, United Kingdom / Computer Programmer, Entrepreneur, Investor, Founder of McAfee Associates, Inc.

Belize

Note: McAfee lived in Belize from 2009 until 2013. While there, he was arrested on a charge of murder.

Belize is so raw and so clear and so in-your-face. There's an opportunity to see something about human nature that you can't really see in a politer society, because the purpose of society is to mask ourselves from each other.

Reported by Joshua Davis in "John McAfee Fled to Belize, but he couldn't escape himself," wired.com, December 24, 2012.

My fragile connection with the world of polite society has, without a doubt, been severed. My attire would rank me among the worst-dressed Tijuana panhandlers. My hygiene is no better. Yesterday, for the first time, I urinated in public, in broad daylight.

Reported by Joshua Davis in "John McAfee Fled to Belize, but he couldn't escape himself," wired.com, December 24, 2012.

I have no illusions. We are tainted by everything we touch.

Reported by Joshua Davis in "John McAfee Fled to Belize, but he couldn't escape himself," wired.com, December 24, 2012.

Computer Viruses

A virus is a computer program created to infect other programs with copies of itself. It has the ability to clone itself, so that it can multiply, constantly seeking new host environments.

John McAfee and Colin Haynes, Computer Viruses, Worms, Data Diddlers, Killer Programs, and Other Threats to Your System (1989).

The reality is so alarming that it would be very difficult to exaggerate. Even if no new viruses are ever created, there are already enough circulating to cause a growing problem as they reproduce. A major disaster seems inevitable.

John McAfee and Colin Haynes, Computer Viruses, Worms, Data Diddlers, Killer Programs, and Other Threats to Your System (1989).

Confidence

Ignorance and confidence are constant companions.

John McAfee, Into the Heart of Truth: The Spirit of Relational Yoga (2001).

Drugs

Note: To the accusation that McAfee had communicated with drug traffickers regarding the designer drug, MDPV, McAfee responded:

It was the most tongue-in-cheek thing in the f***ing world. . . . If I'm gonna do drugs, I'm gonna do something that I know is good. I'm gonna grab some mushrooms, number one, and maybe get some really fine cocaine. But anybody who knows me knows I never do drugs.

Reported by Joshua Davis in "John McAfee Fled to Belize, but he couldn't escape himself," wired.com, December 24, 2012.

Examples

A good example is more irritating than a bad one.

Answer during Q&A following presentation, Munich, Germany, January, 1991.

Facts

If you own the facts, you may distort them as you like.

Roundtable, anti–computer virus conference, 1992.

Going One's Own Way

I think that it's when we step out of the road, step outside the box, become our own person and we walk fearlessly down paths other people wouldn't look at, that true progress comes. And sometimes true beauty as well.

Interview with Leo Kelion, "John McAfee: Addict, Coder, Runaway," BBC News, bbc.com, October 11, 2013.

Government Corruption

I am not implying that our entire Government is corrupt. I am saying that it is corrupt to the point that no-one is untouched by it.

McAfee tweet, June 10, 2019.

History

History is sympathetic to its authors.

John McAfee, Into the Heart of Truth: The Spirit of Relational Yoga (2001).

Hope

Hope is paltry food for living.

John McAfee, Into the Heart of Truth: The Spirit of Relational Yoga (2001).

Individual Opinion

Opinions need a willing ear.

John McAfee, Beyond the Siddhis: Supernatural Powers and the Sutras of Patanjali (2001).

Majority Opinion

If the majority holds something of value, you can be certain it has none.

Presentation, anti–computer virus conference, Sydney, Australia, 1991.

McAfee on McAfee

Note: McAfee's father committed suicide when his son was 15 years old.

Every day I wake up with him. Every relationship I have, he's by my side; every mistrust, he is the negotiator of that mistrust. So my life is f***ed.

Reported by Joshua Davis in "John McAfee Fled to Belize, but he couldn't escape himself," wired.com, December 24, 2012.

I gravitate to the world's outcasts. Prostitutes, thieves, the handicapped . . . For some reason I have always been fascinated by these subcultures.

Reported by Joshua Davis in "John McAfee Fled to Belize, but he couldn't escape himself," wired.com, December 24, 2012.

People kept saying I hyped this, I hyped this. I never contacted the press—they called me.

Reported by Josh Quittner, New York Newsday, April 5, 1992.

If you have the winning cards, why cheat?

Interview, Good Morning America, ABC, June, 1991; in response to accusation he had falsified VirusScan's capabilities.

Note: On October 5, 2020, Spain arrested McAfee at the request of the US, to face fraud charges connected to cryptocurrency promotion. On June 23, 2021, McAfee was found dead in his prison cell near Barcelona.

Getting subtle messages from U.S. officials saying, in effect: "We're coming for you McAfee! We're going to kill yourself." I got a tattoo today just in case. If I suicide myself, I didn't. I was whacked.

McAfee tweet, December 1, 2019.

I am content in here. I have friends. The food is good. All is well. Know that if I hang myself, à la [Jeffrey] Epstein, it will be no fault of mine.

McAfee tweet, October 16, 2020.

I have nothing. Yet, I regret nothing.

McAfee's final tweet, June 16, 2021.

Obedience

Disobedience is the vehicle of progress.

Reported by Josh Quittner, New York Newsday, April 5, 1992.

Power

There are three kinds of power: the power to create, the power to acquire, and the power to destroy. The power to create Is ever with the people. The other two must be removed from Government. We need a Government with zero power, controlled by an all-powerful people.

McAfee tweet. January 19, 2020.

Software

Software production is unlike any other production that preceded it. No raw materials are required, no time is required, and no effort is required. You can make a million copies of a piece of software instantaneously for free. It's a totally new paradigm of production.

Interview, Nerds 2.0.1—A Brief History of the Internet, Volume Three: Wiring the World, television film directed by John Segaller, PBS, 1998.

John McWhorter

John Hamilton McWhorter V / b. 1965 / Professor of Linguistics, Author, Political Commentator, Podcaster

Note: The specific sources of the following quotations are provided where known. Otherwise, quotations may be assumed to derive from McWhorter's numerous writings, commentaries, and podcasts.

Black Americans

[I] would argue that native-born blacks are so vastly less "African" than actual Africans that calling ourselves "African American" is not only illogical but almost disrespectful to African immigrants. Here are people who were born in Africa, speak African languages, eat African food, dance in African ways, remember African stories, and will spiritually always be a part of Africa—and we stand up and insist that we, too, are "African" because Jesse Jackson said so?

I am not "African American"—I am black American.

As far as I'm concerned, and this is a big theme of mine, I'm not interested in white people loving me. It's an unrealistic expectation. Black people don't love anybody but themselves.

Black English

It would be good if teachers could genuinely understand that black English is not mistakes, it's just different English, and that what you want to do is add an additional dialect to black students' repertoire rather than teaching them out of what's thought of as a bad habit, like sloppy posture or chewing with your mouth open.

Ebonics—or black English, as I prefer to call it—is one of a great many dialects of English. And so English comes in a great many varieties, and black English is one of them.

The contribution of West African languages to Ebonics is absolutely infinitesimal. What it actually is is a very interesting hybrid of regional dialects of Great Britain that slaves in America were exposed to because they often worked alongside the indentured servants who spoke those dialects that we often learn about in school.

Black English is something which—it's a natural system in itself. And even though it is a dialect of English, it can be very difficult for people who don't speak it, or who haven't been raised in it, to understand when it's running by quickly, spoken in particular by young men colloquially to each other. So that really is an issue.

Black English is simpler than standard English in some ways; for example, it often gets by with just "be" and drops "am," "is," and "are." That's because black English arose when adult African slaves learned the language.

People think of black English as ungrammatical, but it bears the same relationship to standard English as contemporary Hebrew does to ancient Hebrew.

Drugs

The war on drugs is what makes thugs.

Education

Black boys do commit more violent offenses in public schools than other kids. Period. This means that if we follow these prophets' advice and go easier on black boys, we hinder the education of other black students. The Elect earnestly decry that most black kids go to school with only other black kids, because it fits into their agenda to point out "segregation." But that "segregation" also entails that the black boys they think should be allowed to beat other kids up in school are handing out the beatings to other black kids.

Woke Racism: How a New Religion Has Betrayed Black America (2021).

Electronic Media

"LOL" is one of several texting expressions that convey nuance in a system where you don't have the voice and face to do it the way you normally would.

People banging away on their smartphones are fluently using a code separate from the one they use in actual writing, but a code it is, to which linguists are currently devoting articles.

English

As languages go, English is pretty user friendly. If you look at a tiny language spoken somewhere that most of us have never heard of, chances are it's going to be so complicated that you have a hard time imagining how people can walk around speaking it without having a stroke.

English, however, is kinky. It has a predilection for dressing up like Welsh on lonely nights.

Our Magnificent Bastard Tongue: The Untold Story of English(2008).

Human Nature

A person you excuse from any genuine challenge is a person you do not truly respect.

Losing the Race: Self-Sabotage in Black America (2000).

If you want to learn about how humans differ, study cultures. However, if you want insight as to what makes all humans worldwide the same, beyond genetics, there are few better places to start than how language works.

The Language Hoax (2014).

Language

Language is always evolving, and we should enjoy it for what it is, not use it to divide us.

Language is a technology that's 5,000 years old. We keep using it because it works.

Learning languages makes you more tolerant and understanding of other cultures.

Loving your language means a command of its vocabulary beyond the level of the everyday.

Most languages spoken by a few thousand people are so complicated they make your head swim; a Siberian yak herder's language is much more complicated than a Manhattan bond trader's.

The Power of Babel: A Natural History of Language (2002).

Language overlaps with culture but is not subsumed by it.

Because all languages are and have always been in a state of continual transformation, anything we see in a language today is the result of change.

The Power of Babel: A Natural History of Language (2002).

Don't tell the Scandinavians I said this, but "Swedish," "Norwegian," and "Danish" are all really one "language."

The Power of Babel: A Natural History of Language (2002).

Poetry

Rap and spoken word have reawakened the country to poetry in itself. Texting and Twitter encourage creative uses of casual language, in ways I have celebrated widely. But we've fallen behind on savoring the formal layer of our language.

In the nineteenth century, poetry was a best-selling genre rather than the cultish phenomenon it is now.

Doing Our Own Thing: The Degradation of Language and Music and Why We Should, Like, Care (2003).

For all but the sliver of poetry fans, over the past forty years popular song lyrics have been the nation's poetry.

Doing Our Own Thing: The Degradation of Language and Music and Why We Should, Like, Care (2003).

Poetry that tames language into tight structures and yet manages to move us comes off as a feat, paralleling ballet or athletic talent in harnessing craft to beauty. When poetry is based on a less rigorous, more impressionistic definition of craft, its appeal depends more on whether one happens to be individually constituted to "get it" for various reasons. The audience narrows: poetry becomes more like tai chi than baseball.

Doing Our Own Thing: The Degradation of Language and Music and Why We Should, Like, Care (2003).

Politics

We need the hard left to point us to new ways of thinking. However, we need them to go back to doing this while seated, with the rest of us, rather than standing up and getting their way by calling us moral perverts if we disagree with them and calling this speaking truth to power."

Woke Racism: How a New Religion Has Betrayed Black America (2021).

We must neither behave as children by resisting honesty, nor allow ourselves to be treated as children by having honesty withheld.

Losing the Race: Self-Sabotage in Black America (2000).

Prescriptive Grammar

Languages are not homogenous. There is no such thing as "proper" English. There is no "pure" anything.

Slang is one of the most important aspects of a language.

People have been warning us that language was going to the dogs ever since Latin started turning into French.

As a linguist, I see the arbitrariness of strictures editors force on me as a writer.

Prescriptive grammar has spread linguistic insecurity like a plague among English speakers for centuries, numbs us to the aesthetic richness of non-standard speech, and distracts us from attending to genuine issues of linguistic style in writing.

Word on the Street: Debunking the Myth of "Pure" Standard English (2001).

In an ideal world, the time English speakers devote to steeling themselves against, and complaining about, things like Billy and me, singular they, and impact as a verb would be better spent attending to genuine matters of graceful oral and written expression.

Our Magnificent Bastard Tongue: The Untold Story of English(2008).

Nota bene: linguists savor articulateness in speech and fine composition in writing as much as anyone else. Our position is not—I repeat, not—that we should chuck standards of graceful composition. All of us are agreed that there is usefulness in a standard variety of a language, whose artful and effective usage requires tutelage. No argument there. The argument is about what constitutes artful and effective usage.

Our Magnificent Bastard Tongue: The Untold Story of English(2008).

Linguists traditionally observe that esteemed writers have been using they as a gender-neutral pronoun for almost a thousand years. As far back as the 1400s, in the *Sir Amadace*story, one finds the likes of "*Iche mon in thayre degree*" [Each man in their degree].

Racism

Racism is not dead. Definitely, there are these biases.

The only way that residual racist feelings could affect legislation, in my opinion, is through a lack of priorities, from not doing things.

Social Mores

The difference between educated people and uneducated people is that educated people have been opened up to the notion that you can disagree without fighting; whereas uneducated people, in conversation, seek to always agree—everybody agrees and agrees and that's considered basic social libation.

Victimhood

Every third person in the world is a drama queen. And crying "victim," especially when you're not really a victim in any real way, feels good. It feels good to cry victim if you're not one.

H.L. Mencken

Henry Louis Mencken / 1880–1956 / Baltimore, Maryland, USA / Journalist, Essayist, Cultural Critic

Americans

Nobody ever went broke underestimating the intelligence of the American public.

Chicago Tribune, November 19, 1926.

Conscience

Conscience is the inner voice that warns us somebody may be looking.

A Mencken Chrestomathy (1949).

Cynicism

A cynic is a man who, when he smells flowers, looks around for a coffin.

A Little Book in C Major (1916).

Education

The aim of public education is not] to fill the young of the species with knowledge and awaken their intelligence… Nothing could be further from the truth. The aim … is simply to reduce as many individuals as possible to the same safe level, to breed and train a standardized citizenry, to put down dissent and originality. That is its aim in the United States… and that is its aim everywhere else.

The American Mercury, April, 1924.

It is the classic fallacy of our time that a moron run through a university and decorated with a Ph.D. will thereby cease to be a moron.

Source unknown.

Freedom

But the right to freedom obviously includes the right to be foolish. If what I say must be passed over for its sagacity by censors, however wise and prudent, then I have no free speech. And if what I may believe – about gall-stones, the Constitution or God – is conditioned by law, then I am not a free man.

Christian Science, 1927.

I believe in only one thing: liberty; but I do not believe in liberty enough to want to force it upon anyone.

"The Physician," in Prejudices: Third Series (1922).

Ideology

An idealist is one who, on noticing that roses smell better than a cabbage, concludes that it will also make better soup.

Source unknown.

Law

Injustice is relatively easy to bear; what stings is justice.

Prejudices: Second Series (1920).

A judge is a law student who marks his own examination papers.

A Mencken Chrestomathy (1949).

Life

Life is a constant oscillation between the sharp horns of dilemmas.

Letters of H. L. Mencken (1961).

Marriage

Marriage is a wonderful institution, but who would want to live in an institution?

Source unknown.

Mencken on Mencken

I go on working for the same reason that a hen goes on laying eggs.

Source unknown.

I believe that it is better to tell the truth than a lie. I believe it is better to be free than to be a slave. And I believe it is better to know than to be ignorant.

Minority Report: H.L. Mencken's Notebooks (1956).

Public Affairs

Democracy is the theory that the common people know what they want, and deserve to get it good and hard.

A Little Book in C Major (1916).

Democracy is also a form of worship. It is the worship of Jackals by Jackasses.

Notes on Democracy (1926).

The whole aim of practical politics is to keep the populace alarmed (and hence clamorous to be led to safety) by an endless series of hobgoblins, most of them imaginary.

In Defense of Women (1918).

For every complex problem, there is an answer that is clear, simple, and wrong.

Source unknown.

All government, in its essence, is a conspiracy against the superior man: its one permanent object is to oppress him and cripple him.

The Smart Set, December, 1919.

A good politician is quite as unthinkable as an honest burglar.

Source unknown.

Every decent man is ashamed of the government he lives under.

Source unknown.

It is inaccurate to say that I hate everything. I am strongly in favour of common sense, common honesty, and common decency. This makes me forever ineligible for public office.

Source unknown.

The most dangerous man to any government is the man who is able to think things out for himself, without regard to the prevailing superstitions and taboos.

The Smart Set, December, 1919.

In this world of sin and sorrow, there is always something to be thankful for; as for me, I rejoice that I am not a Republican.

Minority Report: H.L. Mencken's Notebooks (1956).

Puritanism

Puritanism: The haunting fear that someone, somewhere, may be happy.

A Mencken Chrestomathy (1949).

Religious Tolerance

We must respect the other fellow's religion, but only in the sense and to the extent that we respect his theory that his wife is beautiful and his children smart.

Minority Report: H.L. Mencken's Notebooks (1956).

Truth

The men the American people admire most extravagantly are the most daring liars; the men they detest most violently are those who try to tell them the truth.

A Little Book in C Major (1916).

Wisdom

The older I grow, the more I distrust the familiar doctrine that age brings wisdom.

Prejudices: Second Series (1920).

Eric Metaxas

Eric Metaxas / b. 1963 / New York, New York, USA / Speaker, Author, Radio Host, Podcaster

Note: The specific sources of the following quotations are unknown, but presumably derive from Metaxas's very numerous writings, interviews, and podcasts.

Abortion

Ultrasound is instrumental in the fight against abortion precisely because it allows women to make an informed choice by shedding light in a place which, for most of its history, has been shrouded in secrecy.

America

America is fundamentally exceptional. No one in the history of the world had ever done anything to compare with what the Founders did, creating a fragile mechanism by which men and women could actually govern themselves.

If America is an idea, which it is—we're not a nation of ethnic groups that say we're Americans because we have American blood; we have the blood of every nation in our veins—and there's something really beautiful about that, but it means that we are an idea and that we all have to buy into this idea.

I guess I'm concerned that vulgarity has now officially entered the mainstream of our culture, and I think people have to respectfully stand up and say, "No thanks."

For proof that our culture has gone to the dogs, look no further than the bizarrely parental ways many Americans talk about our furry friends.

Often, we have only focused on what we've done wrong as a nation. Of course we should face our sins and our mistakes. But if we get stuck there and don't focus on where we've come from and how we've overcome those sins and mistakes, we are truly to be pitied.

America is the only nation in the world based on an idea—freedom and self-government—so if we don't understand that idea and what sacrifices were made to win that freedom and keep it for over two centuries, how can we possibly continue to keep it?

Being an American is something we need to learn and understand.

One of my favorite things about America is our breathtaking collection of national and state parks, many of which boast wonders the Psalmist would envy.

Angels

The Bible is filled with stories about angels, but many of us have had our view of angels confused by popular misconceptions about them, the principal of which is that angels do not actually exist anymore than fairies do, or wood nymphs or water sprites. But they do exist, and the Bible attests to their existence innumerable times.

Anger

As Christians, we sin with anger because we lack faith in God's ability to provide for or protect us.
We all can do our part to address America's anger mismanagement crisis. And for us Christians, it starts with a little more faith, hope, and love.

The Big Questions

I have no doubt, if people are really seeking the big questions, it will lead them to the Lord.
We're commanded by God to worship God with our mind.

Biography

Perhaps the best thing about biographies is that they enable us to slip the strictures of time and provide a bracing corrective to our tendency to see everything in the dark glass of our own era, with all its blind spots, motes, beams, and distortions.

Children

You can't fool children.
In some sense, there is no such thing as writing for children.

Christianity

Wilberforce, because of his faith, stood up for African slaves. Bonhoeffer, because of his faith, stood up for Jews. That's Christianity to me.
Christians who enjoy and support art and culture, who make it a priority in their lives, and who reach out to those in the arts instead of reflexively pushing them away, can help bring the culture toward a renewed appreciation of goodness, truth, and beauty. And that is good for everyone.
If the main contribution that Christians make to culture is complaining about it, we're doing something wrong.
A Christian worldview impacts every area of life. Including making your house a home.

Faith

Faith is not the absence of doubt, but the courage to believe in spite of it.

Fear of Death

Our longing for immortality is good! It was put there on purpose. We were meant—from the moment of our creation—to live forever.

Fellowship

All of us, believers and non-believers, desire some kind of fellowship and connection.
God designed humans to live in community.
Home is—or should be—a place for companionship, for rearing children and having friends and family over for meals while the dog begs for scraps under the table.

Forgiveness

Thankfully, forgiveness, and the healing it brings in its wake, has nothing to do with "deserve."
The power of forgiveness transcends personal relationships.

Freedom of Religion

I think most people have no idea about what religious freedom means.
Religious liberty is the salt and light that has made us the great nation we are in a whole number of ways.
Religious liberty is misunderstood. It simply means that the Founders said that everyone in America should have the freedom to practice and exercise their religion. Not to be-

lieve it but to exercise our beliefs—to act on our beliefs. It's not about believing privately in your head, privately in that building, or simply about freedom of worship.

Many in our increasingly secular culture want to chase Christians out of the public square altogether.

Freedom of Speech

To try to preemptively shut down debate with name-calling is profoundly un-American and will harm this country.

God

God doesn't always give you what you want, but He always gives you what you need.

No one knows what the future holds, except the One Who holds the future!

Where did God come from? It's certainly more complicated than trying to figure out where, say, Barry Manilow was born.

Most people really have no problem with the idea of a creator God. Their question is just what is this God like, how can I know about him, how can I know him.

People everywhere see the True, the Beautiful, and the Good and long to know their source. And, thank God, He has revealed Himself!

History

Each era has the fatal hubris to believe that it has once and for all climbed to the top of the mountain and can see everything as it is, from the highest and most objective vantage point possible.

Immigration

We've always been the most generous nation in the world when it comes to caring for those outside of our borders.

Language

Language is powerful. Words matter.

Life

Sometimes the things that go wrong in our lives lead us to the things that are right for us.

Don't let fear stop you from pursuing your dreams. Have the courage to take that first step.

True happiness is found not in pursuing our own selfish desires, but in serving others and living a life of purpose.

When you have a biblical idea of men's strength, you know that God only gives us anything good to be used for his purposes and mainly to serve others.

The familiar can feel good—especially with so much uncertainty when we turn on the news. But it doesn't uplift us, challenge us, or inspire anew as truly original work can.

We all have different strengths, different gifts.

Created in the awesome image of God, men and women know that life has a meaning beyond "eat, drink, and be merry, for tomorrow we die."

Marriage

Everyone needs to stop and breathe and look at how redefining marriage will have a hugely chilling effect on religious liberty in America.

The truth is many singles deeply desire and pray for marriage.

Men and Women

Every single cell in each person's body tells us whether that person is a male or a female. There is no human being in history whose cells have some mixture of the two, nor anyone who has ever been able to change that cellular reality.

Young men, more than anything, need good role models in their lives.

Women are, I think, moved by the idea that self-sacrifice is noble and can be the source of great joy.

Men and women are complements to each other, physically and otherwise.

Metaxas on Metaxas

[Re: Metaxas's biography of Dietrich Bonhoeffer]:

Six-hundred-page biographies of German theologians aren't known to fly off the shelves.

I think the fact that I use salty words in my Bonhoeffer book would tip you off that I'm no prude, exactly.

I thought a book on miracles might be a great idea, but just because it's a great idea doesn't mean I'm supposed to do it. But my editor persisted, and eventually I thought, "He's right. I should write this book."

As an undergrad, I was the editor of the Yale humor magazine, and since then, I've published humor in the *New York Times* and *Atlantic*, among other places.

Millennials

For at least a decade, Millennials have been stereotyped as lazy, entitled, and stuck on social media. While that may not be entirely fair, they are notoriously liberal, overwhelmingly supporting left-leaning candidates, and favoring policies like nationalized healthcare and same-sex "marriage."

Miracles

The greatest miracle of all time, without any close seconds, is the universe. It is the miracle of all miracles, one that ineluctably points with the combined brightness of every star to something—or Someone—beyond itself.

If God miraculously created all that is, including you and me, then to say that we need miracles is an understatement. Our only response to that idea should be undying gratitude.

Whether one believes in miracles or the miraculous has mostly to do with the presuppositions one brings to the subject.

Miracles seem to attest to the presence of a loving and compassionate God, one who wants to help us, who wants to speak to us and encourage us.

Miracles are signs, and like all signs, they are never about themselves; they're about whatever they are pointing toward. Miracles point to something beyond themselves. But to what? To God himself. That's the point of miracles—to point us beyond our world to another world.

If you accept my thesis that the universe and this earth are the most outrageous miracles by an infinite margin, then you will understand that simply for us to exist requires a miracle.

Miracles are supposed to point us to Him, but we can get to God without miracles. It is God himself we should long for rather than for the miracles that point to him. To get caught up in wanting miracles is a bit like thinking the destination of a road trip is the highway you're supposed to take.

Nature

Quite simply, our isolation from nature has become isolation from God's Word. Cocooned in our manmade world of climate-controlled homes, cars, subways, and high-rises, we're finding it easier to live as practical atheists.

We may have city lights and the glow of touch screens to obscure our view, but God's world is still near at hand, even right here in New York City where I live.

Politics

Sometimes you have to hold your nose and vote for the person who is going to do the least damage or who is maybe going to pull you back from the brink.

It's one thing to be innocent and another thing to be naive or willfully ignorant.

Part of my life's thesis is that we live in a culture that has bought into the patently silly idea that there is a divide between the secular world and the faith world.

The freedoms we have enjoyed in America —and spread around the world—are incredibly fragile freedoms.

Restricting the religious impulses of Americans is precisely like killing free enterprise with too many regulations.

I think that there are deceptive forces out there that will try to lead us away from God, and we really do need to be careful.

Freedom requires virtue. Virtue requires faith. And faith, in turn, requires freedom. You can't have coerced state-sanctioned religion. It has to be utterly free.

The only leader America should ever have is someone who understands that the people are the government.

You and I must demonstrate love to our gay neighbors, of course, remembering that we are ultimately engaged in spiritual warfare. But we should boldly stand up when our rights as citizens and the demands of our conscience are threatened.

Relativism

The logical conclusion of relativism is absurdity. Non-sense. A worldview that undermines its own premises.

Science

To be labeled a "science-denier" in 2017 often just means you've upset someone who insists on teaching strict, Darwinian orthodoxy in schools or who advocates particular climate legislation or who supports ethically fraught research on embryos.

There was a time when "science" meant the systematic pursuit of knowledge through experimentation and observation. But it's rapidly becoming a synonym for progressive politics and materialist philosophy.

Scripture

Let me tell you something you already know: reading is critically important—especially for Christian believers. God, after all, reveals Himself to us in the written words of Scripture. Think about it: when we read the Word, we place ourselves in the very presence of God.

Even if you aren't a believer, there are incredible stories in the "good book" that I guarantee you will keep you glued to the page. The Bible is no less a part of our cultural heritage than Shakespeare is—and by the way, Shakespeare's plays are absolutely loaded with Biblical references.

Sin

Thinking about the sins of others give us a feeling of moral superiority. But thinking about our own sins is a humbling experience, which is generally much less fun.

Trump

Donald Trump's rise is certainly a symptom of our fading virtue and faith, but ironically, he may well be our only hope for finding our way back to bolder expressions of them.

For many of us, this is very painful, pulling the lever for someone many think odious. But please consider this: A vote for Donald Trump is not necessarily a vote for Donald Trump himself. It is a vote for those who will be affected by the results of this election.

Not to vote is to vote. God will not hold us guiltless.
I came to the conclusion over time that Trump is not the person I feared he was in the beginning when I was against him.
Here's one thing the media and all of us should learn: Trump is not wrong nearly as much as everybody says he's wrong.
Donald Trump is not some great man of virtue, but this much I'll say for him: I think he loves America, and I don't think he wants to line his own pockets.
When Trump says America first, it doesn't mean cheering for America only. It means if you want to care for your neighbors, you have to make sure that you are yourself, first, healthy.

Wilberforce

No politician has ever used his faith to a greater result for all of humanity, and that is why, in his day, Wilberforce was a moral hero far more than a political one.

Work

God gave men and women work to do in the Garden before the Fall.
Work is not optional for those able to do work, and that's most of us. There are to be no shirkers in the Lord's kingdom.
Work allows us to take care of God's creation and bring glory to Him as His stewards.

The World

Doesn't assuming that an intelligence created these perfect conditions require far less faith than believing that a life-sustaining Earth just happened to beat the inconceivable odds to come into being?
The odds against life in the universe are simply astonishing. Yet here we are, not only existing, but talking about existing. What can account for it? Can every one of those many parameters have been perfect by accident? At what point is it fair to admit that science suggests that we cannot be the result of random forces?
There's already a world of evidence that life on Earth is unique and intelligently crafted.

Ludwig von Mises

Ludwig Heinrich Edler von Mises / 1881–1973 / Lemberg, Galicia, Austro-Hungarian Empire (now Lviv, Ukraine) / Economist, Political Philosopher

Action

Economics, as a branch of the more general theory of human action, deals with all human action, i.e., with man's purposive aiming at the attainment of ends chosen, whatever these ends may be.

Source: Human Action: A Treatise on Economics (Yale University Press, 1949).

Action is an attempt to substitute a more satisfactory state of affairs for a less satisfactory one. We call such a willfully induced alteration an exchange.

Source: Human Action: A Treatise on Economics (Yale University Press, 1949).

Most actions do not aim at anybody's defeat or loss. They aim at an improvement in conditions.

Source: Human Action: A Treatise on Economics (Yale University Press, 1949).

Man's striving after an improvement of the conditions of his existence impels him to action. Action requires planning and the decision which of various plans is the most advantageous.

Source: The Ultimate Foundation of Economic Science: An Essay on Method (D. Van Nostrand Company, 1962).

The uncertainty of the future is already implied in the very notion of action. That man acts and that the future is uncertain are by no means two independent matters. They are only two different modes of establishing one thing.

Source: Human Action: A Treatise on Economics (Yale University Press, 1949).

Bureaucracy

A bureaucrat differs from a nonbureaucrat precisely because he is working in a field in which it is impossible to appraise the result of a man's effort in terms of money.

Source: Bureaucracy (Arlington House, 1969).

Only to bureaucrats can the idea occur that establishing new offices, promulgating new decrees, and increasing the number of government employees alone can be described as positive and beneficial measures.

Source: Omnipotent Government: The Rise of the Total State and Total War (Yale University Press, 1944).

The trend toward bureaucratic rigidity is not inherent in the evolution of business. It is an outcome of government meddling with business.

Source: Bureaucracy (Arlington House, 1969).

No private enterprise will ever fall prey to bureaucratic methods of management if it is operated with the sole aim of making profit.

Source: Bureaucracy (Arlington House, 1969).

Capitalism

What the workers must learn is that the only reason why wage rates are higher in the United States is that the per head quota of capital invested is higher.

Source: Planning for Freedom, and Other Essays and Addresses (Libertarian Press, 1952).

There are no means by which the general standard of living can be raised other than by accelerating the increase of capital as compared with population.

Source: Planning for Freedom, and Other Essays and Addresses (Libertarian Press, 1952).

Those politicians, professors and union bosses who curse big business are fighting for a lower standard of living.

Source: Theory and History: An Interpretation of Social and Economic Evolution (Yale University Press, 1957).

Under capitalism, material success depends on the appreciation of a man's achievements on the part of the sovereign consumers. In this regard there is no difference between the services rendered by a manufacturer and those rendered by a producer, an actor or a playwright.

Source: The Anti-Capitalistic Mentality (D. Van Nostrand Company, 1956).

The greater the fund of means of subsistence in a community, the lower the rate of interest.

Source: The Theory of Money and Credit (original German edition, 1912).

Danger

The most serious dangers for American freedom and the American way of life do not come from without.

Source: Economic Freedom and Interventionism: An Anthology of Articles and Essays (Foundation for Economic Education, 1990).

Equality

The worst form of inequality is to try to make unequal things equal.

Source: Human Action: A Treatise on Economics (Yale University Press, 1949).

Government Intervention

Credit expansion can bring about a temporary boom. But such a fictitious prosperity must end in a general depression of trade, a slump.

Source: Planned Chaos (Foundation for Economic Education, 1972).

There is no means of avoiding the final collapse of a boom brought about by credit expansion. The alternative is only whether the crisis should come sooner as the result of a voluntary abandonment of further credit expansion, or later as a final and total catastrophe of the currency system involved.

Source: Human Action: A Treatise on Economics (Yale University Press, 1949).

Inflation and credit expansion, the preferred methods of present day government openhandedness, do not add anything to the amount of resources available. They make some people more prosperous, but only to the extent that they make others poorer.

Source: Bureaucracy (Arlington House, 1969).

Inflation is the fiscal complement of statism and arbitrary government. It is a cog in the complex of policies and institutions which gradually lead toward totalitarianism.

Source: The Theory of Money and Credit (original German edition, 1912).

The essence of the interventionist policy is to take from one group to give to another. It is confiscation and distribution.

Source: Human Action: A Treatise on Economics (Yale University Press, 1949).

Socialism and interventionism. Both have in common the goal of subordinating the individual unconditionally to the state.

Source: Omnipotent Government: The Rise of the Total State and Total War (Yale University Press, 1944).

It is the typical policy of après nous le déluge. Lord Keynes, the champion of this policy, says: "In the long run we are all dead." But unfortunately nearly all of us outlive the short run. We are destined to spend decades paying for the easy money orgy of a few years.

Source: Omnipotent Government: The Rise of the Total State and Total War (Yale University Press, 1944).

Ideas

Only ideas can overcome ideas.

Source: Socialism: An Economic and Sociological Analysis(original German edition, 1922).

The ideas that change the intellectual climate of a given environment are those unheard of before. For these new ideas there is no other explanation than that there was a man from whose mind they originated.

Source: The Ultimate Foundation of Economic Science: An Essay on Method (D. Van Nostrand Company, 1962).

In a battle between force and an idea, the latter always prevails.

Source: Liberalism: In the Classical Tradition (original German edition, 1927).

Ideas live longer than walls and other material artifacts.

Source: Theory and History: An Interpretation of Social and Economic Evolution (Yale University Press, 1957).

No one can escape the influence of a prevailing ideology.

Source: Epistemological Problems of Economics (original German edition, 1933).

Liberty

Liberty is always freedom from the government.

Source: "Liberty and Property," lecture, Princeton University, October 15, 1958.

Progress

Progress of any kind is always at variance with the old and established ideas and therefore with the codes inspired by them. Every step of progress is a change involving heavy risks.

Source: Bureaucracy (Arlington House, 1969).

Value

The buyers do not pay for the toil and trouble the worker took nor for the length of time he spent in working. They pay for the products.

Source: Planning for Freedom, and Other Essays and Addresses (Libertarian Press, 1952).

Michel de Montaigne

Michel de Montaigne / 1533–1592 / France / Essayist
Note: All quotations are taken from Montaigne's Essays [*Essais*], first published in 1580 (with numerous later editions).

Animals

When I play with my cat, who knows if I am not a pastime to her more than she is to me?
II, 12.

Belief

Nothing is so firmly believed as what is least known.
I, 32.

Books

It is more of a job to interpret the interpretations than to interpret the things, and there are more books about books than about any other subject: we do nothing but write glosses about each
other.
III, 13.

Brotherhood of Man

Not because Socrates said so, but because it is in truth my own disposition—and perchance to some excess—I look upon all men as my compatriots, and embrace a Pole as a Frenchman, making less account of the national than of the universal and common bond.
III, 9.

Cannibals

I find that there is nothing barbarous and savage in this nation [of cannibals], by anything that I can gather, excepting, that every one gives the title of barbarism to everything that is not in use in his own country. . . . We may then call these people barbarous, in respect to the rules of reason: but not in respect to ourselves, who in all sorts of barbarity exceed them.
I, 31.

Chance

Our wisdom and deliberation for the most part follow the lead of chance.
III, 8.

Death

I want death to find me planting my cabbages.
I, 20.
Live as long as you please, you will strike nothing off the time you will have to spend dead.
I, 20.
Wherever your life ends, it is all there. The advantage of living is not measured by length, but by use; some men have lived long, and lived little; attend to it while you

are in it. It lies in your will, not in the number of years, for you to have lived enough.

I, 20.

Education

Since I would rather make of him [the child] an able man than a learned man, I would also urge that care be taken to choose a guide [tutor] with a well-made rather than a well-filled head.

I, 26.

Fear

The thing I fear most is fear.

I,18.

Friendship

If you press me to say why I loved him, I can say no more than it was because he was he and I was I.

I, 28.

Hierarchy

No matter that we may mount on stilts, we still must walk on our own legs. And on the highest throne in the world, we still sit only on our own bottom.

III, 13.

Human Nature

The souls of emperors and cobblers are cast in the same mold. ... The same reason that makes us bicker with a neighbor creates a war between princes.

II, 12.

A man may be humble through vainglory.

II, 17.

I find that the best goodness I have has some tincture of vice.

II, 20.

Every man bears the whole stamp of the human condition.

III, 1.

There is no man so good that if he placed all his actions and thoughts under the scrutiny of the laws, he would not deserve hanging ten times in his life.

III, 9.

Inner Self

We must reserve a back shop all our own, entirely free, in which to establish our real liberty and our principal retreat and solitude.

I, 39.

The greatest thing in the world is to know how to belong to oneself.

I, 39.

Man

Truly man is a marvelously vain, diverse, and undulating object. It is hard to found any constant
and uniform judgment on him.

I,1.

Man is certainly crazy. He could not make a mite, and he makes gods by the dozen.

II, 12.

Marriage

It [marriage] happens as with cages: the birds without despair to get in, and those within despair of getting out.

III, 5.

Montaigne Himself

I have seen no more evident monstrosity and miracle in the world than myself.

III, 11.

Montaigne and the *Essays*

Everyone recognizes me in my book, and my book in me.

III, 5.

I have here only made a nosegay of culled flowers, and have brought nothing of my own but the
thread that ties them together.

III, 12.

Mind

It is a thorny undertaking, and more so than it seems, to follow a movement so wandering as that of our mind, to penetrate the opaque depths of its innermost folds, to pick out and immobilize the innumerable flutterings that agitate it.

II, 6.

Nature

Let us give Nature a chance; she knows her business better than we do.

III, 13.

Our utmost endeavours cannot arrive at so much as to imitate the nest of the least of birds, its contexture, beauty, and convenience: not so much as the web of a poor spider. All things, says Plato, are produced either by nature, by fortune, or by art; the greatest and most beautiful by the one or the other of the former, the least and the most imperfect by the last.

I, 31.

Self-Knowledge

I do not speak the minds of others except to speak my own mind better.

I, 26.

Skepticism

This notion [skepticism] is more clearly understood by asking "What do I know?"

II, 12.

Subject of the *Essays*

Had I been seeking public attention, I would have made myself look better and presented myself more carefully. But I want you to see me as I am, in a plain, natural, and ordinary way, free of pretense and artifice. I am the one depicted here. My faults and my very self are exposed for all to see, at least as much as public conventions will let me. Had I lived among those nations, which (they say) still live under the sweet liberty of nature's primitive laws, I assure you I would easily have painted myself quite fully and quite naked. So, reader, here I am, the subject of my book, and I see no reason why you should spend your free time on so unimportant and pointless a topic. Farewell, then!

"To the Reader."

Truth

I speak the truth, not my fill of it, but as much as I dare speak; and I dare to do so a little more as I grow old.

III, 1.

Gordon Moore

Gordon Earle Moore / 1929–2023 / California, USA / Chemist, Applied Physicist, Entrepreneur, Co-Founder of Fairchild Semiconductor Corporation and Intel Corporation

Education

The technology at the leading edge changes so rapidly that you have to keep current after you get out of school. I think probably the most important thing is having good fundamentals.

Interview with Laura Schmitt, Ingenuity magazine, Electrical and Computer Engineering Department, University of Illinois at Urbana–Champaign, 5(2), May, 2000.

Failure

With engineering, I view this year's failure as next year's opportunity to try it again. Failures are not something to be avoided. You want to have them happen as quickly as you can so you can make progress rapidly.

Interview with Laura Schmitt, Ingenuity magazine, Electrical and Computer Engineering Department, University of Illinois at Urbana–Champaign, 5(2), May, 2000.

Fairchild

Fairchild did a lot of pioneering work. The company was really in the right place at the right time. In the first place, we pursued this idea of a diffused silicon transistor that [William] Shockley had been initially going to do. It was something that had been made in the laboratory at Bell Labs but was not a commercial device at all. We were the first ones to bring to the market what's known as a "mesa" transistor and it was a silicon mesa transistor at that time. It was quite a successful device on the scale that we were working at least, but that was only the first of several devices.

That was the first silicon transistor that was built by the batch process—where you made a lot of them on a wafer and then cut them up individually. And it was the first device in manufacturing that used photolithography to produce the structures. So these were fairly important early developments.

Interview with Rob Walker, "Silicon Genesis: Oral Histories of Semiconductor Industry Pioneers," Program in History and Philosophy of Science, Department of History, Stanford University, March 3, 1995.

Moore's Law

The complexity for minimum component costs has increased at a rate of roughly a factor of two per year. . . . Certainly over the short term this rate can be expected to continue, if not to increase. Over the longer term, the rate of increase is a bit more uncertain, although there is no reason to believe it will not remain nearly constant for at least

10 years. That means by 1975, the number of components per integrated circuit for minimum cost will be 65,000. I believe that such a large circuit can be built on a single wafer.

"Cramming more components onto integrated circuits," Electronics, ***38****(8): 114–117, April 19, 1965.*

I had no idea this was going to be an accurate prediction, but amazingly enough instead of 10 [years] doubling, we got nine over the 10 years, but still followed pretty well along the curve.

Press release, "Computer History Museum Presents: The 40th Anniversary of Moore's Law with Gordon Moore and Carver Mead," Computer History Museum, computerhistory.org, September 15, 2005.

I used to give talks about how other industries might have progressed. You know, had the auto industry made progress at the same rate [as silicon microelectronics], you would have gotten a million miles per gallon of fuel, had cars that could go several hundred thousand miles an hour. It'd be more expensive to park [one] downtown for the night than to buy a new Rolls-Royce.

Interview with Rachel Courtland, "Gordon Moore: The Man Whose Name Means Progress," IEEE Spectrum, spectrum.ieee.com, March 30, 2015.

By making things smaller, everything gets better at the same time. The transistors get faster. The reliability goes up. The cost goes down. It's a unique violation of Murphy's Law.

Video interview, "Our Stories—Gordon Moore about Moore's Law," ASML, youtube.com, December 18, 2014.

So, I took this doubling every year and extrapolated it ten years, from 1965 to 1975, from 60 components to 60,000 components on a chip—a pretty wild extrapolation. And It turned out to be ridiculously accurate. . . . One of my colleagues called this "Moore's Law." Rather than just being something that chronicles the progress of the industry, it kind of became something that drove the progress of the industry.

Video interview, "Our Stories—Gordon Moore about Moore's Law," ASML, youtube.com, December 18, 2014.

A: . . . Now, I modified that in 1975, suggesting it was going to slow down to more like a doubling every *two* years and I was a little bit too pessimistic then—we've actually beat that. It doubles something between 18 months and two years.

Q: Yes, and when will it approach the number of atoms in the universe?

[Laughter.]

A: I haven't extrapolated it *that* far. [Laughter.] That's one thing: any exponential like that predicts a disaster if you extrapolate it far enough.

Interview with Rob Walker, "Silicon Genesis: Oral Histories of Semiconductor Industry Pioneers," Program in History and Philosophy of Science, Department of History, Stanford University, March 3, 1995.

Q: You've predicted the end of Moore's Law several times in the past. How long do you think it will continue?

A: Well, I have never quite predicted the end of it. I've said I could never see more than the next couple of [chip] generations, and after that it looked like [we'd] hit some kind of wall. But those walls keep receding. I'm amazed at how creative the engineers have been in finding ways around what we thought were going to be pretty hard stops. Now we're getting to the point where it's more and more difficult, and some of the laws are quite fundamental. . . . the finite velocity of light and the atomic nature of materials. . . . We're very close to the atomic limitation now. We take advantage of all the speed we can get, but the velocity of light limits performance. These are fundamentals

I don't see how we [will] ever get around. And in the next couple of generations, we're right up against them.

Interview with Rachel Courtland, "Gordon Moore: The Man Whose Name Means Progress," IEEE Spectrum, spectrum.ieee.com, March 30, 2015.

Risk-Taking

. . . when you're a startup company you have to bet the company on a lot of the programs you do. When you get bigger you only want to bet half the company if you can do that. You don't want to do something that if it doesn't work, will put you out of business completely.

On the other hand, you gotta keep reaching. If everything you do works, you're probably not trying hard enough.

Interview with Rob Walker, "Silicon Genesis: Oral Histories of Semiconductor Industry Pioneers," Program in History and Philosophy of Science, Department of History, Stanford University, March 3, 1995.

Technological Progress

Some things may have been tried before their time, but if these things don't violate the laws of physics they are likely to prove possible the next time around. Engineering is a series of failures with an occasional success. At least the kind where you are really looking at new technology. You tend to try things. You try things that are extrapolations of what has happened before. A lot of them don't work. Occasionally, you hit one that does. That's the way we make progress. Failures are not something to be avoided. You want to have them happen as quickly as you can so you can make progress rapidly. But, I've known technical people who are very competent but who would avoid doing a critical experiment. They would kind of work around the problem and do the things where the results were relatively straightforward, but they hated to do that experiment that might tell if their whole approach was right or wrong. And these people were relatively nonproductive. Then I've known other people who weren't perhaps as bright as the ones that worked around the problem who jumped right at the heart of the matter. They turn out to be the most productive. So my single piece of advice is don't delay making the critical test. That's the one that will tell you if you are right or wrong and where to go next.

*Interview with Laura Schmitt, Ingenuity magazine, Electrical and Computer Engineering Department, University of Illinois at Urbana–Champaign, **5**(2), May, 2000.*

Q: What happens then, once you've reached those [fundamental physical] limits?

A: Well, things change when we get to that point. No longer can we depend on making things smaller and higher density. But we'll be able to make several billion transistors on an integrated circuit at that time. And the room this allows for creativity is phenomenal.

Interview with Rachel Courtland, "Gordon Moore: The Man Whose Name Means Progress," IEEE Spectrum, spectrum.ieee.com, March 30, 2015.

Akio Morita

Akio Morita / 1921–1999 / Nagoya, Japan / Businessman, Entrepreneur, Co-Founder of Sony Corporation

American Business Culture

In the United States businessmen often do not trust their colleagues. If you trust your colleague today, he may be your competitor tomorrow, because people frequently move from one company to another.

Akio Morita, with Edwin M. Reingold and Mitsuko Shimomura, Made in Japan: Akio Morita and Sony (1986).

I have had my difficulties with the American legal system, and so I feel qualified to talk about it.

Akio Morita, with Edwin M. Reingold and Mitsuko Shimomura, Made in Japan: Akio Morita and Sony (1986).

The American system of management, in my opinion, also relies too much on outsiders to help make business decisions., and this is because of the insecurity that American decision makers feel in their jobs, as compared with most top Japanese corporate executives.

Akio Morita, with Edwin M. Reingold and Mitsuko Shimomura, Made in Japan: Akio Morita and Sony (1986).

. . . the differences between U.S. and Japanese companies go beyond the cultural.

Akio Morita, with Edwin M. Reingold and Mitsuko Shimomura, Made in Japan: Akio Morita and Sony (1986).

Business Philosophy in General

More people are interested in trying to shuffle paper assets around than building lasting assets by producing real goods.

Statement from1989; reported in The Book of Management Wisdom: Classic Writings by Legendary Managers, edited by Peter Krass (2000).

Executives of the company must have the necessary qualities to direct the personnel by showing them the way to do things.

Reported by Mark Fisher in The Millionaire's Book of Quotations (out of print) (1991).

A company will get nowhere if all of the thinking is left to management.

Reported by John Raymond Phillips in The Future of Labor-Management Cooperative Programs (out of print (1994).

What we in industry learned in dealing with people is that people do not work just for money and that if you are trying to motivate, money is not the most effective tool.

Akio Morita, with Edwin M. Reingold and Mitsuko Shimomura, Made in Japan: Akio Morita and Sony (1986).

The investor and the employee are in the same position, but sometimes the employee is more important, because he will be there a long time whereas an investor will often get in and out on a whim in order to make a profit.

Akio Morita, with Edwin M. Reingold and Mitsuko Shimomura, Made in Japan: Akio Morita and Sony (1986).

The important thing in my view is not to pin the blame for a mistake on somebody, but rather to find out what caused the mistake.

Akio Morita, with Edwin M. Reingold and Mitsuko Shimomura, Made in Japan: Akio Morita and Sony (1986).

. . . the remarkable thing about management is that a manager can go on for years making mistakes that nobody is aware of, which means that management can be a kind of a con job.

Akio Morita, with Edwin M. Reingold and Mitsuko Shimomura, Made in Japan: Akio Morita and Sony (1986).

To gain profit is important, but you must invest to build up assets that you can cash in in the future.

Akio Morita, with Edwin M. Reingold and Mitsuko Shimomura, Made in Japan: Akio Morita and Sony (1986).

Advertising and promotion alone will not sustain a bad product or a product that is not right for the times.

Akio Morita, with Edwin M. Reingold and Mitsuko Shimomura, Made in Japan: Akio Morita and Sony (1986).

. . . without an organisation that can work together, sometimes over a very long period, it's difficult to see new projects to fruition.

Akio Morita, with Edwin M. Reingold and Mitsuko Shimomura, Made in Japan: Akio Morita and Sony (1986).

. . . I believe it is a big mistake to think that money is the only way to compensate a person for his work. People need money, but they also want to be happy in their work and proud of it.

Akio Morita, with Edwin M. Reingold and Mitsuko Shimomura, Made in Japan: Akio Morita and Sony (1986).

. . . the company must not throw money away on huge bonuses for executives or other frivolities but must share its fate with the workers.

Akio Morita, with Edwin M. Reingold and Mitsuko Shimomura, Made in Japan: Akio Morita and Sony (1986).

You can be totally rational with a machine. But if you work with people, sometimes logic often has to take a backseat to understanding.

Akio Morita, with Edwin M. Reingold and Mitsuko Shimomura, Made in Japan: Akio Morita and Sony (1986).

Creativity

Once you have a staff of prepared, intelligent, and energetic people, the next step is to motivate them to be creative.

Akio Morita, with Edwin M. Reingold and Mitsuko Shimomura, Made in Japan: Akio Morita and Sony (1986).

. . . the key factor in industry is creativity. I said there are three creativities: creativity in technology, in product planning, and in marketing. To have any one of these without the others is self defeating in business.

Akio Morita, with Edwin M. Reingold and Mitsuko Shimomura, Made in Japan: Akio Morita and Sony (1986).

From a management standpoint, it is very important to know how to unleash people's inborn creativity. My concept is that anybody has creative ability, but very few people know how to use it.

Akio Morita, with Edwin M. Reingold and Mitsuko Shimomura, Made in Japan: Akio Morita and Sony (1986).

My solution to the problem of unleashing creativity is always to set up a target. The best example of this was the Apollo project in the United States.

Akio Morita, with Edwin M. Reingold and Mitsuko Shimomura, Made in Japan: Akio Morita and Sony (1986).

[The] Japanese Government believes that if you have a big laboratory with all the latest equipment and good funding it will automatically lead to creativity. It doesn't work that way.

Akio Morita, with Edwin M. Reingold and Mitsuko Shimomura, Made in Japan: Akio Morita and Sony (1986).

Only with these three kinds of creativity—technology, product planning, and marketing—can the public receive the benefit of a new technology.

Akio Morita, with Edwin M. Reingold and Mitsuko Shimomura, Made in Japan: Akio Morita and Sony (1986).

Engineers

Management of an industrial company must be giving targets to the engineers constantly; that may be the most important job management has in dealing with its engineers.

Akio Morita, with Edwin M. Reingold and Mitsuko Shimomura, Made in Japan: Akio Morita and Sony (1986).

While the United States has been busy creating lawyers, we have been busier creating engineers.

Akio Morita, with Edwin M. Reingold and Mitsuko Shimomura, Made in Japan: Akio Morita and Sony (1986).

Japanese Business Culture

There is no secret ingredient or hidden formula responsible for the success of the best Japanese companies.

Akio Morita, with Edwin M. Reingold and Mitsuko Shimomura, Made in Japan: Akio Morita and Sony (1986).

The most important mission for a Japanese manager is to develop a healthy relationship with his employees, to create a family-like feeling within the corporation, a feeling that employees and managers share the same fate.

Akio Morita, with Edwin M. Reingold and Mitsuko Shimomura, Made in Japan: Akio Morita and Sony (1986).

The "patron saint" of Japanese quality control, ironically, is an American named W. Edwards Deming, who was virtually unknown in his own country until his ideas of quality control began to make such a big impact on Japanese companies.

Akio Morita, with Edwin M. Reingold and Mitsuko Shimomura, Made in Japan: Akio Morita and Sony (1986).

Amenities are not of great concern to management in Japan.

Akio Morita, with Edwin M. Reingold and Mitsuko Shimomura, Made in Japan: Akio Morita and Sony (1986).

We want everybody to have the best facilities in which to work, but we do not believe in posh and impressive private offices.

Akio Morita, with Edwin M. Reingold and Mitsuko Shimomura, Made in Japan: Akio Morita and Sony (1986).

Japanese attitudes toward work seem to be critically different from American attitudes.

Akio Morita, with Edwin M. Reingold and Mitsuko Shimomura, Made in Japan: Akio Morita and Sony (1986).

Japanese Society

The effect of three things—the new laws, the revision of the tax system, and the elimination of the zaibatsu conglomerates—was to make Japan an egalitarian society for the first time.

Akio Morita, with Edwin M. Reingold and Mitsuko Shimomura, Made in Japan: Akio Morita and Sony (1986).

The concept of lifetime employment arose when Japanese managers and employees both realized that they had much in common and that they had to make some long-range plans.

Akio Morita, with Edwin M. Reingold and Mitsuko Shimomura, Made in Japan: Akio Morita and Sony (1986).

Lawyers

. . . if you have so many lawyers, they have to find business, which sometimes they have to create. Sometimes nonsensical lawsuits are generated by lawyers. In this country [the United States] everybody sues everybody.

Akio Morita, with Edwin M. Reingold and Mitsuko Shimomura, Made in Japan: Akio Morita and Sony (1986).

Learning

We all learn by imitating, as children, as students, as novices in the world of business. And then we grow up and learn to blend our innate abilities with the rules or principles we have learned.

Akio Morita, with Edwin M. Reingold and Mitsuko Shimomura, Made in Japan: Akio Morita and Sony (1986).

Morita on Morita

I have always made it a point to know our employees, to visit every facility of our company, and to try to meet and know every single employee.

Akio Morita, with Edwin M. Reingold and Mitsuko Shimomura, Made in Japan: Akio Morita and Sony (1986).

In all my years in business I can recall very few people I have wanted to fire for making mistakes.

Akio Morita, with Edwin M. Reingold and Mitsuko Shimomura, Made in Japan: Akio Morita and Sony (1986).

I often say to my assistants, "Never trust anybody," but what I mean is that you should never trust someone else to do a job exactly the way you would want it done.

Akio Morita, with Edwin M. Reingold and Mitsuko Shimomura, Made in Japan: Akio Morita and Sony (198

Sony

We tell our young managers: "Don't be afraid to make a mistake. But make sure you don't make the same mistake twice."

Reported by Nick Lyons in The Sony Vision: The Remarkable Saga of the Pioneering Electronics Company Whose Innovative, Quality Products Helped Revolutionize the World's View of Japanese Exports (1976).

We want to keep the company healthy and its employees happy, and we want to keep them on the job and productive.

Akio Morita, with Edwin M. Reingold and Mitsuko Shimomura, Made in Japan: Akio Morita and Sony (1986).

. . . I established the rule that once we hire an employee, his school records are a matter of the past and are no longer used to evaluate his work or decide on his promotion.

Akio Morita, with Edwin M. Reingold and Mitsuko Shimomura, Made in Japan: Akio Morita and Sony (1986).

I believe one of the reasons we went through such a remarkable growth period was that we had this atmosphere of free discussion.

Akio Morita, with Edwin M. Reingold and Mitsuko Shimomura, Made in Japan: Akio Morita and Sony (1986).

Of course we have to make a profit, but we have to make a profit over the long haul, not just the short term, and that means we must keep investing in research and development —it has run consistently about 6 percent of sales at Sony—and in service.

Akio Morita, with Edwin M. Reingold and Mitsuko Shimomura, Made in Japan: Akio Morita and Sony (1986).

We made a completely new kind of transistor (the NPN BJT), and in our development work, our researcher, Leo Esaki, demonstrated the electron tunneling effect, which led to the development of the tunnel diode for which he was awarded a Nobel Prize seventeen years later, after he had joined IBM.

Akio Morita, with Edwin M. Reingold and Mitsuko Shimomura, Made in Japan: Akio Morita and Sony (1986).

Charlie Munger

Charles Thomas Munger / b. 1924 / Nebraska, USA / Attorney, Businessman, Investor, Vice Chairman of Berkshire Hathaway, Inc.

Accounting

Obviously, you have to know accounting. It's the language of practical business life. It was a *very* useful thing to deliver to civilization. I've heard it came to civilization through Venice which of course was once the great commercial power in the Mediterranean. However, double-entry bookkeeping was a hell of an invention. And it's not that hard to understand.

But you have to know enough about it to understand its limitations—because although accounting is the starting place, it's only a crude approximation. And it's not very hard to understand its limitations. For example, everyone can see that you have to more or less just guess at the useful life of a jet airplane or anything like that. Just because you express the depreciation rate in neat numbers doesn't make it anything you really know.

> *Speech, "A Lesson on Elementary, Worldly Wisdom As It Relates to Investment Management and Business," Business School, University of Southern California (USC), 1994.*

You can't give the average Wall Street CEO really lenient standards of accounting and expect the figures to be good. The accountant is like the referee in soccer. The accountant has to be the adult that prevents the mayhem. Accountants don't want to be the adults because it causes liability, it causes responsibility, it causes difficulty . . . they failed us terribly.

> *Interview with Ross School of Business, University of Michigan at Ann Arbor, video recording, youtube.com, March 22, 2011.*

Berkshire Hathaway

Our investment style has been given a name—focus investing—which implies ten holdings, not one hundred or four hundred. The idea that it is hard to find good investments, so concentrate on a few, seems to me to be an obvious idea. But 98% of the investment world does not think this way. It's been good for us.

> *Charles T. Munger, Poor Charlie's Almanack: The Wit and Wisdom of Charles T. Munger, edited by Peter D. Kaufman, expanded third edition (2005).*

We don't want to make our money selling things that are bad for people.

> *Statement, 2021 Berkshire Hathaway annual meeting; reported by Yahoo Finance, youtube.com, May 1, 2021.*

A lot of people with high IQs are terrible investors because they've got terrible temperaments. And that is why we say that having a certain kind of temperament is more important than brains. You need to keep raw irrational emotion under control. You need patience and discipline and an ability to take losses and adversity without going crazy.

You need an ability to not be driven crazy by extreme success.

Reported by J. Lukas Neely in Value Investing: A Value Investor's Journey Through the Unknown (2015).

Bitcoin

I see [Bitcoin as] an artificial speculative medium that people are buying just because they think they can sell it to somebody else at a higher price, even though it inherently has no intrinsic value. So, I regard the whole business as anti-social, stupid, immoral. . . . I regard the thing as a combination of dementia and immorality, and I think the people that are pushing it are a disgrace.

Interview with Andrew Serwer, Yahoo Finance, video recording, youtube.com, May 7, 2018.

Business Education

. . . much of what is taught in modern corporate finance courses is twaddle.

Q&A, 1996 Berkshire Hathaway Annual Meeting, video recording, youtube.com, June 28, 2018.

You have to learn all the big ideas in the key disciplines in a way that they're in a mental latticework in your head and you automatically use them for the rest of your life. If you do that, I solemnly promise you that one day you'll be walking down the street and you'll look to your right and left and you'll think "my heavenly days, I'm now one of the few competent people in my whole age cohort." If you don't do it, many of the brightest of you will live in the middle ranks or in the shallows.

Commencement address, Law School, University of Southern California (USC), video recording, genius.com, May 13, 2007.

How do these super-smart people with all these degrees and higher mathematics end up doing these dumb things? I think it's explainable by the old proverb that to the man with a hammer every problem looks pretty much like a nail. They've learned these techniques and they just twist the problem so it fits the solution—which is not the way to do it.

Q&A, 2012 Berkshire Hathaway Annual Meeting, video recording, youtube.com, 2012.

Neither Warren [Buffett] nor I have ever used any fancy math in business—and neither did Ben Graham who taught Warren. Everything I have ever done in business could be done with the simplest algebra and geometry and addition and multiplication and so forth. I never used calculus for any practical work in my whole damn life—and I was a perfect whiz at it when they taught it to me.

Interview with Ross School of Business, University of Michigan at Ann Arbor, video recording, youtube.com, December 20, 2017.

If you don't get this elementary, but mildly unnatural, mathematics of elementary probability into your repertoire, then you go through a long life like a one-legged man in an ass-kicking contest.

Reported by Philip E. Tetlock and Dan Gardner in Superforecasting: The Art and Science of Prediction (2015).

History

. . . I regard it as a cinch that a great nation will in due time be Rome. . . . Where is Rome? Where is Britain in its heyday? They all pass and so our turn is bound to come some day.

Interview with CNBC Television, "Berkshire Hathaway VP Charlie Munger on investing," video recording, youtube.com, February 15, 2019.

There is no better teacher than history in determining the future. . . . There are answers worth billions of dollars in a $30 history book.

Charles T. Munger, Poor Charlie's Almanack: The Wit and Wisdom of Charles T. Munger, edited by Peter D. Kaufman, expanded third edition (2005).

Munger on Munger

In my whole life, I have known no wise people (over a broad subject matter area) who didn't read all the time—none, zero. You'd be amazed at how much Warren reads—and at how much I read. My children laugh at me. They think I'm a book with a couple of legs sticking out.

Charles T. Munger, Poor Charlie's Almanack: The Wit and Wisdom of Charles T. Munger, edited by Peter D. Kaufman, expanded third edition (2005).

It takes character to sit with all that cash and to do nothing. I didn't get to where I am by going after mediocre opportunities.

Charles T. Munger, Poor Charlie's Almanack: The Wit and Wisdom of Charles T. Munger, edited by Peter D. Kaufman, expanded third edition (2005).

All I want to know is where I'm going to die so I'll never go there.

Reported by Peter Atkins in Life is Short and So is This Book: Brief Thoughts on Making the Most of Your Life (2011).

Personal Philosophy

What I would say is the single most important thing, if you want to avoid all the stupid errors, is knowing where you're competent and where you aren't. And that's very hard to do because the human mind naturally tries to make you think you're way smarter than you are.

Interview with Jean-Laurent Rosenthal, California Institute of Technology (Caltech), youtube.com, December 17, 2020.

You fix what can be fixed, and what can't be fixed you endure.

Interview with Yahoo Finance, video recording, youtube.com, February 24, 2021.

Spend each day trying to be a little wiser than you were when you woke up. Day by day, and at the end of the day—if you live long enough—like most people, you will get out of life what you deserve.

Charles T. Munger, Poor Charlie's Almanack: The Wit and Wisdom of Charles T. Munger, edited by Peter D. Kaufman, expanded third edition (2005).

How to find a good spouse? The best single way is to deserve a good spouse.

Charles T. Munger, Poor Charlie's Almanack: The Wit and Wisdom of Charles T. Munger, edited by Peter D. Kaufman, expanded third edition (2005).

Acquire worldly wisdom and adjust your behavior accordingly. If your new behavior gives you a little temporary unpopularity with your peer group . . . then to hell with them.

Charles T. Munger, Poor Charlie's Almanack: The Wit and Wisdom of Charles T. Munger, edited by Peter D. Kaufman, expanded third edition (2005).

What are the secrets of success? One-word answer: "rational."

Charles T. Munger, Poor Charlie's Almanack: The Wit and Wisdom of Charles T. Munger, edited by Peter D. Kaufman, expanded third edition (2005).

I believe in the discipline of mastering the best that other people have ever figured out. I don't believe in just sitting down and trying to dream it all up yourself. Nobody's that smart.

Reported by Tren Griffin in Charlie Munger: The Complete Investor (2015).

Remember that reputation and integrity are your most valuable assets—and can be lost in a heartbeat.

Reported by Tren Griffin in Charlie Munger: The Complete Investor (2015).

The best armor of old age is a well spent life perfecting it.

Charles T. Munger, Poor Charlie's Almanack: The Wit and Wisdom of Charles T. Munger, edited by Peter D. Kaufman, expanded third edition (2005).

Mimicking the herd invites regression to the mean (merely average performance).

Reported by Tren Griffin in Charlie Munger: The Complete Investor (2015).

Politics

Re: US Representative Alexandria Ocasio-Cortez:

I don't think that she knows who Adam Smith was.

Interview with Yahoo Finance, "Charlie Munger's advice on investing and life choices that make a person wealthy," video recording, youtube.com, May 9, 2019.

Rupert Murdoch

Keith Rupert Murdoch / b. 1931 / Melbourne, Australia / Businessman, Investor, Owner of News Corp.

Business and Economics

While it's impossible to be completely prepared for a downturn of this magnitude, we began priming ourselves for a weakening economy earlier last year. We have implemented strict cost cutting measures across all our operations. We have reduced headcount in individual businesses where appropriate and we've scaled back on capital expenditures. Even in plush times, we have never been a company that tolerates fat. So in times like these, we are better positioned to weather this cycle than our competitors.

Reported in "News Corporation F2Q09 (Qtr End 12/31/08) Earnings Call Transcript," SA Transcripts, seekingalpha.com, February 5, 2009.

People are reading news for free on the web; that's got to change.

Reported by David Kravets in "Murdoch Calls Google, Yahoo Copyright Thieves —Is He Right?," wired.com, April 3, 2009.

Fox

Everybody went into a bit of a dip. When there's news more people turn to us. Flat period compared [to last year]. Suddenly in the last week Bill Clinton chose to lose his temper... Fox is up 20 per cent in prime time, 15 per cent in day time, so we're just fine.

Interview with Joshua Chaffin and Alien van Duyn, "Interview transcript: Rupert Murdoch and Roger Ailes," Financial Times, October 3, 2006; accessible at ft.com.

As far as we're concerned all our cable networks are up in double figures in revenue in this coming year. Our stations are the only group of stations that are up, record revenues and record profits, up 8 per cent revenue in September. Putting more news in and are getting increasingly better ratings. It takes time, it takes time, time to mature and get noticed, but every year it builds up, we've doubled in the last two or three years, but since Roger became chairman, we are putting more and more news on our stations. We recognise the future of the stations had to be localism. Put on more and more news. But also doing it better and it's showing to some extent in the ratings and to a big extent in advertising.

Interview with Joshua Chaffin and Alien van Duyn, "Interview transcript: Rupert Murdoch and Roger Ailes," Financial Times, October 3, 2006; accessible at ft.com.

Fox News can now be received in realtime in every corner of the globe. It can be received in 80 countries. I'm not sure if we are putting on Star encrypted or not because we are trying to encrypt things that Indians will pay for, but certainly it is available in all of Europe, just as Sky news is available. Our Indian news channel is fine, there are too many damn news channels there, but it's OK, we have a good partner. We have a 100-percent-owned Italian news channel which is the most respected news channel in Italy by all sides. If we try and start [an international] Fox Channel the way CNN is done, you are going to bleed money. They have hundreds of people in London.

Interview with Joshua Chaffin and Alien van Duyn, "Interview transcript: Rupert Murdoch and Roger Ailes," Financial Times, October 3, 2006; accessible at ft.com.

The real story about Fox is the business story. The real thing is by being fair and balanced by putting on both sides all the time we really have changed the political equation in this country. People think we're conservative but we're not conservative...Bill O'Reilly is not a newscaster, he's a commentator, but he's on both sides...Brit Hume is not a politician.

Interview with Joshua Chaffin and Alien van Duyn, "Interview transcript: Rupert Murdoch and Roger Ailes," Financial Times, October 3, 2006; accessible at ft.com.

Look at the news at 6 oclock at night with Brit Hume, there's no bias in that. There's not an ounce of bias in that.

Interview with Joshua Chaffin and Alien van Duyn, "Interview transcript: Rupert Murdoch and Roger Ailes," Financial Times, October 3, 2006; accessible at ft.com.

Q: The anti-Fox argument is that the political mood is shifting and that that will cap your growth.

A: That's BS. If the government changes to a totally Democratic Washington, all those who don't like it, 48 per cent of the country, will be turning on Fox News.

Interview with Joshua Chaffin and Alien van Duyn, "Interview transcript: Rupert Murdoch and Roger Ailes," Financial Times, October 3, 2006; accessible at ft.com.

Hitler Diaries

Note: In 1983, a document surfaced purporting to be Adolf Hitler's private diaries. Murdoch hired the historian Hugh Trevor-Roper (Baron Dacre of Glanton) to authenticate the diaries. Originally, Trevor-Roper pronounced them authentic, but later changed his mind. Murdoch chose to publish them anyway in the *Sunday Times* and other publications he owned. The alleged diaries were soon exposed as forgeries.

F**k Dacre. Publish.

Reported by Robert Harris in Selling Hitler: The Extraordinary Story of the Con Job of the Century (1986).

After all, we are in the entertainment business.

Reported by Robert Harris in Selling Hitler: The Extraordinary Story of the Con Job of the Century (1986).

Media

Keith Olbermann is trying to make a business out of destroying Bill O'Reilly. He's done certain things to Bill O'Reilly that I believe were way over the line. I think that's bad behavior. But it's okay for him to criticize Bill. And Bill shouldn't be so sensitive. He should ignore that.

Reported by Danny Shea in "Rupert Murdoch on Olbermann-O'Reilly Feud: 'Bill Shouldn't Be So Sensitive,'" huffpost.com, October 13, 2008.

Well, except for ABC, CBS, NBC, MSNBC, CNN, *New York Times*, the *Washington Post*, and about another 100 newspapers, I find little evidence of liberal bias in the media.

Widely cited; however, attribution unconfirmed.

In this country, Fox News has gotten a big, big audience that appreciates its independence. There's passion there, and it's pushed. . . . It has taken a long boot time, but it has now changed CNN because it has challenged them—they've become more centrist in their choice of stories. They're trying to become, using our phrase, more fair and balanced.

Interview with Robert J. Dowling and Paula Parisi, "Dialogue: Rupert Murdoch," Hollywood Reporter, November 17, 2005; accessible at hollywoodreporter.com.

Content is not just king, it is the emperor of all things electronic.

Reported by Michael Gerson in "The 64-gigabyte shape of the future," Washington Post, May 7, 2010; accessible at washingtonpost.com.

One day will get breakthrough and get retransmission money from cable. They say over our dead bodies, but one day someone with nothing to lose like CBS will break through and then everyone will follow.

Interview with Joshua Chaffin and Alien van Duyn, "Interview transcript: Rupert Murdoch and Roger Ailes," Financial Times, October 3, 2006; accessible at ft.com.

I believe people will be watching their TV screens for a long time and that TV channels have a long-term life. Do people want to delay their programme or watch it the next day? Yes, often, if it's their favourite programme. Do they want to pay for that? I don't know. They've certainly been prepared to pay for DVDs at the end of the season for a series, we led the way in that with Fox. There are going to be very many different ways of delivering content and we are here with content. Among the channel business, we like the channels, because it's a convenient way to create an identity. But if someone wants to put it on their DVRs, some shows, it's fine with us, as long as you pay for it.

Interview with Joshua Chaffin and Alien van Duyn, "Interview transcript: Rupert Murdoch and Roger Ailes," Financial Times, October 3, 2006; accessible at ft.com.

I'm going to Japan and Korea in the next few weeks. There are so many things happening, and new ways of delivering things. You have 20mg bits of delivery in Korea, yet TV is flourishing. People are playing games on their TV, young men are, and people are shopping . . . they are not watching their news channels, but they are using their TV's for other things. Broadband is not here just to replace TV. It's a handy way for cable, they need broadband to deliver, as a two-way instrument for people to trade or talk to each other; it's tremendous.

Interview with Joshua Chaffin and Alien van Duyn, "Interview transcript: Rupert Murdoch and Roger Ailes," Financial Times, October 3, 2006; accessible at ft.com.

The CNN international is a different service, it is even more leftist and anti-American than CNN is. That's their business, that's fine, but it can't be getting any revenue. There is no cable network that I know of anywhere in the world other than in America that pays them for their products. Maybe they have some deals with hotels but it's very much a hodgepodge and eats up a tremendous amount of money.

Interview with Joshua Chaffin and Alien van Duyn, "Interview transcript: Rupert Murdoch and Roger Ailes," Financial Times, October 3, 2006; accessible at ft.com.

Most of the media are local monopolies. They've got elitist journalists coming out of journalism school and they look down on their audiences. They are not in touch at all with the average middle class guy with the 50, 60,000 dollar job living out in the exurbs or the suburbs living a normal life. Look at what's happening in long island. The taxes have gone up so much that there is a major flight to the South. Do you get reports about it in the Long Island Newsday – no. The reason for these taxes, I don't know, but there is a major flight away from high taxes, big pieces of their discretionary income are going on this, and much against their will, second, third generation people are moving to the south or the west, not the far west because they would get hit again in California.

Interview with Joshua Chaffin and Alien van Duyn, "Interview transcript: Rupert Murdoch and Roger Ailes," Financial Times, October 3, 2006; accessible at ft.com.

There is a new young middle class who want better for themselves and their children, who aren't happy with inner city education, who were brought up in the row houses of Queens and the Bronx who have moved out to the suburbs, and now their children and moving further out or moving away altogether. These people are not conservatives, or don't think of themselves as conservatives, I would not know how they vote, there're not much in their local newspaper or on CNN that's designed for them.

Interview with Joshua Chaffin and Alien van Duyn, "Interview transcript: Rupert Murdoch and Roger Ailes," Financial Times, October 3, 2006; accessible at ft.com.

Murdoch on Murdoch

News—communicating news and ideas, I guess—is my passion. And giving people alternatives so that they have two papers to read (and) alternative television channels.

Interview with Robert J. Dowling and Paula Parisi, "Dialogue: Rupert Murdoch," Hollywood Reporter, November 17, 2005; accessible at hollywoodreporter.com.

They've started it. We've had bitter, personal attack on some of our people. They tried to destroy our credibility as a network. But it is only natural that the people can stand who were personally attacked and their children were personally attacked should fight back and I support them. I support my people completely.

Reported by Nicole Bell in "Countdown's Worst Person: Threats and Feuds Edition," crooksandliars.com, June 2, 2008.

I was very nervous. I dreaded falling in love —but I knew this would be my last. It better be. I'm happy.

Reported in "Rupert Murdoch to marry for fifth time at 92: 'I knew this would be my last,'" theguardian.com, March 20, 2023.

We're both looking forward to spending the second half of our lives together.

Reported in "Rupert Murdoch to marry for fifth time at 92: 'I knew this would be my last,'" theguardian.com, March 20, 2023.

Politics

The greatest thing to come out of [the Iraq War] for the world economy, if you could put it that way, would be $20 a barrel for oil. That's bigger than any tax cut in any country.

Reported by Julia Day in "Murdoch praises Blair's 'courage,'" theguardian.com, February 11, 2003.

Re: Donald Trump:

What a f**king idiot.

Reported by Michael Wolff in "Donald Trump Didn't Want to Be President," New York magazine, January 7, 2018; accessible at nymag.com.

The current American political debate is profound, whether about education or welfare or economic opportunity. It is crucial that conservatives play an active, forceful role in that debate, but that will not happen if President

Trump stays focused on the past. The past is the past, and the country is now in a contest to define the future.

Reported by Bess Levin in "Rupert Murdoch Tells Trump to STFU about 2020," vanityfair.com, November 17, 2021.

Elon Musk

Elon Musk / b. 1971 / South Africa / Entrepreneur, Co-Founder of PayPal, Founder of Tesla and SpaceX, and Owner of Twitter
Note: Though a native of South Africa, Musk has spent the bulk of his career in the US.

Apple

They [Apple] have hired people we've fired. We always jokingly call Apple the "Tesla Graveyard." If you don't make it at Tesla, you go work at Apple. I'm not kidding. . . . cars are very complex compared to phones or smartwatches. You can't just go to a supplier like Foxconn and say: Build me a car. But for Apple, the car is the next logical thing to finally offer a significant innovation. A new pencil or a bigger iPad alone were not relevant enough.

"All Charged Up in Berlin," Handelsblatt, September 25, 2015.

Artificial Intelligence

AI is much more advanced than people realize. ... Humanity's position on this planet depends on its intelligence so if our intelligence is exceeded, it's unlikely that we will remain in charge of the planet.

"Artificial intelligence: Should we be as terrified as Elon Musk and Bill Gates?," ZDNet, October 25, 2015.

Business Strategy

There's a graveyard of prior attempts, a big graveyard. There's probably some freshly dug graves just waiting to be filled. Our aspiration is to avoid that destination.

Interview, Wired Science, PBS (2007).

When thinking about starting a business, I think it's actually better to start in a trough and come to market in a peak, than the other way around. Frankly, if anything does, and it's almost cliché, space has a long-term future.

Interview, Wired Science, PBS (2007).

When Henry Ford made cheap, reliable cars people said, "Nah, what's wrong with a horse?' That was a huge bet he made, and it worked.

Interview, Wired Science, PBS (2007).

Starting and growing a business is as much about the innovation, drive and determination of the people who do it as it is about the product they sell.

Interview, Wired Science, PBS (2007).

I think it is a mistake to hire huge numbers of people to get a complicated job done. Numbers will never compensate for talent in getting the right answer (two people who don't know something are no better than one), will tend to slow down progress, and will make the task incredibly expensive.

Interview, Wired Science, PBS (2007).

My approach is simply to seek out very talented people, ensure that the environment at SpaceX is as motivating & enjoyable as possible and establish clear and measurable objectives.

Interview, Wired Science, PBS (2007).

When something is important enough, you do it even if the odds are not in your favor.

60 Minutes, CBS, March 18, 2012.

Failure

If things are not failing, you are not innovating enough.

"Hondas in Space," Fast Company magazine, February 1, 2005.

Free Speech

A good sign as to whether there is free speech is, "Is someone you don't like allowed to say something you don't like?

'Elon Musk talks Twitter, Tesla and how his brain works," TED2022, April 14, 2022.

God

I believe there's some explanation for this universe, which you might call God.

Axios, season 1, episode 4: "Technology, Faith and Impact on the Future," HBO, November 25, 2018.

Human Destiny

The long term ultimate objective—the holy grail—is we would like to help make life multi-planetary.

Interview, Wired Science, PBS (2007).

As life's agents, it's on our shoulders.

Interview, Wired Science, PBS (2007).

Sooner or later, we must expand life beyond our little blue mud ball—or go extinct.

Esquire, October 1, 2008.

We need to figure out how to have the things we love, and not destroy the world.

"Driving With Elon Musk," Forbes Life, March 26, 2012.

I think we have a duty to maintain the light of consciousness to make sure it continues into the future.

Attribution unconfirmed.

Internet

In terms of the Internet, it's like humanity acquiring a collective nervous system. Whereas previously we were more like a... collection of cells that communicated by diffusion. With the advent of the Internet, it was suddenly like we got a nervous system. It's a hugely impactful thing.

Interview with Adam Mann, Wired magazine, April 26, 2012.

Musk on Musk

I didn't really expect to make any money [with Tesla]. If I could make enough to cover the rent and buy some food that would be fine. As it turns out, it turned out to be quite valuable in the end.

Interview, Wired Science, PBS (2007).

I like to be involved in things that change the world. The Internet did, and space will probably be more responsible for changing the world than anything else. If humanity can expand beyond the Earth, obviously that's where the future is.

Interview, Wired Science, PBS (2007).

If you have millions of dollars it changes your lifestyle, and anyone who says differently is talking b******t. I don't need to work, from a standard of living point of view, but I do, you know. I work every day and on weekends and I haven't taken a vacation for years.

Interview, Wired Science, PBS (2007).

I'm nauseatingly pro-American. It is where great things are possible.

Interview, Wired Science, PBS (2007).

The heroes of the books I read, *The Lord of the Rings* and the *Foundation* series, always felt a duty to save the world,

"Plugged In: Can Elon Musk lead the way to an electric-car future?," New Yorker, August 24, 2009.

I'd rather be optimistic and wrong; than pessimistic and right.

Attribution unconfirmed.

I would like to die on Mars; just not on impact.

Interview with Ashley Vance, "Elon Musk, the 21st Century Industrialist," Bloomberg, September 12, 2012.

I plan to travel to Mars and make it my home.

Elon Musk, "Foreword," in Marc Kaufman, Mars Up Close: Inside the Curiosity Mission (2014).

For those wondering, I will pay over $11 billion in taxes this year.

"Elon Musk Claims He Will Pay More Than $11 Billion In Taxes This Year," Forbes, December 20, 2021.

Quality Assurance

We're adding a triple sign-off for all work done on the launch pad, on flight components, and flight critical GSE. You have a technician, a responsible engineer, and then quality assurance will sign the final, record all information, and take photographs of all the work that was done, and then make sure that all information is put into our quality assurance database, which is reviewed prior to launch.

Interview, Wired Science, PBS (2007).

Software Development

So, I think the best analogy for rocket engineers, if you want to create complicated software, you can't run as an integrated whole, or run on the computer it's intended to run on, but, first time you run it, it has to run with no bugs. That's the essence of it. So . . . we missed the mark there.

South Africa

I think South Africa is a great country.

Interview, Wired Science, PBS (2007).

I don't have an issue with serving in the military per se, but serving in the South African army suppressing black people just didn't seem like a really good way to spend time.

Interview, Wired Science, PBS (2007).

Space Exploration and SpaceX

There is nothing inherently expensive about rockets. It's just that those who have built and operated them in the past have done so with horrendously poor efficiency.

Interview, Wired Science, PBS (2007).

. . . we're cheaper than the Chinese, cheaper than [the] Russians or anywhere else—and we're doing it in the United States with American labour costs.

Interview, Wired Science, PBS (2007).

I think the reason it's cheaper is, first of all, we are a private entity and we have a very lean system in here. What we have been able to do here at SpaceX is to cherry-pick, you know, the top one or two percent and give them, you know, capital to execute well and a clear mission, which is low cost, reliable access to space, and no other constraints.

Interview, Wired Science, PBS (2007).

I think we've got the risks pretty well characterized. I think we are at least avoiding the mistakes that have been made in the past.

Interview, Wired Science, PBS (2007).

I want to be able to make sure that we have enough capital to survive at least three consecutive failures. If you want to make a small fortune in the launch vehicle business, start with a large one.

Interview, Wired Science, PBS (2007).

If we can build something that is capable of taking people and equipment to Mars, such that it can service a transportation infrastructure for humanity becoming a multi- planet species—which I think is a very, very important objective—then I would consider the mission of SpaceX successful, at that point.

Interview, Wired Science, PBS (2007).

Rocket engineering is not like ditch digging. With ditch digging you can get 100 people and dig a ditch, and you will dig it a hundred times faster if you get 100 people versus one. With rockets, you have to solve the problem of a particular level of difficulty; one person who can solve the problem is worth an infinite number of people who can't.

Interview, Wired Science, PBS (2007).

Although I am new in the business, my team is not. I would say that, person for person, there has never been a better rocket company in existence, in history. I don't think there has ever been a group this talented in one place, in one company, developing a rocket—ever.

Interview, Wired Science, PBS (2007).

Sending large numbers of people to explore and settle Mars in the decades ahead isn't inevitable, but it is entirely possible. The biggest challenge isn't the engineering and spacecraft, however difficult they may be. Instead, it's making sure that a sustained Mars campaign proceeds as a national priority, and that will happen only if the American people are behind it. We have the opportunity now to make this happen. We might not be so fortunate in the future.

Elon Musk, "Foreword," in Marc Kaufman, Mars Up Close: Inside the Curiosity Mission (2014).

Technological Improvement

We are used to things improving every year; we are used to having a better cell phone next year than this year; a better lap top. We are even used to some basic things, like we expect more from your car in next year's model than last year's model. But this is not the case in space; reliability and cost—those are the fundamental parameters of transportation—have not improved.

Interview, Wired Science, PBS (2007).

Twitter

This is not a way to make money. . . . I don't care about the economics at all. This is just my strong, intuitive sense . . . that having a public platform that is maximally trusted and broadly inclusive is extremely important to the future of civilization.

Pete Evans, "Elon Musk launches hostile bid for Twitter claiming free-speech concerns," CBC, Apr 14, 2022.

Is there a conspiracy theory about Twitter that didn't turn out to be true? So far they've all turned out to be true—if not more true than people thought.

Chamath Palihapitiva, "All-In" podcast, December 27, 2022.

Tyranny

If you scare people enough, they will demand removal of freedom. This is the path to tyranny.

Matthew Miller, "Elon Musk tweets ominous warning about 'path to tyranny,'" Washington Examiner, January 28, 2022.

United States

If you wanted to be close to the cutting edge, particularly in technology, you came to North America.

Interview, Wired Science, PBS (2007).

Friedrich Nietzsche

Friedrich Nietzsche / 1844–1900 / Röcken, Province of Saxony, Kingdom of Prussia (now Germany) / Classicist, Philosopher, Author

Abyss

He who fights with monsters should see to it that he himself does not become a monster. And if you gaze long into an abyss, the abyss also gazes into you.

Jenseits von Gut und Böse [Beyond Good and Evil] (1886).

Art

Art is the supreme task and the truly metaphysical activity in this life.

Die Geburt der Tragödie [The Birth of Tragedy] (1872).

Thus the man who is responsive to artistic stimuli reacts to the reality of dreams as does the philosopher to the reality of existence; he observes closely, and he enjoys his observation: for it is out of these images that he interprets life, out of these processes that he trains himself for life.

Die Geburt der Tragödie [The Birth of Tragedy] (1872).

Without art we would be nothing but foreground and live entirely in the spell of that perspective which makes what is closest at hand and most vulgar appear as if it were vast, and reality itself.

Die fröhliche Wissenschaft [The Gay Science] (1882).

Boredom

Against boredom even gods struggle in vain.

Der Antichrist [The Anti-Christ] (1888).

Conscience

What does your conscience say?—"You shall become the person you are."

Die fröhliche Wissenschaft [The Gay Science] (1882).

Education

The surest way to corrupt a youth is to instruct him to hold in higher esteem those who think alike than those who think differently.

Morgenröte [Daybreak] (1881).

Equality

The doctrine of equality! … But there is no more venomous poison in existence: for it appears to be preached by justice itself, when it is actually the end of justice … "Equality to the equal; inequality to the unequal"—that would be true justice speaking: and its corollary, "never make the unequal equal."

Götzen-Dämmerung [Twilight of the Idols] (1888).

Experience

What does not kill me, makes me stronger.

Götzen-Dämmerung [Twilight of the Idols] (1888).

Facts

There are no facts, only interpretations.

Tageücher [Notebooks]; selections first published posthumously in 1901; numerous subsequent editions.

Freedom

Today as always, men fall into two groups: slaves and free men. Whoever does not have two-thirds of his day for himself, is a slave, whatever he may be: a statesman, a businessman, an official, or a scholar.

Menschliches, allzumenschliches [Human, All Too Human] (1878).

God

Have you not heard of that madman who lit a lantern in the bright morning hours, ran to the market place, and cried incessantly: "I seek God! I seek God!"—As many of those who did not believe in God were standing around just then, he provoked much laughter. Has he got lost? asked one. Did he lose his way like a child? asked another. Or is he hiding? Is he afraid of us? Has he gone on a voyage? emigrated?—Thus they yelled and laughed. The madman jumped into their midst and pierced them with his eyes. "Whither is God?" he cried; "I will tell you. *We have killed him*—you and I. All of us are his murderers. But how did we do this? How could we drink up the sea? Who gave us the sponge to wipe away the entire horizon? What were we doing when we unchained this earth from its sun? Whither is it moving now? Whither are we moving? Away from all suns? Are we not plunging continually? Backward, sideward, forward, in all directions? Is there still any up or down? Are we not straying, as through an infinite nothing? Do we not feel the breath of empty space? Has it not become colder? Is not night continually closing in on us? Do we not need to light lanterns in the morning? Do we hear nothing as yet of the noise of the gravediggers who are burying God? Do we smell nothing as yet of the divine decomposition? Gods, too, decompose. God is dead. God remains dead. And we have killed him.

How shall we comfort ourselves, the murderers of all murderers? What was holiest and mightiest of all that the world has yet owned has bled to death under our knives: who will wipe this blood off us? What water is there for us to clean ourselves? What festivals of atonement, what sacred games shall we have to invent? Is not the greatness of this deed too great for us? Must we ourselves not become gods simply to appear worthy of it? . . .

Die fröhliche Wissenschaft [The Gay Science] (1882).

Haste

Haste is universal because everyone is in flight from himself.

"Schopenhauer als Erzieher" [Schopenhauer as Educator], collected in Unzeitgemässe Betrachtungen [Untimely Meditations] (1873).

Humanity

Once upon a time, in some out of the way corner of that universe which is dispersed into numberless twinkling solar systems, there was a star upon which clever beasts invented knowing.

"Über Wahrheit und Lüge im aussermoralischen Sinne" [On Truth and Lies in a Nonmoral Sense], composed in 1873; first published in 1896.

Man has an invincible inclination to allow himself to be deceived and is, as it were, enchanted with happiness when the rhapsodist tells him epic fables as if they were true, or when the actor in the theater acts more royally than any real king.

"Über Wahrheit und Lüge im aussermoralischen Sinne" [On Truth and Lies in a Nonmoral Sense], composed in 1873; first published in 1896.

Life

No one can construct for you the bridge upon which precisely you must cross the stream of life, no one but you yourself alone.

"Schopenhauer als Erzieher" [Schopenhauer as Educator], collected in Unzeitgemässe Betrachtungen [Untimely Meditations] (1873).

For believe me!—the secret for harvesting from existence the greatest fruitfulness and the greatest enjoyment is: to live dangerously!

Die fröhliche Wissenschaft [The Gay Science] (1882).

He who has a Why? in life can tolerate almost any How?

Götzen-Dämmerung [Twilight of the Idols] (1888).

Motivation

One will rarely err if extreme actions be ascribed to vanity, ordinary actions to habit, and mean actions to fear

Menschliches, allzumenschliches [Human, All Too Human] (1878).

Music

Without music, life would be a mistake.

Götzen-Dämmerung [Twilight of the Idols] (1888).

Philosophy

. . . philosophy offers an asylum to a man into which no tyranny can force it way, the inward cave, the labyrinth of the heart.

"Schopenhauer als Erzieher" [Schopenhauer as Educator], collected in Unzeitgemässe Betrachtungen [Untimely Meditations] (1873).

Reality

We believe that we know something about the things themselves when we speak of trees, colors, snow, and flowers; and yet we possess nothing but metaphors for things—metaphors which correspond in no way to the original entities.

"Über Wahrheit und Lüge im aussermoralischen Sinne" [On Truth and Lies in a Nonmoral Sense], composed in 1873; first published in 1896.

Reputation

Some are born posthumously.

Der Antichrist [The Anti-Christ] (1888).

One must pay dearly for immortality; one has to die several times while one is still alive.

Ecce Homo [Ecce Homo] (1888).

I know my fate. One day my name will be associated with the memory of something tremendous—a crisis without equal on earth, the most profound collision of conscience, a decision that was conjured up against everything that had been believed, demanded, hallowed so far. I am no man, I am dynamite.

Ecce Homo [Ecce Homo] (1888).

Socrates

We cannot help but see Socrates as the turning-point, the vortex of world history.

Die Geburt der Tragödie [The Birth of Tragedy] (1872).

State

Everything the State says is a lie, and everything it has it has stolen.

Also Sprach Zarathustra [Thus Spoke Zarathustra] (1883).

Truth

Lessing, the most honest of theoretical men, dared to say that he took greater delight in the quest for truth than in the truth itself.

Die Geburt der Tragödie [The Birth of Tragedy] (1872).

What then is truth? A movable host of metaphors, metonymies, and anthropomorphisms: in short, a sum of human relations which have been poetically and rhetorically intensified, transferred, and embellished, and which, after long usage, seem to a people to be fixed, canonical, and binding.

"Über Wahrheit und Lüge im aussermoralischen Sinne" [On Truth and Lies in a Nonmoral Sense], composed in 1873; first published in 1896.

In the mountains of truth you will never climb in vain: either you will get up higher today or you will exercise your strength so as to be able to get up higher tomorrow.

Menschliches, allzumenschliches [Human, All Too Human] (1878).

Convictions are more dangerous enemies of truth than lies.

Menschliches, allzumenschliches [Human, All Too Human] (1878).

It is not enough to prove something, one has also to seduce or elevate people to it.

Morgenröte [Daybreak] (1881).

Wit

A witticism is an epigram on the death of a feeling.

Menschliches, allzumenschliches [Human, All Too Human] (1878).

Larry Edward Page

Larry Edward Page / b. 1973 / Michigan, USA / Computer Scientist, Entrepreneur

Artificial Intelligence

The Star Trek computer doesn't seem that interesting. They ask it random questions, it thinks for a while. I think we can do better than that.

Reported by Ben Elgin, "Google's Goal: 'Understand Everything,'" BusinessWeek, May 3, 2004.

Dreaming

Sometimes it's important to wake up and stop dreaming. When a really great dream shows up, grab it.

Page's Commencement Address, University of Michigan, 2009.

Impossibility

Have a healthy disregard for the impossible.

Reported by David J.. Hill, "Larry Page: With a Healthy Disregard for the Impossible, People Can Do Almost Anything," singularityhub.com, May 26, 2012.

Research

I have a simple algorithm, which is, wherever you see paid researchers instead of grad students, that's not where you want to be doing research.

Plenary Lecture, annual conference, American Association for the Advancement of Science (AAAS), San Francisco, February, 2007.

YouTube

It's hard to keep things moving. And that's always a big trick. I think for me, the key is setting really big goals. And, you know, with YouTube, I think we've had tremendous leadership, both with the founders and now with Salar [Kumangar], who's been running it.

Interview with Campbell Brown, Zeitgeist Americas 2012 Conference, Arizona, October 16, 2012.

Satchel Paige

Satchel Paige / 1906–1982 / Alabama, USA / Baseball

There ain't no man can avoid being born average. But there ain't no man got to be common.

Source: Lincoln Evening Journal and Nebraska State Journal, July 26, 1958.

Don't pray when it rains if you don't pray when the sun shines.

Source: New York Post, October 4, 1959.

Avoid running at all times. And don't look back—something might be gaining on you.

Source: Collier's Magazine, June 13, 1953.

I never threw an illegal pitch. The trouble is, once in a while I toss one that ain't never been seen by this generation.

Source: New York Times, June 9, 1982.

They said I was the greatest pitcher they ever saw… I couldn't understand why they couldn't give me no justice

Source: New York Times, June 9, 1982.

Dorothy Parker

Dorothy Parker (née Rothschild) / 1893–1967 / Long Branch, New Jersey, USA / Poet, Literary Critic, Satirist

Children

The best way to keep children at home is to make the home atmosphere pleasant, and let the air out of the tires.

"My Home Town," The American Mercury, July, 1937.

Human Nature

Beauty is only skin deep, but ugly goes clean to the bone.

Review of The House of Mirth by Edith Wharton, Vanity Fair, 1918.

You can lead a horticulture, but you can't make her think.

The New Yorker, 1927.

The cure for boredom is curiosity. There is no cure for curiosity.

Interview, "The Paris Review," Spring, 1956.

Literature

This is not a novel to be tossed aside lightly. It should be thrown with great force.

The New Yorker, 1952.

Parker on Parker

That would be a good thing for them to cut on my tombstone: Wherever she went, including here, it was against her better judgment.

The New Yorker, August 22, 1942.

It serves me right for putting all my eggs in one bastard.

Cited in Kevin C. Fitzpatrick, The Algonquin Round Table New York: A Historical Guide (2015).

I don't know much about being a millionaire, but I'll bet I'd be darling at it.

Interview, "The Paris Review," Spring, 1956.

I don't care what is written about me so long as it isn't true.

The New Yorker, March 26, 1927.

I'd like to have money. And I'd like to be a good writer. These two can come together, and I hope they will, but if that's too adorable, I'd rather have money.

Interview, "The Paris Review," Spring, 1956.

What fresh hell is this? (upon hearing her doorbell ring).

Source unknown.

Politics

You can't teach an old dogma new tricks.

Review of Catherine the Great by Zoë Oldenbourg, Esquire, June, 1965.

The Rich

If you want to know what God thinks of money, just look at the people he gave it to.

"The Philosopher," in Not So Deep as a Well (1937).

Take care of the luxuries, and the necessities will take care of themselves.

"Our Lady of Wrath," Esquire, September, 1952.

Romance

Men seldom make passes at girls who wear glasses.

Review of A Portrait of the Artist as a Young Man by James Joyce, Vanity Fair, 1922.

Suicide

Razors pain you;
Rivers are damp;
Acids stain you;
And drugs cause cramp.
Guns aren't lawful;
Nooses give;
Gas smells awful;
You might as well live.

"Resumé," Enough Rope (1926).

Wit

There's a hell of a distance between wisecracking and wit. Wit has truth in it; wisecracking is simply calisthenics with words.

Cited in Marion Meade, Dorothy Parker: What Fresh Hell Is This? (1988).

Writing

This is a funny business we're in. But it's a business.

The New Yorker, July 11, 1953.

Blaise Pascal

Blaise Pascal / 1623–1662 / France / Mathematician, Physicist, Philosopher, Theologian

Beginning

Things are always at their best in their beginning.

Source: Provincial Letters, Letter IV (1656).

Belief

People almost invariably arrive at their beliefs not on the basis of proof but on the basis of what they find attractive.

Source: De l'art de persuader [On the Art of Persuasion] (1658).

Distraction

Distraction.—When I have sometimes considered the various troubles of men and the perils and pains they expose themselves to, in the court, in war, whence flow so many quarrels, passions, and bold and often bad ventures, etc., I have often said that all of men's unhappiness derives from one single thing: that they cannot rest quietly in a room.

Source: Pensées [Thoughts], Léon Brunschvicg ed. #139; first published posthumously in 1670.

Equality

Your soul and your body are, of themselves, indifferent to the state of boatman or that of duke; and there is no natural bond that attaches them to one condition rather than to another.

Source: Three Discourses on the Condition of the Great (written 1660; published 1670).

If you act externally with men in conformity with your rank, you should recognize, by a more secret but truer thought, that you have nothing naturally superior to them.

Source: Three Discourses on the Condition of the Great (written 1660, published 1670).

Friends

I lay it down as a fact that if all men knew what others say of them, there would not be four friends in the world.

Source: Pensées [Thoughts], Léon Brunschvicg ed. #101; first published posthumously in 1670.

God

FIRE.

GOD of Abraham, GOD of Isaac, GOD of Jacob, not of the philosophers and scholars.

Certainty. Certainty. Feeling. Joy. Peace.

Source: "Mémorial" [Remembrance], a parchment found sewn into the lining of Pascal's overcoat after his death, commemorating a an epiphany he experienced between 10:30 pm, November 23, and12:30 am, November 24, 1654, known as the "nuit de feu" [night of fire].

Justice

The justest man in the world is not allowed to be judge in his own cause.

Source: Pensées [Thoughts], Léon Brunschvicg ed. #82; first published posthumously in 1670.

Liberty

It is not good to have too much liberty. It is not good to have all one wants.

Source: Pensées [Thoughts], Léon Brunschvicg ed. #379; first published posthumously in 1670.

Man

What is man in nature? Nothing in relation to the infinite, everything in relation to nothing, a mean between nothing and everything.

Source: Pensées [Thoughts], Léon Brunschvicg ed. #72; first published posthumously in 1670.

The state of man: inconstancy, boredom, anxiety.

Source: Pensées [Thoughts], Léon Brunschvicg ed. #127; first published posthumously in 1670.

Man is but a reed, the most feeble thing in nature; but he is a thinking reed. The entire universe need not arm itself to crush him. A vapour, a drop of water suffices to kill him. But, if the universe were to crush him, man would still be more noble than that which killed him, because he knows that he dies and the advantage which the universe has over him; the universe knows nothing of this.

Source: Pensées [Thoughts], Léon Brunschvicg ed. #347; first published posthumously in 1670.

Meaning of Life

When I consider the brief span of my life absorbed into the eternity which precedes and will succeed it—*Memoria hospitis unius diei praetereuntis**—the small space I occupy and which I see swallowed up in the infinite immensity of spaces of which I know nothing and which know nothing of me, I take fright and am amazed to see myself here rather than there: there is no reason for me to be here rather than there, now rather than then. Who put me here? By whose command and act were this place and time allotted to me?

Source: Pensées [Thoughts], Léon Brunschvicg ed. #205; first published posthumously in 1670.

**"[. . . like as the smoke which is dispersed here and there with a tempest, and] passeth away as the remembrance of a guest that tarrieth but a day" (Wisdom 5:14 KJV).*

Morality

The vanity of the sciences.—The science of external things will not console me for ignorance of morality in time of affliction; but the science of ethics will always console me for ignorance of the external sciences.

Source: Pensées [Thoughts], Léon Brunschvicg ed. #67; first published posthumously in 1670.

Persuasion

The art of persuasion consists as much in that of pleasing as in that of convincing, so much more are men governed by caprice than by reason!

Source: De l'art de persuader [On the Art of Persuasion] (1658).

Reasons

The heart has its reasons which reason knows nothing of.

Source: Pensées [Thoughts], Léon Brunschvicg ed. #277; first published posthumously in 1670.

Self-Importance

How many kingdoms know nothing of us!

Source: Pensées [Thoughts], Léon Brunschvicg ed. #207; first published posthumously in 1670.

Truth

Whilst in speaking of human things, we say that it is necessary to know them before we can love them…the saints on the contrary say in speaking of divine things that it is necessary to love them in order to know them, and that we only enter truth through charity.

Source: De l'art de persuader [On the Art of Persuasion] (1658).

God only pours out his light into the mind after having subdued the rebellion of the will.

Source: De l'art de persuader [On the Art of Persuasion] (1658).

Universe

The eternal silence of these infinite spaces frightens me.

Source: Pensées [Thoughts], Léon Brunschvicg ed. #206; first published posthumously in 1670.

Writing

I would have written a shorter letter, but I did not have the time.

Source: Provincial Letters, Letter XVI (1656).

H. Ross Perot

Henry Ross Perot / 1930–2019 / Texas, USA / Businessman, Founder and CEO of Electronic Data Systems, Third-Party US Presidential Candidate

Economics

Unless we take action now, our nation may confront a situation similar to the Great Depression and maybe even worse. Our economic growth has been sluggish for nearly two decades. The unemployment numbers remain depressing, while the Federal Reserve worries about inflation. . . .

In other words, our economy is perched on the edge of a cliff. Either we work together to climb back to safety, or we must brace ourselves for potential disaster. This book provides a plan to pull our nation back from the brink.

Ross Perot, United We Stand: How We Can Take Back Our Country (1992).

Environment

The activist is not the man who says the river is dirty. The activist is the man who cleans up the river.

Widely cited; however, attribution unconfirmed.

Federal Deposit Insurance Corporation (FDIC)

The institutions we depend on to preserve our financial security are shaky. If they fail, millions of people will be devastated. Banks are already weak. The Federal Deposit Insurance Corporation (FDIC), which we as taxpayers guarantee, may incur liabilities greater than those from the recent Savings & Loan crisis.

Ross Perot, United We Stand: How We Can Take Back Our Country (1992).

National Debt

There's only one way to fix it and that is to face the issue. I mean, if you're in debt, you know what you've gotta do: you've gotta pay it, right?

Interview with Bill Cork, President, Texarkana Chamber of Commerce, April 7, 2015; video accessible at youtube.com.

See, here's the sad thing. The newspapers and television make no effort at all to educate the American people on this, **the** most critical issue facing our country. If they would, then the American people would say "We've gotta fix it," right? "We don't have a choice, we **have** to fix it." It's kind of like the guy that drinks too much, you know? He's gotta put a cork on the bottle. He's gotta quit. We can't stop spending, but we can cut it back to a rational level.

Interview with Bill Cork, President, Texarkana Chamber of Commerce, April 7, 2015; video accessible at youtube.com.

Perot on Perot

I was born on June 27, 1930, in the hospital [in Texarkana]. Outside it was 120 degrees. My dad walked in after I was born—I couldn't remember this, but mother told me —and said: "Well, the devil must have come up to see his handiwork, it's so hot outside." That's the way it all started.

Interview with Bill Cork, President, Texarkana Chamber of Commerce, April 7, 2015; video accessible at youtube.com.

All of my business training was at my father's knee. I sat in his office and watched him deal with the farmers as a cotton broker.

Television interview with Murphy Martin, "A Conversation with Ross Perot," 1992; video accessible at youtube.com.

People have asked me over the years when I first felt rich. I've always said I was born rich. . . . We always saved money. We always got by. Everybody worked when I was a child.

Television interview with Murphy Martin, "A Conversation with Ross Perot," 1992; video accessible at youtube.com.

During the Depression, hobos coming [from] as far away as California would jump off the train there, come up a gravel road to our house, and knock on the door for food. And my mother would always give them food. And one time, one of the people said, "Lady, do you have a lot of people coming up here?" And she said, "Yes, I do." He said, "Did you ever wonder why?" She said, "No." He said, "Would you like me to show you?" She said, "Yes." He showed her the mark on the curb. It meant, "This lady—they'll give you food." And—I'll never forget—when he left I said, "Mother, do you want me to wash that off?" And she looked me in the eye, with no smile at all, and said, "No, son. These are people who are down on their luck, we need to help them." Now that tells you the environment I grew up in.

Interview with Bill Cork, President, Texarkana Chamber of Commerce, April 7, 2015; video accessible at youtube.com.

Re: Perot's wife Margot:

We had a blind date. I was immediately in love. Anybody who ever knows Margo immediately falls in love with her. . . . I had bigtime competition. . . . I talked her into marrying me.

Television interview with Murphy Martin, "A Conversation with Ross Perot," 1992; video accessible at youtube.com.

I've got plenty to work on all day, so I have to come in early and work hard. I've got a wife and four daughters, so i have to work hard to stay even, David.

Telephone interview with David Letterman, Late Night with David Letterman, NBC, April 21, 1992; video accessible at youtube.com.

I was Texas born and Texas bred, and Texarkana raised, and when I die, I'll be Texas dead.

Interview with Bill Cork, President, Texarkana Chamber of Commerce, April 7, 2015; video accessible at youtube.com.

Perot's Supporters

This book is dedicated to the millions of volunteers who accomplished the seemingly impossible task of getting the petitions signed. You did it brilliantly.

You changed American politics in just five months.

You made it clear that the people, not the special interests, own this country.

Everyone in Washington now understands that the American people own this country, have reasserted their roles as owners, and want the country's problems addressed and solved.

The creativity, ingenuity, and focused dedication to this task are unique in American politics.
The founders of our government must be looking down from heaven, smiling on all of you.

Ross Perot, United We Stand: How We Can Take Back Our Country (1992).

Presidential Campaign of 1992

I love the American people and I am sure that you do, too. I owe them a debt I can never repay and so do you. Today, their Government is a mess, and they want it fixed. By joining together as the owners of this great country, they can solve these problems.
As I've said before, it is time to clean out the barn—join us—pick up a shovel. Get to work!

Speech; reported in "How Stupid Do They Think We Are?," New York Times, August 30, 1992; accessible at nytimes.com.

Few people in this country have been able to live the American Dream to the extent that I have. . . . Neither political party has effectively addressed the issues that concern the American people. . . . The American people are good, but they have a government that is a mess.

News conference, October 1, 1992; video accessible at cspan.com.

Re: North Atlantic Treaty Organization (NATO):
If I'm poor and you're rich, and I can get you to defend me that's good. But when the tables get turned, I would do my share. Right now we spend about $300 billion dollars a year on defense, the Japanese spend around $30 billion in Asia, the Germans spend about $30 billion in Europe. For example, Germany will spend about a trillion dollars building infrastructure over the next 10 years. That's kinda easy to do if you don't have to pick up a $30 billion dollar tab to defend your country. The European community is in a position to pay a lot more then they have in the past. . . . Now that they can, they should.

Presidential debate, 1992.

Re: North American Free Trade Agreement (NAFTA):
We've shipped millions of jobs overseas and we have a strange situation because we have a process in Washington where after you've served for a while you cash in and become a foreign lobbyist, make $30,000 a month; then take a leave, work on Presidential campaigns, make sure you got good contacts, and then go back out. Now if you just want to get down to brass tacks, the first thing you ought to do is get all these folks who've got these one-way trade agreements that we've negotiated over the years and say, "Fellows, we'll take the same deal we gave you." And they'll gridlock right at that point because, for example, we've got international competitors who simply could not unload their cars off the ships if they had to comply—you see, if it was a two-way street—just couldn't do it. We have got to stop sending jobs overseas.

Presidential debate, 1992; transcript accessible at nytimes.com.

Re: North American Free Trade Agreement (NAFTA):
We have got to stop sending jobs overseas. It's pretty simple: If you're paying $12, $13, $14 an hour for factory workers and you can move your factory South of the border, pay a dollar an hour for labor, . . . have no health care—that's the most expensive single element in making a car—have no environmental controls, no pollution controls and no retirement, and you don't care about anything but making money, there will be a giant sucking sound going south. . . . When jobs [in Mexico] come up from a dollar an hour to six dollars an hour, and ours go down to six dollars an hour, then it's leveled again. But

in the meantime, you've wrecked the country with these kinds of deals.

Presidential debate, 1992; transcript accessible at nytimes.com.

Success

Something in human nature causes us to start slacking off at our moment of greatest accomplishment. As you become successful, you will need a great deal of self-discipline not to lose your sense of balance, humility and commitment.

Widely cited; however, attribution unconfirmed.

Jordan B. Peterson

Jordan Bernt Peterson / b. 1962 / Edmonton, Alberta, Canada / Clinical Psychologist, Professor of Psychology, Lecturer, Author, Podcaster
Note: Where known, sources are cited. However, no specific sources are known for many of the following quotations, which may appear in multiple writings, lectures, interviews, podcasts, and/or tweets.

Happiness

The pursuit of happiness is a pointless goal.
Happiness is a pointless goal. The more you pursue it, the more you flee it.
12 Rules for Life: An Antidote to Chaos (2018).

Human Nature

If you think tough men are dangerous, wait until you see what weak men are capable of.
People who don't think that their lives are worthwhile and meaningful are likely to be resentful, bitter, dangerous, and destructive.
12 Rules for Life: An Antidote to Chaos (2018).
The very idea of the 'Noble Savage' is a racist concept. It suggests that human beings are so corrupt that only aboriginal people are essentially good. That's nonsense.

Ideology

Ideologies are substitutes for true knowledge, and ideologues are always dangerous when they come to power, because a simple-minded I-know-it-all approach is no match for the complexity of existence.
12 Rules for Life: An Antidote to Chaos (2018).

Life

Order and chaos are the yin and yang of life.
The purpose of life is finding the largest burden that you can bear and bearing it.
The purpose of life is not happiness alone. It is something greater: meaningfulness.
12 Rules for Life: An Antidote to Chaos (2018).
You're not after a secure income, comfortable inaction, and endless leisure. You're after adventure, and adventure is never without risk.
12 Rules for Life: An Antidote to Chaos (2018).
You don't get to choose not to pay a price, you only get to choose which price you pay.
It's in responsibility that most people find the meaning that sustains them through life. It's not in happiness. It's not in impulsive pleasure.
12 Rules for Life: An Antidote to Chaos (2018).

Moral Education

Don't let your kids do anything that makes you dislike them.
12 Rules for Life: An Antidote to Chaos (2018).

The best way to make a tyrant out of someone is to feed and encourage their victim mentality.

You should take care of, you should have some care for, you should have some respect for, the things that are outside of you that are fragile and dying.

It is far better to render Beings in your care competent than to protect them. It is far better to ensure that they are able to take care of themselves.

12 Rules for Life: An Antidote to Chaos (2018).

Public Discourse

In order to think, you have to risk being offensive.

If you don't say what you think then you kill your unborn self.

Self-Improvement

Clean your room.

Compare yourself to who you were yesterday, not to who someone else is today.

12 Rules for Life: An Antidote to Chaos (2018).

To stand up straight with your shoulders back is to accept the terrible responsibility of life, with eyes wide open.

12 Rules for Life: An Antidote to Chaos (2018).

Treat yourself as if you were someone you are responsible for helping.

12 Rules for Life: An Antidote to Chaos (2018).

Aim at the highest good you can conceive and commit to it heart and soul.

Order is not enough. You can't just be stable, and secure, and unchanging because there are still vital and important new things to be learned. Nonetheless, chaos can be too much. You can't long tolerate being swamped and overwhelmed beyond your capacity to cope while you are learning what you still need to know.

12 Rules for Life: An Antidote to Chaos (2018).

You cannot be protected from the things that frighten you and hurt you, but if you identify with the part of your being that is responsible for transformation, then you are always equal or more than equal to the challenge.

12 Rules for Life: An Antidote to Chaos (2018).

Self-Knowledge

You're not as nice as you think. You're not as smart as you think.

You can only find out what you actually believe (rather than what you think you believe) by watching how you act. You simply don't know what you believe, before that. You are too complex to understand yourself.

12 Rules for Life: An Antidote to Chaos (2018).

Suffering

You need a meaning to offset the suffering of life.

Lecture, "The Psychological Significance of the Biblical Stories, Lecture 6: The Flood—Psychological Background" (2017).

The suffering that you will have to endure will have a purpose, even if it is only the learning of what you do not want. And that's a start. That's always a start. Then you can ask yourself, if you dare, what it is that you would like to find instead.

12 Rules for Life: An Antidote to Chaos (2018).

You're going to pay a price for every bloody thing you do and everything you don't do. You don't get to choose to not pay a price. You get to choose which poison you're going to take. That's it.

Lecture, "Personality and Its Transformations, Lecture 18: Biology and Traits —Openness, Intelligence, and Creativity (Part 1)" (2017).

Truthfulness

It's a lot harder to tell the truth than to not, and if you do tell the truth, then you have to be a good person, because otherwise, all that's going to happen to you is that you're going to get walloped.

Vision

Don't underestimate the power of vision and direction. These are irresistible forces, able to transform what might appear to be unconquerable obstacles into traversable pathways and expanding opportunities.

12 Rules for Life: An Antidote to Chaos (2018).

T. Boone Pickens

Thomas Boone Pickens, Jr. / 1928–2019 / Oklahoma, USA / Geologist, Wildcatter, Entrepreneur, Financier, Founder and Chairman of BP Capital Management

Business Philosophy

Don't fall victim to the notion that you have to be a high-priced talent to succeed. That simply isn't true. You can make yourself into a first-rate talent, whatever your chosen field, by hard work and experience.

Twitter post, June 26, 2014.

A plan without action is not a plan. It's a speech.

Speech, National Press Club, 2008; repeated in T. Boone Pickens, The First Billion is the Hardest: Reflections on a Life of Comebacks and America's Energy (2008), and in an interview with Piers Morgan, CNN, October 20, 2011.

A fool with a plan can outsmart a genius with no plan any day.

Reported in New York Times Magazine, August 3, 2008.

Don't fall victim to what I call the ready-aim-aim-aim-aim syndrome. You must be willing to fire.

Speech, Rotary Club of Dallas,1996; reported by Steve Coll in "The Oracle of Oil," The New Yorker, October 16, 2006.

Be willing to make decisions. That's the most important quality in a good leader.

Reported by Katie Couric, "The Best Advice I Ever Got," Time magazine, January 7, 2013.

When you are hunting elephants, don't get distracted chasing rabbits.

Reported in "Boone Pickens' 10 Best Quotes," Forbes magazine, September 12, 2011.

In business, you either have a competitive advantage or you don't. The question is whether you have one that is sustainable.

T. Boone Pickens, Jr., Boone (1987).

If you're not making mistakes, you're not taking risks, and that means you're not going anywhere.

Interview with CNBC, May 2, 2012.

Deepwater Horizon Oil Spill

Q: What is this going to do to BP [British Petroleum]? Do they go out of business?

A: No. They're not going to go out of business. I mean, they are the largest oil producer in the United States. 700,000 barrels a day and 2.5 billion cubic feet of gas a day is what they produce in the United States. So, those assets alone, not counting their marketing and refining, are worth probably $150 billion.

Interview with Larry King, CNN, July 19, 2010; transcript accessible at cnn.com.

Q: What's the danger of other spills?

A: You know, this is the first one in 50 years. And, you know, not to be repetitious, but it has been awhile. But, you know, two pilots qualified, crashed an airliner. You can sure have pilot error and sometimes you do have.

You don't quit—you don't shut down the airlines for that. So here, they should go back to drilling.

Interview with Larry King, CNN, July 19, 2010; transcript accessible at cnn.com.

Q: Does the federal government owe something?

A: No, I don't see the federal government is not—I think they were slow getting the skimmers in there. And that part, they were slow making some decisions, but I don't think the government owes anybody anything.

Interview with Larry King, CNN, July 19, 2010; transcript accessible at cnn.com.

Q: Did we refuse help from other countries?

A: I think we did.

Q: Was that a mistake?

A: Probably.

Q: Why do you think we would refuse someone—

A: I don't know. I don't understand it. We should have taken the help.

Interview with Larry King, CNN, July 19, 2010; transcript accessible at cnn.com.

Energy Policy

Q: How much headway have you made there?

A: Good. I mean, we've made good progress. And I think we'll have an energy plan for America before the year is out, and that will be the first energy plan America has ever had in 40 years. I think that will happen.

Interview with Larry King, CNN, July 19, 2010; transcript accessible at cnn.com.

Q: Why does the Pickens plan only call for reducing dependence on foreign oil?

A: Well, I really—it's even narrower than that. I want to get off the Mid East oil. I want to get off OPEC oil, because I think it's a security issue for the country. But you know, it's exactly what the president said. When he got the nomination at Denver in July of 2008, on energy, he said in ten years, we will not import any oil from the Mid East. And I cheered him for that when he said it. And that's the oil we have to get off of first.

Interview with Larry King, CNN, July 19, 2010; transcript accessible at cnn.com.

Q: And natural gas is still your big thing, right?

A: Well, you got 4,000 trillion cubic feet of natural gas in the United States. And it's 30 percent cleaner than oil. It's cheaper. It sells for 25 percent of the cost of oil—

Q: Seems logical.

A: It sure does. You'd look like an idiot if we don't do it.

Interview with Larry King, CNN, July 19, 2010; transcript accessible at cnn.com.

Pickens on Pickens

The first billion is the hardest.

Interview with Fortune magazine, June 12, 2008; repeated in interview with Forbes magazine, September 8, 2008.

The older you get, the more it's not about what you've accomplished, but what you can accomplish.

Interview with CNBC, October 27, 2017.

The older I get, the more convinced I am that the only way to become a billionaire is to help a billion people.

Twitter post, January 21, 2015.

The older I get, the more convinced I am that the only way to reach your potential is to help others reach theirs.

T. Boone Pickens, The First Billion Is the Hardest: Reflections on a Life of Comebacks and America's Energy (2008).

The older I get, the more convinced I am that the only way to become a better investor is to invest in yourself.

Twitter post, September 22, 2013.

I never made a mistake in my life. I thought I did once, but I was wrong.

Twitter post, November 20, 2017.

The people who invest with me are not looking for safety. They're looking for a big return.

Reported in the New York Times, July 30, 2007.

In any investment, you expect to have fun and make money.

Reported in USA Today, September 14, 2018.

The older I get, the more convinced I am that the only way to get ahead in this world is to be proactive, not reactive.

T. Boone Pickens, The First Billion Is the Hardest: Reflections on a Life of Comebacks and America's Energy (2008).

Q: Could you retire?

A: No. I owe too much money. Thanks.

Interview with Larry King, CNN, July 19, 2010; transcript accessible at cnn.com.

Technology

Q: When can a car go on natural gas?

A: You can get cars now—if [the caller] lived in Paris, France, he could go shopping tonight for a passenger car and look at 40 to 45 cars that are on natural gas. BMWs, Mercedes, GM, Ford, all of them are made there. GM makes 18 and makes none in the United States.

Q: Why?

A: Because they haven't had a market for it. If there had been a market, GM would have made them.

Interview with Larry King, CNN, July 19, 2010; transcript accessible at cnn.com.

Q: [The caller] couldn't convert his car to [natural gas]?

A: I don't advise that. But if—what I'm after are the big users of diesel. And those are the 18-wheelers. There are 8 million of them. If I could get those 8 million on natural gas, I could cut OPEC in half. So, that's what I'm after. What I want the president to do, two things. One, I want him to tell us that he remembers very well what he said about OPEC—Mid East oil, no Mid East oil in ten years. His first step would be all federal vehicles that are—that we buy, the federal government does, would be by federal order, would be on our resources. They could be on battery, hybrid, natural gas, butane, propane, ethanol. I don't care. Just so it's American. The second thing I'd like for him to do is to go to the American people and say this has nothing to do with politics. It's all about us, all Americans. In the next eight years, two of these ten years have gone, so he has eight years to make good on this. He has to put it in place. He isn't going to be here in eight years. But he's got to put it in place for it to happen. I think the American people would rise to the occasion and love every minute of it. They would—what he would tell them is you have to be on natural resource — our resources in the United States. Make your pick. We don't care. But just be on American resources in eight years.

Interview with Larry King, CNN, July 19, 2010; transcript accessible at cnn.com.

Plato

Plato / c. 428–c. 348 BC / city-state of Athens / Philosopher

Beauty

And the true order of going, or being led by another, to the things of love, is to begin from the beauties of earth and mount upwards for the sake of that other beauty, using these steps only, and from one going on to two, and from two to all fair forms to fair practices, and from fair practices to fair notions, until from fair notions he arrives at the notion of absolute beauty, and at last knows what the essence of beauty is.

Symposium.

Beginning

The beginning is the most important part of the work.

Republic, Book I.

Crime and Punishment

Mankind censure injustice fearing that they may be the victims of it, and not because they shrink from committing it.

Republic, Book I.

The greatest penalty of evildoing—namely, to grow into the likeness of bad men.

Laws.

Death

The hour of departure has arrived, and we go our ways—I to die, and you to live. Which is better God only knows.

Apology.

Man is a prisoner who has no right to open the door of his prison and run away. . . . A man should wait, and not take his own life until God summons him.

Phaedrus.

Must not all things at the last be swallowed up in death?

Phaedo.

The soul takes nothing with her to the other world but her education and culture.

Phaedo.

Democracy

Democracy passes into despotism.

Republic, Book VIII.

Education

Bodily exercise, when compulsory, does no harm to the body; but knowledge which is acquired under compulsion obtains no hold on the mind.

Republic, Book VII.

Let early education be a sort of amusement; you will then be better able to find out the natural bent.

Republic, Book VII.

The direction in which education starts a man will determine his future life.

Republic, Book IV.

Gods

And this which you deem of no moment is the very highest of all: that is whether you have a right idea of the gods, whereby you may live your life well or ill.

Laws.

Not one of them who took up in his youth with this opinion that there are no gods ever continued until old age faithful to his conviction.

Laws.

Human Soul

The soul of man is immortal and imperishable.

Republic, Book X.

Old Age

He who is of a calm and happy nature will hardly feel the pressure of age, but to him who is of an opposite disposition youth and age are equally a burden.

Republic, Book I.

One and Many

If a man, fixing his attention on these and the like difficulties, does away with ideas of things and will not admit that every individual thing has its own determinate idea which is always one and the same, he will have nothing on which his mind can rest; and so he will utterly destroy the power of reasoning.

Parmenides.

You cannot conceive the many without the one.

Parmenides.

Philosopher-Kings

Until philosophers are kings, or the kings and princes of this world have the spirit and power of philosophy, and political greatness and wisdom meet in one, and those commoner natures who pursue either to the exclusion of the other are compelled to stand aside, cities will never have rest from their evils—no, nor the human race, as I believe—and then only will this our State have a possibility of life and behold the light of day.

Republic, Book V.

Philosophy

Well, my art of midwifery is in most respects like theirs; but differs, in that I attend men and not women, and I look after their souls when they are in labor, and not after their bodies: and the triumph of my art is in thoroughly examining whether the thought which the mind of the young man brings forth is a false idol or a noble and true birth.

Theaetetus.

Socrates

Someone will say: Yes, Socrates, but cannot you hold your tongue, and then you may go into a

foreign city, and no one will interfere with you? Now I have great difficulty in making you [men of Athens] understand my answer to this. For if I tell you that to do as you say would be a disobedience to the God, and therefore that I cannot hold my tongue, you will not believe that I am serious; and if I say again that daily to discourse about virtue, and of those other things about which you hear me examining myself and others, is the greatest good of man, and that the unexamined life is not worth living, you are still less likely to believe me. Yet I say what is true, although a thing of which it is hard for me to persuade you.

Apology.

Crito made a sign to the servant, who was standing by; and he went out, and having been absent for some time, returned with the jailer carrying the cup of poison. Socrates said: You, my good friend, who are experienced in these matters, shall give me directions how I am to proceed. . . . . Then raising the cup to his lips, quite readily and cheerfully he drank off the poison. And hitherto most of us had been able to control our sorrow; but now when we saw him drinking, and saw too that he had finished the draught, we could no longer forbear, and in spite of myself my own tears were flowing fast; so that I covered my face and wept, not for him, but at the thought of my own calamity in having to part from such a friend. . . . He was beginning to grow cold about the groin, when he uncovered his face, for he had covered himself up, and said—they were his last words—he said: Crito, I owe a cock to Asclepius; will you remember to pay the debt? The debt shall be paid, said Crito; is there anything else? There was no answer to this question; but in a minute or two a movement was heard, and the attendants uncovered him; his eyes were set, and Crito closed his eyes and mouth.

Such was the end, Echecrates, of our friend; concerning whom I may truly say, that of all the men of his time whom I have known, he was the wisest and justest and best.

Phaedo.

Truth and Falsehood

False words are not only evil in themselves, but they infect the soul with evil.

Phaedo.

Everything that deceives may be said to enchant.

Republic, Book III.

Tyranny

The people have always some champion whom they set over them and nurse into greatness. . . . This and no other is the root from which a tyrant springs; when he first appears he is a protector.

Republic, Book VIII.

When the tyrant has disposed of foreign enemies by conquest or treaty, and there is nothing to fear from them, then he is always stirring up some war or other, in order that the people may require a leader.

Republic, Book VIII.

Virtue

No evil can happen to a good man, either in life or after death.

Apology.

Wealth

Wealth is the parent of luxury and indolence, and poverty of meanness and viciousness, and both of discontent.

Republic, Book IV.

Tim Pool

Timothy Daniel Pool / b. 1986 / Chicago, Illinois, USA / Journalist, Political Commentator, Podcaster

Note: Only a couple of the following quotations are sourced; the others presumably come from Pool's numerous online videos, commentaries, interviews, and podcasts.

Citizen Journalism

The only defense you have against police violence is to film it and share it so people are aware of what's happening.

You never know when you might become the most important journalist in the world.

Unbeknownst to me, I started doing journalism, just because I was bearing witness.

I've resisted the tag "citizen journalist"—that's not what I am.

Culture

The culture war is real, and it's affecting every aspect of our society.

Documentary Films

A lot of documentaries are biased—they leave out a lot of information.

Free Speech

What you see from these tech companies—Facebook, YouTube, Twitter—they control the space and they control the speech.

I am terrified of a future where people will not share their opinions because people are being banned or ostracized.

I think information wants to be free, it deserves to be free, and the only way we are going to have a functioning government for the people is if people can see and understand why decisions are made. I hope I am contributing to that.

Life

Bloom beautifully . . . dangerously . . . loudly. Bloom softly. You are the blossom. However you need to—just bloom.

Media

The mainstream media has a credibility crisis, and it's their own fault.

I've seen news organizations outright just take photos from Instagram and use it for news without credit, without permission.

Social media is reshaping the way we consume news and information.

There is no money. Companies are struggling and firing left and right. The companies that are doing well learned that hyper-partisan content shares better than real news.

Life is much more chill and boring than media makes it seem.

Political Discourse

It's better to have a conversation with someone you disagree with than to shout them down.

We need to have more civil discourse and less tribalism in our political discussions.

Look, as far as I'm concerned, if someone who is white feels like people are saying things that are anti-white, sure, you're allowed to feel however you want, and I really don't see the problem with that. However, calling you a white supremacist discredits you beyond just your concerns about what people are saying about white people.

One of the problems with the Democrats and many people on the left—and it's true for everybody, but something I've seen repeatedly among left-wing activists and the far-left—is that they don't think about what the result will actually be.

Pool on Pool

I got started by couch surfing and being broke, homeless, without healthcare.

I've done a lot of the "No Blood for Oil" anti-war marches for whatever political reason that people have for being against war—I just don't like war.

I want people to be able to get their information from me.

There were instances where—I can't name names—but a big show used my content without credit.

I consider myself an activist, but I'm never a protestor.

I am an activist for transparency.

I used to be [an action junkie]. I used to travel all over the world, two flights per week. It's not so much the action—but kind of, you know, definitely an adrenaline junkie, I've been skateboarding my whole life—but it was more so, I want to know why things are happening.

"The Full Tim Pool Interview," John Stossel, Stossel TV, October 29, 2023.

I ultimately didn't really care if I told people what was happening. I wanted to watch it so I *knew*. Because, you know, some people don't trust the media, I don't know who to believe, why don't I just go there and I can see for myself? And as it turns out there is one good way to fund that: Tell people what you saw.

"The Full Tim Pool Interview," John Stossel, Stossel TV, October 29, 2023.

I don't want to stand filming in front of the water cannon and guys with Molotovs. I want to show you what it's like to be there as best I can, even if that ends with me running full-speed into a café and rubbing lemons all over my face after being tear-gassed.

As soon as I saw Google Glass, I realized that it would allow me to do what I always do with this first-person live recording, but my hands would be free.

No one tells me what I can and can't report on, and no one tells me what to say.

The content I produce isn't coming at the behest of a corporation or a government.

I try not to judge people.

Fusion [TV] told me and many other staff to "side with the audience." Which they clarified as young people being liberal or left leaning, so that's the angle we take regardless of the facts. It was not a fun time.

I started to feel an obligation to people who had become loyal to our channel. Those viewers were loyal to me and I am in turn loyal to them.

Truth

The truth doesn't care about your feelings.

We need to have more civil discourse and less tribalism in our political discussions.

WikiLeaks

I am a huge fan of the ideals behind WikiLeaks.

Marcel Proust

Marcel Proust / 1871–1922 / France / Literary Critic, Novelist
Note: All quotations are taken from *À la recherche du temps perdu* [In Search of Lost Time], published in seven volumes between 1913 and 1927.

Adultery

Adultery introduces spirit into the dead letter of marriage.

Vol. 5: La Prisonnière [The Prisoner] (1923).

Art

Less disappointing than life is, great works of art do not begin by giving us all their best.

Vol. 2: À l'ombre des jeunes filles en fleur [In the Shadow of Young Girls in Flower] (1919).

What artists call posterity is the posterity of the work of art.

Vol. 2: À l'ombre des jeunes filles en fleur [In the Shadow of Young Girls in Flower] (1919).

By art alone we are able to get outside ourselves, to know what another sees of this universe which for him is not ours, the landscapes of which would remain as unknown to us as those of the moon. Thanks to art, instead of seeing one world, our own, we see it multiplied and we have as many worlds at our disposal as there are original artists, more different from each other than those which revolve in infinity and which still send us their distinctive ray many centuries after the hearth—be it Rembrandt's or Vermeer's—from which it emanated was extinguished.

Vol. 7: Le temps retrouvé [Time Recovered] (1927).

Body and Spirit

Happiness is beneficial for the body but it is grief that develops the powers of the spirit.

Vol. 7: Le temps retrouvé [Time Recovered] (1927).

Cruelty

Perhaps she would not have thought that evil was a state so rare, so extraordinary, so disorienting, to which it was so restful to emigrate, if she had been able to discern in herself, as in everyone else, that indifference to the sufferings we cause and which, whatever other names we give to it, is the terrible and permanent form of cruelty.

Vol. 1: Du côté de chez Swann [Swann's Way] (1913).

Decisions

We always make definitive decisions because of a state of mind that is not destined to last.

Vol. 2: À l'ombre des jeunes filles en fleur [In the Shadow of Young Girls in Flower] (1919).

Faces

The features of our face are scarcely more than gestures become fixed by habit.

Vol. 2: À l'ombre des jeunes filles en fleur [In the Shadow of Young Girls in Flower] (1919).

Illness

Illness is the doctor to whom we pay most heed. To kindness, to knowledge, we make promises only; pain, we obey.

Vol. 4: Sodome et Gomorrhe [Sodom and Gomorrah] (1922).

Life

We want passionately for there to be another life, in which we would be the same as we are here below. But we do not reflect that, even without waiting for this other life, in this life itself, after a few years, we are unfaithful to what we used to be, to the way we wanted to stay forever.

Vol. 4: Sodome et Gomorrhe [Sodom and Gomorrah] (1922).

The only true voyage, the only Fountain of Youth, would be not to travel toward new landscapes, but to have fresh eyes, to see the universe with the eyes of another person, of a hundred other people, to see the hundred universes that each of them sees, that each of them constitutes.

Vol. 5: La Prisonnière [The Prisoner] (1923).

The bonds between another human being and ourselves exist only in our thought. Memory, as it grows weaker, lets go of them . . . Man is the being who cannot emerge out of himself, who knows others only in himself, and who, when he denies this, lies.

Vol. 6: Albertine disparue [Albertine Gone] (1925).

We do not succeed in changing things according to our desire, but gradually our desire changes. The situation that we hoped to change because it was intolerable becomes unimportant. We have not managed to surmount the obstacle, as we were absolutely determined to do, but life has taken us round it, led us past it, and then if we turn round to gaze at the remote past, we can barely catch sight of it, so imperceptible has it become.

Vol. 6: Albertine disparue [Albertine Gone] (1925).

Love

Earlier, we dream of possessing the heart of the woman we love; later, the feeling that we possess the heart of a woman may be enough to make us fall in love.

Vol. 1: Du côté de chez Swann [Swann's Way] (1913).

In love, happiness is an abnormal state.

Vol. 2: À l'ombre des jeunes filles en fleur [In the Shadow of Young Girls in Flower] (1919).

Like everyone not in love, he imagined that we choose the person we love after endless deliberations and on the basis of various qualities and conventions.

Vol. 4: Sodome et Gomorrhe [Sodom and Gomorrah] (1922).

Love is space and time rendered perceptible to the heart.

Vol. 5: La Prisonnière [The Prisoner] (1923).

There is not one single woman whose possession is as precious to us as that of the truths she reveals to us in making us suffer.

Vol. 6: Albertine disparue [Albertine Gone] (1925).

Memory

As soon as I recognized the taste of the piece of *madeleine* dunked in linden tea that my aunt gave to me (although I did not yet know and had to wait until much later to discover why this memory made me so happy), immediately the old gray house on the street, where her bedroom was located, came to me like a stage set.

Vol. 1: Du côté de chez Swann [Swann's Way] (1913).

The places that we have known belong now only to the little world of space on which we map them for our own convenience. None of them was ever more than a thin slice, held between the contiguous impressions that composed our life at that time; remembrance of a particular form is but regret for a particular moment; and houses, roads, avenues are as fugitive, alas, as the years.

Vol. 1: Du côté de chez Swann [Swann's Way] (1913).

Neurotics

Everything we recognize as great comes to us from neurotics. They, and they alone, have founded religions and composed masterpieces.

Vol. 3: Du côté de Guermantes [The Guermantes Way] (1920).

Personality

. . . our social personality is created by the thoughts of other people.

Vol. 1: Du côté de chez Swann [Swann's Way] (1913).

Pleasure

It is not evil that gave her the idea of pleasure, which seemed to her attractive; it is pleasure that seemed evil.

Vol. 1: Du côté de chez Swann [Swann's Way] (1913).

Suffering

We are healed of a suffering only by experiencing it to the full.

Vol. 6: Albertine disparue [Albertine Gone] (1925).

Time

The time which we have at our disposal every day is elastic. The passions that we feel expand it, those that we inspire contract it, and habit fills up what remains.

Vol. 2: À l'ombre des jeunes filles en fleur [In the Shadow of Young Girls in Flower] (1919).

Virtue

Our virtues themselves are not free and floating qualities over which we retain a permanent control and power of disposal; they come to be so closely linked in our minds with the actions in conjunction with which we make it our duty to practice them, that, if we are suddenly called upon to perform some action of a different order, it takes us by surprise, and without our supposing for a moment that it might involve the bringing of those very same virtues into play.

Vol. 2: À l'ombre des jeunes filles en fleur [In the Shadow of Young Girls in Flower] (1919).

Wisdom

We are not given wisdom, we must discover it for ourselves after a journey that no one can take for us or spare us.

Vol. 2: À l'ombre des jeunes filles en fleur [In the Shadow of Young Girls in Flower] (1919).

Ayn Rand

Ayn Rand, née Alisa Zinovyevna Rosenbaum / 19051982 / St. Petersburg, Russian Empire / Novelist, Essayist, Political Philosopher

Aspiration

Do not let your fire go out, spark by irreplaceable spark in the hopeless swamps of the not-quite, the not-yet, and the not-at-all. Do not let the hero in your soul perish in lonely frustration for the life you deserved and have never been able to reach. The world you desire can be won. It exists . . . it is real . . . it is possible . . . it's yours.

Atlas Shrugged (1957).

Audacity

The question isn't who is going to let me; it's who is going to stop me.

The Fountainhead (1943).

Civilization

Civilization is the progress toward a society of privacy. The savage's whole existence is public, ruled by the laws of his tribe. Civilization is the process of setting man free from men.

The Fountainhead (1943).

The Constitution

The government was set to protect man from criminals—and the Constitution was written to protect man from the government.

"The Nature of Government," in The Virtue of Selfishness (1964).

Contradictions

Contradictions do not exist. Whenever you think you are facing a contradiction, check your premises. You will find that one of them is wrong.

Atlas Shrugged (1957).

Creativity

A creative man is motivated by the desire to achieve, not by the desire to beat others.

"The Nature of Government," in The Virtue of Selfishness (1964).

Egoism

The man who does not value himself, cannot value anything or anyone.

The Romantic Manifesto (1969).

Man's ego is the fountainhead of human progress.

The Fountainhead (1943).

To say "I love you" one must first be able to say the "I."

The Fountainhead (1943).

Freedom

I guard my treasures: my thought, my will, my freedom. And the greatest of these is freedom.

The Fountainhead (1943).

Freedom (n.): To ask nothing. To expect nothing. To depend on nothing.

The Fountainhead (1943).

Human Nature

I am, therefore I'll think.

"The Objectivist Ethics," in The Virtue of Selfishness (1964).

Man's unique reward, however, is that while animals survive by adjusting themselves to their background, man survives by adjusting his background to himself.

The Fountainhead (1943).

In the name of the best within you, do not sacrifice this world to those who are its worst. In the name of the values that keep you alive, do not let your vision of man be distorted by the ugly, the cowardly, the mindless in those who have never achieved his title.

The Fountainhead (1943).

Do not lose your knowledge that man's proper estate is an upright posture, an intransigent mind, and a step that travels unlimited roads.

Atlas Shrugged (1957).

Man's mind is his basic tool of survival.

Atlas Shrugged (1957).

The Individual

The smallest minority on earth is the individual. Those who deny individual rights cannot claim to be defenders of minorities.

"Collectivized 'Rights,'" in The Virtue of Selfishness (1964).

The man who lets a leader prescribe his course is a wreck being towed to the scrap heap.

The Fountainhead (1943).

The only power that can destroy a man is the power that he grants to others. Before you can control a man, you must control his self-esteem.

The Fountainhead (1943).

Money

Money is only a tool. It will take you wherever you wish, but it will not replace you as the driver.

Atlas Shrugged (1957).

Money is the barometer of a society's virtue.

Atlas Shrugged (1957).

Morality

The purpose of morality is to teach you, not to suffer and die, but to enjoy yourself and live.

Atlas Shrugged (1957).

I could die for you. But I couldn't, and wouldn't, live for you.

The Fountainhead (1943).

Achievement of your happiness is the only moral purpose of your life, and that happiness, not pain or mindless self-indulgence, is the proof of your moral integrity since it is the proof and the result of your loyalty to the achievement of your values.

Atlas Shrugged (1957).

The evil of the world is made possible by nothing but the sanction you give it.

Atlas Shrugged (1957).

The spread of evil is the symptom of a vacuum. Whenever evil wins, it is only by default: by the moral failure of those who evade the fact that there can be no compromise on basic principles.

Capitalism: The Unknown Ideal (1966).

Opportunity

The ladder of success is best climbed by stepping on the rungs of opportunity.

"The Nature of Government," in The Virtue of Selfishness (1964).

Reason

Reason is not automatic. Those who deny it cannot be conquered by it. Do not count on them. Leave them alone.

Atlas Shrugged (1957).

Rights

Individual rights are the means of subordinating society to moral law.

"Man's Rights," in The Virtue of Selfishness (1964).

A government is the most dangerous threat to man's rights: it holds a legal monopoly on the use of physical force against legally disarmed victims.

"The Nature of Government," in The Virtue of Selfishness (1964).

The only power any government has is the power to crack down on criminals. Well, when there aren't enough criminals, one makes them. One declares so many things to be a crime that it becomes impossible for men to live without breaking laws.

Atlas Shrugged (1957).

Truth

The truth is not for all men but only for those who seek it.

Atlas Shrugged (1957).

The hardest thing to explain is the glaringly evident which everybody has decided not to see.

The Fountainhead (1943).

Work

There is no such thing as a lousy job—only lousy men who don't care to do it.

The Fountainhead (1943).

Antoine de Rivarol

Antoine de Rivarol /1753–1801 / France / Poet, Essayist, Political Commentator, Journalist, Translator, Aphorist
Note: All quotations are taken from *Pensées inédites* [Unpublished Thoughts] (first published posthumously in 1808).

Heart and Mind

Mind is the partial side of men; the heart is everything.

Ideas

Ideas are a capital that bears interest only in the hands of talent.

Life

Man spends his life in reasoning on the past, in complaining of the present, in fearing future.

Love

The world is governed by love,—self-love.

Modesty

The modest man has everything to gain, and the arrogant man everything to lose; for modesty has always to deal with generosity, and arrogance with envy.

Philosophers

It is easy for men to write and talk like philosophers, but to act with wisdom, there is the rub!

Pity

In general, indulgence for those we know is rarer than pity for those we know not

Silence

Silence never yet betrayed any one!

Society

Of every ten persons who talk about you, nine will say something bad, and the tenth will say something good in a bad way.

Solitude

That which happens to the soil when it ceases to be cultivated by the social man happens to man himself when he foolishly forsakes society for solitude; the brambles grow up in his desert heart.

Thought and Speech

Speech is external thought, and thought internal speech.

Time

Opinions, theories, and systems pass by turns over the grindstone of time, which at first gives them brilliancy and sharpness, but finally wears them out.

Wealth

If poverty makes man groan, he yawns in opulence. When fortune exempts us from labor, nature overwhelms us with time.

Joe Rogan

Joseph James Rogan / b. 1967 / Newark, New Jersey, USA / Comedian, Television Host, Podcaster

Note: None of the following quotations is specifically sourced; most presumably derive from Rogan's long-running and highly popular podcast.

Comedy

It's painful for me to watch someone who isn't funny. It's horrifying to sit in the back and watch some guy who just totally sucks.

Economics

You have to be disciplined, and you have to save, even if you hate our current financial system. Because if you don't save, then you're forever dependent on the system.

Experience

The more you experience, the more you learn; the more you learn, the more you can appreciate.

Friends

It's in the darkest moments that we find our true friends.

Greatness

Greatness and madness are next-door neighbors, and they often borrow each other's sugar.

Happiness

The key to happiness doesn't lie in numbers in a bank account but in the way we make others feel and the way they make us feel.

The key to being happy isn't a search for meaning. It's to just keep yourself busy with unimportant nonsense, and eventually, you'll be dead.

If you're always striving to achieve something, you're not really enjoying what you have.

The only way to be truly satisfied is to do what you believe is great work. And the only way to do great work is to love what you do.

The ego-driven mindset will never be happy because it constantly needs validation from the external world.

You're not gonna be happy because you're successful. You're gonna be successful because you're happy.

Hate

The time you spend hating on someone robs you of your own time. You are literally hating on yourself and you don't even realize it.

Honesty

When someone comes along and expresses him or herself as freely as they think, people flock to it. They enjoy it.

Humility

If you are the greatest, why would you go around talking about it.

Life

The quickest way to become an old dog is to stop learning new tricks.
Life is about the journey, not the destination.
Be the kind of person your dog thinks you are.
One of the most fascinating lessons I've absorbed about life is that the struggle is good.
People want their 15 minutes and are willing to do anything to get it.
Live your life like you're the hero in your own movie.
To really appreciate life you got to know you're going to die.
Work hard, challenge yourself, and learn new things, and in the process, you'll become a better version of yourself.
We're all gonna die. You're gonna die, I'm gonna die. It's a part of life. Get used to it.
It's an incredibly exciting thing, this one, meaningless life of yours.
The most important thing is to be authentic and true to yourself.
Your attitude has a giant effect on how you live your life.
Live your life with passion, because if you're not passionate about what you're doing, then you're not really living.
Life is strange. You keep moving and keep moving. Before you know it, you look back and think, 'What was that?

Morality

Treat everyone as if they were you. If we really are all one, then I am you, and you are me.
Be cool to people. Be nice to as many people as you can. Smile to as many people as you can, and have them smile back at you.
Kindness is one of the best gifts you can bestow . . . and it's free.

Perspective

If you ever start taking things too seriously, just remember that we are talking monkeys on an organic spaceship flying through the universe.

Reality

The problem with the world is that we've lost our understanding of what's real.

Rogan on Rogan

I had a sense of who I was before I got famous.
There's a never-ending ocean of techniques to study and learn, and I'm just trying to find my own way through it.
There's a lot of guys that just get comfortable with their position and rest on their laurels. I had to earn my way.
I'm obsessed with the idea of making things. I can't help it.
It's hard to stay mad when there's so much beauty in the world. Sometimes I feel like I'm seeing it all at once, and it's too much. My heart fills up like a balloon that's about to burst.

Self-Awareness

The people I know that have the most self-awareness, they're constantly checking themselves on their own bulls**t.
The people I respect the least are people that have no self-awareness, that don't have the ability to look at themselves honestly.

Self-Improvement

The best way to improve oneself is to surround oneself with people who are smarter and more accomplished than we are.

Skepticism

Don't let the force of an impression when it first hits you knock you off your feet; just say to it: Hold on a moment; let me see who you are and what you represent. Let me put you to the test.

Success

The universe rewards those who take bold chances.

There's a direct correlation between positive energy and positive results in the physical form.

I love a success story, but even more than a success story, I like a dude who f***s his life up and then gets it back together again story.

We define ourselves far too often by our past failures. That's not you. You are this person right now. You're the person who has learned from those failures.

If you ever have the opportunity to speak with someone who has achieved a high level of success, you'll find out that their early life was one marked by hardship and the simple act of overcoming adversity.

The person who is best prepared for an opportunity is the one who is going to get it.

You are not going to get good at something just by doing it a few times. You have to practice it.

Success is not about how much money you make; it's about the difference you make in people's lives.

The more information you have, the better decisions you can make.

Strive to become the best version of yourself, not in the eyes of others, but in your own eyes.

The ultimate thing is to be able to say, "I made it, I'm successful, and I'm happy." But the only way you can do that is to push the boundaries and try new things.

The Universe

The universe is under no obligation to make sense to you.

Dave Rubin

David Joshua Rubin / b. 1976 / New York, New York, USA / Comedian, Political Commentator, Podcaster
Note: The specific sources of the following quotes are unknown; however, they most likely derive from Rubin's many online commentaries, interviews, and podcasts.

College

Instead of silencing speakers on campus, perhaps do what you're supposed to in college instead: listen to someone who thinks differently than you do.

Comedy

Even though standup seems like one-way conversation, if you're doing it right, it's actually a two-way discussion between the comic and the audience… the audience just happens to be communicating through laughter.
The whole point of real comedy is that you can say something that is true, and by being funny, you can make it tolerable for people, and hopefully they'll laugh at you, too.

Free Speech

We should all be able to express our opinions without fear of being silenced or canceled.
Free speech is the cornerstone of a free society.
I don't have to agree with you to respect your right to speak.
If you don't stand up for free speech when it's under attack from your own side, you don't really believe in free speech.
Ideas are not dangerous; the suppression of ideas is dangerous.
The battle for free speech is the defining issue of our time.
Ideas should be challenged through open dialogue, not silenced.

Gay Marriage

I think for me, as a gay person, I can convince a lot more people to be for gay marriage by not screaming at them and berating them and embarrassing them and belittling them, but by showing them that we're all exactly the same.

Human Rights

You are born free. I was born free. The government can take your freedom away, but it did not give you your freedom. It was your human right. The key part of that is you are free first.

Identity

I don't care about your identity; I care about your ideas.
I don't care who you are or where you come from; if you have a good idea, I'm willing to listen.
The best way to combat hate speech is with more speech, not less speech.

The Left

Sadly, the Left is no longer liberal at all, for it has traded in individualism for collectivism, thus placing us into an oppression Olympics where victimhood is a virtue. This post-modernism—this cultural Marxism or whatever you want to call it—can only destroy; it cannot create.

Everyone that we disagree with is a racist and a homophobe and Islamophobe and a bigot. It's just silly. It's lazy thinking, and I think it gets us nowhere.

The regressive Left ranks minority groups in a pecking order to compete in a kind of 'Oppression Olympics.' Gold medal goes to the most offended.

Just by existing as men, we are automatically guilty of everything in some people's minds. And, on top of that, we've created a situation in the media where men are only allowed to talk about politics and sport.

Prohibiting any words not approved of as "politically correct"—that's not progressive. Putting "trigger warnings" on books, movies, music, anything that might offend people—that's not progressive, either.

Marketplace of Ideas

I believe in the marketplace of ideas. I believe in open dialogue, free speech, and the free exchange of ideas.

In the marketplace of ideas, the best arguments should prevail.

It's important to have conversations with people who disagree with you; that's how we grow and learn.

The battle for free speech is a fight worth having.

The marketplace of ideas is the best tool we have for solving problems and finding truth.

You don't need to agree with someone to have a civil conversation with them.

Media

I think the media has portrayed conservatives as these cold, heartless people who want poor people to die and let half the population starve and all this. They've done that so effectively because they've owned the narrative for so long.

Cable news is force-feeding you an endless back and forth of pundits who consistently get everything wrong, while at the same time, they mask their opinions as facts and argue about the endless minutia of a broken Washington, D.C., instead of arming you with real knowledge and new ideas.

Politics

It's not enough to be against something; you have to be for something.

The most important thing we can do is to engage in honest and open conversations with people who disagree with us.

Ideas don't hurt you. They're just ideas.

Freedom of speech is the bedrock of a free society. Without it, we risk losing all our other freedoms.

The best way to combat bad ideas is to expose them to the light of good ideas.

Open-mindedness and intellectual diversity are crucial for progress.

You are the one who makes the choices that control your fate.

It really is this: you are either for liberty, you're for freedom, and you're for living how you want to live without infringing and impugning on anyone else's rights, or you want the state to deal with everything.

The Right, much more than the Left, believes in the notion of live and let live, and that is the true definition of tolerance.

Speaking out, sharing what you think, and expressing yourself—regardless of sexuality or anything else—is the most important thing you can do as a man, as a human.

It's not about whether we should have a conservative or a liberal. It's about, do we have someone that has the mental acumen to understand what the laws are, and not write laws but defend the laws. That's the whole purpose of three branches of government.

Rubin on Rubin

I'm a classical liberal, which means I believe in individual liberty, limited government, and the importance of free expression.

I would rather stand for what I believe in than bow down and be loved.

I got into politics when I was 12, back when George H.W. Bush was running against Michael Dukakis. We did a mock election in my social studies class, and I remember how so much of what was thought of as liberal made sense to me.

I'm a married gay man, so you might think that I appreciate the government forcing a Christian baker or photographer or florist to act against their religion in order to cater, photograph, or decorate my wedding. But you'd be wrong. A government that can force Christians to violate their conscience can force me to violate mine.

Somehow, defending my liberal values of free speech, liberty, and rights of the individual has become a conservative position.

I'm not a huge parade guy myself.

I firmly believe in individual liberty more than anything else. And that you have to live the life you want for yourself.

One criticism that I hear occasionally is that I am actually not a real liberal, and I am secretly a conservative. Or sometimes they will say I am the only thing worse than a conservative—a dreaded "right-winger."

I'm not even proud to say this, but I've never voted for a Republican in my entire life.

Tolerance

The Right, much more than the Left, believes in the notion of live and let live, and that is the true definition of tolerance.

Seriously, we all need to get over being offended every time someone says something you don't agree with. Guess what? That's life. And I'd rather have that life any day than only hear from people who agree with me.

Do you know people on the Right who are tolerant of people who are for gay marriage and are pro-choice? I actually do, plenty of them. When there is a disagreement, I see way more people on the Right… more often willing to agree to disagree rather than to defriend or to smear.

Trump

The election of Trump threw the chess board up. The pieces are all over the place. That's upsetting to a lot of people, but what I think is there's a lot of fertile ground for good ideas.

Obviously, I agree with Trump on many of his criticisms of the mainstream media. You can absolutely argue that their failure to report honestly, to get outraged before we could, and to collude with the Clinton campaign directly led to the rise of Trump.

Babe Ruth

Babe Ruth (George Herman Ruth, Jr.) / 1895–1948 / Maryland, USA / Baseball

I'm afraid that someday I'll kill some pitcher. It is one thing I've always dreaded. My heart stood still in that game in Detroit when I almost got Ehmke with that drive through the box. I thought for a certainty that the ball would hit him before he got his hands up to protect himself. A couple of pitchers have asked me not to hit the ball back at them, and I always try not to. Why should I try to hurt any ball players? We are all out there trying to make a living, and no man worthwhile would deliberately try to injure another.

Source: The Louisville Courier-Journal, July 18, 1920.

I always swing at the ball with all my might. I hit or miss big and when I miss I know it long before the umpire calls a strike on me, for every muscle in my back, shoulders and arms is groaning, "You missed it." And believe me, it is no fun to miss a ball that hard. Once I put myself out of the game for a few days by a miss like that.

Source: The Chicago Tribune, August 13, 1920.

It just goes to show that people take a lot of things for granted. They don't observe things closely, particularly things about which they feel confident.

Source: Babe Ruth's Own Book of Baseball, Chapter 1 (1928).

For ball players know that it isn't individuals who count. It's the way a team plays as a whole that determines its offensive power or its defensive strength. Smart ball players and smart managers consider offense and defense as units, knowing that it takes nine men to do the fielding and nine hitters to make up a batting order that will score runs.

Source: Babe Ruth's Own Book of Baseball, Chapter 2 (1928).

Pitchers—real pitchers— know that their job isn't so much to keep opposing batsmen from hitting as it is to make them hit it at someone. The trouble with most kid pitchers is that they forget there are eight other men on the team to help them. They just blunder ahead, putting everything they have on every pitch and trying to carry the weight of the whole game on their shoulders. The result is that they tire out and go bad along in the middle of the game, and then the wise old heads have to hurry out and rescue them. I've seen a lot of young fellows come up, and they all had the same trouble. Take Lefty Grove over at Philadelphia, for instance. There isn't a pitcher in the league who has more speed or stuff than Lefty. He can do things with a baseball that make you dizzy. But when he first came into the league he seemed to think that he had to strike out every batter as he came up. The result was he'd go along great for five or six innings, and then blow. And he's just now learning to conserve his strength. In other words, he's learning that a little exercise of the noodle will save a lot of wear and tear on his arm.

Source: Babe Ruth's Own Book of Baseball, Chapter 3 (1928).

Baseball always has been and always will be a game demanding team play. You can have the nine greatest individual ball players in the world, but if they don't play together the club won't be worth a dime.

Source: Babe Ruth's Own Book of Baseball, Chapter 10 (1928).

I have only have one superstition: I make sure to touch all the bases when I hit a home run.

Source: Attribution unconfirmed.

Sheryl Sandberg

Sheryl Kara Sandberg / b. 1969 / Washington, DC, USA / Business Executive, VP of global online sales and operations at Google, COO of Facebook, COO of Meta Platforms, Founder of LeanIn.org

Business Philosophy

What would you do if you weren't afraid?

Sheryl Sandberg, Lean In: Women, Work, and the Will to Lead(2013).

Done is better than perfect.

Sheryl Sandberg, Lean In: Women, Work, and the Will to Lead(2013).

We cannot change what we are not aware of, and once we are aware, we cannot help but change.

Sheryl Sandberg, Lean In: Women, Work, and the Will to Lead(2013).

Fortune does favor the bold and you'll never know what you're capable of if you don't try.

Sheryl Sandberg, Lean In: Women, Work, and the Will to Lead(2013).

But the upside of painful knowledge is so much greater than the downside of blissful ignorance.

Sheryl Sandberg, Lean In: Women, Work, and the Will to Lead(2013).

Option A is not available. so let's just kick the shit out of Option B.

Sheryl Sandberg, Option B: Facing Adversity, Building Resilience, and Finding Joy (2017).

Life is never perfect. We all live some form of Option B.

Sheryl Sandberg, Option B: Facing Adversity, Building Resilience, and Finding Joy (2017).

Being confident and believing in your own self-worth is necessary to achieving your potential.

Sheryl Sandberg, Lean In: Women, Work, and the Will to Lead(2013).

Each one of us is more than the worst thing we've ever done.

Sheryl Sandberg, Option B: Facing Adversity, Building Resilience, and Finding Joy (2017).

Careers

Careers are a jungle gym, not a ladder.

Sheryl Sandberg, Lean In: Women, Work, and the Will to Lead(2013).

If you're offered a seat on a rocket ship, don't ask what seat. Just get on.

Address to Harvard Business School Class of 2012, reported by Jay Yarrow in "Sheryl Sandberg's Full HBS Speech: Get On A Rocketship Whenever You Get The Chance," businessinsider.com, May 25, 2012.

I hope you find true meaning, contentment, and passion in your life. I hope you navigate the difficult times and come out with greater strength and resolve. I hope you find whatever balance you seek with your eyes wide open. And I hope that you—yes, you—have the ambition to lean in to your career and run the world. Because the world needs you to change it.

Sheryl Sandberg, Lean In: Women, Work, and the Will to Lead(2013).

I have never met a woman, or man, who stated emphatically, "Yes, I have it all.'" Because no matter what any of us has—and how grateful we are for what we have—no one has it all.

Sheryl Sandberg, Lean In: Women, Work, and the Will to Lead(2013).

We compromise our career goals to make room for partners and children who may not even exist yet.

Sheryl Sandberg, Lean In: Women, Work, and the Will to Lead(2013).

Diversity

Endless data show that diverse teams make better decisions. We are building products that people with very diverse backgrounds use, and I think we all want our company makeup to reflect the makeup of the people who use our products. That's not true of any industry really, and we have a long way to go.

Interview with Jessica Guynn in "Facebook's Sheryl Sandberg on tech's diversity gap," usatoday.com, March 11, 2013.

At the broadest level, we are not going to fix the numbers for under-representation in technology or any industry until we fix our education system and until we fix the stereotypes about women and minorities in math and science.

Girls are at 18% of computer science college majors. We can't go much above 18% in our coders if there's only 18% coming into the workplace, and at every level, more boys stay in than girls in every industry. In order to move numbers, we all understand that we have to increase the numbers going into the funnel.

Interview with Jessica Guynn in "Facebook's Sheryl Sandberg on tech's diversity gap," usatoday.com, March 11, 2013.

Leadership

There is no perfect fit when you're looking for the next big thing to do. You have to take opportunities and make an opportunity fit for you, rather than the other way around. The ability to learn is the most important quality a leader can have.

Sheryl Sandberg, Lean In: Women, Work, and the Will to Lead(2013).

Marriage

When looking for a life partner, my advice to women is date all of them: the bad boys, the cool boys, the commitment-phobic boys, the crazy boys. But do not marry them. The things that make the bad boys sexy do not make them good husbands. When it comes time to settle down, find someone who wants an equal partner. Someone who thinks women should be smart, opinionated and ambitious. Someone who values fairness and expects or, even better, wants to do his share in the home. These men exist and, trust me, over time, nothing is sexier.

Sheryl Sandberg, Lean In: Women, Work, and the Will to Lead(2013).

When women work outside the home and share breadwinning duties, couples are more likely to stay together. In fact, the risk of divorce reduces by about half when a wife earns half the income and a husband does half the housework.

Sheryl Sandberg, Lean In: Women, Work, and the Will to Lead(2013).

A truly equal world would be one where women ran half our countries and companies and men ran half our homes.

Sheryl Sandberg, Lean In: Women, Work, and the Will to Lead(2013).

Motivation

Motivation comes from working on things we care about. It also comes from working with people we care about.

Sheryl Sandberg, Lean In: Women, Work, and the Will to Lead(2013).

Sandberg on Sandberg

I always tell people if you try to connect the dots of your career, if you mess it up you're going to wind up on a very limited path. If I decided what I was going to do in college —when there was no Internet, no Google, no Facebook . . . I don't want to make that mistake. The reason I don't have a plan is because if I have a plan I'm limited to today's options.

Reported by Shana Montesol Johnson in "I Wouldn't Plan On It," developmentcrossroads.com, August, 2011.

I realized that searching for a mentor has become the professional equivalent of waiting for Prince Charming. We all grew up on the fairy tale "Sleeping Beauty," which instructs young women that if they just wait for their prince to arrive, they will be kissed and whisked away on a white horse to live happily ever after. Now young women are told that if they can just find the right mentor, they will be pushed up the ladder and whisked away to the corner office to live happily ever after. Once again, we are teaching women to be too dependent on others.

Sheryl Sandberg, Lean In: Women, Work, and the Will to Lead(2013).

Let me fall if I must fall. The one I become will catch me.

Sheryl Sandberg, Option B: Facing Adversity, Building Resilience, and Finding Joy (2017).

I don't believe that everyone should make the same choices—that everyone has to want to be a CEO or everyone should want to be a work-at-home mother. I want everyone to be able to choose, but I want us to be able to choose unencumbered by gender choosing for us. I have a 7-year-old son and a 5-year-old daughter. Success for me is that if my son chooses to be a stay-at-home parent, he is cheered on for that decision. And if my daughter chooses to work outside the home and is successful, she is cheered on and supported.

Reported in "'Lean In': Facebook's Sheryl Sandberg Explains What's Holding Women Back," npr.org, March 11, 2013.

Tech Industry

What's holding women back in computer science is the exact same thing . . . that's holding women back in leadership. It's something social scientists call "stereotype threat."

Stereotype threat means that the more we're aware of a stereotype, the more we act in accordance with it. So, stereotypically we believe girls are not good at math. Therefore, girls don't do well at math, and it self-perpetuates. If you ask a girl right before she takes a math test to check off "M" or "F" for male or female, she does worse on that test. The reason there aren't more women in computer science is there aren't enough women in computer science.

Reported in "'Lean In': Facebook's Sheryl Sandberg Explains What's Holding Women Back," npr.org, March 11, 2013.

Women and Business

In the future, there will be no female leaders. There will just be leaders.

Sheryl Sandberg, Lean In: Women, Work, and the Will to Lead(2013).

Women need to shift from thinking "I'm not ready to do that" to thinking "I want to do that- and I'll learn by doing it.

Sheryl Sandberg, Lean In: Women, Work, and the Will to Lead(2013).

There's a special place in hell for women who don't help other women.

Sheryl Sandberg, Lean In: Women, Work, and the Will to Lead(2013).

Success and likeability are positively correlated for men and negatively for women. When a man is successful, he is liked by both men and women. When a woman is successful, people of both genders like her less.

Sheryl Sandberg, Lean In: Women, Work, and the Will to Lead(2013).

Real change will come when powerful women are less of an exception. It is easy to dislike senior women because there are so few.

Sheryl Sandberg, Lean In: Women, Work, and the Will to Lead(2013).

. . . many people, but especially women, feel fraudulent when they are praised for their accomplishments. Instead of feeling worthy of recognition, they feel undeserving and guilty, as if a mistake has been made. Despite being high achievers, even experts in their fields, women can't seem to shake the sense that it is only a matter of time until they are found out for who they really are—impostors with limited skills or abilities.

Sheryl Sandberg, Lean In: Women, Work, and the Will to Lead(2013).

We must raise both the ceiling and the floor.

Sheryl Sandberg, Lean In: Women, Work, and the Will to Lead(2013).

Social gains are never handed out. They must be seized.

Sheryl Sandberg, Lean In: Women, Work, and the Will to Lead(2013).

I want half, half, half across the board. Fifty percent. I would like women to earn 58% of the (computer science) degrees, because women earn 58% of college degrees.

Interview with Jessica Guynn in "Facebook's Sheryl Sandberg on tech's diversity gap," usatoday.com, March 11, 2013.

We call our little girls bossy. Go to a playground: Little girls get called "bossy" all the time, a word that's almost never used for boys. And that leads directly to the problems women face in the workforce. When a man does a good job, everyone says, "That's great." When a woman does that same thing, she'll get feedback that says things like, "Your results are good, but your peers just don't like you as much" or "maybe you were a little aggressive."

Reported in "'Lean In': Facebook's Sheryl Sandberg Explains What's Holding Women Back," npr.org, March 11, 2013.

Peter Schiff

Peter David Schiff / b. 1963 / Connecticut, USA / Stock Broker, Financial Commentator, Author

China

The real bubble in China is in US Treasuries, in US dollars.

Schiff, hosting Wall Street Unspun, March 3, 2010.

. . . it is precisely because it is not a democracy that China will likely be so successful… What is of vital importance for economic success is economic freedom, meaning the protection of private property, the rule of law, and minimal regulation and taxation, not the right to vote.

Peter D. Schiff, with John Downes, Crash Proof: How to Profit From the Coming Economic Collapse (2007).

Consumer Credit

. . . consumer credit does little to increase consumption. All it accomplishes is to pull forward future consumption into the present (while generating a fee for the banker). This is like giving yourself a blood transfusion from your left arm to your right. Nothing is accomplished, except the possibility of spilling blood on the floor. But it's not even that benign.

Schiff, "Debt is No Salvation," BusinessInsider.com, August 4, 2014.

Currency Debasement

While we've been buying time, things have gone from bad to worse. We have debased our currency so much it is already beyond control. We just haven't felt the full impact yet because we have had massive artificial support from abroad.

Peter D. Schiff, with John Downes, Crash Proof: How to Profit From the Coming Economic Collapse (2007).

Inflation is the unhappy result of our monetary mismanagement and the ultimate cause of the coming economic collapse.

Peter D. Schiff, with John Downes, Crash Proof: How to Profit From the Coming Economic Collapse (2007).

. . . the reason the federal government wasn't given that power [to create paper money or issue bills of credit] was because the framers didn't want it to have the power to create inflation. They had just experienced it firsthand with the Continental dollar, which ended up being worth around 10 cents and gave rise to the expression "not worth a Continental."

Peter D. Schiff, with John Downes, Crash Proof: How to Profit From the Coming Economic Collapse (2007).

Economics

Nobody is entitled to someone else's money, that is the bottom line. People think they are entitled to it because they think they paid into it, nobody paid into anything, it was a fraud.

Every single dollar that the gov collected in social security taxes, has already been spent, there is nothing there, there is no money, so the only money the government gets to make current payment is the money it can take from people who are still working. It's a transfer from the working poor in many cases to the retired rich. We don't have the money, I feel bad for the fact people made promises we can't keep, I feel bad for the people that invested with Bernie Madoff and lost their money, but it's the same principle, it's the same Ponzi scheme. We have to put an end to it, we have to find real solution to these problems because if we keep on denying that they exist and keep on spending money, we're going to destroy the value of everyone's benefits.

Schiff's remarks, Republican Town Committee (RTC), Avon, Connecticut, May 10, 2010.

What America has succeeded in creating is not an economy impervious to shocks, but merely one which enables their consequences to be postponed to a later date.

Reported in "US shoppers spend as savings fall," BBC News website, September 1, 2005.

. . . it is the natural tendency of market economies to lower prices that makes them so successful.

Peter D. Schiff, with John Downes, Crash Proof: How to Profit From the Coming Economic Collapse (2007).

Real economic growth emanates from increased productivity, which tends to hold prices down.

Peter D. Schiff, with John Downes, Crash Proof: How to Profit From the Coming Economic Collapse (2007).

Legitimate economic expansions, financed by actual savings, do not need busts. It is only the inflation-induced varieties that sow the seeds of their own destruction.

Peter D. Schiff, with John Downes, Crash Proof: How to Profit From the Coming Economic Collapse (2007).

It is a common misconception that low wages are the main factor influencing prices. The reality is that low capital costs, and the absence of taxation and regulation, are far more important.

Peter D. Schiff, with John Downes, Crash Proof: How to Profit From the Coming Economic Collapse (2007).

Forecasting the 2008 Financial Collapse

By historical standards and given the gloomy corporate profits outlook in an environment of high corporate debt and rising interest rates, the Dow Jones Industrial Average is considerably overvalued at late-2006 levels and should be avoided. I say that, even setting aside the imminent prospect of a collapsed dollar and the recession and hyperinflation that would accompany it.

Peter D. Schiff, with John Downes, Crash Proof: How to Profit From the Coming Economic Collapse (2007).

In the perspective of previous bear markets, notably those of the 1930s and the 1970s, the prospects look even worse. Economic conditions now are as bad as or worse than what existed then.

Peter D. Schiff, with John Downes, Crash Proof: How to Profit From the Coming Economic Collapse (2007).

Government

There are no checks and balances if the gov is wrong. If a private entrepreneur makes a mistake, he goes bankrupt, the losses are cut, if he bets wrong, he loses. If the gov bets wrong, they just get bigger, they just appropriate more money; it's a bottomless pit, because they either get it from the tax payers or run it off a printing press.

Authors@Google: Peter Schiff, YouTube, April 2, 2009.

When private industry makes a mistake, it gets corrected and goes away. As governments make mistakes, it gets bigger, bigger and bigger and they make more, more and more because as they run out of money, they just ask for more and so they get rewarded for making mistakes. In the meantime that is exactly what we are doing by subsidizing companies which are failing, we have a reverse Darwinism, we've got survival of the unfittest, the companies and people that have made terrible mistakes are being rewarded and other people are being punished and being taxed.

Authors@Google: Peter Schiff, YouTube, April 2, 2009.

Paying attention to the CPI and the others is like leaving your house on a rainy day without carrying an umbrella because a government weather report told you it was sunny.

Peter D. Schiff, with John Downes, Crash Proof: How to Profit From the Coming Economic Collapse (2007).

The process of dumbing people down so they'll buy official figures showing inflation "under control" at levels of 1 to 2 percent or so (when it is actually more like 8 to 9 percent) is actually a fairly recent development.

Peter D. Schiff, with John Downes, Crash Proof: How to Profit From the Coming Economic Collapse (2007).

Think about all the rules and regulations American businesses have to deal with. How can we compete with nations that don't impose those excessive burdens? Does anyone think that the United States could ever have become a great power with all the rules, regulations, and taxation that exist today?

Peter D. Schiff, with John Downes, Crash Proof: How to Profit From the Coming Economic Collapse (2007).

Money

The Founding Fathers, those who wrote the Constitution and founded the American Republic, they understood the benefits of sound money and the evils of paper money. They've put America on a gold standard from the very birth of the republic and we should heed their wise—they were very learned men. I think they were much more educated and understanding about economics then the people who lead the U.S. today. So, to try to suggest that we will have less robust economy if we went back to gold standard—mostly, that's propaganda from Central Bankers and politicians, who want to scare us from going back to something that works, because when you go back to free market, the politicians and bankers will lose their power, and they want to maintain their power by scaring people into thinking that if we just go back to freedom and market forces, that's somehow is going to be bad and we have to surrender our freedoms to politicians and bankers because they know much better than the market. They can define the proper rate of interest and they can manage the money supplier, centrally planning the economy, and it's going to be more effective than free market capitalism—and that is just not the case.

Reported by Sophie Shevarnadze in "Blind faith in dollar will lead world to financial Armageddon—leading financial analyst," RT.com, September 26, 2014.

Schiff's 2010 Senate Campaign

Too many people in Connecticut are struggling right now, and the last thing we need is meddling politicians making things worse. Only by cutting deficit spending, reducing burdensome regulations, and letting people keep more of their hard-earned dollars will we get our economy back on track.

Reported by Daniela Altimari, "Peter Schiff criticizes Chris Dodd's plan to overhaul financial regulators," Capitol Watch blog, Hartford Courant, September 22, 2009.

Transferring regulatory authority from one unaccountable agency to another will not solve any problems.

Reported by Daniela Altimari, "Peter Schiff criticizes Chris Dodd's plan to overhaul financial regulators," Capitol Watch blog, Hartford Courant, September 22, 2009.

I think most Connecticut voters know that we need fewer czars in Washington, not more. As long as Fannie and Freddie and Congress are meddling with the economy, changing the structure of the regulators is basically rearranging deck chairs on the *Titanic*.

Reported by Daniela Altimari, "Peter Schiff criticizes Chris Dodd's plan to overhaul financial regulators," Capitol Watch blog, Hartford Courant, September 22, 2009.

I'm interrupting my career. It's not like I want my new career in politics. But I'm willing to interrupt it the same way that somebody interrupted their career and joined World War II and went off to fight the Nazis. I don't think that I'm that heroic, and I don't think I'm risking as much as a soldier. But it's the same principle.

Interview with Frank Ahrens, "Peter Schiff: Hard-Core Free-Marketeer," Outlook and Opinions, washingtonpost.com, October 4, 2009.

Stock Market

Non-dividend-paying growth stocks can be attractive but should be viewed as speculation rather than investing.

Peter D. Schiff, with John Downes, Crash Proof: How to Profit From the Coming Economic Collapse (2007).

If Enron had been forced to pay cash dividends, it could never have pulled that caper off!

Peter D. Schiff, with John Downes, Crash Proof: How to Profit From the Coming Economic Collapse (2007).

It can be argued that the U.S. brokerage and investment banking industry has transformed the modern American stock market into nothing more than a mechanism for transferring wealth from shareholders to management.

Peter D. Schiff, with John Downes, Crash Proof: How to Profit From the Coming Economic Collapse (2007).

If you think mutual funds aren't a flagrant enough example of conflict of interest, try hedge funds.

Peter D. Schiff, with John Downes, Crash Proof: How to Profit From the Coming Economic Collapse (2007).

Trade

Borrowing to build factories is not the economic equivalent of borrowing to buy television sets, and it's amazing just how few modern economists can see the difference… Borrowing to produce is the way poor countries become rich. Borrowing to consume is the way rich countries become poor. A vivid example of the latter is the stream of container ships unloading at U.S. ports and going back empty because we have nothing to ship.

Peter D. Schiff, with John Downes, Crash Proof: How to Profit From the Coming Economic Collapse (2007).

Arthur M. Schlesinger, Jr.

Arthur Meier Schlesinger, Jr. / 1917–2007 / Columbus, Ohio, USA / Historian, Political Activist, Public Servant, Author

American System of Government

The genius of the American system is that it gives you great flexibility to do a lot of things at once.

Interview, The Atlantic, July, 2000.

The genius of the Constitution rests not in any static meaning it might have had in a world that is dead and gone, but in the adaptability of its great principles to cope with current problems and current needs.

The Imperial Presidency (1973).

Our task is not to rediscover our institutions but to reinvent them.

The Disuniting of America: Reflections on a Multicultural Society (1992).

In the United States, the health of the people is the foundation of all the powers of government.

The Age of Roosevelt, Vol. I: The Crisis of the Old Order, 1919–1933 (1957).

Democracy

In a democracy, dissent is an act of faith.

The Disuniting of America: Reflections on a Multicultural Society (1992).

Democracy, if it means anything, means a society in which power, to be legitimate, must be disciplined by the will and judgment of the governed.

The Crisis of Confidence: Ideas, Power, and Violence in America(1969).

Economics

The most important single central fact about a free market is that no exchange takes place unless both parties benefit.

The Age of Jackson (1945).

Extremism

Political extremism involves two prime ingredients: an excessively simple diagnosis of the world's ills, and a conviction that there are identifiable villains back of it all.

The Vital Center: The Politics of Freedom (1949).

Idealism is fine, but as it approaches reality, the costs become prohibitive.

A Thousand Days: John F. Kennedy in the White House (1965).

Freedom

Freedom is fragile and must be protected. To sacrifice it, even as a temporary measure, is to betray it.

The Vital Center: The Politics of Freedom (1949).

History

History is to the nation as memory is to the individual.

The Cycles of American History (1986).

We are not the prisoners of history but its makers. We make our own history by our decisions and our actions.

The Age of Roosevelt, Vol. I: The Crisis of the Old Order, 1919–1933 (1957).

History is an antidote for despair.

The Cycles of American History (1986).

History gives us a kind of chart, and we dare not surrender even a small rushlight in the darkness.

The Age of Roosevelt, Vol. I: The Crisis of the Old Order, 1919–1933 (1957).

To be ignorant of what happened before you were born is to remain forever a child.

The Disuniting of America: Reflections on a Multicultural Society (1992).

Language

The great enemy of clear language is insincerity.

The Vital Center: The Politics of Freedom (1949).

Political Power

Power in America today is control of the means of communication.

The Politics of Hope (1963).

Power confuses itself with virtue and tends also to take itself for omnipotence.

The Imperial Presidency (1973).

In this world, shipmates, sin that pays its way can travel freely, and without passport; whereas Virtue, if a pauper, is stopped at all frontiers.

The Age of Jackson (1945).

I take it to be axiomatic that people are revolted by power, but they are also revolted by the absence of power.

The Imperial Presidency (1973).

Prejudice

The persistence of racial and ethnic prejudice in America indicates that discrimination is an ineradicable part of human society.

The Disuniting of America: Reflections on a Multicultural Society (1992).

Science and Technology

Science and technology revolutionize our lives, but memory, tradition, and myth frame our response.

The Disuniting of America: Reflections on a Multicultural Society (1992).

Science has made gods of us before we have deserved even to be men.

The Crisis of Confidence: Ideas, Power, and Violence in America(1969).

Science, in the very act of solving problems, creates more of them.

The Age of Roosevelt, Vol. I: The Crisis of the Old Order, 1919–1933 (1957).

Welfare

The lessons of history . . . show conclusively that continued dependence upon relief induces a spiritual and moral disintegration fundamentally destructive to the national fiber.

The Age of Roosevelt, Vol. I: The Crisis of the Old Order, 1919–1933 (1957).

Eric Emerson Schmidt

Eric Emerson Schmidt / b. 1955 / Virginia, USA / Software Engineer, Business Executive

Business Philosophy

Playing catch-up with the competition can only ever help you make incremental gains. It will never help you create something new.

Reported in "Eric Schmidt: 'Playing catch-up with the competition will never help you create something new,'" MacDailyNews, August 27, 2014.

Cybersecurity

We have always been the leader in security and in encryption. Our systems are far more secure and encrypted than anyone else, including Apple. They're catching up, which is great.

Reported by Mikey Campbell, "Eric Schmidt says Google 'far more secure' than Apple, denies allegations of harvesting datam," AppleInsider, October 3, 2014.

Disinformation

I fundamentally believe that disinformation becomes so easy to generate, because complexity overwhelms knowledge, that it's in people's interests, if you will, over the next decade, to build disinformation-generating systems. This is true for corporations, for marketing, for governments, and so forth.

In discussion with Julian Assange, June, 2011; reported in Assange's When Google Met Wikileaks (2016).

Global Warming

Everyone understands climate change is occurring and the people who oppose it are really hurting our children and our grandchildren and making the world a much worse place. And so we should not be aligned with such people—they're just, they're just literally lying.

Reported in "'They're just literally lying': Google's Eric Schmidt on cutting ties with conservative group," SFGate, September 22, 2014.

Google

When you use Google, do you get more than one answer? Of course you do. Well, that's a bug. We have more bugs per second in the world. We should be able to give you the right answer just once. We should know what you meant. You should look for information. We should get it exactly right and we should give it to you in your language and we should never be wrong. That's our challenge.

Interview, The Charlie Rose Show, PBS, June 3, 2005.

I actually think most people don't want Google to answer their questions. They want Google to tell them what they should be doing next.

Reported by Holman W. Jenkins, Jr., The Wall Street Journal, wsj.com, August 14, 2010.

The current inclination of the company is to invest heavily . , , we test stuff and, when it works, we put a lot more emphasis on it. So, Google+—all the signs are very positive, so now the whole company is ramping up on top of it.

Reported by Matt McGee, "With 'Millions' of Users and Growing, Google+ Set to Power All Google Products," searchengineland.com, July 9, 2011.

Ultimately, application vendors are driven by volume, and volume is favored by the open approach Google is taking. There are so many manufacturers working so hard to distribute Android phones globally that whether you like [Android 4.0] or not … you will want to develop for that platform, and perhaps even first.

Reported by Stephen Shankland, "Google's Schmidt: Android leads the iPhone," CNET, December 7, 2011.

By the summer of 2012, the majority of the televisions you see in stores will have Google TV embedded.

Reported by Jeff Blagdon, "Eric Schmidt: Google TV on 'majority' of new TVs by summer 2012," The Verge, December 27, 2011.

Government

Technology will move faster than governments, so don't legislate before you understand the consequences . . .

Reported by Stewart Mitchell, "Group calls for ban on spying technology sales," Alphr.com, May 25, 2011.

Openness

If you have something that you don't want anyone to know, maybe you shouldn't be doing it in the first place

Interview with Lee Brodie, "CEO Eric Schmidt Reveals 'Centerpiece' Of Google's 2010 Strategy,'" CNBC, December 3, 2009.

Ultimately, in the Internet, openness has always won. I cannot imagine that the current competitive environment would reverse that.

Reported by John Tozzi, "America's Best Young Entrepreneurs 2010," Bloomberg.com, September 23, 2010.

Arthur Schopenhauer

Arthur Schopenhauer / 1788–1860 / Danzig, Polish-Lithuanian Commonwealth (now Gdańsk, Poland) / Philosopher, Aphorist

Animals

One might say with truth, Mankind are the devils of the earth, and the animals the souls they torment.

Parerga and Paralipomena (1851).

Boundless compassion for all living beings is the surest and most certain guarantee of pure moral conduct,

On the Basis of Morals (1840).

Compassion for animals is intimately connected with goodness of character, and it may be confidently asserted that he, who is cruel to living creatures, cannot be a good man. Moreover, this compassion manifestly flows from the same source whence arise the virtues of justice and loving-kindness towards men.

On the Basis of Morals (1840).

Field of Vision

Every man takes the limits of his own field of vision for the limits of the world.

Parerga and Paralipomena (1851).

Great Minds

It is natural for great minds—the true teachers of humanity—to care little about the constant company of others; just as little as the schoolmaster cares for joining in the gambols of the noisy crowd of boys which surround him. The mission of these great minds is to guide mankind over the sea of error to the haven of truth—to draw it forth from the dark abysses of a barbarous vulgarity up into the light of culture and refinement. Men of great intellect live in the world without really belonging to it.

Parerga and Paralipomena (1851).

Happiness

The two foes of human happiness are pain and boredom.

Parerga and Paralipomena (1851).

Almost all of our sorrows spring out of our relations with other people. There is no more mistaken path to happiness than worldliness.

Parerga and Paralipomena (1851).

Hatred vs. Contempt

Hatred comes from the heart; contempt from the head; and neither feeling is quite within our
control.

Parerga and Paralipomena (1851).

Honor

If people insist that honor is dearer than life itself, what they really mean is that existence and well- being are as nothing compared with other people's opinions. Of course, this may be only an exaggerated way of stating the prosaic truth that reputation, that is, the opinion others have of us, is indispensable if we are to make any progress in the world.

Parerga and Paralipomena (1851).

Intellect

Intellect is invisible to the man who has none.

Parerga and Paralipomena (1851).

Life

He who lives to see two or three generations is like a man who sits some time in the conjurer's booth at a fair, and witnesses the performance twice or thrice in succession. The tricks were meant to be seen only once; and when they are no longer a novelty and cease to deceive their effect is gone.

Parerga and Paralipomena (1851).

Do not shorten the morning by getting up late; look upon it as the quintessence of life, as to a certain extent sacred. . . . Each day is a little life: every waking and rising a little birth, every fresh morning a little youth, every going to rest and sleep a little death.

Parerga and Paralipomena (1851).

If we were not all so interested in ourselves, life would be so uninteresting that none of us would be able to endure it.

Parerga and Paralipomena (1851).

Life is a business that does not cover the costs.

The World as Will and Representation (1819; 1844; 1859).

Mankind

The doctor sees all the weakness of mankind; the lawyer all the wickedness, the theologian all the stupidity.

Parerga and Paralipomena (1851).

Marriage

To marry is to halve your rights and double your duties.

The World as Will and Representation (1819; 1844; 1859).

Memory

It is a curious fact that in bad days we can very vividly recall the good lime that is now no more; but that in good days we have only a very cold and imperfect memory of the bad.

Parerga and Paralipomena (1851).

Mystery of Existence

The more unintelligent a man is, the less mysterious existence seems to him.

The World as Will and Representation (1819; 1844; 1859).

Opinion

Opinion is like a pendulum and obeys the same law. If it goes past the centre of gravity on one side, it must go a like distance on the other; and it is only after a certain time that it finds the true point which it can remain at.

Parerga and Paralipomena (1851).

Parting and Reunion

Every parting gives a foretaste of death; every coming together again a foretaste of the resurrection.

Parerga and Paralipomena (1851).

Talent vs. Genius

Talent hits a target no one else can hit; Genius hits a target no one else can see.

The World as Will and Representation (1819; 1844; 1859).

True Thinker

Every true thinker for himself is so far like a monarch; he is absolute, and recognises nobody above him. His judgments, like the decrees of a monarch, spring from his own sovereign power and proceed directly from himself. He takes as little notice of authority as a monarch does of a command; nothing is valid unless he has himself authorised it. On the other hand, those of vulgar minds, who are swayed by all kinds of current opinions, authorities, and prejudices, are like the people which in silence obey the law and commands.

Parerga and Paralipomena (1851).

Truth

To truth only a brief celebration of victory is allowed between the two long periods during which it is condemned as paradoxical, or disparaged as trivial.

The World as Will and Representation (1819; 1844; 1859).

To free a man from error is to give, not to take away. Knowledge that a thing is false is a truth.

Parerga and Paralipomena (1851).

Truth that is naked is the most beautiful, and the simpler its expression the deeper is the impression it makes.

Parerga and Paralipomena (1851).

Wealth

Wealth is like sea-water; the more we drink, the thirstier we become.

Parerga and Paralipomena (1851).

William Shakespeare

William Shakespeare / 1564–1616 / England / Playwright, Poet

All the World's a Stage

. . . All the world's a stage,
And all the men and women merely players;
They have their exits and their entrances . . .
As You Like It, Act II, Scene VII; Jaques.

Ambition

Glamis thou art, and Cawdor; and shalt be
What thou art promised: yet do I fear thy nature;
It is too full o' the milk of human kindness
To catch the nearest way: thou wouldst be great;
Art not without ambition, but without
The illness should attend it: what thou wouldst highly,
That wouldst thou holily; wouldst not play false,
And yet wouldst wrongly win . . .
Macbeth, Act I, Scene V; Lady Macbeth.

Band of Brothers

And Crispin Crispian shall ne'er go by,
From this day to the ending of the world,
But we in it shall be remember'd;
We few, we happy few, we band of brothers;
For he to-day that sheds his blood with me
Shall be my brother; be he ne'er so vile,
This day shall gentle his condition:
And gentlemen in England now a-bed
Shall think themselves accursed they were not here,
And hold their manhoods cheap whiles any speaks
That fought with us upon Saint Crispin's day.
Henry V, Act IV, Scene III; King Henry V.

Bloody Murder

By the pricking of my thumbs,
something wicked this way comes.
Macbeth, Act IV, Scene I; Second Witch.
Yet here's a spot. . . .
Out, damned spot! out, I say!–One: two: why,
then, 'tis time to do't.–Hell is murky!–Fie, my
lord, fie! a soldier, and afeard? What need we fear who knows it, when none can call our power to
account?–Yet who would have thought the old man
to have had so much blood in him. . . .
Here's the smell of the blood still: all the
perfumes of Arabia will not sweeten this little
hand. Oh, oh, oh!
Macbeth, Act V, Scene I; Lady Macbeth.
Whence is that knocking?
How is't with me, when every noise appalls me?
What hands are here? ha! they pluck out mine eyes.
Will all great Neptune's ocean wash this blood
Clean from my hand? No, this my hand will

rather
The multitudinous seas incarnadine,
Making the green one red.
Macbeth, Act II, Scene II; Macbeth.

Burying Caesar

Friends, Romans, countrymen, lend me your ears;
I come to bury Caesar, not to praise him.
The evil that men do lives after them;
The good is oft interred with their bones;
So let it be with Caesar. The noble Brutus
Hath told you Caesar was ambitious:
If it were so, it was a grievous fault,
And grievously hath Caesar answer'd it.
Julius Caesar, Act III, Scene II; Antony.

Cowards

Cowards die many times before their deaths;
The valiant never taste of death but once.
Julius Caesar, Act II, Scene II; Caesar.

Dissembling

I am settled, and bend up
Each corporal agent to this terrible feat.
Away, and mock the time with fairest show:
False face must hide what the false heart doth know.
Macbeth, Act I, Scene VII; Macbeth.

Fate

Why, man, he doth bestride the narrow world
Like a Colossus, and we petty men
Walk under his huge legs and peep about
To find ourselves dishonourable graves.
Men at some time are masters of their fates:
The fault, dear Brutus, is not in our stars,
But in ourselves, that we are underlings.
Julius Caesar, Act I, Scene II; Cassius.

Fatherly Advice

Neither a borrower nor a lender be;
For loan oft loses both itself and friend,
And borrowing dulls the edge of husbandry.
Hamlet, Act I, Scene III; Polonius.
This above all: to thine ownself be true,
And it must follow, as the night the day,
Thou canst not then be false to any man.
Hamlet, Act I, Scene III; Polonius.

Greatness

. . . be not afraid of greatness: some
are born great, some achieve greatness, and some
have greatness thrust upon 'em. . . .
Twelfth Night, Act II, Scene V; Malvolio.

Just Deserts

. . . use every man
after his desert, and who should 'scape whipping?
Hamlet, Act II, Scene II; Hamlet.

Kingship

Uneasy lies the head that wears a crown.
Henry IV, Part II, Act III, Scene I; King Henry IV.

Literary Immortality

Shall I compare thee to a summer's day?
Thou art more lovely and more temperate:
Rough winds do shake the darling buds of May,
And summer's lease hath all too short a date:
Sometimes too hot the eye of heaven shines,
And too often is his gold complexion dimm'd:
And every fair from fair sometimes declines,
By chance or natures changing course untrimm'd;
By thy eternal summer shall not fade,

Nor lose possession of that fair thou owest;
Nor shall Death brag thou wander'st in his shade,
When in eternal lines to time thou growest:
So long as men can breathe or eyes can see,
So long lives this and this gives life to thee.

Sonnet 18.

Love

Love looks not with the eyes, but with the mind.
And therefore is wing'd Cupid painted blind.

A Midsummer Night's Dream, Act I, Scene I; Helena.

O, she doth teach the torches to burn bright!
It seems she hangs upon the cheek of night
Like a rich jewel in an Ethiope's ear;
Beauty too rich for use, for earth too dear!
So shows a snowy dove trooping with crows,
As yonder lady o'er her fellows shows.
The measure done, I'll watch her place of stand,
And, touching hers, make blessed my rude hand.
Did my heart love till now? forswear it, sight!
For I ne'er saw true beauty till this night.

Romeo and Juliet, Act I, Scene V; Romeo.

If music be the food of love, play on.

Twelfth Night, Act I, Scene I; Duke Orsino.

When, in disgrace with fortune and men's eyes,
I all alone beweep my outcast state,
And trouble deaf heaven with my bootless cries,
And look upon myself and curse my fate,
Wishing me like to one more rich in hope,
Featured like him, like him with friends possessed,
Desiring this man's art and that man's scope,
With what I most enjoy contented least;
Yet in these thoughts myself almost despising,
Haply I think on thee, and then my state,
(Like to the lark at break of day arising
From sullen earth) sings hymns at heaven's gate;
For thy sweet love remembered such wealth brings
That then I scorn to change my state with kings.

Sonnet 29.

Meaning of Life and Death

To be, or not to be, that is the question,
Whether 'tis nobler in the mind to suffer
The slings and arrows of outrageous fortune,
Or to take arms against a sea of troubles,
And by opposing end them? To die: to sleep;
No more; and by a sleep to say we end
The heart-ache and the thousand natural shocks
That flesh is heir to, 'tis a consummation
Devoutly to be wish'd. To die, to sleep;
To sleep: perchance to dream: ay, there's the rub;
For in that sleep of death what dreams may come
When we have shuffled off this mortal coil,
Must give us pause: there's the respect
That makes calamity of so long life;
For who would bear the whips and scorns of time,
The oppressor's wrong, the proud man's contumely,
The pangs of despised love, the law's delay,
The insolence of office and the spurns
That patient merit of the unworthy takes,
When he himself might his quietus make
With a bare bodkin? who would fardels bear,
To grunt and sweat under a weary life,
But that the dread of something after death,
The undiscover'd country from whose bourn
No traveller returns, puzzles the will
And makes us rather bear those ills we have
Than fly to others that we know not of?
Thus conscience does make cowards of us all;
And thus the native hue of resolution

Is sicklied o'er with the pale cast of thought . . .

Hamlet, Act III, Scene I; Hamlet.

As flies to wanton boys, are we to the gods.
They kill us for their sport.

King Lear, Act IV, Scene I; Gloucester.

To-morrow, and to-morrow, and to-morrow,
Creeps in this petty pace from day to day
To the last syllable of recorded time,
And all our yesterdays have lighted fools
The way to dusty death. Out, out, brief candle!
Life's but a walking shadow, a poor player
That struts and frets his hour upon the stage
And then is heard no more: it is a tale
Told by an idiot, full of sound and fury,
Signifying nothing.

Macbeth, Act V, Scene V; Macbeth.

Mercy

The quality of mercy is not strain'd,
It droppeth as the gentle rain from heaven
Upon the place beneath: it is twice blest;
It blesseth him that gives and him that takes:
'Tis mightiest in the mightiest: it becomes
The throned monarch better than his crown;
His sceptre shows the force of temporal power,
The attribute to awe and majesty,
Wherein doth sit the dread and fear of kings;
But mercy is above this sceptred sway;
It is enthroned in the hearts of kings,
It is an attribute to God himself . . .

Merchant of Venice, Act IV, Scene I; Portia.

A Plague on Both Your Houses

. . . A plague o' both your houses!
They have made worms' meat of me . . .

Romeo and Juliet, Act III, Scene I; Mercutio.

Where be these enemies? Capulet! Montague!
See, what a scourge is laid upon your hate,
That heaven finds means to kill your joys with love.
And I for winking at your discords too
Have lost a brace of kinsmen: all are punish'd.

Romeo and Juliet, Act V, Scene III; Prince.

Relativity

. . . for there is nothing
either good or bad, but thinking makes it so . . .

Hamlet, Act II, Scene II; Hamlet

O Romeo, Romeo, wherefore art thou Romeo?
Deny thy father and refuse thy name.
Or if thou wilt not, be but sworn my love
And I'll no longer be a Capulet.
'Tis but thy name that is my enemy:
Thou art thyself, though not a Montague.
What's Montague? It is nor hand nor foot
Nor arm nor face nor any other part
Belonging to a man. O be some other name.
What's in a name? That which we call a rose
By any other name would smell as sweet;
So Romeo would, were he not Romeo call'd,
Retain that dear perfection which he owes
Without that title. Romeo, doff thy name,
And for that name, which is no part of thee,
Take all myself.

Romeo and Juliet, Act II, Scene II; Juliet.

Sleep

Methought I heard a voice cry "Sleep no more!
Macbeth does murder sleep," the innocent sleep,
Sleep that knits up the ravell'd sleeve of care,
The death of each day's life, sore labour's bath,
Balm of hurt minds, great nature's second

course,
Chief nourisher in life's feast, . . .
Still it cried "Sleep no more!" to all the house:
"Glamis hath murder'd sleep, and therefore Cawdor
Shall sleep no more; Macbeth shall sleep no more."

Macbeth, Act II, Scene II; Macbeth.

Unity of Humanity

. . . I am a Jew. Hath
not a Jew eyes? hath not a Jew hands, organs, dimensions, senses, affections, passions? fed with
the same food, hurt with the same weapons, subject
to the same diseases, healed by the same means,
warmed and cooled by the same winter and summer, as
a Christian is? If you prick us, do we not bleed?
if you tickle us, do we not laugh? if you poison
us, do we not die? and if you wrong us, shall we not
revenge?

The Merchant of Venice, Act III, Scene I; Shylock.

What a Piece of Work is Man

What a piece of work is a man! how noble in reason!
how infinite in faculty! in form and moving how
express and admirable! in action how like an angel!
in apprehension how like a god! the beauty of the
world! the paragon of animals! And yet, to me,
what is this quintessence of dust? man delights not
me . . .

Hamlet, Act II, Scene II; Hamlet.

Wild Oats

We have heard the chimes at midnight, Master Shallow.

Henry IV, Part II, Act III, Scene II; Falstaff.

George Bernard Shaw

George Bernard Shaw / 1856–1950 / Ireland (then, United Kingdom of Great Britain and Ireland) / Playwright, Essayist

Action

He who can, does. He who cannot, teaches.

Man and Superman, Appendix: Maxims for Revolutionists (1903).

Ambition

Miss Warren is a great devotee of the Gospel of Getting On.

Mrs. Warren's Profession, Act IV (1893).

You see things; and you say, "Why?" But I dream things that never were; and I say, "Why not?"

Back to Methuselah, Act I (1921).

One man that has a mind and knows it can always beat ten men who haven't and don't

The Apple Cart, Act I (1929).

Circumstances

People are always blaming their circumstances for what they are. I don't believe in circumstances. The people who get on in this world are the people who get up and look for the circumstances they want, and, if they can't find them, make them.

Mrs. Warren's Profession, Act II (1893).

Conscience

Liza: Theres lots of women has to make their husbands drunk to make them fit to live with. You see, it's like this. If a man has a bit of a conscience, it always takes him when he's sober; and then it makes him low-spirited. A drop of booze just takes that off and makes him happy.

Pygmalion, Act III (1913).

Fear

It is not . . . easy for mental giants who neither hate nor intend to injure their fellows to realize that nevertheless their fellows hate mental giants and would like to destroy them, not only enviously because the juxtaposition of a superior wounds their vanity, but quite humbly and honestly because it frightens them. Fear will drive men to any extreme; and the fear inspired by a superior being is a mystery which cannot be reasoned away.

Saint Joan, Preface (1923).

Golden Rule

Do not do unto others as you would that they should do unto you. Their tastes may not be the same.

Man and Superman, Appendix: Maxims for Revolutionists (1903).

Happiness

We have no more right to consume happiness without producing it than to consume wealth without producing it.

Candida, Act I (1898).

A lifetime of happiness! No man alive could bear it: it would be hell on earth.

Man and Superman, Act I (1903).

Honor

Hardly any of us have ethical energy enough for more than one really inflexible point of honor.

The Doctor's Dilemma, Preface (1906).

Hotels

The great advantage of a hotel is that it's a refuge from home life.

You Never Can Tell, Act II (1898).

Humanity

The rich are instinctively crying "Let us eat and drink; for tomorrow we die," and the poor, "How long, O Lord, how long?" But the pitiless reply still is that God helps those who help themselves. This docs not mean that if Man cannot find the remedy no remedy will be found. The power that produced Man when the monkey was not up to the mark, can produce a higher creature than Man if Man does not come up to the mark. What it means is that if Man is to be saved, Man must save himself.

Back to Methuselah, Preface (1921).

Idolatry

The savage bows down to idols of wood and stone: the civilized man to idols of flesh and blood.

Man and Superman, Appendix: Maxims for Revolutionists (1903).

Inhumanity

The worst sin towards our fellow creatures is not to hate them, but to be indifferent to them: that's the essence of inhumanity.

The Devil's Disciple, Act II (1901).

Joy

This is the true joy in life, the being used for a purpose recognized by yourself as a mighty one; the being thoroughly worn out before you are thrown on the scrap heap; the being a force of nature instead of a feverish selfish little clod of ailments and grievances complaining that the world will not devote itself to making you happy.

Man and Superman, Epistle Dedicatory (1903).

Love and Marriage

It's well to be off with the Old Woman before you're on with the New.

The Philanderer, Act II (1893).

The fickleness of the women I love is only equaled by the infernal constancy of the women who love me.

The Philanderer, Act II (1893).

When two people are under the influence of the most violent, most insane, most delusive, and most transient of passions, they are required to swear that they will remain in that excited, abnormal, and exhausting condition continuously until death do them part.

Getting Married, Preface (1908).

Music

Hell is full of musical amateurs: music is the brandy of the damned.

Man and Superman, Act III (1903).

Poverty

The greatest of our evils and the worst of our crimes is poverty.

Major Barbara, Preface (1905).

Religion

There is only one religion, though there are a hundred versions of it.

Plays Pleasant and Unpleasant, Preface (1898).

Morality

An Englishman thinks he is moral when he is only uncomfortable.

Man and Superman, Act III (1903).

Pickering: Have you no morals, man?
Doolittle: Can't afford them, Governor.

Pygmalion, Act II (1913).

Shame

We live in an atmosphere of shame. We are ashamed of everything that is real about us; ashamed of ourselves, of our relatives, of our incomes, of our accents, of our opinions, of our experience, just as we are ashamed of our naked skins. . . . We are ashamed to walk, ashamed to ride in an omnibus, ashamed to hire a hansom instead of keeping a carriage, ashamed of keeping one horse instead of two and a groom-gardener instead of a coachman and footman. The more things a man is ashamed of, the more respectable he is.

Man and Superman, Act I (1903).

Tragedy

There are two tragedies in life. One is to lose your heart's desire. The other is to gain it.

Man and Superman, Act IV (1903).

Virtue

Virtue consists, not in abstaining from vice, but in not desiring it.

Man and Superman, Appendix: Maxims for Revolutionists (1903).

Women

Man is no longer, like Don Juan, victor in the duel of sex. Whether he has ever really been may be doubted: at all events the enormous superiority of Woman's natural position in this matter is telling with greater and greater force.

Man and Superman, Epistle Dedicatory (1903).

Writing

My method is to take the utmost trouble to find the right thing to say, and then to say it with the utmost levity.

Answers to Nine Questions (1896).

Adam Smith

Adam Smith / 1723–1790 / Scotland (Great Britain) / Philosopher

Centralization Folly

The statesman who should attempt to direct private people in what manner they ought to employ their capitals would not only load himself with a most unnecessary attention, but assume an authority which could safely be trusted, not only to no single person, but to no council or senate whatever, and which would nowhere be so dangerous as in the hands of a man who had folly and presumption enough to fancy himself fit to exercise it.

Source: Wealth of Nations, 1776; Book IV, Chapter II.

Customers and Consumption

To found a great empire for the sole purpose of raising up a people of customers, may at first sight appear a project fit only for a nation of shopkeepers. It is, however, a project altogether unfit for a nation of shopkeepers; but extremely fit for a nation whose government is influenced by shopkeepers.

Source: Wealth of Nations, 1776; Book IV, Chapter III, Part II, Chapter VII.

Consumption is the sole end and purpose of all production; and the interest of the producer ought to be attended to only so far as it may be necessary for promoting that of the consumer.

Source: Wealth of Nations, 1776; Book IV, Chapter VIII.

Free Markets

All systems either of preference or of restraint, therefore, being thus completely taken away, the obvious and simple system of natural liberty establishes itself of its own accord. Every man, as long as he does not violate the laws of justice, is left perfectly free to pursue his own interest his own way, and to bring both his industry and capital into competition with those of any other man or order of men.

Source: Wealth of Nations, 1776; Book IV, Chapter IX.

Government Waste

It is the highest impertinence and presumption, therefore, in kings and ministers to pretend to watch over the economy of private people, and to restrain their expense.... They are themselves always, and without any exception, the greatest spendthrifts in the society.

Source: Wealth of Nations, 1776; Book II, Chapter III.

Invisible Hand

Every individual necessarily labors to render the annual revenue of the society as great as he can. He generally indeed neither intends to promote the public interest, nor knows how much he is promoting it.... He intends only his own gain, and he is in this, as in many other cases, led by an invisible hand to promote an end which was no part of his intention.... By pursuing his own interest he frequently promotes that of the society more effectually than when he really intends to promote it. I have never known much good done by those who affected to trade for the public good.

Source: Wealth of Nations, 1776; Book IV, Chapter II.

Monopolies and Cartels

A monopoly granted either to an individual or to a trading company has the same effect as a secret in trade or manufactures.

Source: Wealth of Nations, 1776; Book I, Chapter VII.

People of the same trade seldom meet together, even for merriment and diversion, but the conversation ends in a conspiracy against the public, or in some contrivance to raise prices.

Source: Wealth of Nations, 1776; Book I, Chapter 10.

New Markets

The discovery of America, and that of a passage to the East Indies by the Cape of Good Hope, are the two greatest and most important events recorded in the history of mankind.

Source: Wealth of Nations, 1776; Book I, Chapter XI.

Obscene Wealth

With the greater part of rich people, the chief enjoyment of riches consists in the parade of riches, which in their eyes is never so complete as when they appear to possess those decisive marks of opulence which nobody can possess but themselves.

Source: Wealth of Nations, 1776; Book I, Chapter XI

Self-Interest Drives Economics

It is not from the benevolence of the butcher, the brewer, or the baker that we expect our dinner, but from their regard to their own interest. We address ourselves, not to their humanity but to their self-love.

Source: Wealth of Nations, 1776; Book I, Chapter II.

Lauren Southern

Lauren Cherie Southern / b. 1995 / Surrey, British Columbia, Canada / Political Commentator, Libertarian Party Candidate for the Canadian Parliament, Author, Podcaster

Note: The sources of the following quotations are provided where known; the rest of the quotations presumably derive from Southern's comments as a candidate for public office, as well as her many writings, online commentaries, interviews, and podcasts

American Family and Culture

In a world that has forgotten the importance of family and culture, those who fight for it are labeled as radicals.

Traditionalism offers a lot of stability in people's life; it offers a guide for how to lead them to the happiest life.

You won't see Christians violently attacking people for criticizing their religion like you do with Islam, things like the Charlie Hebdo attack.

Dismissing the guidance built for us over thousands and thousands of years in the form of gender roles, traditional lifestyles, hard work, objectivity, and cultural supremacy was, in fact, painfully stupid.

> <u>*Barbarians: How the Baby Boomers, Immigration, and Islam Screwed My Generation*</u> *(2016).*

Diversity

"Diversity is our strength" is a dangerous myth. True strength comes from unity and shared values, not division.

Down Under

It's a pleasure to land here and see Australia upholding its commitment to free speech and Western culture—something that may not be here for much longer if left-wing Australian politicians continue their pathological worship of multiculturalism.

The reality is, we have had filled rooms wherever we've spoken, and in New Zealand, the left and the right have been coming together and saying, "We believe in free speech."

I think, in Australia, the no-go areas wouldn't be as bad as in Europe because they've got less mass immigration, but I've heard some pretty bizarre stories about riots, attacks.

Freedom

Freedom isn't being able to do what you want; it's being able to do what you should.

Liberty is the right to do what the law permits.

The best way to defeat an idea is with a better idea, not by suppressing it.

Never underestimate the power of free speech. It's the foundation of a free society.

Ideas should be met with debate, not with deplatforming and censorship.

Censorship and silencing of unpopular opinions only breed resentment and further division.

Freedom of speech isn't about protecting popular opinions; it's about protecting unpopular and controversial ones.

The battle for freedom and free expression is ongoing, and it requires constant vigilance.

Government

There are so many people that are offended by debate and free speech that sometimes governments cower. It's just way easier to play into the hands of people who are totalitarian.

The West needs to think of itself as a family again, not as a sugar daddy for other people and their families.

Barbarians: How the Baby Boomers, Immigration, and Islam Screwed My Generation (2016).

Guns

I think the Americans have it right. The idea of having guns is essentially to protect yourself from a totalitarian government.

Immigration

It seems as though our leaders have almost forgotten about legal immigration and are just leaving our borders open, which is a detriment culturally, financially, and in a lot of other realms for native people.

I don't know why legal immigration even exists anymore when I can just put on some bronzer, get on a dingy boat, and just show up at the beaches of Sicily with the Koran in my hand.

People think my position is this horrifying, scary, harsh position to say we need to protect our borders and that people cannot illegally enter our nation. This isn't my opinion —this is the law.

Unchecked immigration is a moral eyesore. It asks our states to fail their most basic obligations by putting the needs of faceless, dubiously friendly strangers over the needs of the citizens they exist to protect and serve.

Barbarians: How the Baby Boomers, Immigration, and Islam Screwed My Generation (2016).

"Islamophobia"

Let's be clear: if the left merely attacked "fear of Islam," this would still be silly, but at least it would be something we could debate. But to brand such a fear as a "phobia" marks it as an a priori irrational fear: in essence, a form of bigotry.

Barbarians: How the Baby Boomers, Immigration, and Islam Screwed My Generation (2016).

The Left

This is because the most fundamental element of New Left thought is a near total rejection of freedom, morality, and of reason in theory, combined with the abuse of all three in practice.

Barbarians: How the Baby Boomers, Immigration, and Islam Screwed My Generation (2016).

We know the future, if left to the hands of the average millennial, is an Ugg boot stomping on a human face, forever.

Barbarians: How the Baby Boomers, Immigration, and Islam Screwed My Generation (2016).

[A] steadily increasing number of millennials are finally beginning to wake up to the choice we face as a civilization, and to the value they've so long overlooked in traditional standards of morality and beauty. They are wondering: is modern culture really so great if it means we substitute Meghan Trainor for Mozart, Emma Sulkowicz for Da Vinci, or bell hooks for Plato? Is it really such a step forward that our civilization, which once shed both blood and ink debating Martin Luther's 95 Theses, is now reduced to considering theses like VICE Magazine's "Dear Straight Guys: It's Time to Start Putting Things in Your Butt"? Is this all there is, or can we do better?

Barbarians: How the Baby Boomers, Immigration, and Islam Screwed My Generation (2016).

Life

The strongest people I've ever met are those who have defeated adversity and known what it's like to struggle.

The Media

The left doesn't win its battles in debate. It doesn't have to. In the twenty-first century, media is everything. The left wins because it controls the narrative. The narrative is controlled by the media. The left is the media. Narrative is everything.

Come out and say it, Zuckerberg—"Our platform that influences billions of people is being used to propagandize left-wing viewpoints."

Multiculturalism

Multiculturalism for any western country is a massive issue. The lack of integration, the increase of crime, violence, and mistrust in society, the segregation created due to mass immigration, these are only the beginning phases of something I fear will almost certainly get more worse and violent.

The first rule of multiculturalism is that you can't talk about multiculturalism.

The experiment of multiculturalism was thought up in the minds of tenured intellectuals, put on paper by virtue signaling politicians, and then enjoyed by big business globalists.

Barbarians: How the Baby Boomers, Immigration, and Islam Screwed My Generation (2016).

Never-Trumpers

With rare, rare exceptions, the anti-Trump "conservatives" were out of touch, boring, lame, ineffective, self-righteous losers without enough flare or original thought to headline an accountants' convention. Except, as their reading of the polls showed us, the accountants are better at math.

Barbarians: How the Baby Boomers, Immigration, and Islam Screwed My Generation (2016).

Political Correctness

In the world of political correctness, a conservative is someone who is winning an argument with a liberal.

Political correctness is just fascism with manners. I wish people would understand that.

Today's SJWs [social justice warriors] fall into two, mutually reinforcing and equally toxic camps: PC Authoritarians and PC Egalitarians.

Barbarians: How the Baby Boomers, Immigration, and Islam Screwed My Generation (2016).

South Africa

This is quite public knowledge. The South African government has said they're doing it. They've started seizing their first couple hundred farms.

Southern on Southern

I judge people based on merit, on personality. I'm totally open to changing my beliefs. I could grow up to be a total communist. I could grow up to be a Neocon. I'm looking to have my views challenged. I'm looking to be corrected.

I don't think the alt-right would call me alt-right. They call me alt-lite, usually. I just consider myself a nationalist or a traditionalist.

When people put effort in life, it's more beautiful. But it doesn't come naturally to me.

I try to surround myself with the people who genuinely believe in changing things, that are angry about it and want to make changes and want to make a change and are willing.

There's this ridiculous idea that I'm a gender traitor because I'm not a feminist. I'm supposed to be part of a sisterhood: you're automatically supposed to support all women just because you have the same genitals as them, which doesn't make sense.

If I were black, I could say I'm proud. If I were Asian, I could say I'm proud. If I were any other ethnicity, I could say I'm proud, because that's how our culture is, but if I'm white and I say I'm proud, the media will go nuts.

I'm happy with being white. I'm fine with being white. I feel zero shame whatsoever in being white.

I was being taught to believe that, first, I was special, unique, important, and great beyond words; second, that I was completely equal to everyone, which is to say average and mediocre.

> *Barbarians: How the Baby Boomers, Immigration, and Islam Screwed My Generation* (2016).

Like many millennials, I had a conventional modern education, and it's only with a lot of painful hindsight and introspection that I can see how deficient it was. Let me give you the biggest, and worst examples: If you asked me in my last year of high school to name five great musicians, I would have probably only got as far as Mozart and Beethoven before drawing a blank. If you asked me to name five great authors, I'd have mentioned Shakespeare and then groped in vain for anything else. If you'd asked me to name five great philosophers, I'm ashamed to say I wouldn't even have got as far as Plato. If you'd asked me about the history of Western civilization, I maybe could have named the Roman Empire, but you couldn't get me to tell you what actually happened while it was around.

> *Barbarians: How the Baby Boomers, Immigration, and Islam Screwed My Generation* (2016).

I was taught that war, when conducted by communists, terrorists, and agitators, is peace. That freedom, when exercised by white cishet men, is slavery. And most horribly of all, that ignorance is strength.

> *Barbarians: How the Baby Boomers, Immigration, and Islam Screwed My Generation* (2016).

Tolerance

You don't have to agree with someone to tolerate their existence.

Tolerance means respecting the right of others to have different opinions, even if you disagree with them.

Triggering

In other words, all those people claiming to be "triggered" aren't lying: they really are rather like overanxious, emotional children with similarly childlike understandings of language and morality.

> *Barbarians: How the Baby Boomers, Immigration, and Islam Screwed My Generation* (2016).

Ukraine War

Even if you hate Russia and want to see it nuked or levelled today, you still need to understand your enemy. You need to understand how they think in order to compete with them.

Interview, "'YOUR WELCOME' with Michael Malice #198: Lauren Southern," March 16, 2022.

[The terrifying thing] is that most of the people commenting on this Ukraine crisis couldn't even point Ukraine on a map a month ago. They have no idea of any of the history. They look at it from a cartoon world view: Putin is just bad, and he's bad because he's bad, of course, and if you disagree with that then you're bad.

Interview, "'YOUR WELCOME' with Michael Malice #198: Lauren Southern," March 16, 2022.

Universities

Not that those professors were blameless angels. Frankly, they'd already been eroding the traditional purpose of a university education for a while when the Boomers showed up: a process that began with the emergence of the Soviet Union, when professors reared on the progressive notions of government-by-expertise fell in love with communism, and fell out with religion.

Barbarians: How the Baby Boomers, Immigration, and Islam Screwed My Generation (2016).

. . . but the most important thing I took away from this class was not my credit, but a strong understanding of what has infected modern education: the curse of the postmodernist, deconstructionist professors making their long march through the institutions.

Barbarians: How the Baby Boomers, Immigration, and Islam Screwed My Generation (2016).

Western Civilization

They'll have to accept that Western ideals have shaped our cultures into some of the greatest, freest, most generous, most decent, most egalitarian, and most peaceful on Earth.

Barbarians: How the Baby Boomers, Immigration, and Islam Screwed My Generation (2016).

Women

I think women need to empower themselves instead of asking for handouts.

Thomas Sowell

Thomas Sowell / b. 1930 / North Carolina, USA / Economist, Political Philosopher

Civil Rights

Civil rights used to be about treating everyone the same. But today some people are so used to special treatment that equal treatment is considered to be discrimination.

Economics vs. Politics

The first lesson of economics is scarcity: There is never enough to satisfy all those who want it. The first lesson of politics is to disregard the first lesson of economics.

Source: Is Reality Optional?, and Other Essays (Hoover Institution Press, 1993).

Education

Ours may become the first civilization destroyed not by the power of our enemies, but by the ignorance of our teachers and the dangerous nonsense they are teaching our children.

The next time some academics tell you how important diversity is, ask how many conservatives there are in their sociology department.

Too often what are called "educated" people are simply people who have been sheltered from reality for years in ivy-covered buildings. Those whose whole careers have been spent in ivy-covered buildings, insulated by tenure, can remain adolescents on into their golden retirement years.

Source: "Random Thoughts," Townhall.com, April 8, 2008.

Greed

I have never understood why it is "greed" to want to keep the money you've earned, but not greed to want to take somebody else's money.

Source: Barbarians Inside the Gates and Other Controversial Essays (Hoover Institution Press, 1999).

Meetings

People who enjoy meetings should not be in charge of anything.

Source: Ever Wonder Why?, and Other Controversial Essays(Hoover Institution Press, 2006).

Parasitism

No society ever thrived because it had a large and growing class of parasites living off those who produce.

Source: The Thomas Sowell Reader (Basic Books, 2011).

What exactly is your "fair share" of what "someone else" has worked for?

One of the sad signs of our times is that we have demonized those who produce, subsidized those who refuse to produce, and canonized those who complain.

Source: The Thomas Sowell Reader (Basic Books, 2011).

One of the consequences of such notions as 'entitlements' is that people who have contributed nothing to society feel that society owes them something, apparently just for being nice enough to grace us with their presence.

Source: Ever Wonder Why?, and Other Controversial Essays (Hoover Institution Press, 2006).

Pragmatism and Pipedreams

Much of the social history of the Western world, over the past three decades, has been a history of replacing what worked with what sounded good.

Source: Is Reality Optional?, and Other Essays (Hoover Institution Press, 1993).

Redistribution

The question is not what anybody deserves. The question is who is to take on the God-like role of deciding what everybody else deserves. You can talk about 'social justice' all you want. But what death taxes boil down to is letting politicians take money from widows and orphans to pay for goodies that they will hand out to others, in order to buy votes to get re-elected. That is not social justice or any other kind of justice.

Source: Controversial Essays (2002).

Responsibility

We seem to be getting closer and closer to a situation where nobody is responsible for what they did but we are all responsible for what somebody else did.

Signs of the Times

One of the sad signs of our times is that we have demonized those who produce, subsidized those who refuse to produce, and canonized those who complain.

Skin in the Game

It is hard to imagine a more stupid or more dangerous way of making decisions than by putting those decisions in the hands of people who pay no price for being wrong.

Source: "Wake Up, Parents," Jewish World Review, August 18, 2000.

Welfare

The welfare state is the oldest con game in the world. First you take people's money away quietly and then you give some of it back to them flamboyantly.

Martha Stewart

Martha Helen Stewart (née Kostyra) / b. 1941 / New Jersey, USA / Businesswoman, Television Host, Author, Publisher

Branding

I said, "Oh, my gosh. I know 20,000 people that will buy this book. I think you better print more." They did. They printed 35,000 copies. It sold out immediately. They had to go back to press. It was a $35 book. It was expensive in those days, too. And yet it was such an instant hit, such an instant gratifying experience for me and I was—I became an expert overnight. And that's what a book does. I mean when you hear all the authors outside, it's that first book that makes you an expert even if it's schlock.

You have to live up to a reputation of excellence. I, of course, was writing nonfiction so I had a grave responsibility to make sure the recipes worked, that the ideas were original, that the inspiration was there, that the photography was beautiful, that the production of the book itself was beautiful. Well, little did I know I was making a brand and that has come much later. I didn't realize about branding until much later, although I had a natural inclination to create a brand. And that doesn't happen very often. I have been told that by many advertising executives, by many Madison Avenue types that what I was doing was really making a brand, developing it, nurturing it, building it, protecting it.

Interview, "Discovering Everyday Good Things," Academy of Achievement, June 2, 1995.

Freedom

The ability, in your waking existence, to go out your front door and not be obstructed in any way. But there are always limitations, and there are limitations that are set by geographical boundaries, territorial boundaries, political boundaries that you have to live with and you have to understand those. We're not so free that we don't have to listen to rules, and laws, and regulations. Those are important. But the spirit, the freedom of the spirit, that's what I think of American Dream, that we are free here to do what we want to do, what we set out to do.

Video, "Martha Bakes," 2016; accessible at harpersbazaar.com.

Health

Loving yourself is good for your health.

Martha Stewart, Martha Stewart's Cupcakes: 175 Inspired Ideas for Everyone's Favorite Treat: A Baking Book (2009).

Landscape Architecture

Re: Stewart's inspirations:

. . . in England, the Humphry Reptons, the William Kents, the Capability Browns; and in France, the René de Girardins, . . .

Martha Stewart, Martha's Flowers: A Practical Guide to Growing, Gathering, and Enjoying (2018).

Male Colleagues

Re: bad behavior by her male colleagues early in Stewart's career:

You had to keep your cool and just do your thing, and brush them away.

Martha Stewart, Martha's Flowers: A Practical Guide to Growing, Gathering, and Enjoying (2018).

Marijuana

Re: the question whether Stewart smokes pot with her friend Snoop Dogg:

What do they call it? A contact high? That's the extent of my getting high with Snoop, is secondhand smoke, which is pretty serious, by the way.

Interview with Jada Yuan, "Martha Stewart Is the Original Influencer," harpersbazaar.com, February 23, 2021.

Philosophy of Life

There is no single recipe for success. But there is one essential ingredient: passion.

Widely cited; however, attribution unconfirmed.

Without an open-minded mind, you can never be a great success. The great artists have been open-minded, even though they may seem, like Picasso, to be very directed, you can be directed and open-minded at the same time. I think you have to be really intensely serious about your work, but not so serious that you can't see the lightness that may also involve your life. You have to have that lightness too. You have to not be so heavy-handed and so ostentatious. It's very important not to be.

Interview, "Discovering Everyday Good Things," Academy of Achievement, June 2, 1995.

Learn something new every day. If you learn something new every day, you can teach something new every day.

Interview with Parents magazine, 2013.

Broaden yourself. You don't have to focus when you're 20. I think the broader you are, the better it is. Later you can focus on your real interests and ideas. The ultimate goal is to be an interesting, useful, wholesome person. If you're successful on top of that, then you're way ahead of everybody.

Interview with Seventeen magazine, 2006.

I've said it so many times, but take your life into your own hands. Don't let other people direct you. Know what you want. I really believe in that.

Interview with Jada Yuan, "Martha Stewart Is the Original Influencer," harpersbazaar.com, February 23, 2021.

Prison

I knew I was strong going in and I was certainly stronger coming out. It was a very serious happening in my life. I take it very seriously. I'm not bitter about it, but . . . My daughter knows all the problems that resulted because of that. There's a lot.

Interview with Jada Yuan, "Martha Stewart Is the Original Influencer," harpersbazaar.com, February 23, 2021.

Reading

We had a lot of chores at our house, a tremendous number of chores, but we were always granted the time to read. . . . I read everything from all the Europeans, the Russians, the English novelists. I read an awful lot of biographies that were very inspiring. In the children's library there were those orange books. I don't know if you remember those orange biographies of everybody, everyone from Harriet Beecher Stowe to the presidents. I read every single one. So that was a good experience.

Video, "Martha Bakes," 2016; accessible at harpersbazaar.com.

Stewart on Stewart

A: Living. Living. Everyday living. At home, in the garden, around the house, with the kids, um, on vacation, and it has always been for me a very serious subject. But to persuade other people that it's a serious subject, not my readers, not my, not my followers, I don't want to call them followers, my friends, but to persuade. . . .

Q: But the world is full of Martha wannabes.

A: Well, that's great because we're all trying to do the same thing. Live well.

Interview with Charlie Rose, PBS, September 15, 1995; accessible on charlierose.com.

Re: hierarchy in Stewart's companies:

There is no hierarchy in my life. I will wash the floor if I have to wash the floor. I'll take out the garbage if nobody else has taken out the garbage. The CEO should be available to everybody at all times, if possible.

Interview with Jada Yuan, "Martha Stewart Is the Original Influencer," harpersbazaar.com, February 23, 2021.

Oh, I love to snowplow. I was out there actually for three hours before I realized it was three hours, and I was semi-frozen to death. But it was fun.

Interview with Jada Yuan, "Martha Stewart Is the Original Influencer," harpersbazaar.com, February 23, 2021.

I'm very inspired by nature—you could say Mother Nature. I look at things around me and get all kinds of inspiration daily. I also look at a lot of art. In New York, I get a tremendous amount of ideas by looking at the paintings and the sculptures, adapting artistic endeavors to crafts. There is a lot of inspiration around us that we can see every day and turn into projects.

Interview with Parents magazine, 2013.

I have been perceived as arrogant. . . . I have sometimes probably forgotten, and I know I have, forgotten to pat the back of someone, or said, thank you, you know, enough times, or even maybe once sometimes. . . . I wish I were perfect. I wish I were just, you know, the nicest, nicest, nicest person on Earth. But I'm a businessperson in addition to a creator of domestic arts. And it's an odd combination. No excuse. But if I were a man, you know, no one would say I was arrogant.

Interview with Larry King, Larry King Live, CNN, 2004.

Q: Are you a perfectionist, or is that just the perception the world has of you?

A: I'm a maniacal perfectionist. And if I weren't, I wouldn't have this company.

Q: So being seen as a perfectionist is not a bad rap?

A: It's the best rap! Nobody's going to fault me for that. I have proven that being a perfectionist can be profitable and admirable when creating content across the board: in television, books, newspapers, radio, videos.

Interview with Oprah Winfrey, "Oprah's Cut with Martha Stewart," O magazine, April 15, 2000; accessible at oprah.com.

I was married for 30 years. Isn't that enough? I've had my share of dirty underwear on the floor.

Interview with Us Weekly magazine.

Oh, I have an experience a day, at least. And it's not like seeing Jesus Christ in a dream or something like that, it's not a religious kind of experience that I experience daily. It's more involving nature, involving natural resources, involving a special quote said by a special person.

Interview, "Discovering Everyday Good Things," Academy of Achievement, June 2, 1995.

Re: Stewart's move from New York City to the suburbs in 1971:
I was living two very distinctly different lives. And the life of the homemaker was more interesting to me than the life on Wall Street.

Interview with Jada Yuan, "Martha Stewart Is the Original Influencer," harpersbazaar.com, February 23, 2021.

I was the girl next door. I was the girl that all parents held up as the example to their daughters. Why can't you be like Martha? Martha is the good girl. Martha is the good student. Martha helps her mom. Martha is the big sister. Martha knows a lot. She can iron a shirt but she can also write an A paper. So it's that kind of thing, which is — I remember all of that very clearly. And my interests— well, I was a big reader. I still am. I was very curious. I still am. I was interested in many, many, many things and I still am.

Video, "Martha Bakes," 2016; accessible at harpersbazaar.com.

A: I had studied a lot of architectural history at Columbia during my Barnard years and I stayed in that library. That's where I did most of my studying. And yet the lure of business was also kind of interesting, so instead of going to architecture school I went to Wall Street and I took a job with a small firm, and I learned not only how to do research in business and analyze companies, but I also learned how to be a super duper institutional stock broker.
Q; How long did you do that?
A: For about seven years. I'm like a grasshopper. I metamorphose every seven years.

Video, "Martha Bakes," 2016; accessible at harpersbazaar.com.

Success

I've tried to figure out why it happens to a person, because I feel that I'm the same person that I've always been. I have grown and become probably smarter in my work, and developed and built a business that's growing, and growing, and growing. But I'm basically the same person. My likes are the same. My tastes may have gotten a little better, or a little bit more educated. But still, I always get up and clean out the kitty litter. You know, I make sure everybody is home, all the animals. I go down through the garden and prune, and pick, and do all those things. I keep grounded, and by keeping grounded you can then see very clearly what's happened to you.

Interview, "Discovering Everyday Good Things," Academy of Achievement, June 2, 1995.

Re: the requirements of success:
For me it's a dedication to your real interests. It's an ability to be open-minded. Without an open-minded mind, you can never be a great success. The great artists have been open-minded, even though they may seem, like Picasso, to be very directed, you can be directed and open-minded at the same time. I think you have to be really intensely serious about your work, but not so serious that you can't see the lightness that may also involve your life. You have to have that lightness too. You have to not be so heavy-handed and so ostentatious. It's very important not to be.

Interview, "Discovering Everyday Good Things," Academy of Achievement, June 2, 1995.

Teachers

I still respect very highly teachers in general and I never allowed my daughter to criticize bitterly her teachers as many students do nowadays. The lack of respect is kind of hideous to me and I think that that lack of respect led to a lot of the problems in the schools and a lot of problems with the occupation of teachers.

Video, "Martha Bakes," 2016; accessible at harpersbazaar.com.

Women

Re: Stewart's first business, a catering business, based in her home:

That came in about 1979 when I realized that the work I was doing, which was original and creative, the preparation of food, the serving of food, the building of a business from a basement, it was just the time when women were finally thinking, oh boy, we better get back to work. I agreed. I agreed that we could —but I agreed—and I thought that we could probably do it from home.

I had to fight town regulations and rules and laws. I had to persuade the health departments that I could cook from my home. I had to fight very difficult neighbor problems. And yet I was sort of paving the way for a lot of women to go back to work.

Interview, "Discovering Everyday Good Things," Academy of Achievement, June 2, 1995.

When I got married and had a child and went to work, my day was all day, all night. You lose your sense of balance. That was in the late '60s, '70s, women went to work, they went crazy. They thought the workplace was much more exciting than the home. They thought the family could wait. And you know what? The family can't wait. And women have now found that out. It all has to do with women, or the homemaker leaving the home and realizing that where they've gone is not as fabulous, or as rewarding, or as self-fulfilling as the balance between the workplace and the home place.

Video, "Martha Bakes," 2016; accessible at harpersbazaar.com.

Writing

Re: Stewart's first book, *Entertaining* (1982).

. . . because I stayed at home, because I still went out and picked the vegetables from my garden, and gathered the eggs from my chickens, and used all those things and the flowering roses and the lilies and everything from my garden, I created a style that I couldn't have done if I hadn't been organically interested in what was going on around me. And that is what gave me my edge and gave me the opportunity to realize that what I was doing was art. It was a kind of art that I could create a book from, and I wrote that landmark book.

Interview, "Discovering Everyday Good Things," Academy of Achievement, June 2, 1995.

I could write. I was prolific. I could write a book a year. To great advantage, I could get it on the bestseller list. My publisher was very happy. And I just kept writing, writing, writing, writing. Working so hard on these books but having the greatest time. And gradually becoming very well known in the country and again what everyone says, you know, she's such a self promoter, but it wasn't about self promotion. It was about filling voids. Every time I wrote a book it was to fill a void that I and my friends had to have filled. So when I wrote a book about *hors d'oeuvres* it was because there wasn't a great book about *hors d'oeuvres*.

Interview, "Discovering Everyday Good Things," Academy of Achievement, June 2, 1995.

J.R.D. Tata

Jehangir Ratanji Dadabhoy Tata / 19041993 / Paris, France / Aviator, Industrialist, Entrepreneur, Chairman of the Tata Group

Note: Tata was born in Paris to a wealthy Indian father and a French mother. The Tata clan—which already included several noted industrialists—were Parsis (Zoroastrians) based in the state of Gujarat.

Business and Economics

There is today hardly any country in the world outside the Communist bloc which does not have a mixed economy. In fact, even countries which call themselves socialist would object to theirs not being described as a mixed economy, for it would imply that it was a totalitarian one, while countries like Germany or Japan, usually thought of as having typically free enterprise economies, would do the same; for, otherwise, it would imply that theirs was a nineteenth century laissez-faire economy.

Address: "Why a Mixed Economy?," Associated Chambers of Commerce and Industry of India, New Delhi, April 4, 1975; reported in J.R.D. Tata, Keynote: Excerpts from his speeches and chairman's statements to shareholders (1986).

Re: The psychology of delay:

Some of the causes of delay in coming to economic decisions in our country seem to lie in the psychological realm. There is such a thing as the psychology of power which motivates people: power of control and patronage, power to delay an application, power to hold up a file, power to keep people waiting in an ante-room, all of which are consciously or subconsciously treated as symbols of prestige and hallmarks of importance.

Report to the Central Advisory Council of Industries, New Delhi, January 3, 1969; reported in J.R.D. Tata, Keynote: Excerpts from his speeches and chairman's statements to shareholders(1986).

Re: Being at the crossroads:

The effective execution of a Plan is what counts and not mere planning on paper; it is not what we put on our plate or even what we eat that provides nourishment and growth, but what we digest.

Report to the Central Advisory Council of Industries, New Delhi, August 13, 1965; reported in J.R.D. Tata, Keynote: Excerpts from his speeches and chairman's statements to shareholders(1986).

India

While I usually came back from meeting Gandhiji elated and inspired but always a bit sceptical, and from talks with Jawaharlal [Nehru], fired with emotional zeal but often confused and unconvinced, meetings with Vallabhbhai [Patel] were a joy from which I returned with renewed confidence in the future of our country. I have often thought that if fate had decreed that he, instead of Jawaharlal, would be the younger of the two, India would have followed a very different path and would be in better economic shape that it is today.

J.R.D. Tata, Keynote: Excerpts from his speeches and chairman's statements to shareholders (1986).

Re: The road to social justice:

The first and perhaps the most important of the factors which have contributed to our failure to make real impact on poverty expressed in terms of total number who live below the poverty line has clearly been the uncontrolled growth of our population. . . . First, we must, at all costs, make a much more earnest effort at controlling the growth of our population. As it is, we are running out of time and there is no longer any possibility of preventing it from exceeding 1,000 million souls by the end of the century.

Address, International Seminar of Economic Journalists, New Delhi, December 5, 1972; reported in J.R.D. Tata, Keynote: Excerpts from his speeches and chairman's statements to shareholders (1986).

I cannot decide how much to borrow, what shares to issue, at what price, what wages and bonus to pay, and what dividend to give. I even need the government's permission for the salary I pay to a senior executive.

J.R.D. Tata, Keynote: Excerpts from his speeches and chairman's statements to shareholders (1986).

I don't want India to be an economic superpower. I want India to be a happy country.

Reported in "The business ethics of J.R.D. Tata," The Hindu, July 29, 2005.

Leadership

To lead men, you have to lead them with affection.

"Believing in Perfection," New India Digest; cited in "Quotations by 60 Greatest Indians," Dhirubhai Ambani Institute Information and Communication Technology, daiict.ac.in.

Not excellence. Perfection. You aim for perfection, you will attain excellence. If you aim for excellence, you will go lower.

"Believing in Perfection," New India Digest; cited in "Quotations by 60 Greatest Indians," Dhirubhai Ambani Institute Information and Communication Technology, daiict.ac.in.

If you want excellence, you must aim at perfection. It has its drawbacks but being finicky is essential.

"Believing in Perfection," New India Digest; cited in "Quotations by 60 Greatest Indians," Dhirubhai Ambani Institute Information and Communication Technology, daiict.ac.in.

Philosophy of Life

Live life a little dangerously.

J.R.D. Tata, Keynote: Excerpts from his speeches and chairman's statements to shareholders (1986).

Never start with difference. Always start with confidence. When you work, work as if everything depends on you.

J.R.D. Tata, Keynote: Excerpts from his speeches and chairman's statements to shareholders (1986).

Science and Technology

No institute of science and technology can guarantee discoveries or inventions, and we cannot plan or command a work of genius at will. But do we give sufficient thought to the nurture of the young investigator, to providing the right atmosphere and conditions of work and full opportunity for development? It is these things that foster invention and discovery.

J.R.D. Tata, Keynote: Excerpts from his speeches and chairman's statements to shareholders (1986).

The essence of air transport is speed, and speed is unfortunately one of the most expensive commodities in the world, principally because of the disproportionate amount of the power required to achieve high speed and to lift loads thousands of feet into the air. This is strikingly illustrated by the fact that while an average cargo ship, freight train and transport aeroplane are each equipped with engines totalling about 2,500 H.P., the ship can carry a load of about 7,000 tons, the train 800 tons and the plane only two and a half tons.

Address, Bombay Rotary Club, November 2, 1943; reported in J.R.D. Tata, Keynote: Excerpts from his speeches and chairman's statements to shareholders (1986).

Tata on Tata

I wish, I were big enough, like Einstein, to do what he did on one occasion. A hundred-dollar-a-plate dinner was organised for him to speak, and leaders of America in all fields, particularly in the field of science, were invited to hear the great man. When his turn came, he rose and said: "I've nothing to say," and sat down. You can imagine the consternation, quite apart from the wasted cost of the dinner! Realising the frightful effect his remarks had on the audience, Einstein got up again and said: "When I've something to say, I'll let you know."

Address, Lions Club of Jamshedpur, August 22, 1963; reported in J.R.D. Tata, Keynote: Excerpts from his speeches and chairman's statements to shareholders (1986).

Peter Thiel

Peter Andreas Thiel / b. 1967 / Frankfurt am Main, Federal Republic of Germany / Hedge Fund Manager, Entrepreneur, Co-Founder of PayPal

Note: Although born in West Germany to German parents, Thiel was brought to the US when he was only one year old. He was educated in the US and in South Africa.

Capitalism and Democracy

I remain committed to the faith of my teenage years: to authentic human freedom as a precondition for the highest good. I stand against confiscatory taxes, totalitarian collectives, and the ideology of the inevitability of the death of every individual. For all these reasons, I still call myself "libertarian." . . . But I must confess that over the last two decades, I have changed radically on the question of how to achieve these goals. Most importantly, I no longer believe that freedom and democracy are compatible… The 1920s were the last decade in American history during which one could be genuinely optimistic about politics. Since 1920, the vast increase in welfare beneficiaries and the extension of the franchise to women—two constituencies that are notoriously tough for libertarians—have rendered the notion of "capitalist democracy" into an oxymoron.

"The Education of a Libertarian," Cato Unbound, April 13, 2009.

Entrepreneurs

Just as the legal attack on Microsoft was ending Bill Gates's dominance, Steve Jobs's return to Apple demonstrated the irreplaceable value of a company's founder. In some ways, Steve Jobs and Bill Gates were opposites. Jobs was an artist, preferred closed systems, and spent his time thinking about great products above all else; Gates was a businessman, kept his products open, and wanted to run the world. But both were insider/outsiders, and both pushed the companies they started to achievements that nobody else would have been able to match.

Zero to One: Notes on Startups, or How to Build the Future(2014).

. . . the phenomenon of serial entrepreneurship would seem to call into question our tendency to explain success as the product of chance.

Zero to One: Notes on Startups, or How to Build the Future(2014).

Future

In politics or culture, for the future to have power over the present, it has to be different from the present. The future has power because it is a time that will look different from the present, and so it can't just be an endless *Groundhog Day*. If it's just always the same, just always repetition, then the future does not have any appeal, and it's not part of any political agenda.

Interview with Peter Robinson, "The World According to Thiel,'" Uncommon Knowledge, with Peter Robinson, Hoover Institution, January 17, 2020.

Looking at Western Europe, I would say, there are . . . basically three plausible futures on offer. Number one is Islamic sharia law, and if you're a woman you get to wear a burqa. Number two is totalitarian AI *à la* China, where the computers track you in everything you do—all the time—and that's kind of creepy. So the Eye of Sauron, to use the *Lord of the Rings* reference, is watching you at all times. And then the third one is hyper-environmentalism, where you drive an e-scooter and you recycle. And even though I'm not a radical environmentalist . . . if those are the three choices, I think you can understand why the Green Movement is winning—because those are the three visions of the future we have. And the challenge on the conservative or libertarian side is to offer something that is a picture of the future that's different from these two dystopian and one somewhat stagnant one.

Interview with Peter Robinson, "Peter Thiel on 'The Straussian Moment,'" Uncommon Knowledge, with Peter Robinson, Hoover Institution, September 23, 2019.

Globalization

My own answer to the contrarian question is that most people think the future of the world will be defined by globalization, but the truth is that technology matters more. . . . In a world of scarce resources, globalization without new technology is unsustainable.

Zero to One: Notes on Startups, or How to Build the Future(2014).

History

I don't think the intellectual battle is ever fully over, because I don't think history is over.

Interview with Peter Robinson, "The World According to Thiel,'" Uncommon Knowledge, with Peter Robinson, Hoover Institution, January 17, 2020.

Innovation

Every moment in business happens only once. The next Bill Gates will not build an operating system. The next Larry Page or Sergey Brin won't make a search engine. And next Mark Zuckerberg won't create a social network. If you are copying these guys, you aren't learning from them.

Zero to One: Notes on Startups, or How to Build the Future(2014).

Unless they invest in the difficult task of creating new things, American companies will fail in the future no matter how big their profits remain today. What happens when we've gained everything to be had from fine-tuning the old lines of businesses that we've inherited? Unlikely as it sounds, the answer threatens to be far worse than the crisis of 2008. Today's "best practices" lead to dead ends; the best paths are new and untried.

Zero to One: Notes on Startups, or How to Build the Future(2014).

Whenever I interview someone for a job, I like to ask this question: "What important truth do very few people agree with you on?" This question sounds easy because it's straightforward. Actually, it's very hard to answer. It's intellectually difficult because the knowledge that everyone is taught in scholl is by definition agreed upon. And it's psychologically difficulty because anyone trying to answer must say something she knows to be unpopular. Brilliant thinking is rare, but courage is in even shorter supply than genius.

Zero to One: Notes on Startups, or How to Build the Future(2014).

Manhattan-Style Projects

Most of our political leaders are not engineers or scientists and do not listen to engineers or scientists. Today a letter from [Albert] Einstein would get lost in the White House mail room, and the Manhattan Project would not even get started; it certainly could never be completed in three years. I am not aware of a single political leader in the U.S., either Democrat or Republican, who would cut health-care spending in order to free up money for biotechnology research—or, more generally, who would make serious cuts to the welfare state in order to free up serious money for major engineering projects.

"The End of the Future," National Review, October 3, 2011.

Money

We're definitely onto something big. The need PayPal answers is monumental. Everyone in the world needs money—to get paid, to trade, to live. Paper money is an ancient technology and an inconvenient means of payment. You can run out of it. It wears out. It can get lost or stolen. In the twenty-first century, people need a form of money that's more convenient and secure, something that can be accessed from anywhere with a PDA or an Internet connection. Of course, what we're calling "convenient" for American users will be revolutionary for the developing world.

Speech delivered in 1999 to PayPal staff; as reported by Eric M. Jackson in The PayPal Wars: Battles with eBay, the Media, the Mafia, and the Rest of Planet Earth (2004).

Progress vs. Progressivism

Men reached the moon in July, 1969, and Woodstock began three weeks later. With the benefit of hindsight, we can see that this was when the hippies took over the country, and when the true cultural war over Progress was lost. Today's aged hippies no longer understand that there is a difference between the election of a black president and the creation of cheap solar energy; in their minds, the movement towards greater civil rights parallels general progress everywhere. Because of these ideological conflations and commitments, the 1960s Progressive Left cannot ask whether things actually might be getting worse.

"The End of the Future," National Review, October 3, 2011.

Teaching Innovation

The paradox of teaching entrepreneurship is that such a formula necessarily cannot exist; because every innovation is new and unique, no authority can prescribe in concrete terms how to be innovative. Indeed, the single most powerful pattern I have notices is that successful people find value in unexpected places. . . .

Zero to One: Notes on Startups, or How to Build the Future(2014).

Trump

[The media] never takes [Trump] seriously, but it always takes him literally. I think a lot of the voters who vote for Trump take Trump seriously, but not literally.

Interview with Thomas Burr, "The Presidential Election of 2016," National Press Club Newsmaker, with Peter Thiel, October 31, 2016.

Universities

The university system in 2014, it's like the Catholic Church circa 1514. . . . You have this priestly class of professors that doesn't do very much work; people are buying indulgences in the form of amassing enormous debt for the sort of the secular salvation that a diploma represents. And what I think is also similar to the 16th century is that the Reformation will come largely from the outside.

Interview with Bill Kristol, "Peter Thiel on Innovation and Stagnation," Conversations with Bill Kristol, July 29, 2014.

Work and Success

It's good to test yourself and develop your talents and ambitions as fully as you can and achieve greater success; but I think success is the feeling you get from a job well done, and the key thing is to do the work.

Caroline Howard, "Peter Thiel: 'Don't Wait to Start Something New,'" Forbes, September 10, 2014.

Hunter S. Thompson

Hunter Stockton Thompson / 19372005 / Louisville, Kentucky, USA / Journalist, Author

Advice

A word to the wise is infuriating.
Hell's Angels (1966).

America

We are turning into a nation of whimpering slaves to Fear—fear of war, fear of poverty, fear of random terrorism, fear of getting down-sized or fired because of the plunging economy, fear of getting evicted for bad debts, or suddenly getting locked up in a military detention camp on vague charges of being a Terrorist sympathizer.
Kingdom of Fear (2003).

In a nation run by swine, all pigs are upward-mobile, and the rest of us are f***ed until we can put our acts together: Not necessarily to Win, but mainly to keep from Losing Completely.
The Great Shark Hunt (1979).

In a closed society where everybody's guilty, the only crime is getting caught. In a world of thieves, the only final sin is stupidity.
Fear and Loathing in Las Vegas (1971).

Weird heroes and mold-breaking champions exist as living proof to those who need it that the tyranny of "the rat race" is not yet final.
The Great Shark Hunt (1979).

Freedom

Freedom is something that dies unless it's used.
The Great Shark Hunt (1979).

Investigative Journalism

I have a theory that the truth is never told during the nine-to-five hours.
Interview with Studs Terkel, in The Great Shark Hunt (1979).

Life

No sympathy for the devil; keep that in mind. Buy the ticket, take the ride . . . and if it occasionally gets a little heavier than what you had in mind, well . . . maybe chalk it up to forced consciousness expansion: Tune in, freak out, get beaten.
Fear and Loathing in Las Vegas (1971).

When the going gets weird, the weird turn pro.
"Fear and Loathing at the Super Bowl," Rolling Stone, 1973.

Life should not be a journey to the grave with the intention of arriving safely in a pretty and well-preserved body, but rather to skid in broadside in a cloud of smoke, thoroughly used up, totally worn out, and loudly proclaiming, "Wow! What a ride!"
Source unknown.

The Edge . . . there is no honest way to explain it because the only people who really know where it is are the ones who have gone over.

Hell's Angels (1966).

We are all alone, born alone, die alone, and —in spite of True Romance magazines—we shall all someday look back on our lives and see that, in spite of our company, we were alone the whole way. I do not say lonely—at least, not all the time—but essentially, and finally, alone. This is what makes your self-respect so important, and I don't see how you can respect yourself if you must look in the hearts and minds of others for your happiness.

The Proud Highway (1997).

When you get into a tight place and everything goes against you until it seems that you cannot hold on for a minute longer, never give up then, for that is just the place and time when the tide will turn.

Source unknown.

For every moment of triumph, for every instance of beauty, many souls must be trampled.

Fear and Loathing in Las Vegas (1971).

Paranoia

There is no such thing as paranoia. Your worst fears can come true at any moment.

Cited in E. Jean Carroll, Hunter: The Strange and Savage Life of Hunter S. Thompson (1993).

Procrastination

A man who procrastinates in his choosing will inevitably have his choice made for him by circumstance.

The Proud Highway (1997).

Television Journalism

The TV business is uglier than most things. It is normally perceived as some kind of cruel and shallow money trench through the heart of the journalism industry, a long plastic hallway where thieves and pimps run free and good men die like dogs, for no good reason.

Generation of Swine (1988).

Thompson on Thompson

I hate to advocate weird chemicals, alcohol, violence or insanity to anyone, but they've always worked for me.

Fear and Loathing in America (2000).

I understand that fear is my friend, but not always. Never turn your back on Fear. It should always be in front of you, like a thing that might have to be killed.

Kingdom of Fear (2003).

Life has become immeasurably better since I have been forced to stop taking it seriously.

The Proud Highway (1997).

It never got weird enough for me.

Source unknown.

Please God, don't let me live long enough to become a Conservative.

The Great Shark Hunt (1979).

Alexis de Tocqueville

Alexis Charles Henri Clérel, comte de Tocqueville / 1805–1859 / France / Politician, Author, Political Philosopher

American Character

As one digs deeper into the national character of the Americans, one sees that they have sought the value of everything in this world only in the answer to this single question: how much money will it bring in?

Letter to Ernest de Chabrol, June 9, 1831.

I know of no country in which there is so little independence of mind and real freedom of discussion as in America.

De la démocratie en Amérique [Democracy in America], Volume 1 (1835).

Americans of all ages, all stations of life, and all types of disposition are forever forming associations… In democratic countries knowledge of how to combine is the mother of all other forms of knowledge; on its progress depends that of all the others.

De la démocratie en Amérique [Democracy in America], Volume 2 (1840).

The first thing that strikes a traveler in the United States is the innumerable multitude of those who seek to emerge from their original condition; and the second is the rarity of lofty ambition to be observed in the midst of the universally ambitious stir of society. No Americans are devoid of a yearning desire to rise, but hardly any appear to entertain hopes of great magnitude or to pursue very lofty aims. All are constantly seeking to acquire property, power, and reputation.

De la démocratie en Amérique [Democracy in America], Volume 2 (1840).

In democratic ages men rarely sacrifice themselves for another, but they show a general compassion for all the human race. One never sees them inflict pointless suffering, and they are glad to relieve the sorrows of others when they can do so without much trouble to themselves. They are not disinterested, but they are gentle.

De la démocratie en Amérique [Democracy in America], Volume 2 (1840).

American Government

The President … may err … Congress may decide amiss … But if the Supreme Court is ever composed of imprudent or bad men, the Union may be plunged into anarchy or civil war.

De la démocratie en Amérique [Democracy in America], Volume 1 (1835).

Democratic Society

The territorial aristocracy of former ages was either bound by law, or thought itself bound by usage, to come to the relief of its serving-men and to relieve their distresses. But the manufacturing aristocracy of our age first impoverishes and debases the men who serve it and then abandons them to be supported by the charity of the public.

De la démocratie en Amérique [Democracy in America], Volume 2 (1840).

Equality

"Equality" is an expression of envy. It means, in the real heart of every Republican, "No one shall be better off than I am"; and while this is preferred to good government, good government is impossible.

In conversation with Nassau William Senior, May 22, 1850.

There is in fact a manly and legitimate passion for equality that spurs all men to wish to be strong and esteemed. This passion tends to elevate the lesser to the rank of the greater. But one also finds in the human heart a depraved taste for equality, which impels the weak to want to bring the strong down to their level, and which reduces men to preferring equality in servitude to inequality in freedom.

De la démocratie en Amérique [Democracy in America], Volume 1 (1835).

God

God does not need to speak for himself in order for us to discover definitive signs of his will; it is enough to examine the normal course of nature and the consistent tendency of events. I know without needing to hear the voice of the Creator that the stars trace out in space the orbits which his hand has drawn.

De la démocratie en Amérique [Democracy in America], Volume 1 (1835).

History

History, it is easily perceived, is a picture-gallery containing a host of copies and very few originals.

L'Ancien Régime et la Révolution [The Ancien Régime and the Revolution] (fourth edition, 1858).

Humanity

Men in general are neither very good nor very bad, but mediocre… Man with his vices, his weaknesses, his virtues, this confused medley of good and ill, high and low, goodness and depravity, is yet, take him all in all, the object on earth most worthy of study, of interest, of pity, of attachment and of admiration. And since we haven't got angels, we can attach ourselves to nothing greater and more worthy of our devotion than our own kind.

Letter to Eugene Stoffels, January 3, 1845.

Law and Morality

The best laws cannot make a constitution work in spite of morals; morals can turn the worst laws to advantage.

"De la supériorité des mœurs sur les lois" [On the superiority of morals over laws] (1831).

Liberty

Even despots accept the excellence of liberty. The simple truth is that they wish to keep it for themselves and promote the idea that no one else is at all worthy of it. Thus, our opinion of liberty does not reveal our differences but the relative value which we place on our fellow man. We can state with conviction, therefore, that a man's support for absolute government is in direct proportion to the contempt he feels for his country.

L'Ancien Régime et la Révolution [The Ancien Régime and the Revolution] (fourth edition, 1858).

He who seeks in liberty anything other than liberty itself is born to serve others.

L'Ancien Régime et la Révolution [The Ancien Régime and the Revolution] (fourth edition, 1858).

Liberty cannot be established without morality, nor morality without faith.

De la démocratie en Amérique [Democracy in America], Volume 1 (1835).

Despotism may govern without faith, but liberty cannot. How is it possible that society should escape destruction if the moral tie is not strengthened in proportion as the political tie is relaxed? And what can be done with a people who are their own masters if they are not submissive to the Deity?

De la démocratie en Amérique [Democracy in America], Volume 1 (1835).

Manners

Nothing seems at first sight less important than the outward form of human actions, yet there is nothing upon which men set more store: they grow used to everything except to living in a society which has not their own manners.

De la démocratie en Amérique [Democracy in America], Volume 2 (1840).

Political Ideology

The last thing abandoned by a party is its phraseology, because among political parties, as elsewhere, the vulgar make the language, and the vulgar abandon more easily the ideas that have been instilled into it than the words that it has learnt.

"France Avant le Consulat" [France Before the Consulate], in Souvenirs politiques de la IIe République [Recollections: The French Revolution of 1848 and Its Aftermath] (1850).

Public Opinion

In the United States, the majority undertakes to supply a multitude of ready-made opinions for the use of individuals, who are thus relieved from the necessity of forming opinions of their own.

De la démocratie en Amérique [Democracy in America], Volume 2 (1840).

Revolution

We are sleeping on a volcano… A wind of revolution blows, the storm is on the horizon.

Speech, Chamber of Deputies, 1848.

It is almost never when a state of things is the most detestable that it is smashed, but when, beginning to improve, it permits men to breathe, to reflect, to communicate their thoughts with each other, and to gauge by what they already have the extent of their rights and their grievances. The weight, although less heavy, seems then all the more unbearable.

Letter to Pierre Freslon, September 23, 1853.

Socialism

As for me, I am deeply a democrat; this is why I am in no way a socialist. Democracy and socialism cannot go together. You can't have it both ways.

Notes for a Speech on Socialism, 1848.

Democracy extends the sphere of individual freedom, socialism restricts it. Democracy attaches all possible value to each man; socialism makes each man a mere agent, a mere number. Democracy and socialism have nothing in common but one word: equality. But notice the difference: while democracy seeks equality in liberty, socialism seeks equality in restraint and servitude.

Speech to the National Constituant Assembly on the question of the right to work, September 12, 1848.

War

No protracted war can fail to endanger the freedom of a democratic country.

De la démocratie en Amérique [Democracy in America], Volume 2 (1840).

Alvin Toffler

Alvin Toffler / 1928–2016 / New York, USA / Editor, Author

You've got to think about big things while you're doing small things, so that all the small things go in the right direction.

Source: Attribution unconfirmed.

Man remains in the end what he started as in the beginning: a biosystem with a limited capacity for change. When this capacity is overwhelmed, the consequence is future shock.

Source: Future Shock (1970).

Freedom of expression is no longer a political nicety, but a precondition for economic competitiveness.

Source: Interview with John Perry Barlow (1997).

Change is not merely necessary to life—it is life.

Source: Attribution unconfirmed.

If industrialism, with its faster pace of life, has accelerated the family cycle, super-industrialism now threatens to smash it altogether.

Source: Future Shock (1970).

Leo Tolstoy

Lev Nikolayevich Tolstoy / 1828–1910 / Imperial Russia / Novelist, Short Story Author, Memoirist, Essayist

Austerlitz

"What's this? Am I falling? My legs are giving way," thought [Prince André] and fell on his back. He opened his eyes, hoping to see how the struggle of the Frenchmen with the gunners ended, whether the red-haired gunner had been killed or not and whether the cannon had been captured or saved. But he saw nothing. Above him there was now nothing but the sky—the lofty sky, not clear yet still immeasurably lofty, with gray clouds gliding slowly across it. "How quiet, peaceful, and solemn; not at all as I ran," thought Prince André—"not as we ran, shouting and fighting, not at all as the gunner and the Frenchman with frightened and angry faces struggled for the mop: how differently do those clouds glide across that lofty infinite sky! How was it I did not see that lofty sky before? And how happy I am to have found it at last! Yes! All is vanity, all falsehood, except that infinite sky. There is nothing, nothing, but that. But even it does not exist, there is nothing but quiet and peace. Thank God!…"

War and Peace, Book III, Chapter 16.

Comet of 1812

It was clear and frosty. Above the dirty, ill-lit streets, above the black roofs, stretched the dark starry sky. Only looking up at the sky did Pierre cease to feel how sordid and humiliating were all mundane things compared with the heights to which his soul had just been raised. At the entrance to the Arbat Square an immense expanse of dark starry sky presented itself to his eyes. Almost in the center of it, above the Prechistenka Boulevard, surrounded and sprinkled on all sides by stars but distinguished from them all by its nearness to the earth, its white light, and its long uplifted tail, shone the enormous and brilliant comet of 1812—the comet which was said to por- tend all kinds of woes and the end of the world. In Pierre, however, that comet with its long luminous tail aroused no feeling of fear. On the contrary he gazed joyfully, his eyes moist with tears, at this bright comet which, having traveled in its orbit with inconceivable velocity through immeasurable space, seemed suddenly—like an arrow piercing the earth—to remain fixed in a chosen spot, vigorously holding its tail erect, shining and displaying its white light amid countless other scintillating stars. It seemed to Pierre that this comet fully responded to what was passing in his own softened and uplifted soul, now blossoming into a new life.

War and Peace, Book VIII, Chapter 22.

Death of Anna Karenina

And all at once she thought of the man crushed by the train the day she had first met Vronsky, and she knew what she had to do.

With a rapid, light step she went down the steps that led from the tank to the rails and stopped quite near the approaching train. . . . She had to wait for the next carriage. A feeling such as she had known when about to take the first plunge in bathing came upon her, and she crossed herself. That familiar gesture brought back into her soul a whole series of girlish and childish memories, and suddenly the darkness that had covered everything for her was torn apart, and life rose up before her for an instant with all its bright past joys. But she did not take her eyes from the wheels of the second carriage. And exactly at the moment when the space between the wheels came opposite her, she dropped the red bag, and drawing her head back into her shoulders, fell on her hands under the carriage, and lightly, as though she would rise again at once, dropped on to her knees. And at the same instant she was terror-stricken at what she was doing. "Where am I? What am I doing? What for?" She tried to get up, to drop backwards; but something huge and merciless struck her on the head and rolled her on her back. "Lord, forgive me all!" she said, feeling it impossible to struggle. A peasant muttering something was working at the iron above her. And the light by which she had read the book filled with troubles, falsehoods, sorrow, and evil, flared up more brightly than ever before, lighted up for her all that had been in darkness, flickered, began to grow dim, and was quenched for ever.

Anna Karenina, *Part Seven, Chapter 31 (1877).*

Families

Happy families are all alike; every unhappy family is unhappy in its own way.

Anna Karenina, *Part One, Chapter I (1877).*

In order to carry through any undertaking in family life, there must necessarily be either complete division between the husband and wife, or loving agreement. When the relations of a couple are vacillating and neither one thing nor the other, no sort of enterprise can be undertaken. Many families remain for years in the same place, though both husband and wife are sick of it, simply because there is neither complete division nor agreement between them.

Anna Karenina, *Part Seven, Chapter 23 (1877).*

Historical Causation

Man's mind cannot grasp the causes of events in their completeness, but the desire to find those causes is implanted in man's soul. And without considering the multiplicity and complexity of the conditions any one of which taken separately may seem to be the cause, he snatches at the first approximation to a cause that seems to him intelligible and says: "This is the cause!" In historical events (where the actions of men are the subject of observation) the first and most primitive approximation to present itself was the will of the gods and, after that, the will of those who stood in the most prominent position—the heroes of history. But we need only penetrate to the essence of any historic event—which lies in the activity of the general mass of men who take part in it—to be convinced that the will of the historic hero does not control the actions of the mass but is itself continually controlled.

War and Peace, *Book XIII, Chapter 1.*

Natural Purpose

A bee settling on a flower has stung a child. And the child is afraid of bees and declares that bees exist to sting people. A poet admires the bee sucking from the chalice of a flower and says it exists to suck the fragrance of flowers. A beekeeper, seeing the bee collect pollen from flowers and carry it to the hive, says that it exists to gather honey. Another beekeeper who has studied the life of the hive more closely says that the bee gathers pollen dust to feed the young bees and rear a queen, and that it exists to perpetuate its race. A botanist notices that the bee flying with the pollen of a male flower to a pistil fertilizes the latter, and sees in this the purpose of the bee's existence. Another, observing the migration of plants, notices that the bee helps in this work, and may say that in this lies the purpose of the bee. But the ultimate purpose of the bee is not exhausted by the first, the second, or any of the processes the human mind can discern. The higher the human intellect rises in the discovery of these purposes, the more obvious it becomes that the ultimate purpose is beyond our comprehension.

All that is accessible to man is the relation of the life of the bee to other manifestations of life. And so it is with the purpose of historic characters and nations.

War and Peace, First Epilogue (1869).

Power

If the realm of human knowledge were confined to abstract reasoning, then having subjected to criticism the explanation of "power" that Juridical science gives us, humanity would conclude that power is merely a word and has no real existence. But to understand phenomena man has, besides abstract reasoning, experience by which he verifies his reflections. And experience tells us that power is not merely a word but an actually existing phenomenon.

War and Peace, Second Epilogue (1869).

Russian Soul

"Go on, Uncle dear," Natásha wailed in an imploring tone as if her life depended on it.

"Uncle" rose, and it was as if there were two men in him: one of them smiled seriously at the merry fellow, while the merry fellow struck a naïve and precise attitude preparatory to a folk dance.

"Now then, niece!" he exclaimed, waving to Natásha the hand that had just struck a chord.

Natásha threw off the shawl from her shoulders, ran forward to face "Uncle," and setting her arms akimbo also made a motion with her shoulders and struck an attitude.

Where, how, and when had this young countess, educated by an *émigrée* French governess, imbibed from the Russian air she breathed that spirit and obtained that manner which the *pas de châle* would, one would have supposed, long ago have effaced? But the spirit and the movements were those inimitable and unteachable Russian ones that "Uncle" had expected of her. As soon as she had struck her pose, and smiled triumphantly, proudly, and with sly merriment, the fear that had at first seized Nicholas and the others that she might not do the right thing was at an end, and they were already admiring her.

She did the right thing with such precision, such complete precision, that Anísya Fëdorovna, who had at once handed her the handkerchief she needed for the dance, had tears in her eyes, though she laughed as she watched this slim, graceful countess, reared in silks and velvets and so different from herself, who yet was able to understand all that was in Anísya and in Anísya's father and mother and aunt, and in every Russian man and woman.

"Well, little countess; that's it—come on!" cried "Uncle," with a joyous laugh, having finished the dance. "Well done, niece! Now a fine young fellow must be found as husband for you. That's it—come on!"

War and Peace, Book IV, Chapter 7.

Self-Consciousness

Consciousness is a source of self-cognition quite apart from and independent of reason.

Through his reason man observes himself, but only through consciousness does he know himself.

War and Peace, Second Epilogue (1869).

Socialization of Young Men

Nothing is so necessary for a young man as the society of clever women.

War and Peace, Book I, Chapter 4.

Truth

"I should never dare to say that I know the truth," said the Mason, whose words struck Pierre more and more by their precision and firmness. *'No one can attain to truth by himself. Only by laying stone on stone with the cooperation of all, by the millions of generations from our forefather Adam to our own times, is that temple reared which is to be a worthy dwelling place of the Great God," he added, and closed his eyes.

War and Peace, Book V, Chapter 2.

War

In war the most deeply considered plans have no significance. . , . All depends on the way unexpected movements of the enemy—that cannot be foreseen—are met, and on how and by whom the whole matter is handled.

War and Peace, Book IX, Chapter 9.

Ted Turner

Robert Edward Turner, III / b. 1938 / Ohio, USA / Businessman, Entrepreneur, Television Producer, Founder of Cable News Network (CNN) and the Turner Broadcasting System (TBS)

Giving

Q: Now one of the messages you've been talking about is that you don't have to be a billionaire to be involved. But obviously, there are people with a great deal less in the way of means than you and the Gates family.
A: Oh, you can do it by dedicating time to help a child who's an orphan and give him some adult supervision and friendship.

Interview with Neal Conan, "Talk of the Nation," NPR, September 20, 2010; accessible at npr.org.

Global Warming

A: I think one individual storm can't be caused by global warming]. But I think that the increasing number of hurricanes and the intensity of the hurricanes—which have about doubled, apparently, over the past 20 years, from the scientific papers that I have read—that the overall trend is caused partially by global warming.
Q: The word "partially" is significant, because we have looked at some of the hurricanes that occurred in the early part of the 1900s. [In 1900] Galveston had a Category 4, 8,000 people dead; 1928 in southeastern Florida, category 4, 2,500 people dead; Florida Keys, a Category 5 in 1935. There were about 10 of them, which were very significant, 3, 4, and 5's, in the early 1900s. And that's before this phenomenon of global warming came up, because all—there are skeptics out there who say global warming has nothing to do with this.
A: Well, global warming sure has a lot to do with the glaciers melting and a lot of other things.
But I think individual storms are like individual weather systems. They are all different. They are all different. And, remember, one reason why those casualties were so great in the early 1900s is, we didn't have nearly as good a communication system. In the Galveston hurricane, I don't think the people were told to evacuate, like they were in New Orleans [which had just been devasted by Hurricane Katrina]. If they hadn't evacuated —most of the people, 90 percent, evacuated. If they hadn't, the death toll would have been much, much higher.

Interview with Wolf Blitzer, "The Situation Room," CNN, September 19, 2005; accessible at cnn.com.

Low-Tech Solution in the Developing World

Q: You're going to be talking tomorrow, with Secretary of State Hillary Clinton, about new cook stoves.
A: Right, we are. The cook stoves that are being used that have fossil fuel as the heating element, when they're used indoors, as they

are in many places, poison the air just like they do poison the air, the atmosphere.

And then we're going to try to get cleaner cook stoves in the developing world that won't kill and harm the people that are cooking dinner.

Q: So this is one of those relatively low-technology improvements like malarial . . .

A: That's right. Twice as many people die, in the world every year, from cook-stove pollution as they do from malaria.

Q: And malaria netting has also been, again, relatively inexpensive and relatively very effective.

A: Absolutely. It's just been a great development.

Q: And how many cook stoves do you hope to get out into the world next year, new ones?

A: As many as we can.

Interview with Neal Conan, "Talk of the Nation," NPR, September 20, 2010; accessible at npr.org.

North Korea

I talked with quite a few of the North Korean leaders and South Korean leaders, too, and spent really the most time with the head negotiator for North Korea. And I was really over there to try and persuade North and South Korea to make the DMZ into an international peace park when they sign a peace treaty, which I anticipate will be fairly soon, now that we have these six-party talks—we have agreement there.

But I had a great time. I am absolutely convinced that the North Koreans are absolutely sincere. There's really no reason—no reason for them to cheat or do anything to violate this very forward agreement. I mean, I think we can put the North Korea and East Asia problems behind us and concentrate on Iran and Iraq, where we still have some ongoing difficulties.

Interview with Wolf Blitzer, "The Situation Room," CNN, September 19, 2005; accessible at cnn.com.

. . . in the Bible, it says you are supposed to forgive seven times 70 or something like that. But just because, you know—I mean, in 1940, the Germans were our enemies; for the last 50 years, they've been our allies. Same with the—the Russians were our enemies before '91, when the Cold War ended.

Interview with Wolf Blitzer, "The Situation Room," CNN, September 19, 2005; accessible at cnn.com.

Personal Philosophy

Whether you're talking about a person or a country, it's okay to be rich and it's okay to be powerful, just as long as you're humble and cooperative. But if you combine being rich and powerful with being arrogant and uncooperative, people won't cut you much slack.

Ted Turner, Call Me Ted (2008).

Turner on Turner

It was now the fall of 1956, and nine years after entering Georgia Military Academy as a scrawny "Yankee" from Ohio, I was now considered a "southerner," enrolling at one of the North's most elite institutions.

Ted Turner, Call Me Ted (2008).

During my first several days there I really did feel like a fish out of water. After years of following a military dress code I wasn't even sure what to wear. The one place I felt like I fit in was out on a boat and, fortunately, trials for the freshman sailing team began right away.

Ted Turner, Call Me Ted (2008).

. . . I just kept up with what was going on technologically, and took advantage of the new equipment and new ways of doing things from the very beginning. In business or in life or in military engagements, which

I'd studied a lot—you know that old saying, "get there firstest with the mostest," and so forth—and that's what I tried to do in business, and I did, because the record speaks for itself. I started with virtually nothing. In 1970, which was my first year in the television business, we had 35 employees at the station in Atlanta and we did $600,000 in business—and 35 employees. And when I merged with Time Warner in 1995, which was 25 years later, we had 12,000 employees and we did two and half billion dollars, and instead of losing a million dollars, which we did the first year, we made close to 250 million dollars' profit. And that was in 25 years.

Interview, Academy of Achievement, October 20, 2007; accessible at youtube.com.

It *was* probably crazy. To take a local station, put it on the satellite—and there were regulations against it. But they changed the regulations. And I was doing some—I started lobbying. A lot of the battles that we fought in the television business were fought to a large degree in Washington against the networks, the broadcasters, against the motion picture studios, against the sports leagues, that didn't want us to take our little station and take the programming and run it all over the country, and basically create a national network that was based on local programming. But we were able to convince Congress that it would be good for business, because it would create competition to the three networks where there was none before.

Interview, Academy of Achievement, October 20, 2007; accessible at youtube.com.

It was okay for people to write negative things about me just as long as they spelled my name right.

Ted Turner, Call Me Ted (2008).

If I only had a little humility, I'd be perfect.

Reported in "At Long Last, He's Citizen Ted," Forbes magazine, January 30, 2003; accessible at forbes.com.

Re: Turner's definition of "success" in philanthropy:

Well, a success for me just to see the world continue to make progress on the critical issues. The ones that concern me the most are getting rid of nuclear weapons and getting a handle on our energy policy and a strong climate change program.

But I'm interested in everything. I'm interested in hunger. A billion people go to bed hungry every night. That's intolerable. I'm on the committee to eliminate poverty or alleviate it, the Millennium Development Goals, and so I'm involved with it from a lot of different angles.

Interview with Neal Conan, "Talk of the Nation," NPR, September 20, 2010; accessible at npr.org.

United Nations

Re: Turner's creation of the $1 billion-endowed United Nations Foundation:

Q: A billion dollars is a lot of money. Thirteen years later, do you think you got your money's worth?

A: Well, it's hard to tell exactly. It's gone into so many different projects, and different aspects. But I'm very happy with it. Yes, I am.

Q: And you could have chosen to give it to one institution. You could have set up a foundation to target one particular issue that you were passionate about. Why did you decide to give it to the UN?

A: Well, because the UN deals with all the problems that we have, from nuclear weapons and refugees and famine and all the other problems, and I figure we've got to handle all the problems if we're going to survive—global climate change.

Q: And this is, you decided this was the best way, the broad-spectrum approach, if you will?

Q: Well, at the time, the United States was two years behind in their dues to the UN. They owed them about a billion dollars, and my first idea was to give the money directly to the UN because they needed the money. They couldn't pay their peacekeepers because the US, who had agreed to pay, just wasn't paying.

Interview with Neal Conan, "Talk of the Nation," NPR, September 20, 2010; accessible at npr.org.

Re: United Nations' integrity:

Well, you know, I've worked with the United Nations almost every day in some way or another, and I don't see that at all. I think that they're aboveboard and up and up. And, you know, there was a little problem with, in the Oil for Food Program, a couple – well, four, five years ago. But that's the only impropriety that I'm aware of in a number of years.

The guys and girls that work over at the U.N. are really, for the most part, really care about what they're doing, and they really work hard for their money.

Interview with Neal Conan, "Talk of the Nation," NPR, September 20, 2010; accessible at npr.org.

United States' Role in the World

. . . you know, we have a long background of being an isolationist country and standing on our own and staying out of—or trying to stay out of—the wars in the rest of the world, which I think was good when we were a small country.

But we're a superpower now, and we have to take our responsibility in the world, seriously, because if we don't do it, nobody else can.

Interview with Neal Conan, "Talk of the Nation," NPR, September 20, 2010; accessible at npr.org.

Mark Twain

Mark Twain (Samuel Langhorne Clemens) / 1835–1910 / Missouri, USA / Novelist, Short Story Author, Lecturer, Publisher

Classic

"Classic." A book which people praise and don't read.

Following the Equator (1897).

Death of the Author

The reports of my death are greatly exaggerated.

Cable from London to the Associated Press, June 1, 1897.

Doing Right

Always do right. This will gratify some people, and astonish the rest.

Card sent to the Young People's Society, Greenpoint Presbyterian Church, Brooklyn, New York, February 16, 1901.

Familiarity

Familiarity breeds contempt—and children.

Notebooks (published posthumously in 1935).

Friends and Enemies

It takes your enemy and your friend, working together, to hurt you to the heart; the one to slander you and the other to get the news to you.

Following the Equator (1897).

Infrastructure and Superstructure

You tell me whar a man gits his corn pone, en I'll tell you what his 'pinions is.

Corn-Pone Opinions (written in 1901, published posthumously in Europe and Elsewhere in 1923).

Life

Why is it that we rejoice at a birth and grieve at a funeral? It is because we are not the person involved.

Pudd'nhead Wilson (1894).

All say, "How hard it is that we have to die"—a strange complaint to come from the mouths of people who have had to live.

Pudd'nhead Wilson (1894).

Whoever has lived long enough to find out what life is, knows how deep a dept of gratitude we owe to Adam, the first great benefactor of our race. He brought death into the world.

Pudd'nhead Wilson (1894).

Majority

Hain't we got all the fools in town on our side? and ain't that a big enough majority in any town?

The Adventures of Huckleberry Finn (1885).

Man

Man is the only animal that blushes. Or needs to.

Following the Equator (1897).

Everyone is a moon, and has a dark side which he never shows to anybody.

Following the Equator (1897).

Noise

Noise proves nothing. Often a hen who has merely laid an egg cackles as if she had laid an asteroid.

Following the Equator (1897).

Punctuality

The widder eats by a bell; she goes to bed by a bell; she gits up by a bell—everything's so awful reg'lar a body can't stand it.

The Adventures of Tom Sawyer (1876).

Reformation

Nothing so needs reforming as other people's habits.

Pudd'nhead Wilson (1894).

I was trying to make my mouth *say* I would do the right thing and the clean thing, and go and write to that n——'s owner and tell where he was; but deep down in me I knowed it was a lie, and He knowed it. You can't pray a lie—I found that out.

So I was full of trouble, full as I could be; and didn't know what to do. At last I had an idea; and I says, I'll go and write the letter—and then see if I can pray. Why, it was astonishing, the way I felt as light as a feather right straight off, and my troubles all gone. So I got a piece of paper and a pencil, all glad and excited, and set down and wrote: Miss Watson, your runaway n—— Jim is down here two mile below Pikesville, and Mr. Phelps has got him and he will give him up for the reward if you send.

I felt good and all washed clean of sin for the first time I had ever felt so in my life, and I knowed I could pray now. But I didn't do it straight off, but laid the paper down and set there thinking—thinking how good it was all this happened so, and how near I come to being lost and going to hell. And went on thinking. And got to thinking over our trip down the river; and I see Jim before me all the time: in the day and in the night-time, sometimes moonlight, sometimes storms, and we a-floating along, talking and singing and laughing. But somehow I couldn't seem to strike no places to harden me against him, but only the other kind. I'd see him standing my watch on top of his'n, 'stead of calling me, so I could go on sleeping; and see him how glad he was when I come back out of the fog; and when I come to him again in the swamp, up there where the feud was; and such-like times; and would always call me honey, and pet me and do everything he could think of for me, and how good he always was; and at last I struck the time I saved him by telling the men we had small-pox aboard, and he was so grateful, and said I was the best friend old Jim ever had in the world, and the *only* one he's got now; and then I happened to look around and see that paper.

It was a close place. I took it up, and held it in my hand. I was a-trembling, because I'd got to decide, forever, betwixt two things, and I knowed it. I studied a minute, sort of holding my breath, and then says to myself:

"All right, then, I'll *go* to hell"—and tore it up.

The Adventures of Huckleberry Finn (1885).

Right Word

The difference between the almost-right word and the right word is really a large matter—it's the difference between the lightning bug and the lightning.

Letter to George Bainton, October 15, 1888.

Temptation

There are several good protections against temptations, but the surest is cowardice.

Pudd'nhead Wilson (1894).

Work

Work consists of whatever a body is *obliged* to do. . . . Play consists of whatever a body is not obliged to do.

The Adventures of Tom Sawyer (1876).

Tom appeared on the sidewalk with a bucket of whitewash and a long-handled brush. He surveyed the fence, and all gladness left him and a deep melancholy settled down upon his spirit. Thirty yards of board fence nine feet high. Life to him seemed hollow, and existence but a burden. Sighing, he dipped his brush and passed it along the topmost plank; repeated the operation; did it again; compared the insignificant whitewashed streak with the far-reaching continent of unwhitewashed fence, and sat down on a tree-box discouraged.

The Adventures of Tom Sawyer (1876).

Luc de Clapiers, Marquis de Vauvenargues

Luc de Clapiers, Marquis de **Vauvenargues** / 1715–1747 / France / Aphorist
Note: All quotations are taken from *Réflexions et maximes* [Reflections and Maxims] (1746).

Achievement

To achieve great things we must live as though we were never going to die.

Belief

As it is natural to believe many things without proof, so, despite all proof, is it natural to disbelieve others.

Beneficence

Give help rather than advice.

Deception

A liar is a man who does now know how to deceive, a flatterer one who only deceives fools.

Emotion and Reason

Emotions have taught mankind to reason.

Fairness

All that is unfair, offends us if it's not beneficial for us.

Faith

Faith is the consolation of the wretched and the terror of the happy.

Hope

More are taken in by hope than by cunning.

Indolence

Indolence is the sleep of the mind.

Intelligent Design

As a house implies a builder, and a garment a weaver, and a door a carpenter, so does the existence of the Universe imply a Creator.

Knowledge

The things we know best are the things we haven't been taught.

Mankind

We should expect the best and the worst from mankind as from the weather.
It is not in everyone's power to secure wealth, office, or honors; but everyone may be good, generous, and wise.

Morality

Our errors and our controversies, in the sphere of morality, arise sometimes from looking on men as though they could be altogether bad, or altogether good.

Necessity

Necessity delivers us from the embarrassment of choice.

Patience

Patience is the art of hoping.

Pleasing Others

The art of pleasing is the art of deception.

Self-Knowledge

We discover in ourselves what others hide from us and we recognize in others what we hide from ourselves.

Servitude

Servitude degrades people to such a point that they come to like it.

Voltaire

Voltaire (François-Marie Arouet) / 1694–1778 / France / Dramatist, Novelist, Essayist

Animals

What a pity and what a poverty of spirit, to assert that beasts are machines deprived of knowledge and sentiment . . .

Source: "Animals," Philosophical Dictionary (1764).

Being Right

It is dangerous to be right in matters where established men are wrong.

Source: The Age of Louis XIV (1751).

Common Sense

It is sometimes said, common sense is very rare.

Source: "Common Sense," Philosophical Dictionary (1764).

Eloquence

One always speaks badly when one has nothing to say.

Source: Commentaires sur Corneille [Commentaries on Corneille] (1764).

Equality

All mortals are equal; it is not their birth,
But virtue itself that makes the difference.

Source: Fanaticism, or Mahomet the Prophet, Act I, Scene IV (1741).

Faith

Faith consists in believing what reason cannot.

Source: "The Flood," Philosophical Dictionary (1764).

Freedom

Man is free at the instant he wants to be.

Source: Brutus, Act II, Scene I (1730).

Virtue supposes liberty, as the carrying of a burden supposes active force. Under coercion there is no virtue, and without virtue there is no religion.

Source: "Du ministère ecclésiastique" [On Ecclesiastical Ministry], Questions sur l'Encyclopédie [Questions on the Encyclopédie] (1771).

Killing

It is forbidden to kill; therefore all murderers are punished unless they kill in large numbers and to the sound of trumpets.

Source: "Droits" [Rights], Questions sur l'Encyclopédie [Questions on the Encyclopédie] (1771).

Nature vs. Culture

Morality is everywhere the same for all men, therefore it comes from God; sects differ, therefore they are the work of men.

Source: "Atheist," Philosophical Dictionary (1764).

Pessimism

If this is the best of possible worlds, what then are the others?

Source: Candide, or Optimism (1759).

Physics

A Frenchman who arrives in London, will find philosophy, like everything else, very much changed there. He had left the world a plenum, and he now finds it a vacuum. At Paris the universe is seen composed of vortices of subtile matter; but nothing like it is seen in London.

Source: Letters Concerning the English Nation, Letter 14 (1733).

Pragmatism

The best is the enemy of the good.

Source: "La Bégueule: Conte Moral" [The Prude: A Moral Tale], Contes en vers [Stories in Verse] (1772).

Religious Tolerance

If there were only one religion in England there would be danger of despotism, if there were two they would cut each other's throats, but there are thirty, and they live in peace and happiness.

Source: Letters Concerning the English Nation, Letter 6 (1733).

Suicide

The man, who in a fit of melancholy, kills himself today, would have wished to live had he waited a week.

Source: "Cato," Philosophical Dictionary (1764).

Trust

Go into the London Stock Exchange—a more respectable place than many a court—and you will see representatives from all nations gathered together for the utility of men. Here Jew, Mohammedan and Christian deal with each other as though they were all of the same faith, and only apply the word infidel to people who go bankrupt. Here the Presbyterian trusts the Anabaptist and the Anglican accepts a promise from the Quaker.

Source: Letters Concerning the English Nation, Letter 6 (1733).

Virtue

Virtue is debased by self-justification.

Source: Oedipus, Act II, Scene IV (1718).

Work

Let us work without reasoning . . . it is the only way to make life endurable.

Source: Candide, or Optimism (1759).

Let us cultivate our garden.

Source: Candide, or Optimism (1759).

Sam Walton

Samuel Moore Walton / 1918–1992 / Oklahoma, USA / Businessman, Founder of Walmart, Inc.

Business Philosophy

Great ideas come from everywhere if you just listen and look for them. You never know who's going to have a great idea.

Sam Walton, with John Huey, Sam Walton: Made In America (1992).

What we guard against around here is people saying, 'Let's think about it.' We make a decision. Then we act on it.

Sam Walton, with John Huey, Sam Walton: Made In America (1992).

If American business is going to prevail, and be competitive, we're going to have to get accustomed to the idea that business conditions change, and that survivors have to adapt to those changing conditions. Business is a competitive endeavor, and job security lasts only as long as the customer is satisfied. Nobody owes anybody else a living.

Sam Walton, with John Huey, Sam Walton: Made In America (1992).

Business is a competitive endeavor, and job security lasts only as long as the customer is satisfied. Nobody owes anybody else a living.

Sam Walton, with John Huey, Sam Walton: Made In America (1992).

Watson, Sr., was running IBM, he decided they would never have more than four layers from the chairman of the board to the lowest level in the company. That may have been one of the greatest single reasons why IBM was successful.

Sam Walton, with John Huey, Sam Walton: Made In America (1992).

. . . could a Wal-Mart-type story still occur in this day and age? My answer is of course it could happen again. Somewhere out there right now there's someone—probably hundreds of thousands of someones—with good enough ideas to go all the way. It will be done again, over and over, providing that someone wants it badly enough to do what it takes to get there. It's all a matter of attitude and the capacity to constantly study and question the management of the business.

Sam Walton, with John Huey, Sam Walton: Made In America (1992).

The small stores were just destined to disappear, at least in the numbers they once existed, because the whole thing is driven by the customers, who are free to choose where to shop.

Sam Walton, with John Huey, Sam Walton: Made In America (1992).

As business leaders, we absolutely cannot afford to get all caught up in trying to meet the goals that some retail analyst or financial institution in New York sets for us on a ten-year plan spit out of a computer that somebody set to compound at such-and-such a rate. If we do that, we take our eye off the ball. But if we demonstrate in our sales and our earnings every day, every week, every quarter, that we're doing our job in a sound way, we will get the growth we are entitled to, and the market will respect us in a way that we deserve.

Sam Walton, with John Huey, Sam Walton: Made In America (1992).

Walmart, Inc. (formerly, Wal-Mart Stores)

Every time Wal-Mart spends one dollar foolishly, it comes right out of our customers' pockets. Every time we save them a dollar, that puts us one more step ahead of the competition—which is where we always plan to be.

Sam Walton, with John Huey, Sam Walton: Made In America (1992).

I don't think any other retail company in the world could do what I'm going to propose to you. It's simple. It won't cost us anything. And I believe it would just work magic, absolute magic on our customers, and our sales would escalate, and I think we'd just shoot past our Kmart friends in a year or two and probably Sears, as well. I want you to take a pledge with me. I want you to promise that whenever you come within ten feet of a customer, you will look him in the eye, greet him, and ask him if you can help him. Now, I know some of you are just naturally shy, and maybe don't want to bother folks. But if you'll go along with me on this, it would, I'm sure, help you become a leader. It would help your personality develop, you would become more outgoing, and in time you might become manager of that store, you might become a department manager, you might become a district manager, or whatever you choose to be in the company. It will do wonders for you. I guarantee it. Now, I want you to raise your right hand—and remember what we say at Wal-Mart, that a promise we make is a promise we keep—and I want you to repeat after me: From this day forward, I solemnly promise and declare that every time a customer comes within ten feet of me, I will smile, look him in the eye, and greet him. So help me, Sam.

Sam Walton, with John Huey, Sam Walton: Made In America (1992).

And like most other overnight successes, it was about twenty years in the making.

Sam Walton, with John Huey, Sam Walton: Made In America (1992).

It is a story about entrepreneurship, and risk, and hard work, and knowing where you want to go and being willing to do what it takes to get there.

Sam Walton, with John Huey, Sam Walton: Made In America (1992).

Walton on Walton

Our last Army posting was in Salt Lake City, and I went to the library there and checked out every book on retailing. I also spent a lot of my off-duty time studying ZCMI, the Mormon Church's department store out there, just figuring that when I got back to civilian life I would somehow go into the department store business.

Sam Walton, with John Huey, Sam Walton: Made In America (1992).

I had to pick myself up and get on with it, do it all over again, only even better this time.

Sam Walton, with John Huey, Sam Walton: Made In America (1992).

What's really worried me over the years is not our stock price, but that we might someday fail to take care of our customers, or that our managers might fail to motivate and take care of our associates. I also was worried that we might lose the team concept, or fail to keep the family concept viable and realistic and meaningful to our folks as we grow. Those challenges are more real than somebody's theory that we're headed down the wrong path.

Sam Walton, with John Huey, Sam Walton: Made In America (1992).

The point I'm trying to make is that we as a family have bent over backward not to take advantage of Wal-Mart, not to press our ownership position unfairly, and everybody in the company knows it.

Sam Walton, with John Huey, Sam Walton: Made In America (1992).

As an old-time small-town merchant, I can tell you that nobody has more love for the heyday of the small-town retailing era than I do. That's one of the reasons we chose to put our little Wal-Mart museum on the square in Bentonville [Arkansas]. It's in the old Walton's Five and Dime building, and it tries to capture a little bit of the old dime store feel. But I can also tell you this: if we had gotten smug about our early success, and said, "Well, we're the best merchant in town," and just kept doing everything exactly the way we were doing it, somebody else would have come along and given our customers what they wanted, and we would be out of business today.

Sam Walton, with John Huey, Sam Walton: Made In America (1992).

If I had to single out one element in my life that has made a difference for me, it would be a passion to compete.

Sam Walton, with John Huey, Sam Walton: Made In America (1992).

We used to get in some terrific fights. You have to be just as tough as they are. You can't let them get by with anything because they are going to take care of themselves, and your job is to take care of the customer. I'd threaten Procter & Gamble with not carrying their merchandise, and they'd say, 'Oh, you can't get by without carrying our merchandise.' And I'd say, 'You watch me put it on a side counter, and I'll put Colgate on the endcap at a penny less, and you just watch me.' They got offended and went to Sam, and he said, 'Whatever Claude says, that's what it's going to be.' Well, now we have a real good relationship with Procter & Gamble. It's a model that everybody talks about. But let me tell you, one reason for that is that they learned to respect us. They learned that they couldn't bulldoze us like everybody else, and that when we said we were representing the customer, we were dead serious.

Sam Walton, with John Huey, Sam Walton: Made In America (1992).

. . . because it was from that experience that I learned a lesson which has stuck with me all through the years: you can learn from everybody. I didn't just learn from reading every retail publication I could get my hands on, I probably learned the most from studying what John Dunham was doing across the street.

Sam Walton, with John Huey, Sam Walton: Made In America (1992).

The two most important words I ever wrote were on that first Wal-Mart sign: "Satisfaction Guaranteed." They're still up there, and they have made all the difference.

Sam Walton, with John Huey, Sam Walton: Made In America (1992).

I always favored the mavericks who challenged my rules. I may have fought them all the way, but I respected them, and, in the end, I listened to them a lot more closely than I did the pack who always agreed with everything I said.

Sam Walton, with John Huey, Sam Walton: Made In America (1992).

I still can't believe it was news that I get my hair cut at the barbershop. Where else would I get it cut? Why do I drive a pickup truck? What am I supposed to haul my dogs around in, a Rolls-Royce?

Sam Walton, with John Huey, Sam Walton: Made In America (1992).

E.B. White

Elwyn Brooks White / 1899–1985 / Mount Vernon, New York, USA / Writer

Christmas

To perceive Christmas through its wrapping becomes more difficult with every year.

"A Winter Diary," Harper's Magazine, December, 1936.

Democracy

Democracy is itself, a religious faith. For some it comes close to being the only formal religion they have.

"Democracy," The New Yorker, July 3, 1943.

Humanity

I would feel more optimistic about a bright future for man if he spent less time proving that he can outwit Nature and more time tasting her sweetness and respecting her seniority.

"Coon Tree," Atlantic Monthly, October, 1937.

Humor

Explaining a joke is like dissecting a frog. You understand it better but the frog dies in the process.

Letter to Mr. Nadeau, March 30, 1959, in Letters of E.B. White(1976).

Libraries

A library is a good place to go when you feel unhappy, for there, in a book, you may find encouragement and comfort. A library is a good place to go when you feel bewildered or undecided, for there, in a book, you may have your question answered.

"The Bookmobile," The New Yorker, March 17, 1956.

Life

We should all do what, in the long run, gives us joy, even if it is only picking grapes or sorting the laundry.

A Slight Sound at Evening," Harper's Magazine, October, 1945.

Literature

I don't know which is more discouraging, literature or chickens.

Letter to James Thurber, February 19, 1956, in Letters of E.B. White (1976).

A poet dares be just so clear and no clearer; he approaches lucid ground warily, like a mariner who is determined not to scrape his bottom on anything solid.

"Poetry," The New Yorker, April 20, 1929.

The Natural World

The world was white as yogurt or a lily or a sheet of typing paper, the new day carved out of a block of ice.

"Blizzard," The New Yorker, January 10, 1948.

We should not see faces in things—only a sense of what might exist in them.

"The Ring of Time," Harper's Magazine, January, 1956.

New York

No one should come to New York to live unless he is willing to be lucky.

Here Is New York (1949).

Prejudice

Prejudice is a great time saver. You can form opinions without having to get the facts.

"Prejudice," The New Yorker, August 17, 1946.

The world is full of people who have never, since childhood, met an open doorway with an open mind.

"Doors," The New Yorker, February 17, 1928.

White on White

If the world were merely seductive, that would be easy. If it were merely challenging, that would be no problem. But I arise in the morning torn between a desire to improve the world and a desire to enjoy the world. This makes it hard to plan the day.

"The Second Tree from the Corner," The New Yorker, May 23, 1947; reprinted in The Second Tree from the Corner (1954).

I don't know what the future holds, but I do know that I'm going to be positive and not wake up feeling desperate.

Letter to Stanley Hart White, June 11, 1977, in Letters of E.B. White (1976).

All that I hope to say in books, all that I ever hope to say, is that I love the world.

"Once More to the Lake," Harper's Magazine (1941).

I would like to say that every sentence I write is a love letter to someone.

Interview with George Plimpton, The Paris Review, Spring, 1969.

Writing

Writing is an act of faith, not a trick of grammar.

The Elements of Style, with William Strunk, Jr. (1959).

A writer who waits for ideal conditions under which to work will die without putting a word on paper.

Letter to a fan, October 3, 1947, in Letters of E.B. White (1976).

I don't believe in the imagination. If you stand out there long enough, the imagination shows up, but if you run out to meet it, it's not there.

Interview with George Plimpton, The Paris Review, Spring, 1969.

Royce White

Royce Alexander White / b. 1991 / Minneapolis, Minnesota, USA / Professional Athlete (Basketball), Mixed Martial Artist, Political Commentator, Author, Podcaster, US Senate Candidate

Note: Sources of the quotations have been provided where known; others presumably derive from White's multiple online commentaries, interviews, and podcasts.

Government

When 2000 people whack up a trillion dollars every single year, we see where the American taxpayer, not having $500 to put together in a crisis, is a real crime of taxation, a real crime of representation, a real misuse of military and defense and security, to make American citizens beg for economic tyranny.

"The Big Neocon," Please Call Me Crazy, Episode 122, October 31, 2023.

Helping Others

Take 30 seconds to encourage everyone you meet today. Everyone. Be genuine and transparent. And do it. Then do it tomorrow. Repeat.

Leadership

Great leaders remove obstacles-including themselves.

Life

The secret to failing isn't failing; the secret to failing is failing forward.

Life is not "either or," it's "both and."

If you don't live in your strengths, you'll die in your weaknesses. Do first and most what you're good at, and bring others along who are good at your weaknesses.

You'll never be great at anything you're not passionate about.

Mental Health

Mental health is a human issue; it's not a white issue, it's not a black issue, it's not a poor issue, it's not a rich issue.

The way we deal with mental health in this country is, honestly, barbaric.

We have to be brave enough to confront the stigmas around mental health and mental illness. It's not a weakness; it's a strength to seek help and speak out.

I have an obligation to my people, to my community, to be a voice for the voiceless when it comes to mental health.

Mental health is just as important as physical health, and we need to start treating it that way.

Mental health should be a fundamental human right, not a privilege for those who can afford it.

Mental illness doesn't discriminate. It doesn't care if you're an athlete, a doctor, or a janitor. It can affect anyone.

Military-Industrial Complex

And when you see it through that lens, you start to understand how people on both sides of the aisle, who are ideologically opposed in every other sense, find their way back to the middle of the row when it comes time to go to war. And so, when I go on Jason [Whitlock] or *Fearless*, or when I go on *War Room* with Steve Bannon, or when I go on*InfoWars* and I emphasize the military-industrial complex, this is why. Because despite all our cultural wedge issues, for some strange reason our politicians, who never really come together for any other premise, any other auspices other than military . . . military . . . and they'll fence it as national defense, they'll fence it as homeland security, they'll fence it as national security, but really, I mean . . . it's getting harder and harder to believe the whole narrative as things unfold.

> *"The Big Neocon," Please Call Me Crazy, Episode 122, October 31, 2023.*

National Basketball Association (NBA)

The amount of NBA players with mental health disorders is*way* over 26 percent. My suggestion would be to ask [former NBA Commissioner] David Stern how many players in the league he thinks have a marijuana problem. Whatever number he gives you, that's the number with mental illness. A chemical imbalance is a mental illness.

There's a crisis of selling out. And what makes me most concerned is that as sports fans we seem not to understand there's a crisis of selling out.

> *Interview, "Royce White: The Washington Post wants to call me a n******!," Fearless with Jason Whitlock, Episode 197, April 28, 2022.*

Please Call Me Crazy

I don't do this for clicks, likes, money, etc. . . . I tell people how they're being lied to and scammed. Which is so rare it sounds crazy! Hence the name—*Please Call Me Crazy*! We live in times where the lies start to sound like the truth and vice versa.

> *Tweet.*

Politics

If you can't change the status quo, make the status quo, change.

And what's the deepest, deepest and ugliest, most dishonest part of the Neocon? The most ugliest part of the Neocon is, it's not really conservative. It's liberal.

> *"The Big Neocon," Please Call Me Crazy, Episode 122, October 31, 2023.*

There are two main budget items that happen, that take place, that are funded every year that always make do. The military, which the Neocons run, and Medicaid-Medicare, which the socialist Democrats run. Uniparty. Always gotta make do. . . . The question is, the question should be in your mind, what does it say that the two parties, who control these two factions, intentionally use legislation to inflate the cost and then make you pay the inflated price? Where I'm from, that would be called "guerilla-pimping." Where I'm from that would be called "guerilla dealing."

> *"The Big Neocon," Please Call Me Crazy, Episode 122, October 31, 2023.*

Relationships

When no one is selfless in a relationship, there is war. When one is selfless, there is peace. When both are selfless, there is joy.

Royce on Royce

It is home. The Twin Cities are home and [Ames] is home. It's definitely always a place that's going to be very special to me.

He [former NBA Commissioner David Stern] told me basically I talked to your agent, stay off of Twitter. No. 1, that's disrespectful and undermining, but No. 2, it showed that what was important was the face value of the brand and not the mental health problem.

Interview with Michael Dunlap, "Royce White's Call For Accountability And Acknowledgement," hoopshabit.com, June 17, 2016.

For the *Washington Post* to call me a white supremacist, a white nationalist, really what they want to say is: "You're crazy." So they should just come out and say it. They want to call me the "N" word, but they know that'd be a little far from their platform. And make no mistake about it, the *Washington Post* is a neoliberal, Marxist, globalist institution.

*Interview, "Royce White: The Washington Post wants to call me a n******!," Fearless with Jason Whitlock, Episode 197, April 28, 2022.*

Here's what I'll say, to go back to this article [in the *Washington Post*] in the broadest sense. The biggest thing I had a problem with is that they said I led protests about police brutality. And that's why I wore the vest here today [pointing to his bullet proof vest with the legend "Enemy"] 'cause it's the same vest I am wearing in the picture, and in the picture we are outside the Federal Reserve. They know that the protest I led was about corporatocracy, which they are in on, 150%. And they still want to try and make it seem like police brutality was the central focus of the protest I led. Why? Because they want to disenfranchise me to the base who they say I'm just pandering to, when really I'm trying to clarify these things for the Republican Party as well. Because there is a Uniparty. There is a two-party Uniparty in our country.

*Interview, "Royce White: The Washington Post wants to call me a n******!," Fearless with Jason Whitlock, Episode 197, April 28, 2022.*

I never supported BLM. I went into . . . I did what many Republicans have forgotten to do, have lost a sense of. Ministry. Ministry. . . . And the reason why we've lost this country is because Republicans have not made it a priority to go back into the inner cities and clean up the narrative that they are not racists.

*Interview, "Royce White: The Washington Post wants to call me a n******!," Fearless with Jason Whitlock, Episode 197, April 28, 2022.*

I'm not afraid to go into the heart of the north side of Minneapolis where crime is the worst and say "You've been lied to." That's why they're afraid of me. Because they know I'm not afraid, like some of my other Republican counterparts, to go into these places that have been abandoned by the genuine conservative, nationalist, American platform and movement and candidates. That's why they're attacking me.

*Interview, "Royce White: The Washington Post wants to call me a n******!," Fearless with Jason Whitlock, Episode 197, April 28, 2022.*

I don't like being called a white nationalist by white liberals.

*Interview, "Royce White: The Washington Post wants to call me a n******!," Fearless with Jason Whitlock, Episode 197, April 28, 2022.*

If I wanted to just make money, I would've kept my mouth shut and still been in the NBA today.

*Interview, "Royce White: The Washington Post wants to call me a n******!," Fearless with Jason Whitlock, Episode 197, April 28, 2022.*

Trust

We learn to trust man when he does what we expect him to do; we learn to trust God when He doesn't do what we expect Him to do.

Jason Whitlock

Jason Lee Whitlock / b. 1967 / Indianapolis, Indiana, USA / Newspaper Reporter, Sports Columnist, Radio Announcer, Podcaster
Note: The specific sources of the following quotes are unknown, but presumably derive from Whitlock's numerous commentaries, interviews, and podcasts

The Black Community

Certain people and groups seem invested in convincing black people that black people are liberal. We've traditionally been conservative, church-going people.

We have allowed our youths to buy into a culture (hip hop) that has been perverted, corrupted, and overtaken by prison culture. The music, attitude, and behavior expressed in this culture is anti-black, anti-education, demeaning, self-destructive, pro-drug dealing, and violent.

There is a business built around racial grievance. And that business is booming at such a level that white people are like hey, I'm going to adopt a whole new identity so I can benefit from being Baby Al Sharpton, Baby Jesse Jackson, and in academia this has been embraced . . .

. . . and that the arming of so many black youths, and loading up our community with drugs, and then just having an open shooting gallery, is the work of people who obviously don't have our best interests [at heart].

Racism is an issue in America but is primarily an issue for the poor. It's not LeBron James's issue.

Black Lives Matter

There's no way you can do any homework on Black Lives Matter and not see that it's a Marxist political organization. It's not about Black Death. It's not about black men. It is a political move. It's a communist political move.

Critical Race Theory

The Colin Kaepernick Kneeling Trojan Horse has turned sports into the victimhood Olympics, the most powerful venue in popular culture to preach critical race excuse-making.

Fear

I think that fear is a mechanism, a tool for control.

If you engage with the police, filled with fear, you're more likely to make really bad decisions that provoke them to take action.

The Democratic Party, the mainstream media are using fear to control people and to control African Americans in particular. You cannot function properly if you live in an irrational fear.

God

God is the embodiment of love and we are a society that seems to be embracing and favoring hate and empowering hate.

Guns

Handguns do not enhance our safety, they exacerbate our flaws, tempt us to escalate arguments, and bait us into embracing confrontation, rather than avoiding it.

Health

Investing in your long-term health means cultivating the skills to prepare your own meals, developing healthy eating habits and a willingness to make time to exercise. The earlier you embrace these habits, the healthier you will be in your 50s, 60s and beyond.

Jim Crow

Jim Crow had unintended benefits. It forced blacks to build and rely on their own economic, educational, and social systems.

Liberalism

In the immediate aftermath of the Civil Rights–movement, Democrats marketed liberalism to us as fashionable, sophisticated, and liberating. Today it needs a surgeon general's warning: hazardous to your family and the values you were taught as a child.

Life

The sacrifices you make in your 20s pay off 30 and 40 years later. The same is true when it comes to financial progress. Every dime saved in your 20s turns into a dollar in your 60s.

You want to be leaders and you're black and I'm here to tell you how to do it. Disconnect from this social media garbage; disconnect from these celebrity athletes who don't really care nothing about you.

It is possible to set your standards too high, which can undermine a man's confidence and ability to perform. Instead of reaching for the stars and settling for the moon, there is considerable evidence that man is better served reaching for a blade of grass and settling for an under-the-table handshake deal.

Self-analysis is the sworn enemy of regret-free living.

Unchecked pride evolves into swagger, a hypnotizing mask of insecurity that can and does compromise our ability to make progress and attain power. Pride stands in the way of forgiveness and a strategic approach to navigating a chessboard rigged to prevent pawns from becoming kings and queens.

The Media

Journalists used to be obsessed with working at a New York magazine or newspaper or TV network. Now the entire industry is obsessed with going viral and how words will be received via social media.

New York and San Francisco are distinctly different. San Francisco is driving the American media, not New York. You have young, microwaved millionaires and billionaires reshaping the American media in a way that reflects San Francisco values.

What has truly impeded ESPN from overcoming its financial mistakes and inability to adapt to technological advances? The decade-long culture war, ESPN lost to Deadspin, a snarky, politically progressive sports blog launched by Gawker's Nick Denton in 2005.

Martin Luther King, Jr.

Martin Luther King Jr. was a Southern, conservative minister who believed in the American promise. His dream was patriotic and traditional. Family, work, self-determination and religion comprised his core values.

Politics

Take your money, pool your resources and support people who actually represent your views and have the time to be full-time involved.

Black people have no reason to fear political free agency.

Poverty

The worst thing to be in America and anywhere on the planet is poor.

Public Discourse

False equivalency is the lifeblood of American public debate.

Words matter, particularly when you're writing a story that could significantly damage a person's or an organization's reputation.

Trust is what leads to the best conversations. People take chances and say what they really think when they trust the person they're engaging with.

You can be authentic without being distasteful or disrespectful.

We have grown comfortable not having our perspective challenged. It's unhealthy.

Sports

You can't be Allen Iverson on a football team. And even Iverson got run out of Philadelphia when he was still a spectacular talent because the Sixers got tired of the headache and his bad attitude.

Men do really dumb things. We see weapons of mass destruction where there are none. We over-emphasize sports. We place athletic achievement ahead of academic achievement. We spoil and pamper child athletes and then complain when they act spoiled and pampered as adults.

Sports culture has long had a major impact on American culture. The values taught and celebrated in sports are conservative.

Far-left political ideologues want to reshape sports culture to their liking.

Professional sports have built themselves on the celebration of Americana, the ideas and values that best exemplify America.

Sports culture is not PC or far left. There are no safe spaces in the field of competition.

Sports culture has long been patriotic, tolerant of diverse backgrounds and perspective and celebratory of meritocracy.

The only place where we're not segregated *en masse* is in sports. You go to a football stadium or a basketball arena, and all of America is there: the wealthy, the poor, the black, white, Latino, conservative, liberal, and we all talk about sports.

Texas

I don't have a beef with Texas. I just don't think Texans know anything about basketball and they don't have a sense of humor. Texans take themselves too seriously.

Wealth

Great wealth creates an arrogance and, to be quite frank, a god complex in some people that they start feeling like they can do no wrong, they own people, they're superior to other people.

Whitlock on Whitlock

My dad didn't graduate high school. My mom is a high school graduate. My mom is a factory worker. My dad owned a bar in the inner city.

I'm not a political partisan. I don't vote.

But at the end of the day, in order for me to reach my full potential, I need an environment that allows me to be me. . . . The executives at Fox Sports get and embrace me. Fox Sports allows me to be real.

Judge my columns, enjoy my tweets. That's my philosophy.

Seriously, I was the wrong fit at ESPN. Definition of insanity is doing the same thing over and over and expecting different results.

Have I been an entertainer, a provocateur, and a humorist? Absolutely.

I'm a bit of a rabble-rouser.

Whatever my critics say, I've been a hardcore journalist all my career.

I didn't brown-nose my way here. I pulled out guns and shot my way here. So people don't mind shooting back. If I'd gotten here brown-nosing and playing all the political games, I'd probably be treated differently.

Personally, I'm not all that interested in making the show appealing to casual sports fans.

I will talk to anybody… You want to talk, let's talk.

I'm a conservative dude from the Midwest. I went crazy out here in LA.

I don't do stand-up anymore. There are no rules in stand-up comedy. Journalists follow plenty of rules.

I eat raw vegetables. But my "30 for 30" documentary better include sit-down interviews with Ronald McDonald, Colonel Sanders, and Little Debbie.

I've been a solo act, a columnist, and worked from home, only relying on myself. Now I'm part of a team, a leader, and I have to fit in at a big corporation and deal with all the moving parts, all the different personalities. That has been a challenge, to be quite honest, that I've embraced.

Oscar Wilde

Oscar Wilde / 1854–1900 / Ireland (then, United Kingdom of Great Britain and Ireland) / Poet, Dramatist, Short Story Writer, Novelist, Essayist

Advice

It is always a silly thing to give advice, but to give good advice is absolutely fatal.

"The Portrait of Mr. W. H.," Blackwood's Magazine (1889); reprinted in subsequent editions of Oscar Wilde, Lord Arthur Savile's Crime and Other Stories, originally published in 1891.

America

We have really everything in common with America nowadays, except, of course, language.

"The Canterville Ghost," The Court and Society Review (1887); reprinted in Oscar Wilde, Lord Arthur Savile's Crime and Other Stories (1891).

Animals

There is no mode of action, no form of emotion, that we do not share with the lower animals. It is only by language that we rise above them, or above each other—by language, which is the parent, and not the child, of thought.

"The Critic as Artist," The Nineteenth Century, 1890; reprinted in Oscar Wilde, Intentions (1891).

Art

The more we study Art, the less we care for Nature.

Intentions (1891).

Art finds her own perfection within, and not outside of herself. She is not to be judged by any external standard of resemblance. She is a veil, rather than a mirror.

Intentions (1891).

We spend our days, each one of us, in looking for the secret of life. Well, the secret of life is in art.

"The English Renaissance of Art," public lecture, New York City, 1882; reprinted in Oscar Wilde, Essays and Lectures, edited by Robert Ross (1908).

Life imitates art far more than art imitates Life.

"The Decay of Lying" (1889); reprinted in Oscar Wilde, Intentions(1891).

. . . alone, without any reference to his neighbours, without any interference, the artist can fashion a beautiful thing; and if he does not do it solely for his own pleasure, he is not an artist at all.

"The Soul of Man Under Socialism," Fortnightly Review,February, 1891.

Calendars

Most modern calendars mar the sweet simplicity of our lives by reminding us that each day that passes is the anniversary of some perfectly uninteresting event.

"A New Calendar," The Pall Mall Gazette, February 17, 1887.

Consistency

Consistency is the last refuge of the unimaginative.

"The Relation of Dress to Art," The Pall Mall Gazette, February 28, 1885; reprinted in Oscar Wilde, Aristotle at Afternoon Tea: The Rare Oscar Wilde, edited by John Wyse Jackson (1991).

Cynic

A man who knows the price of everything and the value of nothing.

Lady Windemere's Fan, Act III (1892); Lord Darlington.

Fashion

And, after all, what is a fashion? From the artistic point of view, it is usually a form of ugliness so intolerable that we have to alter it every six months.

"The Philosophy of Dress," The New-York Tribune, 1885.

Genius

I put all my genius into my life; I put only my talent into my works.

In conversation with André Gide in Algiers, reported by Gide in a letter to his mother dated January 30, 1895.

Greatness

Be warned in time, James, and remain, as I do, incomprehensible: to be great is to be misunderstood.

Letter to James McNeill Whistler, February 23, 1885.

History

Anybody can make history. Only a great man can write it.

"The Critic as Artist," The Nineteenth Century, 1890; reprinted in Oscar Wilde, Intentions (1891).

Ideas

An idea that is not dangerous is unworthy of being called an idea at all.

Intentions (1891).

Income

It is better to have a permanent income than to be fascinating.

"The Model Millionaire," The World, 1912; reprinted in Oscar Wilde, Lord Arthur Savile's Crime and Other Stories (1891).

Life

To live is the rarest thing in the world. Most people exist, that is all.

"The Soul of Man Under Socialism," Fortnightly Review,February, 1891.

"Know thyself" was written over the portal of the antique world. Over the portal of the new world, "Be thyself" shall be written.

"The Soul of Man Under Socialism," Fortnightly Review,February, 1891.

We are all in the gutter, but some of us are looking at the stars.

Lady Windemere's Fan, Act III (1892); Lord Darlington.

Love

The mystery of love is greater than the mystery of death.

Salome: A Tragedy in One Act (1893).

Yet each man kills the thing he loves
By each let this be heard,
Some do it with a bitter look,
Some with a flattering word,
The coward does it with a kiss,
The brave man with a sword!

"The Ballad of Reading Gaol" (1898).

Man

Man is least himself when he talks in his own person. Give him a mask, and he will tell you the truth.

"The Critic as Artist," The Nineteenth Century, 1890; reprinted in Oscar Wilde, Intentions (1891).

Orphans

To lose one parent may be regarded as a misfortune … to lose both seems like carelessness.

The Importance of Being Earnest, Act I (1895); Lady Bracknell.

Poetry

A poet can survive everything but a misprint.

"The Children of the Poets," The Pall Mall Gazette, October 14, 1886.

Popular Opinion

For to disagree with three-fourths of the British public on all points is one of the first elements of sanity, one of the deepest consolations in all moments of spiritual doubt.

"The English Renaissance of Art," public lecture, New York City, 1882; reprinted in Oscar Wilde, Essays and Lectures, edited by Robert Ross (1908).

Prison

The vilest deeds like poison weeds
Bloom well in prison-air;
It is only what is good in man
That wastes and withers there;
Pale Anguish keeps the heavy gate,
And the Warder is Despair.

"The Ballad of Reading Gaol" (1898).

Religious Conversion

How else but through a broken heart
May Lord Christ enter in?

"The Ballad of Reading Gaol" (1898).

Socialism

The true perfection of man lies, not in what man has, but in what man is.

"The Soul of Man Under Socialism," Fortnightly Review,February, 1891.

The trouble with socialism is that it takes up too many evenings.

Attribution unconfirmed.

Tastes

I have the simplest tastes. I am always satisfied with the best.

In conversation with Edgar Saltus, reported in the Saltus's book, Oscar Wilde: An Idler's Impression (1917).

Teaching

. . . everybody who is incapable of learning has taken to teaching.

"The Decay of Lying" (1889); reprinted in Oscar Wilde, Intentions(1891).

Temptation

I can resist everything except temptation.

Lady Windemere's Fan, Act I (1892); Lord Darlington.

Thinking

A man who does not think for himself does not think at all.

"The Soul of Man Under Socialism," Fortnightly Review,February, 1891.

Tragedy

In this world there are only two tragedies. One is not getting what one wants, and the other is getting it.

Lady Windemere's Fan, Act III (1892); Mr. Dumby.

Truth

I have said to you to speak the truth is a painful thing. To be forced to tell lies is much worse.

De Profundis (1897).

Oprah Winfrey

Oprah Gail Winfrey / b. 1954 / Mississippi, USA / Actress, Television Talk Show Host and Producer, Businesswoman

Free Speech

Re: Winfrey's acquittal of libel for criticizing the beef industry:

I will continue to use my voice. I believed from the beginning that [the lawsuit] was an attempt to muzzle my voice, and I come from a people who have struggled and died in order to have a voice in this country. And I refused to be muzzled.

Reported in "Oprah: 'Free speech rocks': Texas cattlemen lose defamation suit," cnn.com, February 26, 1998.

Philosophy of Life

What other people label or might try to call failure, I have learned is just God's way of pointing you in a new direction.

Commencement address, Howard University, May 12, 2007; accessible on youtube.com.

I believe that every single event in life happens in an opportunity to choose love over fear.

Reported by Tuchy Palmieri in Oprah, in Her Words: Our American Princess (2008).

All the energy that you spend, trying to hurt somebody else, that energy will turn around and slap you in the face. The same thing is true, Love, what I know is that the energy that put out everyday with the best of intentions that it would reach you where you really live in heart of yourself has come back to me from all of you in full force. So that what we've learnt on this show; You are responsible for your life and when you get that, everything changes, my friends. So don't wait for somebody else to fix you, to save you or complete you. . . .

The Oprah Winfrey Show Finale, May 25, 2011; reported by Cynthia McFadden in "Oprah's Final Farewell," ABC News; accessible on youtube.com.

Turn your wounds into wisdom.

Interview with Piers Morgan, "Piers Morgan Tonight," CNN, January 17, 2011; accessible on cnn.com.

Your life is not static. Every decision, setback, or triumph is an opportunity to identify the seeds of truth that make you the wondrous human being that you are. I'm not talking just about what you do for a living. When you pay attention to what feeds your energy, you move in the direction of the life for which you were intended. Trust that the Universe has a bigger, wider, deeper dream for you than you could ever imagine for yourself.

Oprah Winfrey, The Path Made Clear: Discovering Your Life's Direction and Purpose (2019).

Politics

Re: Barack Obama's election as Senator from Illinois:

It felt like a new day.

Obama interview, "Man of the Moment," The Oprah Winfrey Show, oprah.com, January 19, 2005.

Re: Pedophiles:

You want motivation? You still don't understand what our children are up against? Let me read you something that was posted on our message boards from someone who claims to be a member of a known pedophile network. He said this: he doesn't forgive, he does not forget, his group has over nine thousand penises and they're all raping children. So, I want you to know: they're organized, and they have systematic ways of hurting children and they use the internet to do it. These are the predators that are molesting and raping our children. They're trading the photos and videos online, and I want to stress again: this is not about politics, it's about giving the dedicated men and women of law enforcement who are trying to catch these predators the resources they need.

The Oprah Winfrey Show, 2008.

Re: the mass shooting in Las Vegas, Nevada, on October 1, 2017:

I feel like my soul is aching for the country. . . . There's not a day that goes by where I'm not putting on my shoes, or brushing my teeth, where I just think about the ordinariness of, people who just went to a concert, or the ordinariness of the day from people from 9/11, who were just doing an ordinary thing, and then you never get home. . . . So, I would say that these days of crisis and tragedy are to remind us all to be present in the ordinariness of our lives, that actually turns out to be extraordinary, when the person you love doesn't come home at night. . . . I would say, we can't allow ourselves to be frightened into not living our lives, and I think that we have to keep going and we have to keep going with the faith that thing will get better. . . . And things will get better when we make them better.

Interview with Entertainment Tonight; reported in "Oprah Winfrey Offers Words of Wisdom in Wake of Deadly Las Vegas Shooting," KTVB-TV, Boise, Idaho, October 2, 2017; accessible on ktvb.com.

Winfrey on Winfrey

I never think about what I want. It's about what you want to give to other people.

Reported by Egbert Sukop in The Money Adventure (1998).

What I learned at a very early age was that I was responsible for my life. And as I became more spiritually conscious, I learned that we all are responsible for ourselves, that you create your own reality by the way you think and therefore act. You cannot blame apartheid, your parents, your circumstances, because you are not your circumstances. You are your possibilities. If you know that, you can do anything.

Reported in O Magazine, January, 2007.

Re: Winfrey's friendship with Gayle King:

I understand why people think we're gay. There isn't a definition in our culture for this kind of bond between women. So I get why people have to label it—how can you be this close without it being sexual?

Reported in "Oprah: Gayle and I Are Not Gay," Peoplemagazine, July 16, 2006.

Re: the 2006 film, *The Secret*:

I think that, uh, you know, I'm really happy that the message, or at least some of the message of *The Secret* is reaching mass consciousness in a way that people realize that they can begin to, uh, positively affect their lives. That's why when I was on the show and said "I've lived this way my whole life", and people who watched our show for years know that I've been talking about how you take responsibility for your life and the choices that you make. Empower your life. And so, when I say that, you know, um, that's how I live my life, the message of *The Secret*, that's what I mean. I *also* believe, that, uh, medical healing or healing comes in lots of forms. You know that adage about the guy being lost and God sent him a boat—then he gets to heaven and says "Why didn't you help me?" And God's, "I sent you the boat, fool!" So, that's the way I look at medical healing.

The Oprah Winfrey Show, March, 2007; accessible on youtube.com.

People often ask me: "*What is the secret to the success of the show?*" "*How it lasted 25 years?*" I jokingly say: "My team and Jesus," because nothing but the Hand of God has made this possible for me. For all of you who get railed up when I mentioned God and you wanna know which God am I talking about, I am talking about the same one you talk about, I am talking about the Alpha and Omega, the Omniscience, the Unprecedented, the Ultimate Consciousness, the Source, the Force, the all of everything that is, The One and Only G-O-D, that's what I am talking about. . . .

The Oprah Winfrey Show Finale, May 25, 2011; reported by Cynthia McFadden in "Oprah's Final Farewell," ABC News; accessible on youtube.com.

I know where my lane is, and I know how to stay in my lane. My lane is evolving the consciousness of people.

Interview with Piers Morgan, "Piers Morgan Tonight," CNN, January 17, 2011; accessible on cnn.com.

The thing that I do best is "Be Here. Be Now."

Interview with Piers Morgan, "Piers Morgan Tonight," CNN, January 17, 2011; accessible on cnn.com.

Growing up in the church, one of my favorite Bible parables was about the mustard seed: If you have faith, even if it's as little as a mustard seed, you can move mountains. Anything is possible. As a child, listening from my seat in church, this brought me so much comfort—just as it did when I was struggling as a reporter in Baltimore and as it still does today.

Oprah Winfrey, The Path Made Clear: Discovering Your Life's Direction and Purpose (2019).

Years ago, I interviewed a grieving mother whose adult son had died after a long illness. You could have heard a pin drop in the studio when she so beautifully told the story of their final moment together. The mother had climbed into bed with her son. She could barely hear him, but her head was on his chest. As he took his last breath, he whispered, "Oh Mom, it is all so simple. It's so simple, Mom." He then closed his eyes and died. I got chills when I heard that. I realized then, just as it resonates with me now: We allow life to get so complicated—when it's really so very simple. From that day forward I resolved to continually ask myself, *How am I making things more difficult than they need to be?* Your answer to that same question is the next step in your path. It's that simple. Imagine what lies just around the bend. Can you see it? I can. Love, Oprah.

Oprah Winfrey, The Path Made Clear: Discovering Your Life's Direction and Purpose (2019).

Tom Wolfe

Thomas Kennerly Wolfe, Jr. / 1930–2018 / Richmond, Virginia, USA / Journalist, Novelist, Essayist

The Art World

One of the few universal observations in the world of art is that you can always tell a major artist by the size of his entourage.

"The New Journalism," New York Magazine, February 14, 1972; reprinted in The New Journalism (1973).

The modern notion of art is an essentially religious or magical one in which the artist is viewed as a holy beast who in some way, big or small, receives flashes from the godhead, which is known as creativity.

"The Painted Word," in The Painted Word (1975).

The notion that the public accepts or rejects anything in modern art is merely romantic fiction. The game is completed and the trophies distributed long before the public knows what has happened.

"The Painted Word," in The Painted Word (1975).

Babies

That baby is a very sentient creature. . . . That baby sees the world with a completeness that you and I will never know again. His doors of perception have not yet been closed. He still experiences the moment he lives in.

The Electric Kool-Aid Acid Test (1968).

Challenging Oneself

If you aren't already in over your head, how do you know how tall you are?

Source unknown.

Cults

A cult is a religion with no political power.

Interview with Ken Auletta, The New Yorker, June, 1996.

Fathers

Sherman made the terrible discovery that men make about their fathers sooner or later… that the man before him was not an aging father but a boy, a boy much like himself, a boy who grew up and had a child of his own and, as best he could, out of a sense of duty and, perhaps love, adopted a role called Being a Father so that his child would have something mythical and infinitely important: a Protector, who would keep a lid on all the chaotic and catastrophic possibilities of life.

The Bonfire of the Vanities (1987).

Human Nature

The whole conviction of my life now rests upon the belief that loneliness, far from being a rare and curious phenomenon, is the central and inevitable fact of human existence.

"Mau-Mauing the Flak Catchers," in Radical Chic & Mau-Mauing the Flak Catchers (1970).

The surest cure for vanity is loneliness.

The Electric Kool-Aid Acid Test (1968).

Everybody, everybody everywhere, has his own movie going, his own scenario, and everybody is acting his movie out like mad, only most people don't know that is what they're trapped by, their little script.

The Electric Kool-Aid Acid Test (1968).

One's destination is never a place, but a new way of seeing things.

Source unknown.

Sometimes we don't even realize what we really care about, because we get so distracted by the symbols.

The Electric Kool-Aid Acid Test (1968).

One of the few freedoms that we have as human beings that cannot be taken away from us is the freedom to assent to what is true and to deny what is false. Nothing you can give me is worth surrendering that freedom for.

A Man in Full (1998).

Language

The language of our time has also been driven to the wall, as language always is in a tyranny.

"My Three Stooges," in Hooking Up (2000).

Las Vegas

Las Vegas is the only town in the world whose skyline is made up neither of buildings, like New York, nor of trees, like Wilbraham, Massachusetts, but signs.

"The First Tycoon of Teen," New York Herald Tribune Sunday Magazine, 1965; reprinted in Hooking Up (2000).

Lies

A lie may fool someone else, but it tells you the truth: you're weak.

Source unknown.

Meaning

Everything in everybody's life is . . . significant. And everybody is alert, watching for the meanings.

The Electric Kool-Aid Acid Test (1968).

New York

One belongs to New York instantly, one belongs to it as much in five minutes as in five years.

The Bonfire of the Vanities (1987).

Non-Fiction

The problem with fiction, it has to be plausible. That's not true with non-fiction.

Interview with George Plimpton, The Paris Review, Summer, 1992.

Political Allegiance

If a conservative is a liberal who's been mugged, a liberal is a conservative who's been arrested.

In Our Time: Memoir of a Revolution (1980).

Prime of Life

One's prime is elusive. You little girls, when you grow up, must be on the alert to recognize your prime at whatever time of your life it may occur. You must then live it to the full.

Commencement address, Boston University, May 21, 2000.

The Sixties

The world was simply and sheerly divided into 'the aware', those who had the experience of being vessels of the divine, and a great mass of "the unaware," "the unmusical," "the unattuned."

The Electric Kool-Aid Acid Test (1968).

Radical Chic, after all, is only radical in Style; in its heart it is part of Society and its traditions.

"Radical Chic: That Party at Lenny's," New York Magazine, 1970; reprinted in Radical Chic & Mau-Mauing the Flak Catchers(1970).

Universities

The idea was that these kids, though they were so bright, were also supposed to be imbued with the spirit of the age.

I Am Charlotte Simmons (2004).

War

I went to see the Beatles last month... And I heard 20,000 girls screaming together at the Beatles... and I couldn't hear what they were screaming, either . . . But you don't have to... They're screaming Me! Me! Me! Me! . . . I'm Me! . . . That's the cry of the ego, and that's the cry of this rally! . . . Me! Me! Me! Me! . . . And that's why wars get fought . . . ego . . . because enough people want to scream Pay attention to Me... Yep, you're playing their game . . .

The Electric Kool-Aid Acid Test (1968).

Wolfe on Wolfe

I'd rather be a lightning rod than a seismograph.

The Electric Kool-Aid Acid Test (1968).

Writing

What I write when I force myself is generally just as good as what I write when I'm feeling inspired. It's mainly a matter of forcing yourself to write.

Source unknown.

To me, the great joy of writing is discovering. Most writers are told to write about what they know, but I still love the adventure of going out and reporting on things I don't know about.

Source unknown.

Steve Wozniak

Stephen Gary ("Woz") Wozniak / b. 1950 / California, USA / Electronics Engineer, Computer Programmer, Inventor, Co-Founder of Apple Computers, Inc.

Apple

Creative things have to sell to get acknowledged as such. Steve Jobs didn't really set the direction of my Apple I and Apple II designs but he did the more important part of turning them into a product that would change the world. I don't deny that.

"General Questions Answered," Letters, woz.org, August 15, 2000; reprinted in Steve Wozniak, with Gina Smith, iWoz: Computer Geek to Cult Icon: How I Invented the Personal Computer, Co-Founded Apple, and Had Fun Doing It (2006).

The transition to a GUI, and eventually to one close to a Macintosh, was a far greater step than refinements since. Some of these are just simple alternatives, which can't be over-valued due to increasing the complexity of having less consistency in how things are done. Others of these are more akin to rearranging the furniture. The great change was in becoming a modern GUI machine. In that sense, virtually every machine is a 'Macintosh' now.

"General Questions Answered," Letters, woz.org, August 15, 2000; reprinted in Steve Wozniak, with Gina Smith, iWoz: Computer Geek to Cult Icon: How I Invented the Personal Computer, Co-Founded Apple, and Had Fun Doing It (2006).

All of a sudden, we've lost a lot of control,. We can't turn off our internet; we can't turn off our smartphones; we can't turn off our computers. You used to ask a smart person a question. Now, who do you ask? It starts with g-o, and it's not God.

Interview with Mark Milian, "Apple's Steve Wozniak: 'We've lost a lot of control,'" cnn.com, December 8, 2010.

Our first computers were born not out of greed or ego, but in the revolutionary spirit of helping common people rise above the most powerful institutions.

Interview, "An Evening with Steve Wozniak at Margaret Court," Margaret Court Arena, Melbourne, Australia, theculturetrip.com, July 27, 2016.

. . . a lot of people confuse that story with Apple's, saying that we started Apple in a garage. Not true. HP started in a garage, true. But in the case of Apple, I worked in my room at my apartment and Steve worked in his bedroom in his parents' house. We only did the very last part of assembly in his garage.

Steve Wozniak, with Gina Smith, iWoz: Computer Geek to Cult Icon: How I Invented the Personal Computer, Co-Founded Apple, and Had Fun Doing It (2006).

Computer Design as Artistry

Artists work best alone. Work alone.

Steve Wozniak, with Gina Smith, iWoz: Computer Geek to Cult Icon: How I Invented the Personal Computer, Co-Founded Apple, and Had Fun Doing It (2006).

It had to be that artistically perfect, because it represents yourself when you do a great design.

Interview, "Steve Wozniak Debunks One of Apple's Biggest Myths," bloomberg.com, December 4, 2014.

. . . this early learning of how to do things one tiny little step at a time. I learned to not worry so much about the outcome, but to concentrate on the step I was on and to try to do it as perfectly as I could when I was doing it.

Steve Wozniak, with Gina Smith, iWoz: Computer Geek to Cult Icon: How I Invented the Personal Computer, Co-Founded Apple, and Had Fun Doing It (2006).

I hope you're as lucky as I am. The world needs inventors–great ones. You can be one. If you love what you do and are willing to do what it really takes, it's within your reach. And it'll be worth every minute you spend alone at night, thinking and thinking about what it is you want to design or build. It'll be worth it, I promise.

"General Questions Answered," Letters, woz.org, August 15, 2000; reprinted in Steve Wozniak, with Gina Smith, iWoz:Computer Geek to Cult Icon: How I Invented the Personal Computer, Co-Founded Apple, and Had Fun Doing It (2006).

Hacking

A lot of hacking is playing with other people, you know, getting them to do strange things.

Keynote address, 5th HOPE (Hackers on Planet Earth) Conference, New York City, July 10, 2004.

Happiness

Years ago, I was thinking about the definition of success in business, and I had a moment–just seconds long–where I compared that kind of life to one of playing pranks with my friends. Life is not about extrinsic symbols of success; life is about how happy you have been. So my formula was created right then. H = S – F: Happiness equals smiles minus frowns. As with my designs, I like the simplicity of that formula. From then on I'd do what I could to build humor and fun into all my productive work. As for frowns, I would not argue. If someone has different beliefs, they are right in their world and I am right in mine. The only person I had to convince was myself. This carries over to the way computers and more could be designed.

Interview with Micah Solomon, "Steve Wozniak On How To Launch A Startup, Give A Keynote Speech And Be Happy," forbes.com, September 27, 2017.

Hardware

When you don't have the hardware resources, you have to take advantage of what you have inside the chip.

Steve Wozniak, with Gina Smith, iWoz: Computer Geek to Cult Icon: How I Invented the Personal Computer, Co-Founded Apple, and Had Fun Doing It (2006).

Patience

And thanks to all those science projects, I acquired a central ability that was to help me through my entire career: patience. I'm serious. Patience is usually so underrated. I mean, for all these projects, from third grade all the way to eighth grade, I just learned things gradually, figuring out how to put electronic devices together without so much as cracking a book . . . I learned to not worry so much about the outcome, but to concentrate on the step I was on and to try to do it as perfectly as I could when I was doing it.

Steve Wozniak, with Gina Smith, iWoz: Computer Geek to Cult Icon: How I Invented the Personal Computer, Co-Founded Apple, and Had Fun Doing It (2006).

Personnel

Wherever smart people work, doors are unlocked.

Keynote address, 5th HOPE (Hackers on Planet Earth) Conference, New York City, July 10, 2004.

Platforms

I'm surprised at the extent of the bigotry. But it really plays out when companies or schools take a side and prohibit the other platform at all. We Mac users should be good even when the other side is bad. We should do what we can to accept the other platforms. All the best people in life seem to like LINUX.

"General Questions Answered," Letters, woz.org, August 15, 2000; reprinted in Steve Wozniak, with Gina Smith, iWoz: Computer Geek to Cult Icon: How I Invented the Personal Computer, Co-Founded Apple, and Had Fun Doing It (2006).

Social Impact

When we started Apple, Steve Jobs and I talked about how we wanted to make blind people as equal and capable as sighted people, and you'd have to say we succeeded when you look at all the people walking down the sidewalk looking down at something in their hands and totally oblivious to everything around them!

Post on reddit.com, March 16, 2016.

Woz on Woz

I wanted my own computer my whole life.

Interview, "Steve Wozniak Debunks One of Apple's Biggest Myths," bloomberg.com, December 4, 2014.

I also like to ride Segways. How much fun that is! Anybody think that's fun? I hope so… There's an awful lot of people in the world that sneer at Segways because other people are having *fun*. There must be something bad about it. But I always tell people, that hey, these Segways are so environmentally conscious. I carry four of them in the trunk of my Hummer.

Keynote address, 5th HOPE (Hackers on Planet Earth) Conference, New York City, July 10, 2004.

Some great people are leaders and others are more lucky, in the right place at the right time. I'd put myself in the latter category. But I'd never call myself a normal designer of anything.

"General Questions Answered," Letters, woz.org, August 15, 2000; reprinted in Steve Wozniak, with Gina Smith, iWoz:Computer Geek to Cult Icon: How I Invented the Personal Computer, Co-Founded Apple, and Had Fun Doing It (2006).

I never lie, even to this day. Not even a little. Unless you count playing pranks on people, which I don't. That's comedy. Entertainment doesn't count. A joke is different from a lie, even if the difference is kind of subtle.

"General Questions Answered," Letters, woz.org, August 15, 2000; reprinted in Steve Wozniak, with Gina Smith, iWoz:Computer Geek to Cult Icon: How I Invented the Personal Computer, Co-Founded Apple, and Had Fun Doing It (2006).

Soldering things together, putting the chips together, designing them, drawing them on drafting tables—it was so much a passion in my life. And to this day, I'll go stay at the bottom of the org chart being an engineer, because that's where I want to be.

Interview, "Steve Wozniak Debunks One of Apple's Biggest Myths," bloomberg.com, December 4, 2014.

If you read the same things as others and say the same things they say, then you're perceived as intelligent. I'm a bit more independent and radical and consider intelligence the ability to think about matters on your own and ask a lot of skeptical questions to get at the real truth, not just what you're told it is.

Steve Wozniak, with Gina Smith, iWoz: Computer Geek to Cult Icon: How I Invented the Personal Computer, Co-Founded Apple, and Had Fun Doing It (2006).

As soon as he said it was okay to do engineering, that really freed me up. My psychological block was really that I didn't want to start a company. Because I was just afraid. In business and politics, I wasn't going to be a real strong participant. I wasn't going to tell other people how to do things. I wasn't going to run things ever in my life. I was a non-political person and I was a very non-forceful person. It dated back to a lot of things that happened during the Vietnam War. But I just couldn't run a company.

"Interview: Steve Wozniak," foundersatwork.com, 2009.

Marguerite Yourcenar

Marguerite Yourcenar (née Marguerite de Crayencour) / 1903–1987 / Belgium / Poet, Short Story Writer, Novelist, Essayist, Translator, Memoirist

Birthplace

The true birthplace is the one where we first cast an intelligent eye upon ourselves; my first fatherlands were books.

Mémoires d'Hadrien [Memoirs of Hadrian] (1951).

Common Sense

. . . in every contest between fanaticism and common sense, the latter rarely has the upper hand.

Mémoires d'Hadrien [Memoirs of Hadrian] (1951).

Courage

All of us would be transformed if we had the courage to be what we are.

Alexis (1929).

Death

Little soul, tender and floating soul, companion of my body, which was your host, you are going to descend into the pale, hard, and naked regions where you will have to give up the games of days gone by. For one more moment, let us look together at the familiar shores, at the objects which no doubt we will never see again . . . Let us try to enter into death with open eyes . . .

Mémoires d'Hadrien [Memoirs of Hadrian] (1951).

Destiny

I believe that a stroke of madness is almost always required to construct a destiny.

Les yeux ouverts: Entretiens avec Matthieu Galey [Open Eyes: Conversations with Matthieu Galey] (1980).

He had arrived at that moment in life, different for each person, where the human being gives in to his personal *daemon*, or *genius*, and follows a mysterious law which orders him either to destroy or to surpass himself.

Mémoires d'Hadrien [Memoirs of Hadrian] (1951).

Freedom

One is not free so long as one desires, so long as one wants, so long as one fears, so long, perhaps, as one lives.

L'Œuvre au noir [Opus nigrum; alchemical term] (1968).

Governing

I do not despise men. If I did, I would have no right, nor any reason, to try to govern them. I know them to be vain, ignorant, greedy, anxious, capable of almost anything to succeed, to shine, even in their own eyes, or simply to avoid suffering. I know. I am like them, at least from time to time, or I could have been.

Mémoires d'Hadrien [Memoirs of Hadrian] (1951).

Greek

Everything that is best that men have said has been said in Greek.

Mémoires d'Hadrien [Memoirs of Hadrian] (1951).

Happiness

Every happiness is a masterpiece. The smallest mistake falsifies it, the least hesitation transforms it, the slightest heaviness ruins it, the tiniest foolishness renders it imbecilic.

Mémoires d'Hadrien [Memoirs of Hadrian] (1951).

Hope

The unfortunate thing is that, because wishes sometimes come true, the agony of hoping is perpetuated.

Denier du rêve [Dream Coin] (1934).

Human Heart

May it please him who perhaps Is to expand the human heart until it equals all of life.

L'Œuvre au noir [Opus nigrum; alchemical term] (1968); inscription on Yourcenar's tombstone.

Humanity

A man who reads, or who thinks, or who calculates, belongs to the species and not to a sex. In his best moments, he eludes even the human.

Mémoires d'Hadrien [Memoirs of Hadrian] (1951).

Innocence

We believe ourselves pure as long as we despise what we do not desire.

Alexis (1929).

Laws

Our civil laws will never be supple enough to adapt to the immense and ever-changing variety of facts. They change more slowly than customs. Although laws are dangerous when they lag behind customs, they are more dangerous still when they undertake to advance ahead of them.

Mémoires d'Hadrien [Memoirs of Hadrian] (1951).

Leisure

Moments of free time. Each well-regulated life has some, and whoever does not know how to find them does not know how to live.

Mémoires d'Hadrien [Memoirs of Hadrian] (1951).

Libraries

I often think of the beautiful inscription that Plotinus had placed at the entrance to the library he established in the middle of Trajan's Forum: "Hospital of the Soul."

Mémoires d'Hadrien [Memoirs of Hadrian] (1951).

To found libraries is construct still more public granaries, to build up reserves against a winter of the spirit . . .

Mémoires d'Hadrien [Memoirs of Hadrian] (1951).

Love

One day, God will erase from men's hearts all the laws except love.

L'Œuvre au noir [Opus nigrum; alchemical term] (1968).

I did not love less; I loved more. But the weight of love, like that of an arm tenderly stretched across a chest, little by little became heavy to bear.

Mémoires d'Hadrien [Memoirs of Hadrian] (1951).

Memory

The memory of most men is an abandoned cemetery where lie the unsung dead they have ceased to cherish.

Mémoires d'Hadrien [Memoirs of Hadrian] (1951).

Music

Every silence is composed of nothing but unspoken words. Perhaps that is why I became a musician. Someone had to express this silence, make it render up all the sadness it contained, make it sing as it were.

Alexis (1929).

Purpose of Life

To perfect oneself is the principal goal of living.

Les yeux ouverts: Entretiens avec Matthieu Galey [Open Eyes: Conversations with Matthieu Galey] (1980).

Routine

I knew that good and bad are both a matter of routine, that the temporary prolongs itself, that what is outside infiltrates the inside, and that the mask finally becomes the face itself.

Mémoires d'Hadrien [Memoirs of Hadrian] (1951).

Scientific Spirit

The skirmishes with the theologians had had their charm, but he knew well that no lasting accord exists between those who seek, ponder, and dissect and pride themselves on being capable of thinking tomorrow other than they do today, and those who accept the Faith, or declare that they do, and oblige their fellow men to do the same, on pain of death.

L'Œuvre au noir [Opus nigrum; alchemical term] (1968).

Stars

It is not difficult to nourish admirable thoughts when the stars are present.

Alexis (1929).

Suicide

I won't kill myself. The dead are so quickly forgotten.

Mémoires d'Hadrien [Memoirs of Hadrian] (1951).

Travel

Who would be so foolish as to die without having made at least the tour of his prison?

L'Œuvre au noir [Opus nigrum; alchemical term] (1968).

True Birth

Nothing is slower than the true birth of a man.

Mémoires d'Hadrien [Memoirs of Hadrian] (1951).

Understanding Human Beings

Like everyone else, I have had access to only three means of evaluating human existence: the study of myself, the most difficult and the most dangerous, but also the most fruitful method; observation of men, who manage most often to hide their secrets from us or else to make us believe they have secrets;

books, with their particular errors of perspective, which rise up from between the lines.

Mémoires d'Hadrien [Memoirs of Hadrian] (1951).

Vegetarianism

At this period of his existence, meat and blood, entrails, and all that had ever lived and breathed disgusted him as food, for an animal dies in pain just as man does, and it repelled him to be digesting death's agony.

L'Œuvre au noir [Opus nigrum; alchemical term] (1968).

Virtues

Our great mistake is to try to obtain from each individual the virtues he does not possess and to neglect to cultivate the ones he does.

Mémoires d'Hadrien [Memoirs of Hadrian] (1951).

Wisdom

There is more than one kind of wisdom, and all of them are essential to the world. It is not a bad thing that they should take turns.

Mémoires d'Hadrien [Memoirs of Hadrian] (1951).

Words and Gestures

The written word has taught me to hear the human voice, just as the grand, motionless attitudes of statues have taught me to appreciate gestures.

Mémoires d'Hadrien [Memoirs of Hadrian] (1951).

Muhammad Yunus

Muhammad Yunus / b. 1940 / village near Chittagong, Bangladesh (then the British Raj) / Economist, Banker, Social Entrepreneur, Founder of Grameen Bank

COVID-19

What happens to the rest of the world? It's as if the rest of the world will be forgotten. . . . This is a vaccine that is needed by 8 billion people. What happens to poor people? What happens to poor countries who cannot afford to pay the prices that they'll be charging in the rich countries? With social business, shareholders don't want to make any profit out of it so no dividend is taken from the company and we can reduce the cost and produce anywhere.

Reported by Darnell Christie in "Nobel winners call for coronavirus vaccines to be available for all," Thomson Reuters Foundation, London, June 29, 2020.

I believe that, ultimately, the only way to definitively eradicate the pandemic is to have a vaccine that can be administered to all inhabitants of the planet. . . . The effectiveness of the upcoming vaccination campaign will depend on its universality. To ensure the availability of the vaccines to all people on the planet almost at the same time, it has to be free from ownership. To do so we intend to make a global pharmaceutical social business operational as soon as possible. I am looking for partners to help us achieve this goal. . . . It has to be freed from commercial interest. The polio vaccine was declared as a common good, not owned by anybody. Why not (have) the corona vaccine follow the same path?

Reported by Shehab Sumon in "Bangladeshi Nobel laureate says COVID-19 vaccine must be free from commercial interests," arabnews.com, July 4, 2020.

Governance

I believe that "government," as we know it today, should pull out of most things except for law enforcement and justice, national defense and foreign policy, and let the private sector, a "Grameenized private sector," a social-consciousness-driven private sector, take over their other functions.

Muhammad Yunus, Banker to the Poor: Micro-Lending and the Battle Against World Poverty (1999).

Another way to achieve [develppment] is to let a business earn profit that is then taxed by the government, and the tax can be used to provide services to the poor. But in practice it never works that way. In real life, taxes only pay for a government bureaucracy that collects the tax and provides little or nothing to the poor. And since most government bureaucracies are not profit motivated, they have little incentive to increase their efficiency. In fact, they have a disincentive: governments often cannot cut social services without a public outcry, so the behemoth continues, blind and inefficient, year after year.

Muhammad Yunus, Banker to the Poor: Micro-Lending and the Battle Against World Poverty (1999).

The challenge I set before anyone who condemns private-sector business is this: If you are a socially conscious person, why don't you run your business in a way that will help achieve social objectives?

Muhammad Yunus, Banker to the Poor: Micro-Lending and the Battle Against World Poverty (1999).

When you can hold the world in your palm and see it from a bird's eye view, you tend to become arrogant—you do not realize that when looking from such a great distance, everything becomes blurred, and that you end up imagining rather than really seeing things.

Muhammad Yunus, Banker to the Poor: Micro-Lending and the Battle Against World Poverty (1999).

Grameen Bank

Poor people always pay back their loans. It's us, the creators of institutions and rules, who keep creating trouble for them.

Reported by Asif Dowla and Dipal Barua in The Poor Always Pay Back: The Grameen II Story (2006).

I will not spend the money for myself. I will rather spend it in special business on a no-profit-no-loss policy. We will also establish an eye hospital where even beggars will be given treatment at the cost of Taka 10–20. (**Note**: the Taka is the Bangladeshi currency.)

Reported in The Daily Star (Dhaka), October 14, 2006.

I did something that challenged the banking world. Conventional banks look for the rich; we look for the absolutely poor. All people are entrepreneurs, but many don't have the opportunity to find that out.

Reported in The Guardian, UK, 2010.

Grameen is a private-sector self-help bank, and as its members gain personal wealth they acquire water-pumps, latrines, housing, education, access to health care, and so on.

Muhammad Yunus, Banker to the Poor: Micro-Lending and the Battle Against World Poverty (1999).

I profoundly believer, as Grammen's experience over twenty years has shown, that personal gains is not the only possible fuel for free enterprise. Social goals can replace greed as a powerful motivational force. Social-consciousness-driven enterprises can be formidable competitors for the greed-based enterprises. I believe that if we play our cards right, social-consciousness-driven enterprises can do very well in the marketplace.

Muhammad Yunus, Banker to the Poor: Micro-Lending and the Battle Against World Poverty (1999).

International Aid

When we want to help the poor, we usually offer them charity. Most often we use charity to avoid recognizing the problem and finding the solution for it. Charity becomes a way to shrug off our responsibility. But charity is no solution to poverty. Charity only perpetuates poverty by taking the initiative away from the poor. Charity allows us to go ahead with our own lives without worrying about the lives of the poor. Charity appeases our consciences

Muhammad Yunus, Banker to the Poor: Micro-Lending and the Battle Against World Poverty (1999).

I learned that things are never as complicated as we imagine them to be. It is only our arrogance which seeks to find complicated answers to simple problems.

Muhammad Yunus, Banker to the Poor: Micro-Lending and the Battle Against World Poverty (1999).

The direct elimination of poverty should be the objective of all development aid. Development should be viewed as a human rights issue, not as a question of simply increasing the gross national product (GNP).

Muhammad Yunus, Banker to the Poor: Micro-Lending and the Battle Against World Poverty (1999).

Population Growth

I believe that the emphasis on curbing population growth diverts attention from the more vital issue of pursuing policies that allow the population to take care of itself.

Muhammad Yunus, Banker to the Poor: Micro-Lending and the Battle Against World Poverty (1999).

UN studies conducted in more than forty developing countries show that the birth rate falls as women gain equality. . . . I believe income-earning opportunities that empower poor women . . . will have more impact on curbing population growth that the current system of "encouraging" family planning practices through intimidation tactics.. Family planning should be left to the family.

Muhammad Yunus, Banker to the Poor: Micro-Lending and the Battle Against World Poverty (1999).

Power

Financial power is not the only power in the world. There is also the power of ideas, of nonviolence, of democracy, of respect, of love. These true powers can be used against the power of guns and bombs.

Muhammad Yunus, Banker to the Poor: Micro-Lending and the Battle Against World Poverty (1999).

Women

If you are born into a poor family, if you are a woman you have seen the worst of poverty. In a cultural way in the families in Bangladesh it's the women who eats last. So if you have a scarcity in the family ... she misses out so everything comes in the raw deal for her. So , given a chance she works very hard to make a change to improve her life. And by training she is the most efficient manager of scarce resources. Because with the little resource she has, she has to stretch it as much as she can to look after the children, look after the family and everything else . . . unlike men—men want to enjoy right away. Whatever he got, whatever tiny bit of thing he got he doesn't care for much what's coming up.

Interview with Australian Broadcasting Corporation, March 25, 1997.

When a destitute mother starts earning an income, her dreams of success invariably center around her children. A woman's second priority is the household. She wants to buy utensils, build a stronger roof, or find a bed for herself and her family. A man has an entirely different set of priorities. When a destitute father earns extra income, he focuses more attention on himself. Thus money entering a household through a woman brings more benefits to the family as a whole.

Muhammad Yunus, Banker to the Poor: Micro-Lending and the Battle Against World Poverty (1999).

World Poverty

Once poverty is gone, we'll need to build museums to display its horrors to future generations. They'll wonder why poverty continued so long in human society—how a few people could live in luxury while billions dwelt in misery, deprivation and despair.

Muhammad Yunus, Creating a World without Poverty: Social Business and the Future of Capitalism (2008).

People . . . were poor not because they were stupid or lazy. They worked all day long, doing complex physical tasks. They were poor because the financial institution in the country did not help them widen their economic base.

Muhammad Yunus, Banker to the Poor: Micro-Lending and the Battle Against World Poverty (1999).

If you go out into the real world, you cannot miss seeing that the poor are poor not because they are untrained or illiterate but because they cannot retain the returns of their labor. They have no control over capital, and it is the ability to control capital that gives people the power to rise out of poverty.

Muhammad Yunus, Banker to the Poor: Micro-Lending and the Battle Against World Poverty (1999).

To me poor people are like bonsai trees. When you plant the best seed of the tallest tree in a flower-pot, you get a replica of the tallest tree, only inches tall. There is nothing wrong with the seed you planted, only the soil-base that is too inadequate. Poor people are bonsai people. There is nothing wrong in their seeds. Simply, society never gave them the base to grow on. All it needs to get the poor people out of poverty for us to create an enabling environment for them. Once the poor can unleash their energy and creativity, poverty will disappear very quickly.

Muhammad Yunus, Creating a World without Poverty: Social Business and the Future of Capitalism (2008).

The poor themselves can create a poverty-free world—all we have to do is to free them from the chains that we have put around them.

Muhammad Yunus, "Eliminating Poverty Through Market-Based Social Entrepreneurship," Global Urban Development Magazine, Volume 1, Issue 1, May, 2005; accessible at globalurban.org.

Poverty has been created by the economic and social system that we have designed for the world. It is the institutions that we have built, and feel so proud of, which created poverty.

Muhammad Yunus, "Eliminating Poverty Through Market-Based Social Entrepreneurship," Global Urban Development Magazine, Volume 1, Issue 1, May, 2005; accessible at globalurban.org.

All human beings have an innate skill—survival skill. The fact that poor are still alive is a proof of their ability to survive. We do not need to teach them how to survive. They know this already.

Reported in "Profile of Yunus," North American Bangladesh Info Center.

Zhang Zai

Zhang Zai (Chang Tsai) / 1020–1077 / China / Scholar-Official, Philosopher

Man's Place in Nature

Heaven is my father and Earth is my mother, and even such a small creature as I finds an intimate place in their midst.
Therefore that which fills the universe I regard as my body and that which directs the universe I consider as my nature.
All people are my brothers and sisters, and all things are my companions.

Source: Xi ming [Western Inscription]; translated by Wing-tsit Chan, Sourcebook in Chinese Philosophy (Princeton UP, 1963); p. 497.

Benefit of Learning

The great benefit of learning is to enable one to transform his physical nature himself. Otherwise he will have the defect of studying in order to impress others, in the end will attain no enlightenment, and cannot see the all-embracing depth of the sage.

Daily Activities

In one's words there should be something to teach others. In one's activities there should be something to serve as model for others. In the morning something should be done. In the evening something should be realized. At every moment something should be nourished. And in every instant something should be preserved.

Developing One's Nature

One who can fully develop his nature can also develop the nature of other people and things. He who can fulfill his destiny can also fulfill the destiny of other people and things, for the nature of all men and things follows the Way and the destiny of all men and things is decreed by Heaven.

Enlightenment

By "sincerity resulting from enlightenment" is meant to develop one's nature fully through the investigation of things to the utmost, and by "enlightenment resulting from sincerity" is meant to investigate things to the utmost through fully developing one's nature.

Great Man's Nature

One's nature is the one source of all things and is not one's own private possession. It is only the great man who is able to know and practice its principle to the utmost. Therefore, when he establishes himself, he will help others to establish themselves. He will share his knowledge with all. He will love universally. When he achieves something, he wants others to achieve the same.

Human Nature

The heavenly endowed nature in man is comparable to the nature of water in ice. It is the same whether the ice freezes or melts. Water's reflection of light may be much or little, dark or bright, but in receiving the light, it is the same in all cases.

Kinds of Knowledge

Knowledge coming from seeing and hearing is knowledge obtained through contact with things. It is not knowledge obtained through one's moral nature. Knowledge obtained through one's moral nature does not originate from seeing or hearing.

Life and Death

Only through fully developing one's nature can one realize that he possesses nothing in life and loses nothing at death.

Limits of Empirical Science

While material force is integrated, how can one not say that it is temporary? While it is disintegrated, how can one hastily say that it is non-being? For this reason, the sage, having observed phenomena and examined above and below, only claims to know the causes of what is hidden and what is manifest but does not claim to know the causes of being and non-being.

Nature vs. Ability

Nature connotes what one can do by natural endowment. Ability connotes what one can do through his own planning. In fully developing his nature, the great man does not consider the ability endowed by Heaven to be ability but considers man's planning to be ability.

Peace and Joy

Peace and joy are the beginning of the Way. Because it is peaceful, it can be great, and because it is joyous, it can be lasting. The nature of Heaven and Earth is nothing other than being great and lasting.

Power of the Mind

The mind commands man's nature and feelings.

Spirit

When material force is clear, it penetrates; and when it is turbid, it obstructs. When clearness reaches its limit, there is spirit. When spirit concentrates, it penetrates like the breeze going through the holes (of musical instruments), producing tones and carrying them to great distances. This is the evidence of clearness. As if arriving at the destination without the necessity of going there, penetration reaches the highest degree.

Virtue

He who understands virtue will have a sufficient amount, that is all. He will not allow sensual desires to be a burden to his mind, the small to injure the great, or the secondary to destroy the fundamental.

Source: Zheng meng [Correction of Youthful Ignorance]; translated by Wing-tsit Chan, Sourcebook in Chinese Philosophy (Princeton UP, 1963); pp. 503–517.

Mark Zuckerberg

Mark Elliot Zuckerberg / b. 1984 / New York, USA / Software Developer, Entrepreneur, Co-Founder of Facebook

Business Philosophy

It is better to buy than compete.

"'It's better to buy than compete': The FTC is using Mark Zuckerberg's own words against him," Business Insider, 2008.

Understanding who you serve is always a very important problem, and it only gets harder the more people that you serve. We try to pay a lot of attention to this by a combination of very rigorous quantitative and qualitative feedback. But if you're serving 1.2 billion people, it's very hard.

Interview with Farhad Manjoo, "Can Facebook Innovate? A Conversation With Mark Zuckerberg," nytimes.com, April 16, 2014.

Change

Change starts local. Even global changes start small—with people like us. In our generation, the struggle of whether we connect more, whether we achieve our biggest opportunities, comes down to this—your ability to build communities and create a world where every single person has a sense of purpose.

Zuckerberg's Commencement Address, Harvard University, Harvard Gazette, May 25, 2017.

Creativity

The idea of a single eureka moment is a dangerous lie. It makes us feel inadequate since we haven't had ours. It prevents people with seeds of good ideas from getting started.

Zuckerberg's Commencement Address, Harvard University, Harvard Gazette, May 25, 2017.

Equality

Every generation expands its definition of equality. Previous generations fought for the vote and civil rights. They had the New Deal and Great Society. Now it's our time to define a new social contract for our generation.

Zuckerberg's Commencement Address, Harvard University, Harvard Gazette, May 25, 2017.

Facebook

Zuck: Yeah so if you ever need info about anyone at Harvard

Zuck: Just ask.

Zuck: I have over 4,000 emails, pictures, addresses, SNS.

[**Name of Friend Redacted**]: What? How'd you manage that one?

Zuck: People just submitted it.

Zuck: I don't know why.

Zuck: They "trust me."

Zuck: Dumb f***s.

Instant messages from 2003, reported by Business Insider, May 13, 2010.

I think that some decisions that we made early on to localize the website and keep it separate for each college on the network kept it really useful, because people could only see people from their local college and friends outside. That made it so people were comfortable sharing information that they probably wouldn't otherwise, which made it useful in the long term for people to look up information about other people on the site.

Interview with Bambi Francisco, Vator, YouTube, 2005.

My goal was never to make Facebook cool.

"Facebook Founder Mark Zuckerberg First Public Q&A!," MyNextGadget, YouTube, November 6, 2014.

We were just building stuff 'cause we thought it was cool. I do remember having these specific conversations with my friends where we thought, you know, someone is gonna build this. Someone is gonna build something that makes it so that people can stay connected with their friends and their family, but no way would we be the ones who were contributing to, kinda, leading the whole Internet in this direction.

Reported by "Mark Zuckerberg and Facebook: What's Next?," 60 Minutes, cbsnews.com, December 1, 2010.

If you want to build a service which is not just serving rich people, then you need to have something that people can afford. . . . At Facebook, we are squarely in the camp of the companies that work hard to charge you less . . . I think it's important that we don't all get Stockholm syndrome and let the companies that work hard to charge you more convince you that they actually care more about you.

Cited in "Mark Zuckerberg calls Tim Cook's comments on Facebook 'extremely glib,'" The Verge, April 2, 2018.

I want make sure that our products are used for good. At the end of the day, other people blaming us or not is actually not the thing that matters to me. It's not that every single thing that happens on Facebook is gonna be good. This is humanity. People use tools for good and bad, but I think that we have a clear responsibility to make sure that the good is amplified and to do everything we can to mitigate the bad.

Interview with Kara Swisher in "Zuckerberg: The Recode interview," Recode website, July 18, 2018.

Human History

We understand the great arc of human history bends towards people coming together in ever greater numbers—from tribes to cities to nations—to achieve things we couldn't on our own.

Zuckerberg's Commencement Address, Harvard University, Harvard Gazette, May 25, 2017.

National Purpose

Every generation has its defining works. More than 300,000 people worked to put a man on the moon—including that janitor. Millions of volunteers immunized children around the world against polio. Millions of more people built the Hoover dam and other great projects. These projects didn't just provide purpose for the people doing those jobs, they gave our whole country a sense of pride that we could do great things.

Zuckerberg's Commencement Address, Harvard University, Harvard Gazette, May 25, 2017.

Social Media

It's not unusual for us to receive an email from somebody saying, "I spend all of my time on your website and now I have less of a social life than I had before." We would much rather have people meet people through the website and go out and party than stay at home on a Friday night reading other people's profiles. And it's surprising, but we have actually received far less complaints about stalking than we otherwise would have expected.

Interview, Current Magazine, November 30, 2004.

It takes courage to choose hope over fear. As I look around the world, I'm starting to see people and nations turning inward, against the idea of a connected world and a global community. The path forward is to bring people together, not push them apart. I hear fearful voices calling for building walls and distancing people they label as "others." I hear them calling for blocking free expression, for slowing immigration, for reducing trade, and in some cases even for cutting access to the internet.

Zuckerberg Keynote Address, Facebook's F8 developers event, developers.facebook.com, April 12, 2016.

I'm Jewish, and there's a set of people who deny that the Holocaust happened. I find that deeply offensive. But at the end of the day, I don't believe that our platform should take that down because I think there are things that different people get wrong. I don't think that they're *intentionally*getting it wrong. It's hard to impugn intent and to understand the intent. I just think, as abhorrent as some of those examples are, I think the reality is also that I get things wrong when I speak publicly. I'm sure you do. I'm sure a lot of leaders and public figures we respect do too, and I just don't think that it is the right thing to say, "We're going to take someone off the platform if they get things wrong, even multiple times." What we will do is we'll say, "Okay, you have your page, and if you're not trying to organize harm against someone, or attacking someone, then you can put up that content on your page, even if people might disagree with it or find it offensive." But that doesn't mean that we have a responsibility to make it widely distributed in News Feed.

Interview with Kara Swisher in "Zuckerberg: The Recode interview," Recode website, July 18, 2018.

Zuckerberg on Zuckerberg

I really want to clear my life so that I have to make as [few] decisions as possible about anything except how to best serve this community.

Reported by Andrew Trotman in "Facebook's Mark Zuckerberg: Why I wear the same T-shirt every day," The Telegraph, November 7, 2014.

I think the reality is that writing code and building a product and then building a company actually is not a glamorous enough thing to make a movie about.

Reported by Madeline Boardman in "Mark Zuckerberg Says The Social Network Was 'Hurtful,' Parts Were 'Made Up,'" Us Weekly, November 7, 2014; regarding the movie The Social Network (2010).

The question I ask myself like almost every day is, "Am I doing the most important thing I could be doing?" . . . Unless I feel like I'm working on the most important problem that I can help with, then I'm not going to feel good about how I'm spending my time.

Reported by Marcia Amidon Lusted in Mark Zuckerberg: Facebook Creator (2011).

www.ingramcontent.com/pod-product-compliance
Lightning Source LLC
LaVergne TN
LVHW060016210926
848481LV00013B/3721